THE OXFORD HANDBOOK OF

SCHOPENHAUER

THE OXFORD HANDBOOK OF

SCHOPENHAUER

Edited by

ROBERT L. WICKS

OXFORD
UNIVERSITY PRESS

OXFORD
UNIVERSITY PRESS

Oxford University Press is a department of the University of Oxford. It furthers
the University's objective of excellence in research, scholarship, and education
by publishing worldwide. Oxford is a registered trade mark of Oxford University
Press in the UK and certain other countries.

Published in the United States of America by Oxford University Press
198 Madison Avenue, New York, NY 10016, United States of America.

Library of Congress Control Number: 2020932224

ISBN 978-0-19-066005-5

1 3 5 7 9 8 6 4 2

Printed by Sheridan Books, Inc., United States of America

Contents

PART III AESTHETIC EXPERIENCE, MUSIC, AND THE SUBLIME

PART IV HUMAN MEANING, POLITICS, AND MORALITY

PART V RELIGION AND SCHOPENHAUER'S PHILOSOPHY

PART VI SCHOPENHAUER'S INFLUENCE

LIST OF CONTRIBUTORS

Urs App is Professor Emeritus of Buddhism at Hanazono University, Kyoto, and presently Senior Research Fellow of the École Française d'Extrême-Orient in Paris. He has written extensively on the history of the Western discovery of Asian religions and philosophies; see his *The Birth of Orientalism* (University of Pennsylvania Press, 2010) and *The Cult of Emptiness* (Universitymedia, 2012). His work on Schopenhauer includes, apart from numerous articles, *Schopenhauer's Kompass* (Universitymedia, 2011) and its enlarged English translation *Schopenhauer's Compass* (Universitymedia, 2014).

Stephan Atzert is Senior Lecturer in German Studies in the School of Languages and Cultures at the University of Queensland in Brisbane, Australia. To date Dr. Atzert has contributed two monographs to the study of the reception of Schopenhauer's philosophy. His first book, *Schopenhauer in the Works of Thomas Bernhard: The Critical Appropriation of Schopenhauer's Philosophy in Thomas Bernhard's Late Novels*, was published in German in 1999. Since then, Dr. Atzert has contributed to the international scholarship on Schopenhauer with journal articles and book chapters, with a focus on Schopenhauer's role in the development of psychoanalysis and for the understanding of Buddhism in Europe. His second monograph in German, *In Schopenhauer's Shadow* (Königshausen & Neumann, 2015), investigates the role of Schopenhauer's philosophy in the writings of Friedrich Nietzsche, Paul Deussen and Sigmund Freud. At present (2019) he is developing a monograph on K. E. Neumann's reception of Schopenhauer in his translations of the Pali discourses into German.

Douglas L. Berger is Professor of Global and Comparative Philosophy and Director of the Centre for Intercultural Philosophy at Leiden University in the Netherlands. He is the author of two monographs, *"The Veil of Māyā": Schopenhauer's System and Early Indian Thought* (Global Academic Publications, 2004) and *Encounters of Mind: Luminosity and Personhood in Indian and Chinese Thought* (SUNY Press, 2015) as well as co-editor, with Jee-Loo Liu, of the collection *Nothingness in Asian Philosophy* (Routledge, 2014). He has written dozens of essays and book chapters in the fields of Brāhmiṇical, Indian Buddhist, Confucian, Daoist, and Chinese Buddhist thought as well as on nineteenth-century German philosophy and cross-cultural hermeneutics. He is currently the editor of the University of Hawai'i book series *Dimensions of Asian Spirituality* and former president of the Society of Asian and Comparative Philosophy.

Paul Bishop is William Jacks Chair of Modern Languages at the University of Glasgow, Scotland. He has written on various topics in German intellectual history (including Cassirer, Goethe, Thomas Mann, Nietzsche, and Schopenhauer) and has recently published *German Political Thought and the Discourse of Platonism: Finding the Way Out of the Cave* (Palgrave Macmillan, 2019), *Ludwig Klages and the Philosophy of Life: A Vitalist Toolkit* (Routledge, 2017), and *On the Blissful Islands: With Nietzsche & Jung in the Shadow of the Superman* (Routledge, 2017).

Maria Lucia Mello Oliveira Cacciola is Professor of Philosophy at the University of São Paolo and President of the Schopenhauer Society in Brazil, a branch of the Schopenhauer Gesellschaft based in Germany. After graduating in Legal Sciences, she earned a second degree in philosophy at the University of São Paulo and thereafter joined the master's program to finish with a dissertation entitled "The Critique of Kant's Reason in Schopenhauer's Thought," on the relation between Schopenhauer and Kant concerning the knowledge and distinction between phenomenon and thing-in-itself. Her PhD thesis was published as a book, *Schopenhauer and the Question of Dogmatism*, and she has since published essays on Kant, Schopenhauer, and other post-Kantians, among which are "Is Schopenhauer a True Disciple of Kant?" in *Aurora*; "Aesthetic Contemplation: Schopenhauer and Mondrian," in *Dois Pontos*; "Immanenter Dogmatismus," in *Schopenhauer Jahrbuch*. She is also coordinator of Classical German Philosophy studies at the University of São Paolo.

David E. Cartwright is Professor of Philosophy Emeritus at the University of Wisconsin-Whitewater and the former director of the North American Division of the Schopenhauer Society. In addition to numerous articles on Kant, Nietzsche, and Schopenhauer, he is the author of *Schopenhauer: A Biography* (Cambridge University Press, 2014) and (Scarecrow Press, 2004) and *Historical Dictionary of Schopenhauer's Philosophy* (2004). He has also edited and co-translated various books on and by Schopenhauer.

David Carus is an independent scholar living in the United States and returning long term to Germany. He completed his PhD on Schopenhauer's and Aristotle's concept of will, translated Schopenhauer's main work *The World as Will and Presentation* with Richard E. Aquila, and worked as Assistant Professor in philosophy at the University of Freiburg. More recently he has had the opportunity to dedicate himself solely to writing in the history of philosophy.

Adrian Del Caro is Distinguished Professor of Humanities and Head of Modern Foreign Languages and Literatures at the University of Tennessee at Knoxville. In addition to numerous articles and books since 1980 on Nietzsche, Hölderlin, Hofmannsthal, and Celan, he is the translator of *Thus Spoke Zarathustra* (Cambridge University Press, 2006), *Beyond Good and Evil and On the Genealogy of Morality* (Stanford University Press, 2014), and Schopenhauer's *Parerga and Paralipomena: Short Philosophical Essays, Vol. 2* (Cambridge University Press, 2015). His last monograph on Nietzsche was the ecocritical *Grounding the Nietzsche Rhetoric of Earth* (Walter de

Gruyter, 2004); a monograph in progress is on *Spirit* and *Earth Spirit* in Goethe's *Faust*. Along with Alan Schrift and Duncan Large, Del Caro is editor of the Stanford University Press critical edition *The Complete Works of Friedrich Nietzsche*.

Yolanda Estes is an independent scholar living in Quito, Ecuador. After teaching many years at Mississippi State University, she retired to Quito, where she continues to engage in scholarly investigations of German idealism and ethical philosophy. She specializes particularly in the philosophy of J. G. Fichte and the philosophy of sex and love. Her works include *J. G. Fichte: The Atheism Dispute* (Routledge, 2010). Most recently, she is co-editing (with David Wood) an anthology addressing Fichte's philosophy of religion.

Sebastian Gardner is Professor of Philosophy at University College London. He is the author of books and articles on the philosophy of psychoanalysis, Kant, Sartre, and other figures in modern European philosophy, among which are *The Transcendental Turn* (edited) (Oxford University Press, 2015), *Sartre's "Being and Nothingness"* (Continuum, 2009), *Art and Morality* (edited) (2003), *Kant and the "Critique of Pure Reason"* (Routledge, 1999), and *Irrationality and the Philosophy of Psychoanalysis* (Cambridge University Press, 1993).

Benedikt Paul Göcke, Dr. Phil, Dr. Theol., is a Research Fellow at the Ian Ramsey Centre for Science and Religion and a member of the Faculty of Theology at University of Oxford. He is also Professor for Philosophy of Religion and Philosophy of Science at Ruhr-Universität Bochum, Germany. Göcke is author of *A Theory of the Absolute* (Macmillan, 2014), *Alles in Gott?* (Friedrich Pustet, 2012), and, together with Christian Tapp, editor of *The Infinity of God* (Notre Dame, 2018). He has published articles in *The International Journal for Philosophy of Religion*, *Zygon*, *Sophia*, *Faith and Philosophy*, *The European Journal for Philosophy of Religion*, and *Theologie und Philosophie*, among others.

Jacob Golomb is Emeritus Professor of Philosophy at the Hebrew University of Jerusalem and a philosophical editor of the Hebrew University Magnes Press. He was a visiting professor of philosophy at Penn State University and a member of Wolfson College, Oxford. Among his many vices are some books: *Nietzsche's Enticing Psychology of Power* (Iowa State Press, 1989), *In Search of Authenticity: From Kierkegaard to Camus* (Routledge, 1995), *Nietzsche in Zion* (Cornell University Press, 2004), *Nietzsche and Jewish Culture* (edited) (Routledge, 1997), *Nietzsche and the Austrian Culture* (edited) (Wien, 2004), and *Nietzsche, Godfather of Fascism?* (co-edited) (Princeton University Press, 2002). His recent article was "Will to Power: Does It Lead to the 'Coldest of All Cold Monsters'?" *The Oxford Handbook of Nietzsche* (2013). He has also published extensively on Kierkegaard, Sartre, Camus, psychoanalysis and the philosophy of Judaism and Zionism.

Paul Gordon is Professor of Comparative Literature/Humanities at the University of Colorado, Boulder. Earlier work includes numerous essays and books on Nietzsche

(*Rapturous Superabundance: Tragedy after Nietzsche,* University of Illinois Press, 2001), Freud and Hitchcock (*Dial "M" for Mother,* Fairleigh Dickenson Press, 2009). His most recent book was a study of *Art as the Absolute: Art's Relation to Metaphysics in Kant, Fichte, Schelling, Hegel and Schopenhauer* (Bloomsbury Press, 2015). *Synaesthetics: Art as Synaesthesia* (Bloomsbury, in press).

Robert Guay is Associate Professor of Philosophy at Binghamton University. He is the editor of the recently published *Dostoevsky's Crime and Punishment: Philosophical Perspectives* (Oxford University Press, 2019) and is currently completing a commentary on Nietzsche's *On the Genealogy of Morality.*

Christopher A. Howard is an anthropologist with a research interest in the changing relations between humans, technology, and environment. He is currently Senior Researcher at the New Zealand Ministry of Business, Innovation, and Employment, and Lecturer in cultural anthropology at Chaminade University of Honolulu. He is the author of numerous articles, reviews, and the monograph, *Mobile Lifeworlds* (Routledge, 2015).

Christopher Janaway is Professor of Philosophy at the University of Southampton. He has written extensively on the philosophy of Nietzsche and Schopenhauer and on aesthetics. His books include *Self and World in Schopenhauer's Philosophy* (Oxford University Press, 1989), *Schopenhauer: A Very Short Introduction* (Oxford University Press, 2002), and *Beyond Selflessness: Reading Nietzsche's "Genealogy"* (Oxford University Press, 2007). He is general editor of the Cambridge Edition of the Works of Schopenhauer, and, in 2007–10, was principal investigator on the AHRC-funded project "Nietzsche and Modern Moral Philosophy" at Southampton.

Kevin C. Karnes is Professor of Music at Emory University (Atlanta). His recent work includes *Arvo Pärt's Tabula Rasa* (Oxford University Press, 2017) and *Korngold and His World* (co-edited with Daniel Goldmark; Princeton University Press, 2019). He is also Editor-in-Chief of the *Journal of the American Musicological Society.* He is currently co-authoring a book with Andrew J. Mitchell (Philosophy, Emory) on Wagner's conception of subjectivity and redemption.

Pilar López de Santa María is Professor of Philosophy at the University of Seville (Spain). Her main field of research is Contemporary Philosophy, especially Schopenhauer and Wittgenstein. Along with numerous articles, she is the author of a book on Wittgenstein, *Sujeto, mente y conducta* (Herder, 1983) and has translated into Spanish Schopenhauer's *The Two Fundamental Problems of Ethics* (Siglo XXI, 1993), *The World as Will and Representation,* Volumes I and II (Trotta, 2003 and 2004), *Parerga and Paralipomena,* Volumes I and II (Trotta, 2006 and 2009), *On Vision and Colors* (Trotta, 2013), and, most recently, *The Fourfold Root of the Principle of Sufficient Reason* (Alianza, 2019).

Gerard Mannion[†] **(1970–2019)** held the Joseph and Winifred Amaturo Endowed Chair in Theology at Georgetown University, where he was a Senior Research Fellow of the

Berkley Center for Religion, Peace, and World Affairs and founding Co-director of the Global Irish Studies Initiative. Educated at the Universities of Cambridge and Oxford, he held visiting professorships and fellowships at universities such as Tübingen (Germany); the University of St Michael's College, Toronto (Canada); the Australian Catholic University; the Institute of Religious Sciences in Trento (Italy); and at the Katholieke Universiteit Leuven (in Belgium). He served as chair of the Ecclesiological Investigations International Research Network and published numerous books and articles, particularly in fields such as ethics, social justice, ecclesiology, and ecumenical and interreligious dialogue, in addition to other aspects of systematic theology and philosophy.

Raymond B. Marcin is Professor Emeritus, the Catholic University of America School of Law. He is the author of *In Search of Schopenhauer's Cat: Arthur Schopenhauer's Quantum-Mystical Theory of Justice* (Washington, DC: Catholic University of America Press, 2006).

Mark Migotti teaches in the department of philosophy at the University of Calgary and has published on Nietzsche and Schopenhauer, Peirce and pragmatism, and the nature of promising and penalties. He is the co-author (with Richard Sanger) of *Hannah's Turn*, a play about the romantic liaison between Hannah Arendt and Martin Heidegger that premiered at the Summerworks Theatre Festival in Toronto, Canada, in August 2011. His long-run projects include a book on Nietzsche's early philosophical development and a book on his critique of morality.

Andrew J. Mitchell is Winship Distinguished Research Professor in Philosophy at Emory University (Atlanta), specializing in nineteenth- and twentieth-century German thought. He is the author of *The Fourfold: Reading the Late Heidegger* (Northwestern University Press, 2015) and *Heidegger Among the Sculptors: Body, Space, and the Art of Dwelling* (Stanford University Press, 2010). He is currently co-authoring a book with Kevin Karnes (Music, Emory) on Wagner's conception of subjectivity and redemption.

Judith Norman is Professor of Philosophy at Trinity University in San Antonio, Texas. She has written on Nietzsche and Schopenhauer as well as on early German Romanticism. She has co-translated many works of Nietzsche and Schopenhauer and is co-editing *Schopenhauer's "The World as Will and Representation": A Critical Guide* for Cambridge University Press. Her current project is doing philosophy with children in the San Antonio public schools.

Richard Reilly is Professor Emeritus of Philosophy at St. Bonaventure University and specializes in ethics, metaphysics, philosophy of Buddhism, and comparative philosophy. He is the author of *Ethics of Compassion* (Rowman and Littlefield, 2008) and of more than three dozen conference papers/journal articles in ethics and action theory. He continues to serve as the founding President of the Olean Meditation Center.

Christopher Ryan is Senior Lecturer in Philosophy and Education at London Metropolitan University. He has written mainly on Schopenhauer and Indian thought, and he is the author of *Schopenhauer's Philosophy of Religion: the Death of God and the Oriental Renaissance* (Peeters, 2010). He is currently writing a monograph on the philosophy of education.

Severin Schroeder is Associate Professor in Philosophy at the University of Reading. He has written three monographs on Wittgenstein: *Wittgenstein: The Way Out of the Fly Bottle* (Polity, 2006), *Wittgenstein Lesen* (Frommann-Holzboog, 2009), and *Das Privatsprachen-Argument* (Schöningh/Mentis, 1998). He is the editor of *Wittgenstein and Contemporary Philosophy of Mind* (Palgrave, 2001) and *Philosophy of Literature* (Wiley-Blackwell, 2010). He is currently working on a book on Wittgenstein's philosophy of mathematics (Routledge).

Sandra Shapshay is Professor of Philosophy at Hunter College, City University of New York (CUNY). She works primarily on the history of ethics and aesthetics in the nineteenth century, with a particular focus on Schopenhauer and Kant, and she aims to bring the insights of this history to bear on contemporary debates. She is the author of *Reconstructing Schopenhauer's Ethics: Hope, Compassion, and Animal Welfare* (Oxford University Press, 2019) and is the editor of the *Palgrave Schopenhauer Handbook* (2018). With Levi Tenen, she recently edited a special issue of the *Journal of Aesthetics and Art Criticism* titled "The Good, The Beautiful, The Green: Environmentalism and Aesthetics" (2018).

R. Raj Singh is Professor of Philosophy at Brock University and specializes Contemporary Continental Philosophy, Heidegger, Schopenhauer, and Philosophies of India, Vedanta, Buddhism, and Gandhi. His publications include *Bhakti and Philosophy* (Rowman and Littlefield, 2006), *Death, Contemplation and Schopenhauer* (Ashgate, 2007), *Schopenhauer: A Guide for the Perplexed* (Continuum, 2010), and *Heidegger, World and Death* (Rowman and Littlefield, 2013), as well as numerous articles and book chapters on Indian thought.

Ivan Soll is Emeritus Professor of Philosophy at the University of Wisconsin-Madison. He has also taught in Italy, Germany, England, Hungary, New Zealand, and Turkey. His philosophical work is principally concerned with figures in the Continental tradition, particularly Kant, Hegel, Schopenhauer, Nietzsche, Sartre, and Freud, and with issues in aesthetic theory, philosophical psychology, and the philosophy of life. He has also been active as an author, designer, and publisher of fine-press book art.

Tom Stern is Associate Professor of Philosophy at University College London. He is the author of *Nietzsche's Ethics* (Cambridge University Press, forthcoming) and *Philosophy and Theatre* (Routledge, 2013) and the editor of *The New Cambridge Companion to Nietzsche* (Cambridge University Press, 2019).

Bart Vandenabeele is Professor of Aesthetics and Philosophy of Art at Ghent University, Belgium. His research interests include (the history of) aesthetics, Schopenhauer, Nietzsche, Kant, and post-Kantian philosophy. He is the author of *The Sublime in Schopenhauer's Philosophy* (Palgrave Macmillan, 2015) and the editor of *A Companion to Schopenhauer* (Wiley-Blackwell, 2012). He is a member of the international advisory board of the *Schopenhauer-Gesellschaft*, past Vice-Chair of the Philosophy of Communication Section of European Communication Conference (ECREA), and past Vice-President of the *Dutch Association of Aesthetics*.

Alistair Welchman is Professor of Philosophy at the University of Texas at San Antonio. He co-translated both volumes of Schopenhauer's *World as Will and Representation* for Cambridge University Press and is co-editing *Schopenhauer's "The World as Will and Representation": A Critical Guide*, also for Cambridge. He has published a wide variety of articles on German Idealism and contemporary French philosophy.

Robert L. Wicks is Professor of Philosophy at the University of Auckland, New Zealand. He is the author of *Schopenhauer* (Blackwell, 2008), *Schopenhauer's "The World as Will and Representation"* (Continuum, 2011), *Kant on Judgment* (Routledge, 2007), and *Introduction to Existentialism: From Kierkegaard to "The Seventh Seal"* (Bloomsbury, 2020), among other books and articles on Kant, nineteenth-century European philosophy, aesthetics, Buddhism, and existentialism.

LIST OF ABBREVIATIONS

There is a variety of translations of Schopenhauer's works into English, with some authors preferring certain translations over others. In view of this, the following abbreviations for Schopenhauer's works will be used throughout this volume. The more frequently encountered translations have been included in this list, using differentiating letters to distinguish between alternative translations of the same work, as in the case of *The World as Will and Representation*. In the essays, the references to quotations from Schopenhauer's main works will be given in-text, using the abbreviations here; the references to quotations from other authors and works will be given in each essay's reference notes. If the publication date for any particular work differs from the one cited here—there are several different publication dates for *Sämtliche Werke in 7 Bänden* (SW), for example—the essays will indicate this. Some authors have chosen to include references to the original German text in conjunction with the reference to the English translation.

EFR	*The Fourfold Root of the Principle of Sufficient Reason* [1813], first edition, published as *Schopenhauer's Early Fourfold Root—Translation and Commentary*, translated by F. C. White. Aldershot: Avebury, 1997.
FR	*On the Fourfold Root of the Principle of Sufficient Reason* [1847], second edition, published in *On the Fourfold Root of the Principle of Sufficient Reason and other Writings,* translated and edited by David E. Cartwright, Edward R. Erdmann, and Christopher Janaway. Cambridge: Cambridge University Press, 2012.
FR$_{[P]}$	*On the Fourfold Root of the Principle of Sufficient Reason* [1847], second edition, translated by E. F. J. Payne. La Salle, IL: Open Court Press, 1974.
VC	*On Vision and Colours* [1816], published in *On the Fourfold Root of The Principle of Sufficient Reason and Other Writings,* translated and edited by David E. Cartwright, Edward R. Erdmann, and Christopher Janaway. Cambridge: Cambridge University Press, 2012.
WWR1	*The World as Will and Representation, Volume One* [1818], translated and edited by Judith Norman, Alistair Welchman, and Christopher Janaway. Cambridge: Cambridge University Press, 2010.
WWR1$_{[P]}$	*The World as Will and Representation, Volume I* [1818], translated by E. F. J. Payne. New York: Dover Publications, 1969.
WWR1$_{[AC]}$	*The World as Will and Presentation, Volume One* [1818], translated by Richard E. Aquila in collaboration with David Carus. New York: Person Longman, 2008.
WWR2	*The World as Will and Representation, Volume Two* [1844], translated and edited by Judith Norman, Alistair Welchman, and Christopher Janaway. Cambridge: Cambridge University Press, 2018.

WWR2$_{[P]}$ *The World as Will and Representation, Volume II* [1844], translated by E. F. J. Payne. New York: Dover Publications, 1966.

WWR2$_{[AC]}$ *The World as Will and Presentation, Volume Two*, translated by David Carus and Richard E. Aquila. New York: Longman, 2011.

WN   *On Will in Nature* [1836], published in *On the Fourfold Root of the Principle of Sufficient Reason and other Writings*, translated and edited by David E. Cartwright, Edward R. Erdmann, and Christopher Janaway. Cambridge: Cambridge University Press, 2012.

WN$_{[P]}$ *On Will in Nature* [1836], translated by E. F. J. Payne, edited by David E. Cartwright. Oxford: Berg 1999.

FW   *Prize Essay on the Freedom of the Will* [1839], published in *The Two Fundamental Problems of Ethics*, translated and edited by Christopher Janaway. Cambridge: Cambridge University Press, 2009.

FW$_{[C]}$ *Prize Essay on the Freedom of the Will* [1839], published in *The Two Fundamental Problems of Ethics*, translated by David E. Cartwright and Edward E. Erdmann. Oxford: Oxford University Press, 2010.

FW$_{[P]}$ *Prize Essay on the Freedom of the Will* [1839], translated by E. F. J. Payne, ed. Günter Zöller. Cambridge: Cambridge University Press, 1999.

FW$_{[K]}$ *Essay on the Freedom of the Will* [1839], translated by Konstantin Kolenda. Indianapolis, IN: The Bobbs-Merrill Company, 1960.

BM   *Prize Essay on the Basis of Morals* [1840], published in *The Two Fundamental Problems of Ethics*, translated and edited by Christopher Janaway. Cambridge: Cambridge University Press, 2009.

BM$_{[C]}$ *Prize Essay on the Basis of Morals* [1840], published in *The Two Fundamental Problems of Ethics*, translated by David E. Cartwright and Edward E. Erdmann. Oxford: Oxford University Press, 2010.

BM$_{[P]}$ *On the Basis of Morality* [1840], translated by E. F. J. Payne. Indianapolis, IN: The Bobbs-Merrill Company, Inc. 1965.

PP1   *Parerga and Paralipomena, Short Philosophical Essays, Volume 1* [1851], translated and edited by Sabine Roehr and Christopher Janaway. Cambridge: Cambridge University Press, 2014.

PP1$_{[P]}$ *Parerga and Paralipomena, Volume 1* [1851], translated by E. F. J. Payne. Oxford: Oxford University Press, 1974.

PP2   *Parerga and Paralipomena. Short Philosophical Essays. Volume 2* [1851], translated and edited by Adrian Del Caro and Christopher Janaway. Cambridge: Cambridge University Press, 2015.

PP2$_{[P]}$ *Parerga and Paralipomena, Volume 2* [1851], translated by E. F. J. Payne, Oxford, Oxford University Press, 1974, 227 (SW6, 242)

SW1, SW2, etc.   *Sämtliche Werke in 7 Bänden*, edited by Arthur Hübscher, Leipzig: F. A. Brockhaus, 1988.

HN1, HN2, etc.   *Der handschriftliche Nachlaß in fünf Bänden*, edited by Arthur Hübscher. Frankfurt am Main: Kramer, 1966–75.

MR1, MR2, etc.   *Manuscript Remains in Four Volumes*, translated by E. F. J. Payne. Oxford/New York/Hamburg: Berg, 1988.

GB   *Gesammelte Briefe*, edited by Arthur Hübscher. Bonn: Bouvier, 1978.

INTRODUCTION

ROBERT L. WICKS

ARTHUR Schopenhauer (1788–1831) is popularly known as a "pessimist," a characterization that refers commonly to those who harbor a downbeat and defeatist attitude of resignation when hope should still remain alive. His work can induce this interpretation, for he indeed states that it would have been better in the first place had this world never existed. Schopenhauer's practical message, though, is to do one's best to live at peace, both with oneself and others; to feel compassion for other living things; to appreciate the beauty of art and music; to try to rise more objectively and tranquilly above the petty disputes, desires, and concerns that tend to absorb the lives of so many; to apprehend that we are all essentially of the same substance and endure the same kinds of sufferings; and, ultimately, to achieve a transcendent state of consciousness of such profundity that it renders into unimportance the ordinary spatio-temporal world in which we live, laugh, suffer, and die.

Schopenhauer stands distinctively among nineteenth-century philosophers for his honest sensitivity to the human condition and his culturally sophisticated manner of expressing hope for an enhanced understanding of ourselves, other people, and the world around us. Born in 1788, he was twelve years old at the turn of the century, and, as a highly intelligent, avid learner with a strong sense of originality, he published his magnum opus, *The World as Will and Representation* in 1818, by the time he had reached the age of thirty. A quarter of a century later, he published a second, complementary volume to this work, and, in 1851, nine years before his death, another two-volume work, *Parerga and Paralipomena*, which precipitated his long-awaited fame.

The second volume of *The World as Will and Representation* appeared in 1844, the year, coincidentally, in which Friedrich Nietzsche was born, whose philosophy was notably influenced by his reading of Schopenhauer when in his early twenties. At the end of his own period of intellectual productivity, after developing a contrasting outlook that prescribed an unconditional affirmation of life, Nietzsche looked back on Schopenhauer's philosophy and described it memorably in his own autobiographical work, *Ecce Homo* (1888), as pervaded by a "cadaverous perfume." In its funereal suggestions of death, beauty, stillness, and the macabre, Nietzsche's phrase is moderately suitable, for Schopenhauer referred to the daily world as a phantasmagoria, invoking the image of the early horror theaters called "phatasmagorias," initially popular in Paris of the 1790s, that featured magic lanterns whose painted glass slides projected upon darkened walls images of demons, ghosts, and skeletons to scores of terrifically astonished audiences.

Schopenhauer's vision of the world can stimulate scenes of carnival nights, Halloween costumes, and Gothic horror stories—it is not pure coincidence that Mary Shelley's *Frankenstein* was published in 1818, the same year as *The World as Will and Representation*—but he is serious about how we often fail to appreciate the suffering of others. His philosophy cannot be understood without comprehending how the experience of compassion allows the exceedingly painful nature of life to touch us first-hand. As an ideal, he presents us with an image of Jesus as someone who, as some describe him, absorbed the depth of everyone's suffering by shouldering the totality of the world's sins. Schopenhauer also brings us to a beachhead in Java, where hundreds of giant turtles emerge yearly from the water to lay their eggs only to be torn apart by packs of wild dogs. As a paradigm, he holds up the image of the bulldog ant, which, when cut in half, viciously attacks itself, with head and tail fighting each other to the death.

Such is the cannibalistic nature of life for Schopenhauer, where every living being is the living grave of thousands of others. As a lesson on how disappointment is concealed in our most powerful drive to reproduce and preserve ourselves, he recalls the story of a man hopelessly consumed with a passionate attraction for a particular woman, who discovers at the culmination of his seduction that the shapely body beneath her garments had been hideously consumed by cancer. Shaken to the core and alienated from his fleshly desires, the man subsequently became a monk.

Schopenhauer grew up in an affluent family—his father was a wealthy merchant—and he traveled throughout Europe at an early age. Having a more reflective and sensitive nature, impressing him indelibly during his travels was the widespread suffering he witnessed for it quickly led him to question the existence of God and the meaning of human life. His philosophy consequently speaks to us all: he does not dwell on refined conceptual technicalities or the analysis of life's merely local aspects; his concern is with the nature of existence and, as he put it, solving the riddle of the world. Religious thought inevitably enters into his reflections, in particular that of Christianity, Hinduism, and Buddhism—a religion whose aim is the enlightened release from suffering through the minimization of desire.

Our volume reflects on Schopenhauer's philosophy with authors from a variety of backgrounds, presently living and working in places as diverse as Australia, Belgium, Brazil, Canada, Ecuador, England, France, Germany, Israel, the Netherlands, New Zealand, Scotland, Spain, and the United States. It begins with a group of essays that attend to influences on Schopenhauer that have been less explored, such as his relationship with Johann Wolfgang von Goethe, his understanding of F. W. J. Schelling's philosophy, his presence at Johann Gottlieb Fichte's lectures when enrolled as a student at the University of Berlin, and, significantly underappreciated, the philosophical impact of his having been the neighbor of Karl Christian Friedrich Krause while he was writing *The World as*

Will and Representation in Dresden. Important as well and described here is Schopenhauer's advanced knowledge of texts, religions, and philosophies from Asia.

Just as Richard Wagner was a father figure to Friedrich Nietzsche, J. W. F. Goethe—a friend of Schopenhauer's mother, Johanna—was a father figure to Schopenhauer. Their relationship was tense, however, as Adrian del Caro shows. Goethe enlisted the young Schopenhauer as an advocate of his controversial theory of light, but, to Goethe's frustration, Schopenhauer's way of earning Goethe's respect was to show how well he could sharply criticize and correct Goethe's theory. Schopenhauer's disposition toward the more well-known German Idealists—Fichte, Hegel, and Schelling—was similarly tension-ridden and, with respect to Fichte and Hegel, relentlessly antagonistic. Judith Norman and Alistair Welchman show that although he criticized Schelling, Schopenhauer had stronger affinities to his philosophy than he tended to admit. In relation to Fichte, who Schopenhauer repeatedly portrayed as a humbug and charlatan, Yolanda Estes reveals the intersecting points between their views and what Schopenhauer owed to Fichte.

Among the German Idealists, Karl Christian Friedrich Krause is a relatively unfamiliar philosopher despite his having been an early advocate of panentheism—a position now popular in the philosophy of religion and theology—not to mention an influential figure in educational theory in Spain and Latin America for a doctrine that became known as "Krausism." Benedikt Paul Göcke describes Krause's views and adds some supportive perspective to Krause's claim that Schopenhauer had adopted some of his key ideas without acknowledgment. On the side of greater familiarity, Schopenhauer is distinguished for his interest in Asian thought. Urs App's essay presents this aspect of Schopenhauer's intellectual background in a manner that ranges comprehensively across Schopenhauer's lifetime, explaining how, due to the lack of scholarly concentration on the actual journals and books on Asian thought that Schopenhauer read, studied, and annotated (such as the Latin translation of the Upanishads, the *Oupnek'hat*) this aspect of Schopenhauer studies is still in its infancy.

A constitutive influence on Schopenhauer is Immanuel Kant's theory of knowledge as expressed in the *Critique of Pure Reason*. To this day, scholars debate about the extent of that influence in view of the question of whether we can know the nature of ultimate reality. To begin the second part of our volume, on Schopenhauer's metaphysics and epistemology, Sandra Shapshay argues that Schopenhauer was more Kantian than has typically been recognized, contrary to how he has been frequently interpreted as asserting straightforwardly that the nature of ultimate reality is a blind, senseless urge that can be called "will." Her view is that Schopenhauer's characterization of ultimate reality as will is best understood as a metonym that stands interpretively open, rather than as a literal, final, and definitive characterization. Ivan Soll writes in the same interpretive vein, presenting the position that although Schopenhauer's metaphysical thesis that ultimate reality is will may be questionable, he can be read as saying epistemologically and more convincingly that we inevitably must conceive of all natural forces as varying forms of what we experience in ourselves as will. David Carus's essay relates to this by considering Schopenhauer's conception of "force" and how it cannot be cognized by natural science. Severin Schroeder then attends to our concept of causality, in reference to which Schopenhauer claims that our own agency provides us with an understanding. Schroeder develops this view, modifying it with considerations that issue from our bodily encounters with material objects.

Continuing with how Schopenhauer's philosophy relates to physical phenomena—in this case, unusual ones—David Cartwright explores Schopenhauer's interest in telepathy, clairvoyance, and magic. Schopenhauer believed that although natural science cannot easily explain extrasensory phenomena, his own metaphysics indeed can, thereby supporting his conviction that his metaphysics is thoroughly comprehensive. Elaborating on some of the more mystery-filled aspects of Schopenhauer's view, Pilar López de Santa María explains along a variety of dimensions and with historical perspective how, in Schopenhauer's philosophy, the ultimate source of freedom is unfathomable.

Schopenhauer's aesthetic theory looks into both the past and the future. Continuing in the long classical tradition that associates beauty with idealized forms, his account of the visual and verbal arts reinforces how beauty is aligned with perfection and transcendence. Anticipating what was to come, his theory of music as the formal expression of human feeling stands among the foundations of modern music, having inspired composers such as Richard Wagner, Johannes Brahms, Antonín Dvořák, Gustav Mahler, and Arnold Schönberg. In our volume's third part, on Schopenhauer's aesthetics, Robert Wicks (the present author) begins by trying to resolve a puzzle in Schopenhauer's theory of beauty—namely, how beautiful portraiture can be related to truth—when his metaphysics implies that virtually everyone is an unattractive, tortured soul. Maria Lucia Cacciola's essay follows with an examination of Schopenhauer's theories of beauty and genius, comparing and contrasting them with Kant's. She explains how Schopenhauer challenges Kant's aesthetics by claiming that it depends too heavily on theoretical abstractions.

Complementing the notion of beauty is the *sublime*—an aesthetic category that Kant also features in his aesthetics. Adding to the comparisons and contrasts to Kant's aesthetics, Bart Vandenabeele focuses on Schopenhauer's account of the sublime, presenting some ways to understand Schopenhauer's solution to the general question of how we can derive aesthetic enjoyment from a sublime experience when one of its essential components is the involvement of feelings of insignificance and fear. In the final essay of this part, Paul Gordon presents Schopenhauer's theory of beauty as the sensuous presentation of Platonic Ideas in its relation to his theory of music and explains how music's position is more continuous with Schopenhauer's theory of beauty than has been previously thought.

As mentioned at the outset, Schopenhauer is commonly associated with pessimism, a standpoint that is usually deprecated but which, on Schopenhauer's own understanding of the word, is the only view that is sufficiently sensitive to the widespread suffering in the world. The next part of our volume accordingly contains essays on human meaning and the associated theme of morality, which lead to considerations of law as well as the nature of compassion. Christopher Janaway begins by questioning the often-accepted proposition that Schopenhauer believes that the spatio-temporal world is essentially meaningless and argues that, through his advocacy of Christian values, Schopenhauer ascribes to the world a moral meaning—one that points us away from the world toward asceticism and salvation. Mark Migotti then examines the exact meaning of Schopenhauer's conception of pessimism, which he shows to derive from the meaning of optimism in philosophies prior to Schopenhauer's, as in Leibinz's theism. His position is that the significance of Schopenhauer's pessimism is best understood through his discussion of suicide. Looking closely at Schopenhauer's moral philosophy, Robert Guay asks the probing question within the Schopenhauerian framework of what could be worth doing or what must be done when, ultimately, nothing makes any sense. He then develops the idea that, via compassion, morality can be understood as a way of manifesting metaphysical knowledge.

There remains the question of how law and legalities stand within Schopenhauer's view. Raymond Marcin addresses this by describing Schopenhauer's conception of law, which relates to our daily activity in the spatio-temporal world—a world where egoism prevails—in juxtaposition with his conception of justice, which relates to our more enlightened, transcendent awareness of the ultimate unity of what is. He argues that Schopenhauer's view has the virtue of being able to reconcile two pairs of theorists—namely, the legal economists and public-choice theorists—with the civic republicans and other communitarians who would otherwise remain opposed. Following the discussion on law and justice, and concluding this part of the volume, are essays by Richard Reilly and Douglas Berger, both on compassion. Richard Reilly critically surveys a variety of philosophical understandings of what compassion is and articulates the Buddhistic aspects of Schopenhauer's account of compassion. Douglas Berger discusses compassion in connection with the twelfth-century Confucian master Zhu Xi, who Schopenhauer, when writing in the 1830s, feared he would be accused of having plagiarized. We learn that Schopenhauer's and Zhu Xi's outlooks are very different, although they agree that compassion provides a means to understand the foundations of human existence.

Despite his atheism, Schopenhauer was a religiously attuned thinker, interested in expressing in a less mythologically imagistic and more philosophical form the essence of Christianity, Hinduism, and Buddhism. Opinions differ on the degree to which each of these religions has a presence in his thought, for Schopenhauer's philosophy is like a prism that, when turned in one direction, displays a more Christian light and, when turned in another, a more Hindu one, and then again from another angle, a more Buddhist quality. Christopher Ryan's essay on the Diamond Sutra begins the volume's fourth part, on Schopenhauer and religion, taking as its interpretive center Schopenhauer's concluding words in *The World as Will and Representation* that the ultimate level of enlightenment compares to the "Prajna-Paramita of the Buddhists, the state of being 'beyond all knowledge,'" where Schopenhauer quotes the orientalist, Isaac Jacob Schmidt (1779–1847).

R. Raj Singh, in his essay on Schopenhauer and Hindu thought, takes a critical approach, working through some of the nuances of Indian philosophy to show where

Schopenhauer understood it accurately and where he did not, underscoring how Schopenhauer's enthusiasm for Hindu thought never waned. Gerard Mannion's essay on Christianity reveals how permeating and extensively Christian Schopenhauer's literary sources actually were, despite his endorsement of Hindu and Buddhist thought. Concluding the group of essays on Schopenhauer and religion, Jacob Golomb addresses a subject that many Schopenhauer scholars have avoided and for which clarification is overdue: namely, Schopenhauer's attitude towards Judaism—a religious outlook that Schopenhauer associates pejoratively with realism and optimism. Hitler quoted Schopenhauer in his own anti-Semitic writings, and this guilt by association is awkward for those who find value in Schopenhauer's thought. Working with the concept of Schopenhauer's "metaphysical anti-Judaism," Golomb explains Schopenhauer's position and puts it into balance, showing that Schopenhauer was more of an anti-Theist than an anti-Semite.

The volume's final part contains essays on Schopenhauer's intellectual reception, concentrating mainly on his more immediate influence during the nineteenth century. Although attention is given to celebrated thinkers such as Nietzsche and Freud, there is an accompanying interest in enhancing the appreciation of less well-known philosophers such as Eduard von Hartmann, Philipp Mainländer, and Julius Bahnsen. Sebastian Gardner's essay surveys Schopenhauer's influence on von Hartmann, Mainländer, Bahnsen, Nietzsche, and Freud, showing how each thinker reacts to a problem inherent in Schopenhauer's philosophy: namely, how it can be legitimate to use reason to convey a metaphysically oriented philosophy when reason itself is brought under suspicion. Tom Stern then develops Schopenhauer's influence on Nietzsche along the dimensions of psychology, history, life, and style using the concept of *Mitleid* (compassion/pity) as it bears on the question of whether life is worth living. Stephan Atzert discusses von Hartmann, Mainländer, and Freud, but from the standpoint of how the notion of the unconscious was slowly popularized in the later nineteenth century. Adding substance to the Schopenhauer–Nietzsche connection, Kevin Karnes and Andrew J. Mitchell illustrate Schopenhauer's influence on Nietzsche's father figure, Richard Wagner, in view of his essays and characters in his operas.

Further exploring the history of Schopenhauer's influence in areas that are relatively less intellectually traveled, Paul Bishop presents in culturally rich detail Schopenhauer's extensive *fin de siècle* reception in Austria—an influence that issued from an attraction to Schopenhauer's pessimism and his account of aesthetic experience. He looks comprehensively at Schopenhauer's influence in music, psychoanalysis, gender- and misogyny-themed writings, literature, philosophy, and the visual arts. Concluding our volume is an essay by Christopher A. Howard that brings Schopenhauer into the twenty-first century. He reviews the Buddhistic affinities between Schopenhauer and the contemporary French writer and filmmaker Michel Houellebecq (b. 1956), with a special attention to his novels.

PART I

BIOGRAPHICAL CONTEXT AND PHILOSOPHICAL INFLUENCES

CHAPTER 1

SCHOPENHAUER'S INTELLECTUAL RELATIONSHIP WITH GOETHE

An Ambivalent Affinity

ADRIAN DEL CARO

"INCIDENTALLY, I hate everything that merely instructs me without enhancing my activity, or directly animating it."[1] This is the Goethe quote Nietzsche used in 1874 to open *On the Use and Disadvantage of History for Living*, the second of four *Unfashionable Observations* that would be joined by a third in the same year: *Schopenhauer as Educator*. The triad Nietzsche, Schopenhauer, Goethe represents an intellectual-historical continuum; while only Schopenhauer and Goethe form the basis of this chapter, the invocation of Goethe by the Schopenhauer disciple Nietzsche illustrates how German thinkers of the modern era signal their intellectual colors—Goethe is a historical benchmark and a national, indeed supranational, treasure. The encounter between Schopenhauer and Goethe, meanwhile, may serve as a metaphor for the rich Goethean tradition that eschews mere instruction but embraces activity and its enhancement, for while Nietzsche only *knew of* Goethe (1749–1832), Schopenhauer actually collaborated with Goethe on color theory in such a way that it profoundly impacted his formation.

The age of Faust that gave rise to the first Faust legend printed by Johann Spies in 1587, later adapted for stage by Marlowe in the 1590s and published as *Doctor Faustus* (1604), reflected the emergence of the Renaissance man, the enterprising, individualistic man of action informed by science versus the traditional man of the Middle Ages who led the *vita contemplativa* (life of contemplation). Young Goethe in the 1770s was well on his way to demonstrating by his own example that a modern individual could fulfill both the active and contemplative life; he commenced writing on *Faust* in 1774 and worked on this masterpiece until his death in 1832. *The Sorrows of Young Werther* became a best-seller when it was published in 1774, so Goethe was already an internationally famous and highly regarded novelist, playwright, and poet and a newly minted *juris doctor* when he was invited to join the court of Duke Karl August of Weimar-Saxony in 1775. In addition to his lifelong service to the Duke in the capacity of councilman, minister, adviser, and chief of finance, Goethe conducted his own scientific studies in botany, geology, physics, meteorology, and zoology. He also served as director of the Weimar theater and flourished as an internationally revered poet, playwright, novelist, scientist, and philosopher.

In 1810, Goethe published *On the Theory of Colors* (*Zur Farbenlehre*) in two volumes, having worked on it for twenty years. His motivation was anything but academic or theoretical—color theory was of direct and lasting significance for his philosophy overall. As Paul Lauxtermann explains, Goethe was repulsed by Newton's method of experimentation, specifically the way he manipulated light through prisms, putting "Nature on the rack" to make it conform to his hypotheses; a related expression of Goethe's rejection of scientific approaches that force, compel, or otherwise abuse nature is his reverence for pure math but his contempt for its application to natural phenomena in such a way that nature is "crucified."[2] Goethe and his romantic contemporaries preferred a holistic, empirical approach to nature, as succinctly demonstrated in the penultimate strophe of Wordsworth's "The Tables Turned" (1798): "Sweet is the lore which Nature brings; / Our meddling intellect / Misshapes the beauteous forms of things— / We murder to dissect."[3]

The editor of the correspondence between Schopenhauer and Goethe, Ludger Lütkehaus, offers a compelling synopsis of why Goethe rejected Newtonian methods. The pressing of light through tiny openings, effectively shattering its unity in order to demonstrate a preconceived hypothesis, smacked to Goethe of Francis Bacon's inquisitorial torture and subjugation of nature. Goethe's attacks on Newton are therefore "a secular rebellion against the experimental spirit of scientific-technical modernism," a new aggressive spirit that "robs human beings of their domicile in the world, in their living environment," destroying the unity of nature and the harmony between nature and the subject. If this all sounds a bit reverential toward nature, perhaps even a bit *contemporary* in environmentalist terms, Lütkehaus explains that Goethe's stand has been referred to by some as "color theology" (*Farbentheologie* vs. *Farbentheorie*).[4]

Some critics maintain that Goethe regarded the theory of color as centrally important to his works overall and more important even than all his poetry, such that the correspondence between Goethe and Schopenhauer on this subject constitutes a unique document of scientific-historical, biographical, psychological, and philosophical importance.[5] For Goethe, colors are expressions of two *Urphenomene* or primal phenomena—namely, light and darkness—such that the history of color theory could serve as a microcosm of intellectual history in general, as Matthew Bell suggests, and while Goethe was not aiming exclusively to replace Newton's theory of light, "The *Farbenlehre* contains an attempt to prescribe a methodology in science on the basis of the way in which, given the constitution of our mental organs and our concrete situation in the world, our knowledge organizes itself most readily."[6] By "most readily" here I infer "most naturally," with the least disruption of the unity of nature and in such a way that science does not serve as a mindless tool for "vexing," splintering, or subduing nature.

These were the years of the Napoleonic wars; Goethe welcomed Napoleon despite the opposition of his Grand Duke and, according to Rüdiger Safranski, even compared himself to Napoleon: the revered emperor would bring light to the dark aftermath of the French Revolution, while Goethe would restore light (literally) to its proper place and remedy Newton's erroneous color theory. But for all the work he had put into his theory, a full twenty years' worth, it was, Safranski continues, as if the mountain had been in labor all this time only to produce a mouse: "His friends dispensed praise; a few painters, among them Runge in particular, took inspiration. But the scientific world waved him off, 'connoisseurs will find nothing new here,' observes the *Gotha Scholarly Review* laconically." Thus, by the time Goethe decided he would approach young Schopenhauer, "he felt misunderstood in what for him was the main thing."[7] Niklas Sommer details how Goethe's book on color theory had been out for three years when he turned his attention to a promising young PhD whom he had described in letters as "remarkable and interesting," with a "certain perspicacious stubbornness." For several years before he published his work, Goethe had shared his insights with only a select few, among them Schiller (d. 1805). He was willing to make this particular overture to Schopenhauer for the sake of his friendship with Johanna Schopenhauer, Arthur's mother and a popular writer who had settled in Weimar after the apparent suicide of her husband; but he was also intrigued by the fact that this young Schopenhauer was a neophyte in matters of color theory, a blank slate, so to speak, who presented Goethe with the opportunity to introduce him to his own theory and viewpoint without having to disabuse him first of the prejudices of Newtonian physics.[8] It turned out to be a fateful decision indeed, for Goethe highly miscalculated the true degree of Schopenhauer's stubbornness, perspicacity, and complete lack of modesty.

If the Newtonian science was to be overturned, Goethe would need to enlist the aid of disciples who could be trusted with bringing about his theory's eventual triumph.[9] Clearly one such disciple seemed almost to have fallen from the sky when Goethe received a copy of Schopenhauer's doctoral dissertation, *On the Fourfold Root of the Principle of Sufficient Reason* in 1813; suddenly, the boy he had virtually ignored all these years in Weimar, where he had grown up in the shadow of his mother's celebrity, resembled a potential disciple. Goethe was immediately struck by the strong emphasis in Schopenhauer on *Anschauung*, intuition, and without giving too much thought to how Schopenhauer's use of the term might differ from his own, Goethe embarked on what Lütkehaus poignantly calls "this productive misunderstanding" by inviting Arthur to participate in experiments in color theory.[10] At the time, Goethe had hoped to find in Schopenhauer a significant disciple, if not the heir to his anti-Newtonianism.[11] What these two men did not know about each other has already contributed many volumes to the world's libraries.

And yet, they were at very different stations in their respective lives, complicating matters in particular for Arthur, whose father appeared to have committed suicide and happened to be around the same age as Goethe. Lütkehaus formulates how fraught the relationship would become: "The long-since world famous Olympian, whose Achilles heel is color theory, encounters a self-confident young philosopher who is on his way to his own system, to what is for him *the* system. The letters reveal Goethe's wisdom about human beings and Schopenhauer's ruthless frankness—in a biographical situation whose 'familial' substratum is laid bare. These are, if not Goethe's letters to a soon prodigal son, then at least Schopenhauer's letters to his (second) father, though naturally one must not reduce their significance to shallow 'Oedipal' clichés."[12] Arguably, as we shall see, Goethe's need for a son was not an issue, and he managed to keep his famous distance, though far more warmly and humanely than in previous cases in which he had been implicated as either a father or an authority figure.

While the function of the theory of color has been described as no less than central to Goethe's life (see note 5), he was advancing toward old age by the time he engaged Schopenhauer, and the latter had his whole life ahead of him. His biographer asserts that without the encounter with Goethe, Schopenhauer would certainly not have taken up the problem of colors, but his reverence for Goethe and his desire to assist him against Newton were compelling.[13] Ever the loner, Schopenhauer embarked on the "one exceptional collaboration" of his career, not as a disciple but in fact convinced of the superiority of his own thinking on the matter.[14] Pessimistic by nature, still he devoted "loving interest" to certain things, among them art and color theory.[15] He distinguished himself from others who had collaborated with Goethe or admired him from a distance by acknowledging the elder's authority without letting it inhibit him; he experienced none of the anxiety or intimidation that affected others. After all, Goethe was known to react with "annihilating sharpness" to genuine or perceived opponents, yet he responded with exceptional patience and mildness to Schopenhauer. For his part, Schopenhauer would have liked to continue the relationship, but there was none of the positive energy that characterized Goethe's earlier relationship with Schiller.[16] However unschooled or unmotivated he may have been in the beginning regarding color theory, once he had written his own theory under the title *On Vision and Colors* (published 1816) and submitted it to Goethe in the hope of engaging him as editor or at least as endorser, it soon became apparent that his own contribution to color theory took hold of him, even took over, as seen in his letters to Goethe.

"I know from you personally," he wrote on September 3, 1815, "that for you, literary activity has always been secondary, while real life has been the main thing. It's just the opposite with me: what I think, what I write, this has value for me and is important: what I experience personally and what happens to me is secondary."[17] Schopenhauer makes this confession in an effort to coax some substantive response from Goethe, who has remained silent, much to Schopenhauer's frustration. When Goethe responds by suggesting that his acquaintance Dr. Seebeck would be in a good position to confer with Schopenhauer on color theory, clinging to his explanation that he has no time to immerse himself in it now, Schopenhauer responds with an extremely lengthy letter (ten pages in print) that surely doomed any chances he might have had of winning over Goethe. Now it has become personal to him; he explains that he will have no rest, no peace of mind due to the high demands of honesty he imposes on himself; the birthing process of his own color theory is painful, and he stands before his own intellect "like a relentless judge before a prisoner who is being tortured, making him answer until there is nothing left to ask." This same honesty now gives him assurance and compels him to speak "frankly and freely to Your Excellency." Here Schopenhauer draws a strong conclusion: surely Goethe must be upset over some minor quibbles, and, insofar as he refuses to inform Schopenhauer of his errors, he can only conclude that he is right, and Goethe is wrong—after all, Schopenhauer's theory is a unified whole, from which no single stone could be removed, while Goethe's work is "the systematic collection of many and manifold facts" distorted and concealed by Newtonian errors: "which means a small error could easily have occurred."[18] Goethe had invited Schopenhauer to join him as a disciple and a teacher of Goethean color theory, but, in fact, Goethe had on his hands not a pupil, not a sympathetic ally but an opponent who demanded that Goethe acknowledge the superiority of Schopenhauerian color theory, maintaining all the while that he remained a faithful and devoted servant of the master!

Before concluding his stunningly bold letter, reminiscent in some respects of the undelivered letter Kafka had written to his father (*Letter to His Father*), Schopenhauer goes on to make utterly extravagant and outrageous claims, alternating between despair and defiance, between bravado and desperate rhetorical pleas for understanding. These need only be sketched here: he surveys the field from on high, seeing everything, while Goethe struggles below to draw a map; he knows with perfect certainty that he has delivered the first true theory of color in the history of science; he had intentionally highlighted the errors of Goethe's theory only to demonstrate that he is not a blind follower; Goethe succeeded in proving Newton wrong, but he had nothing to replace him with; Goethe's theory is a pyramid, while Schopenhauer's is the apex thereof; he doesn't need Dr. Seebeck, he demands *Goethe's* authority; sarcastically he jabs "Your Excellency has other preoccupations now, is perhaps in the higher region of the creative arts"; a proper response regarding Schopenhauer's mistakes shouldn't take him long, since it took Schopenhauer only "a couple weeks" to write his theory; Goethe should at least look Schopenhauer's "little baby" in the eyes before he declines to serve as its godfather.[19] Surprisingly, Goethe responded with two more letters, maintaining his poise, and, unsurprisingly, Schopenhauer even in his final letter to Goethe took a defiant stance: "instead of weakening my good opinion of my work and crushing my courage, your lack of sympathy seems almost to have elevated them both."[20]

When we reflect on what happened, it becomes clear that color theory not only took over in Schopenhauer's mind, he also took extraordinary pains to appropriate it—*and may have felt empowered by Goethe's own words*: "What you received but as your father's heir, / Make it your own to gain possession of it!"[21] When Schopenhauer used this *Faust* verse so many years later in PP2, he provided this interpretation: "It is of great value and use to discover, independently and before we know it, what thinkers before us have already discovered…and when later one finds it among earlier thinkers, one unexpectedly gains strong endorsement from external, recognized authority, that testifies to its truth; through which, subsequently, one gains confidence and steadfastness for championing it against any contradiction" (PP2, 18). Schopenhauer proposed a counter-theory, or what he regarded as the first actual theory of color to Goethe's, manifesting *independence* in this arduous exchange, as well as confidence, steadfastness, and advocacy for his own truth.

For his part, Goethe held his counsel, never revealing the "evidence" Schopenhauer demanded of him, never acknowledging the "superiority" of the young philosopher's views, and, though he was sorely used and practically poked with a sharp stick by Schopenhauer, Goethe never lost his composure. Lütkehaus suggests that Goethe the Olympian, the expert in the history of myths and families, would surely have understood the message.[22] Safranski tells us that others who approached Goethe as suitors, notably Lenz and Kleist, were nearly broken by the experience, but not Schopenhauer: he remained true to himself and his philosophy, maintained his veneration for the master, and lost himself neither in veneration nor in spasms of self-confidence.[23] Let us recall that the theory of color and Goethe's needs at the time were the only reasons these two men became collaborators. Schopenhauer had plans for himself without Goethe— he had just published his dissertation after all, and *The World as Will and Representation* was already beginning to occupy his thinking. The opportunity allowed Schopenhauer to measure himself not only against Goethe's best scientific writing, the passion of two decades of dedication, but also against Goethe *himself*: Schopenhauer was convinced of his own superiority vis-à-vis Goethe's color theory, and though he clearly did not measure up as a man, as a human being, still the experience did not kill him, as Nietzsche would say, and it seemed to make him stronger.

Safranski relates an episode that illustrates how light as a phenomenon was regarded quite differently by Goethe and Schopenhauer, especially since the latter had just radicalized Kantian transcendentalism in his dissertation. Many years after their collaboration Schopenhauer recounted: "But this Goethe...was so entirely a *realist* that it simply would not dawn on him that *objects* as such only exist insofar as they are *represented* by the cognizing subject. 'What!' he said to me once, staring at me with his Jupiter eyes, 'light is supposed to exist only insofar as you see it? No, *you* wouldn't exist if light did not see *you.*'"[24] This anecdote should be borne in mind whenever Schopenhauer professes his "complete agreement" with Goethe and belabors the "complete correctness" of Goethe's theory—Goethe held a fundamentally different position, they both knew it virtually from the moment Goethe read Schopenhauer's manuscript, but Schopenhauer wanted to assert himself *and* win over Goethe at the same time—a task doomed to failure.

In briefly reviewing some of the technical aspects of Goethe's color theory, readers can gauge for themselves where he stood and how Schopenhauer responded, bearing in mind that the collaboration was invited by Goethe and was intended to serve the propagation of his findings. The details of their *competing* theories, as Goethe must have viewed them, or of their complementary theories as Schopenhauer purported, reveal opposing worldviews informed by science.

In the introduction to *On the Theory of Colors*, Goethe makes this striking assertion: "The eye owes its existence to light. From indifferent animal organs, light summons forth an organ that will become its equal, and so the eye forms itself from light for light, so that the inner light is able to approach the outer."[25] I translate *seinesgleichen* as "its equal," but the main thing is that Goethe wants us to know that light affects humans as beings whose existence is light-dependent and light-produced. The "inner light" residing in humans is reminiscent of how Christianity speaks of light in the New Testament, of how Meister Eckhart referred to the "divine spark" in us, or, more commonly, of the expression "his eyes lit up"; it is half of the German word for vision, *Augenlicht*. But Goethe is not making a theological statement here; instead, he emphasizes the interaction that must take place between humans and nature as our light "approaches" the outer light. The inference is that we are supposed to be approaching the outer light, however we might choose to interpret this action philosophically.

If there is a moral dimension to humans approaching the light, then it is certainly in the secular, Enlightenment sense that recognizes light as the root of enlightenment. The alternative is darkness in historical and intellectual terms, from which the historical Enlightenment has liberated us, and, of course, Goethe was fond of binaries: "colors develop in opposition," and "they are what they are only in their interrelationship: one color is no color."[26] The polar opposite colors are blue and yellow, from which "all other colors can be derived through intensification of one, or through the union of two of them."[27] The polarization is not limited to colors, as illustrated in Goethe's pairing of *The Elective Affinities* (1809) and *On the Theory of Colors* (1810), and the effect of light on colors and emotions is similar: Goethe maintained that when our intellect gazes through "our beclouded inner life" toward the light, our emotions are love and hope, but when we gaze through this same medium toward the dark, our emotions are hate and fear.[28] Thus whereas Newton attributed color to the properties of light rays, and Schopenhauer regarded it as a physiological effect stemming from the eye, Goethe held a middle position stressing the importance of the physical media encountered by light on its way from the source to the beholder.[29] Goethe's physical medium, which he technically referred to as *das Trübe* or in Greek *skieron*, is shadowy or gray, and we perceive colors through this medium—Goethe's theory thus positions human beings at the receiving end of light filtered through the *skieron*.

Today Goethe's color theory is not regarded as a viable competitor with Newton's, though, according to Böhme, its emphasis on subjective perception demonstrated that there is a regularity to color phenomena that had previously been regarded as random optical illusions. Böhme characterizes him as a "systematically working lover of nature" compared to Newton and "the scientific professionals," though he concedes that, in terms of data, method, law, explanation, and theory, Goethe's efforts conform to those of modern science.[30] Goethe influenced later writers on color theory, including Purkinje (1819), Müller (1826), and, of course, Schopenhauer (1816),[31] and as T. J. Reed explains, he was "no dilettante ... But essentially he was operating with the eye of the imagination" which, Reed adds, can "carry a science forward at a critical juncture in its history."[32]

A similar brief review of Schopenhauer's position on colors starts with his proposition that "colours are not intrinsic properties of objects, but pertain to the perceiver alone" (FR, xxxviii). Whereas for Goethe white and black were primal phenomena, for Schopenhauer they are "modifications of the eye. Lightness or white is the full activity of the retina. Darkness or black is the inactivity of the retina; whereas, colour is the qualitatively divided activity of the retina." Moreover, again as distinguished from Goethe, the numerical fractions corresponding to activity of the retina are an "innovation that allows him to demonstrate the production of white from colours" (VC, xl–xli). These are already major differences, but there is more: Schopenhauer praises Goethe in language that damns with faint praise, claiming that Goethe's first great service had been to "break the old spell of Newton's incorrect theory," the second "he delivered in full measure what the title promised: data *for* a theory of colour. There are important, complete, significant data, rich material for a future theory of colour. However, he did not undertake to provide this theory itself" (VC, 207–08). So, in addition to differing with Goethe on key points, Schopenhauer displaced Goethe as the alternative to Newton—this alternative in the form of a real theory was Schopenhauer's achievement. We must try to imagine what Goethe felt and thought in reading these transparently condescending phrases—after all, he had labored over his color theory for twenty years, only to be instructed now by the young philosopher that his labors amounted to a bunch of useful data.

As galling as the assertions themselves are, consider the effusive, almost fawning praise that accompanies them: "If we (here, I mean very few) also see Newton's incorrect theory completely refuted by Goethe, partially by the polemical part of his work, partially by the correct presentation of colour phenomena of every kind, which Newton's theory had falsified, then this victory is not complete until a new theory appears in the place of the old" (VC 209). Or "conversely, the urphenomenon presented by Goethe also perfectly and most satisfactorily meets the requirements regarding the *skieron*" (VC 268), or "in this now we have a complete *a priori* proof of the truth of the Goethean urphenomenon and the correctness of his whole theory of colors, which I ask the reader to consider" (VC, 269). This manner of partial praising, of effusive praising and hyperbole while picking apart the weaknesses of Goethe's work, had specific purposes; Schopenhauer surely realized that Goethe could see through this soupy muddle. A few pages later we find: "my theory compels me to differ from Goethe in just two points, specifically with regard to the true polarity of colours…and with respect to the production of white from colours, for which latter, Goethe never forgave me; however, neither in conversation nor correspondence has he ever advanced an argument against it" (VC, 278).

Clearly, then, Goethe's theory was not wholly correct, and Newton's incorrect theory was not "completely refuted" by Goethe. Schopenhauer must have felt trapped. For one thing, he truly revered Goethe, in the inimitable fashion of Schopenhauerian reverence at least, and the elder had approached him with an agenda that Schopenhauer was honor-bound to respect. He also had to market his theory as compatible and complementary to Goethe's simply to avoid being seen as an upstart, turn-coat, and ingrate. Goethe quickly concluded that Schopenhauer had become an opponent and revealed as much when Schopenhauer published his book, writing to Schultz on July 19, 1816, that he had been betrayed by his disciple.[33] Perhaps Schopenhauer reasoned that as long as the reading public could see him openly praising the master, he could garner their support. The very fact that it never came to an open, public feud or scandal, or to outright banishment by Goethe, suggests Schopenhauer may have been at least partially effective. Furthermore, in order to succeed in becoming "the first" to provide a theory of color, he would have needed Goethe's imprimatur, and this he could clearly not earn by means of rudeness and mockery alone—qualities Schopenhauer enjoyed venting in his writings generally. Where he is strong and assertive, it is in order to "vindicate" himself, just as he had said he would in his letter to Goethe of February 7, 1816.[34] Finally, Schopenhauer knew he was playing the long game, and, just as Goethe has reasoned that it would be useful to have Schopenhauer working on his behalf, the young philosopher calculated that he would need to have Goethe working for him for many decades to come—this turned out to be the case in more ways than one, inasmuch as Goethe never broke the staff over him, Schopenhauer assiduously mined Goethe's literary works for wisdom and illustrative effect, and, toward the end of his days, he revealed himself as an almost fanatic Goethe admirer who surely knew how to profit from his former collaboration and continuing linkage with the Olympian. Fame came late to Schopenhauer, *but it came* nonetheless. Had he burned his bridges with Goethe, it is doubtful indeed whether Germany would have clasped him to her bosom as she did finally in the 1850s and 1860s.

In the late work *Parerga and Paralipomena* (1851) we have another fine example of how Goethe was simultaneously elevated and debased—indeed one of the cleverest, most spiteful yet playful formulations of the Schopenhauer-Goethe conundrum. He embarks on a critical discussion of how excessively objective Goethe had been; instead of explaining, Goethe mostly described things:

> Accordingly the most universal and supreme truth of his entire theory of colour is an explicit, objective fact that he himself quite properly calls *urphenomenon*. With that he considered everything done; a proper "it is so" was for him everywhere the ultimate goal, without his having craved an "it must be so," and indeed this enabled him to mock:
>
> Enter: Philosopher, and lo!
>
> He proves to you it must be so.
>
> Now that is why he was a poet after all and not a philosopher, i.e., not animated or possessed, as you wish, by a striving for the ultimate grounds and the innermost relation of things. And for precisely this reason he had to leave me the best harvest, as gleanings, insofar as the ultimate satisfaction and the key to everything that Goethe teaches are to be found in me alone.   (PP2, 164)

This passage cries out for exegesis as a clue to the intellectual relationship between Schopenhauer and Goethe; indeed, here Schopenhauer proves too clever even for himself. He would have his readers believe that Goethe is mocking the philosophers here in *Faust I*, lines 1928–29, without revealing that the speaker is Mephistopheles, the nihilist, "the spirit which eternally denies" (line 1338). Mephistopheles has disguised himself in Faust's academic regalia in order to take over for him as academic adviser. There is some comic relief in this scene, with Mephisto holding forth on all the available disciplines of study: logic, metaphysics, law, theology, medicine. He finally paints a lurid picture of the medical profession, capturing the student's imagination for the first time with splendid sexual innuendo, thus getting the student to eagerly declare medicine as his major. The serious point of this entire scene, and certainly also of the lines that lampoon the logician (1928–29), is to demonstrate how Mephistopheles and his kind thrive on the undermining of true learning, on the peddling of fake news. As Faust exits, and just before Mephistopheles begins his "advising session," the devil says: "Go, spurn intelligence and science, / Man's lodestar and supreme reliance, / Be furthered by the liar-in-chief / In works of fraud and make-believe, / And I shall have you dead to rights" (lines 1851–1855). These dark sentiments are not Faust's, nor are they Goethe's— Schopenhauer might have known better.

Instead, he uses this masterful passage from *Faust* to first elevate Goethe by display- ing his masterpiece, then to take a poke at him by reminding his philosophical readers that Goethe had been a mere poet—and a disrespectful one at that, daring to mock the philosophers. "Enter" the philosopher Schopenhauer to pick up the gleanings of the poet Goethe, and "lo!"—"the key to everything that Goethe teaches are to be found in me alone." But why does the philosopher boast, at this point, of serving as the poet's heir, as the "key" to the poet's teaching? Surely these gleanings must be precious and con- cealed, or Schopenhauer would not be promising to unlock them for our collective ben- efit as only *he* can. The philosopher appears to suffer from poet envy.[35]

We have taken samples of the different color theories of Goethe and Schopenhauer, as well as analyzed both how Schopenhauer applied his own philosophical system to colors and how at times he articulated his disagreements in a baffling tone of voice. Safranksi reviewed the Lütkehaus book on the Goethe–Schopenhauer correspondence, conclud- ing: "Here we have Schopenhauer in his best moments. And Goethe, too, is entirely himself in this constellation."[36] A closer look at the hole Schopenhauer dug for himself is warranted, since Goethe did what he could to keep the relationship friendly and even-keeled.

In the megaletter, Schopenhauer acknowledges that his phenomena stand solidly and implacably on Goethe's foundation, such that his theory is completely incompatible with Newton's but "corresponds most highly" with Goethe's. Now, he insists, the "publi- cation of my theory must lead to the collapse of Newton's." He draws on his floweriest rhetoric to describe Newton's science as an old fortress under siege by Schopenhauer; he has planted a powerful mine capable of blowing up the whole structure; all he needs is for Goethe to light the fuse—"may you not be deterred," adds Schopenhauer, "if a few of your own siege works, which are superfluous now in any case, might suffer a little damage." The disciple (as seen by Goethe) is here instructing the master on how he, the master, can assist in toppling Newton. Goethe shouldn't be worried about the collateral damage to his own siege works—these aren't needed anymore once Schopenhauer achieves in one swift, powerful stroke what Goethe could never achieve. Observe that here, too, Schopenhauer begins by claiming complete compatibility with Goethe's work, but again ends up demonstrating that Goethe is merely in the way. By the end of the letter, having expended all his fantasies and recriminations, Schopenhauer simply requests that Goethe return the manuscript and inform him as to whether he has shared it with anyone, Dr. Seebeck in particular, because he fears he will be plagiarized.[37] If the manuscript itself had not already convinced Goethe that his new collaborator was in fact a rival, this long, strange letter would have left no doubt.

On November 16, 1815, Goethe responds with the equanimity of a god: "Much indeed, my most esteemed friend, am I thankful to you for desiring by means of your friendly and thorough letter to successfully dispel the distance that separates us. I can only respond partially to it and therefore assure you above all regarding the question: whether anyone has seen your essay? and to this I can sincerely reply: no one!" Because Schopenhauer had disagreed with him regarding the origin of violet, he added to this letter a full page of justifications for his views, in which he also includes a paragraph on the production of white—Schopenhauer was in this sense wrong to claim Goethe never provided him with counter-arguments or explanations. However, the most significant passage in this letter occurs toward the end, before the addendum of explanations for violet, and it merits a closer look. Goethe reiterates that he has an "unconquerable aversion" to becoming involved now in anything remotely related to publicly participating in the color debate, yet he also feels he owes it to Schopenhauer to disclose his views of the work to him: "Whoever is himself inclined to construct the world from the subject, will not reject the observation that the subject, in its phenomenon, is always merely the individual and therefore requires a certain share of truth and error in order to maintain its characteristic. But nothing separates human beings more than the fact that the portions of these two ingredients are mixed according to different proportions."[38] Here Goethe offers an explanation for his response without joining the color debate or providing anything beyond the addendum on violet. Schopenhauer is the one who constructs the world from the subject; he should know that the subject is individual and therefore flawed, an admixture of truth and error. So far, Goethe has merely reminded Schopenhauer to be consistent with his own truths. A second step provides what could be the main reason this "distance" will never be bridged; namely, the proportions of truth and error in individuals vary so much that two individuals may never come to an understanding without obliterating what is characteristic of them or peculiar to them (*Eigenthümlichkeit*). Goethe is signaling again that it is perfectly understandable to allow these differences and distances.[39]

Schopenhauer's elevation of tragedy to the highest form of writing corresponds with the pessimistic worldview, but before we move on from Goethe's classicist, universalist justification of his response to Schopenhauer, a summary of the latter's view on tragedy is provided by Barbara Neymeyr, who outlines the three possibilities for precipitating the great misfortune that leads to catastrophe: extraordinary malice of character, blind fate (chance, error), and, third, the constellation of characters that is conditioned by the intersecting striving wills of individuals. Not surprisingly, Schopenhauer explicitly embraces the third possibility for catastrophe.[40] This makes perfect sense because Schopenhauer knows better than most how frail, limited, and lost we are in the principle of individuation. The other two forces for catastrophe don't possess the individual human factor that so effectively illustrates our futility. When Goethe reminded Schopenhauer in 1815 of how fraught and feckless we are as individuals, he helped to avert a catastrophe in their relationship, such that only a few short years later, Schopenhauer would champion not only tragedy, but conduct a fierce and compelling critique of the individual in relation to the whole. This is Goethe material, for this is what Goethe had been illustrating through *Faust* these many decades; namely, the presence of the universal in the particular.

As one might expect from a polyglot lover of great literature, Schopenhauer's works are replete with quotations, often in the original language, and he used *Faust* in particular to good effect. Schopenhauer seems to use his literary sources as allies to validate his own positions, but he also uses them more authentically to provide examples of specific points he is trying to make—few philosophers are as keen to provide examples generally, and even fewer had his command of literature. So for example when he quotes Goethe's poem *Rechenschaft* (Accountability), it is because the phrase "only scoundrels are modest" directly supports his argument that "the virtue of modesty has only been invented as a weapon against envy." He even cross-references here to WWR1 and explains that the Goethe quote has a predecessor in Cervantes (PP2, 416). We saw a similar dynamic at work in the *Faust* lines exhorting us to "make our own" what we merely inherit from the father (PP2, 18). The didactic component of the Goethe quotes is generally joined with a self-elevating gesture, as if to demonstrate that he and Goethe were like-minded. Neymeyr sees another dimension to these quotes; namely, that he mediates between generalizing abstraction and concrete individual works to provide evidence for his theses. She directs our attention to WWR1 Books 3 and 4 because they contain frequent examples from Goethe's works in order to illustrate matters of aesthetics, the will, and ethics, with a similar pattern in PP.[41] Nietzsche clearly followed Schopenhauer's example in dipping richly into Goethe's works, beginning with *The Birth of Tragedy* but including *Thus Spoke Zarathustra*, in which the intertextuality problematizes Goethe's legacy as a poet (see "On Poets").

Schopenhauer mined Goethe's works in his use of Tasso, the Italian poet-genius depicted in Goethe's tragedy, *Torquato Tasso* (1790), a work with autobiographical overtones stemming from Goethe's life at the court of Weimar-Saxony. Schopenhauer was able to leverage both the proximity of genius and madness and the doomed nature of artistic genius in society in the practical affairs of life.[42] While tragedy was his favorite genre and garnered most of his attention, he was fond of quoting lyric poems and made a point of calling it the "easiest" genre, where a successful effect could be produced by "even someone who is not particularly distinguished." Now we might quibble with Schopenhauer about his explanation for the seemingly "easy" emergence of lyric poems; he attributes this to "some strong, external source of inspiration…because all that is needed for this is a lively intuition of his own state in the moment of exhilaration" (WWR1, 276). Nietzsche was much more convincing in his lyric theory in *The Birth of Tragedy*, pointing out that the lyrist is *least inclined* to be "in his own state" because he has been absorbed, embodied by the primal unity (in Schopenhauerian parlance, his principle of individuation has been disrupted).

Understandably, most Goethe quotes stem from *Faust*, a pattern repeated in writers who invoke Goethe. Neymeyr attributes Schopenhauer's interest to the fact that, as a protagonist, Faust displays prominent features of Schopenhauer's philosophy, and she appears to agree with critics who generally limit his use of *Faust* to Part I.[43] But before we invest too much in the equation of who influenced whom on the question of striving, we should be clear that striving is proto-Goethean material and characteristic of the *Faust* temperament and ethos. Matthew Bell details how Goethe, already in 1801, wrote to Schiller regarding four "constant and irreducible properties of humankind," namely enjoyment, striving, resignation, and habit.[44] Another substantive intellectual link is the existence of the *labyrinth* as metaphor for existence. Schopenhauer speaks in PP2 of "the great herd of the human race" requiring leaders, guides, counselors, and higher types generally, who acquire "an overview of this labyrinth" (PP2, 223). The labyrinth is already stated in *Faust* line 14 of the Dedication, and it is central to Goethe, Schopenhauer, and Nietzsche,[45] as is the importance of higher humans who can survey from high ground.

Stated summarily in terms of affinity, intellectual traits, or inclinations shared by Goethe and Schopenhauer are reliance on intuition versus rational reflection[46]; polarized structure of their works reflecting the polarities in nature[47]; intercultural mediators to the West in matters of Eastern thought and religion[48]; the deduction of scientific comparability from analogous relationships ascertained by a non-neutral (nonobjective) observer[49]; pioneers of life-affirmation on the basis of the critique of idealism and metaphysics; embrace of the open, contradictory, and nonclosure versus a system of absolutes; elaboration of ancient Greek philosophy as a model for opposing modern academic professionalism[50]; and a critical stance vis-à-vis mathematics as a panacea.[51] This list is of course not exhaustive, and additional affinities have already been discussed earlier.

Goethe himself erred in seeing affinity with his scientific views, probably because he raced to engage Schopenhauer as a disciple. Among the real differences between them are that Goethe champions activity while Schopenhauer reveals its futility and opts for asceticism; Schopenhauer ultimately stresses the primacy of philosophy over poetry, whereas Goethe remains open and eclectic[52]; Schopenhauer's subjective turn is at odds with Goethe's realism (VC, xxxix); Schopenhauer's color theory was substantially incompatible with Goethe's, largely because Schopenhauer's views actually aligned better with Newton's[53]; and they differed profoundly in character and temperament, along the axis of life-affirmation versus pessimism.[54]

When Schopenhauer late in life reviewed his collaboration with Goethe, it was important to him to claim that he remained and always had been a champion of Goethe's superior science—he belabors the point, comes across as disingenuous, and persists in claiming that he was correct while Goethe was wrong. We understand why Schopenhauer cherished this relationship. In the end, given his acerbic temperament, his relative isolation, and his very late epiphany as a philosophical authority, one may conclude that Goethe's qualified friendship had been a highpoint. On balance no other thinker or writer of note could claim to have stood up to Goethe while maintaining that revered idol's respect; the brief, fraught partnership remains a consequential encounter of modern intellectual history since it imparted direction to Schopenhauer's work by cementing his self-confidence. He could also suggest that his affinity rested on the fact that both he and Goethe endured silence, indeed were shunned by the critics— Goethe with respect to his color theory, Schopenhauer with respect to his philosophy generally.[55] This counter-current becomes a key feature of the romantic-existential push against the splintering of the modern self, in which the forces of technology and academic specialization appear to be in league with nihilism.

The afterimage of this compelling intellectual relationship can be sketched as follows in its contemporary significance. If it is true that Goethe's *Farbenlehre* made a come-back late in the twentieth century based on its consideration of physiological and psychological aspects of color, this would follow from our aversion or indifference to modern theoretical physics.[56] It would be part of the search for "the qualitative whole-ness of the phenomenon" that Reed admires in Goethe, "which science ought not to dissolve into quantitative abstraction." But Reed appropriately points back to the early twentieth century to highlight the dangers of attacking scientific objectivity and ration-ality: "One need only recall that in 1933 the poet and Nazi fellow-traveler Gottfried Benn, who had pretensions to scientific knowledge, publicly glorified Goethe's science as 'the first rejection of European intellectualism' and of the Newtonian 'objective world' in favour of an 'existential and transcendent world' which alone mattered."[57] More on Reed's point in a moment.

Goethe never flirted with the spirit of fascism, which is in effect the political-ideological triumph of nihilism among the masses; in fact, he warned against it—we saw this in Mephistopheles's remark "Go, spurn intelligence and science" (line 1851). When Goethe takes up this theme again in Part II he introduces Baccalaureus, a character now based on Schopenhauer, enabling Mephistopheles to reprise his role as professor. *Baccalaureus is the same student* Mephistopheles "advised" as a freshman; now brash, confident, disrespectful, utterly full of himself: "One who is thirty years or over / Already is as good as dead / It would be best if you were put away" (lines 6787–89). The student speaks thus to the professor (Mephistopheles) to illustrate how Mephistopheles's nihilism corrupts minds, how youth in particular can be deluded into thinking "the world was not, until I made it be" (line 6794), an allusion to Schopenhauer's subjectivism.[58] It is one thing for Goethe to critique the fragmenting effect of science; it is quite another to condemn science outright. Goethe is placing the spirit of Schopenhauer under the negating aegis of Mephistopheles. For any who might doubt whether Schopenhauer could harbor sympathies of this kind, a telling passage is: "Between the spirit of Graeco-Roman paganism and that of Christianity the real contrast is that of affirmation and negation of the will to life, according to which, in the final analysis, Christianity is basically right" (PP2, 282). Here "negation" is the called-for response, not Faustian-Goethean affirmation of life. Goethe concluded as did Nietzsche, but a good half century sooner: the "ultimate yes-sayer" to life later condemned Schopenhauer's denial of life as "a paradigm of nihilism."[59]

Now let us pick up the thread of T. J. Reed's observation regarding the historical consequences of denying science. For Goethe it is not a matter of denying science per se, only how science gets done and to what uses it is put. He did not refute Newtonian theory, but he did shatter its claim to irrefutability.[60] Science and scientific method were two activities embraced by both Goethe and Schopenhauer—the whole color theory debate reinforces this point—yet they remained far apart as individuals. The binding tie between them is science: it is the arena in which they contested their theories and communicated with one another despite serious differences. While our information-overloaded society struggles to find direction, as our youth, absorbed by insidious hand-held devices, learn to navigate the labyrinth of information and misinformation under the "guidance" of glib nihilists who claim it's all one and the same—the tumultuous intellectual relationship between Goethe and Schopenhauer serves as a parable, as a warning, as a beacon—good, smart people can agree on the sublime value of science even as they disagree on whether the ultimate laurels belong to literature or to thought.

Notes

1. Friedrich Nietzsche, *Vom Nutzen und Nachteil der Historie für das Leben*, in *Friedrich Nietzsche: Sämtliche Werke. Kritische Studienausgabe in 15 Einzelbänden*, edited by Giorgio Colli and Mazzino Montinari (Berlin: Walter de Gruyter, 1988), vol. 1, 245. Translations from German are my own, except for Schopenhauer who is quoted from the Cambridge University Press editions, edited by Christopher Janaway, and Goethe's *Faust* in English, quoted from the Arndt translation. These words are from Goethe's letter to Schiller on December 19, 1789.
2. Paul F. H. Lauxtermann, "Schopenhauer's Color Theory," in *A Companion to Schopenhauer*, edited by Bart Vandenabeele. (Oxford: Blackwell, 2012), 63.
3. William Wordsworth, "The Tables Turned," in *The Norton Anthology of English Literature* (3rd edition), edited by M. H. Abrams (New York: W. W. Norton & Company, 1975), 1371.
4. Ludger Lütkehaus, ed., *Arthur Schopenhauer. Der Briefwechsel mit Goethe und andere Dokumente zur Farbenlehre* (Zürich: Haffmans Verlag, 1992), 84. See also Adrian Del Caro, *Grounding the Nietzsche Rhetoric of Earth* (Berlin: Walter de Gruyter, 2004), 298–300, where Bacon's "new language" of nature exploitation is discussed.
5. Lauxtermann, "Schopenhauer's Color Theory," 64; Lütkehaus, *Arthur Schopenhauer*, 79, 84, 80.
6. Matthew Bell, *Goethe's Naturalistic Anthropology: Man and Other Plants* (Oxford: Clarendon Press, 1994), 267, 289.
7. Rüdiger Safranski, *Schopenhauer und Die wilden Jahre der Philosophie. Eine Biographie* (München: Carl Hanser Verlag, 1987), 268–69.
8. Niklas Sommer, "Der physiologische Idealismus. Die Apologie der Farbenlehre," in *Schopenhauer und Goethe. Biographische und philosophische Perspektiven*, edited by Daniel Schubbe and Søren R. Fauth (Hamburg: Felix Meiner Verlag, 2016), 359.
9. Lauxtermann, "Schopenhauer's Color Theory," 63.
10. Lütkehaus, *Arthur Schopenhauer*, 81–82.
11. Lauxtermann, "Schopenhauer's Color Theory," 63.

12. Lütkehaus, *Arthur Schopenhauer*, 79. The title of the critical essay that accompanies the letters is *Who/Whom Sees the Light… The Deeds and Sorrows of the Color Teachers* (Wer/ Wen das Licht sieht…Die Taten und Leiden der Farbenlehrer), emphasizing the diametrically opposed views of the two: for Goethe, the light sees us, sees all, and is primary; for Schopenhauer, we see light. The subtitle, in turn, shifts the emphasis away from theory (*Lehre*) to teachers (*Lehrer*) because the teachers do battle and suffer here. The subtitle is also reminiscent of Goethe's *The Sorrows of Young Werther* (Die Leiden des jungen Werther). Lütkehaus also points out that Schopenhauer's sister Adele was allowed to call Goethe "father" (p. 81). Here I thank Robert Wicks for reminding me, since my essay begins with Nietzsche, that Wagner was the same age as Nietzsche's deceased father, creating a parallel to the Schopenhauer–Goethe case, whereby father figures were simultaneously embraced and resisted by prodigal sons.

13. Safranski, *Schopenhauer*, 278.

14. Christopher Janaway, *Schopenhauer* (Oxford: Oxford University Press, 1994), 5.

15. Wolfgang Wittkowski, "Goethe and Schopenhauer: A Phenomenology of the Final Vision in *Faust II*," *Analecta Husserliana* 37 (1991), 383–408, 385.

16. Michael Dirrigl, *Goethe und Schopenhauer. Mit zwei Exkursen: Giacomo Leopardi— August Graf von Platen-Hallermünde. Ein Vademecum für Wahlverwandte* (Regensburg: Universitätsverlag Regensburg, 2000), 11–12.

17. Lütkehaus, *Arthur Schopenhauer*, 10.

18. Ibid., 15–18.

19. Ibid., 20–23.

20. Ibid., 33.

21. Johann Wolfgang von Goethe, *Faust. A Tragedy*, translated by Walter Arndt, edited by Cyrus Hamlin (2nd edition). (New York: W. W. Norton, 2001), 20. This translation will be quoted henceforth in parentheses by line number.

22. Lütkehaus, *Arthur Schopenhauer*, 80. By contrast: though Goethe was able to respond with mildness and composure to young Schopenhauer, Wagner had greeted Nietzsche's attempt in 1876 to engage him for Brahms's *Triumphlied* with "fuming rage." See Curt Paul Janz, *Friedrich Nietzsche Biographie*. 3 vols. (Munich: Carl Hanser Verlag, 1978), vol. 1, 585.

23. Safranski, *Schopenhauer*, 278.

24. Ibid., 275–76, also Arthur G. Zajonc, "Facts as Theory: Aspects of Goethe's Philosophy of Science," in *Goethe and the Sciences: A Reappraisal*, edited by Frederick Amrine, Francis J. Zucker, and Harvey Wheeler. (Boston: D. Reidel Publishing Company, 1987), 240; 219–45.

25. Johann Wolfgang von Goethe. *Naturwissenschaftliche Schriften* in *Goethes Werke. Hamburger Ausgabe in 14 Bänden*, edited by Dorothea Kuhn, Vol. XIII (Hamburg: Christian Wegner Verlag, 1955), 323.

26. Gernot Böhme, "Is Goethe's Theory of Color Science?," in *Goethe and the Sciences: A Reappraisal*, edited by Frederick Amrine, Francis J. Zucker, and Harvey Wheeler (Boston: D. Reidel Publishing Company, 1987), 151.

27. Lauxtermann, "Schopenhauer's Color Theory," 61.

28. Douglas E. Miller, "Goethe's Color Studies in a New Perspective" in *Goethe and the Sciences: A Reappraisal*, edited by Frederick Amrine, Francis J. Zucker, and Harvey Wheeler (Boston: D. Reidel Publishing Company, 1987), 102; 101–12.

29. Lauxtermann, "Schopenhauer's Color Theory," 67.

30. Gernot Böhme, "Is Goethe's Theory of Color Science?" 148, 154, 170; 147–73.

31. Frederick Amrine, *Goethe and the Sciences*, 432.

32. T. J. Reed, *Goethe* (Oxford: Oxford University Press, 1984), 48.

33. Frederick Burwick, *The Damnation of Newton*, 68.

34. Lütkehaus, *Arthur Schopenhauer*, 33. But "vindicate" was really too strong a word: Goethe had not done anything to damage Schopenhauer at this point, so if he suffered any injured pride or reputation, then only in his own mind. This choice of words reveals how obsessed Schopenhauer had become with being right, with receiving his due.

35. Barbara Neymeyr ("Das 'Labyrinth des Lebens' im Spiegel der Literatur. Zur exemplarischen Funktion der *Faust*-Tragödie und anderer Werke Goethes in Schopenhauers Ästhetik und Willensmetaphysik," in *Schopenhauer und Goethe*, 299–335) briefly discusses this misreading or deliberate obfuscation of the *Faust* lines, stressing that "one must differentiate on principle between the credo of the author and the speeches of the characters in his work" (317).

36. Safranski, "Du bist mein lieber Sohn," *ZeitOnline* (1993 10 September), http://www.zeit. de/1993/37/du-bist-mein-lieber-sohn/komplettansicht. Accessed July 11, 2016.

37. Lütkehaus, *Arthur Schopenhauer*, 21–22, 24.

38. Ibid., 26.

39. Goethe makes this quite clear in his final letter of January 28, 1816, when he writes: "And so I saw all too clearly then that it would be a futile effort for us to try to come to a mutual understanding" (Lütkehaus, *Arthur Schopenhauer*, 42). Safranski (*Schopenhauer*) offers that, in order for their relationship to remain in balance, Schopenhauer felt he had to have something in which he surpassed his father figure: "Arthur wants to earn his blessing by proving that he can give something to the 'father.' But Goethe does not submit to the demand for such fatherhood, how could he, given that he could only tolerate even his real son in the role of secretary" 285.

40. Neymeyr, "Das 'Labyrinth,'" 314.

41. Ibid., 304.

42. Ibid., 306–07; she also points to several inconsistencies in Schopenhauer's lyric theory and his improper use of Goethe's poems as examples thereof, 310–11.

43. Ibid., 316. Wittkowski, "Goethe and Schopenhauer," also lays emphasis on the futile striving of Faust, implying a direct borrowing from Schopenhauer and a close reading of WWR that most critics dispute.

44. Matthew Bell, *Goethe's Naturalistic Anthropology: Man and Other Plants* (Oxford: Clarendon Press, 1994), 265.

45. See Adrian Del Caro, "Margarete-Ariadne: Faust's Labyrinth," *Goethe-Yearbook* 18 (2011), 223–43; and Neymeyr, "Das 'Labyrinth,'" 319.

46. Daniel Schubbe, "'Gegengewicht im Zeitgeist'. Schopenhauer, Goethe und die Polarität des Denkens: Zur Einleitung des Bandes," in *Schopenhauer und Goethe. Biographische und philosophische Perspektiven*, edited by Daniel Schubbe and Søren R. Fauth (Hamburg: Felix Meiner Verlag, 2016), 14.

47. Ibid., 17.

48. Thomas Regehly, "'Licht aus dem Osten'. Wechsellektüren im Zeichen des *Westöstlichen Divans* und anderer Werke Goethes und Schopenhauers," in *Schopenhauer und Goethe. Biographische und philosophische Perspektiven*, edited by Daniel Schubbe and Søren R. Fauth (Hamburg: Felix Meiner Verlag, 2016), 82–83.

49. Steffen W. Lange. "Lebendiges Wort? Schopenhauers und Goethes Anschauungen von Sprache im Vergleich" in *Schopenhauer und Goethe. Biographische und philosophische*

Perspektiven, edited by Daniel Schubbe and Søren R. Fauth (Hamburg: Felix Meiner Verlag, 2016), 197.

50. Alexander Roth, "Das Dynamische," in *Schopenhauer und Goethe. Biographische und philosophische Perspektiven*, edited by Daniel Schubbe and Søren R. Fauth (Hamburg: Felix Meiner Verlag, 2016), 204, 209, 215.

51. Lauxtermann, "Schopenhauer's Color Theory," 63.

52. Wittkowski, "Goethe and Schopenhauer," 393; Neymeyr, "Das 'Labyrinth,'" 317.

53. Lütkehaus, *Arthur Schopenhauer*, 83, 87–90, 95; Brigitte Scheer, "Goethes und Schopenhauers Ansichten vom Verhältnis zwischen Wissenschaft und Kunst," in *Schopenhauer und Goethe. Biographische und philosophische Perspektiven*, edited by Daniel Schubbe and Søren R. Fauth (Hamburg: Felix Meiner Verlag, 2016) 143; Theda Rehbock, "Hat Schopenhauer Goethes Farbenlehre verstanden?," in *Schopenhauer und Goethe*, 371.

54. I tend to agree with Roth, "Das Dynamische," that, despite Schopenhauer's pessimism, his capacity to direct human striving and to embrace the quality of personal experience through art and meditation positions him in the counter-current to rationalist alienation and modern fragmentation of the self, 204, 212, 214.

55. Lütkehaus, *Arthur Schopenhauer*, 60.

56. Dennis L. Sepper, "Goethe Against Newton: Towards Saving the Phenomenon," in *Goethe and the Sciences: A Reappraisal*, edited by Frederick Amrine, Francis J. Zucker, and Harvey Wheeler (Boston: D. Reidel Publishing Company, 1987), 175.

57. Reed, *Goethe*, 50, 52.

58. Lütkehaus, *Arthur Schopenhauer*, 97, 103.

59. Ken Gemes and Christopher Janaway, "Life-Denial versus Life-Affirmation: Schopenhauer and Nietzsche on Pessimism and Asceticism," in *A Companion to Schopenhauer*, 289.

60. Theda Rehbock, "Hat Schopenhauer Goethes Farbenlehre verstanden?", 371.

FURTHER READING

Allert, Beate. "'*Trübe*' as the Source of New Color Formations in Goethe's Late Works *Entoptische Farben* (1817–20) and *Chromatik* (1822)." *Goethe Yearbook* 19 (2012): 29–47.

Amrine, Frederick, Francis J. Zucker, Harvey Wheeler, eds., *Goethe and the Sciences: A Reappraisal*. Boston: D. Reidel Publishing Company, 1987.

Bell, Matthew. *Goethe's Naturalistic Anthropology: Man and Other Plants*. Oxford: Clarendon Press, 1994.

Böhme, Gernot. "Is Goethe's Theory of Color Science?" In *Goethe and the Sciences: A Reappraisal*, edited by Frederick Amrine, Francis J. Zucker, and Harvey Wheeler. Boston: D. Reidel Publishing Company, 1987, 147–73.

Burwick, Frederick. *The Damnation of Newton: Goethe's Color Theory and Romantic Perception*. Berlin: Walter de Gruyter, 1986.

Cartwright, David E. *Schopenhauer: A Biography*. Cambridge University Press, 2010.

Del Caro, Adrian. *Grounding the Nietzsche Rhetoric of Earth*. Berlin: Walter de Gruyter, 2004.

Del Caro, Adrian. "Margarete-Ariadne: Faust's Labyrinth." *Goethe-Yearbook* 18 (2011): 223–43.

Dirrigl, Michael. *Goethe und Schopenhauer. Mit zwei Exkursen: Giacomo Leopardi—August Graf von Platen-Hallermünde. Ein Vademecum für Wahlverwandte*. Regensburg: Universitätsverlag Regensburg, 2000.

Gemes, Ken, and Christopher Janaway. "Life-Denial Versus Life-Affirmation: Schopenhauer and Nietzsche on Pessimism and Asceticism." In *A Companion to Schopenhauer*. Oxford: Wiley-Blackwell, 280–99.

Goethe, Johann Wolfgang von. *Faust. A Tragedy*, translated by Walter Arndt and edited by Cyrus Hamlin (2nd edition). New York: W. W. Norton, 2001.

Goethe, Johann Wolfgang von. *Naturwissenschaftliche Schriften* in *Goethes Werke. Hamburger Ausgabe in 14 Bänden*, edited by Dorothea Kuhn. Vol. XIII. Hamburg: Christian Wegner Verlag, 1955.

Janaway, Christopher. *Schopenhauer*. Oxford: Oxford University Press, 1994.

Janz, Curt Paul. *Friedrich Nietzsche Biography*. 3 vols. Munich: Hanser, 1978.

Lange, Steffen W. "Lebendiges Wort? Schopenhauers und Goethes Anschauungen von Sprache im Vergleich." In *Schopenhauer und Goethe. Biographische und philosophische Perspektiven*, edited by Daniel Schubbe and Søren R. Fauth. Hamburg: Felix Meiner Verlag, 2016, 184–98.

Lauxtermann, Paul F. H. "Hegel and Schopenhauer as Partisans of Goethe's Theory of Color." *Journal of the History of Ideas* 51, no. 4 (1990): 599–624.

Lauxtermann, Paul. F. H. "Schopenhauer's Color Theory." In *A Companion to Schopenhauer*, edited by Bart Vandenabeele. Oxford: Wiley-Blackwell, 60–69.

Lütkehaus, Ludger, ed. *Arthur Schopenhauer. Der Briefwechsel mit Goethe und andere Dokumente zur Farbenlehre*. Zürich: Haffmans Verlag, 1992.

Miller, Barbara L. "'He' Had Me at Blue: Color and Visual Art." *Leonardo* 47, no. (2014): 461–65.

Miller, Douglas E. "Goethe's Color Studies in a New Perspective." In *Goethe and the Sciences: A Reappraisal*, edited by Frederick Amrine, Francis J. Zucker, and Harvey Wheeler. Boston: D. Reidel Publishing Company, 1987, 101–12.

Neymeyr, Barbara. "Das 'Labyrinth des Lebens' im Spiegel der Literatur. Zur exemplarischen Funktion der *Faust*-Tragödie und anderer Werke Goethes in Schopenhauers Ästhetik und Willensmetaphysik." In *Schopenhauer und Goethe. Biographische und philosophische Perspektiven*, edited by Daniel Schubbe and Søren R. Fauth. Hamburg: Felix Meiner Verlag, 2016, 299–335.

Nietzsche, Friedrich. "Vom Nutzen und Nachteil der Historie für das Leben." In *Friedrich Nietzsche: Sämtliche Werke. Kritische Studienausgabe in 15 Einzelbänden, Vol. 1*, edited by Giorgio Colli and Mazzino Montinari. Berlin: Walter de Gruyter, 1988.

Reed, T. J. *Goethe*. Oxford: Oxford University Press, 1984.

Regehly, Thomas. "'Licht aus dem Osten.' Wechsellektüren im Zeichen des *Westöstlichen Divans* und anderer Werke Goethes und Schopenhauers." In *Schopenhauer und Goethe. Biographische und philosophische Perspektiven*, edited by Daniel Schubbe and Søren R. Fauth. Hamburg: Felix Meiner Verlag, 2016, 59–97.

Rehbock, Theda. "Hat Schopenhauer Goethes Farbenlehre Verstanden?" In *Schopenhauer und Goethe. Biographische und philosophische Perspektiven*, edited by Daniel Schubbe and Søren R. Fauth. Hamburg: Felix Meiner Verlag, 2016, 371–408.

Roth, Alexander. "Das Dynamische der Erkenntnis. Goethe, Schopenhauer und die Anfänge der Lebensphilosophie." In *Schopenhauer und Goethe. Biographische und philosophische Perspektiven*, edited by Daniel Schubbe and Søren R. Fauth. Hamburg: Felix Meiner Verlag, 2016, 199–222.

Safranski, Rüdiger. "Du bist mein lieber Sohn," *ZeitOnline* (1993, 10 September). http://www.zeit.de/1993/37/du-bist-mein-lieber-sohn/komplettansicht. Accessed July 11, 2016.

Safranski, Rüdiger. *Schopenhauer und Die wilden Jahre der Philosophie. Eine Biographie.* München: Carl Hanser Verlag, 1987.

Schubbe, Daniel, and Søren R. Fauth, eds. *Schopenhauer und Goethe. Biographische und philosophische Perspektiven.* Hamburg: Felix Meiner Verlag, 2016.

Schubbe, Daniel. "'Gegengewicht im Zeitgeist'. Schopenhauer, Goethe und die Polarität des Denkens: Zur Einleitung des Bandes." In *Schopenhauer und Goethe. Biographische und philosophische Perspektiven*, edited by Daniel Schubbe and Søren R. Fauth. Hamburg: Felix Meiner Verlag, 2016, 11–28.

Sepper, Dennis L. "Goethe Against Newton: Towards Saving the Phenomenon." In *Goethe and the Sciences: A Reappraisal*, edited by Frederick Amrine, Francis J. Zucker, and Harvey Wheeler. Boston: D. Reidel Publishing Company, 1987, 175–93.

Sommer, Niklas. "Der physiologische Idealismus. Die Apologie der Farbenlehre." In *Schopenhauer und Goethe. Biographische und philosophische Perspektiven*, edited by Daniel Schubbe and Søren R. Fauth. Hamburg: Felix Meiner Verlag, 2016, 351–70.

Vandenabeele, Bart, ed. *A Companion to Schopenhauer.* Oxford: Blackwell, 2012.

Wicks, Robert. *Schopenhauer.* Oxford: Blackwell, 2008.

Wittkowski, Wolfgang. "Goethe and Schopenhauer: A Phenomenology of the Final Vision in *Faust II*." *Analecta Husserliana* 37 (1991): 383–408.

Wordsworth, William. "The Tables Turned." In *The Norton Anthology of English Literature* (3rd edition), edited by M. H. Abrams. New York: W. W. Norton & Company, 1975, 1371.

Zajonc, Arthur G. "Facts as Theory: Aspects of Goethe's Philosophy of Science." In *Goethe and the Sciences: A Reappraisal*, edited by Frederick Amrine, Francis J. Zucker, and Harvey Wheeler. Boston: D. Reidel Publishing Company, 1987, 219–45.

CHAPTER 2

KARL CHRISTIAN FRIEDRICH KRAUSE'S INFLUENCE ON SCHOPENHAUER'S PHILOSOPHY

BENEDIKT PAUL GÖCKE

ARTHUR Schopenhauer and Karl Christian Friedrich Krause shared the same address in Dresden from Michaelmas 1815 to September 1818. Although Krause is not mentioned in Schopenhauer's *oeuvre*, Schopenhauer is mentioned a few times both in Krause's diary and in some of the letters and notes written by his sons, Karl Erasmus and Wilhelm. These notes indicate that Krause and Schopenhauer had intense discussions concerning their systems of philosophy, the importance of Indian philosophy, Plato, and Kant. Since the fundamental architecture of Krause's system of philosophy did not change substantially during Krause's life, these discussions must have been quite useful to Schopenhauer who, at the time, was working on *The World as Will and Representation*. Because Krause complained in 1821 that *The World as Will and Representation* contained ideas Schopenhauer had been informed about by Krause in 1817, and because Schopenhauer's system of philosophy reveals an astonishing similarity to Krause's panentheistic philosophy at the center of which is not *Will*, but *Essence*, it is plausible to assume that Krause influenced Schopenhauer in a significant way.

2.1 Who Was Karl Christian Friedrich Krause?

Karl Christian Friedrich Krause was born on May 6, 1781, in Eisenberg, Thuringia, seven years before Schopenhauer's birth in 1788.[1] He enrolled at the University of Jena in 1797, where he heard lectures by Jacobi, Fichte, Schelling, and Schlegel.[2] He was awarded the degree of Doctor of Philosophy in 1801, and, in 1802, he passed his *Habilitation* with the work *De philosophiae et matheseos notione et earum intima conjunctione*. In the next two years, Krause offered lectures in logic, natural law, and pure mathematics. Even though these lectures had not been announced in advance, he found an audience for all of them.

In 1804, Krause left Jena and briefly settled in Rudolstadt—the city in which Schopenhauer would later write his PhD thesis in 1813. In April 1805, Krause moved to Dresden, where he needed to keep himself afloat through giving private lessons. He worked on writings about Freemasonry, sculpture, philosophy, architecture, painting, music, the natural sciences, mathematics, geography, politics, society, ethics, natural law, and linguistics.[3] Although today these topics are classified as independent areas of science, it was clear to Krause that together they make up a single science: "That I am dealing with all sorts of things, is my psychological motivation. It is nothing without unity, and there is nothing here that is not necessary to my main work, the system. I have still not exhausted this wealth of knowledge, and I cannot do anything else."[4]

Krause's residence in Dresden was not of long duration. After just a few years he moved to Tharandt and remained there for several months before moving to Berlin in December 1813. However, after some seeming initial success at von Humboldt University, he failed to obtain a permanent position and moved back to Dresden in 1815. Since, again, he could not obtain a permanent position, Krause moved to Göttingen in 1823, to make a fresh start. After initial success at the University of Göttingen, however, the number of students attending his lectures was below his expectations and the intellectual climate at the university wore him out. Krause often looked back with nostalgia at the beginning of his career in Jena.

> If I had not withdrawn from university teaching in the year 1804, or had even just remained vigorous and up to date as a writer, I would now be in a position of outstanding effectiveness, which certainly a Fries or a Hegel . . . would not know how to see beyond.[5]

Krause's difficult situation was exacerbated by an awkward political mishap, when he was unjustly suspected of having been involved in the Göttingen student and civil rebellion January 8–16, 1831. To spare Krause being prosecuted by the police and the legal authorities, and because Krause had long planned to leave Göttingen, he was asked, as an ultimatum, to do so immediately. Krause obeyed and moved to Munich, where he had as little prospect of a secure existence as in Göttingen. He stood without bread or wages and had to begin to sell his books and pawn other property.

In the shock of his life, he was forced by a police decree to leave Munich on March 17, 1832. It was thrown at him that he acted with depravity toward the students who were affiliated to him.[6] However, due to the intervention of, among others, Franz von Baader, the king lifted the expulsion order and Krause was allowed to stay in Munich. On September 27, 1832, Karl Christian Friedrich Krause died impoverished and without, in his own lifetime, being able to bring about the good he had hoped: to lead humanity to a better future through philosophy.

Krause left an impressive *oeuvre* of 256 books and articles, covering most branches of philosophy, the humanities, and science.[7] Through his pupil Julián Sanz del Río he has gained considerable popularity in Spain and Latin America, where his philosophy goes by the name "Krausismo" (Krausism), and, next to Alexander von Humboldt, he is sometimes claimed as the greatest German thinker.[8]

In recent Anglo-Saxon philosophy, he is known mainly for devising the term "pan-entheism."[9] Apart from this slight fame, anglophone understanding of Krause is impressionistic, contains mistakes, and is incomplete. For example, it is said that his philosophy is "mystical and spiritualistic,"[10] that he was "an obscure...figure"[11] who "expressed himself in an artificial and often unfathomable vocabulary which included... monstrous neologisms...which are untranslatable into German, let alone English."[12] It is said that he was "under the influence...of Schelling"[13] and "a student of Hegel."[14]

However, it is straightforwardly false that Krause was a student of Hegel[15] or that, apart from his first years as a student in Jena, he was under the influence of Schelling,[16] and it is inadequate to characterize his philosophy as mystical or obscure. One might wonder how such statements could be justified, given that there are no English translations of Krause's relevant works, and even the German works are hardly ever cited.

2.2 KRAUSE AND SCHOPENHAUER IN DRESDEN

According to Robert Wicks,[17] Krause and Schopenhauer might have crossed paths in Berlin in 1812–1813: "Krause and Schopenhauer were both at the University of Berlin in 1812–13, were involved in philosophical studies at the university and were connected to Fichte as either present or former students." However, although it is true that both Krause and Schopenhauer were students of Fichte at different times, it is unlikely that they met in Berlin in 1812–1813. This is not supported but rather denied by the available historical sources: Schopenhauer left Berlin on May 2, 1813,[18] whereas Krause moved to Berlin from Tharandt, in the hope of starting a career at von Humboldt University, not before December 15, 1813.[19] Because Krause did not obtain a permanent position in Berlin, and after Fichte's death was not elected as Fichte's successor, he saw no more future for himself in Berlin and moved back to Dresden around Michaelmas 1815.

Krause settled at the Große Meißnische Gasse.[20] This house was not only within walking distance of the *Japanischer Palais*, in which the Royal Library with its collection of Indian and Asiatic Philosophy was accommodated and where the Masonic lodge *Asträa* held their meetings, but, for our purpose most interestingly, it was also the home of Arthur Schopenhauer, who had been living there since April 1814.[21]

While Schopenhauer lived the quiet life of a bachelor, Krause moved in with his wife Amalie and nine children. One can imagine that the Große Meißnische Gasse 35 suddenly was livelier, and maybe this was too much trouble and noise for Schopenhauer: we know that from 1816 onward, he rented a second flat in Dresden, in the Ostra-Allee 897, without giving up his flat in the Große Meißnische Gasse 35.[22] Schopenhauer was therefore in the comfortable position of being able to freely choose whether to stay in the house with Krause, close to the Royal Library, or to stay in his second flat in a quieter part of town where he mainly worked on his *The World as Will and Representation*.[23]

Krause and Schopenhauer's shared time in the Große Meißnische Gasse ended when Schopenhauer traveled to Italy on September 24, 1818, and was only interrupted once, by Krause's journey to Italy from Easter 1817 to January 1818. When Schopenhauer returned from Italy in 1819, he did not come back to the flat in the Große Meißnische Gasse and started to live exclusively in the Ostra-Allee 897 until he left Dresden in 1819 to pick up his new position in Berlin. Meanwhile Krause also decided to move into a more affordable flat in a house in the Reitbahngasse in Dresden, where he stayed until he moved to Göttingen in 1823.[24]

Although we do not know about their personal contact after 1818, we know that, during their shared time in the Große Meißnische Gasse, Krause and Schopenhauer had intense conversations and saw each other on a regular basis. As Cartwright states, "Schopenhauer was naturally drawn to [Krause]..., due to their mutual passion for mysticism and Eastern thought."[25]

We know that they exchanged books. This is witnessed by a letter written by Krause's son Karl Erasmus on September 22, 1818: "Schopenhauer has fetched his book on Saturday, and wanted to come back on Monday to speak to you, but will now be gone."[26]

We know that Schopenhauer visited Krause to join the audience of some of the lectures Krause delivered in his flat to his friends and family. This is shown by the lecture notes composed by Krause's son, Wilhelm. He mentions the following: "Beautiful prose arises verbally in beautiful society, but one must not be too methodical and pedantic. Schlegel says that one should not speak like a book, and that is true, e.g. Schopenhauer."[27] As Riedel states, this note refers to one of Krause's private lectures on Schlegel and only makes sense if Krause's son in fact listened to Schopenhauer quite often, who thus must have been present on a regular basis: "It was only appropriate when Krause's children in fact had heard Schopenhauer several times, and this was probably not long ago, otherwise the example would not have been recommended by experience."[28]

Third, we know that both philosophers took an immense interest in Indian philosophy and stayed at the Royal Library for several hours per day.[29] As Riedel argues,

> ...when [Krause] again crossed Schopenhauer's path before or in the Japanese Palais, the only two philosophers in Dresden who were looking for India with their

soul, had to come into conversation with each other. Both were deeply impressed by the Upanishads that had been published under the title *Oupnekhat* by Anquetil Duperron in Latin based on a Persian translation.[30]

Furthermore, since Krause could read Sanskrit and since he was reading and collecting books on Indian philosophy from as early as 1807, it is likely that "through Krause's private library Schopenhauer became acquainted with Sanskrit originals and their recent translations."[31]

2.3 HISTORICAL EVIDENCE FOR KRAUSE'S INFLUENCE ON SCHOPENHAUER

Based on the fact that they knew each other quite well, it is surprising that Cartwright assumes that "Krause's philosophy itself probably was outside Schopenhauer's philosophical concerns."[32] This is surprising because quite the contrary seems to be the case. As Wicks states, "it is difficult to avoid speculating that Krause significantly influenced Schopenhauer and that his presence in Dresden affected the philosophical outlook Schopenhauer expressed in *The World as Will and Representation*."[33]

Two considerations speak in favor of the assumption that Schopenhauer himself did not significantly influence Krause: we know that the architecture and insights of Krause's panentheistic system of philosophy were already formulated and expressed in Krause's lectures as early as 1803–1806. Although the final expression of his system of philosophy was published as late as 1828, as his *Vorlesungen über das System der Philosophie*, the system itself had changed only in terminology and detail. As Krause himself remarks in 1827: "I am convinced that my system of philosophy, which I presented as an academic teacher in Jena as early as 1803–1804, and on which I have since been working without a change of structure, will contribute to the solution of the [task of philosophy]."[34]

Furthermore, before he met Schopenhauer in 1815, Krause was already aware of the importance of Indian philosophy and, in 1816, stated clearly that in his view Indian philosophy contains the main insights of philosophy.

> It was not until 1815 that I began to read mystical writings…and in 1807 partly *Oupnekhat*. It is remarkable how many images and doctrines and true propositions, which I have previously found for myself, and, to a greater extent, clearer and better, I also found in the mystics, for example, in *Oupnekhat*.[35]

Since Schopenhauer started reading the *Oupnekhat* probably not before 1814,[36] and since there is no revision but instead a continuous development of Krause's thinking during the years 1815–1818, it is implausible to assume that Schopenhauer himself did have significant impact on Krause's thinking, either in respect to his philosophical system or in respect to his stance on the importance of Indian philosophy.

That Krause in turn most likely had significant influence on Schopenhauer can be reconstructed from some of Krause's remarks on the importance of Indian philosophy. On January 11th, 1819, Krause wrote the following:

> That the reunion of the European people with the Indians and with Indian philosophy and art would cause a more important change…than the so-called restoration of the sciences after the conquest of Constantinople by the Turks, I had already thought of in 1807 and even clearer in 1814 and 1815, where I obtained even more exact knowledge of Indian books.[37]

Although Krause wrote this after 1818 (i.e., after his time with Schopenhauer), he may be relied upon since he already was aware of the importance of Indian philosophy in 1807: Krause was convinced that important philosophical insights could be found in Indian philosophy, and, in fact, he considered his own system of philosophy to be the first to relate them to philosophical insights of Plato and Kant.[38]

Since we know that Krause and Schopenhauer met frequently to discuss philosophical matters, it is hard to avoid speculating that in their discussions Krause not only stated *what* he thought about Indian philosophy, Plato, and Kant, but also expressed quite explicitly the reasons *why* he considered it necessary to establish a system of philosophy that unites Indian philosophy with the insights provided by Plato and Kant, and *why*, in his eyes, the system of philosophy he worked on was the first that truly achieved this task. In other words, Krause will have acquainted Schopenhauer with the structure of his (Krause's) panentheistic system of philosophy, its distinguishing features, and the arguments speaking in its favor. If this is true, then Schopenhauer, who back then was working on *The World as Will and Representation*, must have been quite aware of the structure of Krause's panentheism and the arguments in its favor.

However, and this is exciting, on February 4, 1821, after reading *The World as Will and Representation*, Krause complained that Schopenhauer had taken over his ideas and published them as his own. To his comment on the importance of Indian philosophy, he added the following remark: "I gave this thought to Dr. Schopenhauer in 1817, who has now printed this in his book *The World as Will and Representation*."[39] For someone like Krause, this comes as close to an accusation of plagiarism as it gets.[40] And indeed, Krause must have been surprised to find himself not even mentioned when, for instance, he read what Schopenhauer wrote in his *opus magnum* in August 1818:

> If [the reader] has shared in the benefits of the *Vedas*, access to which, opened to us by the *Upanishads*, is in my view the greatest advantage which this still young century has to show over previous centuries, since I surmise that the influence of Sanskrit literature will penetrate no less deeply than did the revival of Greek literature in the fifteenth century [that is, through the conquest of Constantinople in 1453]; if, I say, the reader has also already received and assimilated the divine inspiration of ancient Indian wisdom, then he is best of all prepared to hear what I have to say to him. (WWR1$_{[P]}$, xv)

Although, then, Krause recognized some of his ideas in Schopenhauer's *The World as Will and Representation*, he did not consider Schopenhauer's system of philosophy to be an adequate unification of Plato and Kant with Indian philosophy. As Krause noted in December 1819, he considered Schopenhauer's system as only containing the seed of truth.

> Brahmanism has attracted half-scientific minds that are on their way to obtain a full intuition of fundamental reality, but to them it is still a pitfall leading to unjustified propositions,... like it is for Schopenhauer.[41]

Krause's assessment of Schopenhauer's philosophy is plausibly assumed to be based on the fact that, already in the years 1812–1813, Krause lectured about what can be identified as some of the key features of Schopenhauer's *The World as Will and Representation*. In his *Vernunftwissenschaft*, published from Krause's *Nachlass* in 1886, Krause argued that an adequate system of science must be based on insight into the nature and existence of the ultimate ground of empirical reality that is recognized as being, in itself, everything that there is. This insight into the nature and existence of the ultimate ground, according to Krause, cannot be deduced logically within the system of science but has to be obtained in and through an immediately certain act of self-observation, in which the I directly intuits the nature and existence of this ultimate ground. As Krause argues,

> If, therefore, there is knowledge of something which in an unlimited way is all that there is, this insight entails that this something is without a ground (*ohne Grund*). Consequently, the insight into the nature and existence of this something is without a ground as well, it is unprovable and not in need of a proof.... If there is such an insight, it must be immediate and not mediated through any other insight or item of knowledge. And although not everyone will be able to obtain it without instruction, it must be possible to instruct every spirit to obtain this insight for themselves.[42]

We find a very similar idea expressed in Volume 1 of Schopenhauer's *The World as Will and Representation*.

> No science can be capable of demonstration throughout any more than a building can stand in the air. All its proofs must refer to something perceived, and hence no longer capable of proof, for the whole world of reflection rests on, and is rooted in, the world of perception. All ultimate, i.e., original, evidence is one of intuitive perception, as the word already discloses.   (WWR1$_{[P]}$, 65)

In his *Vernunftwissenschaft*, Krause continues to argue that, through self-observation, every subject can obtain the immediately certain insight that what it is, concerning its nature and existence, is *will*.

> I, myself, am willing, or, objectively conceived, will.[43]

Schopenhauer will formulate this in Volume 1 of *The World as Will and Representation*, in one of its various formulations, as follows:

> To the subject of knowing, who appears as an individual only through his identity with the body, this body is given in two entirely different ways. It is given in intellect perception as representation, as object among objects, liable to the laws of these objects. But it is also given in quite a different way, namely as that which is known immediately to everyone, and is denoted by the word *will*.   (WWR1$_{[P]}$, 100)

Krause then argues that "we can only become aware of other things in so as far as these things are ourselves, and we are in these things ourselves."[44] Furthermore, "we can make an inference to the beings outside us, under the form: as true as I am myself, as I observe myself, there is also this or that being."[45] Krause, in other words, argues that, through self-observation, we can use what is discovered as the true nature of the I to account for the ultimate ground of empirical reality. Schopenhauer, in turn, will express this idea in Volume 2 of *The World as Will and Representation*, and in a similar way: "What is directly known to us must give us the explanation of what is only indirectly known, not conversely" (WWR2$_{[P]}$, 196). That is, as formulated in *On the Will in Nature*:

> ...if we had the same internal relation to any natural phenomenon that we have to our own organism, the explanation of any natural phenomenon and all the properties of any body would ultimately be traced back in the same way to a will manifesting itself in them [i.e., that which is discovered as the nature of the I in self-observation].   (WN, 346)[46]

Based on his onto-epistemological assumption about the relation between what is revealed in self-observation as the true nature of the I and what is constitutive of the nature and existence of empirical reality, Krause argues in his *Vernunftwissenschaft* that if the I were nothing over and above will, then empirical reality would be nothing over and above a manifestation of will. Here, Krause deploys the terms "will" and "pure activity" as synonyms.

> If we were pure activity (*reine Tätigkeit*), an unlimited idealism would be decided by the fact that all objects [according to their true nature] were only opposing manifestations of will (*entgegengesetzte Tätigkeit*), and, indeed, pure activities.[47]

Schopenhauer will refer to this insight as the key feature of his system of philosophy. In *On the Will in Nature*, he summarizes the idea as follows:

> ...the core and principal point of my theory, its metaphysics proper;...what *Kant* called the *thing in itself* as opposed to mere *appearance*...; I say this substratum of all appearances and hence of all nature, is nothing other than that with which we are immediately acquainted and precisely intimate, that which we find on our innermost selves as *will*.   (WN, 324)

Krause, however, resumes by arguing that, although the I recognizes itself in an immediately certain act of self-observation, as will, it does not follow that the I is nothing over and above pure activity.

> If I find myself as nothing else but activity, it does not follow from this that I am nothing but activity, not even that I will not find myself in the future as something else.[48]

On Krause's own account, ultimately, the immediately certain self-observation of the nature and existence of the I shows that the I is will, but also *more* than will: the I is discovered as a finite, same and whole, willing, feeling, and knowing manifestation of the one same and whole, willing, feeling, and knowing infinite Essence.[49] Because Krause does not assume that self-observation shows that the I is nothing over and above will, he does not assume that empirical reality is only a manifestation of will, and consequently he does not conclude that the ultimate ground of empirical reality is nothing over and above will: Krause assumes that will is an *essential*, but not the only relevant, feature that reveals itself in an immediately certain act of self-observation, as an attribute of the ultimate ground of empirical reality.

In Volume 2 of *The World as Will and Representation*, Schopenhauer will agree with this.

> Meanwhile it is to be carefully noted, and I have always kept it in mind, that even the inward observation we have of our own will still does not by any means furnish an exhaustive and adequate knowledge of the thing-in-itself.   (WWR2$_{[P]}$, 196)

Since it is very hard to believe that in their discussions about Indian philosophy, Plato, and Kant, Krause would not have mentioned what he had lectured about a few years earlier (viz., the nature and existence of will), and since we find these ideas in Schopenhauer's system of philosophy, it is understandable both that, in Krause's mind, Schopenhauer's early emphasis on the will as the single ultimate ground of empirical reality is inadequate and that Krause would complain that in his *The World as Will and Representation*, Schopenhauer published thoughts he had been informed about by Krause.

2.4 SYSTEMATIC EVIDENCE FOR KRAUSE'S INFLUENCE ON SCHOPENHAUER

Both Krause and Schopenhauer assumed that an adequate system of philosophy has to integrate the insights provided by Indian philosophy, Plato, and Kant. To integrate the insights of Kant, to them, meant acknowledging that in the everydayness of being we do not perceive ultimate reality directly—the *Ding an sich*—but, instead, perceive empirical reality as structured by our transcendental constitution; that is, our forms of intuition and the categories of the Understanding. To integrate the insights of Plato meant to adhere to the idea that, although we do not normally perceive ultimate reality as such, there is an ultimate ground of empirical reality that accounts for its true nature and existence in an intelligible way. To integrate the insights of Indian philosophy meant developing a system of philosophy in which the relation between empirical reality and the ultimate ground of empirical reality is not one of opposition and separation, but one of ultimate nonduality, or unity, in which the ultimate ground of empirical reality in one way or the other *is*, or *shows* itself *as*, empirical reality.[50] Based on the fact that Krause's system of philosophy did not change much during his life, and based on the fact that Schopenhauer's most creative years were 1814–1818, which includes his time with Krause, we should expect a significant similarity between their attempts to develop a system of philosophy that integrates these insights if Krause influenced Schopenhauer's thinking.[51] And, in fact, there is an astonishing similarity between the overall architecture of Krause's and Schopenhauer's systems of philosophy. This can be seen if we now look at some of the key common features of their thinking.

First, Krause and Schopenhauer, apparently independently from one another,[52] concluded that the principle of sufficient reason (*Satz vom Grunde*) is the most fundamental transcendental principle constitutive of empirical reality. They both maintained that it is open to different interpretations in different contexts of use and that the system of science, which they both understood to be an adequate mapping of empirical reality, is structured by this principle. Based on these shared assumptions, it comes as no surprise that Krause and Schopenhauer deploy essentially the same concept of science. According to Krause, science is a system of true findings, differentiated within itself, in which all parts

> ...exist in relation to each other, not merely as a whole, in which parts are next to one other, collected in a mere aggregate, but as a whole in which the parts are all in, with and through one other (*in, mit und durch einander*), are all only in, with and through, the whole thing. Everything is essentially joined to form a whole which contains parts, each of which, although something specific, and exists for itself, nevertheless exists only for itself, by, and as long, as it is in a certain connectedness, and interaction, with all other members of that structure (*Gliedern*), which also account for the organism.[53]

In his *On the Fourfold Root of the Principle of Sufficient Reason*, Schopenhauer fully agrees on the adequacy of such a concept of science.

> *Science* specifically means a *system* of findings [*Erkentnissen*], i.e., a unity of connected findings in opposition to a mere aggregate of the same. But what else than the principle of sufficient reason connects members of a system? The very thing that distinguishes any science from a mere aggregate is that each of a science's findings follows from another as its ground.   (FR, 9–10)

Based on this understanding of science, Krause and Schopenhauer struggled with the question of how such a system, as a mapping of empirical reality, relates logically to the ultimate ground of empirical reality. Krause argued that the ultimate ground of empirical reality cannot be deduced within the system of science itself, but has to be intuited by the I in an immediately and certain act of self-observation that is beyond the realm of the principle of sufficient reason. As Krause states in 1813,

> My chief principle is that all science rests upon the intuition of an infinite substance, which intuition can not be proven according to the principle of sufficient reason, but can only be shown as present in the human mind. All that is, is this substance, and in this substance, and all scientific knowledge must also be grounded in that intuition, and through it.[54]

Schopenhauer agrees with this demand. In 1814, he wrote the following concerning the need for immediate insight: "A principal defect of all *philosophy* hitherto existing, which is connected with its being sought as *science*, is that mediate knowledge, i.e., knowledge from *reasons* or *grounds*, was also sought where immediate knowledge is given" (MR1, 228–229). In Volume 1 of *The World as Will and Representation*, Schopenhauer argues for this:

> That all science in the real sense, by which I understand systematic knowledge under the guidance of the principle of sufficient reason, can never reach a final goal or give an entirely satisfactory explanation. It never aims at the inmost nature of the world; it can never get beyond the representation; on the contrary, it really tells us nothing more than the relation of one representation to another.   (WWR1$_{[P]}$, 28)

Both Krause and Schopenhauer assumed that ultimate reality can only reveal itself in an immediately certain act of self-observation. The question, then, is how to account for this immediately certain intuition of ultimate reality. Both assumed that it must be possible for every subject to obtain this intuition. But, since the ability to obtain this intuition is not proved as the conclusion of any argument, it becomes a didactical and hermeneutical task to lead oneself and other people to the execution of this intuition. In characterizing this task, both philosophers assumed that there is a helpful traditional distinction between an analytic-inductive and a synthetic-deductive method of science: the analytical-ascending part of science is the way up to this insight into the nature and existence of the ultimate ground. The synthetic-descending part putatively shows how a system of science relates logically to what is perceived in this insight. As Krause says,

> In the first [part of science], from the first certain knowledge which is found in every consciousness, all of it certain, but particular and conditioned, becomes knowledge by self-observation.... And, at the same time, it steadily becomes ever higher, to the discovery of that fundamental knowledge (*der Grunderkenntnis*), which must show itself in this way if a system of science is to be possible for the human mind.... The second main part of the system of human science then forms in, and through, the fundamental knowledge, that is; in and through the principle of all special, conditioned, knowledge, as an organism.[55]

Schopenhauer agrees with this specification of the two methods of science and suggests specifying them in a way in which Krause had specified them already.

> The analytical method goes from the facts, the particular, to the propositions, the universal, or from consequents to grounds; the other method proceeds in the reverse direction. Therefore it would be much more correct to name them the inductive and deductive methods [which Krause did, BPG], for the traditional names are unsuitable and express the matter badly.   (WWR2$_{[P]}$, 122)

Let us briefly pause. So far, Krause and Schopenhauer agree on the architecture of an adequate system of philosophy: a system of philosophy is a system of science, which in turn is a harmonic whole in which the parts and the whole are all interrelated. To establish a system of science, to account for that *in virtue of which* the system is adequate to the ultimate ground of empirical reality, an intuition or self-observation is needed that is not subject to the principle of sufficient reason and therefore cannot be deduced in the system of science itself. Instead, this intuition has to be immediately certain and can only be obtained by each and every individual for themselves, although it is possible, in the analytic part of science, to lead other subjects, through instructing phenomenological reflection, to a level where they can obtain this intuition.

Based on this common outlook on the system of philosophy, Krause and Schopenhauer argued that the ultimate ground of empirical reality that is discovered in self-observation cannot be opposed to or separated from empirical reality in the manner that a cause is related to its effect in empirical reality. That is, both agreed that the ultimate ground of empirical reality cannot be addressed as the cause of empirical reality if by "cause" we refer to any kind of cause with which we are empirically familiar because this interpretation of "cause" is only applicable *within* the system of science and is subject to the principle of sufficient reason.

Instead, empirical reality, in Krause's words, has to be understood *panentheistically* as being *in* the ultimate ground, while, in Schopenhauer's words, it has to be understood as a *manifestation* of the ultimate ground. Although different in name, both doctrines arguably express the same concept: that B is *in* A means that, according to its true nature and existence, B is completely and inseparably determined by the true nature and existence of A. As Krause states,

> Following present linguistic usage, I use "in" here … of finite essences and essentialities, and mean by it that this finite thing is the higher whole [i.e., Essence] as part of it. So this finite thing, as a part of the same, is, however, bounded by the whole of pure Essentiality. So, indeed, the limit of the finite is in common with that of its whole, but this boundary does not limit or circumscribe (*begrenzt oder umgrenzt*) the whole as a whole.[56]

That B *is a manifestation of* A means the same. What Schopenhauer says about the relation between the ultimate ground of empirical reality and empirical reality itself therefore fits well with Krause's panentheistic definition of the world's being in its ultimate ground.

Now this is all very well, yet to me, when I consider the vastness of the world, the most important thing is that the essence in itself [57] ... is present whole and undivided in everything in nature, in every living being.... [T]rue wisdom ... is acquired by thoroughly investigating any individual thing, in that we try thus to know and understand perfectly its true and peculiar nature.[58]   (WWR1$_{[P]}$, 129)

The only *prima facie* major difference between the architecture of Krause's and Schopenhauer's systems is their apparently different interpretations of *what* is revealed as the true nature and existence of the I in an immediately certain act of self-observation. Once he rejected will as the single ultimate ground of empirical reality, Krause argued that self-observation leads to the recognition that the ultimate ground of empirical reality is Essence. Essence is the one infinite and unconditioned principle of fact and knowledge that holds the world within itself and determines everything, both in its being and its being-recognized. For Krause, whoever intuits Essence as the one infinite fact and knowledge principle of science, or as the "absolutely independent, and absolutely whole, and one essence,"[59] has successfully fulfilled the task of self-observation.[60]

Schopenhauer apparently argued that will is the single ultimate ground of empirical reality that manifests itself as empirical reality.

The reader will recognize that same will not only in those phenomena that are quite similar to his own, in men and animals, as their innermost nature, but continued reflection will lead him to recognize the force that shoots and vegetates in the plant, indeed the force by which the crystal is formed, the force that turns the magnet to the North Pole, the force whose shock he encounters from the contact of metals of different kinds, the force that appears in the elective affinities of matter as repulsion and attraction, separation and union, and finally even gravitation, which acts so powerfully in all matter, pulling the stone to the earth and the earth to the sun; all these he will recognize as different only in the phenomenon, but the same according to their inner nature. He will recognize them all as that which is immediately known to him so intimately and better than everything else, and where it appears most distinctly is called *will*.   (WWR1$_{[P]}$, 109–110)

However, Schopenhauer seems to be at least ambivalent concerning the determination of will as the single ultimate ground of empirical reality. Sometimes, in Volume 1 of *The World as Will and Representation*, Schopenhauer seems to argue that the act of self-observation shows that the nature of the ultimate ground of empirical reality is nothing over and above will, and consequently, he argues, pessimistically, that the "absence of all aim, of all limits, belongs to the essential nature of the will in itself, which is an endless striving" (WWR1$_{[P]}$, 109–110). But then, in Volume 2 of *The World as Will and Representation*, Schopenhauer argues that he is open to the possibility that what he identifies as will has further qualities.

Accordingly, even after this last and extreme step, the question may still be raised what that will, which manifests itself in the world and as the world, is ultimately and absolutely in itself; in other words, what it is, quite apart from the fact that it manifests itself as will, or in general appears, that is to say, is known in general. This question can never be answered, because, as I have said, being-known of itself contradicts being-in-itself, and everything that is known is as such only phenomenon. But the possibility of this question shows that the thing-in-itself, which we know most immediately in the will, may have, entirely outside all possible phenomenon, determinations, qualities, and modes of existence which for us are absolutely unknowable and incomprehensible, and which then remain as the inner nature of the thing-in-itself.   (WWR2$_{[P]}$, 198)[61]

This, however, is precisely what Krause argued for already in his 1812/1813 lectures, with the only difference being that Krause, in contrast to Schopenhauer, assumed that these further qualities, modes, and determinations are accessible in the immediately certain act of self-observation and therefore have to be taken into account by an adequate system of philosophy. The major difference between Krause and Schopenhauer, after all, might therefore be smaller than appears.

2.5 Krause's Influence on Schopenhauer's Philosophy

Krause and Schopenhauer had frequent contact during 1815 and 1818. The historical evidence suggests that Schopenhauer was aware of Krause's system of philosophy and of Krause's analysis of the will as a fundamental philosophical principle that, if taken as a single principle of philosophy, entails an idealism of opposing manifestations of will. Seen in this light, the fact that the architecture of Schopenhauer's philosophy is almost indistinguishable from Krause's system of philosophy and the fact that Schopenhauer apparently was open to the possibility that the ultimate ground of empirical reality might be more than blind will (which would have impact on his ethics) provides considerable grounds for concluding that Krause indeed significantly influenced Schopenhauer's thinking.

Notes

1. For an excellent biography of Krause's life, see Enrique M. Ureña, *Karl Christian Friedrich Krause: Philosoph, Freimaurer, Weltbürger. Eine Biographie* (Stuttgart: frommann-holzboog, 1991). Throughout this chapter, the translations of the German quotations are my own; the references are to the German text. I am grateful to Daniel Came and Stephen Priest for their comments on an earlier version of this paper.
2. Ibid., 30.
3. Ibid., 269.
4. Karl C. F. Krause, *Der Briefwechsel Karl Christian Friedrich Krauses: zur Würdigung seines Lebens und Wirkens. Aus dem handschriftlichen Nachlass*, Vol. 1, edited by Paul Hohlfeld and August Wünsche (Leipzig, 1903), 190.

5. Karl C. F. Krause, *Der Menschheitbund: nebst Anhang und Nachträgen aus dem handschriftlichen Nachlasse von Karl Christian Friedrich Krause*, edited by Richard Vetter (Berlin, 1900), 330.

6. Ureña, *Karl Christian Friedrich Krause*, 622

7. According to Ureña (lxx) there are only two translations of Krause's work into English. The first one is Karl Christian Friedrich Krause, *The Ideal of Humanity and Universal Federation.: A Contribution to Social Philosophy* (Edinburgh: T. & T. Clark, 1900a); the second one is Karl Christian Friedrich Krause, *The Family: A Pansophic ideal* (Willits, CA: Universal Pansophic Society for North America and Mexico, 1933).

8. See Arnulf Zweig, "Karl Christian Friedrich Krause," *The Encyclopedia of Philosophy*, Vol. 4, edited by Paul Edwards, 365: "Krause's philosophy, while not very influential in Germany, found considerable support in Spain, where, for a time, 'Krausism' flourished. This was largely due to the efforts of Julian Sanz del Rio, the minister of culture, who visited Germany and Belgium in 1844 and came into contact with a number of Krause's disciples, notably Heinrich Ahrens in Brüssels and Hermann von Leonhardi in Heidelberg."

9. See John W. Cooper, *Panentheism: The Other God of the Philosophers. From Plato to the Present* (Grand Rapids: Baker Academic, 2006), 26: "Panentheism literally means 'all-in-God-ism.' This is the Greek-English translation of the German term Allingottlehre, 'the doctrine that all is in god.' It was coined by Karl Krause (1781–1832), a contemporary of Schleiermacher, Schelling, and Hegel, to distinguish his own theology from both classical theism and pantheism."

10. Arnulf Zweig, "Karl Christian Friedrich Krause," 4:363.

11. Neil McInnes, "Spanish Philosophy," in *The Encyclopedia of Philosophy*, Vol. 7, edited by Paul Edwards, 514.

12. Arnulf Zweig, "Karl Christian Friedrich Krause," 4:363.

13. Ibid.

14. Charles Hartshorne, "Pantheism and Panentheism," in *The Encyclopedia of Religion*, Vol. 11, edited by Mircea Eliade (New York: Macmillan, 1987), 169.

15. Hegel and Krause had been colleagues for some time in Jena, lecturing at the same time. See Karl C. F. Krause, *Das Eigentümliche der Wesenlehre, nebst Nachrichten zur Geschichte der Aufnahme derselben, vornehmlich von Seiten Deutscher Philosophen: Aus dem hand-schriftlichen Nachlasse des Verfassers*, edited by Paul Hohlfeld and August Wünsche (Leipzig: Otto Schulze, 1890), 16: "Fries and Hegel knew me personally, and I lectured simultaneously with them in Jena in the years 1802–1804."

16. Krause visited some of Schelling's lectures but did not like either them or Schelling much. See Krause: *Der Briefwechsel Karl Christian Friedrich Krauses*: "I like Schlegel very much, but not Schelling" (7) and "I am pleased with Schelling's lecturing, as I am with his philos-ophy.... In his philosophy of nature I find propositions, which I already discovered for myself, following Fichte's system" (11). For an analysis of Schelling's influence on Krause and his independence of Schelling, see Thomas Bach and Olaf Breidbach, "Einleitung: Naturphilosophie als Systemdeduktion" in *Entwurf des Systems der Philosophie: Erste Abtheilung enthaltend die allgemeine Philosophie, nebst einer Anleitung zur Naturphilosophie*, edited by Thomas Bach and Olaf Breidbach, Ausgewählte Schriften 1 (Stuttgart-Bad Cannstatt: frommann-holzboog, 2007), 3–43.

17. Robert Wicks. *Schopenhauer* (Oxford: Blackwell, 2008), 6.

18. Rüdiger Safranski, *Schopenhauer und die wilden Jahre der Philosophie* (Frankfurt am Main: Fischer, 2016), 547.

19. Ureña, *Karl Christian Friedrich Krause*, 328–29.

20. Siegfried Wollgast, *Karl Christian Friedrich Krause: Aspekte von Leben, Werk, Wirkung* (Berlin: Weidler Buchverlag, 2016), 25.

21. The house was destroyed during WWII. See Walther Rauschenberger, "Schopenhauers Wohnungen während seines Lebens," *Schopenhauer-Jahrbuch* 25 (1938), 286: "The house, now called Kaiser-Wilhelm-Platz 6, was located in the immediate vicinity of the Japanese Palace, where the Royal Library was accommodated, which Schopenhauer has diligently used."

22. Walther Rauschenberger, "Schopenhauers Wohnungen: Ein Nachtrag," *Schopenhauer-Jahrbuch* 26 (1939), 387: "Schopenhauer lived in Dresden on Große Meißnische Gasse 35 III, and most likely until 1816. He then moved to Ostra-Allee 897 and lived there until the end of the stay in Dresden. However, after he had moved to Ostra-Allee, he probably kept his first apartment on Große Meißnische Gasse, because he still addressed his letters to his apartment there." See also Rauschenberger, "Schopenhauers Wohnungen während seines Lebens," 286: "All the letters addressed to Schopenhauer from the years 1814–1818 corresponded to this address [in the Große Meißnische Gasse 35], so that it cannot be doubted that Schopenhauer actually lived there." Therefore, as Rauschenberger concludes, "In this case, he had two apartments" (288).

23. It was in the Ostra-Allee, not in the Große Meißnische Gasse, where Schopenhauer mainly worked on his *opus magnum*: "At that time, Schopenhauer lived in a friendly garden-house far from the noise of the street at Ostra-Allee, and when he had finished his work, he wrote the following words in a window-pane of his working-room in Latin language: 'Schopenhauer lived here from 1816 to 1819, and wrote his four books of the world'" (Rauschenberger, "Schopenhauers Wohnungen: Ein Nachtrag," 388).

24. It is not true that "on Michaelmas 1818, Krause left to seek his fortunes in Berlin," David E. Cartwright, *Schopenhauer: A Biography* (Cambridge: Cambridge University Press, 2010), 283.

25. Ibid.

26. Karl Christian Friedrich Krause, *Nachlass von K. C. F. Krause, K. H. v. Leonhardi und Paul Hohlfeld*, 25 [DH in the following]. Ureña, *Karl Christian Friedrich Krause*, 530

27. DH, 33.

28. Kurt Riedel, "Schopenhauer bei Karl Christian Friedrich Krause," *Schopenhauer-Jahrbuch* 37 (1956), 17–18.

29. Arthur Hübscher, *Arthur Schopenhauer: Gespräche* (Stuttgart-Bad Cannstatt: frommann-holzboog, 1971), 38.

30. Riedel, "Schopenhauer bei Karl Christian Friedrich Krause," 18.

31. Claus Dierksmeier, "Eastern Principles within Western Metaphysics: Krause and Schopenhauer's Reception of Indian Philosophy," in *Conversations in Philosophy: Crossing the Boundaries*, edited by F. Ochieng'-Odhiambo, Roxanne Burton, and Ed Brandon (Cambridge: Cambridge Scholars Publishing, 2008), 63–64. See also Safranski, *Schopenhauer und die wilden Jahre der Philosophie*, 302: "Krause, unlike Schopenhauer, mastered Sanskrit and produced his own translations. Schopenhauer looked for professional advice from his neighbor, who was an Indian scholar, borrowed books, and used to meet him frequently."

32. Cartwright, *Schopenhauer*, 284.

33. Wicks, *Schopenhauer*, 7.

34. Karl C. F. Krause, *Zur Geschichte der neueren philosophischen Systeme: Aus dem handschriftlichen Nachlass*, edited by Paul Hohlfeld and August Wünsche (Leipzig: Otto Schulze, 1889a), 3. The lectures Krause gave in Dresden in 1805–1806 already contain the basic architecture of the system that Krause continuously worked on until he died in 1832. The

Dresden Lectures are found in Karl C. F. Krause, *Philosophische Abhandlungen: Aus dem handschriftlichen Nachlass*, edited by Paul Hohlfeld and August Wünsche (Leipzig: Otto Schulze, 1889), 106–61. See also Krause. Der Menschheitbund, 143–44: "I can actually regard myself as the first continuator of Kant, but I was this originally, without intending it. For what appears to be a continuation of Kant was already finished in 1803, before I could fully understand the relationship between my own and the Kantian research, because I had only very little read and thought of Kant`s writings. On the other hand, my system, which had already been completed in 1805 and 1806, was the key to the Kantian aspirations, and made it possible for me to understand Kant's intention and to appreciate his system from the highest position."

35. Karl C. F. Krause, *Anschauungen oder Lehren und Entwürfe zur Höherbildung des Menschheitlebens: Aus dem handschriftlichen Nachlasse des Verfassers*, Vol. 1, edited by Paul Hohlfeld and August Wünsche (Leipzig: Otto Schulze, 1890a), 184.

36. Hübscher, *Arthur Schopenhauer*, 38.

37. Karl C. F. Krause, *Anschauungen oder Lehren und Entwürfe zur Höherbildung des Menschheitlebens: Aus dem handschriftlichen Nachlasse des Verfassers*, Vol. 2, edited by Paul Hohlfeld and August Wünsche (Leipzig: Otto Schulze, 1891), 270.

38. See Krause, *Zur Geschichte der neueren philosophischen Systeme*, 478: "We are convinced that in our system, the principles of which have been repeatedly described by us, and the partial execution of which we have published in a series of works, the task of scientific research and scientific education (*Wissenschaftsforschung und Wissenschaftsbildung*), in its main points, is satisfactorily carried out. For, inasmuch as the recognition and acknowledgment of the principle is gained by the, analytic-subjective, self-knowledge of spirit (*Geistes*), the whole structure of science can be pictured in law-like and organic progress. And so the task of Socrates and Plato, as well as Kant, Fichte, and Schelling, is generally solved." It is interesting that, in 1816, Schopenhauer also claimed to have been the first to achieve this: "I confess, by the way, that I do not believe that my doctrine ever might arise before the Upanishads, Plato, and Kant could simultaneously throw their rays into a human spirit" (HN1, 422).

39. Krause, *Anschauungen oder Lehren und Entwürfe zur Höherbildung des Menschheitlebens*, 270.

40. Ureña, *Karl Christian Friedrich Krause*, 530: "In his diary, Krause once raised the accusation that Schopenhauer had borrowed ideas from him and declared them as his own."

41. Krause, *Anschauungen oder Lehren und Entwürfe zur Höherbildung des Menschheitlebens*, 292.

42. Karl Christian Friedrich Krause, *Reine Allgemeine Vernunftwissenschaft oder Vorschule des Analytischen Hauptteiles des Wissenschaftgliedbaues* (Leipzig: Otto Schulze, 1886), 9.

43. Ibid., 37.

44. Ibid., 66.

45. Ibid., 75.

46. Furthermore: "the two originally different sources of our cognition, the outer and the inner, must be connected through reflection. Comprehension of nature and that of our own self arises solely from this connection: but then the interior of nature is disclosed to our intellect, to which on its own only the exterior is otherwise accessible, and the secret that philosophy has so long sought is revealed" (WN, 398).

47. Krause, *Reine Allgemeine Vernunftwissenschaft*, 52.

48. Ibid., 52.

49. See Benedikt Paul Göcke, *Alles in Gott? Zur Aktualität des Panentheismus Karl Christian Friedrich Krauses* (Regensburg: Pustet, 2012).

50. See Benedikt Paul Göcke, *A Theory of the Absolute* (Basingstoke: Palgrave Macmillan, 2014), for a modern development of the architecture of such a system of philosophy based partly on Krause's insights.

51. For further analysis of Krause's system of philosophy, see Benedikt P. Göcke, *Alles in Gott? Zur Aktualität des Panentheismus Karl Christian Friedrich Krauses* (Regensburg: Pustet, 2012); Benedikt P. Göcke, "On the Importance of Karl Christian Friedrich Krause's Panentheism," *Zygon* 48, no. 2 (2013); Benedikt P. Göcke, "Gott und die Welt? Bemerkungen zu Karl Christian Friedrich Krause's System der Philosophie," *Theologie und Philosophie*, no. 87 (2012a); and Wollgast, *Karl Christian Friedrich Krause*.

52. See Johann Baptist Rieffert, *Die Lehre von der empirischen Anschauung bei Schopenhauer* (Halle an der Saale: Max Niemeyer, 1914), 218–20.

53. Karl Christian Friedrich Krause, *Der zur Gewissheit der Gotteserkenntnis als des höchsten Wissenschaftsprinzips emporleitende Theil der Philosophie*, Vorlesungen über das System der Philosophie 1 (Prague: Tempsky, 1869), 4.

54. Krause, *Der Briefwechsel Karl Christian Friedrich Krauses*, 362f.

55. Krause, *Reine Allgemeine Vernunftwissenschaft*, 4.

56. Furthermore: "Of course, all the words in our ordinary language (*Volkssprache*) which designate relations between things are first derived from space, as 'in,' 'beside,' 'on,' 'below,' 'beside,' 'out.' Or, rather, in the ordinary pre-scientific consciousness they are mostly understood only from space. But all these words must be spiritualised (*vergeistigt*), and taken in a way that transcends sense (*übersinnlich*), when they are used in connection with (*Zusammenhange*) philosophical science. It is, therefore, not permitted to distort these words of the philosopher, as if he were speaking of spatial relations, if he also uses these words, to denote the relation of the finite to the infinite." Krause, *Der zur Gewissheit der Gotteserkenntnis*, 307–08.

57. It is here interesting to observe that "Essence" (Wesen) is Krause's *terminus technicus* for ultimate reality.

58. As Wicks, *Schopenhauer*, 53 says, "when 'A manifests itself as B,' A and B can be identical; when 'A causes B,' they cannot. The manifestational relationship preserves a fundamental unity between the items in relation, the causal relationship sharply separates them. The former is appropriate for a monistic metaphysics that asserts 'all is essentially one.'"

59. Krause, *Der zur Gewissheit der Gotteserkenntnis als*, 204.

60. As Siegfried Wollgast, *Karl Christian Friedrich Krause: Anmerkungen zu Leben und Werk*, Sitzungsberichte der Sächsischen Akademie der Wissenschaften zu Leipzig. Philologisch-historische Klasse 129. 5 (Berlin: Akademie Verlag, 1990), 22, summarizes Krause's insight: "Human self-knowledge, and therefore all knowledge, presupposes an absolute principle, 'Essence', which first makes the unity of thought and being (Sein) possible. The subject, searching for indubitable knowledge, and so reflecting on itself, presupposes the Absolute, knows that it always already finds itself within the Absolute, that it can know itself and the Absolute only through the Absolute." Krause has therefore, to his mind, succeeded in uniting the Platonic-Neoplatonic efforts to recognize God as the supreme Essence (*oberste Wesen*) with the insight of Kant, that only transcendental knowledge can ground science. For Krause, transcendental knowledge of the Ego is nothing other than supreme tran-scendent knowledge applied to the Ego. In and through the Ego, Essence knows itself. See also Krause, *Das Eigentümliche der Wesenlehre, nebst Nachrichten zur Geschichte der Aufnahme derselben, vornehmlich von Seiten Deutscher Philosophen*, 13: "Because my system,

throughout, from its very first seed, is cultivated in independent, self-sufficient, research, and in the formation of the pure and fully grasped principle, it has not departed from this, and could not depart from this, to approximate to some other philosophical system, or unite itself to already existing conflicting systems. But, among other old tasks, that of liberating Platonism and Aristotelianism from their one-sidedness, and unifying them by means of their opposing essentials has also come to pass, as the main thing; but as far as that task has its meaning as a repetition of the Kantian task but at a higher level, and as the dissolution of the latter."

61. According to Robert Wicks (*Schopenhauer*, ch. 6), Schopenhauer is here referring to some of his notes (see MR3, 40–41 [HN, 36]) written down no later than 1821).

FURTHER READING

Bach, Thomas, and Olaf Breidbach. "Einleitung: Naturphilosophie als Systemdeduktion." In *Entwurf des Systems der Philosophie: Erste Abtheilung enthaltend die allgemeine Philosophie, nebst einer Anleitung zur Naturphilosophie*, edited by Thomas Bach and Olaf Breidbach. Karl Christian Friedrich Krause. Ausgewählte Schriften 1. Stuttgart-Bad Cannstatt: frommann-holzboog, 2007, 3–44.

Cartwright, David E. *Schopenhauer: A Biography*. Cambridge: Cambridge University Press, 2010.

Cooper, John W. *Panentheism: The Other God of the Philosophers. From Plato to the Present*. Grand Rapids: Baker Academic, 2006.

Dierksmeier, Claus. "Eastern Principles Within Western Metaphysics: Krause and Schopenhauer's Reception of Indian Philosophy." In *Conversations in Philosophy: Crossing the Boundaries*, edited by F. Ochieng'-Odhiambo, Roxanne Burton, and Ed Brandon. Cambridge: Cambridge Scholars Publishing, 2008, 63–72.

Edwards, Paul, ed. *The Encyclopedia of philosophy*. New York: The Macmillan Company & The Free Press, 1967.

Göcke, Benedikt P. "Gott und die Welt? Bemerkungen zu Karl Christian Friedrich Krause's System der Philosophie." *Theologie und Philosophie* 87 (2012): 25–45.

Göcke, Benedikt P. *Alles in Gott? Zur Aktualität des Panentheismus Karl Christian Friedrich Krauses*. Regensburg: Pustet, 2012.

Göcke, Benedikt P. "On the Importance of Karl Christian Friedrich Krause's Panentheism." *Zygon* 48, no. 2 (2013): 364–79.

Göcke, Benedikt P. *A Theory of the Absolute*. Basingstoke: Palgrave Macmillan, 2014.

Hartshorne, Charles. "Pantheism and Panentheism." In *The Encyclopedia of Religion*. Vol. 11, edited by Mircea Eliade. New York: Macmillan, 1987, 165–71.

Hübscher, Arthur. *Arthur Schopenhauer: Gespräche*. Stuttgart-Bad Cannstatt: frommann-holzboog, 1971.

Krause, Karl C. F. *Anschauungen oder Lehren und Entwürfe zur Höherbildung des Menschheitlebens: Aus dem handschriftlichen Nachlasse des Verfassers*, Vol. 1, edited by Paul Hohlfeld and August Wünsche. Leipzig: Otto Schulze, 1890a.

Krause, Karl C. F. *Nachlass von K. C. F. Krause, K. H. v. Leonhardi und Paul Hohlfeld*.

Krause, Karl C. F. *Zur Geschichte der neueren philosophischen Systeme: Aus dem handschriftlichen Nachlass*, edited by Paul Hohlfeld and August Wünsche. Leipzig: Otto Schulze, 1889a.

Krause, Karl C. F. *Der zur Gewissheit der Gotteserkenntnis als des höchsten Wissenschaftsprinzips emporleitende Theil der Philosophie. Vorlesungen über das System der Philosophie 1*. Prague: Tempsky, 1869.

Krause, Karl C. F. *Reine Allgemeine Vernunftwissenschaft oder Vorschule des Analytischen Hauptteiles des Wissenschaftgliedbaues.* Leipzig: Otto Schulze, 1886.

Krause, Karl C. F. *Philosophische Abhandlungen: Aus dem handschriftlichen Nachlass,* edited by Paul Hohlfeld and August Wünsche. Leipzig: Otto Schulze, 1889.

Krause, Karl C. F. *Das Eigentümliche der Wesenlehre, nebst Nachrichten zur Geschichte der Aufnahme derselben, vornehmlich von Seiten Deutscher Philosophen: Aus dem handschriftlichen Nachlasse des Verfassers,* edited by Paul Hohlfeld and August Wünsche. Leipzig: Otto Schulze, 1890.

Krause, Karl C. F. *Anschauungen oder Lehren und Entwürfe zur Höherbildung des Menschheitlebens: Aus dem handschriftlichen Nachlasse des Verfassers,* Vol. 2, edited by Paul Hohlfeld and August Wünsche. Leipzig: Otto Schulze, 1891.

Krause, Karl C. F. *Der Menschheitbund: nebst Anhang und Nachträgen aus dem handschriftlichen Nachlasse von Karl Christian Friedrich Krause,* edited by Richard Vetter. Berlin, 1900.

Krause, Karl C. F. *Der Briefwechsel Karl Christian Friedrich Krauses: zur Würdigung seines Lebens und Wirkens. Aus dem handschriftlichen Nachlass,* Vol. 1, edited by Paul Hohlfeld and August Wünsche. Leipzig, 1903.

McInnes, Neil. "Spanish Philosophy." In *The Encyclopedia of Philosophy.* Vol. 7, edited by Paul Edwards. New York: Macmillan Publishing Co., Inc., 1967, 511–6.

Rauschenberger, Walther. "Schopenhauers Wohnungen während seines Lebens." *Schopenhauer-Jahrbuch* 25 (1938): 281–93.

Rauschenberger, Walther. "Schopenhauers Wohnungen: Ein Nachtrag." *Schopenhauer-Jahrbuch* 26 (1939): 385–87.

Riedel, Kurt. "Schopenhauer bei Karl Christian Friedrich Krause." *Schopenhauer-Jahrbuch* 37 (1956): 15–21.

Rieffert, Johann B. *Die Lehre von der empirischen Anschauung bei Schopenhauer.* Halle an der Saale: Max Niemeyer, 1914.

Safranski, Rüdiger. *Schopenhauer und die wilden Jahre der Philosophie.* Frankfurt am Main: Fischer, 2016.

Ureña, Enrique M. *Karl Christian Friedrich Krause: Philosoph, Freimauerer, Weltbürger. Eine Biographie.* Stuttgart: frommann-holzboog, 1991.

Ureña, Enrique M. *Die Krause-Rezeption in Deutschland im 19. Jahrhundert.: Philosophie - Religion-Staat.* Stuttgart: frommann-holzboog, 2007.

Wicks, Robert. *Schopenhauer.* Oxford: Blackwell, 2008.

Wollgast, Siegfried. *Karl Christian Friedrich Krause: Anmerkungen zu Leben und Werk.* Sitzungsberichte der Sächsischen Akademie der Wissenschaften zu Leipzig. Philologisch-historische Klasse 129. 5. Berlin: Akademie Verlag, 1990.

Wollgast, Siegfried. *Karl Christian Friedrich Krause: Aspekte von Leben, Werk, Wirkung.* Berlin: Weidler Buchverlag, 2016.

Zweig, Arnulf. "Karl Christian Friedrich Krause." In *The Encyclopedia of philosophy,* edited by Paul Edwards. New York: Macmillan, 1967, 363–65.

....

CHAPTER 3

SCHOPENHAUER'S UNDERSTANDING OF SCHELLING

....

JUDITH NORMAN AND ALISTAIR WELCHMAN

SCHOPENHAUER's philosophical brilliance and famous stylistic virtuosity is matched by his equally famous and frequent displays of petty, personal name-calling and mud-slinging. No one vexed him more than the German Idealists: Fichte, Schelling, and Hegel, and none were more frequent targets of his spiteful diatribes. Indeed, Brian Magee writes: "In intensity and amount, this highly personal abuse of named contemporaries or near-contemporaries has no equal in the history of philosophy."[1] Schopenhauer calls them sophists, windbags, charlatans, frauds, dishonest peddlers of nonsense, delirium, and crazy twaddle; he accuses them of being careerists using philosophy as simply a means of advancing professional status, using obscurantist, mystifying language. Their words are "senseless," he writes (SW5, 508 [PP2, 508]). They are injurious to students, whom they lead astray by "vandalizing the legacy of Kant";[2] they are guilty of perversity, "driveling," and plagiarism. In Volume 1 of *Parerga and Paralipomena*, Schopenhauer refuses to include any of the three in his lengthy essay on the history of philosophy—and goes out of his way, in an appendix, to ensure that the reader has noticed the omission (SW5, 22f [PP2, 23f]).

Of his three Idealist adversaries, Schopenhauer was most ambivalent about Schelling. He often dismissed Fichte in a fairly perfunctory way, while Hegel was the object of a pure and self-assured hatred, lacking any nuance. Schopenhauer's relationship to Schelling, by contrast, was more complicated: in *The Fourfold Root of the Principle of Sufficient Reason*, for instance, Hegel is "thoroughly contemptible"[3] while Schelling is merely an "impudent, cocky gasbag" (SW1, 11–12 [FR, 16]).

In his published works, Schopenhauer intersperses cautious and occasional praise for Schelling in his typical invective, calling him, in PP1, "definitely the most talented among the three [Idealists]" (SW5, 26 [PP1, 25]), and even declaring, in Volume 2 of *Parerga and Paralipomena*, "…where Schelling stands on Kant's shoulders he says much that is good and worth remembering" (SW6, 118 [PP2, 102]). In the same discussion, he concedes some of Schelling's scientific insights to be valuable.

In this chapter, we look at some features of this ambivalent relationship: the nature of Schopenhauer's engagement with Schelling and some possible motivations for its occasional virulence. We argue that the ambiguous attitude Schopenhauer entertains toward Schelling can be explained by Schopenhauer's awkward consciousness of how much his project genuinely resembled that of Schelling. At the same time, if we take seriously the virulence of his self-distancing from Schelling (and the pejorative terms in which he often describes his evil twin), we can illuminate some of the distinctiveness of Schopenhauer's metaphysics.

3.1 ANXIETY OF INFLUENCE

Recent scholarship has called some much-deserved attention to the contemporaneity of Schopenhauer and Schelling.[4] To their contemporaries, Schelling was an obvious point of reference for Schopenhauer. Indeed, almost all of the first reviews of *The World as Will and Representation* note the similarities between the systems, a comparison that infuriated Schopenhauer. The first two published reviews of WWR1 indicated widespread points of sympathy between Schopenhauer's thought and that of Schelling.[5] The second review expressed particular surprise at Schopenhauer's hostility to Schelling, as its (anonymous) author claimed that Schopenhauer's main ideas were simply a rehashing of themes in Schelling. A further review, by the prominent philosopher, Johann Friedrich Herbart, noted Schopenhauer's proximity to Schelling in one respect; namely, that Schopenhauer is susceptible to the same criticism he made of Schelling, that of falling into transcendent metaphysical speculation rather than remaining within the bounds of knowledge established by Kant.[6] Yet another reviewer was struck simply by how "unbefitting a scholar" Schopenhauer's insulting language concerning Schelling really was.[7]

Schopenhauer was particularly irritated by the suggestion that his central philosophical insight was anticipated by Schelling, who in his middle-period works (roughly 1809–1813) developed a metaphysics of will as supersensuous ground of reality and wrote in his 1809 essay, *Philosophical Investigations into The Essence of Human Freedom*, that "Willing is primal being."[8] We know from Schopenhauer's notes that he had read this text particularly carefully in the years prior to the publication of Volume 1 of *The World as World in Representation* in 1818. In PP1, he has three points of rebuttal to the claim that Schelling anticipated his philosophy with this insight into the primacy of will, each of which is worth consideration.

Schopenhauer's first strategy is to deny that there is any direct lineage from Schelling's thought to his own—but that both were influenced jointly by Kant—and so any apparent similarities can be accounted for in this way.

The root of my philosophy already lies in the Kantian philosophy, especially in the doctrine of empirical and intelligible character...[and] as soon as Kant throws more light on the thing in itself, it looks out through its veil as will...[and consequently] my philosophy is only the thinking-through-to-the-end of his. Thus we should not be surprised when traces of the same fundamental thought can be found in the philosophemes of Fichte and Schelling, which also start out from Kant, although there they occur without consistency, connection, and completion, and are thus to be seen as a mere foreshadowing of my doctrine.   (SW5, 142 [PP1, 122])

He then develops a surprisingly long and colorful list of images to illustrate this notion of foreshadowing and motivate his claim that, although Schelling's ideas anticipated those of Schopenhauer, Schopenhauer has a prior right to them.

In general it needs to be said about this point that of every great thought, before it has been discovered, an anticipation makes itself known, a presentiment, a faint image, as in a fog, and a futile attempt to grasp it.... However only that person is the author of a truth who has recognized it from its ground.... However, that at one time or another...it has been uttered half-consciously and almost as if speaking in one's sleep...means not much more than if it were written in just so many letters, even if it is written in just so many words—in the same way that the finder of a thing is only that person who, in recognizing its value, picked it up and kept it, but not the one who accidentally took it in his hand and dropped it again; or, in the way that Columbus is the discoverer of America, but not the first shipwrecked person washed up there by the waves.   (SW5, 142–3 [PP1, 122])

Finally, Schopenhauer enumerates a series of older writers who privileged will over intellect as evidence that the idea was not original to Schelling either—that Schelling was not even the first shipwrecked sailor upon this particular shore (SW5, 143 [PP1, 122]). (In his marginal notes to the *Freedom* essay, Schopenhauer accuses Schelling of being derivative but of another source: the whole essay is "almost only a recasting of Jacob Boehme's *Mysterium magnum*, in which practically every sentence and every expression can be identified" [MR2, 354]).

Schopenhauer's argument is curious here, and it shares something of the logic of Freud's famous joke about the cracked kettle: "I am original and neither was Schelling." For one thing, the Columbus metaphor is unconvincing—a polished work of philosophy is a poor candidate for the sort of semi-conscious stammering of an idea that would be a candidate point of comparison to the shipwrecked person. But more importantly, the two-way relationship between the shipwrecked party and Columbus doesn't extend very easily to the three-way relations among Kant, Schopenhauer, and Schelling. Schopenhauer appears to be arguing that he is original with respect to Schelling at being unoriginal with respect to Kant. Kant, in the terms of this odd metaphor, would have to be the country, not the voyager; the source of truth, not the seeker after it.

The conclusion Schopenhauer wants his readers to draw is clear even if his arguments are not: Schelling is not the true proprietor of the good ideas that occasionally appear in his writings. That honor goes, variously, to Kant, Schopenhauer himself, and Jakob Boehme. But this conclusion is of a piece with the distinctive set of insults that Schopenhauer persistently uses in describing Schelling's philosophical project. Looking carefully, we can see that Schopenhauer's insults are not simply poisoned darts but in fact cohere on a specific critical judgment: Schelling himself has nothing to say. His thoughts (when they truly are his own, as opposed to his many incompetent borrowings) are empty, meaningless, full of air, a faint or perverse echo of a truth, lacking sense and substance.

But poisonous as these darts certainly are, we might speculate that their affective intensity is the result of another form of the anxiety of influence. Not only does Schopenhauer worry that his philosophy is not as original as he clearly wants it to be—he often takes pride in telling historical stories that insert him into the canon of philosophical greats while omitting his contemporaries—but he may also be worried that he is doing *just what he is criticizing Schelling for doing*, a classic case of Freudian projection. Specifically, he may be worried that his attacks on Schelling's use of intellectual intuition as a means of doing metaphysics might also apply to his own metaphysics: both, after all, appear to seek to go beyond experience to the thing in itself. To see this, we need to get beyond the insults and look more closely at the substantive content of Schopenhauer's complaints against Schelling: first, his critique of Schelling's metaphysics and second, his critique of Schelling's epistemology.

3.2 THE SUBSTANCE OF THE CRITIQUE: METAPHYSICS

Schopenhauer had a number of substantial criticisms of Schelling's philosophy, but most of them are centered on the notion that Schelling transgressed the epistemological boundaries established by Kant and illicitly applied representational forms to areas beyond the jurisdiction of the principle of sufficient reason, and specifically to the thing in itself. In his marginal notes to Schelling's philosophy, Schopenhauer records this response to a reading of Schelling's 1800 *System of Transcendental Idealism*:

> It is one of the craziest excesses of the human mind that, after Kant's appearance, it has been possible for it to presume to demonstrate according to laws of spatiality and to others valid for experience that which is said to be the supersensuous ground of all consciousness, for which experience is first possible.   (MR2, 384–85)

In similar vein, Schopenhauer writes this about the (1809) *Freedom* essay:

> Everything comes down to the fact that, underlying man's phenomenal appearance in time, there is something outside all time as well as outside all the conditions of the

phenomenon. If we try to adapt these conditions to the otherwise correct concept of that something, then we get *monstra*.   (MR2, 353)

The most mendacious aspect of that claim, in Schopenhauer's opinion, was the idea of a discrete intellectual faculty that bypassed the understanding, the faculty of intellectual intuition. Schopenhauer regards intellectual intuition as a sort of cheap circus trick, secret evidence on behalf of the cause, an unverifiable, unteachable special sense. "Here is the breastwork behind which Fichte and Schelling hide from all arguments; they assert that they see something apart which no one sees except them and their mob" (MR2, 381). We will address the problem of intellectual intuition at greater length momentarily, but Schopenhauer's great proof against it was that he detected in the reported results of such an intuitive grasp of metaphysical truths a mere reproduction of the structures of phenomenal knowledge, or even, as we shall see, something worse: "That their observations [taken from intellectual intuition] of the transcendental ego's way of acting are false is seen from their describing that way of acting as occurring according to the laws of the empirical ego" (MR2, 381).

Accordingly, Schelling's supposed descriptions of metaphysical reality are simply a warmed-over duplication of empirical reality. In contrast to his own method (to which we will soon turn), Schopenhauer accuses Schelling of "secretly abstracting metaphysics ahead of time from the empirical sciences and then…finding a priori what it had learned a posteriori." (SW4, 2 [WN, 323]).[9] Schopenhauer applies a form of this same criticism to Schelling's ethical reasoning which, Schopenhauer argues, betrays a misunderstanding of the relation between the transcendent and the empirical registers. While acknowledging the independence of the human essence from temporality, Schelling nevertheless attributes change to it: he "speaks of punishment that is a consequence of the soul's deed, of its future state and so on. In short, he presents the entire world as an event in accordance with finite laws, an event that flows out of an action of God and has a final purpose" (MR2, 376).

Schopenhauer's criticism of Schelling's earlier Identity philosophy hangs on the specific accusation that Schelling has imported the subject–object distinction, which is a feature (the defining feature) of representational consciousness, into the transcendent realm of the thing in itself. Schelling's philosophical project involved deriving first the subjective world of consciousness and second the objective world of nature from a prior and grounding identity or Absolute. "The basis of our consciousness, its falling apart into subjective and objective, is '*explained*' by that philosophy trying to refer it to laws according to which it must be so and not otherwise. But where do these come from? From the understanding!" (MR2, 378). Schelling offends both when he imports concepts of the understanding wholesale into the transcendent realm—such as the concepts of causation and, more generally, temporality and change, which are needed to grasp the derivation of the object from the subject and vice versa—and when he modifies concepts of understanding to indicate the distinctiveness of the metaphysical—such as when he entertains the thought of an absolute subject, an object-less subject, which Schopenhauer considers nonsense. The Identity philosophy does not provide Schelling the philosophical resources to develop and articulate an appropriate conception of the supersensible. Again, Schelling tries to resolve the problem with the magical solution of intellectual intuition (or rational intuition, as Schopenhauer sometimes calls it), to which Schopenhauer replies:

> Very little is clear to me about this method, but enough to know that it proceeds according to the principle of sufficient reason in its various forms [i.e., it doesn't successfully transcend experience]. Since rational intuition has passed me by completely, I forgo the deep wisdom that such construction contains....Indeed, this is true to such an extent that—strange to say—whenever someone is teaching this deep wisdom, it is as if I can hear only the dronings of atrocious and extremely tedious windbags.   (SW2, 31 [WWR1, 48])

Schopenhauer hints, moreover, that intellectual intuition is not just a projection of the empirical on the transcendental but also projects a specifically *religious* metaphysics, thus connecting his critique with Kant's. For instance, he describes Schelling's "Absolute" unity of subject and object as "reverend [*ehrwürdig*]" (2:30) and refers to the public record of Schelling's philosophy (as opposed to the private deliverances of his "intellectual intuition") as something accessible, by contrast, to "the laity [*uns Profanen*]" (2:31). We will return to this important point later.

In his middle-period system, with the *Freedom* essay, Schelling had abandoned the conception of an Absolute as subject–object identity for a metaphysical conception of primal will, which plays the role of God's material "ground." Schopenhauer has limited praise for this move: "Schelling himself later realized that metaphysical problems cannot be dismissed through peremptory assertions [and] he provided a real metaphysical attempt in his treatise on freedom." But Schopenhauer does not by any means think Schelling has overcome his methodological difficulties, describing the essay as "a mere fantasy, a tall tale" (SW5, 29 [PP1, 28]). In BM, Schopenhauer reports that the *Freedom* essay contains

> ...an extensive report on a god with whom the esteemed author betrays an intimate acquaintance, since he even describes his coming into existence; it is only to be regretted that he does not mention in a single word how he came to this acquaintance.   (SW4, 84 [FW, 99])

Although Schopenhauer's critical concerns are not without merit, they do not seem to warrant the level of invective he displays. The complaint that Schelling illicitly applied transcendental categories to transcendent experience can be equally urged against Kant, as Schopenhauer himself noted: he roundly condemns Kant for asserting that the thing in itself "affects" the subject with sensations, which are the raw material of cognition. This inference is based on the law of causality, whose proper sphere of operation is *within* experience, not *between* experience and the thing in itself (SW2, 516–17 [WWR1, 463]). And Kant was certainly also liable to the charge of smuggling theological pieties into metaphysics. So, this error on its own cannot explain the virulence of Schopenhauer's critique.

But, more significantly, it is not at all clear that Schopenhauer has resources any different from intellectual intuition for discovering and articulating what lies outside experience. In his notes, after rejecting Schelling's intellectual intuition Schopenhauer wrote, in the context of Kant's thing = x (i.e., thing in itself),

> Instead of this [x], the genuine, that is to say the critical, philosopher should do the-oretically what the virtuous man does practically. Thus the latter does not make the desire attaching to him through his sensuous nature into an absolute desire, but follows the better will in him without associating it with that desire, as for example with a reward, and thus to want only relatively and not absolutely what is good. In just the same way, the genuine critical philosopher separates his better knowledge from the conditions of empirical knowledge and does not carry these over into the former knowledge (as does the sensuous man his sensuous pleasures into paradise because he himself does not like to enter this without them). He does not use these as a bridge to unite the two worlds (like the sensuous believer who uses reward as a bridge to virtue). On the contrary, he coldly and imperturbably leaves behind the conditions of his empirical knowledge, content to have clearly separated the better knowledge from that other, and to have recognized the twofold nature of his being.
>
> (HN2, 328 [MR2, 376–77])

Schopenhauer clearly articulates a will to depart from the empirical into the metaphysical, but the mechanism for doing so—the "better knowledge" [*beßre Erkenntniß*]—remains undefined. Schopenhauer largely abandoned the term "better knowledge" in his pub-lished writings, using other vocabulary to explore the question of epistemic access. But it remains as yet an open question how this is distinct from an intellectual intuition. We think that Schopenhauer need not be anxious on this account: he does in fact have a dis-tinct method, and one that is not subject to the criticisms he makes of Schelling's use of intellectual intuition. It is to this notion of intellectual intuition that we now turn.

3.3 THE SUBSTANCE OF THE CRITIQUE: INTELLECTUAL INTUITION

Schopenhauer has a ready vocabulary of abuse against Schelling for his metaphysical speculations and his favored instrument of intellectual intuition. We have looked at Schopenhauer's justified philosophical concerns with Schelling's metaphysics, but we have not yet seen him provide a philosophically motivated critique of intellectual intu-ition. But if we are to see how his own method of epistemic access to the metaphysical truths avoids the problems of intellectual intuition, we need to do so now.

Schopenhauer's critique of Kant in BM is helpful in this regard. This critique is different from that offered in the long Appendix to WWR1. There, he focuses on theoretical issues, including the one discussed briefly earlier criticizing Kant's illicit projection of the concept of cause onto the thing in itself (SW2, 515–17 [WWR1, 462–64]). Here, by contrast, Schopenhauer is interested in practical issues, and he introduces his discussion with brief genealogy of the concept of intellectual intuition.

Schopenhauer explains that the idealist tradition derives the value it gives to intellectual intuition from Kant's categorical imperative, and specifically from the notorious "fact of reason [*Faktum der Vernunft*]."[10] In the extensive critique of Kant's ethics Schopenhauer offers in §6 of BM, he starts by making it clear that Kant should not be read (as the "fact of reason" obviously suggests) as arguing that morality has some empirical basis. In the first place, Schopenhauer focuses the rays of his attack precisely on the implausibility of a completely a priori account of morality, which would have to be based on "*pure concepts a priori*, i.e., concepts that as yet have no content," in other words, "mere shells without a core" (SW4, 130 [BM, 134]). (It is noteworthy that Schopenhauer repeats exactly this reproach of emptiness against Schelling.) At first, Schopenhauer's critique of Kant seems to be just as rhetorical as his blasts against Schelling: he goes on to wonder how "a couple of totally abstract, utterly substanceless concepts . . . [could] have the power to bring bit and bridle to bear upon the stress [*Drang*] of desires, the storm of passion, the gigantic structure of egoism." "Now that is something we would like to see" (SW4, 130 [BM, 134]) he adds, sarcastically.

But a corollary of Kant's view gestures at a more significant difference: if the ground of morality really must be *a priori*, then it must be a principle of reason. And if reason itself is pure (i.e., unmixed with any empirical components), then it cannot be confined to merely human reason but extended to all rational beings, or even to a being that is nothing but reason: "This *pure* reason, then, is not taken as a cognitive power of *human beings*, which is all that it really is, but *hypostasized as something subsisting in itself*" (SW4, 131 [BM, 134]). Here Schopenhauer offers a proto-Nietzschean diagnostic[11]: Kant is tacitly appealing to theology ("dear little angels") and supposing that the "inner, eternal essence of the human being consists in *reason*" (SW4, 132 [BM, 135]). This is, of course, the precise opposite of Schopenhauer's view: that the in-itself of human being is will and that reason is decisively subordinate to the will (e.g., SW3, 233–36 [WWR2, 219–22]). Here, though, two things are important: (1) the implications of Schopenhauer's view not for the will, but for his conception of reason; and (2) the consequences of Kant's (or rather Kant's followers') mistaken "hypostasis" of reason.

Kant's followers forget Kant's own stringent claims that morality must be a priori and not empirical. Thus, the "categorical imperative increasingly appears as a hyperphysical fact" (SW4, 146 [BM, 148]), and thus the "fact of reason" is the genealogical forebear of the notion of intellectual intuition, as Schopenhauer conceives it. As Schopenhauer paints it: from Kant's modest (although mistaken) "fact of reason" there "sprang . . . doctrines of a reason that at first just faintly 'detected', then clearly 'perceived', and finally had full-bodied 'intellectual intuition of' the 'supersensible' " (SW4, 147 [BM, 148]).

This genealogy sheds considerable light on Schopenhauer's conception of intellectual intuition; it brings out the fact that Schopenhauer is concerned with the manner in which it is primarily *intellectual*, which is to say bound up with *reason*. Intellectual intuition is not just any ability to make contact with the thing in itself; it is specifically a *rational* faculty with the ability to grant cognition of the supersensible. The "fact" of Kant's "fact of reason" can make it look as if it has an empirical element. But this is a mistake, Schopenhauer argues, as can be seen by looking more carefully (the idealists did not do this) at Kant's own tough-minded rejection of an empirical or a posteriori element in morality: that is why the "fact" is in quotation marks, and Kant himself qualifies it as "strange."[12] The "factuality" of intellectual (rational) intuition is an illusion: all there is to it is a priori conceptual reasoning; but the concepts involved do not actually have any factual content; they are, as Schopenhauer repeatedly emphasizes, "empty."

There is another, more subtle, aspect to Schopenhauer's understanding of intellectual intuition. It is not just that intellectual intuition is a conception of reason that lays claim to hyperphysical cognitive access; it is also that Schopenhauer, in his model of intellectual intuition (and perhaps tacitly), treats the *content* of what it accesses as also essentially rational; there we find specifically the moral law (i.e., the law of practical reason), but generally (as the doctrine of intellectual or rational intuition expands) we find *noumena* (i.e., objects of thought, intelligible objects).[13] Moreover, if the noumenal aspect of something is its in-itself, then we, as phenomena with a noumenal aspect, are also in ourselves rational. This is one of the reasons why Schopenhauer only uses the term "thing in itself" and never noumenon; what we are in our cores is not reason, but will.[14]

Schopenhauer understands intellectual intuition as involving the pretense that our intellectual or rational faculties have unmediated access to things in themselves. Modesty about reason is very important to Schopenhauer.[15] There are several reasons why this is the case. Most importantly, reason is ultimately the "servant" of the will (SW3, 238 [WWR2,220). Secondarily, but still importantly, despite the importance he attaches to Kant, Schopenhauer is strongly influenced by the empiricist tradition, and especially the significance of perceptual knowledge, for which he adopts the Kantian term *Anschauung*, which is customarily translated into English as "intuition." Intuitions are, to a first approximation, spatio-temporal particulars, and, although the English term "intuition" is in some ways misleading, Schopenhauer does think that we grasp such particulars directly and that they have a vivid impact on us. But intuitions clearly go beyond mere perceptual particularity. First, Schopenhauer argues that causal relations are part of intuitive perception; by contrast, Kant thinks that causation is a conceptual determination. This leads Schopenhauer to claim that intuitive perception is as impor-tant as reasoning in science, in some ways more important: intuitive cognition "of cause and effect is indeed intrinsically deeper, more complete, and more exhaustive than an abstract thought of cause and effect" (SW2, 63 [WWR1, 78]). Second, it is intuitive perception and not reason that is the touchstone of Schopenhauer's thought: the two commanding heights of his philosophy, the theory of aesthetic experience and of morality, are both resolutely counter-conceptual in orientation. As Schopenhauer aphoristically expresses it: "Virtue is as little taught as genius: indeed, concepts are just as barren for it [virtue] as they are for art" (SW2, 319–20 [WWR1, 298]).

But the third and most salient motivation for Schopenhauer's modesty about reason is that concepts get their content from intuitive perceptions. Schopenhauer defines a concept as a "representation of a representation" (*Vorstellung einer Vorstellung* [SW2, 49; WWR1, 64]; *Vorstellungen aus Vorstellungen* [SW1, 98; FR, 94]). This definition is upwardly recursive (i.e., a concept can be used to represent a group of existing concepts) and so concepts are naturally arranged in a hierarchy; but it rests finally upon intuitive perceptions so that first-level concepts are representations of intuitive perceptions (SW2, 48–49 [WWR1, 63–64]). Thus, ultimately, concepts get their content or meaning from intuitive perceptions. In a familiar Kantian slogan, concepts without intuitions are empty; although, by contrast, Schopenhauer does not think that intuitions without concepts are blind, as does Kant. Indeed, one of his main critiques of Kant is that Kant fails to admit the possibility of intuitive knowledge.

Schopenhauer is particularly emphatic about his modest conception of reason because he thinks that the term "reason" also underwent a kind of genealogical shift in the work of Kant and the Idealists, and he is returning it to its original philosophical meaning. Prior to Kant, he argues in FR, the term meant more or less what he means by it; that is, abstract, conceptual knowledge and inference (SW1, 110 [FR,105]). But Kant uses the term "understanding [*Verstand*]" to mean "conceptual cognition," thus freeing up the term "reason" to designate something else. What is this something else? Well, at least in the hands of the post-Kantian idealists[16]:

> They needed the place and name of *reason* for an invented, fabricated, or ... completely fictitious faculty that was supposed to rescue them from the perils in which *Kant* had put them, a faculty for immediate, metaphysical knowledge, i.e., one going beyond all possibility of experience, one grasping the world of things in themselves and its relations, hence a faculty that is above all a "consciousness of God", i.e., one that knows the Lord God immediately ... a "faculty of the supersensible" ... designed immediately for *metaphysics* ... an immediate rational intuition of the absolute.
> (SW1, 111–12 [BM, 106–07])

Why don't we have a faculty of intellectual intuition, according to Schopenhauer? Because "concepts ... must obtain their *material* and *content* from *intuitive* cognition" (SW1, 115 [BM, 109]). Intellectual intuition is therefore supposed to be a modification of reason that gives reason direct cognitive contact with things in themselves. But there is no such faculty because concepts have meaning only in relation to ultimately intuitive cognitive content. Without this, they are empty or meaningless.

Intellectual intuition therefore involves the reification of speculative pre-critical metaphysics; that is, the assumption of the existence of a special faculty for conceptual argumentation that transcends the possibility of experience. But because of Schopenhauer's rearrangement of transcendental idealism, he has no need for any a priori concepts, and hence subscribes to the empiricist doctrine of concept-empiricism (i.e., the claim that all concepts must trace back to intuitions).[17]

3.4 Meaningless Concepts

It is worth dwelling for a minute on the notion of empty and meaningless concepts. Strictly speaking, for Schopenhauer, there *are* no empty concepts. This follows from his definition of a concept as a representation of a representation: if there is no intuition for a (conceptual) representation to be a representation *of*, then there can be no conceptual representation.[18] Most philosophers prior to the linguistic turn did not consider language as methodologically significant or an object of interesting independent investigation: for Kant words more or less represent or are tokens for concepts, and analysis can be taken up at the level of concepts without loss. Schopenhauer, however, appears to use language in a philosophically significant way, to address the problem of abstraction in the empiricist tradition. The obvious way in which concepts can arise from intuitions is that a representative or canonical intuition is used to represent a type (i.e., as a concept). A representative intuition of a dog might stand for the concept DOG, for instance. But it is not obvious how we can distinguish between the intuition that is serving a conceptual role and a regular intuition without presupposing that we can already distinguish concepts from intuitions, in which case concepts must have their origin elsewhere than in intuitions. Schopenhauer's modern-sounding solution is that we use language.

> [R]epresentations that are sublimated, and thereby decomposed into abstract concepts, have forfeited all their intuitive quality, they would completely escape consciousness and would thus have no value for the intended operations of thought if they were not fixed and held fast in our senses by arbitrary signs: these signs are words. Therefore insofar as they make up the contents of the lexicon, that is, of language, words always refer to *general* representations, concepts, never to intuitive things.   (SW1, 99 [BM, 94–95])[19]

It does not seem to be too strong a reading of the passage to suggest that words are necessary for conceptuality: without words, we would have no epistemic access to concepts. While therefore (strictly) Schopenhauer thinks that there cannot be empty concepts, it does seem to be consistent with his view that there can be meaningless words, words precisely for (nonexistent) concepts that purport to go beyond experience (i.e., beyond any intuitive content).

Schopenhauer's polemics against Schelling's notion of intellectual intuition are therefore quite motivated from a philosophical point of view: Schelling's use of intellectual intuition involves concepts that lack (even possible) intuitive content. Such concepts are literally meaningless, "empty verbiage" (SW3, 68 [WWR2, 70]) or "empty shells" (SW3, 92 [WWR2, 91]; SW2, XX [WWR1, 14]). It is this accusation that drives the content (if not the affect) of Schopenhauer's frequent accusation that Schelling is a "windbag" (SW2, 31 [WW1, 48]), for, if his words are empty, then they are equally just wind as they are "meaningless" marks (e.g., SW2, 40 [WWR1, 56], about Fichte). The critique of intellectual intuition also grounds Schopenhauer's account of boring books (SW3, 77–79 [WWR2, 77–80]), an accusation he often throws at the idealists (e.g., Fichte at SW2, 40

[WWR1, 56], and a priori philosophizing at SW5, 139 [PP1, 119]). This sounds like a simple insult, but in fact has a special technical application. Boring books are those that are based only on concepts rather than intuitions. And books based on concepts can do nothing other than elaborate the implicit content of those concepts explicitly, so they do not "introduce any really new cognition" (SW3, 78 [WWR2, 78], see also SW1, 103–04 [FR, 98–99]). Only intuition can do that.

Moreover, it is precisely this lack of anchoring content in Schelling's conceptuality that allows it to function as an effective screen on which to project his own fantasy content. But Schopenhauer does not think Schelling is projecting a *personal* content; rather, Schelling becomes a conduit for the projection of generalized cultural content (i.e., Christian dogma).

This, then, is the reason that Schopenhauer rejects intellectual intuition and abuses those who claim it for an epistemological tool. But we need to be cautious about the conclusions we can draw from this critique for Schopenhauer's own positive philosophy. For instance, we believe that Julian Young draws too sweeping a conclusion from the vehemence of Schopenhauer's critique in arguing that, in rejecting the idealists' faculty for metaphysical insight into the supersensible, Schopenhauer also rejected the project of metaphysics. Young argues that Schopenhauer's critique of the notion of intellectual intuition shows that the "traditional" reading of Schopenhauer must be incorrect. This traditional reading sees him "as basing his own metaphysics on direct encounters with the thing in itself; on what is in fact if not in name, intellectual intuition"[20]; but endorsing intellectual intuition would be a "betrayal of Kant" and his intellectual heritage.[21] Young is certainly right that Schopenhauer connects his attacks on his German Idealist "band of brothers" with his intellectual fealty to Kant. Indeed, the affective structures of Schopenhauer's reception of the idealists comprise in some ways the prototype of modern analytic philosophy's reception of the idealists. But Young interprets this as evidence in support of the view that Schopenhauer in fact *does* want to respect Kant's epistemic constraints and therefore that his claims that the thing in itself *is* will should be understood as falling short of a transcendent metaphysics.

This interpretation, or set of interpretations, is common in the literature.[22] And Schopenhauer can reasonably be construed as conflicted on the matter. On the one hand, he clearly states that "the will is *thing in itself*" (SW2, 131 [WWR1, 135]). On the other, especially in WWR2, he appears equally clearly to deny this, arguing that the thing in itself only "*appears*, which is to say is cognized, as *will*" (SW3, 221 [WWR2, 209]).[23]

But, whichever is the case, Schopenhauer's critique of intellectual intuition is *not* a reason for thinking that Schopenhauer himself is not trying to develop a transcendent metaphysics in which the Kantian thing in itself is identified as will. The problem with intellectual intuition, as we have shown, is not that it promises the impossible—access to the transcendent—but rather that, *as a specific cognitive strategy*, it is misplaced. And this leaves the door open to the possibility that there are other, legitimate, cognitive strategies that *can* yield metaphysical knowledge, for there may be a species of *nonintellectual* intuition that constitutes or provides the bridge to the thing in itself. Schopenhauer may be denying the *intellectual* not the *intuition*. This view is indeed prima facie plausible because of Schopenhauer's critique of the role of the intellect in general, especially in comparison with his contemporaries.

To be sure, Schopenhauer never claimed we have an intuition of the thing in itself. When he introduces the "deduction" of the will as thing in itself in WWR1, he contrasts our external cognition of our bodies with the special "inner" cognition or awareness we have of our bodies as will. But he consistently uses the term "intuition" to refer to our external, representational cognition, for example:

> The *will* makes itself known as the essence in itself of our own body, as that which it is *besides being an object of intuition.*   (SW2, 126 [WW1, 130]; emphasis added)

And in WWR2 he clearly states that "cognition of the will in self-consciousness is...not an *intuition* of the will" (SW3, 280 [WW2, 260]). In some ways, it is clear why Schopenhauer does this. He probably has in mind Kant's seamless view of experience, where inner experience (although structured only temporally) is not qualitatively distinct from outer experience (despite the fact that the latter is structured spatiotemporally): they both yield only knowledge of things—including ourselves—as *appearances*, not how they are in themselves. Such a seamless view of experience is probably the tacit presupposition governing the inference of those, like Young, who assume that Schopenhauer's rejection of intellectual intuition must entail a rejection of any transcendent metaphysics.

It is clear that Schopenhauer *wants* to break with Kant on this issue: he summarizes Kant's view (SW3, 219 [WWR2, 207]) and then immediately qualifies it by saying "I accept this for everything except the cognition everyone has of his own *willing*: this is neither an intuition (because all intuition is spatial), nor is it empty." He clearly thinks we have *some* form of access to ourselves (or rather our bodies) as will in inner awareness. He sometimes terms this "cognition [*Erkenntnis*]" (e.g., SW2, 121 [WW1, 126]). He is pretty clear that, whatever it is, it is "direct" and not mediated. But the term "cognition" is obviously going to raise similar Kantian issues, and so he often equivocates, terming it a form of "consciousness [*Bewußtsein*]" (SW2, 123 [WWR1, 128]) or, in perhaps the best term he developed, a "wholly immediate awareness [*Innewerden*]" (SW3, 280 [WWR2, 260]). But he does not hesitate about at least one thing: the philosophical task involves "raising immediate consciousness, concrete cognition, to rational knowledge or transferring it to abstract cognition" (SW2, 122 [WWR1, 127]) In other words, whatever the *sui generis* inner awareness of ourselves (bodies) as will *is*, it is functionally equivalent to an intuition in that it plays the same content-determining role as intuitions do in relation to concepts.

Schopenhauer's critique of intellectual intuition in Schelling is therefore not (on its own) evidence that Schopenhauer must be interpreted as giving up access to the thing in itself and as offering only a "hermeneutic" interpretation of experience as a whole. Schopenhauer, correctly understood, has a consistent way of rejecting Schelling and asserting his own metaphysics. Of course, there remain other objections, alluded to briefly earlier, operating from the Kantian axiom that the seamlessness of inner and outer experience entails the blanket inaccessibility of the thing in itself.

It is possible to resist these objections, and there is currently a lively debate on the issue in the literature.[24] Robert Wicks mentions, for instance, a kind of "veil of perception" model in which subtraction of transcendental forms of space and causality leaves inner awareness closer to the thing in itself than fully transcendentally realized intuitions: inner awareness of the will has fewer "veils," as it were.[25] Without being able to settle the issues here, this kind of interpretation could see Schopenhauer as an early practitioner of a kind of "phenomenology of the extreme" in which unusual "experiences" break through the ordinary and give us more fundamental insight.

On the other hand, the best evidence that Schopenhauer really does take his strictures on Schelling's intellectual intuition seriously is his own use of hermeneutic vocabulary to characterize the ultimate status of the will, what Young calls ("with some reservations") "the hermeneutic Schopenhauer."[26] The "deduction" of the will in WWR1 §18 relies on a thought experiment in which the world would "pass by us strange and meaningless" (SW2, 113 [WWR1, 119]) if it were only representation, suggesting that will provides the "meaning" of the world; will is therefore the "solution to a riddle" (SW2, 119 [WWR1, 124]), the "riddle of existence" (SW2, 168 [WWR1, 166]). Similarly, in WWR2 he presents metaphysics as (or on an analogy to) "deciphering" the meaning of a text (SW3, 204f [WWR2, 193]).

But is this really evidence that Schopenhauer ultimately realizes that his metaphysical task is too much like Schelling's intellectual intuition and should be (re)construed hermeneutically, not literally? It is not obvious, for the *metaphysical* understanding of will is able to give "meaning" to the world as representation precisely because it provides its content. The hermeneutic view of the will depends precisely on the metaphysical: intuitive representations give "meaning" to conceptual representations in the same way that the will gives meaning to *all* representation.

3.5 CONCLUSION

Schopenhauer's abusive language toward Schelling is, as we earlier quoted one contemporary as saying, "unbefitting a scholar." And indeed it is redundant, in that Schopenhauer was perfectly capable of framing his critical objections in legitimately scholarly language: in other words, the debate could easily have been conducted on much higher ground. That said, we have tried to show that attending to the nature and vehemence of the insults yields genuinely interesting results. On the one hand, the accusations of meaninglessness and "windbaggery" reinforce the legitimate criticism that Schelling's epistemic methods derive from a hypertrophied conception of reason. On the other hand, the intensity and tedious repetition of Schopenhauer's abusive language point perhaps more to the proximity of his philosophy to that of Schelling than to the distance. Indeed, both are developing metaphysics (a metaphysics, as Schelling comes to conceive it, of will) with full and conflicted awareness of the Kantian epistemic strictures against metaphysics.

In view of this, Schopenhauer is particularly concerned to mark his own project as legitimate by highlighting the manner in which he avoids Schelling's errors. Schelling was, perhaps, too close for comfort.

NOTES

1. Bryan Magee, *The Philosophy of Schopenhauer* (Oxford: Oxford University Press, 1983), 249.
2. Ibid., 248.
3. Indeed, his essay *On the Basis of Morality* was rejected for a prize by the Danish Royal Society in 1837, in part for the harsh things he had to say about Hegel. Not unexpectedly, this elicited an even more furious tirade in Schopenhauer's preface to the published version in 1841 (SW4, XVIIf [BM, 13f]).
4. See, for instance, Matthias Koßler, "Empirischer und intelligibler Charakter: von Kant über Fries und Schelling zu Schopenhauer," *Schopenhauer Jahrbuch* 76 (1995), 195–201; Lore Hühn, "Die intelligible Tat, zu einer Gemeinsamkeit Schillings und Schopenhauer," in *Selbstbesinnung der philosophischen Moderne: Beitrage zur kritische Hermeneutik ihrer Grundbegriffe*, edited by Christian Iber and Romano Pocai (Cuxhaven & Dartford: Junghans, 1998), 55–94; Andrew Bowie, *Aesthetics and Subjectivity: From Kant to Nietzsche* (Manchester: Manchester University Press, 2003), 261–70; many of the essays in *Die Ethik Arthur Schopenhauer im Ausgang vom Deutschen Idealismus (Fichte/Schelling)*, edited by Lore Hühn (Würzburg: Ergon Verlag, 2006); Lars-Thade Ulrichs, "Das Ganze der Erfahrung. Metaphysik und Wissenschaften bei Schopenhauer und Schelling," in *Internationales Jahrbuch des Deutschen Idealismus/International Yearbook of German Idealism: Philosophie und Wissenschaft/Philosophy and Science* 8(2010), 251–81; *L'héritage de Schelling/Das Erbe Schellings*: Interprétations aux XIXème et XXIème siècles/Interpretationen des 19. und 20. Jahrhundert, edited by Lore Hühn and Philipp Schwab (Freiburg/Munich: Verlag Karl Alber, 2015); and Marcello Ruta, *La Deuxième voie du postkantisme: Temporalité et éternité dans les philosophies de Schopenhauer et Schelling* (Paris: Éditions L'Harmattan, 2017). Of these, only Bowie's short section is available in English.
5. Indeed, the first review was written, albeit anonymously, by the Schellingian, Friedrich Ast. See David Cartwright, *Schopenhauer, A Biography* (New York: Cambridge University Press, 2010), 380.
6. Johann Friedrich Herbart *Hermes oder kritisches Jahrbuch der Literatur*, no. 3, 1820; reprinted in *Sechstes Jahrbuch der Schopenhauer-Gessellschafte* (1917), 89–117.
7. Cartwright, *Schopenhauer*, 388.
8. F. W. J. Schelling, *Philosophical Investigations into the Essence of Human Freedom*, translated by Jeff Love and Johannes Schmidt (Albany: State University of New York Press, 2006), 7:350. Pagination refers to F. W. J. Schelling, *Friedrich Wilhelm Joseph Schellings Sämtliche Werke*, edited by K. F. A. Schelling, I Abtheilung Vols. 1–10. Stuttgart: Cotta, 1856–1861. We will refer to this work using the standard designation as "the *Freedom* essay."
9. See also SW6, 62 [PP2, 57]).
10. *Critique of Practical Reason* [henceforth "second Critique"], translated by Lewis White Beck (New York: Macmillan, 1956), Ak. 5:47. Page references are to the "*Akademie*" [henceforth "Ak."] edition of Kant's works, Immanuel Kant, *Gesammelte Schriften* (Berlin: De Gruyter, 1902) by volume and page number. Schopenhauer is far from alone in thinking there is something amiss with this doctrine. See the introduction to Owen Ware, "Rethinking

Kant's Fact of Reason," *Philosophers' Imprint* 14, no. 32 (November 2014), 1–21, who himself defends Kant on the issue.

11. A few pages further on, Schopenhauer declares of a moral system that depends, like Kant's, on imperatives (rather than, like his, on virtue) "What a slave-morality! [*Sklavenmoral*]" (SW4, 134 [BM, 137]). See also Alistair Welchman, "Schopenhauer," in *The Cambridge History of Moral Philosophy*, edited by Sacha Golob and Jens Timmerman (Cambridge: Cambridge University Press), 448–58.

12. Ware, *Rethinking*, 16.

13. Kant affirms this connection while, of course, denying the existence of intellectual intuition, arguing that a noumenon should not be interpreted as "a special *intelligible object*" unless we have intellectual intuition (*Critique of Pure Reason*, translated by Paul Guyer and Allen Wood [Cambridge: Cambridge University Press, 1998], A256/B311-2; see also B307). Page references are to the standard A and B editions. Schopenhauer discusses this passage in WWR1 (SW2, 565 [WWR1, 505]).

14. Schopenhauer remarks that Kant had this insight, too, but "disregarded it" (SW4, 133 [BM, 136]). See Alistair Welchman, "Deleuze and Schopenhauer," in *At the Edges of Thought: Deleuze and Post-Kantian Philosophy*, edited by Craig Lundy and Daniella Voss (Edinburgh: Edinburgh University Press, 2015), 213–52.

15. This summary reworks some of Alistair Welchman, "Schopenhauer's Two Metaphysics: Transcendental and Transcendent," in *The Palgrave Schopenhauer Handbook*, edited by Sandra Shapshay (London: Palgrave/Macmillan), 129–49.

16. We have already seen how Kant laid the ground for this move with his "fact of reason."

17. See Julian Young, *Schopenhauer* (London: Routledge, 2005), 46–48; Young, *Willing and Unwilling: A Study of the Philosophy of Arthur Schopenhauer* (Dordrecht: Nijhoff, 1987), 23–25.

18. This is more or less equivalent to saying that concepts cannot go beyond *actual* rather than *possible* experience, even though Schopenhauer uses the latter phrase frequently. Young (*Schopenhauer*, 49) points this out as a problem.

19. See SW2, 46f [WWR1, 62f] where Schopenhauer remarks that if we did use intuitions or "images" to represent concepts in general, then our heads would be full of such pictures: "What a tumult there would be in our heads while listening to a speech or reading a book!" It seems likely that this passage influenced Wittgenstein's famous account of reading (and rejection of a mentalistic account of semantic content) in the *Philosophical Investigations*, translated by G. E. M. Anscombe (Oxford: Blackwell, 1953). It is worth noting that Schopenhauer later appears to deny the dependence of concepts on words (e.g., SW3, 67 [WWR2, 69]). Severin Schroeder, "Schopenhauer's Influence on Wittgenstein," in *A Companion to Schopenhauer*, edited by Bart Vandenabeele (Oxford: Blackwell, 2012), 367–84, at 379, notes the similarities but argues that Schopenhauer has not in fact seen the philosophical problem at all.

20. Young, *Schopenhauer*, 51.

21. Ibid., 90.

22. See John E. Atwell, *Schopenhauer on the Character of the World* (Berkeley: University of California Press, 1995), chapters 3 and 4; Julian Young, *Schopenhauer*; Sandra Shapshay, "Poetic Intuition and the Bounds of Sense: Metaphor and Metonymy in Schopenhauer's Philosophy," *European Journal of Philosophy* 16 (2008), 214–16; Sandra Shapshay "The Enduring Kantian Presence in Schopenhauer's Philosophy" (in this volume, Chapter 6); and Christopher Janaway, "Will and Nature," in *The Cambridge Companion to Schopenhauer*, edited by Christopher Janaway (Cambridge: Cambridge University Press, 2006), 138–70, for a summary.

23. *"Demnach ist zwar der Willensakt nur die nächste und deutlichte Erscheinung des Dinges an sich."*

24. See earlier discussion.

25. Robert Wicks, *Schopenhauer* (Oxford: Blackwell, 2008), 67f. See SW2, 130–31 (WWR1, 134–35) and SW3, 220f (WWR2, 208–09).

26. Ibid., 94.

FURTHER READING

Atwell, John E. *Schopenhauer on the Character of the World.* Berkeley: University of California Press, 1995.

Bowie, Andrew. *Aesthetics and Subjectivity: From Kant to Nietzsche.* Manchester: Manchester University Press, 2003.

Cartwright, David. *Schopenhauer: A Biography.* New York: Cambridge University Press, 2010.

Gardner, Sebastian. "Schopenhauer's Contraction of Reason: Clarifying Kant and Undoing German Idealism." *Kantian Review* 17, no. 3 (2012): 375–401.

Herbart, Johann Friedrich. Hermes oder kritishces Jahrbuch der Litteratur, no. 3, 1820. From Sechstes Jahrbuch der Schopenhauer-Gessellschafte (1917).

Hühn, Lore. "Die intelligible Tat, zu einer Gemeinsamkeit Schillings und Schopenhauer." In *Selbstbesinnung der philosophischen Moderne: Beitrage zur kritische Hermeneutik ihrer Grundbegriffe*, edited by Christian Iber, Romano Pocai, 55–94. Cuxhaven & Dartford: Junghans, 1998.

Hühn, Lore, ed. *Die Ethik Arthur Schopenhauer im Ausgang vom Deutschen Idealismus (Fichte/Schelling).* Würzburg: Ergon Verlag, 2006.

Hühn, Lore, and Philipp Schwab, eds. *L'héritage de Schelling/Das Erbe Schellings*: Interprétations aux XIXème et XXIème siècles/Interpretationen des 19. und 20. Jahrhundert. Freiburg/Munich: Verlag Karl Alber, 2015.

Jacquette, Dale. "Schopenhauer's Proof that the Thing-in-Itself Is Will." *Kantian Review* 12, no. 2 (2007): 76–108.

Janaway, Christopher. *Self and World in Schopenhauer's Philosophy.* Oxford: Clarendon Press, 1998.

Janaway, Christopher. "Will and Nature." In *The Cambridge Companion to Schopenhauer*, edited by Christopher Janaway. Cambridge: Cambridge University Press, 2006, 138–70.

Kant, Immanuel. 1782/87. *Critique of Pure Reason*, translated by Paul Guyer and Allen Wood. Cambridge: Cambridge University Press, 1998.

Kant, Immanuel. 1788. *Critique of Practical Reason*, translated by Lewis White Beck. New York: Macmillan, 1956.

Kant, Immanuel. *Gesammelte Schriften.* Berlin: De Gruyter, 1902.

Kosch, Michelle. *Freedom and Reason in Kant, Schelling and Kierkegaard.* Oxford: The Clarendon Press, 2006.

Koßler, Matthias. "Empirischer und intelligibler Charakter: von Kant über Fries und Schelling zu Schopenhauer," *Schopenhauer Jahrbuch* 76 (1995): 195–201.

Magee, Bryan. *The Philosophy of Schopenhauer.* Oxford: Oxford University Press, 1983.

Norman, Judith. "The Idea of Intellectual Intuition from Kant to Hegel." PhD dissertation University of Wisconsin–Madison, 1995.

Pippin, Robert B. *Hegel's Idealism: The Satisfactions of Self-Consciousness.* Cambridge: Cambridge University Press, 1989.

Ruta, Marcello. *La Deuxième voie du postkantisme: Temporalité et éternité dans les philosophies de Schopenhauer et Schelling*. Paris: Éditions L'Harmattan, 2017.

Schelling, F. W. J. *Friedrich Wilhelm Joseph Schellings Sämtliche Werke*, ed. K.F.A. Schelling, I Abtheilung, Vols. 1–10; II Abtheilung Vols. 1–4. Stuttgart: Cotta 1856–1861.

Schelling, F. W. J. *Philosophical Investigations into the Essence of Human Freedom*, translated by Jeff Love and Johannes Schmidt. Albany: State University of New York Press, 2006.

Schroeder, Severin. "Schopenhauer's Influence on Wittgenstein." In *A Companion to Schopenhauer*, edited by Bart Vandenabeele. Oxford: Blackwell, 2012, 367–84.

Shapshay, Sandra. "Poetic Intuition and the Bounds of Sense: Metaphor and Metonymy in Schopenhauer's Philosophy." *European Journal of Philosophy* 16 (2008): 214–16.

Shapshay, Sandra. "The Enduring Kantian Presence in Schopenhauer's Philosophy," (in this volume, Chapter 6).

Ulrichs, Lars-Thade. "Das Ganze der Erfahrung. Metaphysik und Wissenschaften bei Schopenhauer und Schelling." *Internationales Jahrbuch des Deutschen Idealismus/International Yearbook of German Idealism: Philosophie und Wissenschaft/Philosophy and Science*, 8, (2010): 251–81.

Ware, Owen. "Rethinking Kant's Fact of Reason." *Philosophers' Imprint* 14, no. 32 (November 2014): 1–21.

Welchman, Alistair. "Deleuze and Schopenhauer." In *At the Edges of Thought: Deleuze and Post-Kantian Philosophy*, edited by Craig Lundy and Daniella Voss. Edinburgh: Edinburgh University Press, 2015, 213–52.

Welchman, Alistair. "Schopenhauer's Two Metaphysics." In *The Palgrave Companion to Schopenhauer*, edited by Sandra Shapshay. London: Palgrave/Macmillan, 2017, 129–49.

Welchman, Alistair. "Schopenhauer." In *The Cambridge History of Moral Philosophy*, edited by Sacha Golob and Jens Timmerman. Cambridge: Cambridge University Press, 2017, 448–58.

Wicks, Robert. *Schopenhauer*. Oxford: Blackwell, 2008.

Wittgenstein, Ludwig. *Philosophical Investigations*. Translated by G. E. M. Anscombe. Oxford: Blackwell, 1953.

Young, Julian. *Willing and Unwilling: A Study of the Philosophy of Arthur Schopenhauer*. Dordrecht: Nijhoff, 1987.

Young, Julian. *Schopenhauer*. London: Routledge, 2005.

CHAPTER 4

FICHTE AND SCHOPENHAUER ON KNOWLEDGE, ETHICS, RIGHT, AND RELIGION

YOLANDA ESTES

4.1 INTRODUCTION: SCHOPENHAUER AND TRANSCENDENTAL IDEALISM

SCHOPENHAUER said little about what he owed to Johann Gottlieb Fichte. Nonetheless, a careful reader will discern some commonalities between transcendental philosophers such as Kant, Fichte, (the young) Schelling, and Schopenhauer. Not only does he share the transcendental approach with his predecessors, the concept of subjectivity remains central in his philosophy—a concept crucial to the philosophy of transcendental idealism.[1] In 1811, Schopenhauer moved to Berlin, where he remained until 1813. He devoted considerable attention to Kant during this time, but he also became familiar with Fichte, attending his lectures on *The Facts of Consciousness* (1812) and the *Wissenschaftslehre* (1812).[2] Moreover, he read many of Fichte's earlier works, including *System of Ethics: According to the Principles of the Wissenschaftslehre* (1798) and *Foundations of Natural Right: According to the Principles of the Wissenschaftslehre* (1796/97).[3] In addition to these more academic lectures and writings, he read one of Fichte's last popular works, *Way to the Blessed Life: Or also, the Religionslehre* (1806).[4]

During his years as a student, Schopenhauer managed to familiarize himself with the main parts of the *Wissenschaftslehre*: theoretical philosophy, practical philosophy, and philosophy of the postulates.[5] He kept notes—found in his *Manuscript Remains*—of his sojourns in Fichte's transcendental idealism, or *Wissenschaftsleere* as he deridingly called it. In later years, he returned to Fichte's philosophy—sometimes explicitly and sometimes implicitly—in the *Basis of Morality* (1840) and the *World as Will and Representation* (1859). In this chapter, I use both Schopenhauer's early notes in the *Manuscript Remains* and his later published writings to show how he understood Fichte's transcendental idealism, where he disagreed with it, and where he (sometimes grudgingly) acknowledged its value.

4.2 Fichte and Schopenhauer on the Theory of Cognition, or the Theoretical *Wissenschaftslehre*

Fichte's theoretical philosophy (of cognition), which he usually just called *Wissenschaftslehre*, was the part of his philosophy that accounted for the possibility of knowledge. It included his deductions of space, time, and what we normally call the categories of the understanding. The theoretical philosophy is supposed to explain how we must think about the natural world and our relation to it as free but limited human subjects. As mentioned earlier, Fichte gave a series of lectures on the *Facts of Consciousness* and the *Wissenschaftslehre* proper in 1812 that Schopenhauer attended, where the former lectures served as a preliminary to the latter.

Unlike early versions of the *Wissenschaftslehre* that address the pure I and its appearance in the sensible world as an individual I, the *Wissenschaftslehre* of 1812 addresses Absolute *Sein*, or Being, and its appearance as Absolute Knowledge within *Dasein*, existence or consciousness. Nonetheless, the concepts of the pure I and the individual I do make an occasional appearance in this version of the *Wissenschaftslehre*.

In the *Facts of Consciousness*, Fichte introduces the idea of philosophy. Philosophical knowledge, or *Wissenschaftslehre*, explains the ground of all knowledge: it is knowledge about knowledge. As such, it must assume a higher standpoint of abstraction than any other form of knowledge. The transcendental philosopher must survey the field of inquiry from the standpoint of philosophy, or the standpoint of absolute thought (*Besonnenheit*).

From the standpoint of absolute thought, the transcendental philosopher observes consciousness, or the I, which posits itself as principle, or the form of knowledge. This I-form (*Ich-form*) is the representer of the world. It is the principle of the synthetic unity of apperception that unites all of its representations as its own. Moreover, the I is a principle of reality—of real being—so it is a practical principle. As an active I that affects the world of which it is a part, consciousness is always arranging the world in new and different ways, but always, at the same time, it is working on a world of material things that it was given in intuition.

Consciousness is guided in its activity by the concept of a goal, which it constructs in consequence of a drive to activity, conceives through its ideal (thinking) activity, and realizes through its real (practical) activity. Each successive action changes the world and, thus, the drive reemerges as an endless series of impulses compelling the I to construct new concepts of goals that satisfy its demands. The resulting endless series of actions on the part of the I, says Fichte, is the revelation of Absolute Being, which is described by the I as an ever-changing image (*Bild*). The I reflects on its drive and formulates it as a practical law for itself—an ought (*Sollen*)—that commands unconditionally for the I to express Being through a series of images. Through the interactions between the pure I's real and ideal activities, the sensible world of ordinary consciousness—the factual world—comes to exist for the individual I. However, the factual world is not the object of philosophical knowledge.

As Fichte had said of earlier presentations of his philosophy, so he says of the *Wissenschaftslehre* of 1812 that philosophical knowledge is really one concept that contains a series of concepts. The concept whereby philosophy begins is Being. The *Wissenschaftslehre* begins with the concept of Being and is concerned with the relation between Being, God, and consciousness. God cannot be expressed through any positive description, but the essence of God does appear in consciousness through the actions of the moral-religious subject.

Being appears in consciousness as knowledge (*Wissen*), which assumes the form of a self, or I, as principle. The entire *Wissenschaftslehre* is, according to Fichte, an analysis of this I, or freedom. The various relations between Being and consciousness are resolved within a central fivefold synthesis of substance, accident, principle (willing), principiate (product), and an ought, which is ultimately revealed to be the Categorical Imperative (or the law that consciousness *ought* to construct an image of Being) and which is ultimately fulfilled by the *Wissenschaftslehre* itself. Consciousness, guided by a concept of a goal that satisfies its fundamental drive to activity, constructs this image of being through its activity, which appears in the factual world as willing.

In the process of explaining this expression of Being as consciousness, Fichte attempts to derive the categories of the understanding and to show the reciprocal relationship between the sensible, visible world, and the supersensible, invisible world. He also argues that consciousness must find itself as an individual within a system of other I's. The concept of God and the concept of the *Wissenschaftslehre* are actually empty according to Fichte. They clarify—they create a space for—one thing alone: the will. The *Wissenschaftslehre* serves a higher purpose, which is to prepare the ground for morality. The true work (and worth) of philosophy remains to be accomplished after the theoretical *Wissenschaftslehre* is completed.

It appears that when Schopenhauer attended Fichte's lectures on the *Facts of Consciousness* and the *Wissenschaftslehre*, he followed Fichte's admonition to avoid taking detailed notes during class. He seems to have completed fairly close transcriptions of Fichte's lectures from memory after returning home, faithful to what Fichte actually said during the lectures. Sadly, the younger philosopher's reactions are overwhelmingly negative, aphoristic, and sarcastic. As a result, we learn more about the *Wissenschaftslehre* of 1812 than we do about its possible influence on Schopenhauer. There is room, of course, for speculation (in the nontechnical sense). It does seem that Schopenhauer's interests were piqued enough to keep him engaged with Fichte's lectures and texts for some time to come.

Schopenhauer's own ideas about the relation between willing and representation seem hardly to have developed in a vacuum. He most definitely regarded sensible existence as a result of willing. Despite his tendency to give greater credit to the Sage of Königsberg than to Fichte, there are much stronger idealistic, and existentialist, elements— such as those we discover in *The World as Will and Representation*—to be found in the *Wissenschaftslehre* of 1812 than in the *Critique of Pure Reason*.

In Fichte's philosophy, we find the explicit discussion of the relation between the one pure I, the system of I's, and the individual I. Schopenhauer does not extract these ideas from Fichte's work and simply insert them into his own, but there seems to have been some influence on his notions of the one noumenal will, the many interconnected wills, and the individual will. Like Fichte, he regards sensible consciousness as a manifestation of ultimate reality.

Most of all, Fichte and Schopenhauer would agree that the problem of philosophy is to show that willing is the ground of the sensible world order. Although Schopenhauer argues that selfless virtue is produced by a good disposition rather than through abstract moral philosophy, he does not regard moral philosophy as useless. Moral philosophy concerns the thing-in-itself that reveals itself in its phenomenon, the individual will. Ultimately, he regards philosophy as providing a path to and an understanding of moral life as well.

4.3 Fichte and Schopenhauer on the Theory of Ethics, or the Practical Wissenschaftslehre (Sittenlehre)

The practical *Wissenschaftslehre*, or *Sittenlehre*, considers the universal and necessary laws of reason to which the willing of every rational subject must conform.[6] Fichte's first written formulation of his *Sittenlehre* appeared as the *System of Ethics According to the Principles of the Wissenschaftslehre*. In the *Manuscript Remains*, *The Basis of Morality*, and *The World as Will and Representation*, Schopenhauer criticizes many aspects of this work. He rejects the Categorical Imperative as the basic principle of morality, the concept of practical reason, the role of duty as a moral motive, and the idea of sensibility as an aspect of the moral world. Nonetheless, like Fichte, he emphasizes the form of moral willing, the motive of moral action, and the role of feeling in moral consciousness.

The first part of the *Sittenlehre*, or the "Deduction of the Principle of Morality," is not a traditional derivation that purports to *prove* the reality of the Categorical Imperative or its supremacy as an ethical foundation. Instead, it contains a transcendental argument which shows that the principle of morality conditions individual self-consciousness. The deduction begins with a problem, or postulate. The reader, or would-be transcendental philosopher, must follow Fichte's request to "think oneself, merely as oneself, i.e., separated from everything that is not ourselves."[7] This act of thinking leads to the discovery that a rational individual becomes conscious of itself only insofar as it becomes conscious of its willing activity.[8] Since a rational subject is necessarily self-conscious, individual self-consciousness is necessarily conditioned by the subject's discovery of its willing activity.[9] However, if the rational subject can perceive its willing, it must be a determinate willing that seeks to produce some alteration in a possible object. The act of willing presupposes some object outside of the willing subject. A rational subject never perceives itself as it is *in itself*, but only as it is *related to external things*.

If the I is considered in abstraction from external things, its essential characteristic is a tendency to self-activity for its own sake. The rational subject intuits this tendency as itself, so it posits itself as possessing a "power of causality by means of mere concepts," or freedom.[10] This tendency appears as a drive within the entire I, which grounds its real self-activity. The entire I, however, is both subjective and objective—a subject-object—which neither the rational individual nor the transcendental philosopher can grasp *as* the identity of subject and object.[11]

The I must be considered as subject and object separately: first, by thinking of the objective side being dependent on the subjective and, second, by thinking of the subjective side being dependent on the objective. This reflection on the two sides of consciousness yields two claims. *Feeling* is the unification of the subjective and the objective in the I insofar as the subjective side of the I is dependent on the objective. *Willing* is the unification of the subjective and the objective in the I insofar as the objective side of the I is dependent on the subjective. Because of the appearance of the drive to self-activity within consciousness, the I thinks of itself as having duties.

The thought of duty can be considered with regard to its form and content. With regard to its *form* it is an aspect of the entire I, which conditions all other thinking (i.e., it is only conditioned and determined through itself). In this regard, the thought of duty is absolute. Ordinary consciousness, which includes moral consciousness, begins with this thought. It is an *intellectual intuition*; specifically, it is the *real* intellectual intuition, which occurs in all rational beings whenever they become aware of their duties and without which the *philosophical* intellectual intuition would not be possible.[12] With regard to its *content*, this thought is also absolute. Its content is that the rational subject must give itself the unbreakable law of self-activity.

The subjective and objective sides of the I are reciprocally determining. Self-legislation occurs when the rational subject thinks of itself as free; the rational subject thinks of itself as free when it imposes the law of self-activity on itself. In form and content the thought of self-legislation is the absolute principle of the I's essence. If any rational being is assumed, it must think of itself as self-sufficient and, thus, as free under the law of self-sufficiency. Considered as such, a rational being is absolute and self-sufficient, is purely and simply its own ground—is nothing apart from its own agency: it must make itself into what it is *and* is nothing that it does not make itself to be. The concept of freedom and the law of self-sufficiency stand in a reciprocal relation within one synthesis.[13]

The derived law of self-sufficiency, or principle of morality, is the "necessary thought of the intellect that it ought to determine its freedom in accordance with the concept of self sufficiency, absolutely and without exception."[14] The "Deduction of the Principle of Morality" accounts for the general form and content of the concept of duty and how it is related to the possibility of individual consciousness. It does not describe the ordinary moral consciousness of the non-philosopher who does not normally think about its duties by means of abstract, universal reasoning. Moreover, it does not imply that any rational individual becomes aware of the principle of morality without engaging in some kind of reflection, philosophical or otherwise.

Within ordinary consciousness, if a rational individual thinks that a particular action is free, then that individual also thinks that action ought to be regulated in some way, even if only for other people. However, whether the principle of morality—and concomitant concept of freedom—is considered from the philosophical or the ordinary standpoint, neither the transcendental philosopher nor the moral individual "is *permitted*" to doubt it. No theoretical reason can be offered for refusing to question moral conviction, but a practical reason can be given that consists in "the firm resolution to grant *primacy* to *practical reason*, to hold the moral law to be the true and ultimate determination of our essence, and not to transform it into an illusion by means of sophistical reasoning."[15]

Fichte's concept of practical reason indicates no power of thought that is entirely distinct from theoretical reason but, rather, the practical employment of one and the same reason that can also be used in a theoretical capacity. No type of reasoning is "mere ratiocination," but rather all reasoning is self-intuiting acting, so all reason is practical in essence. However, because reason is finite, its activity is limited, or determinate. This determinacy appears as an *ought*, which pure reason imposes on itself and which occurs in theoretical philosophy as a hypothesis, or *qualitas occulta*, and within practical philosophy as the Categorical Imperative. All thinking—whether it is *ideal* thinking about duty or *real* thinking about objective things, all consciousness—whether it is of the intelligible world of *doing* or the sensible world of *being*, and all acting—whether it is real *efficacious* activity or ideal *representing* activity—follows from this original, autonomous activity of one, single reason.[16]

Through the *feeling* of respect, the ethical "drive for freedom simply for freedom's sake" becomes conscious.[17] If the moral individual clarifies this feeling in reflection, it formulates the demand for free activity as the Categorical Imperative. Consequently, the principle of morality is the moral subject's own product, or concept, based on a real intellectual intuition of its freedom in willing. The moral individual produces this principle by reflecting on its own freedom and thus even the most basic moral consciousness requires activity on the individual's part.

The ethical drive demands reasons's self-sufficiency as its end. In subordinating its freedom to the law of self-sufficiency, the moral individual must do "what duty demands, *because duty commands* it."[18] However, in order to act dutifully, the moral subject needs a criterion to discern what duty requires. If dutiful acting is possible, there must be such a criterion because the moral law never demands the impossible. However, the moral law is not a power of thinking. It cannot cognize the concept of some specific action that satisfies the ethical drive. The ethical drive compels the *theoretical* power of *reflective judgment* to search for some particular action, which promotes reason's self-sufficiency, until the moral subject develops a firm *conviction* that it has discovered the requisite action. This conviction must be tested by the *practical* power of *conscience*.

When reflective judgment has discovered an action that conscience can confirm, the concept of the proposed action coincides with the demand of the ethical drive. This harmony produces a *feeling* of "cold approval," which is the voice of conscience and the ultimate criterion of duty.[19] An action is morally obligatory if and only if conscience confirms it as such. Every moral individual must consider its judgment against its own feeling because "there is absolutely no external criterion for the binding force of an ethical command."[20] Individual moral conviction is not a condition of passivity but reason's free submission to the practical power of conscience. Although each moral individual must answer to its own conscience, developing its own convictions, all moral individuals should engage in reciprocal interactions with others in an effort to reach "communally shared practical convictions" because the end of the moral law is not the individual, who is but "one of the instruments of its realization in the sensible world," but reason as a whole.[21]

If it is true that the moral individual is "a tool of the moral law in the sensible world," it is equally true that the "entire sensible world is supposed to come under the dominion of reason, to be a tool of reason in the hands of rational beings," which requires continuous reciprocal interactions among the moral individual, other rational beings, and the sensible world.[22] The sensible world is a condition for the possibility of the intelligible world and morality. Indeed, there is no intelligible world apart from the sensible (and no sensible world apart from the intelligible). Ultimately, the goal of reason is to thoroughly integrate the intelligible world within every aspect of the sensible world.

Unlike Fichte or Kant, Schopenhauer does not offer a doctrine of duty based on an unconditional ought. He argues instead that ethics is concerned with what human beings actually do rather than with what they ought to do. The task of ethical theory is to discover the origins of moral and immoral actions. Ethics is an empirical inquiry that explains morally worthy deeds, such as disinterested justice and kindness, by accounting for the incentives that compel people to perform them.

Egoism, malice, and compassion are the three basic motives for all human activity in Schopenhauer's view. Egoism is the human essence, which consists in the drive for life and prosperity. The egoistic individual prioritizes its own needs and desires without regard for others. Although egoism is a powerful—and by far the most common— incentive for human behavior, there are others. For example, malice makes others' suffering an end in itself, whereas compassion makes others' well-being an end in itself. Schopenhauer claims that only actions motivated by compassion have moral worth.

According to Schopenhauer, anything that motivates the will is connected to the well-being of a subject (insofar as it either conforms to or conflicts with that subject's will). Most actions promote the rational individual's own well-being, but moral actions promote another person's well-being. In order for the idea of another person's well-being to influence the moral individual's will, the individual must experience the other person's suffering and desire. The moral individual must identify with the other person in such a manner that the usual differences between them become irrelevant. This occurs when *compassion* alters the individual's concept of the other person.

Schopenhauer's basic principle of morality is: "Harm no one; rather help everyone to the extent that you can" (BM, 162). The virtues of justice (refraining from harming others) and loving-kindness (endeavoring to help others) follow from this principle. The other virtues can be explained on the basis of these two. Nonetheless, compassion itself remains a mystery that defies rational explanation. In some sense, egoism and malice are as mysterious as compassion because reason cannot account for the proportions of egoism, malice, and compassion that exist within any particular moral individual.

Egoism, malice, and compassion determine the relative weight of the potential motives that operate on the moral subject. They form its *empirical* character, which appears discursively through its deeds as a phenomenal individual in time and space. The *intelligible* character of the moral subject is determined by the one will, or thing-in-itself. The moral subject is meritorious or blameworthy on account of its essence, which is inalterable and manifest in time as its individuality. Thus, Schopenhauer argues that the moral individual is both entirely determined by its nature but entirely responsible for its actions.

Whatever conforms to the desire of the individual will is *good* (for that individual) and whatever conflicts with it is *bad* (for that individual). The person who promotes others' interests is a *good* person. The good person exhibits the virtues of justice and loving-kindness in response to compassion or the direct participation in the well-being or suffering of others. Essentially, the good person (who possesses compassion and is less egoistic) makes less distinction between itself and others, whereas the *bad* person (who lacks compassion and is more egoistic, or even malicious) makes more distinction between itself and others.

Viewed from the empirical standpoint, the bad, or egoistic, person is justified, but the plurality of wills experienced at the empirical standpoint is merely the consequence of the *Principium Individuationis*, which is only operative at the level of space and time. True comprehension of the nature of ultimate reality, or the thing-in-itself, obliterates this distinction between individual wills and is the metaphysical basis of compassion, which the philosopher conceives at the transcendental standpoint and which the moral individual grasps intuitively.

Conscience gives the moral subject insight into the ultimate relation between itself and others. It is a presentiment, revealed through feeling, that the distinction between individual wills at the empirical standpoint is illusory. Through conscience the individual comes to know its unchanging intelligible character by observing its ongoing empirical deeds. It experiences its conscience through feelings of dissatisfaction or satisfaction that arise when it thinks about its own behavior.

Schopenhauer believed that Kant's greatest contribution to ethics was the elimination of eudaemonism, which gives precedence to the production of happiness. He also commended Kant for showing that the moral worth of human action did not depend on the laws of the phenomenal world but rather on those of the noumenal world. Likewise, he praised Kant's recognition that morality was the link to the intelligible world (*mundus noumenôn*). Nonetheless, Schopenhauer reserved some of his sharpest criticism for

Kant, and many of his objections to Kant's ethics apply to Fichte's ethics as well. Indeed, he regards Fichte's ethics as "a magnifying glass for the errors of the Kantian," which should "convince anyone of the worthlessness of Kant's ethical foundation" (BM, 124–25).

Schopenhauer denies both Kant's and Fichte's characterization of the moral law as an absolute, or unconditional, "ought" because he regards obedience to any command as conditioned by some presupposed reward or punishment. Moreover, he claims that an autonomous will cannot be subject to a moral law that dictates the content of willing. He condemns most of Kant's formulations of the Categorical Imperative as covert hypothetical imperatives that appeal to egoistic inclinations. Indeed, he accuses Kant of eudaemonism and egoism insofar as Kant's concept of the highest good connects virtue and happiness.

Schopenhauer also rejects the idea that the moral law commands respect for the rational being as an end-in-itself. Fichte claimed that the rational being's potential to serve as an instrument of the moral law—its capacity for freely determined action—should be respected as an end-in-itself, which possesses absolute, or immeasurable worth. Schopenhauer counters that ends are always motives relative to some will and thus that there can be no ends-in-themselves. Moreover, he argues that since worth is always comparative, the notion of immeasurable worth is contradictory.

Ultimately, Schopenhauer believes the "ought" functions in Fichte's ethics as a type of moral fate that determines the moral subject to act only on maxims sanctioned by the Categorical Imperative, but which is never satisfied insofar as it compels the moral subject to engage in ceaseless and aimless striving. He points to several passages in the *Sittenlehre* that he believes illustrate this fatalism, but he claims it is also evident in the *Wissenschaftslehre* of 1812. Although Schopenhauer mocks Fichte's conception of the ought as a principle that uses individuals as its vehicle, some scholars have argued that he also admits this relation between moral law and the individual will.[23]

Schopenhauer claims "Practical Reason is not what Fichte regarded it as: i.e., a special faculty, *qualitas occulta*, moral instinct" (BM, 61). Instead, he argues that all reason is practical insofar as it is merely a tool of the will. "Practical reason" is simply prudence, or reflection on the best means for accomplishing any goal, regardless of its moral implications. The supreme law of practical reason is thus not the moral law but the principle of sufficient reason, which the moral subject disregards in an effort to promote other individuals' causes that might run counter to its own interests. Schopenhauer also counters Fichte's claim that the theoretical and practical powers are two capacities of one reason by appealing to Kant's assertion that the unity of theoretical and practical reason cannot be found within the I's activity.

Schopenhauer believes Fichte's account of moral judgment is flawed. He suggests that we do not always have time for moral reflection. Moreover, he claims that the moral law reveals what should be done immediately and that reflection on duty is often an attempt to find an excuse for not performing an action the moral law has already commanded. He raises many of the objections commonly addressed to deontological ethics as well. Schopenhauer asks, for instance, about the possibility of an action undertaken sincerely that is based on a mistaken judgment or the case of the reformed criminal who is suddenly transformed into a good person despite his past. He considers the confusion often befuddling the moral agent, who wonders which of two actions is right. He proposes the possibility of a collision of duties that must be compared to each other as well as the question of the limits of imperfect duties and how each is to be weighed against the other. Ultimately, he claims that Fichte proposes a free indifferent choice based on trivial and frivolous reasons (BM, 127).

Schopenhauer objects to Fichte's stipulation that morally worthy action must be motivated by respect for the moral law or the concept of duty rather than inclinations or emotions, including sympathy. He is dissatisfied with Fichte's de-emphasis of sympathy in morality since he believes that genuine moral virtue requires the motive of compassion. Indeed, Schopenhauer thinks that Fichte condemns actions inspired by sympathy and kindness because he says that the desire to promote the goals of reason should motivate acts of charity. Overall, he believes that Fichte offers a frail substitute for the sentiment of loving-kindness. He also argues that Fichte misunderstands the basic nature of morality, which is concerned with "what we do" (i.e., willing, rather than with what is done; i.e., the deed).[24]

Although Schopenhauer rejects many aspects of Kant's ethics, including his Categorical Imperative, he congratulated Kant for limiting reason by postulating a supersensible realm wherein the principle of morality, rather than the principle of sufficient reason, applied. He argues that Fichte violates this limitation by treating the intelligible and the sensible realms as interdependent. Schopenhauer rejects this interdetermination of morality and sensibility in Fichte's ethics, insisting instead on a sharp delineation between the sensible individual and the one, noumenal will. He also views Fichte's claims about the "comprehensibility" of the moral law as violating the boundary between the sensible and supersensible realms. Indeed, Schopenhauer objects to Fichte's use of the term "ordinary consciousness" (i.e., nonphilosophical, natural consciousness) to refer to moral consciousness.

Despite their differences, the moral theories of Fichte and Schopenhauer share several features. In their ethics, it is not the particular deeds or results that matter but rather the form that willing takes within the individual. Specifically, willing must be the free product of the moral subject's activity. In Schopenhauer's case, this means that the subject's intelligible character is the author of its action. Although Fichte and Schopenhauer would disagree about the proper motivation for moral activity, each regards the motive of willing as determining the moral worth of an action. Fichte believes that morally worthy actions are motivated by respect for duty, whereas Schopenhauer believes they are motivated by compassion. In both cases, they would argue that only morally worthy actions—as they define them—gain the approval of conscience, which is manifest in *feeling*.

Both Fichte and Schopenhauer stress the role of feeling and intuition in moral consciousness. Conscience expresses its approval and disapproval through feeling. Despite their differences regarding conscience and its role in ethics, Fichte and Schopenhauer both claim that the moral subject feels satisfaction or dissatisfaction in response to its moral activities. For Fichte, the moral law is not a feeling or intuition, *but*, through the feeling of respect, the ethical drive becomes conscious (and if reflected upon allows for the formulation of the moral law). Schopenhauer believes that both moral consciousness and the philosophical account for ethics require intuitive knowledge of the relation between individuality and the will in-itself. Although Fichte's idea of intellectual intuition is very different from Schopenhauer's idea of intuitive knowledge, he does believe that moral consciousness is related to a real intellectual intuition of freedom.

4.4 Fichte and Schopenhauer on the Theory of Right, or the *Rechtslehre*

Fichte's *Sittenlehre* deals with reason as a whole, but reason appears within many individuals who can and do come into conflict. The goal of reason must be accomplished through the unification of these many different wills, so their individual freedom must be restricted to ensure that each person's freedom can be expressed. The theory of right, or the *Rechtslehre*, addresses this task. The *Rechtslehre* is part of the "philosophy of the postulates," which deals with the postulate that theory gives to practice, or freedom: many free individuals must unite in peaceful relations.

In the *Foundations of Natural Right: According to the Principles of the Wissenschaftslehre* (1796/1797), Fichte first articulated his *Rechtslehre*. Schopenhauer read this work and kept detailed notes on it, which are preserved in the *Manuscript Remains*. In his later writings, he returned to the subject of right, but generally elided any direct critique of Fichte's *Rechtslehre*. He disagrees with Fichte about numerous issues, the most important of which are the *Aufforderung*, or summons; the theoretical ground of the *Rechtslehre*; and the practical goals of society. He does, however, grant Fichte that the decision to enter into community with others rests on a hypothetical imperative and thus that there is no overarching moral obligation to establish a social contract.

In the *Rechtslehre*, Fichte's initial project is to deduce the concept of right, or the necessary relations between rational subjects. Doing this requires answering the question, "How can the subject find itself as an object?"[25] In order to discover itself as something real, the rational subject must posit itself (i.e., must become self-conscious). However, a rational being cannot become self-conscious without attributing a free efficacy to itself, which requires it to posit an object that opposes its efficacy; it cannot posit an object, though, if it is not really efficacious. Thus, Fichte's argument appears circular. He explains that "the reason the possibility of self-consciousness cannot be explained without always presupposing it as already actual lies in the fact that, in order to be able to posit its own efficacy, the subject of self-consciousness, must have already posited an object, simply as an object."[26]

To extricate himself from this difficulty, Fichte introduces the hypothesis that the rational being's efficacy must be precisely this "already posited" object. However, the rational being feels the object as a determinate limitation on its activity, but the object and the subject are supposed to be united, so the subject must find itself as constrained and free simultaneously, which seems contradictory. Fichte argues that the rational being can find itself in this manner only if "we think of the subject's being-determined as *its being-determined to be self-determining*, i.e., as a summons [*eine Aufforderung*] to the subject, calling upon it to resolve to exercise its efficacy."[27]

An *Aufforderung* from another rational subject initiates the rational being's self-awareness without undermining its freedom because, in grasping the summons, the subject chooses freely to act or not to act in deference to another subject. The subject's self-concept is necessarily connected to the thought of reciprocal interaction between individuals—a relation of mutual determination—whereby, "a particular sphere is allotted to the subject as the sphere of its possible activity."[28] The *principle of right* enjoins: "I must in all cases recognize the free being outside me as a free being, i.e., I must limit my freedom through the concept of the possibility of his freedom."[29]

Unlike Kant (and Schopenhauer), Fichte does not think that the *Rechtslehre* is grounded in the *Sittenlehre*. Although the theories of morality and right are ultimately derived from the same principle of intellectual intuition, which originally appeared as a theoretical hypothesis, or *qualitas occulta*, in the theoretical *Wissenschaftslehre* they constitute separate parts of philosophy. Moreover, the summons to act freely, which appears as the Categorical Imperative—the *principle of morality*—in the *Sittenlehre*, appears as a hypothetical imperative—the *principle of right*—in the *Rechtslehre*.[30]

Fichte claims that the *Sittenlehre* and the *Rechtslehre* have different objectives. The principle of morality commands the moral subject to respect freedom in itself and others as an end in itself. The principle of right solicits the rational subject to defer to the freedom of others as a condition for recognizing and preserving its individual freedom. To be sure, if everyone followed the moral law and agreed about its commands, then the state would be superfluous. Since this is not so, right makes it possible for moral subjects to realize their freely chosen moral goals by providing them (*qua* juridical subjects) with a sphere of formal freedom wherein they can act efficaciously.

The main and most important practical goal of society is to provide the juridical subject with an education whereby it develops as an individual in reciprocal relations with others. As Fichte says, "the summons to engage in free activity is what we call up-bringing [*Erziehung*]" and "all individuals must be brought up to be human beings, otherwise they would not be human beings."[31] In other words, the summons is best construed as a communal process rather than a particular invitation from one individual to another. While education involves reciprocal activity between individuals, no one particular encounter constitutes an education. This education begins within the family, specifically, within the reciprocal activities between woman and man, as well as those between mother and child. Sexual relations, reproduction, and childrearing provide a transition between nature and ethics, which the state protects but does not control.

The state does not merely protect citizens from harm or provide them with the conveniences of civil society: it cultivates and preserves the formal freedom necessary for their efficacious, self-determined activity. The freedom enjoyed by the juridical subject within society is different in kind from its natural liberty in isolation from other rational individuals. Only in community with others can the rational subject truly develop as a human being.

Following Kant, Schopenhauer regards morality as the ground of social and political justice. The same pangs of conscience that accompany wrongdoing (and indicate to the perpetrator that its victim is only different *qua* phenomenon but not *qua* noumenon) are the basis of natural right. According to Schopenhauer, the social contract consists in a mutual agreement to renounce the "pleasure of doing wrong in order to be spared the pain of suffering wrong" (WWR1$_{[P]}$, 343) (i.e., of enduring bodily injury or compulsion at another's hand). Wrongdoing is motivated by egoism, which the social contract counters by restricting the juridical subject's will to its own body. Thus, the worst effects of natural egoism are curbed by appealing to the rational individual's egoistic motivations.

At the phenomenal level of egoistic interactions between individuals, "well-being in one place is merely suffering in another" (WWR1$_{[P]}$, 354). The mutual agreement to forgo harming others mediates between juridical subjects within the state, which is the source of *temporal justice*. Temporal justice is relative to the future. The state employs the principle of sufficient reason to balance out the right and wrong actions performed by many different individuals. Offenses are followed by punishments (which presumably ward off future wrongdoing).

At the noumenal level of the thing-in-itself, the perpetrator and the victim of wrongdoing are the same, so every offense is simultaneously its own punishment. The thing-in-itself, or one will to life, is the source of *eternal justice*. The will *wills* the world to be as it is, and, within this world, there is balance between the harms inflicted and endured. Of course, the juridical individual does not comprehend eternal justice, which is only grasped by a person with intuitive knowledge of the metaphysical underpinnings of the phenomenal world, but the juridical subject has a presentiment, felt as dread, that absolute justice governs the world as a whole.

Schopenhauer criticizes Fichte's characterization of the I as well as his concept of the *Aufforderung*, objecting to Fichte's characterization of the I as "an acting on itself." According to Schopenhauer, this is a relation of spontaneous causality that thus includes cause and effect, or a relation between two objects. Moreover, he complains that Fichte describes the I as an acting without an actor, which he takes to be impossible. Schopenhauer argues that an acting on itself would involve the identity of cause and effect, which is likewise impossible since this understanding of the self results in an infinite regress. He accuses Fichte of self-contradiction because Fichte says that the I does not become conscious of its acting, but likewise that there is no I without consciousness and thus no action of the I without consciousness and yet no I without activity.

Schopenhauer regards Fichte's acknowledgment of circularity within the basic argument of the *Rechtslehre* as an admission of failure. He believes that resolving the seeming contradiction with the *Aufforderung* presupposes the consciousness of another rational being (and thus of an object), which begs the question. Moreover, he claims that Fichte infers from the rational being's moral freedom an obligation to *allow* others their freedom, which, he objects, can neither be given nor taken.

Although Schopenhauer does not discuss the issue, his views about the obligations of the state to its citizens and the scope of its power differ very much from Fichte's. The state that Schopenhauer envisions exists primarily to protect individuals from harms inflicted by other individuals. Redistribution of resources to promote the well-being of less fortunate individuals within the society would be a separate moral issue, motivated by compassion and thus not compelled by the state. Fichte, in contrast, argues that the state is obliged to provide its citizens with the means to develop as human beings. This entails additional obligations for juridical subjects who must contribute to the development of their fellow citizens as well.

Despite their many differences regarding the philosophy of right, Fichte and Schopenhauer would agree that society must offer an incentive that moves every juridical subject to cooperate regardless of its level of moral development. Although Fichte's principle of right is not equivalent to Schopenhauer's renouncing the pleasure of doing wrong in order to be spared the pain of suffering wrong, it does appeal to the juridical subject's egoistic interest in recognizing and preserving itself as a free individual. To be sure, Fichte would claim that a just society provides the juridical subject with an opportunity to become something more than an egoistic individual.

4.5 FICHTE AND SCHOPENHAUER ON THE THEORY OF RELIGION, OR THE *RELIGIONSLEHRE*

The philosophy of religion, or *Religionslehre*, is the part of the philosophy of the postulates that deals with the postulate that reason addresses to nature, "which by means of a supersensible law is supposed to accommodate itself to the goal of morality."[32] Fichte laid out his concept of God in "On the Ground of Our Belief in a Divine World-Governance" (1798) and expanded on it in subsequent writings during the *Atheismusstreit*, or atheism dispute (1798–1800). He returned to this topic in *The Way to the Blessed Life, or Also the Religionslehre* (1806). Schopenhauer was familiar with this latter text and included notes on it, which can be found in his *Manuscript Remains*. In later works, he offered his own account of religion and salvation.

For Fichte, salvation consists in renouncing the sensible result of willing, whereas for Schopenhauer, it consists in renouncing willing itself. He denies Fichte's claim that human contentment can be achieved within the present world, but he agrees that human despair originates in the pursuit of sensible satisfaction. Like Fichte, he produces an account of religion and salvation that does not depend on God's existence. Both philosophers follow Kant in asserting that moral activity very often results in unhappiness because the human subject is divided: it is both a sensible being with carnal desires and a rational being with intelligible interests. For Fichte, human salvation depends on reconciling sensibility and reason, or happiness and virtue, which he regards as possible within human life. Schopenhauer denies this possibility.

Fichte's *Way to the Blessed Life* provides an empirical guide to achieving a blessed state; that is, a morally upright life of peace and contentment. According to Fichte, beatitude depends on the divided, finite subject's love, striving, and drive to unite with the eternal—*Sein*—or God. The individual perceives and enjoys itself (as a free being) and the world through the objects of its love, which its drives and interests determine and which it strives to accomplish. The subject loves itself and believes in its personal individual freedom, but the objects in which the developing individual seeks its satisfaction establish the nature of its consciousness and life.

At the level of *sensibility*, the sensuous individual's self-love expresses itself as desire for particular sensible objects. When the sensuous subject enjoys the desired objects, it feels itself to be free, but the sensuous gratification is never forthcoming, so it seeks new, different, and better objects, with its own nature changing with every passing desire. The sensuous individual finds itself as dependent and dissipated—unfree and unhappy—because it disperses its thinking and energy among a multitude of unsatisfactory things. Sensibility negates itself by destroying the individual's interest in itself and the world, leading it to hope for future worlds that it might earn through "virtuous" behavior or receive by God's "grace."

At the level of *legality*, love of law replaces sensuous self-love. The stoic individual submits itself to an ethical law in an attempt to become self-sufficient. Although the subject escapes sensuous desires and compulsions, the resulting sense of freedom is merely negative, empty, and formal because its freedom consists in the ability merely to obey or disobey the law. The stoic individual acts only to avoid self-condemnation, but its activity provides no positive gratification. To the extent that it resists desire, it feels free, but its freedom is aimless. Moreover, every personal inclination threatens the stoic individual's freedom, so it renounces happiness. Insofar as it freely chooses to obey the law, it holds forth the possibility of opposing the law, and, thus, the law appears as an external will, which is the source of a categorical imperative.

By determining its will according to the Categorical Imperative, the stoic individual renounces its individual, personal will and thus the level of *higher morality* replaces legality. At this level of development, the moral subject views its individuality as an expression of the external will—a pure will—which it adopts as its own will and loves as its own self. Immediate consciousness reveals to each individual a vocation wherein the divine will, the individual will, and desire coincide. Although the moral subject's freedom and desire coincide in its inner intelligible willing, it wants its will to be efficacious in the sensible world. To the extent that the subject succeeds in producing the intended sensible result, the individual feels contented, but it feels failure as an affront to its freedom and as a frustration of its desire. Nonetheless, this feeling of limitation compels the moral individual to reflect on itself and thereby to clarify its intelligible goal.

Insofar as the moral subject recognizes that its goal consists in developing the intelligible world, by engaging in moral willing, it believes that it succeeds. Moral willing implies this belief and the concomitant belief in the sensible sphere of free activity. Self-conscious faith in the ultimate success of intelligible willing distinguishes the level of *religion* from morality. The moral-religious individual views the sensible world and its own personality as means to a life of faith in action. It strives within the world without needing to change the world because faith reveals a new intelligible world within the sensible world.

The moral-religious individual realizes that the outer result of its willing depends partly on others' free activities, which it ought not to thwart, and, thus, it wills a sensible result conditionally as a temporal manifestation of the divine life. It promotes others' freedom because its ultimate task is to cultivate freedom in itself and others. The moral-religious individual acts in the sensible world, but it loves the intelligible world, or namely, freedom itself.

According to Fichte, moral activity is complete in itself and, thus, despite individual failure and death, the moral-religious subject believes in its fellow individuals and hopes for their future. It treats others as if they were already what they ought to be and as it expects them to become. The moral-religious individual has immediate conviction of its vocation, so it does not fear the future. It devotes itself wholly to its present activity, so it does not mourn the past.

Schopenhauer views Fichte's effort to reconcile sensibility and reason as futile. Because happiness as he understands it requires satisfaction of the will, while virtue requires denial of the will, he believes the virtuous individual cannot be happy. Moreover, like Kant, he thinks that the moral subject cannot trust itself to know whether sensibility or reason has determined its actions. Even when the moral subject believes that it has done the right thing for the right reasons, it may be subject to self-deception. At best, the moral subject can hope to live a prudent life wherein it uses the understanding to curb sensible desire, but a reconciliation of sensibility and reason is not possible in this world.

Schopenhauer argues that virtuous activity arises only occasionally during the moral subject's life, which is mostly spent alternating between the throes of sensible compulsion and the pangs of rational regret. Since the conflict between sensibility and reason cannot be overcome, and since the demands of both are insatiable, even the most contented and virtuous of moral subjects experiences a life of futile and painful struggle. Therefore, every moral subject hopes for a better life after death, whether or not it is rational to expect one, and every rational subject hopes for an end to its present life.

According to Schopenhauer, salvation consists in the renunciation of desire, striving, and, ultimately, of the will to live. The egoistic subject must gradually disabuse itself of its delusion that happiness is the purpose of its life. Schopenhauer thinks that, during the course of an ordinary human existence, little observation is needed to convince the individual that sensible striving never leads to genuine or lasting satisfaction. Once the subject achieves its goals, it ceases to value them. Everywhere there is misery and grief, which spoils the individual's appetite for pleasure and for life itself. This is a disguised boon because suffering hastens the subject's recognition that it must abandon the cycle of desiring and willing. Moreover, the remorse that accompanies indulgence and egoism exposes the subject to intuitive knowledge of the intelligible underpinnings of the sensible world and thus to virtue.

Virtue, according to Schopenhauer, appears in the moral subject's compassionate activities. Nonetheless, he does not regard moral self-improvement as the purpose of human existence. Since compassion requires feeling others' suffering, virtue necessarily increases the moral subject's suffering. Empathic suffering produces knowledge that the will to live is the source of all striving and suffering. Comprehending the futility of striving and renouncing the will to live prepares the moral subject for the true aim of its existence: the recognition that the life of willing is a terrible mistake that must be remedied through asceticism.

Despite their many differences, there are similarities to be found in Fichte's and Schopenhauer's explanations of religion and salvation. Neither philosopher's account depends on the existence of God or an afterlife. Fichte employs the concept of *Sein* or God in the *Way to the Blessed Life*, but this concept is only realized in the moral-religious activities and relationships of *Dasein*, or individual self-consciousness. His description of salvation involves the moral-religious subject's attitude toward itself, the moral community, and the sensible results of its moral willing. Schopenhauer claims that the moral subject cannot but hope for a better life after death, but he does not suggest it has any good reason to expect one. True virtue and holiness, as well as ultimate denial of the will and resignation, do not require belief in God or an afterlife.

Both Fichte and Schopenhauer claim that the sensuous subject's egoistic willing leads to despair. Likewise, both claim that the legalistic willing of the stoic individual results in despair as well. Moreover, they argue that despair can be an incentive to reflection, which allows the moral individual to better comprehend its relation to the sensible world. For Fichte, this means that the moral-religious individual renounces the sensible results of its willing, whereas for Schopenhauer, this means that the moral-religious individual renounces willing itself.

Fichte and Schopenhauer argue that the moral subject's individuality must be subsumed within a larger spiritual whole. Fichte claims that the moral-religious subject is able to abandon its desire to control others in order to produce its moral objectives because ultimately the goals of reason are accomplished by promoting the freedom of others even if they might make the wrong moral choices. Schopenhauer asserts that recognition that one will underpins all individual willing and that the suffering of one individual in the world amounts to the suffering of all others undermines natural egoism, thus allowing the moral-religious subject to empathize with others and promote their well-being. In both cases, the moral-religious subject recognizes that its willing, moral or otherwise, must not thwart or undermine the goals of other individuals in the moral community. Fichte and Schopenhauer both believe that salvation ultimately involves a type of knowledge.

4.6 CONCLUSION: IDEALISTIC PHILOSOPHY

In conclusion, there are several issues about which Fichte and Schopenhauer would wholeheartedly agree. Both think that philosophy represents the highest standpoint from which life may be viewed. Each uses supersensible willing as the basis for a philosophical account of sensible experience. Moreover, they claim idealism is the sole viable philosophy because realism (materialism) cannot account for moral activity, which is a fundamental aspect of human subjectivity.[33]

Fichte and Schopenhauer also share certain basic ideas about what it means to be a human subject. They would agree that the subject first discovers itself as one willing individual among others in a sensible world. As striving in general characterizes humanity, so striving after particular goals defines the human individual. They would also acknowledge that striving causes diremption that can be manifest as conflict and despair. The individual's striving separates it from others because they do not share its goals. Furthermore, striving divides the individual from itself because it has not yet accomplished its goals.

Despite their general accord about human subjectivity, Fichte and Schopenhauer differ markedly about the nature and value of the human will. Fichte regards the will as essentially rational. Hence, his account of human striving is optimistic. He celebrates humanity's infinite progress toward moral perfection. Schopenhauer views the will as fundamentally irrational. Hence, his description of human striving is pessimistic. He deplores humanity's perpetual failure to remedy its too obvious and too painful imperfection.

NOTES

1. For detailed discussion of Schopenhauer's relation to Fichte and German idealism, see Günter Zöller, "Schopenhauer's Fairy Tale about Fichte: The Origin of the *World as Will and Representation* in German Idealism," in *Blackwell Companions to Philosophy: A Companion to Schopenhauer*, edited by Bart Vandenabeele (Oxford: Wiley-Blackwell, 2012), 384–402. For discussion of his relation to transcendental idealism in particular, see Douglas McDermid, "Schopenhauer and Transcendental Idealism," in *A Companion to Schopenhauer*, edited by Bart Vandenabeele (Oxford: Wiley-Blackwell, 2012), 70–86.

2. *Ueber die Tatsachen des Bewußtseyns. Fichte's Vorlesungen über das Studium der Philosophie; aus dem Gedächtniß nach dem Kollegio niedergeschrieben* and *Ueber die Tatsachen des Bewußtseyn und die Wissenschaftslehre bey Fichte* in HN2 (Munich: Deutscher Taschenbuch, 1985), 16–216. Schopenhauer's transcripts of Fichte's lectures can also be found as *Fichtes Vorlesungen über das Studium der Philosophie. Nachschrift Schopenhauer* and *Ueber die Thatsachen des Bewußtseyns. Nachschrift Schopenhauer* in *J. G. Fichte Gesamtausgabe der Bayerischen Akademie der Wissenschaften*, edited by Reinhard Lauth, Hans Jacob, and Hans Gliwitzky (Stuttgart-Bad Cannstatt: Frommann, 1964–2012) section IV, Vol. 4, 59–67 and 195–237.

3. *Das System der Sittenlehre nach den Principien der Wissenschaftslehre (1798)* in *Fichtes Werke*, edited by Immanuel Hermann Fichte (Berlin: Walter de Gruyter and Co., 1971) Vol. IV, 1–365 (Henceforth FW IV); *System of Ethics According to the Principles of the Wissenschaftslehre*, edited and translated by Daniel Breazeale and Günter Zöller (Cambridge: Cambridge, 2005) (Henceforth SE); *Grundlage des Naturrechts nach Principien der Wissenschaftslehre (1796–97)* in *Fichtes Werke*, edited by Immanuel Hermann Fichte (Berlin: Walter de Gruyter and Co., 1971), Vol. III, 1–384 (henceforth FW III); *Foundations of Natural Right According to the Principles of the Wissenschaftslehre*, edited by Frederick Neuhouser and translated by Michael Baur (Cambridge: Cambridge, 2000) (henceforth FNR).

4. *Die Anweisung zum seligen Leben, oder auch die Religionslehre* (1806), edited by Fritz Medicus (Hamburg: Meiner, 1910) (henceforth RL). For a discussion of the distinction between a popular and a philosophical exposition of truth, see RL, 32–33. Compare Fichte's *Vocation of Man*, edited and translated by Peter Preuss (Indianapolis: Hackett, 1987) (henceforth VM), 1–2 (*Die Bestimmung des Menschen* in *Fichte Gesamtausgabe der Bayerischen Akademie der Wissenschaften*, edited by Reinhard Lauth, Hans Jacob, and Hans Gliwitzky (Stuttgart-Bad Cannstatt: Frommann, 1964–2012) section I, Vol. 6, 189–90).

5. *Foundations of Transcendental Philosophy (Wissenschaftslehre) nova methodo* (1796/99), edited and translated by Daniel Breazeale (Ithaca and London: Cornell, 1992) (Henceforth FTP). FTP is the English translation of Fichte's lectures on the *Wissenschaftslehre nova methodo*. It is based on *Wissenschaftslehre nova methodo* (1796-98), *Krause Transcript*, edited by Erich Fuchs (Hamburg: Meiner, 1982) (henceforth WLnm[K]) and *J. G. Fichte Gesamtausgabe der Bayerischen Akademie der Wissenschaften*, edited by Reinhard Lauth, Hans Jacob, and Hans Gliwitzky (Stuttgart-Bad Cannstatt: Frommann, 1964–2012) section IV, Vol. 2 (henceforth GA IV, 2).

6. FTP, 470 (Wlnm[K], 242 and GA IV, 2, 263–64).

7. SE, 24 (FW IV, 18–19).

8. SE, 25–26 (FW IV, 19–21). This is followed by a proof based on the concept of the I (SE, 27–28 [FW IV, 21–23]). This proof also appears in FNR, 18–21 (FW III, 17–20).

9. SE, 29 (FW IV, 23–24). See also FTP, 358–463 (Wlnm[K[, 234–38 and GA IV, 2, 255–59).

10. SE, 33–44 (FW, IV, 28–29).

11. SE, 45 (FW IV, 41–42). See also, *J. G. Fichte: Introductions to the Wissenschaftslehre and Other Writings*, edited and translated by Daniel Breazeale (Indianapolis: Hackett, 1994) (henceforth IWL), 74 (*Versuch einer neuen Darstellung der Wissenschaftslehre, J. G. Fichte Gesamtausgabe der Bayerischen Akademie der Wissenschaften* (henceforth Versuch), edited by Reinhard Lauth, Hans Jacob, and Hans Gliwitzky (Stuttgart-Bad Cannstatt: Frommann, 1964–2012) section I, Vol. 4 (henceforth GA I, 4).

12. SE, 50 (FW IV, 47–48). See FTP, 110 (Wlnm[K], 28). See also, IWL, 48–50 and 106–108 (GA, I, 4, 219–20 and 521–23).

13. SE, 55 (FW IV, 52–53). As Fichte points out, Kant also associates conviction of freedom with awareness of the moral law. See Immanuel Kant, *Critique of Practical Reason*, edited and translated by Mary Gregor (Cambridge: Cambridge University Press, 1996), 178–79.

14. SE, 60–63 (FW IV, 58–63).

15. SE, 56–60 and 156–57 (FW IV, 54–59 and 164–66).

16. SE, 56 and 90 (FW IV, 54–55 and 92–93). For a detailed discussion of the relation between the intellect and the will in Fichte's philosophy, see Günter Zöller, *Original Duplicity: The Original Duplicity of Intellect and Will in Fichte's Philosophy* (Cambridge: Cambridge, 1998).

17. SE, 181 (FW IV, 190–91).

18. SE, 181 and 147 (FW IV, 190–91 and 154–55). See also, *Groundwork of the Metaphysics of Morals, Practical Philosophy*, edited by Mary J. Gregor and Allen Wood, translated by Mary J. Gregor (Cambridge: Cambridge University Press, 1996), 84–85 and 102.

19. SE, 155–65 (FW IV, 163–74). See also, 166, 185, and 197 (FW IV, 174–75, 194–95, 207–08). For an excellent discussion of these issues in Fichte's practical philosophy, see Owen Ware, "Fichte on Conscience," *Philosophical and Phenomenological Research* 95, no. 2 (September 2017), 376–94. This is a matter of controversy among Fichte scholars. Some Fichte scholars argue that conscience determines the content of moral duty for Fichte. See Daniel Breazeale, "In Defense of Fichte's Account of Ethical Deliberation," *Archiv für Geschichte der Philosophie* 94: 178–207; and Günter Zöller, "The Choice of the Philosopher," comments

on Michelle Kosch, "Agency and Self-Sufficiency in Fichte's Ethics," refereed symposium session, Pacific APA, 2013.

20. SE, 168–98 (FW IV, 176–209).

21. SE, 224–25 (FW IV, 235–37).

22. SE, 248 (FW IV, 259–60). See also, SE, 262 (FW IV, 274–75) and FNR, 29–37 (FW III, 30–39).

23. Zöller, "Schopenhauer's Fairy Tale About Fichte," 399.

24. See SE, 245–47 (FW IV, 257–58). This is a peculiar objection since Fichte stresses the form of moral willing in his ethics.

25. FNR, 32 (FW III, 33).

26. FNR, 30–38 (FW III, 31–40).

27. FNR, 30–38 (FW III, 31–40).

28. Ibid.

29. FNR, 49 (FW III, 52–53).

30. See FTP, 338 and 437 (Wlnm[K], 169–70 and 220–21 and GA IV, 2, 168, and 240–41); SE, 68–71 (FW IV, 68–70); FNR, 37–39 (FW III, 39–41).

31. FNR, 38, 132, 310–19 (FW, III, 39–40, 147–48, 359–68).

32. FTP, 471. See FNR, 1–2 and 18–19 (FW III, 1–3 and 17).

33. McDermid, "Schopenhauer and Transcendental Idealism," 79.

FURTHER READING

Breazeale, Daniel. "Fichte's nova methodo phenomenologica: On the Methodological Role of 'Intellectual Intuition' in the Later Jena Wissenschaftslehre." *Revue International de Philosophie* [Brussels] no. 206 (1998): 587–616.

Estes, Yolanda. "Intellectual Intuition, the Pure Will, and the Categorical Imperative." In *New Essays on Fichte's Later Jena Wissenschaftslehre*, edited by Daniel Breazeale and Tom Rockmore. Evanston, IL: Northwestern, 2002, 209–25.

Estes, Yolanda. "Morality, Right, and Philosophy in the Jena Wissenschaftslehre." In *Rights, Bodies, and Recognition: New Essays on Fichte's Foundations of Natural Right*, edited by Tom Rockmore and Daniel Breazeale. Aldershot, UK: Ashgate, 2006, 59–70.

Estes, Yolanda. "After Jena: Fichte's Religionslehre." In *After Jena: New Essays on Fichte's Later Philosophy*, edited by Daniel Breazeale and Tom Rockmore. Evanston, IL: Northwestern, 2008, 99–114.

Estes, Yolanda. "J. G. Fichte's Account of Human Sexuality: Gender Difference as the Basis for Equality in a Just Society." *Social Philosophy Today: Gender, Diversity, and Difference* 25 (2009): 63–74.

Kamata, Yasuo. *Der Junge Schopenhauer. Genese des Grundgedankens der Welt als Wille und Vorstellung.* Freiburg and Munich: Alber, 1988.

La Vopa, Anthony J. *Fichte: The Self and the Calling of Philosophy.* Cambridge: Cambridge University Press, 2001.

McDermid, Douglas. "Schopenhauer and Transcendental Idealism." In *Blackwell Companions to Philosophy: A Companion to Schopenhauer*, edited by Bart Vandenabeele. Oxford: Wiley-Blackwell, 2012, 70–86.

Miodoński, Leon. "Kontinuität oder Wandlung. Schopenhauer und das Paradigma de deutschen Idealismus." In *Schopenhauer in Kontext. Deutsch-polnisches Schopenhauer Symposium 2000*, edited by D. Birnbacher, A. Lorenz, and L. Miondoński. Würzburg: Königshausen and Neumann, 2002, 113–19.

Safranski, Rüdiger. *Schopenhauer and the Wild Years of Philosophy*. Cambridge, MA: Harvard University Press, 1987.

Schöndorf, Haral. *Der Leib im Denken Schopenhauers und Fichtes*. Munich: Johannes Berchmanns, 1982.

Zöller, Günter. *Original Duplicity: The Original Duplicity of Intellect and Will in Fichte's Philosophy*. Cambridge: Cambridge University Press, 1998.

Zöller, Günter. "German Realism: The Self-Limitation of Idealist Thinking in Fichte, Schelling, and Schopenhauer." In *Cambridge Companion to Schopenhauer*, edited by Christopher Janaway. Cambridge: Cambridge, 2000, 18–43.

Zöller, Günter. "Schopenhauer's Fairy Tale About Fichte: The Origin of the World as Will and Representation in German Idealism." In *Blackwell Companions to Philosophy: A Companion to Schopenhauer*, edited by Bart Vandenabeele. Oxford: Wiley-Blackwell, 2012, 384–402.

CHAPTER 5

••

SCHOPENHAUER AND
THE ORIENT

••

URS APP

DURING Schopenhauer's lifetime (1788–1860), Western interest in the Orient and its philosophies and religions exploded. Information about the region beyond the Middle East that had hitherto been mainly furnished by missionaries and early travelers came to be gradually replaced by the results of academic research based on the discovery of monuments and the study of original sources in languages such as Sanskrit, Pali, Chinese, Mongolian, and Tibetan.[1] In the course of the eighteenth century, the focus of European interest in China (for example by Leibniz, Bayle, and Malebranche[2]) was substituted by an infatuation with India, fueled by best-selling authors such as Voltaire and Constantin Volney who portrayed India as the world's oldest civilization and fount of ancient wisdom.[3] The Indian Vedas came to be regarded as far older than the Old Testament, and a largely invented "Oriental Philosophy" was laboriously described in influential publications by Pierre Bayle, Johann Lorenz Mosheim, Johann Jakob Brucker, and, subsequently, in Diderot/d'Alembert's *Encyclopédie* and other encyclopedias of the Age of Enlightenment.[4]

Four years prior to Schopenhauer's birth, a new era of Oriental studies began with the foundation by William Jones of the Asiatic Society. The first volume of the Society's journal, the *Asiatick Researches*, appeared in Calcutta in the very year of the philosopher's birth.[5] Around the turn of the century, seminal articles in the large volumes of this journal and various translations into English of Sanskrit sources came to be retranslated and studied all over Europe, fueling an Indomania[6] that, in the first decades of nineteenth-century Germany, inspired romantic authors and mythologists such as Friedrich Schlegel, Joseph Görres, and Friedrich Creuzer. In 1814, when Schopenhauer began his independent research on Oriental philosophies and religions, Europe's first chair of Sinology was established in Paris, followed in 1815 by the first chair of Sanskrit. In 1817, the first Western book about Buddha and Buddhism appeared in Paris[7]; and, from the 1820s, continental researchers familiar with Asian languages such as Sanskrit, Pali,

Chinese, Mongolian, and Tibetan began to publish, apart from books, an increasing number of research articles in specialized journals such as the *Journal Asiatique* (founded in 1822). By the time of Schopenhauer's death in 1860, the scholarly output in German, French, and English was already substantial and included not only translations from original sources but also a flood of studies on the religions and philosophies of Asia and their history.

Schopenhauer was an avid reader of such publications, so much so that he may be regarded as one of the best informed among Europe's nonspecialized readers of such materials in the first six decades of the nineteenth century. From his youth to his death he consulted and collected publications in Latin as well as in modern European languages. Apart from the writings published in his lifetime, we can today follow his course of study using the copious notes in his philosophical notebooks, jottings in the margins of his books, letters (including book orders), and library lending records and thus gain a detailed picture of the development of his interest in the Orient and in particular of Oriental influences on his thought. For this purpose, the study of the sources that were actually used by the philosopher is indispensable.

However, much of the extant scholarly literature about Oriental influences on Schopenhauer actually consists of comparisons of his thought with modern knowledge about Asian philosophies and religions.[8] Though such comparative studies can be of great interest, they generally contribute little to the question of influence because this question necessitates the use not of our *present-day* sources and knowledge but rather of sources used by Schopenhauer and the information available *in his time*. The most conspicuous example of this dead angle of Schopenhauer research is certainly the philosopher's favorite book: the Latin translation of the Upanishads known as *Oupnek'hat*. Already in 1816, just before he began to write *The World as Will and Representation*, Schopenhauer listed the Upanishads as the first of three main influences: "I confess that I do not believe that my doctrine could ever have formed before the Upanishads, Plato, and Kant cast their rays simultaneously into one man's mind" (HN1, 422, §623).[9] Thirty-five years later, he even called the *Oupnek'hat* "the most rewarding and uplifting reading possible in the world: it has been the solace of my life and will be that of my death" (PP2, §184; SW5, 421). Surprisingly, in more than 150 years of Schopenhauer research only two authors have studied the influence of this work,[10] and even recent studies on Schopenhauer and Indian thought are generally based on modern translations and present-day knowledge.[11]

This shows that research about Oriental influences on Schopenhauer is still in its infancy. Arthur Hübscher has published a list of Orientalia in Schopenhauer's library (HN5, 319–52) that, in spite of some imperfections (for instance regarding collections, references in the *Manuscript Remains*, and Schopenhauer's remarks in the margins of materials he owned), can still serve as a guide to Schopenhauer's Asia-related sources. In this chapter, only some of the most important sources and influences will be mentioned, and most attention will be paid to the least-researched but most crucial phase: namely, the period prior to the publication of Schopenhauer's major work of 1819, *The World as Will and Representation*.

5.1 FIRST PHASE (1800–1819)

Already as a fifteen-year-old teenager, Schopenhauer wandered around Amsterdam in search of a laughing Chinese Putai figure and instead found beautiful Buddha statues ("pagodas").[12] The young university student exhibited interest in Asian cultures and history, as shown by his extensive notes from the ethnology lectures of Professor A. H. L. Heeren (1760–1817) at the University of Göttingen.[13] Professor Heeren had a special interest in India,[14] and his student missed almost none of the ethnography lectures. Schopenhauer noted, for example, that the religion of Buddha is prevalent in countries such as Burma (Myanmar) and Japan and that professor Heeren was not certain if the faith of the Lamas in Tibet and the "religion of Fo" in China form part of the same Buddhist religion.[15]

The first sign of Schopenhauer's independent interest in Asian thought is his borrowing of the two volumes of Julius Klaproth's *Asiatisches Magazin*[16] from the Weimar ducal library in late 1813. This occurred during a prolonged stay in Weimar just after obtaining his doctorate, a time when he frequented Goethe and held long discussions with him about the theory of vision and colors[17] that inspired Schopenhauer's first book publication, *Über das Sehn und die Farben* (On Vision and Colors). In these volumes he found not only a German version of the earliest translation of a Buddhist sutra in a Western language, the *Forty-Two Section Sutra*,[18] but also the German translation (from English) by his indophile friend, Friedrich Majer, of the *Bhagavad Gita*[19] from which Schopenhauer made two interesting excerpts.[20] Among Schopenhauer's next Asia-related borrowings from Weimar's ducal library in the spring of 1814 we already find the *Oupnek'hat*, Schopenhauer's favorite book, whose profound influence on the genesis of Schopenhauer's philosophical system has only recently been documented.[21]

The *Oupnek'hat*[22] is Abraham-Hyacynthe Anquetil-Duperron's (1731–1805) richly annotated Latin translation of fifty Indian Upanishads. Rather than relying on the Sanskrit originals of these fundamental philosophico-religious texts of India, Anquetil used manuscripts of a Persian translation finished in 1656 under the supervision of the reigning Mughal dynasty's crown prince, Dara Shikoh (1615–1659), the firstborn son of emperor Shah Jahan (1592–1666). Prince Dara's mother was Shah Jahan's beloved wife Mumtaz Mahal (1593–1631) whose mausoleum is the famous Taj Mahal in Agra.

Since his youth Prince Dara had been interested in Islamic mysticism. He had not only studied and practiced under the guidance of Sufi masters but also authored several books about Sufism and Hinduism.[23] The translation from Sanskrit into Persian of fifty Upanishads, entitled *Sirr-I akbar* (The Great Secret), was prepared by the prince with the help of a team of India's most learned *pandits* and mystics. Woven into the Persian translation we find (sometimes extensive) Sufism-inspired commentaries that likely stem from the pen of Prince Dara and also explanations of his expert team that are often based on Shankara's vedantic Upanishad commentaries.[24] Anquetil's Latin translation of the Persian *Sirr-I akbar*, the *Oupnek'hat* of 1801–1802, contains not only the rendering of Upanishadic texts with (mostly imperceptibly) interwoven commentaries but also Anquetil's commentary and lengthy explanatory essays. According to my estimate[25] only about one-third of Schopenhauer's favorite book consists of Upanishad translation. Even without taking into account Schopenhauer's markup and the interesting handwritten comments in the margins of his extant two *Oupnek'hat* volumes,[26] this fact alone is striking evidence for the necessity of studying this Latin work rather than modern Upanishad translations from Sanskrit (see Figure 5.1).

Anquetil's volumes that had such a fundamental impact on the genesis of Schopenhauer's philosophical system thus contain not the Upanishads known to modern readers but are rather the work of an inspired Sufi adept and his learned Indian translation team as translated and commented upon by the Frenchman Anquetil-Duperron, who regarded it, like most of his readers, as a very literal translation of the Upanishads and the philosophical essence of India's ancient Vedas. Schopenhauer's reliance on such a "tarnished" text has often been lamented, and the *Oupnek'hat* is not only almost never used but often not even mentioned in studies on Schopenhauer and India.[27] But just as Meister Eckhart's sermons contain much more than biblical text and are of interest just because of that, the *Oupnek'hat* contains much more than fifty Upanishads, and Schopenhauer's markup further increases the interest. Rather than a *secretum tegendum* (secret to be safeguarded), as Anquetil wrote in his *Oupnek'hat* title, this work should be a *secretum legendum*: required reading for students of the genesis of Schopenhauer's philosophy.

Marco Piantelli first noticed the importance of the Islamic concept of *ishq* in the *Oupnek'hat*: the primordial desire of Allah to reveal himself in creation.[28] Prince Dara repeatedly quoted the famous saying of the Islamic *hadith* tradition: "I was a hidden treasure, then I desired to be known; so, I brought the creation into existence."[29] Dara linked this primordial desire or will with *maya*.

> For Dara creation is an act of desire and love (*ishq*) by the absolute, and simultaneously a veiling (*maya*) of the absolute through the illusion of diversity and multiplicity. Creation simultaneously reveals and hides; as long as there is an "I" that is looking at "the world," the One remains hidden in the Many. Prince Dara thus portrays the treasure, which was revealed through love, as a treasure hidden underneath the veil of *maya*.... The absolute can only be revealed through "the annihilation and disappearance of all particularities" whereby one can know "everything in this world as One."[30]

In the margins of Schopenhauer's copy of the *Oupnek'hat* we find numerous comments that clearly show his understanding. For example, on page 395 of volume 1, where Dara explains that the multiplicity of the world including all concepts and forms is an illusion (*maya*), Schopenhauer jotted in the margin: "Ding an sich u. Erscheinung" [thing-in-itself and representation].[31] Schopenhauer's comments and countless underlinings of the words "voluntas" (will), "volle" (willing), and "nolle" (not-willing) in the *Oupnek'hat*, along with his remarks in his philosophical notebooks, are indicative of

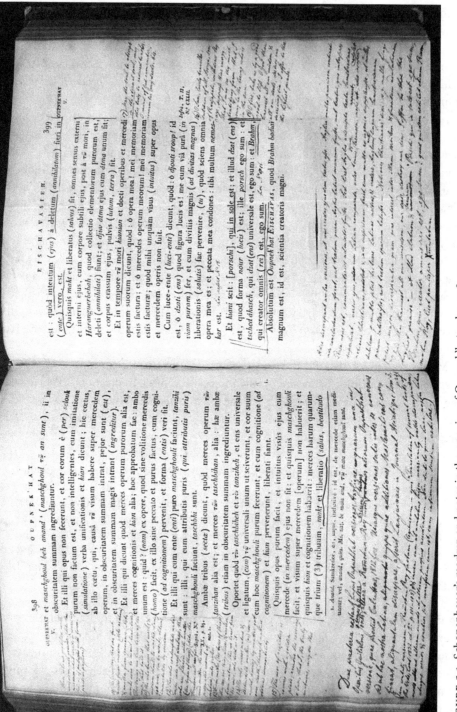

FIGURE 5.1 Schopenhauer's markup and notes in the margins of Oupnek'hat vol. 1, 398–399.

Photo by Urs App. Archivzentrum der Universitätsbibliothek J.C. Senckenberg, Bestand: Na 50 – Nachlass Arthur Schopenhauer—"Schopenhauer-Archiv."

the profound influence of this work, in particular of Prince Dara's conflation of will-*ishq-maya* and of his ideal of the death of the ego (*fanā*) in the annihilation of will: "The impure heart is that which has will; the pure heart is that which has absolutely none."[32] In this light, Schopenhauer's remark of 1816 (HN1, 422 [§623]) about the crucial influence of the Upanishads on the genesis of his system gains profile.

Subsequent to his purchase of the *Oupnek'hat* in the summer of 1814, Schopenhauer read, between November of 1815 and May of 1816, the first nine volumes of the *Asiatick Researches*. These volumes, published in Calcutta between 1788 and 1807 and reprinted in England, mark the beginning of modern indology. They were stored in the Dresden library's "Indienschrank" (India book case) in whose vicinity another passionate admirer of the *Oupnek'hat*, Karl Christian Friedrich Krause, often studied. Schopenhauer filled an entire notebook with excerpts from the *Asiatick Researches*.[33] His notes deal, among numerous other topics, with key concepts such as *maya* and *brahman*, with texts such as the Vedas and Upanishads, with Indian philosophical currents such as Vedanta, and with figures such as Shankara and Buddha.[34] An example is Schopenhauer's excerpt from volume 5 which confirmed his interpretation of *brahman* as universal force or will.

> On that effulgent power, which is *Brahme himself*, & is called the light of the radiant sun, do I meditate; governed by the mysterious light which resides *within me*, for the purpose of thought; that very light is the earth, the subtle ether & all which exists within the created sphere; it is the threefold world containing all which is fixed or moveable; *it exists internally in my heart, externally in the orb of the Sun, being one & the same with that effulgent power. I myself am an irradiated manifestation of the supreme Brahme.*[35]

Already, in May of 1814, soon after first borrowing the *Oupnek'hat* in Weimar, Schopenhauer called the approach via the subject "die indische Methode" (the Indian method) and explained in his notebook: "The wiser Indians started from the subject, from Atma, Djiv-Atma. The fact that the subject has mental representations [*Vorstellungen*] is what is essential, not the connection of representations among themselves. If we, after the manner of the Indians, set out from the subject then the world, and with it the principle of sufficient reason ruling in it, stands there in one fell swoop" (HN1, 107 [§189]). Already, one month later, this "method of the Indians" was described as Schopenhauer's own method which allows one to "seize the entire problem of empirical consciousness by the topknot" (HN1, 136 [§192]).

Schopenhauer's excerpts and notes about Colebrooke's seminal treatise on the Vedas in volume 8 of the *Asiatick Researches* are of similar significance. They show that, in the spring of 1816, when his system was already well established but not yet written down, he regarded it as congruent with Indian doctrine.[36] He summarized Colebrooke's argument as follows: "That from which all things are created and through which they live when they are born; that through which they subsist; and that into which they dissolve: that you must search, because that is *brahman*." In the margin next to this note Schopenhauer commented: "The will-to-live is the source and essence of things."[37] Such remarks confirm that Schopenhauer interpreted *brahman, parabrahman*, and similar terms as *will* or *will to live*, and they point to his explanation of 1833 about his choice of *will* as key concept of his system: "I have named the *thing-in-itself*, the inner essence of the world, after that of it with which we are *most intimately familiar: will.* Admittedly this is a term chosen subjectively, i.e., with regard to the *subject of knowing*; but this regard is essential since we are communicating *knowledge.* Therefore it is infinitely better than having named it *brahman* or *Brahma*, world-soul, or something of the kind" (HN4, 143 [§148]).

During his study of the *Asiatick Researches* in the spring of 1816, Schopenhauer also made copious excerpts and notes about Buddhism. They show his interest in eight major themes related to Buddhism: (1) the identity of its founder, (2) metempsychosis or the transmigration of souls, (3) the fact that the perfect beings of the Buddhists are merely men, (4) the existence of a large body of Buddhist texts, (5) the large geographical extension of the religion, (6) the atheist nature of Buddhism, (7) its excellent system of morality, and (8) its ideal of *nieban* or *nirvana.*[38] He noted that "The Sect of *Gotama* esteem [sic] the belief of a divine being, who created the universe, as highly impious"[39] and remarked that the Buddhists have a good system of morality in spite of being "ignorant of a supreme Being, the creator & preserver of the Universe." Schopenhauer was especially fascinated by the ideal of this religion, *Nieban* (nirvana), "the most perfect of all states" that consists "in a kind of annihilation."[40] He noted that nirvana does not signify total annihilation but rather liberation from the miseries of "weight, old age, disease, and death": "No thing, no place, can give us an adequate idea of *Nieban*: we can only say that to be free from the 4 above mentioned miseries, & to obtain salvation, is *Nieban.*"[41]

A few months after this note about nirvana, in the fall of 1816, Schopenhauer explained the goal of his new metaphysics of will as follows: "The turning, the abolition of the will is therefore identical with the abolition of the world. We call that which is left *nothing*, and our nature revolts against this transition into nothing" (HN1, 411, §612). This remark opens Schopenhauer's early draft of the final passage of *The World as Will and Representation* that was published two years later. Whereas the Europeans pull back from this *nothing* with childish fear and repress the "transition into nothing," the Indians posit, as does Schopenhauer, this transition as the goal. Unlike the Europeans who fear and evade this *nothing* entirely, the Indians only choose different words for it. According to Schopenhauer, the Indians could just as well have refrained from mincing words and called *nothing* by its name. Thus Schopenhauer wrote in the 1816 draft of the passage that was to conclude his major work,

> In this manner—through the observation of the life and conduct of saints…we wish to banish the somber impression of that nothing which hovers as the ultimate goal behind all virtue and saintliness and which, like children who fear darkness, we seek to drive away instead of circumscribing it, as the Indians do, through myths and bland words such as the Brahmans' "reabsorption into primeval spirit" or the Buddhists' Nieban (see *asiatick researches* and Upnek'hat). For those who still will,

what remains after the abolition of will is indeed *nothing*. But for those whose will has turned, this oh-so-real world of ours with all its suns and galaxies, is—nothing.

(HN1, 411–12 [§612])[42]

The impact on Schopenhauer of his study of the *Oupnek'hat* and of the *Asiatick Researches* is also apparent in a striking claim in the preface to the first edition of *The World as Will and Representation*:

> But if the reader has enjoyed the blessing of the Vedas, access to which through the Upanishads to my mind constitutes the greatest advance of our still young century over previous ones (and I expect the influence of Sanskrit literature to have as profound an effect as the revival of Greek literature in the fourteenth century)—if the reader, I say, has already received initiation into ancient Indian wisdom and has been receptive to it: then he will be best prepared to hear what I have to say to him. Then it [viz., the Indian Wisdom as presented in the *Oupnek'hat*] will not strike him, as it strikes many others, as foreign or even inimical, for would it not sound too conceited, I would even like to claim that each of the individual and disconnected utterances that form the Upanishads could be deduced as a consequence from the thoughts I am about to communicate, though conversely my thoughts are certainly not already contained there.   (WWR1, Preface to the First Edition)

Schopenhauer was convinced that he had not only laid bare and presented the core of Plato's and Kant's philosophy but also that of the Indian Upanishads. This claim is also implied in a note from mid-1816, where Schopenhauer linked his three main influences in a table (HN1, 392 [§578] [MR1, 434]).

	Universal	Particular
Metaphysics	Platonic Idea	That which becomes, never is.
	Kant's thing-in-itself	Phenomenon.
	Wisdom of the Vedas	Maya.

By contrast, when writing his major work in 1817 and 1818, Schopenhauer had with regard to Chinese philosophy and religion hardly gone beyond the information gained in Professor Heeren's ethnology course of 1811 and in Klaproth's *Asiatisches Magazin*.

5.2 Second Phase (1819–1836)

Whereas Schopenhauer's lecture manuscripts of the early 1820s describe some topics of Asian philosophies and religions in somewhat greater detail, they furnish not much new information. However, his notebook of 1822 features a few quotations from the

Chinese-English dictionary of Morrison[43] regarding the relationship of the "great ultimate" (Ch. *taiji* 太極) of Chinese philosophy and religion to theism, the dating of Buddha's life, and yin-yang polarity (HN3, 55).[44] Four years later, in 1826, Schopenhauer made a discovery that was bound to occupy him for the remaining thirty-four years of his life. He wrote in his notebook:

> In the seventh volume of *Journal Asiatique*, Paris 1825, there are rather elaborate and exceedingly beautiful portrayals of the life and esoteric teaching of *Fo* or *Budda*, or *Schige-Muni*, Schakia-Muni, which are in wonderful agreement with my system. In volume 8, this is continued with the exoteric teaching that, however, is very mythological and much less interesting. Both are by *Deshauterayes*, who died in 1795.
>
> (HN3, 161)

Though only published in 1825, Deshauterayes's articles and translations stem from the second half of the eighteenth century. After the *Forty-Two Section Sutra*, which Schopenhauer had already read in the winter of 1813/14, Deshauterayes's text is one of the earliest European translations of a Chinese Buddhist scripture.[45] Even in his old age, Schopenhauer did not tire to retell its Buddha biography with tears in his eyes.[46]

At a time when the Europeans completely ignored his philosophy and when he wondered what he should do with the rest of his life, Schopenhauer suddenly saw his doctrine confirmed not only by the oldest philosophy of India but also by Asia's largest religion: Buddhism. The Chinese text that Michel-Ange-André le Roux Deshauterayes (1724–1795) had partially translated has been identified as the *Dazang yilan* 大藏一覽, *The Buddhist Canon at a Glance*, of 1157, and it is of interest to note that both this text and Schopenhauer's version of the *Forty-Two Section Sutra* form part of the Chinese Zen (Chan 禪) tradition.[47] In the "esoteric doctrine" of Buddha described by Deshauterayes, Schopenhauer found a striking presentation of his doctrine of negation of will and of the *nothing* at the end of his major work. In particular, he was impressed by the following passage that he copied in his notebook:

> With my Buddha-eyes I consider all perceptible beings of the three worlds; nature is in me, and it is by itself unencumbered and free of all bonds: I look for something real in all three worlds but cannot find anything: and because *I have put my root into nothing*, also the trunk, the branches and the leaves are annihilated: so as soon as someone is freed or liberated from ignorance, he is also liberated from old age and death.   (HN3, 305)[48]

Already in 1817, Schopenhauer had hailed metempsychosis as "the *non plus ultra* of mythical description."

> Of all myths that have ever been devised, the *myth of transmigration of souls* is by far the deepest, most significant, and nearest to philosophical truth—so much so that I regard it as the *non plus ultra* [the supreme achievement] of mythical description. This is why Pythagoras and Plato have revered and used it; and the people with

whom it prevails as a popular, general creed and exerts distinct influence on daily life, is for this very reason to be regarded as the most *mature*, in addition to being the most ancient.   (HN1, 479 [§686])

In Deshauterayes's article he now found "love" (*ai* 愛), which in Chinese Buddhist texts commonly has the connotation of "attachment" or "cupidity" rooted in desire, portrayed as the driving force and basis of transmigration or metempsychosis.

> From all eternity, the inclination to good as well as love, cupidity and concupiscence are found naturally in everything that is born. From this comes the transmigration of souls. Everything that is born, in whatever way this happens—from an egg, a mother's bosom, from rot, or from transformation—takes its nature and its life from the concupiscence to which cupidity leads love; so it is in love that the transmigration of souls has its origin.... From love comes concupiscence, and from concupiscence comes life. All living beings, by loving life, also love its origin. Love induced to concupiscence is the cause of life; love of life is its effect.   (HN3, 305–06)[49]

Schopenhauer also saw his doctrine of all-oneness confirmed by all three major religions of China—Buddhism/the religion of *Fo* (佛 Buddha), Daoism/the religion of *Taossee* (道士 Daoshi), and Confucianism/the philosophers—and he wrote the following observation by Deshauterayes in his notebook:

> These three sects (in China, that is, the Hochang bonzes—sectarians of Fo—, the Taossee bonzes, and the philosophers) all agree about the principle that *all things are but one*, that is to say: since the matter of each particular being is a portion of the primary matter [matière première], their forms are also only parts of the universal soul [âme universelle] that constitutes nature and that fundamentally is not at all really distinct from matter.   (HN3, 306)

In 1828, Schopenhauer found in volume 22 (1826) of the renowned *Asiatic Journal and Monthly Register for British India and its Dependencies* an unsigned article entitled "Chinese theory of the Creation" and wrote excerpts in his 1828 notebook (HN3, 389).[50] He was particularly struck by the statement attributed to an unnamed Chinese philosopher to the effect that "*the mind of heaven is deducible from what is the will of mankind*." In 1836, in his "Sinology" chapter of *The Will in Nature*, Schopenhauer explained why: he was afraid of being accused of plagiarism (SW4, 138).[51] Had some Chinese philosopher discovered long before him that one can understand the nature of everything by using man's will as a lead? Motivated by the need to defend his originality and by the "wonderful agreement" between Buddhism and his own doctrine that he had detected in Deshauterayes's articles (HN3, 161), Schopenhauer read, between 1826 and 1836, numerous publications about Buddhism: Chinese Buddhism (Abel-Rémusat's *Mélanges* 1, HN5, [§1172]), Mongolian and Tibetan Buddhism (Isaak Jakob Schmidt, HN5, No. 1186), Nepalese Buddhism (Hodgson, HN5 [§1128]), and Ceylonese Buddhism (Upham; HN5 [§1204]). The more Schopenhauer read, the closer he felt to this religion and its founder—so much so that in 1832 he jotted in his notebook,

At age seventeen, without any advanced schooling, I was as overwhelmed by the *wretchedness of life* as the Buddha in his youth when he saw illness, old age, pain, and death. Soon enough, the truth, proclaimed loudly and clearly by the world, overcame the Jewish dogmas that I had also been indoctrinated with, and the result for me was that this world cannot be the work of an all-good being but rather of a devil who had brought creatures into existence in order to gloat over the sight of their anguish. This is what the data indicated; and my belief that this is the case gained the upper hand.   (HN4, 96)

The Will in Nature of 1836 is a collection of essays furnishing a variety of scientific evidence in support of Schopenhauer's system. Its Sinology chapter was designed to not only defend the author against the charge of plagiarism but, more importantly, to claim the support of the world's most populous nation and of Asia's largest religion for Schopenhauer's doctrine that was then still almost totally unknown. He noted that Buddhism "reigns in the majority of Asian countries and has, according to its latest researcher Upham, 300 million adherents, which makes it the largest among all religions on this globe" (SW4, 129). Although Schopenhauer had read numerous other books and articles, he recommended only three in the 1836 edition of his Sinology essay:

> For general knowledge about his [the Buddha's] life and teaching I especially recommend the beautiful biography of him, as it were the gospel of the Buddhists, by Deshauterayes in French in vol. 7 of the Journal Asiatique Par[is] 1825.—Likewise one finds much valuable information about Buddhaism in the Mélanges Asiatiques by Abel-Rémusat Vol. 1 1825—as well as in J. J. Schmidt's History of the East Mongols 1829.—And now that the Asiatic Society of Paris finally has taken possession of the Gandschur or Kaghiour we can with joyful expectation look forward to a presentation of Buddhism on the basis of these canonical books themselves.   (SW4, 130)

Schopenhauer also collected all new Upanishad translations that he could get hold of. As they were usually based on Sanskrit texts, they were quite different from the *Oupnek'hat*. Comparing such translations to the *Oupnek'hat*, Schopenhauer declared them to be worse or even totally unusable and accused some translators of having no more mastery of Sanskrit than an average German middle school student has of ancient Greek (SW5, 421). Many excerpts of such translations in Schopenhauer's hand are found in the margins of his *Oupnek'hat* volumes. He also studied early translations of Sufi texts (HN5, §§1199, 1200), but it was Buddhism—the religion of which he still knew very little when writing *The World as Will and Representation*—that now attracted his keenest interest.

5.3 THIRD PHASE (1837–1860)

For Schopenhauer's understanding of Buddhist philosophy, the most influential author was certainly Isaak Jakob Schmidt (1779–1847), a Russo-German scholar who had not only translated texts from the Mongolian and Tibetan traditions into German but had also authored grammars and dictionaries. Schopenhauer was very selective in his use of publications that he ordered from booksellers in various countries and sometimes purchased from auctions of late orientalists' libraries. In Schmidt's publications, one of which he had already recommended in *The Will in Nature* of 1836 (see earlier quotation), Schopenhauer learned much about Mahayana philosophy. This led him to proclaim in the second volume of *The World as Will and Representation* (1844) that

> [w]ere I to take the results of my philosophy as the measure of truth, I would have to prefer Buddhism to all other [religions]. At any rate, I cannot but be pleased to see such great agreement between my teaching and the majority religion on earth, the religion that counts more adherents than any other. This accord [*Uebereinstimmung*] must be all the more pleasing to me as in my philosophizing I have certainly not been under its influence. Until 1818, when my work appeared, only very few, highly imperfect and poor reports about Buddhism were to be found in Europe; they were almost entirely limited to a few papers in the earlier volumes of the *Asiatick Researches* and dealt mainly with the Buddhism of the Burmese. Since then, more knowledge about this religion has gradually reached us, mainly in form of the well-founded and instructive treatises of the meritorious academician of St. Petersburg, J. J. Schmidt, in the *Denkschriften* of his academy. May this great specialist of Central Asian languages soon communicate from the treasure trove of the complete Buddhist libraries that are available to him, and whose content is open to his under-standing, some chosen translations from the original texts themselves.   (SW3, 186)

While continuing his broad research on Oriental religions and philosophies,[52] Schopenhauer studied a surprising amount of pioneering works about Buddhism. Relying primarily on authors renowned for their mastery of Oriental languages, he acquired knowledge of a breadth that few if any nonspecialized Europeans of his time could match. Of particular importance were—apart from Schmidt's books and articles (HN5, Nos. 1183–93)[53]—the Frenchman Eugène Burnouf's revolutionary study of Indian Buddhism and Buddhist history based on Sanskrit texts (HN5 [§1102]); the long and informative articles about the Tibetan Buddhist canon and Mahayana doctrine by the Hungarian Csoma de Körös in *Asiatick Researches* vol. 20 (1836; HN5 [§1091]); Carl Friedrich Köppen's two-volume *Die Religion des Buddha und ihre Entstehung* (HN5 [§1139]); and the works by Robert Spence Hardy (HN5 [§1121, §1122]), which focused on Theravada Buddhist practices and beliefs in Sri Lanka.

In Schopenhauer's works of the 1840s and 1850s we find ever more effusive praise of Buddhism, which he came to regard as the best of all possible religions. In the second edition of *The Will in Nature* of 1854, the number of entries in his bibliography of recom-mended works on Buddhism jumped from three to twenty-three, and, in the following years, he added more references in the margins of his working copy (SW4, 131).[54] In order to underline Buddhism's importance he once again emphasized the enormous number of its adherents: "This religion which, both on account of its inner excellence and truth and of the superior number of its adherents must be regarded as the noblest on earth, reigns in the largest part of Asia and counts, according to its most recent researcher Spence Hardy, 369 million faithful, which is far more than any other religion" (SW 4, 130).

The *Oupnek'hat*, Schopenhauer's most important Oriental inspiration and the "solace" of his life and death, always lay open in the Frankfurt study of the aged philosopher. However, this was not his only solace. While his favorite book was either completely ignored or severely criticized by scholars familiar with Sanskrit Upanishad texts or translations thereof, Schopenhauer's study was illuminated by the gleam from the window sill of a Burmese Buddha statue that he had ordered from Paris and had gilded in Frankfurt (Figure 5.2).[55]

Schopenhauer's exuberant praise of Buddhism first incited disciples like Adam von Doß[56] and artists like Richard Wagner[57] to read about Buddhism, and later it inspired authors of the caliber of Tolstoi and Kafka, early Theosophists like Helena Blavatsky, and many early European and American Buddhists. The influence of his enthusiastic evaluation of Buddhism even reached remote countries like Japan where, in the late nineteenth century, several students of philosophy credit Schopenhauer with having inspired them to become Buddhist scholars.[58]

FIGURE 5.2 Schopenhauer's Buddha?

Photo by Urs App. Print stored at the Archivzentrum der Universitätsbibliothek
J. C. Senckenberg—"Schopenhauer-Archiv."

Shortly before his death in 1860, after having received Schmidt's article on *prajñā pāramitā*, the supreme wisdom of Mahayana Buddhism, Schopenhauer scribbled the following comment underneath the final word "nothing" in his working copy of *The World as Will and Representation*: "Just this is also the Pratschna Paramita of the Buddhists, the 'yonder of all cognition,' i.e., the point where subject and object are no more. (See J.J. Schmidt, 'Ueber das Mahajana und Pratschna-Paramita')" (SW2, 638).

NOTES

1. For facets of the historical development of Oriental studies in nineteenth-century France and Germany, see the recent studies of Christine Maillard, *L'Inde vue d'Europe. Histoire d'une rencontre (1750–1950)* (Paris: Albin Michel, 2008); Pascale Rabault-Feuerhahn, *L'archive des origines. Sanskrit, philologie, anthropologie dans l'Allemagne du XIXe siècle* (Paris: Cerf, 2008); Sabine Mangold, *Eine "weltbürgerliche Wissenschaft"—Die deutsche Orientalistik im 19. Jahrhundert* (Stuttgart: Franz Steiner Verlag, 2004); Andrea Polaschegg, *Der andere Orientalismus. Regeln deutsch-morgenländischer Imagination im 19. Jahrhundert* (Berlin: de Gruyter, 2005).

2. See Virgile Pinot, *La Chine et la formation de l'esprit philosophique en France (1640–1740)* (Geneva: Slatkine Reprints, 1971).

3. See Urs App, *The Birth of Orientalism* (Philadelphia: University of Pennsylvania Press, 2010), in particular chapter 1 on Voltaire (pp. 15–76) and chapter 8 (pp. 440–80) on Volney.

4. For the history of this invention from the sixteenth to the beginning of the eighteenth century, see Urs App, *The Cult of Emptiness. The Western Discovery of Buddhist Thought and the Invention of Oriental Philosophy* (Rorschach/Kyoto: UniversityMedia, 2012). On Bayle, see pp. 219–37.

5. Asiatic Society, *Asiatick Researches*, vol. 1 (Calcutta: Manuel Cantopher, 1788).

6. See Thomas Trautmann, *Aryans and British India* (Berkeley: University of California Press, 1997); and Douglas McGetchin, *Indology, Indomania, and Orientalism: Ancient India's Rebirth in Modern Germany* (Madison/Teaneck: Fairleigh Dickinson University Press, 2009).

7. Michel-Jean-François Ozeray, *Recherches sur Buddou ou Bouddou, instituteur religieux de l'Asie orientale; précédées de considérations générales sur les premiers hommages rendus au Créateur; sur la corruption de la religion, l'établissement des cultes du soleil, de la lune, des planètes, du ciel, de la terre, des montagnes, des eaux, des forêts, des hommes et des animaux* (Paris: Brunot-Labbé, 1817). Schopenhauer owned this book (HN5, §1158). For an analysis of its content, the French text, and its English translation, see Michel-Jean-François Ozeray and Urs App, *The First Western Book on Buddha and Buddhism* (Wil, Switzerland/ Paris: UniversityMedia, 2017).

8. The most interesting recent books of this "comparative" genre are Lakshmi Kapani, *Schopenhauer et la pensée indienne. Similitudes et différences* (Paris: Hermann, 2011), and Stephen Cross, *Schopenhauer's Encounter with Indian Thought: Representation and Will and Their Indian Parallels* (Honolulu: University of Hawaii Press, 2013).

9. Unless otherwise noted, all translations of non-English sources are mine. The section numbers will be those used in MR.

10. Mario Piantelli, "La 'Mâyâ' nelle 'Upanishad' di Schopenhauer," *Annuario filosofico* (1986), 163–207; and, with much more detail and scope, Urs App, *Schopenhauer's Compass. An*

Introduction to Schopenhauer's Philosophy and Its Origins (Wil, Switzerland: UniversityMedia, 2014).

11. See, for instance, Douglas Berger, *The Veil of Maya: Schopenhauer's System and Early Indian Thought* (Binghamton, NY: Global Academic Publications, 2004), and Kapani, *Schopenhauer et la pensée indienne.*

12. See the entry in Schopenhauer's Travel Diaries: Arthur Schopenhauer, *Die Reisetagebücher,* edited by Ludger Lütkehaus (Zürich: Haffmans Verlag, 1988), 51, and the explanations of Urs App, "Schopenhauer and China: A Sino-Platonic Love Affair," *Sino-Platonic Papers* 200 (2010), 1–4.

13. See the transcriptions and English translations of Schopenhauer's Asia-related lecture notes in Urs App, "Notizen Schopenhauers zu Ost-, Nord- und Südostasien vom Sommersemester 1811," *Schopenhauer-Jahrbuch* 84 (2003), 13–39; and Urs App, "Schopenhauer's India Notes of 1811," *Schopenhauer-Jahrbuch* 87 (2006), 15–31.

14. Arnold Hermann Ludwig Heeren, *Ueber die Indier* (Göttingen: Vandenhoeck und Ruprecht, 1815).

15. App, "Notizen Schopenhauers zu Ost-, Nord- und Südostasien," 39.

16. Julius Klaproth, ed., *Asiatisches Magazin*, 2 vols. (Weimar: Industrie-Comptoir, 1802).

17. For a detailed account of Schopenhauer's meetings with Goethe and his contact with Asia experts in Weimar see Urs App, "Schopenhauer's Initial Encounter with Indian Thought," *Schopenhauer-Jahrbuch* 87 (2006), 35–76.

18. See Urs App, "Schopenhauers Begegnung mit dem Buddhismus," *Schopenhauer-Jahrbuch* 79 (1998a), 35–58, here 42. For the history of this text and its impact in the West, see App, *The Birth of Orientalism,* 223–37.

19. App, "Schopenhauer's Initial Encounter with Indian Thought," 58–60.

20. Ibid., 68–75. On Friedrich Majer and his role in introducing Schopenhauer to Indian thought, see pp. 40–44.

21. Urs App, *Schopenhauers Kompass* (Rorschach/Kyoto: UniversityMedia, 2011). The book's English version *Schopenhauer's Compass. An Introduction to Schopenhauer's Philosophy and Its Origins* (Wil, Switzerland: UniversityMedia, 2014), contains a new appendix on the *Oupnek'hat,* 265–99.

22. Abraham Hyacinthe Anquetil-Duperron, *Oupnek'hat (id est, secretum tegendum),* 2 vols. (Argentorati: Levrault, 1801–1802).

23. App, *Schopenhauer's Compass,* 130–40.

24. See Albrecht Weber, "Analyse der in Anquetil du Perron's Uebersetzung enthaltenen Upanisad," *Indische Studien, Zeitschrift für die Kunde des indischen Alterthums* (1850), 247–302, 380–456; (1853), 1–111, 170–236; (1865), 1–54; and Erhard Göbel-Gross, *Die persische Upaniṣaden-Übersetzung des Moġulprinzen Dārā Šukoh* (Marburg: Erich Mauersberger, 1962). For graphic examples of additions to Upanishad text, see App, *Schopenhauer's Compass,* 270 and 279.

25. App, *Schopenhauer's Compass,* 290–94.

26. Arthur Hübscher listed only three examples: Arthur Hübscher, *Arthur Schopenhauer: Der handschriftliche Nachlass in fünf Bänden* (München: Deutscher Taschenbuch Verlag, 1985), vol. 5, 338, but I found traces of Schopenhauer's study on about 840 pages of the two *Oupnek'hat* volumes (i.e., on almost every second page). See App, *Schopenhauer's Compass,* 269.

27. For example, the doctoral dissertation by Werner Scholz, *Arthur Schopenhauer—ein Philosoph zwischen westlicher und östlicher Tradition* (Frankfurt/Bern: Peter Lang, 1996),

does not even list the *Oupnek'hat* in its bibliography, and Vecchiotti's 600-page book on the genesis of Schopenhauer's doctrine and its relationship with Indian philosophy fails to mention it even once: Icilio Vecchiotti, *La dottrina di Schopenhauer. Le teorie schopenhaueriane considerate nella loro genesi e nei loro rapporti con la filosofia indiana* (Roma: Ubaldini, 1969). My thanks to Prof. Francesca Gambarotto for procuring this book.

28. Piantelli, "La 'Mâyâ' nelle 'Upanishad' di Schopenhauer."

29. M. Mahfuz-ul-Haq, *Majima'-ul-Bahrain or the Mingling of the Two Oceans, by Prince Muhammad Dârâ Shikûh* (Calcutta: Asiatic Society of Bengal, 1929; repr., Karachi: Royal Book Company, 1990), 39.

30. App, *Schopenhauer's Compass*, 138.

31. Ibid., 142.

32. Ibid., 161–62, 248.

33. These notes are transcribed and, where necessary, translated into English in Urs App, "Notes and Excerpts by Schopenhauer Related to Volumes 1–9 of the Asiatick Researches," *Schopenhauer-Jahrbuch* 79 (1998), 11–33.

34. App, "Notes and Excerpts," 15–21.

35. Ibid., 19. Emphases by Schopenhauer.

36. Ibid., 27–33.

37. Ibid., 31.

38. See the transcription and translation of all of Schopenhauer's excerpts and notes in App, "Notes and Excerpts," 15–33. For references to specific pages in the *Asiatick Researches*, see App, "Schopenhauer and China," 13–14.

39. App, "Notes and Excerpts," 20.

40. Ibid., 21.

41. Ibid., 21. For the development of Schopenhauer's view of Nirvana see Urs App, "Schopenhauers Nirwana," in *Die Wahrheit ist nackt am schönsten. Arthur Schopenhauers philosophische Provokation*, edited by Michael Fleiter (Frankfurt: Institut für Stadtgeschichte/Societätsverlag, 2010), 200–08.

42. See Schopenhauer's edited final passage, published in 1819, in WWR1 (SW2, 321 [WWR1, 299]). See also Urs App, "NICHTS. Das letzte Wort von Schopenhauers Hauptwerk," in *Das Tier, das du jetzt tötest, bist du selbst…Arthur Schopenhauer und Indien*, edited by Jochen Stollberg, Frankfurter Bibliotheksschriften Band 13 (Frankfurt: Vittorio Klostermann, 2006b), 51–60, and the different view of Moira Nicholls, "The Influences of Eastern Thought on Schopenhauer's Doctrine of the Thing-in-Itself," in *The Cambridge Companion to Schopenhauer*, edited by Christopher Janaway (Cambridge/New York: Cambridge University Press, 1999), 171–212.

43. Robert Morrison, *Dictionary of the Chinese Language, in Three Parts* (Macao: East India Company Press, 1815–1818).

44. See App, "Schopenhauer and China," 16–19.

45. Ibid., 20f.

46. Arthur Hübscher, *Arthur Schopenhauer: Gespräche* (Stuttgart: Friedrich Frommann Verlag, 1971), 104, 147, 236, 311.

47. App, "Schopenhauer and China," 10f, 22f.

48. Michel-Ange-André le Roux Deshauterayes, "Recherches sur la religion de Fo, professée par les bonzes *Ho-chang* de la Chine," *Journal Asiatique* 7 (1825), 150–73, here 171. Schopenhauer (HN3, 305) copied Deshauterayes's French text. For the Chinese text, Deshauterayes's French translation, and an English translation of both, see App, "Schopenhauer and China," 31.

49. For the original Chinese text, Deshauterayes's French translation used by Schopenhauer, and an English translation of both, see App, "Schopenhauer and China," 29.

50. See App, "Schopenhauer and China," 34–35.

51. Ibid., 36. For the first edition of the Sinology essay (1836), see pp. 37–42; for the second edition, pp. 43–50; and for a synoptic English translation of both editions, pp. 124–40.

52. See HN5, §§1092–1095, 1104, 1115, 1116, 1119, 1127, 1129, 1130, 1141, 1161, 1162, and 1210.

53. For Schopenhauer's view and study of Tibetan Buddhism, see Urs App, "The Tibet of Philosophers: Kant, Hegel, and Schopenhauer," in *Images of Tibet in the 19th and 20th Centuries, Vol. 1*, edited by Monica Esposito (Paris: Ecole Française d'Extrême-Orient, 2008), 42–60.

54. See also App, "Schopenhauer and China," 126–28.

55. See Robert Wicks, "Arthur Schopenhauer's Bronze Buddha: Neither Tibetan nor Thai, but Shan," *Schopenhauer Jahrbuch* 92 (2011), 307–15; and Jochen Stollberg, "Arthur Schopenhauer über seinen Buddha in Gesprächen und Briefen," in *Das Tier, das du jetzt tötest, bist du selbst... Arthur Schopenhauer und Indien*, edited by Jochen Stollberg (Frankfurt: Vittorio Klostermann, 2006), 163–72.

56. Hübscher, *Arthur Schopenhauer: Gespräche*, 149.

57. Urs App, *Richard Wagner and Buddhism* (Rorschach/Kyoto: UniversityMedia, 2011).

58. Takeo Shioya, "Schopenhauer in Japan," *Jahrbuch der Schopenhauer-Gesellschaft* 53 (1972), 156–67.

FURTHER READING

App, Urs. "Schopenhauers Begegnung mit dem Buddhismus." *Schopenhauer-Jahrbuch* 79 (1998): 35–58.

App, Urs. "Notizen Schopenhauers zu Ost-, Nord- und Südostasien vom Sommersemester 1811." *Schopenhauer-Jahrbuch* 84 (2003): 13–39.

App, Urs. "Schopenhauer's India Notes of 1811." *Schopenhauer-Jahrbuch* 87 (2006): 15–31.

App, Urs. "NICHTS. Das letzte Wort von Schopenhauers Hauptwerk." In *"Das Tier, das du jetzt tötest, bist du selbst...," Arthur Schopenhauer und Indien*, edited by Jochen Stollberg. Frankfurt: Vittorio Klostermann, 2006, 51–60.

App, Urs. "Schopenhauer's Initial Encounter with Indian Thought." *Schopenhauer-Jahrbuch* 87 (2006): 35–76.

App, Urs. "The Tibet of Philosophers: Kant, Hegel, and Schopenhauer." In *Images of Tibet in the 19th and 20th Centuries*, edited by Monica Esposito. Paris: Ecole Française d'Extrême-Orient, 2008, 11–70.

App, Urs. *The Birth of Orientalism*. Philadelphia: University of Pennsylvania Press, 2010.

App, Urs. "Schopenhauers Nirwana." In *Die Wahrheit ist nackt am schönsten. Arthur Schopenhauers philosophische Provokation*, edited by Michael Fleiter. Frankfurt: Institut für Stadtgeschichte/Societätsverlag, 2010, 200–08.

App, Urs, "Schopenhauer and China: A Sino-Platonic Love Affair," *Sino-Platonic Papers* 200 (2010): 1–160 (http://www.sino-platonic.org/complete/spp200_schopenhauer.pdf).

App, Urs. *Schopenhauers Kompass*. Rorschach/Kyoto: UniversityMedia, 2011.

App, Urs. *Richard Wagner and Buddhism*. Rorschach/Kyoto: UniversityMedia, 2011.

App, Urs. *The Cult of Emptiness. The Western Discovery of Buddhist Thought and the Invention of Oriental Philosophy*. Rorschach/Kyoto: UniversityMedia, 2012.

App, Urs. "Required Reading: Schopenhauer's Favorite Book." *Jahrbuch der Schopenhauer-Gesellschaft* 93 (2012): 65–86.

App, Urs. "Asiatische Philosophien und Religionen." In *Schopenhauer Handbuch. Leben—Werk—Wirkung*, edited by Daniel Schubbe and Matthias Koßler. Stuttgart/Weimar: J. B. Metzler, 2014, 187–92.

App, Urs. *Schopenhauer's Compass. An Introduction to Schopenhauer's Philosophy and Its Origins*. Wil, Switzerland: UniversityMedia, 2014.

Barua, Arati. *Schopenhauer and Indian Philosophy: A Dialogue Between India and Germany*. New Delhi: Northern Book Centre, 2008.

Barua, Arati, Michael Gerhard, and Matthias Koßler, eds. *Understanding Schopenhauer through the Prism of Indian Culture. Philosophy, Religion and Sanskrit Literature*. Berlin/Boston: Walter de Gruyter, 2013.

Berger, Douglas. *The Veil of Maya: Schopenhauer's System and Early Indian Thought*. Binghampton, NY: Global Academic Publications, 2004.

Brucker, Johann Jacob. *Historia critica philosophiae*. Leipzig: Christoph Breitkopf, 1742–1744.

Creuzer, Georg Friedrich. *Symbolik und Mythologie der alten Völker, besonders der Griechen*. 2 völlig umbearb. Ausg. ed. Leipzig & Darmstadt: Heyer & Leske, 1819–1821.

Cross, Stephen. *Schopenhauer's Encounter with Indian Thought: Representation and Will and Their Indian Parallels*. Honolulu: University of Hawaii Press, 2013.

Deshauterayes, Michel-Ange-André le Roux. "Recherches sur la religion de Fo, professée par les bonzes Ho-chang de la Chine." *Journal Asiatique* 7 (1825): 150–73.

Diderot, Denis, and Jean le Rond d'Alembert. *Encyclopédie ou dictionnaire raisonné des sciences, des arts et des métiers, Vol. 1*. Paris, 1751.

Esposito, Monica. *Images of Tibet in the 19th and 20th Centuries*. 2 vols. Paris: Ecole Française d'Extrême-Orient, 2006.

Gerhard, Michael. "Suspected of Buddhism—Śaṅkara, Dārāṣekoh and Schopenhauer." In *Understanding Schopenhauer through the Prism of Indian Culture. Philosophy, Religion and Sanskrit Literature*, edited by Arati Barua, Michael Gerhard, and Matthias Koßler. Berlin/Boston: Walter de Gruyter, 2013, 31–62.

Göbel-Gross, Erhard. *Die persische Upaniṣaden-Übersetzung des Moġulprinzen Dārā Šukoh*. Marburg: Erich Mauersberger, 1962.

Görres, Joseph. *Mythengeschichte der asiatischen Welt, Vol. 1* (2 vols.). Heidelberg: Mohr und Zimmermann, 1810.

Gurisatti, Giovanni. *Arthur Schopenhauer. Il mio oriente*. Milano: Adelphi, 2007.

Heeren, Arnold Hermann Ludwig. *Ueber die Indier*. Göttingen: Vandenhoeck und Ruprecht, 1815.

Hübscher, Arthur. *Arthur Schopenhauer: Gespräche*. Stuttgart: Friedrich Frommann Verlag, 1971.

Hübscher, Arthur. *Arthur Schopenhauer: Der handschriftliche Nachlass in fünf Bänden*. München: Deutscher Taschenbuch Verlag, 1985.

Kapani, Lakshmi. *Schopenhauer et la pensée indienne. Similitudes et différences*. Paris: Hermann, 2011.

Klaproth, Julius. *Asiatisches Magazin* (2 vols.). Weimar: Industrie-Comptoir, 1802.

Koßler, Matthias, ed. *Schopenhauer und die Philosophien Asiens*. Wiesbaden: Harrassowitz, 2008.

Mahfuz-ul-Haq, M. *Majima'-ul-Baḥrain or the Mingling of the Two Oceans, by Prince Muhammad Dârâ Shikûh*. Calcutta: Asiatic Society of Bengal, 1929. Reprint, Karachi: Royal Book Company, 1990.

Maillard, Christine. *L'Inde vue d'Europe. Histoire d'une rencontre (1750–1950)*. Paris: Albin Michel, 2008.

Mangold, Sabine. *Eine "weltbürgerliche Wissenschaft"—Die deutsche Orientalistik im 19. Jahrhundert*. Stuttgart: Franz Steiner Verlag, 2004.

McGetchin, Douglas. *Indology, Indomania, and Orientalism: Ancient India's Rebirth in Modern Germany*. Madison/Teaneck: Fairleigh Dickinson University Press, 2009.

Morrison, Robert. *Dictionary of the Chinese Language, in Three Parts*. Macao: East India Company Press, 1815–1818.

Mosheim, Johann Lorenz. *Dissertationes ad historiam ecclesiasticam pertinentes* (2nd ed.). Altona/Flensburg: Korte, 1743.

Nicholls, Moira. "The Influences of Eastern Thought on Schopenhauer's Doctrine of the Thing-in-Itself." In *The Cambridge Companion to Schopenhauer*, edited by Christopher Janaway. Cambridge/New York: Cambridge University Press, 1999, 171–212.

Ozeray, Michel-Jean-François. *Recherches sur Buddou ou Bouddou, instituteur religieux de l'Asie orientale; précédées de considérations générales sur les premiers hommages rendus au Créateur; sur la corruption de la religion, l'établissement des cultes du soleil, de la lune, des planètes, du ciel, de la terre, des montagnes, des eaux, des forêts, des hommes et des animaux*. Paris: Brunot-Labbé, 1817.

Ozeray, Michel-Jean-François, and Urs App. *The First Western Book on Buddha and Buddhism*. Wil, Switzerland/Paris: UniversityMedia, 2017.

Piantelli, Mario. "La 'Mâyâ' nelle 'Upanishad' di Schopenhauer." *Annuario filosofico* 2 (1986): 163–207.

Pinot, Virgile. *La Chine et la formation de l'esprit philosophique en France (1640–1740)*. Genève: Slatkine Reprints, 1971. Reprint, Geneva: Slatkine, 1971.

Polaschegg, Andrea. *Der andere Orientalismus. Regeln deutsch-morgenländischer Imagination im 19. Jahrhundert*. Berlin: de Gruyter, 2005.

Rabault-Feuerhahn, Pascale. *L'archive des origines. Sanskrit, philologie, anthropologie dans l'Allemagne du XIXe siècle*. Paris: Cerf, 2008.

Schlegel, Friedrich von. *Über die Sprache und Weisheit der Indier*. Heidelberg: Mohr und Zimmer, 1808.

Scholz, Werner. *Arthur Schopenhauer—ein Philosoph zwischen westlicher und östlicher Tradition*. Frankfurt/Bern: Peter Lang, 1996.

Schubbe, Daniel, and Matthias Koßler, eds. *Schopenhauer Handbuch. Leben—Werk—Wirkung*. Stuttgart/Weimar: J. B. Metzler, 2014.

Shioya, Takeo. "Schopenhauer in Japan." *Jahrbuch der Schopenhauer-Gesellschaft* 53 (1972): 156–67.

Stollberg, Jochen. "Arthur Schopenhauers Annäherung an die indische Welt." In *"Das Tier, das du jetzt tötest, bist du selbst...," Arthur Schopenhauer und Indien*, edited by Jochen Stollberg. Frankfurt: Vittorio Klostermann, 2006, 5–34.

Stollberg, Jochen. "Arthur Schopenhauer über seinen Buddha in Gesprächen und Briefen." In *"Das Tier, das du jetzt tötest, bist du selbst...," Arthur Schopenhauer und Indien*, edited by Jochen Stollberg. Frankfurt: Vittorio Klostermann, 2006, 163–72.

Trautmann, Thomas. *Aryans and British India*. Berkeley: University of California Press, 1997.

Vecchiotti, Icilio. *La dottrina di Schopenhauer. Le teorie schopenhaueriane considerate nella loro genesi e nei loro rapporti con la filosofia indiana*. Roma: Ubaldini, 1969.

Volney, Constantin-François. *Les Ruines, ou méditation sur les révolutions des empires*. Paris: Desenne, 1791.

Voltaire. *Fragmens sur l'Inde, sur le Général Lalli, sur le progrès du Comte de Morangiés, et sur plusieurs autres sujets*. London, 1774.

Weber, Albrecht. "Analyse der in Anquetil du Perron's Uebersetzung enthaltenen Upanisad," *Indische Studien, Zeitschrift für die Kunde des indischen Alterthums* (1850): 247–302, 380–456; (1853): 1–111, 170–236; (1865): 1–54.

Wicks, Robert. "Arthur Schopenhauer's Bronze Buddha: Neither Tibetan nor Thai, but Shan." *Schopenhauer Jahrbuch* 92 (2011): 307–15.

PART II

METAPHYSICS OF WILL AND EMPIRICAL KNOWLEDGE

CHAPTER 6

THE ENDURING KANTIAN PRESENCE IN SCHOPENHAUER'S PHILOSOPHY

SANDRA SHAPSHAY

Schopenhauer's system bears a complicated yet faithful relationship to Kant's transcendental idealism, or so I shall argue in this chapter.[1] Following Kant, he espouses what I would regard as the three fundamental tenets of transcendental idealism: (1) that our experience is ineluctably structured by our cognitive faculties, (2) that the mediation of experience through our cognitive faculties necessarily puts an epistemic barrier between ourselves and the world as it is in itself, and thus (3) we can never know things as they are in themselves. However, while Schopenhauer's explicit aim was to "take up directly from Kant" (WWR1, 443), it seems that he radically breaks with him in his identification of the Kantian thing-in-itself with "will" in Book II of his main work, thus abandoning the third tenet of transcendental idealism above.

Accordingly, most commentators hold (in a variety of ways) that Schopenhauer really departs from transcendental idealism and utilizes two senses of "metaphysics" in his system: a *transcendental* one (à la Kant) that sees "metaphysics" as equivalent to knowledge of the synthetic a priori in our cognition and a *transcendent* one, his metaphysics of will.[2] This latter sense constitutes a positive (albeit partial) account of the thing-in-itself, something Kant never thought possible. Given this second sense of metaphysics, contra my opening statement, it certainly seems that Schopenhauer departs radically from transcendental idealism.

What I would like to do in this chapter is first to examine a particularly interesting, recent interpretation by Alistair Welchman that reads Schopenhauer in just this sort of "two metaphysics" way, and then I shall suggest that we need not and—textually speaking—should not read Schopenhauer as breaking from transcendental idealism despite his identification of the thing-in-itself with will. This is because his *identification should be understood as metonymic,* and the *second sense of metaphysics* at work in his system should be understood as *hermeneutic.* That is, he is not giving a transcendent metaphysical doctrine so much as an immanent "interpretation" of the inner meaning of the world—along the lines of an interpretation of the meaning of a work of art.[3] This interpretation of the world is proffered in the spirit of meeting the human need for metaphysics (*das metaphysiche Bedürfnis*); that is, the need for an explanation of the *meaning* of the world, and one that gives a person some orientation within it, but without going transcendent.

On my view, then, the second sense of metaphysics that Schopenhauer offers is not a claim to *transcendent* knowledge, but is rather a claim to *an always-immanent decipher-ing or interpretation of the world* that, he believes, accords best with the philosophical and empirical evidence and which can provide some orientation for life. This second, hermeneutic, sense of metaphysics is circumscribed by and remains consistent with his allegiance to Kant's transcendental idealism.[4]

6.1 WELCHMAN'S TWO SENSES OF "METAPHYSICS" IN SCHOPENHAUER

In a recent paper, Alistair Welchman has advanced an interpretation that does see two senses of "metaphysics" in Schopenhauer's oeuvre.[5] As described earlier, the first is the familiar Kantian sense of metaphysics; namely, the synthetic a priori cognition that makes experience possible. Welchman writes that "[t]his is Schopenhauer's *transcendental* metaphysics, which he never officially abandons, but which is much more prominent in his earliest work, like the 1813 FR." However, by the time of his main work, according to Welchman, Schopenhauer offers us a *transcendent* metaphysics that "increasingly comes to supplant the first, even to the extent that the transcendental idealism on which the first is based becomes less significant."[6]

The declining significance of transcendental idealism in Schopenhauer's thought, according to Welchman, is due to his offering a transcendent metaphysics of intrinsic and extrinsic properties of objects, one that is similar to a recent interpretation of Kant given by Rae Langton.[7] As an interpretation of Kant's metaphysics, this view connects the pre-Critical, realist, Leibnizian substance metaphysics to the Critical writings to a greater extent than most commentators had done before. As an interpretation of Schopenhauer, it divorces his talk of the essence of things from transcendental idealism. That is to say, rather than seeing the inner essence of objects as tantamount to the "unconditioned" essence of any given representation, for Welchman, Schopenhauer's transcendent metaphysics derives from a separate set of concerns, namely, from Schopenhauer's anxiety that "our experience of objects leaves us alienated from their intrinsic properties because it gives us access only to their extrinsic [relational] proper-ties, not primarily because they are only representations."[8] Thus, the second sense of metaphysics—and the identification of the thing-in-itself with will—on Welchman's view "can be formulated much more independently of transcendental idealism"[9] and is based instead on Schopenhauer's uneasiness with the idea that the world of representation—a world in which all properties are entirely relational—is all that there is. On this basis, he formulates a transcendent metaphysics of the inner, nonrelational, substantial essence of things.[10]

One might think that by distinguishing an outer and inner side of things, Schopenhauer stays firmly in a Kantian lane, echoing the distinction between appearances and things as they are in themselves, but for Welchman Schopenhauer shows himself to be "unKantian" by identifying "the inner essence of things with fundamental forces"[11] of nature, rather than pointing to unknowable things-in-themselves. And then, in order to gain more information on these fundamental forces, he looks to first-personal experience to furnish evidence as to what they are like from the inside.

Welchman's is a fresh and intriguing interpretation of the two senses of metaphysics at work in Schopenhauer's mature writings. It has the further advantage of connecting it to newer currents in Kant scholarship (Langton), as well as to contemporary currents in metaphysics such as panpsychism. But I would like to suggest, by contrast, that Schopenhauer's allegiance to the three tenets of Kant's transcendental idealism was more steadfast throughout his writings than Welchman recognizes and to offer a reading of Schopenhauer's second sense of metaphysics that is not only inspired by transcendental idealism, but remains faithful to it as well.

6.2 One Certain Thing

In the first book of WWR, Schopenhauer employs the Kantian, transcendental sense of metaphysics, but in Book II, he seems to most commentators to be offering a transcendent metaphysics. According to Robert Wicks, for example, Schopenhauer goes transcendent by identifying the Kantian thing-in-itself with will on the strength of the unique, only very thinly veiled by the form-of-time insight into our own acts of will.[12]

And, as sketched earlier, on Welchman's recent view, he goes transcendent by separating intrinsic and extrinsic properties of objects and identifying those intrinsic properties with fundamental forces. On either of these views, he is dropping the Kantian, transcendental-idealist claim that we must remain ignorant of things as they are in themselves. But let us look closely at the text to see if Schopenhauer really does depart from transcendental idealism in his identification of the thing in itself with will.

At the start of Book II, he sums up the problem we are left with after Book I: Is the world nothing more than the world of representation? Does it have any meaning beyond this? He holds that we look to the natural sciences and mathematics in vain for an answer to these questions for all that they will give us are etiological explanations that boil down to "a catalogue of inexplicable forces and an authoritative specification of the rule according to which they emerge, succeed one another, and displace one another in space and time" (WWR1, 122). These etiological explanations do not satisfy the need to know what the world of representation really means, however.

> [W]e want to know the meaning [*Bedeutung*] of those representations: we ask if this world is nothing more than representation; in which case it would have to pass over us like an insubstantial dream or a ghostly phantasm, not worth our notice; or in fact whether it is something else, something more, and if so, what this could be.
> (WWR1, 123)

This compressed bit of reasoning takes the form of a *modus tollens* and goes as follows: If the world were nothing more than representation, then we wouldn't care so much about it. But we clearly do care a lot about it! Thus, the world *must* be something in addition to representation.[13] So what is it?

In the search for the "meaning" [*Bedeutung*] of the world of representation, Schopenhauer takes one Cartesian-style point of certainty as his point of departure. "[T]his much is certain" he writes, "what we are looking for would have to be wholly and completely different from representation, and so its forms and laws could be nothing at all like those of representation" (WWR1, 123). But a question naturally arises about this; namely, what licenses him to start from this "certain" claim in his search for the meaning of the in-itself of the world?

The answer is…*transcendental idealism*. Recall the three tenets of transcendental idealism adumbrated at the start of this chapter: (1) that our experience is ineluctably structured by our cognitive faculties, (2) that this mediation of experience through cognitive faculties inevitably puts an epistemic barrier between ourselves and the world as it is in itself, and thus (3) we can never know things as they are in themselves. The second tenet is the guiding one, giving Schopenhauer the *one certain clue* as to the nature of the in-itself of the world as representation for it says that the cognitive conditioning we impose on representations (space, time, and causality) *necessarily* impose an epistemic barrier between us and the way things are in themselves. That is to say, the way the world is in itself *cannot* be like the way we represent it since the conditions we impose in representing it are *exclusively subjective*. Contra the representational realist, then, who believes that our cognitive faculties just give us the way the world really is in itself, the transcendental idealist—at least according to Kant and Schopenhauer–holds that the cognitive conditioning we impose on representations *must obscure* the way things are in themselves: since the forms we impose on our experience are *exclusively subjective*, the way things are in themselves *cannot be like* the way they appear to us.

The Kantian assumption of *the exclusive subjectivity* of spatio-temporal form was famously criticized by Adolf Trendelenburg (and also in Kant's lifetime by H. A. Pistorius).[14] In what has come to be called his "neglected alternative" objection, Trendelenburg held that Kant neglected the possibility that spatiotemporal form could be a subjective cognitive condition *as well as* an objective property of the way things are in themselves. On this view, our cognitive conditions would not obscure the way things are themselves (let alone *necessarily* obscure them from us); rather, they would track or reflect the way things really are in themselves. Leaving aside whether or not this objection to the second tenet of transcendental idealism is potent, what is important for this inquiry is that Schopenhauer was aware of the objection and, along with Kant, held on to the *exclusive subjectivity* of spatiotemporal form, thinking it frankly absurd that a subjective form of our cognition could also be an actual property of things as they are in themselves.

On my view, Schopenhauer embraces the position Kant takes in the *Prolegomena*, where he responds to the charge that he is a Berkeleyan idealist who does away with an extra-mental world entirely. In responding to this charge, Kant responds implicitly to the "neglected alternative," writing,

> I would very much like to know how then my claims must be framed so as not to contain any idealism. Without doubt I would have to say: that the representation of space not only is perfectly in accordance with the relation that our sensibility has to objects, for I have said that, but that it is even fully similar to the object; an assertion to which I can attach no sense [*keinen Sinn verbinden kann*], any more than to the assertion that the sensation of red is similar to the property of cinnabar that excites this sensation in me.[15]

I take the key premise in Kant's reasoning here to be based on Berkeley's "likeness principle," which is somewhat ironic since he is intent to argue that he is not a Berkeleyan idealist in this section of the *Prolegomena*. For Berkeley, our ideas of sensible qualities cannot resemble those qualities themselves, for "an idea can be like nothing but an idea; a color or figure can be like nothing but another color or figure."[16] In the preceding passage, I take Kant to interpret the likeness principle in the following manner: properties that belong to a representation *in virtue of its character as representation* cannot "resemble" or "be similar to" the properties in the object which excite the representation. Thus, with respect to the "cinnabar" in the preceding quote, it is logically impossible for the sensation of red (a property that belongs to one's representation *in virtue of its being a representation*) "to be similar" to the objective property in the cinnabar that excites the sensation in the subject.

If my interpretation of this passage is accepted, we may reconstruct the following Kantian argument for the non-spatiotemporality of the thing in itself, or what amounts to the same thing, the *exclusive* subjectivity of spatiotemporal form, as follows:

1. Properties that belong to a representation in virtue of its character as representation cannot logically be similar to the properties in the object which excite the representation.
2. Spatiotemporal form is a property of representations in virtue of their representational character.
3. Thus, things as they are in themselves must be non-spatiotemporal.[17]

Schopenhauer was an admirer of the *Prolegomena*, and I believe he is on board with Kant's reasoning in *Prolegomena* 13 (Ak. 4:290), writing that Kant had "proved [*daß er bewies*] space as well as time to be a mere form [*sei eine bloße Form*] of our intuition or perception, which in consequence [*die folglich*] does not belong to things-in-themselves" (WWR2$_{[P]}$, 7).[18] Connecting this back to our main discussion, by taking as his one, certain starting point that the way things are in themselves "would have to be wholly and completely different from representation" (WWR1, 123), Schopenhauer shows himself to be a faithful follower of Kant's transcendental idealism for he is using one of its central tenets as a guide.

Yet perhaps one might think that he drops this allegiance once he actually hits on the crucial metaphysical insight; namely, the way to identify the thing in itself with will through one's own bodily awareness. Perhaps then and only then does he decide to go transcendent? Let us delve further into Schopenhauer's reasoning for the identification of the thing-in-itself as will to see if he finally goes transcendent in due course.

For Schopenhauer, it is the fact that we are not just "disembodied" knowers of the world who can view even our own bodies from a purely objective standpoint, but that we are also rooted in the world as desiring, feeling, and willing individual bodies that gives us the "solution to the riddle" (WWR1, 124). This "double cognition" of our own body—as an object like any other object that we learn about through observation, but also first-personally, more immediately, from the inside—is the "key to the essence of every appearance in nature" which we may judge "on the analogy with our body..." (WWR1, 129). But the reason why our first-personal experience of our bodies *counts as affording such insight* into the essence of ourselves and world as a whole in the first place is, again, transcendental idealism. He is guided toward this insight by seeking a kind of knowledge that bypasses, to the largest extent possible, the necessarily *distorting* cognitive conditions we place on all of the objects of our experience—*distorting*, that is, if one wants to know how things are in themselves.

Since the consciousness of ourselves as willing is the "most immediate thing in our consciousness, and thus has not passed completely into the form of representation in which object and subject stand opposed to each other" (WWR1, 134), it counts as a monumentally significant insight. In other words, because we have an insight that is *more immediate* and *less cognitively conditioned* than any other—that is to say, conditioned by those forms which *necessarily distort* the way things are in themselves—we therefore have an insight that has bypassed to a great extent the distorting "veils" between the cognizing subject and the way things are in themselves. So Schopenhauer is guided in his search for a "way into the fortress" of the thing-in-itself precisely by the aforementioned first two tenets of transcendental idealism.

Furthermore, Schopenhauer is careful to note that while the cognition one has of his or her own will is "the most immediate cognition there is" (WWR1, 127), it is still cognitively conditioned by the form of time, "time being the form in which my body (like every other object) appears" (WWR1, 216). So we have gotten very close to immediate access to the thing in itself, and, in WWR2, Schopenhauer characterizes this insight as "a kernel of the phenomenon different from the phenomenon itself." Yet, a veil is still a veil, and this insight "can never be entirely separated from the phenomenon, and be regarded by itself as an *ens extramundanum*" (WWR2$_{[P]}$, 183). Accordingly, we still do not have a Schellingian "intellectual intuition" of the in-itself of the world even in our most immediate experience of our own acts of will. So why does Schopenhauer think that he can go ahead and identify the thing-in-itself with will on the strength of this *most-but-not-entirely* immediate first-personal insight?

On my view, Schopenhauer knows he *cannot* justify making this identification as a piece of transcendent metaphysical doctrine for he recognizes that the thing-in-itself can never be a true object of knowledge: "This *thing in itself* (we will retain the Kantian expression as a standing formula) can never be an object, because an object is only its appearance and not what it really is" (WWR1, 135).

However, if we want to "think objectively" about it, if we want to take a stab at solving the riddle of the world, then our best bet is to use the clue we have from the *most imme-diate* cognition we have. Schopenhauer certainly wants to offer a solution to the riddle of the world, he wants to decipher it, and so he names the thing in itself "will." But note in the following passage how he qualifies this identification; he writes:

> It is nonetheless fair to say that we are only using a denomination from the superior term [a *denonimatio a potiori*] that gives the concept of will a broader scope than it had before.... Accordingly, I will name the genus [the thing in itself] after its most important species [the human will]; the more intimate and immediate cognition we have of this species leads to the mediated cognition we have of all the others.
>
> (WWR1, 135–36)

By signaling that he is "only using a denomination from the superior term [a *denonimatio a potiori*]" to identify the thing itself as "will," he signals that he is not using the "is" of ordinary predication (e.g., "S is P"). Rather, he announces that he is only using a poetic device to name the thing in itself "will." According to dictionaries of Schopenhauer's day, "*denominatio a potiori*" meant something like "after or according to the main part or feature does a thing get its name."[19] The Meyers Konversations-Lexikon (edition 1885–1892: 1, 695), for example, glosses "*a potiori*" as: "*seinem Hauptteil nach erhält ein Ding seine Benennung.*" This device is one that I call "metonymic" insofar as it names the whole (*das Ding*) according to one of its parts (typically the best known part) (*ein Hauptteil*). This is the kind of identification at work when, for example, one says that "the crown" set out on horseback to meet the Spanish armada. Here, "the crown" is a part that stands for the whole, Queen Elizabeth I, or perhaps for a less tangible whole, the determination or the power of the monarch. Similarly, Schopenhauer uses the term "will" (the best known part) to stand for the whole (the thing in itself) in order to think objectively about what strictly speaking cannot be known as an object.[20]

In the preceding quotes, then, we see that Schopenhauer is carefully qualifying the knowledge claim involved in the identification of the thing in itself with the term "will": first, the thing in itself can never be an actual *object* of cognition; second, if we try to think of it objectively, we'll need to use a figurative device, the *denominatio a potiori* or metonymy, naming what cannot be a direct object of knowledge after its best known part; and third, even our access to its best known part—to one's own will—is mediated through the form of time, and so that access is not entirely immediate.

These caveats demonstrate abiding Kantian epistemic scruples, yet Schopenhauer's metaphysical pronouncements can at times seem quite bold, as in the following:

> Only the will is *thing in itself*: as such, the will is by no means a representation, it is quite different in kind from representation: all representations, all objects are the appearance, the visible manifestation, the objecthood of the will. The will is the innermost, the kernel of every individual thing and likewise of the whole.
>
> (WWR1, 135)

While it sounds here as if Schopenhauer is offering a transcendent metaphysical doctrine, what I'd like to suggest is that we take him in such passages as being less careful than he should be, given the interpretation offered here. Sometimes it seems that Schopenhauer gets carried away by his own rhetoric and goes off the rails, but, in his more careful moments, I believe that what he is offering is not metaphysics in a transcendent sense, but rather an immanent *metaphysics in a hermeneutic sense*. Greater evidence for this hermeneutic sense of metaphysics can be found in a lengthy discussion of "Man's Need for Metaphysics" (WWR2, ch. 17) to which I now turn.

6.3 THE METAPHYSICAL NEED

Recall that, for Kant, the one legitimate sense of metaphysics is the *transcendental* one, knowledge of the synthetic a priori conditions of experience; with this, according to Kant, we should be humble and satisfied. On moral grounds, we may legitimately *hope* that there is a God, a soul, and an afterlife in which happiness will be proportionate to moral desert, but we cannot have theoretical knowledge of these and other traditional themes of metaphysics. Because Kant's arguments relegated such transcendent meta-physical speculation to the "dustbin of history" (to quote Marx anachronistically), he received the moniker "*der Alleszermalmende Kant*" (the all-destroying Kant) from his friend, Moses Mendelssohn.[21]

Schopenhauer agrees that Kant has crushed traditional metaphysics as it had been done by Spinoza, Leibniz, and Wolff, but he also recognizes that there is a universal, human desire to have such traditional metaphysical questions addressed, and he does not think that human beings will ever be satisfied with Kantian humility about the nature of the world as it is in itself. Unlike non-human animals, where will and intellect are closely aligned, Schopenhauer sees that in human beings they are sufficiently separated such that we feel "surprised" at our own existence (WWR2$_{[P]}$, 160). We wonder at our own works, at our inevitable death, at the apparent vanity and fruitlessness of human effort, and at the existence of evil, wickedness, and suffering (WWR2$_{[P]}$, 171). From this wonder arises a "metaphysical need," a need for "an interpretation" of the world. This need also explains why "the really materialistic as well as the absolutely sceptical systems have never been able to obtain a general or lasting influence..." (WWR2$_{[P]}$, 162). In terms of popular appeal, materialism and skepticism have long lost out to metaphysical philosophies and even more so to religions, which not only meet the metaphysical need but also perform the dual function of being "guiding star of their action" as well as "the indispensable consolation of the deep sorrows of life" (WWR2$_{[P]}$, 167).

Testimony to this metaphysical need can be found in the "[t]emples and churches, pagodas and mosques, [that exist] in all countries and ages, in their splendor and spaciousness" (WWR2$_{[P]}$,162). The task for philosophers, as Schopenhauer sees it, is not to rest with Kantian humility but rather to furnish an interpretation of the world that is based in experience and well-supported by the philosophical and empirical evidence. Accordingly, he describes his own metaphysical endeavor as follows:

> The whole of experience is like a cryptograph, and philosophy is like the deciphering of it, and the correctness of this is confirmed by the continuity and connection that appear everywhere. If only this whole is grasped in sufficient depth, and inner experience is connected to outer, it must be capable of being *interpreted, explained,* from itself.   (WWR2$_{[P]}$, 182)

The model of metaphysics that he outlines as the proper one is that of "deciphering" or "interpretation" of the world in which the philosopher uses all of the phenomenological resources of inner and outer experience and seeks confirmation by the interpretation's ability to make sense of phenomena as a whole. Thus, appropriate philosophy (metaphysics) is similar to offering a well-justified interpretation of a work of art. Like an artistic interpretation, it should stand or fall on how well it accords with the evidence in that work (in the case of the world, the empirical evidence, both first and third-personal) and with how well it makes sense of the work as a whole. Now, one can offer an interpretation of the world that *is also* transcendently metaphysical, and this is the way the standard view would read Schopenhauer. But as I will argue in what follows, Schopenhauer is intent on offering an interpretation of the world—thus meeting the metaphysical need— that nonetheless remains immanent and is always bound up with the phenomena that are to be explained.[22]

To illustrate the difference between my *hermeneutic* reading of Schopenhauer's approach to metaphysics and the traditional reading of Schopenhauer as a more old-style, transcendent sort of metaphysician, it is helpful to look at how Robert Wicks frames the Schopenhauerian identification for the thing-in-itself with Will. Wicks writes,

> If the thing-in-itself is not essentially Will, however, then there is no reason *to expect* that the world as representation will present a violent appearance. This is the problem. As we know, Schopenhauer accounts for the daily world's violence in reference to a single, blind Will that our PSR divides into individuals that stand against each other. Individuals selfishly and aggressively oppose each other owing to the metaphysical fact that their inner nature is blind Will, not because the nature of reality merely

appears to us to be in itself Will, or because Will is only one of possibly an infinite number of the thing-in-itself's other dimensions.[23]

Here, Wicks presents Schopenhauer as utilizing his key breakthrough—the thing-in-itself is will—as a "metaphysical fact." This secure fact then leads us "to expect" that the world as representation will present as violent. According to Wicks's characterization here, Schopenhauer's methodology seems to be foundationalist: get the metaphysical facts straight, and then they will be able to predict the character of the phenomena.

By contrast, instead of seeing Schopenhauer as foundationalist in his methodology, I see him as a coherentist: starting from the arguments in favor of transcendental idealism and then adding to this his breakthrough first-personal insight into oneself as will, he names (metonymically) the thing in itself "will." In this, we have *a key* (rather than a "metaphysical fact") for interpreting the phenomena. But we should not then take the key itself as predictive; rather, we must look to experience of the phenomenal world to confirm or disconfirm it. Happily, for Schopenhauer, experience does confirm that he is on the right track and much of *On Will in Nature* consists of detailing how the best science of his day does actually confirm the "key" to interpreting the world. However, the major difference between Wicks's view and mine is that, on my view, it is the *evidence from experience* that gives us good reason to think the key is right and not the key on its own that gives us predictive power about the phenomenal world. Thus, I think it is a live possibility for Schopenhauer that the empirical evidence might *disconfirm* the key. My view has the advantage of making sense of Schopenhauer's many assertions about the importance of his *On Will in Nature* as providing the empirical "confirmation" that the key is correct.

Further evidence for reading Schopenhauer as having a back-and-forth, coherentist method between philosophical argument/insight and experience of the phenomenal world comes in his criticism of Kant for not trying to address nagging metaphysical questions at least in part with empirical evidence.

> But does it not rather seem positively wrong-headed that, in order to solve the rid-dle of experience, in other words, of the world which alone lies before us, we should close our eyes to it, ignore its contents, and take and use for our material merely the empty forms of which we are a priori conscious?   (WWR2$_{[P]}$, 181)

Similarly, he faults those who have tried to address metaphysical questions for lack of consistency between their theories and the empirical evidence.

> Thus, for example, the optimism of Leibniz conflicts with the obvious misery of existence; Spinoza's doctrine that the world is the only possible and absolutely nec-essary substance is incompatible with our wonder and astonishment at its existence and essential nature; Wolff's doctrine that man has *existentia* and *essentia* from a will foreign to him runs counter to our moral responsibility for actions.
>
> (WWR2$_{[P]}$, 184)

In contrast to foundationalist thinkers like Spinoza, Leibniz, and Wolff, the "key" to deciphering the "riddle" of the world consists in "combining at the right place outer experience with inner, and making the latter the key to the former" (WWR2$_{[P]}$, 181), but confirmation that one has deciphered the world of phenomena correctly comes from the fact that it allows us to "perceive agreement and consistency in the contrasting confusion of the phenomena of this world" (WWR2$_{[P]}$, 185).

It is important to underscore, however, that throughout this endeavor to decipher the world correctly, Schopenhauer shows himself to be faithful to transcendental idealism. The right sort of metaphysics, he writes,

> ... *remains immanent, and does not become transcendent*; for it never tears itself entirely from experience, but remains the mere interpretation and explanation thereof, as it never speaks of the thing-in-itself otherwise than in its relation to the phenomenon. This, at any rate, is the sense in which I have attempted to solve the problem of metaphysics, taking into general consideration the limits of human knowledge which have been demonstrated by Kant.   (WWR2$_{[P]}$, 183, emphasis added)

From this quote, one sees that Schopenhauer himself did not conceive of his metaphysical enterprise as transcendent but rather thought of it as immanent and always circumscribed by and consistent with Kant's transcendental idealism.

6.4 CONCLUSION

While I believe the textual evidence favors the *metonymic* interpretation of Schopenhauer's identification of the thing in itself with will as well as the immanent *hermeneutic* interpretation of Schopenhauer's metaphysical enterprise, there are some prima facie philosophical problems with this view that might make it unattractive, viz. Wicks's more traditional interpretation or Welchman's more forward-looking interpretation.

First, on the hermeneutic interpretation, Schopenhauer's "deciphering" of the world is likened to the "deciphering" of the meaning of a work of art. But the analogy between the world as representation and a work of art is a strained one. A work of art—even if it is one of Duchamp's readymades—has *an artist* who presumably has intentions to convey some kind of meaning through the work. But Schopenhauer's philosophy is decidedly atheistic: there is no sense here of a Celestial Artist of the world who tries to convey a meaning to us through the world-as-artwork.

I think the way to assuage this worry, however, is to recognize that the "deciphering" language is meant to track *a similarity in interpretative process* that takes place in legitimate metaphysics and in the interpretation of a work of art without the assumption that the object of interpretation in each case is similarly intentional and meaningful.

In fact, in the end of WWR1, Book IV, Schopenhauer suggests that the "meaning" of the world as representation is really nothing more than blind striving that, while *purposive*, is ultimately *purposeless*. This actually makes the world as representation sound very much like a beautiful natural object—one which exhibits purposiveness without a purpose (on Kant's aesthetics)—rather than a work of art. So while the approach to interpretation is similar in each case, the object to be interpreted varies fundamentally. Ultimately, for Schopenhauer, the divergence of the world of representation from a work of art—it seems to lack an intelligent author/designer, it seems to lack actual purpose and meaning—should come as a rather unpleasant shock to the system of anyone who grasps this fully.

Another worry is that perhaps my hermeneutic interpretation makes Schopenhauer's view less interesting than, say, Welchman's interpretation that connects Schopenhauer with currents in contemporary metaphysics and forward-thinking Kant scholarship. This may be the case, and I respect those who would like to read Schopenhauer with an eye to contemporary philosophical trends, but I do think that my interpretation makes Schopenhauer interesting from a *methodological* perspective. Reading Schopenhauer's metaphysics as pulling off a difficult balancing act between addressing the human meta-physical need and remaining faithful to transcendental idealism shows him as a very resourceful thinker. In my view, he utilizes the following resources:

1. Kantian transcendental argument (though mostly in his earliest work, FR)
2. Close attention to experience (both inner and outer)
3. Careful phenomenological description of various sorts of experience (conative, disinterested-aesthetic, sublime, moral, ascetic, mystical)
4. Evidence from the best science of his day
5. Inference to the best explanation

Schopenhauer attempts to put all of this together in a kind of Rawlsian "reflective equi-librium" *avant la lettre*. While Rawls tries to offer a theory of justice that best comports with our moral intuitions and empirical evidence (from economics, sociology, etc.), Schopenhauer tries to offer an interpretation of the meaning of the world—an immanent metaphysics—that best comports with transcendental idealism and inner and outer experience. By looking closely at actual experiences, he finds the "key"—the notion of the essence of the world as will—to deciphering the meaning of the world as representation.

But the key is not deployed in a top-down fashion. He checks that key insight against scientific findings (especially in *On Will in Nature*), finding empirical confirmation of his interpretation of the essence of the world. He also checks it against deep intuitions from ordinary experience, such as the feeling of moral responsibility at the end of *On the Freedom of the Will*, which supports the Kantian intelligible/empirical character distinc-tion. And he checks the interpretation against the evidence of genuine compassion and the sense that only the motive of compassion gives an action moral worth (in *On the Basis of Morality*). Finally, he checks it in light of the experience of aesthetic and ascetic will-lessness (in Books III and IV of WWR1).

After a careful back and forth between transcendental idealism and the "key" it affords through inner experience to deciphering the meaning of the world as representation, he searches around in a wide variety of human experiences, in the cutting-edge natural science of his day, in works of art, music, and perhaps even a little bit of history, to see whether it all fits together into a coherent interpretation. Ultimately, Schopenhauer is satisfied with his interpretation for he thinks he has hit on an epistemically virtuous equilibrium, writing,

> I must deny that any doctrine of my philosophy could honestly be added to such a list [of problematic metaphysical doctrines], just because each one has been thought out in the presence of perceived reality, and none has its root in abstract concepts alone.... The discovered answer to a riddle shows itself as the right one by the fact that all the statements of the riddle are consistent with it. Thus my teaching enables us to perceive agreement and consistency in the contrasting confusion of the phenomena of this world, and solves the innumerable contradictions which, seen from every other point of view, are presented by it.   (WWR2$_{[P]}$, 184–85)

Although Schopenhauer is satisfied that he has hit upon the correct interpretation of the world as representation, one that enables us to "perceive agreement and consistency" in the world and resolves the "innumerable contradictions" that arise from other doctrines, if there should be recalcitrant facts that don't square with his system, or puzzles and contradictions that his own system cannot resolve, or new scientific findings that cast facets of his system into doubt, then, by the lights of *his own methodological advice*, we should keep working on a better interpretation.

Are there recalcitrant facts of experience that Schopenhauer's system does not address? Surely there are. What about the experience of positive joy in the world that seems to conflict with this theory of pleasure as being merely a privation? What about the fact that *striving* can actually be enjoyable and engaging rather than relentlessly painful? What about the evident role of reason in morality, a role that seems badly undertheorized in his view of compassion as the source of all morally worthy actions?[24]

Are there scientific facts that don't square well with his system? Indeed, a Darwinian view of species does not fit well at all with the Platonic Ideas as the levels of objectification of the will. Are there puzzles and contradictions that his system does not resolve? Surely there are: How exactly are we to square the Platonic Ideas with the notion of a monistic world as will? How can the intelligible character act in the world if it is not in time? How is it possible for an individual to renounce the will, apparently, through an act of will?

It may be possible to deal successfully with these challenging questions, but my point here is simply that *on Schopenhauer's own methodological grounds*, they should spur us on to seek out an improved interpretation. It could be that some of these contradictions might be so severe that we should actually give up on one of the key tenets of transcendental idealism (like that worrisome tenet 2 perhaps). But, to his credit, on the hermeneutic interpretation, Schopenhauer himself offers up a methodology that points us in a fruitful direction for further philosophical inquiry.

Notes

1. I am grateful to Robert Wicks, Alistair Welchman, and Jens Lemanski for helpful discussion of the themes in this chapter.

2. David Cartwright helpfully lays out the 20th c. critical landscape on this issue in his "Two Senses of the 'Thing-in-Itself' in Schopenhauer's Philosophy," *Idealistic Studies* (2001): 31–54. He also characterizes the standard view as follows: "Schopenhauer claimed that the will (*Wille*) is the thing-in-itself, and since metaphysical knowledge is knowledge of the thing-in-itself, Schopenhauer also claimed metaphysical knowledge" (p. 31).

3. My interpretation of Schopenhauer's second sense of metaphysics as hermeneutic is similar to recent views put forward by Daniel Schubbe in his book *Philosophie des Zwischen: Hermeneutik und Aporetik bei Schopenhauer*. Würzburg: Königshausen u. Neumann, 2010. See also Daniel Schubbe, "Schopenhauers Hermeneutik—Metaphysische Entzifferung oder Explikation 'intutiver' Erkenntnis?" *Schopenhuaer-Jahrbuch*, 93 (2012), 409–424, and Thomas Regehly & Daniel Schubbe *Schopenhauer und die Deutung der Existenz: Perspectiven auf Phänomenologie, Existenzphilosophie und Hermeneutik*. Stuttgart: J.B. Metzler, 2016, especially Peter Welsen, "Schopenhauers Hermeneutik des Willens" pp. 157–170 in this volume. For some recent studies that resist such a reading, see Manja Kisner, *Der Wille und das Ding an sich. Schopenhauers Willensmetaphysik in ihrem Bezug zu Kants kritischer Philosophie und dem nachkantischen Idealismus*. Würzburg, Königshausen u. Neumann, 2016 and Alessandro Novembre, *Il Giovane Schopenhauer: L'Origine Della Metafisica Della Volontà* (Milan: Memesis, 2018), especially Chapter 12.

4. My interpretation of Schopenhauer's second sense of metaphysics as hermeneutic is also similar to that offered by Julian Young in his *Willing and Unwilling: A Study of the Philosophy of Arthur Schopenhauer* (Dordrecht: Nijhoff, 1987) and John Atwell, *Schopenhauer and the Character of the World: The Metaphysics of Will* (Berkeley: University of California Press, 1995). However, my interpretation differs from theirs in that they downplay the identification that Schopenhauer actually makes between the Kantian thing-in-itself and will. I acknowledge that Schopenhauer makes this identification, but hold that it is metonymical.

5. Alistair Welchman, "Schopenhauer's Two Metaphysics: Transcendental and Transcendent," in *The Palgrave Schopenhauer Handbook*, edited by Sandra Shapshay (London: Palgrave-Macmillan, 2017), 129–49.

6. Ibid., 146.

7. It should be noted, though, that Welchman and I are operating with somewhat different understandings of transcendental idealism. He thinks of it as claim (1) plus the inference that things in themselves must be non-spatiotemporal or causal. Following Langton, Welchman holds that one can be a transcendental idealist in this narrower sense *and remain neutral* about epistemic access to things in themselves, and he offers an interpretation of Schopenhauer as holding on to this narrower view of transcendental idealism and claiming that we can know something about the thing-in-itself.

8. Welchman, "Schopenhauer's Two Metaphysics," 146.

9. Ibid., 130.

10. Ibid., 140.

11. Ibid., 134.

12. Robert Wicks canvasses alternative, more Kantian views like the one I am urging in this chapter but defends this traditional, transcendent metaphysical view of Schopenhauer in chapter 6 of his *Schopenhauer* (Oxford: Blackwell, 2008). Wicks writes, "[w]hen Schopenhauer claims that the thing-in-itself is Will, it seems to be an absolute and exhaustive

characterization of the basis of things. This would locate him squarely among the more optimistic post-Kantian philosophers who maintain that since the thing-in-itself is knowable, traditional metaphysics is possible and achievable" (67).

13. This reasoning may also be characterized as a *modus tollendo ponens* or disjunctive syllogism or perhaps even more accurately as an exclusive disjunctive syllogism. I am grateful to Jens Lemanski for discussion on this point.

14. For Trendelenburg's famous objection, which stirred a lively debate with the great historian of philosophy, Kuno Fischer, see F. A. Trendelenburg, *Logische Untersuchungen* (2nd edition) (Leipzig, 1862) and his *Kuno Fischer und sein Kant* (Leipzig, 1869) for the original formulation of this objection. According to Hans Vaihinger, the "neglected alternative" was actually first suggested by a contemporary of Kant's, H. A. Pistorius. See Vaihinger, *Commentar zu Kants Kritik der reinen Vernunft, Vol. 2* (Stuttgart, 1922), 134–51.

15. Immanuel Kant, *Prolegomena to any Future Metaphysics*, edited and translated by Gary Hatfield (Cambridge: Cambridge University Press, 2004), 41, Ak. 4: 289f.

16. George Berkeley, *A Treatise Concerning the Principles of Human Knowledge*, edited by C. M. Turbayne (Indianapolis, IN: Hackett, 1970), section 8, 249.

17. For the full argument for this claim, see Sandra Shapshay, "Did Schopenhauer Neglect the 'Neglected Alternative' Objection?" *Archiv für Geschichte der Philosophie* 93, 3 (2011): 321–48.

18. Desmond Hogan takes issue with my Berkeleyan interpretation of how Kant (and following him, Schopenhauer) thought he was entitled to dismiss the so-called neglected alternative. According to Hogan, Schopenhauer held that the Transcendental Aesthetic's argument from synthetic *a priori* knowledge to the non-spatiotemporality of things in themselves was successful and was not susceptible to Trendelenburg's famous objection. For his alternative proposal on Kant and Schopenhauer's handling of the "neglected alternative," see "Schopenhauer's Transcendental Aesthetic" in *The Sensible and Intelligble Worlds: New Essays on Kant's Metaphysics and Epistemology*, edited by Karl Schafer and Nick Stang (Oxford: Oxford University Press, forthcoming).

19. Dale Jacquette, in his "Schopenhauer's Proof that the Thing-in-Itself Is Will," *Kantian Review* 12, 2 (2007), 76–108, presents a reconstruction of what he terms Schopenhauer's second (later) argument for the identification of the thing-in-itself as will that is similar to mine, except that he does not draw as much attention to the part–whole identification that I am calling "metonymic" and he does not think that Kantian epistemic scruples hold Schopenhauer back from claiming transcendent metaphysical knowledge.

20. For the full argument for this metonymical identification, see Sandra Shapshay, "Poetic Intuition and the Bounds of Sense: Metaphor and Metonymy in Schopenhauer's Philosophy," *European Journal of Philosophy* 16, 2 (2008), 211–29, reprinted in *Better Consciousness: Schopenhauer's Philosophy of Value*, edited by Christopher Janaway and Alex Neill (London: Blackwell, 2009).

21. See the preface to Moses Mendelssohn, *Morgenstunde oder Vorlesungen über das Daseyn Gottes*, in *Gesammelte Schriften*. Band 3.2 (Berlin, 1929). First published in (Berlin: Christian Friedrich Voß, 1785).

22. I am grateful to Alistair Welchman for pressing me on this point.

23. Wicks, *Schopenhauer*, 131 (emphasis added).

24. For more on this please see Chapter 5 of my *Reconstructing Schopenhauer's Ethics: Hope, Compassion and Animal Welfare* (Oxford: Oxford University Press, 2019).

FURTHER READING

Atwell, John. *Schopenhauer and the Character of the World: The Metaphysics of Will*. Berkeley: University of California Press, 1995.

Cartwright, David. "Two Senses of the 'Thing-in-Itself' in Schopenhauer's Philosophy." *Idealistic Studies* 31, 1 (2001): 31–54.

Hogan, Desmond. "Schopenhauer's Transcendental Aesthetic" in *The Sensible and Intelligble Worlds: New Essays on Kant's Metaphysics and Epistemology*, edited by Karl Schafer and Nick Stang. Oxford: Oxford University Press, forthcoming.

Jacquette, Dale. "Schopenhauer's Proof that the Thing-in-Itself Is Will." *Kantian Review* 12, 2 (2007): 76–108.

Kisner, Manja. *Der Wille und das Ding an sich. Schopenhauers Willensmetaphysik in ihrem Bezug zu Kants kritischer Philosophie und dem nachkantischen Idealismus*. Würzburg: Königshausen u. Neumann, 2016.

Novembre, Alessandro. *Il Giovane Schopenhauer: L'Origine Della Metafisica Della Volontà*. Milan: Mimesis, 2018.

Regehly, Thomas, and Daniel Schubbe. *Schopenhauer und die Deutung der Existenz: Perspectiven auf Phänomenologie, Existenzphilosophie und Hermeneutik*. Stuttgart: J.B. Metzler, 2016.

Schubbe, Daniel. "Schopenhauers Hermeneutik—Metaphysische Entzifferung oder Explikation 'intutiver' Erkenntnis?" *Schopenhuaer-Jahrbuch* 93, (2012): 409–24.

Schubbe, Daniel. *Philosophie des Zwischen: Hermeneutik und Aporetik bei Schopenhauer*. Würzburg: Königshausen u. Neumann, 2010.

Shapshay, Sandra. *Reconstructing Schopenhauer's Ethics: Hope, Compassion, and Animal Welfare*. Oxford: Oxford University Press, 2019.

Shapshay, Sandra. "Did Schopenhauer Neglect the 'Neglected Alternative' Objection?" *Archiv für Geschichte der Philosophie* 93, 3 (2011): 321–48.

Shapshay, Sandra. "Poetic Intuition and the Bounds of Sense: Metaphor and Metonymy in Schopenhauer's Philosophy." *European Journal of Philosophy* 16, 2 (2008), 211–29.

Welchman, Alistair. "Schopenhauer's Two Metaphysics: Transcendental and Transcendent." In *The Palgrave Schopenhauer Handbook*, edited by Sandra Shapshay. London: Palgrave-Macmillan, 2017, 129–49.

Welsen, Peter. "Schopenhauers Hermeneutik des Willens" in Thomas Regehly & Daniel Schubbe. *Schopenhauer und die Deutung der Existenz: Perspectiven auf Phänomenologie, Existenzphilosophie und Hermeneutik*. Stuttgart: J.B. Metzler, 2016, 157–70.

Wicks, Robert. *Schopenhauer*. Oxford: Blackwell, 2008.

Young, Julian. *Willing and Unwilling: A Study of the Philosophy of Arthur Schopenhauer*. Dordrecht: Nijhoff, 1987.

....

CHAPTER 7

SCHOPENHAUER ON THE WILL AS THE WINDOW TO THE WORLD

....

IVAN SOLL

IN this essay, I try to show how Schopenhauer's theory of the will is developed, in great part, as a response to Kant's philosophy, particularly to Kant's denial that we can ever know things as they really are, and also how his theory addresses certain problems in the Cartesian dualism between body and mind. Then I critically assess Schopenhauer's views and arguments concerning the experience of one's own will. After finding some of his *metaphysical theses* about the true nature of the will and the world to be unjustified, I argue that he also propounds a *transcendental thesis* about how we must experience and think about the world and the will, which is separable from his metaphysical position, and which has considerably more merit. I conclude with a short defense of Schopenhauer against possible charges that he is a proponent of a crude and untenable *panpsychism*. Of course, in order to evaluate Schopenhauer's ideas, I shall have to directly and critically engage with some of the philosophical and psychological issues involved.

Schopenhauer defends several related but distinct theses about the nature of the will and our experience of it:

1. The *thesis of the uniqueness of our experience of our own will*: that our experience of our own will is radically different from all of our other experiences of the world.
2. The *thesis of the epistemologically privileged nature of the experience of one's own will*: that it is epistemologically privileged in the sense that it provides us with a type knowledge that no other experience does.
3. The thesis of the *metaphysically privileged nature of the experience of one's own will*: that it is our only experience of something as it really is rather than as it appears to be, the only experience unencumbered by the distorting structures we otherwise impose upon whatever we confront in the world. In the Kantian

terminology that Schopenhauer adopts, it is an experience of oneself as a "thing-in-itself" rather than as an empirical "representation."[1]

4. The *cosmological extension of the metaphysical thesis of the will*: that we must understand the real, undistorted nature of everything—not only of ourselves, but also of other people, animals, living organisms, and even inorganic nature—as being variations of the will that we experience in ourselves; that the experience of one's own will is the window to the true nature of the rest of the world.

I have here initially formulated these theses in a somewhat rough, provisional manner, but I shall refine them in the course of this chapter. Since each of them represents a philosophically significant and problematic position, I believe they all merit careful and critical consideration.

7.1 THE KANTIAN CONTEXT OF SCHOPENHAUER'S THEORY OF THE WILL

In the first book of *The World as Will and Representation*, Schopenhauer adopts and adapts Kant's basic epistemological and metaphysical position from *The Critique of Pure Reason*. Following Kant, he argues that the world as we normally experience it is not the world as it really is "in-itself," but rather the world as we "represent" it to ourselves and that this process of representing the world to ourselves inevitably involves changing and distorting it. Kant had argued that certain universal and unvarying structural features of the world as we normally experience it are not actually structures of the world itself, but rather structures we necessarily impose upon the world in the process of experiencing it. He held that they are needed to enable us to organize the dauntingly inchoate and overwhelming mass of raw data with which the world confronts us. He claims that we need to impose them to make some sense of this world (i.e., to experience the world as a coherent whole that can be comprehended).

Among the structures that we universally and necessarily impose on the world of our experience are *space, time, causality,* and *substance*. We experience everything that exists or happens in the world as existing or happening somewhere and at some time and as taking up some space and existing or occurring for some time. The world we experience is also composed and constituted by substances or things, which are complex unities of various distinct qualities and which somehow retain their identities over time and through certain sorts of change. According to Kant, we do not initially experience the world as a plethora of fleeting and unconnected impressions, as the British empiricists had held, but immediately, as composed of qualitatively complex but nevertheless unified entities that endure through qualitative change. And we experience every event that occurs as having a cause, even when we do not experience the cause or nevercome to know what it is.

Kant had argued that the very universality and necessity of such structural features of our experience show that we contribute them to the world rather than simply encountering them there. He pointed out that it is impossible to be absolutely certain of what the external world will confront us with in our future encounters with it. Yet, we are nevertheless certain that all of the experience we shall have in the future, or could possibly have, will be characterized by such structural features as space, time, causality, and substance. How can we account for this certainty? Only, says Kant, if they are not features of the world that confronts us, for we can never be sure of what we are going to encounter, but structures that we shall inevitably impose upon whatever we happen to encounter in the world. So the spatial, temporal, causal, and substantial structure of the world we experience is not true of the world as it is "in-itself," but only of the world as we experience it or "represent" it to ourselves. This, in brief, is Kant's famous "Copernican Revolution" in philosophy, the idea that these omnipresent structural features of the world as we experience it are really not features of the world in itself, as we have usually supposed them to be, but only features of the way we structure our experience of the world. It is a *constructivist* view in that it holds that the world of our everyday experience is one we actively construct rather than simply receive and record.

Schopenhauer accepts the basic idea of Kant's "Copernican Revolution in philosophy," of Kant's constructivism, but makes several significant amendments: First, he calls attention to a structure of the world of our experience that he claims is so basic that Kant simply overlooked it, namely, that every experience we have of the world is one in which we as subjects are aware of an object (WWR1$_{[P]}$, 1). On this view, even many of the reflexive experiences of our own selves involve the self as a conscious subject and the self as object of this consciousness. Second, he streamlines Kant's philosophy, jettisoning most of the more than a dozen universal structures that Kant had claimed we apply to all of our experience of the world, retaining only three basic ones: space, time, and causality.[2] Third, he unifies the three basic structures by arguing that it would be impossible to have any of them without having all of them (i.e., that they form an inseparable unity). In this way, he reinforces Kant's claim for the necessity of organizing our experience in just the way that we do (WWR1, §4).[3] Fourth, he focuses on the fact that, in our experience of the world, we are able to distinguish *pluralities of individual instances of the same kind*. And he asks how do we do this, particularly in cases in which we do not or cannot distinguish them qualitatively; for example, how are we able to see six bottles of the same beer or the proverbial pluralities of peas in a single pod without noting any discernible qualitative differences among them. He argues that we obviously do this by considering the differences in their positions in space and time. Since he views space and time as structures we impose upon the world of our representative experience, he views the "*individuation*" of particular things in our experience to be the consequence of these imposed structures and thus not a characteristic of the world as it is in itself.[4]

Having embraced the basic Kantian position that the world as we usually experience it is not the world as is really is "in-itself," Schopenhauer, like other German philosophers of the late eighteenth and early nineteenth centuries, was challenged by Kant's daunting denial of the possibility of ever knowing reality as it really is. Like several thinkers of the period (such as Fichte, Schelling, Jacobi, and Hegel), Schopenhauer sought a way to accept Kant's conclusions concerning our normal way of experiencing the world and yet find a special way to achieve a deeper or truer knowledge of reality.

Intuitionists, like Jacobi, had claimed that, while Kant's *constructivist* view is valid for ordinary experience, we can also access the world through special acts of "*intellectual intuition*," in which we suspend the distorting constructions that we usually impose on the world and simply take it in as it really is. *Dialecticians*, like Hegel, while denying the existence and possibility of such acts of nondistorting intellectual intuitions, argued that we can transcend ordinary experience toward a deeper and truer understanding of reality by utilizing a *dialectical method*, which was not bound by the limiting restraints of ordinary logic and thought.

Schopenhauer rejected these solutions, but his theory of the will represents yet another attempt to accept most of the basic tenets of Kant's thought while devising a way of circumventing Kant's denial that we can ever know reality as it really is. Schopenhauer proposes that we can know reality undistorted by the structures of normal experience in and through some of our experiences of ourselves specifically through our experiences of our own will, that is, through our experiences of our own willful acts, of our own agency.

Schopenhauer does this principally in the second book of *The World as Will and Representation*, titled *The World as Will, the First Consideration: The Objectification of the Will*. Here he claims that one's experience of one's own will is radically different from one's experience of everything else. He formulates this point by asserting that one's experience of one's own will is "totally different" from all of our other experience and "comparable with no other" (WWR1$_{[P]}$, 103). Indeed, he says that it is different "*toto genere*" (WWR1$_{[P]}$, 102), which might suggest that Schopenhauer wants to claim that one's experience of one's own will is entirely different, *different in every respect* from all of one's other experiences. But he soon after modulates this overly simple and robust initial statement of his position by admitting that our experience of our own will, while still *radically different* from all other experience, is not different in absolutely every way. Nevertheless, he continues to suggest that the experience of one's own will is characterized by the absence of, if not all, at least most of the distorting structures ubiquitous in all other experience. And he concludes from this that one's experience of oneself as will, even if it is still just a bit distorted, is at least an experience that gets much closer to capturing something it as it really is than any other experience one can have. In either version, he presents it as an epistemologically and metaphysically privileged experience and as one that escapes or circumvents, either totally or for the most part, the limitations Kant had placed on human knowledge, which had so sorely challenged the traditional metaphysical aspirations of philosophers to know reality as it really is.

7.2 PERSPECTIVAL VERSUS METAPHYSICAL DUALISM

Like Descartes, Schopenhauer describes human beings as composed of two components. For Descartes a human being is both a spirit (or mind) and a body; for Schopenhauer each of us is, and indeed experiences oneself, both as a will and as a physical body. But these two dualisms are fundamentally different in nature. Descartes's two elements are *two completely distinct substances or entities*, a mind and a body, a nonphysical substance and a physical one, which are somehow mysteriously connected to each other. In contrast, Schopenhauer's two elements are rather *two perspectives on (or aspects of) a single entity, the body.* While Descartes propounds a *metaphysical dualism*, Schopenhauer propounds a *perspectival dualism.* This perspectival dualism allows Schopenhauer implicitly to embrace a *metaphysical monism* with respect to the being of humans. Each of us is nothing but a body, which we can experience either in the way we necessarily experience all other bodies—that is, as a representation, from the outside, through our senses of sight, touch, etc.—or in the way that we can only experience ourselves, "from the inside," that is, as will.

Schopenhauer boldly states his *perspectivally dualistic* thesis early in the second book of *The World as Will and Representation.*

> Whereas in the first book we were reluctantly forced to declare our own body to be a mere representation of the knowing subject, like all other objects of this world of perception, it has now become clear to us that something in the consciousness of everyone distinguishes the representation of his own body from all others that are in other respects quite like it. This is that the body occurs in consciousness in quite another way, *toto genere* different, that is denoted by the word *will.* It is just this double knowledge of our own body which gives us information about that body itself, about its action [*Wirken*] and movement following upon motives, as well as about its suffering through outside impressions [*Einwirkung*], in a word, about what it is, not as representation, but as something over and above this, and hence what it is *in itself.*[5]   (WWW1[P], 103)

Schopenhauer's shift from a metaphysical to a perspectival dualism serves at least two purposes. First, it removes one of the problems besetting Descartes's metaphysical dualism, "the mind–body problem," or "the problem of interaction": How can a mind, which is not at all physical, influence a physical body, as it seems to do when we, for example, voluntarily move our bodies? And how can the physical body affect a nonphysical mind, as it seems to do in perception, when changes in our physical sensory system cause us to have new mental experiences? Since, on Schopenhauer's view, the will is *not only an embodied will, but is the body itself experienced in a different way*, the problem of how the will interacts with and influences the body does not even arise.

Second, to posit one's own body as an entity that we know in two distinct ways supplies the necessary structure for Schopenhauer's claim that our experience of our own will is an experience of ourselves as we really are in ourselves, indeed our only direct experience of anything as it is *in itself.* For to make the claim that an experience of something is an experience of that thing as it really is, we must be able to contrast that experience with *an experience of the same thing* not as it is in itself, but only as it appears to be.[6]

In support of the idea that every act of will involves a movement or act of the body, Schopenhauer argues that resolutions or intentions concerning future actions are not in themselves acts of will but only "deliberations of reason," "mere intentions that can be altered" (WWR1[P], 100). For Schopenhauer, wishful thinking is not willing. To will something, it is not enough to think that you would like it to be the case. To will what you would like to be the case, you must also take some action toward the realization or achievement of that end. The action taken need not result in successfully achieving what one wills to achieve. It need not even get close to achieving it. But if no action of any sort is undertaken to realize a desired end, this end has not been actually willed.

7.3 TWO PROBLEMS WITH SCHOPENHAUER'S IDENTIFICATION OF WILLING WITH BODILY ACTION

Schopenhauer's distinction between just considering something to be desirable and actually trying to bring it about, and his identification of willing with the latter, seem plausible. Yet, this theory is also fraught with some difficulties.

First, if acts of will are identified with the bodily actions taken to bring about what is willed, how can it account for cases in which we try to achieve an end by trying to think about ways we might do this, but we do not succeed in finding any strategy that seems feasible? We might even figure out a way the desired result might be achieved but not have the means to even begin to carry it out. It seems that thinking about how one might achieve a desired end, even without a bodily movement or action toward that end, is still an expression of the will. It seems that not all acts of will involve movements of the body, or at least that not all acts of the will are accompanied by *bodily actions that we can perceive as such.* Using a metaphysically dualistic Cartesian idiom we could easily describe such cases. We could say that in such cases we do not move from mental acts of the will (mental activity directed toward the realization of some end) to any bodily movement toward that same end. But Schopenhauer, given his rejection of Cartesian dualism, cannot account for such phenomena in this way.

To defend Schopenhauer's view, one could argue that, though not all acts of will involve perceptible bodily movement, they all still involve bodily activity, in as much as they involve brain activity. But even if I believe that all mental activity is also activity of the brain, which is part of my body, in experiencing the workings of my mind I do not experience them *as* the workings of my brain, *as* bodily actions. My experience of my own mental activity, in cases in which I am actively considering how to achieve a desired end without undertaking any other actions toward that end, *does not seem to involve any direct awareness of the physiological activity of my brain as such.* In such cases, I seem to have an experience of my mental activity that seems to involve my will but does not contain the experience of a bodily component *as such.*

Conversely, just as there is a problem concerning activity of the will that is perceived as not involving bodily activity, there is also a problem concerning bodily action perceived as not involving the will, a problem concerning what appear to be *involuntary bodily actions*. If an act of will is really nothing but an aspect of all bodily movement and nothing separate from it, we are left with the problem of how there could be any involuntary actions.[7]

In addressing this problem, we should distinguish between two kinds of involuntary movement: the first is movement that is caused by an outside force (e.g., someone pushes my hand and it moves); the second is movement that I initiate but is not experienced as consequent on any wish of mine. This second types includes both involuntary twitches (e.g., the doctor taps the shin of my bent leg and my leg moves by reflex) and also actions I catch myself doing "by habit" without any awareness of wanting to do them—perhaps even despite an awareness of not wanting to do them. Actions of the first type present no great problem, for one can simply deny that they are actions at all. But what can Schopenhauer say about actions of the second type? Though they seem to be actions in that they are experienced not just as movements of our bodies, but as actions that we initiate and that move toward ends or goals, we do not experience any sort of willing supporting them.[8] Indeed some of them seem to occur in opposition to one's willing.

7.4 THE EXPERIENCE OF ONE'S OWN WILL AS FREE FROM ALL (OR MOST) OF THE STRUCTURES THAT DISTORT ALL OF OUR OTHER EXPERIENCE

Schopenhauer's bold claim in section 19 of WWR1, that the experience of our own will or agency is "*toto genere* different" from all of our other experiences, including both our experiences of other objects in the world and our other sorts of experiences of ourselves, is unfortunately not accompanied by any closer analysis of the experience of one's own will or any arguments to support his claim about its thoroughgoing uniqueness.

One could read the claim that the will is "*toto genere* different" in two ways: as the more modest claim, that it is in *some fundamental way* different in kind from our other experience, or as the more robust claim, that it is different *in every way*.[9] But since he bases his claim that this is the only experience we have of something as it really is in itself on its radical difference from all our other experience, he is clearly suggesting that its difference lies in its being free, or free for the most part, of the distorting structures that shape all other experiences. Thus, he is suggesting that it is free of all (or at least most) of those structures, like time, space, and causality, that he assumes we universally and necessarily impose upon all of our other experience.

However, Schopenhauer himself admits that we still experience our own will as a series of acts that take place in time, so he is forced to conclude that one's experience of one's will is still fraught with the structure of time.

Finally, the knowledge I have of my own will, although an immediate knowledge, cannot be separated from that of my body. I know my will not as whole, not as a unity, not completely according to its own nature, but only in its individual acts, and hence in time, which is the form of my body's appearing, as it is of every body.[10]

(WWR1$_{[P]}$, 101–02)

Given Schopenhauer's reduced list of the basic structures we impose uponour experience, the continued presence of time in this experience leaves only the possible absence of space or causality to differentiate the experience of one's own will from all other experiences.

But is it plausible for Schopenhauer to suggest that the structures of space and causality are absent from one's experience of one's own will, especially given his view that the will is an aspect of the body? Schopenhauer asserts that the will is always experienced not only as an *embodied will*, as necessarily somehow connected to a body, but as the body itself observed in a different way. For Schopenhauer, there are no acts of will that are not also acts of the body: for him, every act of will *is an act of the body*, just viewed in another way. Given the bodily nature of the will, it becomes extremely difficult to conceive of it as not being in space. The awareness of a voluntary act of one's own body seems to entail an awareness of the location of one's body in space. It does not seem possible to separate my consciousness of my willing to move my body in a particular way, which for Schopenhauer involves a consciousness of my actually moving my body, from an awareness of the spatial nature of my body.

Moreover, one experiences one's body as an individual body separate and distinct from other bodies. Likewise, one experiences one's own will as the individual will of one's individual body, distinct from other wills. But Schopenhauer holds that the individuation of bodies of any sort depends on their position in both time and space. So he cannot consistently deny that our experience of our own individual will is also characterized and distorted by both space and time.[11]

This leaves only the structure of causality as a possible locus of the deep difference between the experiences of the world as representation and as will. According to the Kantian-Schopenhauerian conception of causality as a structure of representation imposed by us upon the world, it makes us experience everything that happens, every event, as causally determined, whether or not we have any experience of what caused the event or even any notion of what that cause might be. It might be argued, however, that in our experience of our own acts of willing, we have a strong sense that we are choosing our own ends rather than having these ends totally determined for us by our given intrinsic nature, our past history, and our present situation in the world. So, although we may view all events in the world, including our own actions, as causally determined when we view them "as representation," we do not have any direct sense of our being causally determined in experiencing our own volitions and actions. On the contrary, we seem to have a strong sense that we ourselves must decide and guide our actions, even when this experienced autonomy is felt to be onerous and unwanted. The structure of causality, *in the sense* of *causal determinism*, present in all other experience, is thus arguably absent in our experience of ourselves as will.

However, the experience of one's own will, even if it is not characterized by *an immediate sense of one's will being causally determined*, is essentially characterized by a *sense of being causally efficacious*. When I experience myself willing something or voluntarily acting toward some end, I also experience my willing or acting as having some degree of efficacy. It is difficult to imagine what it would even mean to try to do something if I did not feel that my trying to do it had some efficacy, had some chance of success, however remote. So it seems that our experience of our own will is still characterized by some sort of causality.[12]

Indeed, it seems that our experience of our own will is still fraught with almost all of the basic distorting structures we impose on our experience of the world as representation: time, space, the individuation that arises from the conjunction of the two, and at least one aspect of causality. Schopenhauer himself admits the presence of one of these structures, that of time, in our experience of our own will. But, as I have here argued, it seems that actually most of them are still there. Yet Schopenhauer nevertheless continues to claim that this experience is different *toto genere* from all of our other experience. Moreover, in basing his claim, that the experience of one's own will is epistemologically and metaphysically privileged on its radical difference from the rest of one's experience, he strongly suggests that this difference consists precisely in its unique freedom from the structures that distort all of our other experience. The persistence of these structures in one's experience of one's own will undermines his claim that the experience of one's own will is our only experience of something as it really is.

7.5 THE VARIETIES OF SELF-AWARENESS: THE SUBJECT AS OPPOSED TO ITSELF AS OBJECT; THE SUBJECT AS IDENTICAL WITH ITSELF AS OBJECT

There still remains one structural feature of representation to consider, one Schopenhauer considered to be the most basic structural feature of all representation and one that had been overlooked by Kant: that every representational experience is characterized by a subject–object dichotomy, that it is an experience in which a subject is aware of an object that is distinct from it. This is clearly the case in our experiences of objects in the external world, but what about the experiences one has of oneself? Many of the experiences we have of ourselves seem to be clearly representational and characterized by this subject–object polarity: for example, many experiences of my own body, looking at it either directly or in a mirror, or attentively listening to my own voice as I speak.[13] Even in such experiences of myself, Schopenhauer holds, there is a subjective "I" who does the looking and listening and an objective "me" who is looked at and listened to.

Schopenhauer insists, however, that my experience of my own will, of my own willed actions, is radically different from my other experiences of myself and of the external world in that it contains no separation or distinction between myself as subject and myself as object. He says that in experiencing our own will, we experience "the object coinciding with the subject, in other words, ceasing to be object" (WWR1$_{[P]}$, 102). Since for Schopenhauer the subject–object dichotomy is the most fundamental structure of all representation, it is crucial for him to claim that it is absent in one's experience of one's own will if he is to claim that this experience is not representational. He suggests that an introspective consideration of our experience of our acts of will support this claim.[14]

But does it? The separation I feel between my subjective self and the other bodies I experience in the world is arguably more robust than the separation I feel between my subjective "I" and my objective "me" when I reflectively experience my own body. And there does seem to be a separation between the subject and object of our consciousness when we reflect on physical aspects of our bodies, one that is not present when we are conscious of our willed actions. It should be noted that this diminution of the sense of separation also occurs not only with respect to acts of will but also with respect to other mental states and processes, such as my reflective awareness of my own emotions, sense experiences, and processes of reasoning. But it still seems that even in my reflections on my own willed actions, I still experience *some sort of* distinction between myself as the reflecting subject and the acts of will I reflect upon.[15]

The way we experience ourselves both as subjects and as objects of our own will or agency may well be different from the way we experience this duality in our other experiences of ourselves. But this difference does not seem to be as simple or stark as Schopenhauer claims it is. Though he presents the subject–object polarity, as a structure that is either fully present or totally absent, it seems that it can vary in degree and kind in a number of ways across different sorts of experiences, including different sorts of experiences of oneself. With respect to this matter, there seems to be more variety and nuance than can be handled by any simple and neat dichotomy.[16]

7.6 THE WILL AS THE ONLY "NATURAL FORCE" WE EXPERIENCE

There is, however, another and more promising line of argumentation in Schopenhauer for the radical difference of our experience of our own will from all other experience. It is an argument concerning the experience of what he calls "natural forces" (WWR1, §18). Here, he does not rest his claim for the radical difference and epistemological superiority of one's experience of oneself on the *purported absence* in it of the structures that organize and distort all of our other experience. Instead, he bases it on the *purported presence* in it of a fundamental feature that is absent in all of our other experience. He argues that only in experiencing the efficacy of our own will to initiate our own bodily action do we ever have a direct experience of a "*natural force*," namely, that of the will's efficacy.

This thesis implicitly consists of two separate claims: a positive claim, that in experiencing the efficacy of our own will we do directly experience a "*natural force*," and a negative claim that we do not directly experience "*natural forces*" in any of our other experiences.

Let us first examine the negative claim. Do we not usually experience all sorts of natural forces at work when we observe the world? What are these "*natural forces*" that, according to Schopenhauer, we do not directly experience in most of our experience of the world? They are the efficacious forces we claim to observe at work when we see what we take to be relations of cause and effect in the world.

However, as David Hume had forcefully argued, what we actually experience in cases of experiencing cause and effect in the world is never the efficacious force itself, *the force which actually causes the effect*, but only the event that we take to be the cause *followed by* the event which we take to be its effect. Hume had argued that when we experience one sort of event or occurrence being *repeatedly and regularly followed* by another sort of event, we tend to *infer* that the two sorts of events are causally connected, but we do not ever *directly experience* the force that connects them.

Hume had also argued that since all of our inferences of causal connections are based on the observation of the constant conjunction of two types of events, there is always the possibility that such apparent constant conjunction will turn out upon further observation not to hold up. Thus, we can never be certain about any of our attributions of causality, neither those with respect to individual cases nor those with respect to specific laws of nature.

Kant, who was intent on locating certainties that could serve as a firm foundation for a knowledge and science of nature, argued that there was still something absolutely certain about causality; namely, what he called the "*causal maxim*," that every event we experience necessarily will be experienced as having a cause, even in cases in which we have no idea of what the cause is. Yet he did not really challenge Hume's views relevant to the attribution of specific causal connections between individual events and the formulation of particular causal laws. Thus, Kant's view seems to be that though we are always absolutely sure that any event has a cause, we can never be absolutely sure about what is its specific cause. Kant does not really challenge Hume's view that our specific attributions of causality are always *indirect inferences* based on the experience of a repeated pattern of a constant conjunction between two types of events.

Schopenhauer, in opposition to both Hume and Kant, argues that there is one case in which we do *directly experience* efficacious forces at work in the world, namely, in experiencing the efficacy of our own will. On Schopenhauer's view, in experiencing the efficacy of my own will to initiate and carry out actions, I do not need to *infer* that my will somehow caused me to act in that way based on the repeated experience of that sort of willing followed by that sort of acting. I *directly experience* the connectedness of the willing and acting in the particular case. I directly experience *the efficacy of my will itself*, the actual connection between my willing and the bodily action that I will.

He argues that no experience of a repeated sequence of events or inference is involved. Moreover, he claims that I do not experience two distinct events—an act of will and act of the body, a cause followed by an effect—but rather one event, my willfully acting. According to him, when I, for example, willfully raise my arm, I do not experience a mental act of willing to raise my arm *followed or even accompanied by* the physical act of my arm going up, but rather a single action or event: *me willfully raising* my arm.

Since we conceive of a causal connection as one between two distinct events, a cause and its effect, Schopenhauer claims that the *efficacious connection* between the willing and the bodily action is not experienced as a causal connection. Willfully acting involves my will and my body, not as two separate entities, but as one: my body viewed as will rather than as representation.

This contrasts sharply with our experience of causality in the world outside ourselves, which, according to Schopenhauer, conforms to the Humean model of being based on the repeated experience of one kind of event followed by another, without any direct experience of their causal connection. If this is true, then our experience of our own willing is different from all of our other experience in a fundamental way. It is the only direct experience we have of an *efficacious connection*, of what Schopenhauer refers to as a "natural force," like all those other forces that make things happen in the world.[17]

This line of argument for the uniqueness of one's experience of one's own will at work is much more promising. It does indeed seem that we experience our own willing as actually effecting action, not just regularly preceding it. Moreover, when I raise my arm, I do not experience my willing as preceding the action and as distinct from it, but as occurring for the most part simultaneously with the action and inseparable from it.[18] Moreover, I do not even experience two distinct, simultaneous events, a cause and an effect—my willing to raise my arm and my arm going up—but one: my willfully raising my arm.[19] Thus, Schopenhauer supplies a serious challenge to Hume's well-entrenched theory that we never directly experience the sort of efficacious connection that we infer to be operative in individual cases of causality in the external world.

This line of argument does not at all depend on Schopenhauer's dubious claim that the experience of one's own will is free of all or most of those distorting structures which we otherwise impose upon the world we confront. Rather than claiming that the experience of one's own willing is free of all or most of the basic structural features of all of our other experience, it claims only that it possesses a fundamental feature that other experiences lack. While this argument, if correct, would still show that one's experience of one's own will is fundamentally different from all of one's other experience, it does not need to attempt to show that it is different in every way, or even almost every way. And while this argument would support the claim that this experience is *epistemologically privileged* in furnishing us with our only direct experience of a "force" of nature," it would not support nor depend on the claim that it is *metaphysically privileged* in being free of, or for the most part free of, the structures that distort our other sorts of experience.

7.7 The Experience of One's Own Will as the Window to the World: The Transcendental Thesis Versus the Metaphysical Thesis

Having argued that it is only in the experience of our own willing that we can directly experience a force of nature at work, Schopenhauer goes on to argue that we must understand all "forces of nature" as being varying forms of the will that we experience in ourselves. Given that we can never directly experience the forces of nature that we take to be operative in the world outside of ourselves, we must conceive of them *as being somehow like* the only force of nature that we can and do directly experience, that of our own will. Otherwise, he argues, we could not form any conception of them whatsoever, for our conception of those natural forces that we never directly experience must be based on the only force that we do directly experience.

It is important to note that this argument does not in itself make any claims about the true nature of all natural forces but only about how we must conceive of them if we are to conceive of them at all. Its conclusion is, in a somewhat extended Kantian sense, a *transcendental* rather than a *metaphysical* thesis in that it does not even assert that all natural forces are in fact like the force of the will, but only that we can only conceive of them as such.

But when Schopenhauer goes on to assert the *metaphysical thesis*, that our experience of our own will is an experience—indeed our only direct experience—of anything as it truly is in-itself and not merely as we represent it to ourselves, his theory of the will takes a *metaphysical turn*. He holds not only that the experience of one's own will is the only possible model for conceiving of all other efficacious forces in the world, but also our only experience of these natural forces and of reality in general *as they really are*. The experience of one's own will becomes our only window to the reality of the rest of the world as it really is "in-itself."

Thus, Schopenhauer ends up maintaining that the experience of one's own will is not only *epistemologically privileged* in that it is less distorted than our other experience or that it uniquely provides access to certain aspects of reality, but also that it is *metaphysically privileged* in that, despite some relatively minor residual distortion, it is nevertheless on the whole an experience of reality as it really is and indeed our only such experience. He ends up arguing that the self as will is the only thing we experience fundamentally as it is in-itself without changing and distorting its essential nature it in the process. Schopenhauer claims that this experience does not involve most of the processing, structuring, and consequently distorting of the world that characterizes our other experience. The claim that this experience is metaphysically privileged is far stronger and more problematic than the claim that it is epistemologically privileged. To show that an experience is epistemologically privileged Schopenhauer has to show only that it is epistemologically privileged *in some way*; that it affords some insights that no other experience does. If it alone affords us a direct experience of a natural force or efficacious connection in the world, as Schopenhauer argued, that would be sufficient to show that it is epistemologically privileged. But even if this were so, it would not be enough to show that the experience of one's own will presented one with an experience of something as it really is "in-itself, undistorted by any of the ways we "represent" the world in all of our other experience. Even if the experience of one's own will is epistemologically privileged in this way, it could still be fraught, not only with stubborn residues of distortions from normal representational experience, as Schopenhauer concedes, but with some distortional structures of its own. As I have tried to show, this experience seems to be fraught with most of the representational structures that are present in other experiences. Moreover, the experience of the will's efficacy itself could be a construction of a different sort. And many recent psychological studies have given us reasons to believe that our experience of our own acts of will and of the will's efficacy, our experience of ourselves as acting on decisions that we have made, may well be constructions and thus to some extent illusory.[20]

But even if our experience of our own agency should turn out to be a representation that is to some extent illusory, it would not at all affect the validity of Schopenhauer's *transcendental thesis*—that we must base our conception of all forces of nature on our experience of our own agency—for his argument does not require that what he asserts to be *the necessary model of all natural forces* be free of construction and illusion. We still may have to base our conception of the forces of nature on our experiences of our own willed actions even if these experiences are somewhat illusory. However, his *metaphysical thesis*—that the experience of one's own agency is not a form of representation but the only direct experience we have of something as it really is, as a "thing-in-itself"—is undermined by any illusory or distortive aspects of this experience, both by any residues of the distortive structures of our ordinary experience of the external world that remain in it and by any illusory aspects of our sense of agency that are peculiar to it.

One is naturally led to ask why Schopenhauer so carelessly overlooked the illusory structures that the experience of one's own will seems to share with our other experiences? Why was Schopenhauer so quick to embrace the idea that the experience of one's own will is an unconstructed and undistorted experience of something as it is "in-itself"?

First, like other German philosophers of the time who were hell-bent on finding a way around Kant's denial of the possibility of experiencing and knowing things as they really are in themselves, Schopenhauer might have been eager to believe that he had found a window to metaphysical knowledge, even where this conclusion was not fully warranted.

Second, Schopenhauer might also have embraced his metaphysical thesis concerning the experience of the will more readily because of his conviction that all representations are characterized by exactly the same set of distortive structures. As I have previously pointed out, he had supplemented and strengthened Kant's claim that space, time, substance, and causality are universal and necessary features of all representations of the world by arguing that this set of qualities must be present as a whole, if it is to be present at all.

Schopenhauer's *thesis of the inseparability and invariability of the structures of representational experience* strengthens the Kantian claim that *all of them* are universally and necessarily present in all representational experience of the world for it suggests that the presence of any of them entails the presence of all of them. But it also entails that an experience that is free of any these structures should be free of all of them. So it predisposes Schopenhauer to believe that an experience that differs with respect to any of these structural features must differ with respect to all of them.

Given his starkly dichotomous view of the possible kinds of experience and his view that the experience of one's own agency seems to possess a structural characteristic that clearly distinguishes it from our other representational experiences—namely, the presence in it of an efficacious connection—Schopenhauer was inclined to conclude (1) that it is not a representation at all and thus (2) that it *must be* free of all of the typical structures of representational experience. This may explain why he seems to conclude that this experience lacks almost all of the structural features of normal representational experience, without carefully looking to see if this is true and even ignoring the fairly obvious presence of several of these structures.

Schopenhauer tends to approach all human experience as falling into one of two possible basic categories: the representational experience of the world outside myself and the nonrepresentational experience of my own will or agency, the first constructed and consequently distorted *in an unvarying manner*, the second completely, or for the most part, unconstructed and undistorted. Given this dichotomous approach, he tended to infer from some features of our experience of our own agency that distinguish it from our experiences of the world outside of ourselves that it must be an experience that involves no construction and distortion—or very little. He fails to see that there may be more than one way we construct our experience and that our experience of our own agency may be another way of doing this.[21]

However, these flaws in Schopenhauer's argument for his *metaphysical thesis* do not at all negatively affect his *transcendental thesis*, his idea that we must conceive of all efficacious connections in the world as somehow like or analogous to the connection between our own willing and acting, for this *transcendental thesis* in itself makes no metaphysical claims and has no metaphysical implications. It asserts nothing about the actual nature of the world outside of ourselves. It is a thesis about how we must understand reality, *no matter how flawed or illusory this understanding may be*, and not a thesis about the nature of reality itself.[22]

7.8 PROJECTION VERSUS PANPSYCHISM

Schopenhauer can easily be misunderstood as advocating an objectionable *"panpsychism,"* the attribution of minds or peculiarly mental traits, like consciousness, to beings who seem clearly not have them. Since, on Schopenhauer's view, we must project from the experience of our own human selves to our understanding of all other entities, one might worry that this entails the projection of peculiarly human traits, like abstract thinking or conscious deliberation, onto all other entities, other animals, plants, and even inorganic matter. But this objection would be ill-founded. Schopenhauer makes it quite clear that he is not arguing that we must project *all* the traits of our own minds and wills onto all other beings, but only what is essential to our willing: namely, movement or impetus toward some end. He makes it clear that action or movement toward some end, though often accompanied by consciousness and deliberation in ourselves, need not be accompanied by the same sort of consciousness or deliberation in other forms of life, and certainly not in the will as it manifests itself in its nonorganic forms. Schopenhauer argues that *this striving or impetus toward some end is the essence of willing* and that it can occur blindly, not requiring any direction by a mind or consciousness of any sort.[23] Thus Schopenhauer cannot be faulted for propounding an indefensible *panpsychism* that ascribes mental attributes peculiar to human beings to all other animals, plants, and even inanimate matter.[24]

7.9 CONCLUSION

Schopenhauer's *transcendental thesis* that we must conceive of all efficacious connections, all "natural forces," as being varying forms of what we experience in ourselves as will, neither entails nor depends on any of his more problematic metaphysical theses about the true nature of all reality. And it does not entail any crude and problematic panpsychism that views animals, plants, and inorganic matter as having minds, consciousness, or thoughts. His *transcendental thesis* could be easily detached from the dubious metaphysical speculations that accompany it in his philosophy. Considered on its own, it is an idea that merits serious consideration.

NOTES

1. We shall see that Schopenhauer modulates his initial statement of this view, admitting that our experience of ourselves as will is still just a bit distorted, but much less distorted than our other experiences.
2. Kant had claimed that there are fourteen of these structures that we all invariably apply to all of our experience of the world: two "pure" forms of intuition, space and time, and a dozen "a priori categories or concepts of the understanding," among which are causality and substance. In rejecting many of Kant's categories as otiose, Schopenhauer was following in the wake of several philosophers of the time who, despite their great admiration for Kant's basic ideas, found most of his twelve "a priori categories of the understanding" to be otiose. To some of them, only substance and causality, along with space and time, seemed to be essential structures of the world as we experience it. Schopenhauer's version of this reduction and simplification of Kant's inventory of a priori structures is unusually austere

in reducing this short list of four to only three: space, time and causality. Yet he does not really reject the idea that one of the essential features of the world as we experience it is that it is composed of substances, its *substantiality*. He argues rather that this substantiality is a necessary consequence of the other three structures, not a distinct, additional structure (WWR1[ₚ], 11).

3. See Section 7.7 for a discussion of how this idea influences Schopenhauer's views of the will.

4. Schopenhauer's rejection of the reality of individuation aligns him with the metaphysical views of Plato, who argued that what most truly exists are the "forms," the natural types or kinds of things, not the individual exemplifications of those types.

   Schopenhauer viewed his overall philosophical project as an amalgam of Plato's and Kant's philosophies. His argument for the illusory nature of individuation exemplifies this project in that it depends on using a Kantian constructivism in a new way to reach Platonic conclusions. Schopenhauer's Platonism also emerges strongly in WWR1, Book III, in his discussion of art and the experience of beauty, both of which he thinks involve transcending our normal experience of a world composed of individuals toward an experience of the forms that are exemplified by these individuals.

5. It is significant that Schopenhauer uses the word "*Wirken*" rather than "*Handeln*." *Handeln* refers to action in a general way. *Wirken* refers more particularly to the efficacious aspect of action. It is the substanivized form of the verb, *wirken*, which means *to act on, to effect*. Thus, in talking about the will's "Wirken," he is talking about its power to have effects in the world of bodies. To experience the "Wirken" of one's own will is to experience its efficacy on one's own bodily action and through that on the world in general.

6. Schopenhauer characterizes our consciousness of ourselves as a "twofold and completely heterogeneous knowledge of one and the same thing" (WWR1[ₚ], 103).

7. On the Cartesian view, such actions might simply be accounted for by defining voluntary bodily actions as those accompanied or guided by a mental act of the will and involuntary actions as those not so accompanied. But Schopenhauer's views preclude this way of describing these sorts of acts.

8. (a) One could suggest, as Schopenhauer sometimes does, that such actions are willed but not consciously willed, that they are vegetative or inorganic manifestations of the will that exist in us alongside conscious ones. But then the claims that these sorts of human actions are willed is no longer based on an examination of our experience of them. And Schopenhauer claims that his theory of the will is based on our direct experience of our own acts of willing.

   (b) Analogously, though I may believe that all of my acts of willing involve bodily activity, or that they essentially are forms of bodily activity, how I directly experience them is another matter and the one that is relevant to Schopenhauer's claims to base his theory of the will on our direct experience of our own will.

9. His other descriptions of this experience as "*ganz anderes*" (translated by Payne as "totally different") and as "completely heterogeneous" suggest the more robust interpretation.

10. When Schopenhauer asserts that knowing the will "only in its individual acts" and "not as a whole" involves an illusory distortion, he is drawing on his idea that there exists only a single world will—and not a plurality of individual wills. (This point is further explained in note 12.)

    There is also, however, the question of the unity of each single personal will, which embraces and unites a plurality individual acts of will. Schopenhauer does not distinguish or address this problem here. But since he holds that the substantial structure of the world of our experience (namely, the fact that it is composed of qualitatively complex but unified substances that endure through time and change) only arises as an inevitable consequence of space, time, and causality all taken together, the disappearance of any of them in our experience of our own will should have the consequence that we do not experience the individual personal will as a complex and enduring unity of its individual acts of will.

However, we arguably still do experience our own individual wills not simply as a series of acts of volition, but as complex and enduring unities, each of which engages in a series of willings, that is, as a *substance that wills*. Moreover, since Schopenhauer has argued that the substantial structure of our world is the result of space, time, and causality working together, the substantiality of the self we experience should suggest that all three of these distortive structures are still present and functioning in the experience of one's own will.

11. Schopenhauer believes that the apparent plurality of individual wills is only an illusory diffraction of a single world will created by the distorting spatio-temporal structure of representation. He bases this striking conclusion not on any claim that we experience our individual wills as part of a single world will, but only on the logical implications of his belief that the plurality of individual wills, indeed any plurality of any sort of individuals, can only arise and indeed must arise in the omnipresent, necessary, but distortive grid created by space and time taken together. He does not claim that we experience the one-ness of the world as will, but that we must *infer* its oneness, that is, its lack of any plurality, from the illusoriness of the spatio-temporal framework which creates all such individuation.

This counterintuitive thesis of the unity or nonplurality of the will is very important to Schopenhauer for he uses it to justify morality. He argues that the basis of the claim that we should treat others like oneself, which he takes to be the heart of all moral sentiment and action, can only be that there really is no difference between the other and oneself, that behind the apparent plurality of individual wills there is really just one world will. He holds that the only justification for the maxim that one should treat others like oneself is that "they" really are not distinct from oneself.

12. Nevertheless, the sense of *causal efficacy* that attaches to the experience of one's own will is still somewhat different from the sense *causal determinism* that structures our other experiences. So there still seems to be a difference between the kind of causality that characterizes the experience of one's own will and the kind that characterizes one's other experiences. The notion of an experience being informed by causality is not as simple, unvarying, and monolithic as Schopenhauer, and Kant before him, present it to be. I suspect that the same would prove to be true of the other organizing structures of our experience that they cite, such as space and time.

13. Nowadays there is also the common experience of seeing myself in recorded images, such as photos and videos, or hearing my recorded voice.

14. Schopenhauer's thesis that it is only in my experience of myself *as will* that the subject–object polarity disappears allows and even implies that the polarity might persist even in one's other reflexive experiences of one's other mental states, such as one's awareness of one's sensations, emotion, and thoughts.

15. Schopenhauer himself indirectly acknowledges some of the murkiness surrounding his notion of "the object coinciding with the subject" in the experience of one's own will by referring to it as a "miracle" (WWR1[p], 102).

16. While Schopenhauer argues that the experience of oneself as will is the only experience of oneself in which the subject–object polarity is absent, he does later make the same claim

about the aesthetic experience of art and nature, which he also presents as transcending, albeit in somewhat different manner, some of the structures that usually distort normal "representational experience" (see WWR1, Book III).

17. I use the term, *efficacious connection*, to avoid *mis*-describing the will's connection to its actions as causal and to capture what is common to (1) the directly perceived connection between one's own willing and the actions of my own body which it *effects* and (2) the connections between those causes and their effects in the world outside of myself, which I can never directly experience but only infer. It is this commonality that allows Schopenhauer to argue that we can use one of these connections to understand the other despite the great difference in the way we can experience and know the two of them.

18. Hume had held that a fundamental feature of all causal relations is that the cause precedes the effect.

19. For Schopenhauer, the efficacious connection between willing and acting is not a connection between two events, but between two aspects of the same event.

20. For examples of works by philosophers who make use of such psychological studies and argue that notion of a self that is the unified seat of our consciousness and agency is a myth or illusion, see Daniel Dennett, *Conscious Explained* (Little Brown and Company, 1991) and Thomas Metzinger, *The Ego Tunnel: The Science of the Mind and the Myth of the Self* (Basic Books 2009).

21. It should be noted that even the presence of the structure of time in our experience of our own agency, which Schopenhauer does grudgingly admit, undermines his thesis that this set of structures must occur all together or be entirely absent. And it seriously calls into question his simplistic, dichotomous view that there are two and only two possible types of experience. It is one of Nietzsche's great contributions to have adopted the Kantian-Schopenhauerian constructivist position with respect to our experience and then further developed it by freeing it from its rigidly dichotomous form.

22. Unfortunately, Schopenhauer obscures the nonmetaphysical character of his transcendental thesis by immediately attaching his metaphysical thesis to it.

23. "We have first of all to get to know more intimately this inner nature of the will, so that we may know how to distinguish from it what belongs not to it itself, but to its phenomenon, which has many grades.... Such for example the circumstance of its being accompanied by knowledge, and the determination by motives.... Therefore, if I say that the force which attracts a stone to the earth is of its nature, in itself apart from all representation, will, then no one will attach to this proposition the absurd meaning that the stone moves itself according to a motive, because it is thus that the will appears in man" (WWR1[$_p$], 105).

24. Note that I deny only that Schopenhauer advocates a panpsychism of a certain crude and objectionable sort. Whether he is a "panpsychist" in any sense of the term is a different matter. The term has been used to refer to a considerable spectrum of views, some ascribing only a very attenuated form or analogue of mind to all reality. Schopenhauer may well be a proponent of "panpscyhism" defined in another less objectionable way. For a survey of the various historical and contemporary forms of "panspychism," see the article on panpsychism in the *Stanford Encyclopedia of Philosophy*. For a lively discussion and endorsement of Schopenhauer's "panpsychism," see Barbara Hannan, *The Riddle of the World: A Reconsideration of Schopenhauer's Philosophy* (Oxford, 2009, ch. 2). Some may find Schopenhauer's idea of a striving or impetus devoid of any consciousness to be itself problematic. However, the potential problem with it is not that it promotes panpsychism, but, on the contrary, that it fails to limit striving, which seems to be an exclusively psychic phenomenon, to its appropriate psychic realm.

FURTHER READING

Dennett, Daniel. *Consciousness Explained*. New York, Boston, London: Little Brown and Company, 1991.

Hannan, Barbara. *The Riddle of the World: A Reconsideration of Schopenhauer's Philosophy*. Oxford: Oxford University Press, 2009.

Metzinger, Thomas. *The Ego Tunnel: The Science of the Mind and the Myth of the Self*. New York: Basic Books, 2009.

Popper, Karl R. "Some Remarks on Panpsychism and Epiphenomenalism." *Dialectica* 31, no. 1/2 (1977): 177–86.

CHAPTER 8

···

FORCE IN NATURE

Schopenhauer's Scientific Beginning

···

D. G. CARUS

ACCORDING to Schopenhauer, natural science is concerned essentially with the constitution and alteration of material states, which are traced back to causes (WWR1, 51 [SW2, 34]). Yet this question of cause, which inevitably seeks an initial cause,[1] does not lead to the essence of appearances (WWR1, 53f [SW2, 36f]). Appearances, as the object of natural science, are understood only within the constraints of the endless concatenation of causality. Schopenhauer considered this beginningless chain of causality to be the insurmountable limitation placed on natural science: "This application of heat is again occasioned by a preceding alteration, e.g., the sun's rays falling on a burning lens, this perhaps by a cloud's moving away from the direction of the sun, this by wind, this by uneven density of air, this by other states, and so on to infinity" (FR, 38 [SW1, 34f]. Natural science attempts to explain matter on the basis of states of matter and their relationship to each other. It traces back effects to a cause, which is a previous state of matter in time; a cause that can thus in turn be viewed as an effect (FR, 38f [SW1, 35f]).

This boundary of natural science in fact determines Schopenhauer's metaphysics: "[By pursuing its own paths,] in all of its branches, physics, and thus natural science in general, must ultimately reach a point at which its explanations come to an end: this is precisely the metaphysical, which physics only perceives as its boundary, beyond which it cannot extend, but within which it must remain, and then it relinquishes its object to metaphysics" (WN, 325 [SW4, 4]). By wishing to transcend natural science through metaphysics, it must not be overlooked that Schopenhauer necessarily connects his philosophy to natural science. In fact, both depart from perceptible and empirical reality: "What does this entire world of representation mean? What in this appearance is the essence, what appears, the thing in itself?—This question is the principal problem of philosophy."[2] Hence, Schopenhauer takes appearance as given and enquires after its "essence."[3] Philosophy poses the question of the inner essence of appearance and therefore, importantly, at the beginning (and end)[4] of Schopenhauer's philosophical development, of force, which makes all alteration and causality possible in the first place

(FR, 47 [SW1, 45]). As we will see, Schopenhauer initially also considers matter an essence of appearance but discards this possibility in the further course of his investigation.

This chapter will in this context examine (1) Schopenhauer's concept of "force"—a concept which, according to Schopenhauer, cannot be recognized through natural science, and (2) force as the boundary point between Schopenhauer's conception of natural science and of metaphysics. The fact that the boundary of natural science constitutes the foundation of Schopenhauer's metaphysics has often been treated as an object of investigation (e.g., by Morgenstern or Young),[5] but what Schopenhauer determined as the concept of force therein has not. Furthermore, neither has the correlation between force and will, which is systematically necessary for an understanding of either term, been explicated.[6] Schopenhauer contends, namely, that to understand force as the essence of appearance, as "thing in itself," we must look to another motive force, the human will within us, which is known to us more intimately than all other things. The question is thus essentially: In what sense does his concept of force become the backbone for his concept of will in nature, and to what extent does he differentiate force from the metaphysical conception of will? Does he adequately differentiate the two, or does this very problem of defining force, as the essence of appearance, turn out to be the crux of his metaphysical dilemma of will? Is this the reason Schopenhauer turned to mysticism?

8.1 SCHOPENHAUER'S UNDERSTANDING OF NATURAL SCIENCE

8.1.1 The Principle of Sufficient Reason

The principle of sufficient reason is divided into four genera according to the law of homogeneity and specification, and this is the only manner in which something can become an object to us (EFR, 13–14, [SW7, 18]). The fourfold root of the principle of sufficient reason serves to understand (a) experience and (b) science. In science, the four roots are to be viewed in isolation from one another, insofar as only one root uniquely determines the path of one science (FR, 149 [SW1, 157]). Hence, every science has a ground upon which all consequences rest, and thus all knowledge is to be traced back to this underlying principle. For example, arithmetic and geometry are recognized on the basis of the formal application of space and time, as Schopenhauer illustrates by drawing on the example of a triangle (FR, 124 [SW1, 131]). He terms the principle responsible for this form of knowledge, in regard to the relation between "the parts" of space and time, the principle of the sufficient reason of being. The principle of sufficient reason that concerns us is that of becoming, as it is concerned with causality, thus with alteration and in turn with force.

8.1.2 Alteration as the Object of the Principle of the Sufficient Reason of Becoming

Natural science is viewed through the principle of the sufficient reason of becoming. Within this context, Schopenhauer divides natural science into two fields of enquiry. *Morphology* describes static shapes and material formation and is therefore concerned, according to Schopenhauer, with the history of nature. *Etiology*, on the other hand, seeks an explanation for the dynamic succession of the states of matter according to laws (WWR1, 120 [SW2, 114]). Schopenhauer does not examine morphology in a more detailed fashion, and alteration only plays a role therein in terms of the genesis of permanent shapes and forms. Hence etiology is consulted with regard to the question of force as the ultimate "cause" of alteration. Etiology's concern for the doctrine of alterations in nature, or as stated, the succession of the states of matter, leads Schopenhauer to see a point of contact with the question of the essence of occurrences: yet this point of contact cannot be resolved positively.[7] Cause and effect is, in view of alteration as appearance, exclusively related to the states of real objects (i.e., to those of intuition), which are questioned with regard to their cause. But this line of questioning cannot lead to a first cause, and hence the question can be posed ad infinitum: "They know it: a first cause is just as inconceivable as is a point at which space has an end or a moment when time takes its beginning" (FR, 41 [SW1, 38]). For this reason, natural science is caught in an endless chain of further-questioning alteration.

Causality cannot lead us to a primary or absolute cause and hence cannot lead us to the essence. Yet the law of causality is the basis for two further laws a priori: the law of inertia and the law of the persistence of substance (FR, 45 [SW1, 42]). The law of inertia states that every state of a body stays in the same state of motion for as long as there is no cause to alter it, and Schopenhauer links this law to his concept of force.[8] However, this law plays no further role in founding his concept of force itself. The second law of the persistence of substance asserts that matter itself remains untouched by change: "the law of causality, which alone is the form under which we are able to think of alterations at all, still always applies to the states of bodies, never to the existence of the bearer of all states, matter. For this reason, I assert the principle of the permanence of substance as a corollary of the causal law" (FR, 46 [SW1, 43]). In other words, through his exposition on causality Schopenhauer recognizes that causality, in order to be a cognition of our mind, must have some kind of precondition in the objective intuitive world: the alteration of the state of matter as cause and effect can only be thought if matter as matter persists. For how, as Schopenhauer contends, could our understanding grasp alteration (e.g., of shape) and enquire after a cause if it does not presuppose that only the quality of matter has altered, but not that it is there? This leads Schopenhauer to two conclusions that are decisive for his epistemology: namely, that two essences, matter and natural forces, are untouched by alteration (FR, 47 [SW1, 45]). Both become essential for Schopenhauer's philosophy: matter itself, which is also termed "substance"[9] and force, which is termed the "essence" of alteration.[10] The persistence of matter is a transcendental cognition and, consequently, a cognizance that makes all experience possible, as we will see later. Yet, as it turns out, matter must, as a concept, be ascribed to experience. Force, however, remains outside the realm of experiential conceptualism.

8.1.3 Matter and Force as Essence

The principle of sufficient reason, which is the form of all representation, prevents natural science from ever gaining knowledge of the "objective source" of the law of causality, which is recognized in its expression. At first, Schopenhauer posits both natural force and matter as essences, which are not subject to change or alteration and must therefore be ontologically prior to the empirical application of the law of causality. However, while natural force develops into a metaphysical and essential question pertaining to the "objective source," matter as a concept is ascribed to cognition and only exists in the world of representation. Schopenhauer inferred the inalterability of matter from causality; the law of causality could not be thought without something that persists through all alteration. Yet he also infers the inalterability of natural force on the basis that it grants the law of causality general and inexhaustible validity (FR, 47 [SW1, 45]). Both are inferred back from the empirical validity of the law of causality and postulated as a necessity for its existence and validity; both concepts gain their status as inalterable essences on the basis of being this foundation or essence of causality. However, the relation between the empirical application of the law of causality and the concepts of (1) matter and (2) natural force now establishes that causality, with regard to matter as its objective correlate, is representation, yet that natural force, which gives causality its causation, is not appearance but instead the essence thereof. Why?

8.1.4 Matter as Appearance and Thought, Not as Essence

Schopenhauer distinguishes between two forms of matter: namely, "mere matter" and what he selectively terms an "element of matter." The former is only a thought: "For this reason, of mere matter there is only a concept, no perception. It enters into every external experience as a necessary constituent thereof, yet can be given in none, but is rather only thought: as the absolutely inert, inactive, formless, propertyless, which is, however, the bearer of all forms, properties and effects" (WWR2$_{[AC]}$, 347 [SW3, 347]). Yet matter, because it is recognized inductively and sensibly, is also known a posteriori (i.e., through sense experience), and this he terms an "element" of matter.

> However, the difference, that matter must, in this respect, be first arbitrarily posited as existing, already indicates that it does not belong as entirely and unqualifiedly to the *formal* part of our cognizance as space and time do, but rather at the same time contains an element that is only given *a posteriori*. It is in fact the point of connection between the empirical and the pure and *a priori* part of our cognizance, hence the cornerstone peculiar to the world of experience.   (WWR2$_{[AC]}$, 348 [SW3, 348])

This element in Schopenhauer is the object of the experiential world, which is given "materially" (i.e., cognized as a property and expression of matter). Mere matter itself is, because it can only be thought, a mere form of the intellect.[11] Hence, matter forms the bond between a priori knowledge and a posteriori knowledge; both, however, are a part of the world as representation. Yet there is a further point Schopenhauer makes concerning matter. Matter makes the reality of experience possible; the world of representation is "the result" or the "facticity" or the "manifestation" of will.

> Consequently, matter is that whereby *will*, which constitutes the inner essence of things, enters into perceptibility, becomes perceptible, *visible*. Thus, in this sense, matter is the mere *visibility* of will, or the bond between the world as will and the world as representation. It belongs to the *latter*, insofar as it is the product of the intellect's functions, to the *former* insofar as that which manifests itself in all material beings, i.e. phenomena, is *will*. Thus, every object is as thing in itself, will, and as phenomenon, matter.   (WWR2$_{[AC]}$, 349 [SW3, 349])

The object of our cognition, as matter, however, can only be attributed to appearance and not to the "thing in itself." Hence, matter is a precondition for the fact that the will becomes manifest and that experience is possible—yet, in the manner in which we know it, does not belong to the essence itself—even though all effectuality, which is *essentially* will, is not possible without matter. Matter belongs only to the empirical world since its expression can only be known through a derivation from the empirical.

8.1.5 The Concept of Force Derived from a Methodological Investigation of Natural Science

In his investigation of force and matter in relation to singular appearances, Schopenhauer concludes that matter is bound by the realm of appearance as an object of the senses and as the visibility of will in nature posited through the intellect[12] while force is what constitutes matter as form and is responsible for its further configuration and movement as well as for its efficacy (FR, 47 [SW1, 45]).[13] Since alterations subdivide into different species—for example, locomotion, change of consistency, growth—so, too, this formal aspect of matter as force, which is "the means by which alterations or effects are possible at all" (FR, 47 [SW1, 45]), is divided into different species related to them. Schopenhauer states that these natural forces are not subject to alteration as they are the reason that alterations are at all possible.

> Cause and effect are the *alterations* connected to necessary succession in time. In contrast, the forces of nature, the means by which all causes operate, are exempted from all change [*Wechsel*]; thus, in this sense, they exist beyond all time, but just because of this, they exist always and everywhere, omnipresent and inexhaustible, always ready to manifest themselves.   (FR, 47 [SW1, 45])

Natural science can never, since it only investigates the expressions of force (i.e., the changes and alterations of matter), address force itself:[14] "Consequently, even the best aetiological explanation of the whole of nature would really be nothing more than a catalogue of inexplicable forces and an authoritative specification of the rule according to which they emerge, succeed one another, and displace one another in space and time" (WWR1, 122 [SW2, 116f]). Force is therefore what Schopenhauer views as "extrinsic" to natural science and terms the "essence of appearance." It is this problem of the essence of appearance that Schopenhauer considers the principal question of philosophy. Force must be taken as a given for all explanations in natural science, and this force as an x, y, z cannot be known. But what does this mean—that force cannot be known? As we said earlier, force, surely, must have to be treated in the same way as the concept of matter since its expression can only be known through a derivation from the empirical, just as that of matter as matter.

8.1.6 Force in Relation to Cause: The Problem with the Schopenhauerian Concept of Force

As shown earlier, Schopenhauer comprehends the concept of force as follows: first, force itself is not subject to change but instead is that which facilitates change or alteration; second, force cannot be known through the question of causality; and third, it appears in nature in different species that cannot be traced back to each other. Schopenhauer is confronted with the problem of how the principle of causality relates to force, where force is not itself known through causality. In this context, he offers a fourth determination of force, one that he had already hinted at in the preceding quotes from his dissertation and terms natural force the "causal nature of a cause" (WWR1, 136 [SW2, 133]).[15] Hence, through these four "definitions" Schopenhauer purports to have strictly distinguished cause, which is compatible with matter as appearance, from natural force. Yet force appears to be related directly to and derived from causality. Gerhard Klamp, who follows on from Schopenhauer, maintains that the strict *distinction* between natural force and cause is a precondition for natural science. He explains for his own part here how Schopenhauer could have arrived at a possible distinction between the two.

> Natural forces, however, are also not causes, which the proponents of today's physics still do not appear to know or have grasped, since they continue, without further thought, to speak of forces as causes of movements, as if Schopenhauer's theory had never existed. To be sure, there is an especially close relationship between force and causality, but only insofar and to the extent that force is what first gives a cause its persisting efficacy. Yet at the same time force is, therefore, not simply cause itself. Causes are, just as effects that equate to them, never something other than states of change and moments of continuation within a flowing occurrence of change, the flow of the effectuality of a causality strictly bound to time, which as such possesses steadfast necessity.[16]

Hence, both Schopenhauer and Klamp attempt to separate force entirely from cause: in this case Klamp asserts, similarly to Schopenhauer, that "persisting efficacy" singles out force from cause. Yet how else could physics grasp the different species of force if they did not classify the general species of causes of movement as species of force? On this theme, Martin Morgenstern writes that Schopenhauer does in fact treat natural forces as "causes" since Schopenhauer asserts that the possibility of efficacy [*Wirken*] arises owing to force.[17] Schopenhauer's distinction between force and cause and the assertion that force is not a cause leads Schopenhauer, according to Morgenstern, to irresolvable paradigms. Morgenstern therefore purports that Schopenhauer "would have done more justice to his fundamental thought by recognizing forces as causes,"[18] which, according to Morgenstern, he did not do owing to his metaphysics; forces do not appear and must be considered indestructible.

Schopenhauer attempts to determine certain general and fundamental causes for movement as forces (in the plural) in the sense of qualitative species. Yet force itself, Schopenhauer contends, cannot be determined by a *particular* cause and effect, as if one could establish through the particular cause of a particular effect which force had caused the cause. For this reason, he traces force back to a principle which does not appear in the causal chain itself.

This principle is not subject to appearance and cannot be known further than by simply positing it as an unknown factor of causes. In this process, Schopenhauer makes the mistake of not determining force as a *general form* of causality and sticking by this, but instead he seeks a "principle" which cannot be explained through "something else" and is thus a "*qualitas occulta.*"[19] Force differs, of course, from the concept of causality, but is an entity related to matter, in space and time, and explains a particular type of relation between cause and effect insofar as something is moved. For example, there is a force involved in picking up a pair of shoes, which is in turn related to power (i.e., the strength of our muscles to move the object), whereby the counterforce is the force of gravity (now thought to be a relationship between masses), which bears on the mass of the shoes. In other words, a change has taken place in time and space that was only possible through force but that can at the same time simply be determined as a singular action according to a specific and singular cause and effect (someone picking up the shoes).[20] The cause and the ensuing effect occurred, in one sense, according to force and can also be explained in this way; yet, in another sense, the specific cause of the particular action was, in this case, the person who picked up the shoes. The cause can be arbitrarily posited at a certain point in time in accordance with the effect, for it does not describe matter itself (i.e., how materiality constitutionally acts), but instead describes a state in time in view of an effect. For example, one could ascribe the cause for lifting the shoes to the birth of that person or the cause would be more directly said to be the person who walked into the hallway, saw the shoes, and thought of going for a walk.

Force describes a *type* of cause for an effect with regard to the *universal activity of matter* in space and time. The force describes a condition for the change in movement of an object in a particular direction. Force itself is an explanation for causes in general, and a necessary one, since force explains how something singular could have caused what it caused in terms of a general theory of the movement of matter. Force is therefore (a) a *universal* determination of a certain possibility and law of the causality of matter, whereby (b) no cause can appear singularly without force as a cause in general. Force is, in this second sense, the universal material condition for the explanation or determination of a specific cause. In the first sense, it describes the general condition of every instance of cause in relation to an effect. Change or alteration can therefore either be traced back to a cause or to force as a general natural law; both are relevant for the understanding of occurrences.

8.2 The Transition from Force to Will

8.2.1 The Relation Between the Principle of Sufficient Reason of Becoming and of Acting

According to Schopenhauer, the concept of force, which in natural science is postulated *ex negativo*, is in philosophy the principle of thought. Schopenhauer now turns his attention to resolving this metaphysical problem of force, the principle that underlies all appearance, by seeking a "path" to its inner essence. For the investigation of force, underlying the principle of sufficient reason of becoming, the principle of the sufficient reason of action (also termed the *law of motivation*) now becomes essential. Schopenhauer addresses the *subject* of motivation as possible "access" to the problem of the hidden cause of causes, which he had identified *objectively* as force. This law of motivation is essential for an understanding of the boundary point between the object of the principle of sufficient reason of becoming and the essence of appearance, which is now investigated from the *subjective* side; for, according to Schopenhauer, "motivation is causality seen from within" (FR, 137 [SW1, 145]). On this basis, *force* is to be postulated analogically to *will* in self-consciousness.[21] This analogy, which Schopenhauer terms *denomenatio a potiori* (WWR1, 135 [SW2, 132]) is what Schopenhauer views as the means of positing will in nature or of understanding force.[22] Motivation is based on an unknown *x* when viewed from the outside, yet is the most intimately and immediately known "object" to us and hence serves as access to the "essence" of the world as will.[23] In fact, the correlation between the law of motivation and that of causality is the cornerstone, as Schopenhauer himself states, of his entire philosophy.[24] In other words, the essence of his philosophy lies in the relation between the ground of becoming and the ground of action, better still in the *x* underlying them.

Schopenhauer henceforth equates the *essence of change*, which he had sought in natural science and attributed to the concept of force in nature, with *will* in the human being. Schopenhauer therefore understands will as a motive force that causes movement:

"whenever we become aware of something originally moved by an immediate, primary force, we are compelled to think of its inner essence as will" (WN, 391 [SW 4, 83]). Hence, Schopenhauer terms this source of movement "will" and parallels it with force as the source of change in nature. But in order to recognize this will as thing in itself, which underlies all things uniformly, it must be possible to recognize it stripped of all forms of representation. Will must be recognized "immediately" if we are to find true access to the inner essence of the world, independent of representation and the principle of sufficient reason. To recognize the will immediately, Schopenhauer turns his attention to bodily movement. He initially asserts that the body is an immediate object to us and thus an immediate expression of will.[25] He hereby asserts an immediate relation between the act of will (*Willensakt*) and the action of the body (*Leibesaktion*), which he claims facilitates a moment of immediate cognition of will in self-consciousness. This claim of immediacy is, however, owing to the later realized representational cognition of body, revised and delegitimated by Schopenhauer in his main work of 1819, in the *Will in Nature* of 1836, and in his revised edition of the *Fourfold Root* of 1847. Yet if will cannot be known immediately through the body, it cannot serve as the inner essence of the material, objective world of appearance.

This change in his cognitive theory leads to an essential paradigmatic problem: Schopenhauer cannot postulate knowledge of the will independently of the mediate and representational cognition of the body and will can thus itself not be recognized independently of representation. He writes with view to this correlation between will and body:

> As a result, we then say that even where the most palpable cause produces an effect, the mysterious something, the x, the real interior of the process, the true agent, the 'in itself' of appearance is still at hand—given to us after all only as representation, according to the forms and laws of representation—and it is essentially the same as that which is given to us in the actions of our body as intuition and representation, known to us intimately and immediately as *will*.   (WN, 399 [SW 4, 92f])

This immediate knowledge of will, which he now seeks to explain through an "immediate view" of will itself as the object of self-consciousness (in isolation from the necessary simultaneous bodily movement), can, however, also not be recognized independently of the form of time. Schopenhauer states: "I do not have cognition of my will as a whole, in its unity, in perfect accordance with its essence; rather I cognize it only in its individual acts, which is to say in time, time being the form in which my body (like every other object) appears" (WWR1, 126 [SW 2, 121].[26] In other words, the term "immediate knowledge" of will used by Schopenhauer in the preceding quote is incorrect (i.e., he states something which he himself denies). What force itself and will is cannot be recognized through science since force and will always appear singularly in representation and can only be recognized as a generality by inference. Essentially, Schopenhauer terms this generalized something, ascertained through inference, derived from the singularly existing, the essence of appearance.

8.2.2 The Essence of Appearance and Its Knowability in Schopenhauer's Philosophy

According to Schopenhauer, philosophy seeks to grasp and know something which in natural science cannot be known. In fact, as it turns out, the knowledge of this uncognizable essence is what can be known in Schopenhauer; what the essence is, the will itself, cannot be known. By paralleling the will as a source of movement in the human being with force in nature, Schopenhauer attempts to link force to human introspection and thereby make it explainable and knowable.[27] He termed the transference of will to natural objects as force and the explanation of force on that basis, a *denominatio a potiori* (i.e., transferring by analogy that which is most knowable to that which is less knowable). He maintains that in our own introspection we can gain the "most immediate" knowledge of will (the source of movement and causation), yet this, too, is mediated by the form of time, as well as by the representation of body, as he later recognizes (WWR1, 135 [SW2, 132]).[28] Thus, his attempt to know the "inner essence of the world" fails in view of the fact that there is no access to it beyond the principle of sufficient reason. He goes on to state that we do not have access to the will as thing in itself other than through various "approaches" to "will as thing in itself," which are, however, not linked to knowledge[29] (i.e., to the term "will" as a motive force). What force is, which marked the boundary line of natural science as an object and principle of Schopenhauer's question of the relation between material appearance and the essence of appearance as such, cannot, in Schopenhauer's philosophy, be answered through a form of knowledge, but instead must remain forever mystical (i.e., unknowable).

NOTES

1. This is the nature of the question of causation, according to Schopenhauer. Owing to the fact that a cause is only a state prior to the effect and that a different state must necessarily have been prior to any and this given state, the question of cause can be posed ad infinitum.

2. Arthur Schopenhauer, *Vorlesung über die gesammte Philosophie [Lecture on the whole of Philosophy]*, edited by Karsten Worm (Berlin: InfoSoftware, 2008), ch. 2, X20. Only available in German.

3. Schopenhauer's philosophy and question therein originally begins with and relates entirely to empirical consciousness, which departs from appearance since this is the only true source of knowledge: "The material provided for every philosophy is accordingly none other than empirical consciousness, which is divided into the consciousness of one's own self (self-consciousness) and the consciousness of other things (external perception). For this alone is what is immediate, what is actually given" (WWR2[AC], 89f).

4. Schopenhauer's two main works on philosophy's relation to natural science are his dissertation, *On the Fourfold Root of the Principle of Sufficient Reason* (EFR and FR) of 1813 (revised 1847) and the later *On the Will in Nature* (WN) of 1836.

5. Julian Young considers the determination of the boundary of natural science to be the cornerstone of Schopenhauer's philosophy. He views natural science and metaphysics as necessarily interlinked and considers the task of philosophy to lie in determining force: "So the task of philosophy is quite specifically defined. It is that of providing an account of the nature of original forces in terms which are experiential but yet do not appeal to spatial structure" (Julian Young, *Willing and Unwilling: A Study in the Philosophy of Arthur Schopenhauer*, [Dordrecht: Springer, 1987], 46f). See also Martin Morgenstern, *Schopenhauers Philosophie der Naturwissenschaft* (Bonn: Bouvier, 1985), 167.

6. This is bizarre, considering the fact that it is the self-proclaimed crux of Schopenhauer's philosophy, as we will see. Schopenhauer makes a lot of "overarching" and superlative statements, but this statement in his dissertation of 1847 is undoubtedly, and with a view to the content of his entire philosophy, one of the most serious ones (FR, 138 [SW1, 145]). However, this statement concerning the necessity of understanding will within us to understand force in nature is dependent on the original postulation of the "immediate" recognition of body (for the essential knowledge of will) in 1813, which, as we will see, Schopenhauer recants. On body as immediate object see *On the Fourfold Root of the Principle of Sufficient Reason* (1813) (EFR, 19, 26f, 54 [SW7, 25f, 36, 74]).

7. On the relationship between morphology and etiology, and the impossibility of the knowledge of forces in etiology, Schopenhauer explains: "Morphology on the whole essentially forgoes all explanation; it only describes in a well-ordered manner, what is there, and does not attempt to show why or how it has arisen or will arise. Aetiology explains what occurs and what will occur: but how? Mechanics, physics, chemistry, teach the rules and laws according to which the forces of impenetrability, weight, cohesion, rigidity, fluidity, elasticity, warmth, light, elective affinity, magnetism, electricity etc. are effectual, i.e. they show us the law, the rule, which these forces, in accordance with every one of their appearances in space and time, are governed by: the forces themselves, however, remain qualitates occultae. And have to: for it is in fact the thing in itself, which, by appearing, expresses that phenomenon, but is itself entirely different from it; it is of course in its appearance subject to the principle of ground, as the form of representation, but it is itself never to be traced back to this form and therefore these appearances cannot be explained to the last aetiologically either, can never be fathomed entirely" (Arthur Schopenhauer, *Vorlesung über die gesamte Philosophie* (1820) [*Lecture on the Whole of Philosophy*], edited by Karsten Worm (Berlin: InfoSoftware, 2008), ch. 10, X93). In other words, the forces can never be fathomed, never be known—this is what Schopenhauer terms *qualitates occultae*. See John E. Atwell on *qualitas occulta* in *Schopenhauer on the Character of the World: The Metaphysics of Will* (Berkeley: University of California Press), 1995, 63f.

8. See FR, 45 (SW1, 42f.). Schopenhauer does not draw on the law of inertia to found his concept of force, but it is clear that inertia is itself a force, essentially because it is the force that makes something capable of continuing on its given motive path. One can see that he considers inertia a force here: "simple and uniform effectual forces, such as gravitation and inertia, in unresisting space" (PP2, 116 [SW6, 135]). See also PP2, 39 (SW6, 41).

9. On matter as substance and change, see WWR1, 31 (SW2, 12).

10. Schopenhauer states: "The endless chain of causes and effects produces all *alterations*, yet it never extends beyond these, so two things remain untouched. These are, on the one hand, *matter*, because, as has just been shown, matter is the *bearer* of all alterations or it is just that *in which* such alterations take place; and on the other hand, the original *forces of nature*, because these forces are the means *by which* alterations or effects are possible at all—the means by which causes first receive causality, i.e., efficacy" FR, 47 (SW1, 45).

11. Helmut Primer explicated in no uncertain terms Schopenhauer's contradictory use of the concept of matter: "Schopenhauer says himself that matter is more of a metaphysical than a physical principle of explanation and in the second volume of the Parerga it is even a *natura naturans*, i.e. as such entirely identical with the will. On the other hand, matter is, however, also *natura naturata*, for otherwise physics would be placed on the throne of metaphysics. This indistinction peculiar to Schopenhauer subverts and undermines the entire system" (Helmut R. A. Primer, *Das Problem des Materialismus in der Philosophie Arthur Schopenhauers* [Frankfurt: P. Lang, 1984], 38). Emil Schill also notes the problematic function of the term "matter" in Schopenhauer's philosophy and indeed its contradictory use: "This function [of connecting the world as will with the world as representation through the visibility of will and linking this to causality] is perfectly fulfilled by matter; but to this end Schopenhauer had to violate its essence, in that he turned it into an abstraction and mere effectuality, by which, however, he could in no way do justice to its real, substantial ontological content" (Emil Schill, *Das Problem der Materie bei Schopenhauer*, PhD Diss, Freiburg i.Br. 1940, 60).

12. See WN, 369 (SW4, 56): "for matter is the mere visibility of will.... Pure matter, absolutely without form and properties, which we think of as the material of a natural product, merely exists in thought [*ist bloß ein ens rationis*] and cannot occur in experience."

13. See also WN, 369 (SW4, 56): "Because in a natural product matter is the mere visibility of form, we also see form appear empirically as the mere offspring of matter, issuing forth from within matter, in crystallization, in vegetable and animal spontaneous generation, which is at least not to be doubted among epizoa.—For this reason, it can be assumed that nowhere, on no planet or satellite, can matter lapse into a state of endless rest; rather, its intrinsic forces (i.e. will, of which it is the mere visibility) will always put to an end any rest that occurs, always awaken from their sleep, in order to begin their acting anew as mechanical, physical, chemical, organic forces, since these always await their opportunity."

14. Schopenhauer writes: "what aetiology calls a natural law is the unchanging constancy with which such a force expresses itself, whenever its known conditions are present. But all that it knows or could ever know is this natural law, these conditions, this emergence at a particular time and place. The force that is itself expressed, the inner essence of the appearances that emerge according to these laws will remain an eternal mystery to it, something as entirely foreign and unfamiliar in the simplest phenomena as in the most complicated" (WWR1, 121f [SW2, 116]).

15. The German is "*Das Ursachsein der Ursache*." Alternative translations are "causal being of a cause" and "cause's being as a cause."

16. Gerhard Klamp, "Kettenreaktion und Kausalkraft," in *Schopenhauer-Jahrbuch*, edited by Arthur Hübscher (Frankfurt: Waldemar Kramer, 1948), 248–56, at 253.

17. Martin Morgenstern also maintains that the natural forces can only be recognized through the natural laws (i.e., by means of causality). Martin Morgenstern, *Schopenhauers Philosophie der Naturwissenschaft* (Bonn: Bouvier, 1985), 164.

18. Ibid., 167.

19. See John E. Atwell, *Schopenhauer on the Character of the World*, 63.

20. For a brief sketch of the relationship between force and cause in Schopenhauer, and a proposed general distinction in terms of causation, see Barbara Hannan, *The Riddle of the World: A Reconsideration of Schopenhauer's Philosophy* (New York: Oxford University Press, 2009), 7f. She refers back to Fred Dretske here. Fred Dretske, *Explaining Behavior: Reason in a World of Causes* (Cambridge, MA: MIT Press, 1988), 42.

21. Schopenhauer addresses this theme with renewed enthusiasm in his later main work, *The World as Will and Representation*. This theme was dubbed a change from his metaphysics of ground to that of will by Rudolf Malter. See Rudolf Malter, "Wesen und Grund: Schopenhauers Konzeption eines neuen Typus von Metaphysik," in *Schopenhauer Jahrbuch* (Frankfurt: Waldemar Kramer, 1988), 29–41, at 36. Schopenhauer returns to his original theme from his dissertation once again after *The World as Will and Representation* (1819) in his later work "On Will in Nature" (1836). I cover this work toward the end of this chapter.

22. On the relationship between the law of motivation and the law of causality see §43 of the *Fourfold Root* of 1847. This key passage essentially underscores Schopenhauer's entire philosophy; that is, the relationship between the outer world of appearances and the notion of a will that underlies them.

23. Schopenhauer writes: "Precisely because the subject of willing is immediately given in self-consciousness, what willing is cannot be further defined or described; moreover, it is the most immediate of all of our cognitions, and indeed, the fact that it is immediate must ultimately cast light on all remaining cognitions, which are mediated" (FR, 136 [SW1, 144]). He contends that the motivations themselves can only be known through a subject in relation to a subject, since actions and occurrences are only ever viewed as outer appearances: "In the physical world alterations are bound together, since the cause is the condition, coming from without, of any event. In contrast, the interior of such events remains a secret to us, since we always remain on the outside" (FR, 137 [SW1, 144]).

24. This cornerstone is crucial to his explanation of "will in nature"; that is, the correspondence between will in the individual human being and the transference of the will to all natural objects. Schopenhauer explains: "From a different perspective, with reference to my philosophy in general, I add here that [the way in which] the law of motivation is related to the law of causality given in § 20 above, [is the same way in which] this fourth class of objects for the subject, and thus that of the will which is perceived in ourselves, is related to the first class. This insight is the cornerstone of my whole metaphysics" (FR, 138 [SW1, 145]). He repeats this claim, yet at the same time explicating the problem of cognizing will as thing in itself at WWR1, 126f (SW2, 121f). The body itself is now merely representation, but the subject is to view itself as will in an attempt to grasp the inner essence of world. However, in terms of knowledge, Schopenhauer himself ends up recognizing that there is no form of knowledge of will.

25. In his dissertation of 1813, Schopenhauer determined the body as an immediate object and therefore attempted to grasp it as will. However, Schopenhauer writes, in his own revision of his dissertation in 1847, that the body is only immediate in the sense that it is the objectivation of will and that one can recognize the act of will through the action of the body; however, the body is, as an object among other objects, entirely subject to representation: "Now insofar as the organic body is the starting point for the intuition of all other objects and thus is the mediation of these, in the first edition of this essay I had called the body the immediate object. This expression, however, can only apply in a quite non-literal sense. For although perception of its sensations is absolutely immediate, it does not present itself as an object at all, but so far everything still remains subjective, that is, sensation.... The body is objectively cognized (that is, as an object) only mediately, because it, like all other objects, presents itself in the understanding, or in the brain (which is the same), as a cognized cause of a subjectively given effect" (FR, 81f [SW1, 84]).

26. On this theme, see D. G. Carus, *Die Gründung des Willensbegriffs* (Wiesbaden: Springer, 2016), Introduction (part 1), 14, 31f.

27. "But until now, people have not recognized the identity . . . between the will and the essence of all the striving and acting [wirkenden] forces in nature" (WWR1, 135 [SW2, 132]).

28. He realizes in the course of his examination in *The World as Will and Representation* that there is no immediate cognition of will in self-consciousness, within us, and states in no uncertain terms in 1844, in Volume 2 of *The World as Will and Representation*, "the form of *time* still remains, along with that of being cognized and cognizing in general. Accordingly, in this inner cognizance the thing in itself has certainly for the most part cast off its veils but still does not emerge entirely naked. In consequence of the form of time that is still attached to the thing in itself, everyone is cognizant of his will only in its successive individual *acts*, but not as a whole, in and for itself. . . . Nevertheless, the perception in which we take cognizance of the stirrings and acts of our own will is far more immediate than any other: it is the point where the thing in itself most immediately makes its appearance and is most closely illuminated by the cognizant subject; this is precisely why that intimately cognized occurrence is simply and solely suited to becoming the interpreter of every other" (WWR2[AC], 220f).

29. As with the denial of the will for life in the ascetic. Yet these "forms" of "recognition" of will as thing in itself are not an instance of the cognition of will, but instead express some form of willinglessness, again no longer linked to the concept of willing or, in turn, to force. See WWR1, 407f (SW2, 449f).

FURTHER READING

Atwell, John E. *Schopenhauer on the Character of the World: The Metaphysics of Will.* Berkeley: University of California Press, 1995.

Bloch, Kurt. "Schopenhauer und die moderne Naturwissenschaft." In *Die Naturwissenschaften.* Berlin: Springer, 1950, 145–50.

Dretske, Fred. *Explaining Behavior: Reason in a World of Causes.* Cambridge, MA: MIT Press, 1988.

Hannan, Barbara. *The Riddle of the World: A Reconsideration of Schopenhauer's Philosophy.* New York: Oxford University Press, 2009.

Hartmann, Hermann. "Schopenhauer und die heutige Naturwissenschaft." In *Schopenhauer-Jahrbuch.* Frankfurt: Waldemar Kramer, 1964, 13–22.

Klamp, Gerhard. "Kettenreaktion und Kausalkraft." In *Schopenhauer-Jahrbuch.* Frankfurt: Waldemar Kramer, 1948, 248–56.

Malter, Rudolf. "Wesen und Grund: Schopenhauers Konzeption eines neuen Typus von Metaphysik." In *Schopenhauer-Jahrbuch.* Frankfurt: Waldemar Kramer, 1988, 29–41.

Morgenstern, Martin. "Die Grenzen der Naturwissenschaft und die Aufgabe der Metaphysik bei Schopenhauer." In *Schopenhauer-Jahrbuch.* Frankfurt: Waldemar Kramer, 1986, 71–95.

Morgenstern, Martin. *Schopenhauers Philosophie der Naturwissenschaft.* Bonn: Bouvier, 1985.

Primer, Helmut R. A. *Das Problem des Materialismus in der Philosophie Arthur Schopenhauers.* Frankfur: P. Lang, 1984.

Rhode, Wolfgang. *Schopenhauer heute. Seine Philosophie aus Sicht naturwissenschaftlicher Forschung.* Rheinfelden/Berlin: Schäuble, 1991.

Schill, Emil. "Das Problem der Materie bei Schopenhauer." PhD Dissertation, Freiburg i.B., 1940.

Seelig, Wolfgang. "Wille und Kraft." In *Schopenhauer-Jarhbuch.* Frankfurt: Waldemar Kramer, 1979, 136–47.

Young, Julian. *Willing and Unwilling: A Study in the Philosophy of Arthur Schopenhauer.* Dordrecht: Springer, 1987.

CHAPTER 9

SCHOPENHAUER AND HUME ON WILL AND CAUSATION

SEVERIN SCHROEDER

9.1 THE WORLD IS WILL

"*THE World is Will*" is the slogan with which Arthur Schopenhauer sums up his metaphysics. And metaphysics it is in the richest sense, offering an answer to the quasi-religious quest for the meaning of life. The world-will is meant to take God's place in an account of the world, explaining why things are as they are and, following from that, recommending an appropriate attitude towards life and the world. However, I will not be going into these big issues now. I shall deal merely with some of the things Schopenhauer says *on the way* to his grand metaphysical destination.

The first two major steps in Schopenhauer's reasoning are these:

1. I am not merely an intellect: I am essentially an embodied creature with a will (i.e., striving to survive, to flourish, and to produce offspring).
2. My first-hand knowledge of willing allows me to reach a deeper understanding of the world as also essentially driven by will.

The first point may seem trivial, but it was not in the historical context in which Schopenhauer made it. "I am a will" (meaning: an *embodied* will) is a direct reply to Descartes, who proclaimed: "I am only a mind: an immaterial thinking thing"—a claim that was widely accepted among post-Cartesian philosophers. The British Empiricists, and Kant, too, tended to regard a human being as essentially just a mind. But Schopenhauer's merit here is not just that he gave a timely reminder of what should have been obvious anyway. He did not merely say that we have a body and non-rational desires; he argued that rationality is not at the core of human nature. He assembled an impressive array of observations to show that our nature and character are to a far lesser degree governed by our intellect than was commonly assumed.

Schopenhauer's second step (from "I am will" to "the world is will") is more problematic. It seems quite appropriate as far as the animal kingdom is concerned. In fact, wildlife is the area where Schopenhauer's vision of perennial strife and struggle appears most obviously correct. But to maintain that even vegetable life and the forces of inanimate nature manifest a will looks like a blatant instance of (what Ruskin called) the *pathetic fallacy*: the projection of our emotions into our environment. Schopenhauer's apparent determination to commit that fallacy is neatly expressed in this passage:

> Spinoza says that if a stone projected through the air had consciousness, it would imagine it was flying of its own will. I add merely that the stone would be right.
> (WWR1$_{[P]}$, 126)

And Schopenhauer goes on, unblushingly, to apply psychological terms like "persistence," "determination," "keen desire," or "longing" [*Sehnsucht*] to inanimate things such as magnets, pieces of iron, or electric poles (WWR1$_{[P]}$, 117f). Of course in poetry, the pathetic fallacy is not a fallacy at all; it is an effective means of expressing a subject's feelings towards the world. But it *would* appear to be a fallacy in philosophy—unless philosophy, too, is regarded as a kind of poetry, distinguished from other poetry perhaps by a more austere form and a more abstract subject matter. Occasionally, Schopenhauer expressed such a view. And it is noteworthy that among his most famous admirers were novelists, such as Tolstoy, Hardy, Proust, and Mann, who admired him as a poet-philosopher; as someone who offered a comprehensive picture of the world that allows one to redescribe a great many phenomena in an illuminating, satisfying, or at any rate stimulating way.

However, what makes Schopenhauer particularly interesting is that, besides being an eminent example of a poet-philosopher, there is also a good deal of the analytical philosopher in him. And his doctrine that the world is will is a case in point.

On closer inspection, it is not as fancifully animistic as it might at first appear. For Schopenhauer makes it quite clear that the will he sees active in inanimate nature is not *conscious* will:.

> [I]f I say that the force which attracts a stone to the earth is of its nature…will, then no one will attach to this proposition the absurd meaning that the stone moves itself according to a known motive, because it is thus that the will appears in man.
> (WWR1$_{[P]}$, 105)

The will that pervades the whole world is, in itself, just a blind force. Only in animals this force is conjoined with consciousness or (in human beings) even with self-consciousness. Why, then, does Schopenhauer not simply say: "The world is force, or energy," thus avoiding the pathetic fallacy?—Because (he explains in WWR1$_{[P]}$, 111–12) he wants to make a point about the origin of some of our understanding of the world. The point is that from an experience of our voluntary actions we learn to understand how things happen in the world, and not the other way round. But what exactly is it that our actions can teach us about events in the world? — They provide us with a concept, or full understanding, of causation:

> I say we recognize first the identical essence of causality in the different forms it must assume at the different levels... [Then we consider the case] when we ourselves are the ones moved and so we know the inner nature of the process intimately and thoroughly..., if we connect this new internal cognition with the external cognition, its key, we will recognize...the identity of our will with that formerly unknown *x* that remains in all explanations of causes.   (WN, 399)

So, here, we have a perfectly sober-minded reading of Schopenhauer's doctrine that the world is will:

(W)   Our own agency provides us with a full understanding of causation which then permeates and structures our experience of the world in general.

9.2 TWO CONCEPTS OF CAUSATION

But now an objection must be raised: Does (W) not contradict Schopenhauer's often repeated doctrine that the concept of causality is a priori: a form of our understanding, not derived from experience?

We have to distinguish two concepts of causation. They are both present in Hume's famous discussion of causation. There is first the rich concept of causation Hume is looking for but cannot find and, secondly, the meager concept of causation, which (Hume concludes) is all experience provides us with. The meager concept of causation is that of constant conjunction. According to this concept, "A causes B" means simply: "A-type events are always followed by contiguous B-type events." Hume claims that that is all experience can ever give us an idea of. But what he had hoped for was a fuller understanding of causation: an understanding of the *necessary* connection between A and B; why, given A, it was absolutely necessary for B to follow. As it is, experience may have taught us that A-events have always been followed by B-events, but that seems to be just a brute fact. It might have been otherwise. We do not see anything in A that makes it absolutely necessary for it to lead to B, only repeated observation tells us that it does. Or so Hume claims.[1]

We re-encounter these two concepts of causation in Schopenhauer. When he says that causation is an a priori form of the understanding, he seems to be operating with a meager or Humean concept of causation, as constant conjunction. He seems to mean two things: first, that we have an innate disposition to pick up regularities and, secondly, that we can be certain a priori that all our experience will be subject to such regularities. (It is doubtful whether for this second claim Schopenhauer has any convincing argument.) So far, a priori, we have only a meager or Humean concept of causation. Following the a priori nature of our understanding, we experience the world as regular. Events must be preceded and followed by other events in regular ways. It is true that as an a priori truth the causal principle holds with necessity and is not just a contingent generalization (as Hume thought); but it does not, for that matter, afford us the full comprehension of specific causal connections that Hume sought: it does not explain why a given event *A* must lead to another event *B* (rather than *C* or *D*).

But then we move on to a fuller understanding of this ubiquitous causality. And it is our own agency that is supposed to give us such a fuller understanding. As Schopenhauer says with reference to his classification of representations in *On the Fourfold Root of the Principle of Sufficient Reason*:

> [T]he first class of representations [viz., material objects] finds its explanation, its solution, only in the fourth class enumerated in that essay [viz., the will]...accordingly, we must learn to understand the inner nature of the law of causality valid in the first class, and of what happens according to this law, from the law of motivation governing the fourth class.   (WWR1$_{[P]}$, 102)

9.3 THE VOLITIONAL THEORY

This idea that our own agency teaches us about causation is not new. It was put forward by Locke, adopted by Berkeley,[2] and critically discussed and dismissed by Hume. Locke wrote:

> [O]bserving in ourselves that we do and can think, and that we can at pleasure move several parts of our bodies...we...get the idea of power.[3]

Hume denied that the experience of one's voluntary actions yields any real understanding of causal power:

> The will being here consider'd as a cause, has no more a discoverable connexion with its effects, than any material cause has with its proper effect. So far from perceiving the connexion betwixt an act of volition, and a motion of the body; 'tis allow'd that no effect is more inexplicable from the powers and essence of thought and matter. Nor is the empire of the will over our mind more intelligible.[4]

As far as an experience of power is concerned, voluntary action is in no way more revealing than the observation of any other apparent case of causation in the world. All we can observe is a succession of two events: an act of will and, say, some bodily movement, while a connection that would make one an effect—that is (for Hume), an inevitable consequence of the other[5]—eludes us. Therefore, Hume insisted, the only possible source of the concept of causation is the observation of regularity: constant conjunction—that one type of event is always seen to follow another.

Hume follows Descartes and Locke in giving a *volitional* account of voluntary action. A voluntary bodily action is construed as a bodily movement caused by a volition; that is, a mental act of willing. And Hume argues that voluntary action cannot give us an understanding of causation because there is never an absolutely necessary link between a volition and its upshot. In a way, Schopenhauer accepts this latter point, but he draws a very different conclusion from it; namely, that there is something wrong with the volitional theory.

Any mental event that might be thought of as a volition (something like a wish, a self-command, or a decision) could occur *without* being followed by the intended action. And not only because I might suddenly be paralyzed but, more revealingly, because whatever I wish or decide to do may not really be what I want, as shown by my *psychological* inability to carry out my resolve. Schopenhauer mentions cases where we become ourselves doubtful about our ability to act according to our resolution:

> Thus, if we have formed some great and bold resolution—which, however, as such is only a promise given by the will to the intellect—there often remains within us a slight, unconfessed doubt whether we are quite in earnest about it, whether, in carrying it out, we shall not waver or flinch, but shall have firmness and determination enough to carry it through.   (WWR2$_{[P]}$, 210–11)

Obviously, as a volition, one would not normally envisage such a *long-term* resolution, but rather one about the immediate future, the next moment, in which case there would not be any time for such doubts. Still, the main point holds regardless of the temporal distance between decision and planned action: namely, that a decision may not be carried out because we find (perhaps to our own surprise) that we have not got the pluck or desire to do it after all. Schopenhauer takes that to show that, in the end, our actions do not really depend on any decisions of the mind. Such a decision of the mind is not yet a genuine manifestation of the will; a genuine manifestation of the will is only the action itself. A decision, or resolution, in the mind can only be a prediction of what, under the circumstances, we will do, i.e., which of all our motives and desires will in the end prevail.

Of course, such predictions (at least with regard to our behavior in the immediate future) will almost always prove correct. They are highly reliable, but (as Schopenhauer stresses) not infallible (WWR2$_{[P]}$, 248). They are reliable for two reasons. For one thing, because we know ourselves (our character: our will) quite well. We have a pretty accurate idea of how certain motives affect us. For example, I may know from experience that learning that I am in a café renowned for the quality of its strawberry ice cream will cause me to order some. And, for another thing, as Schopenhauer himself remarks, decisions, even if they are only mental occurrences, are themselves manifestations of our will (or character) (WWR2$_{[P]}$, 251). It is the same will (or character) that manifests itself in my decisions and (more definitely) in my actions. That makes it a priori probable that the two will usually be in agreement. If I am the kind of person who *resolves* to have a double portion of ice cream, it is quite likely that I am also the kind of person who *does* have a double portion of ice cream, and vice versa. However, I may occasionally miscalculate the effect certain motives will have on me, and there may occasionally be a discrepancy between my decisions and my actions. It is 7:30 A.M.; I have to go to work soon; I seriously decide to get out of bed—and do not. Or again: I am up on the 10-foot diving board and command myself to take the plunge. And do I jump? No, I do not. "The spirit indeed is willing, but the flesh is weak" (Matthew 26:41).

And it is not just in omissions that one can see the flesh's weakness (or stubbornness) overrule the spirit's intentions. I am asked a somewhat impertinent question; at the very moment of opening my mouth in reply, a sincere resolve to remain polite crosses my mind; and yet, the next moment, I find myself making a rude retort. On a volitional account, in such cases where I mentally "will" to do A but then find myself doing B, neither my doing B (making a rude remark), nor my omission of A (not getting up; not jumping off the diving board) could count as a voluntary action. Schopenhauer saw that that is wrong. We can and do hold people (notably ourselves) responsible for what they do or fail to do even if no mental resolve preceded the action; indeed, even if the agent honestly decided on a contrary (and perhaps more virtuous) course of action. Hence, voluntariness cannot lie in any mental act distinct from the action. There is no willing distinct from the actual doing.

So much for Schopenhauer's rejection of the volitional theory. In the twentieth century, further arguments have been added to Schopenhauer's observations, notably by Gilbert Ryle, which could be used to clinch Schopenhauer's case.[6] But I shall not pursue them now.

9.4 ACTIONS AS ACTS OF WILL

With the volitional theory out of the way, what is Schopenhauer's own account of voluntary action?

> Every true act of [the subject's] will is also at once and inevitably a movement of his body; he cannot actually will the act without at the same time being aware that it appears as a movement of the body. The act of will and the action of the body do not stand in the relation of cause and effect, but are one and the same thing, though given in two entirely different ways, once quite immediately and once in perception for the understanding.   (WWR1$_{[P]}$, 100–01)

Schopenhauer held on to the expression "act of will." That is understandable for, in his philosophy, the will has indeed a very active role ("will" becomes a shorthand for our non-intellectual nature); but it is somewhat misleading, for this expression is a hangover from the discarded volitional account. The redundancy of acts of will, as distinct mental acts, is precisely Schopenhauer's highly plausible negative point: when I raise my arm, I do just that and nothing more. I need not perform any other act besides raising my arm. Hence, if one is determined to keep using the term "act of will," then raising my arm is what it must refer to for there is no other act involved. The act of will and the bodily action are identical. And saying that is just a somewhat artificial way of saying that I raised my arm voluntarily. And what is more, I am immediately aware of my agency. As Schopenhauer puts it: a bodily action is perceived "in self-consciousness as an immediate, actual act of will" (WWR2$_{[P]}$, 248). I *know* that it was I who raised my arm. *How* do I know that? — Schopenhauer gives no answer, and rightly so, for there is no answer. This kind of case was to become a prominent theme in twentieth-century philosophy of mind. Such first-person authority is typically not based on any evidence, neither introspective nor observational. There is no interesting answer to the question "How do you know that you are in pain?" nor to the question "How do you know that you raised your arm voluntarily?"

Ludwig Wittgenstein, in his *Philosophical Investigations*, discusses this issue:

> "How do you know that you have raised your arm?"—"I feel it." So what you recognize is the feeling? And are you certain that you recognize it right?[7]

"I feel it" is the answer one would be inclined to give. If pressed, Schopenhauer might well have given the same reply. But, of course, as Wittgenstein's questions make us realize, our certainty about our agency is not really based on the recognition of sensations for it is not based on any evidence. Wittgenstein continues:

> You are certain that you have raised your arm; isn't this the criterion, the measure, of the recognition?
>   …So one might say: voluntary movement is marked by the absence of surprise. And now I do not mean you to ask "But *why* isn't one surprised here?"[8]

Of course, there is no awareness, let alone discussion, of the peculiarities of first-person authority in Schopenhauer. The simple fact is that he could not think of any further explanation of voluntariness apart from saying (in his terminology) that the agent is somehow immediately aware of it, independently of any possible mental acts preceding the action. However, by drawing on Wittgenstein's considerations, one can show that Schopenhauer's reticence on this point can be justified.

9.5 MOTIVATION AS CAUSATION SEEN FROM WITHIN

Agency is supposed to give us an idea of causation. But where do we find causation in human action if it is not caused by volitions? According to Schopenhauer, voluntary action is always caused by motives (i.e., reasons, perceptions, or thoughts that induce us to act).[9] And from the intimate experience of motivation in us we derive a proper understanding of causation: "*Motivation* (Schopenhauer says) *is causation seen from within*" (FR, 137).

The idea is that the experience of acting on motives gives us an understanding of causation that goes beyond what Hume had to offer and what Schopenhauer thought we could establish a priori to be generally applicable; namely, a concept of causation as constant conjunction. That is to say, what we are looking for inside is a link between cause and effect that is not merely inductive; not just a hypothesis of constant conjunction to be confirmed by repeated observation. Does motivation provide us with such an experience?

Consider an example of an action whose cause can be cited as a "motive": I hear the doorbell ring and get up to open the door. Now, is it only on inductive grounds that I could claim a causal link between that motivating perception and my action? I think not. My claim (that it was the doorbell that made me get up) is neither based on observed regularities nor does it await confirmation or refutation through future experiments.

9.6 HUME'S OBJECTIONS

But let us now return to Hume, and consider his more specific objections to the idea that our own agency might provide an understanding of causation, to see if, after some necessary modifications, those objections are not equally applicable to Schopenhauer's modified version of the view. (Remember that Hume's original discussion was directed at a volitional theory of voluntary action, which Schopenhauer replaced by a different account.)

First, Hume would probably object (to Schopenhauer) that we do not really understand why a certain "motive" produces a certain action and not another one. But, in many cases, that seems quite wrong: we do understand that kind of link. If the sound of the doorbell made me wiggle my toes, we would be puzzled. That indeed would look like an entirely contingent link that we might accept only as a hypothesis. But it is perfectly understandable why the sound of a doorbell should make a rational creature with certain beliefs and interests get up and open the door. It is a *reasonable* reaction.

Secondly, Hume mentions the case of a "man suddenly struck with a palsy in the leg or arm."[10] In this case a reason, say, hearing the doorbell, will not produce the normal response: the man finds himself unable to get up and open the door. Hume might continue thus:

> Here he is as much conscious of [the] power [of his reason to stir him into action], as a man in perfect health is conscious of [such a power]. But consciousness never deceives. Consequently, neither in the one case nor in the other, are we ever conscious of any power.[11]

Hume assumes that perceiving an object's causal powers must enable you to predict exactly what it will cause. But that is false. You may know exactly what power a certain fork-lift has: it can lift weights up to three tons. So will it lift that big box over there? Obviously, you cannot tell if you do not know the weight of that box. Likewise, if you do not know whether you are paralyzed or not, you cannot tell whether a certain reason will make you get up. But that does not prove your ignorance about the motive's causal powers.

We all know that the same cause can have different effects under different circumstances. So all Hume could reasonably expect to be discoverable in a cause is a power to produce a certain effect *under certain conditions*. Can such a *conditional* causal power be found in a motivating perception?—I think it can. There is a conceptual interdependence among a creature's beliefs, desires, capacities, and actions. If you know what an animal wants, what it is able to do, and what it does, you can infer (or even perceive) what it believes. If you know what an animal believes, is able to do, and does, you can infer (or even perceive) what it wants. Similarly, if you know sufficiently well what an animal believes, wants, and is able to do, you can very often predict what it will do. In other words, at least of some beliefs, you can say that, conjoined with certain other beliefs, desires, and capacities, they will lead inevitably to a certain kind of behavior. For example, the belief that a dangerous enemy is approaching will result in flight provided that the creature is desirous to remain unharmed, believes itself unable to fight off the predator, yet is able and in a position to outrun it.

A belief is not an occurrence but more like a disposition, so it might perhaps be said that it is not very well suited to play a causal role. That is why in my (doorbell) example I did not choose a belief, but a sense perception as a "motive." A sense perception is a datable event, and, as the cause of a certain belief, it can also be cited as a cause of that belief's possible behavioral manifestations. But insofar as it is identified partly in terms of the belief it engenders, it is analytic to say that it is a cause of any possible manifestation of that belief. Now, I hear that the doorbell is ringing. On Schopenhauer's behalf and against Hume, it can be claimed that in this sense-perception I can detect the causal power to make me open the door *under certain conditions*, roughly: that I am familiar with the function of doorbells, that I want to speak to people who call at my house, that I believe opening the door is the only appropriate way of doing so, that I know I am able to open the door, and that I have no reason or inclination not to open the door. In general, it is analytic that

> If a person A has an all-in desire to φ if p, and knows that he is able to φ and in no way prevented from φ-ing, then perceiving that p will make A φ.

If A does not φ on seeing that p, we can conclude that not all of the conditions were fulfilled.

Thirdly, Hume might object that we cannot experience a motivating perception's bringing about an action because there is no *direct* causal connection between them. All the reason really causes is some movement in our nerves, passed on to other nerves and then to some muscles which eventually cause some bodily movement.—The reply is that even if Hume's original argument had some plausibility in the context of a volitional account, there is no such indirectness in the causation envisaged by Schopenhauer. For the motivating perception is not said to cause a bodily movement, a mere *event*, but a voluntary *action*—say, a person's opening the door. And the physiological occurrences Hume mentions are not causes of the action, intervening between motivating perception and action; they are involved *in* the action, features of it on another level of description.

9.7 INANIMATE CAUSES

To recapitulate so far: Schopenhauer seems to be right (contra Hume) that our intentional actions afford us an insight into causation that goes beyond a mere registration of regularities. But could a concept of causation derived from our voluntary actions be applied to anything but voluntary actions? Could, in other words, an experience of our own voluntary actions really help us to understand the actions of non-conscious or even inanimate agents? Berkeley, for one, denied that, and he bravely accepted the consequence that we could not make sense of any action or causation in the world that was not due to a conscious agent,[12] which (for Berkeley) means that if something is not caused by one of us, it must be caused by God. But, of course, that was not Schopenhauer's view, who had not the slightest inclination to deny inanimate agency. So we must consider whether the transfer from the intentional to the inanimate is licit. Again, we can draw on Hume for the contrary view. In a footnote in his *Enquiry Concerning Human Understanding*, Hume says that people are prone to transfer descriptions of voluntary causation to the inanimate realm. And he makes it clear that he regards that as a bad mistake:

> No animal can put external bodies in motion without the sentiment of a *nisus* or endeavour; and every animal has a sentiment or feeling from the stroke or blow of an external object, that is in motion. These sensations...we are apt to transfer to inanimate objects, and to suppose, that they have some such feelings, whenever they transfer or receive motion.[13]

The absurdity of this assumption—that, for example, a stone feels the exertion of breaking a window—is probably the kind of absurdity many people are inclined to see in Schopenhauer's doctrine of the world as will: namely, a preposterous animism. But Schopenhauer makes it clear that that is not his view. He is not concerned with the *feelings* accompanying our actions, but with the immediacy with which we realize that a certain force is activated by certain circumstances. The claim is that what we witness here is essentially what happens everywhere, though not always witnessed by anybody, nor accompanied by any feelings.

Here we encounter once more Schopenhauer's first claim, "I am a will," and his radical break with Cartesian mentalism. As noted earlier, the word "will" in Schopenhauer in its primary psychological application to human beings and animals does not stand for a faculty of the conscious mind. Although we are mostly aware of our desires, that is merely because in us the will is conjoined with an intellect. On its own, the will has no consciousness. It is a blindly striving force. What is Schopenhauer's evidence for this claim, which anticipates some of Freud's teachings? It is the same kind of evidence you find in Freud: the fairly common phenomena of behavior that can be appropriately described by saying that it manifests emotions or desires the agent was not previously aware of; or again, the fact that we can occasionally be surprised by our own behavior.

> We often do not know what we desire or fear. For years we can have a desire without admitting it to ourselves or even letting it come to clear consciousness, because the intellect is not to know anything about it, since the good opinion we have of ourselves would inevitably suffer thereby. But if the wish is fulfilled, we get to know from our joy, not without a feeling of shame, that this is what we desired; for example the death of a near relation whose heir we are.... we are often entirely mistaken as to the real motive from which we do or omit to do something, till finally some accident discloses the secret to us.... For example, as we imagine we omit to do something for purely moral reasons; yet we learn subsequently that we were deterred merely by fear, since we do it as soon as all danger is removed.
>
> (WWR2$_{[P]}$, 209–10)

To this Schopenhauer adds examples of instinctive behavior: animals are frequently driven by their instincts to do certain things without any understanding of why they do them. (One of Schopenhauer's favorite examples was that "The larva of the stag-beetle gnaws the hole in the wood, where it will undergo its metamorphosis, twice as large if it is to become a male beetle as if it is to become a female, in order in the former case to have room for the horns, though as yet it has no idea of these" [WWR1$_{[P]}$, 114]).

But even if we are prepared to accept that the driving force that manifests itself in our actions is not all that different from other forces in nature, there remains a worry about the way it is normally set in motion, namely, by motives. Schopenhauer acknowledges the differences between causation by motive, stimulus, and purely physical cause (WWR1$_{[P]}$, 115–17; cf. WWR1$_{[P]}$, 105, quoted earlier). Does such a difference in the kind of cause not set voluntary action too far apart from events in the inanimate world for the latter to be comprehensible as essentially like the former? I do not think so. Even if voluntary action provides us only with a concept of a rather special kind of causation, causation it is, and so it will do to overcome Hume's professed inability to experience a causal link in any particular instance. A more general concept of causation may then be constructed by abstraction.[14]

9.8 MOTIVATION PRESUPPOSES AN UNDERSTANDING OF CAUSATION

However, there is another and more serious objection to Schopenhauer's account, namely, that as a *source* of the concept of causation motivation comes too late.

To act is to bring something about. Certainly to act on other objects is to have a causal impact on them. Hence to act on other objects *intentionally* is to act with the intention of having a causal impact on them. But (to take my example again) for the sound of the doorbell to make me *intentionally* get up and open the door, I must already *have* an understanding of what I am thus causing to happen. (Otherwise the perception would not motivate me to act in such a way.) Motivation *presupposes* an understanding of causation and thus cannot be its source.

Nor could one argue that all it presupposes is a Humean concept of causation as constant conjunction. For *that* concept is not really applicable to agent causation. Consider: if *I* cause my arm to go up (rather than a volition doing it), then there are not two kinds of events involved that could be found to be constantly conjoined. Furthermore, even where we have a causal impact on other objects by our moving our body, it is often quite obvious that we are actually unable to construe that as an instance of constant conjunction. We would have to say, for example, "Whenever I move my hands in a certain way, my shoelaces get tied." But the only identifying description we can actually give of that movement is that it is the movement of tying our shoelaces.

9.9 SENSORY EXPERIENCE OF CAUSATION

So where *do* we get our (non-Humean) concept of causation? There is a very straightforward (empiricist) answer: *We can feel causation in our encounters with material objects.* We can feel our impact on other bodies and their impact on us. When pushing a heavy obstacle out of our way we feel, that is, perceive by touch, how the object puts up some resistance that is gradually overcome.

Now this direct sensory experience of causation is exactly what Hume thought was impossible to have. But that is because Hume was hampered by an unduly narrow conception of sense-experience. Following Descartes and Locke, Hume was inclined to construe all sense experiences as bodily sensations; that is, as experiences of one's own subjective states, located in one's own body, which only *indirectly* could tell us anything about the outside world. Consider again the passage from the *Enquiry* quoted earlier:

> No animal can put external bodies in motion without the sentiment of a *nisus* or endeavour; and every animal has a sentiment or feeling from the stroke or blow of an external object, that is in motion. These sensations. . .we are apt to transfer to

inanimate objects, and to suppose, that they have some such feelings, whenever they transfer or receive motion.[15]

Now, of course inanimate things cannot possibly have such feelings. But inanimate things do have causal powers. So, Hume rightly concludes, causation cannot be explained in terms of such feelings, i.e., in terms of what we feel *in our body*.

But the word "feeling" can also be used in a different sense. We can also feel things outside our body. Schopenhauer gives a pertinent example:

> [W]e feel directly and immediately how a burden, which hampers our body by its gravitation toward the earth, incessantly presses and squeezes this body in pursuit of its one tendency. (WWR1$_{[P]}$, 118)

Unfortunately, Schopenhauer failed to see how close he was here to a better explanation of our understanding of causation. For here is something we feel which we *can* take as a paradigm of causation and attribute even to inanimate things because, although felt, it is not a feeling. It is a physical process: our bodily impact on an object, or vice versa.

9.10 CONCLUSION

To conclude, Schopenhauer was right to insist on agency as a source of a non-Humean understanding of causation. Moreover, he was right in his account of voluntary action to get rid of volitions. Arguably, he was also right to locate an immediate experience of causation where he did: between at least some kinds of motivating perceptions and our consequent actions. But he was wrong in suggesting that this experience might be the source of our understanding of causation; intentional action already presupposes that understanding and cannot provide it. Although in many respects Schopenhauer pioneered breaks with the Cartesian tradition, here, he was still too much in the grip of it. Like Hume, he was too inclined to limit the range of our experiences to what we are aware of *within ourselves*.

NOTES

1. David Hume, *Enquiry Concerning Human Understanding*, in *Enquiries Concerning Human Understanding and Concerning the Principles of Morals* (3rd edition), edited by L. A. Selby-Bigge, revised by P. H. Nidditch (Oxford: Clarendon Press, 1975), 34–35.
2. George Berkeley, *De Motu/Of Motion*, in *The Works of George Berkeley, Bishop of Cloyne*, Vol. 4, edited by A. A. Luce and T. E. Jessop (London: Thomas Nelson, 1951), 1–52; §25.
3. John Locke, *An Essay Concerning Human Understanding*, edited by P. H. Nidditch (Oxford: Oxford University Press, 1975), 2.7.8.
4. David Hume, *Treatise of Human Nature* (2nd edition), edited by L. A. Selby-Bigge (Oxford: Oxford University Press, 1978), 632.

5. Hume, *Enquiry*, 63.
6. See Gilbert Ryle, *The Concept of Mind* (London: Hutchinson, 1949), 62–69; also see Anthony Kenny, *The Metaphysics of Mind* (Oxford: Clarendon Press, 1989), 32.
7. Ludwig Wittgenstein, *Philosophical Investigations*, translated by G. E. M. Anscombe (Oxford: Blackwell, 1958), $625.
8. Wittgenstein, *Philosophical Investigations*, $$625 and 628.
9. Whereas in English the word "motive" is used mainly for emotions or attitudes inspiring an action (pity, hatred, revenge, etc.), Schopenhauer applies the term "*Motiv*" to all perceptions or thoughts that motivate our actions (FN, chapter III). Thus, in the case of intentional action "reason" might be a better translation, but then, strictly speaking, what causes me to act (e.g., to seek shelter) is not the reason (e.g., the fact that it is raining), but the occurrence it identifies (e.g., the rain). As Schopenhauer says that "motives" are *Vorstellungen*, I shall sometimes translate the term as "motivating perception."
10. Hume, *Enquiry*, 66.
11. Adapted from Hume, *Enquiry*, 66.
12. George Berkeley, *Philosophical Commentaries*, in *The Works of George Berkeley, Bishop of Cloyne, Vol. 1*, edited by A. A. Luce and T. E. Jessop (London: Thomas Nelson, 1948), 1–139; $$499; 699.
13. Hume, *Enquiry*, 78n.
14. In addition, there is reason to believe that the non-inductive awareness of causation is not peculiar to causation by motives. A sudden noise makes me start, contact with a hot surface causes a reflex to withdraw. These are examples of the stimulus–response type.
15. Hume, *Enquiry*, 78n.

Further Reading

Berkeley, George. *De Motu/Of Motion*. In *The Works of George Berkeley, Bishop of Cloyne, Vol. 4*, edited by A. A. Luce and T. E. Jessop. London: Thomas Nelson, 1951, 1–52.
Berkeley, George. *Philosophical Commentaries*. In *The Works of George Berkeley, Bishop of Cloyne, Vol. 1*, edited by A. A. Luce and T. E. Jessop. London: Thomas Nelson, 1948, 1–139.
Hume, David. *Enquiry Concerning Human Understanding*. In *Enquiries concerning Human Understanding and Concerning the Principles of Morals* (3rd edition), edited by L. A. Selby-Bigge, revised by P. H. Nidditch. Oxford: Clarendon Press, 1975, 5–165.
Hume, David. *Treatise of Human Nature* (2nd edition), edited by L. A. Selby-Bigge. Oxford: Oxford University Press, 1978.
Kenny, Anthony. *The Metaphysics of Mind*. Oxford: Clarendon Press, 1989.
Locke, John. *An Essay Concerning Human Understanding*, edited by P. H. Nidditch. Oxford: Oxford University Press, 1975.
Ryle, Gilbert. *The Concept of Mind*. London: Hutchinson, 1949.
Wittgenstein, Ludwig. *Philosophical Investigations*, translated by G. E. M. Anscombe. Oxford: Blackwell, 1958.

···

CHAPTER 10

SCHOPENHAUER'S HAUNTED WORLD

The Use of Weird and Paranormal Phenomena to Corroborate His Metaphysics

···

DAVID E. CARTWRIGHT

[L]ike a magician, it calls into visibility things that for us are of the greatest reality, but that in respect of the will are merely reflections of its essence.[1]

DRIVEN by a steadfast commitment to the genius of his intuitions, an unbridled curiosity, cosmopolitan sensibilities, a dedication to track the scent of truth wherever the trail led, an unrelenting desire for discovering sources substantiating his philosophy, coupled with a forty-eight-year-long philosophy career, Arthur Schopenhauer explored varied and various subjects, common and weird, acceptable and taboo, normal and paranormal. Friedrich Nietzsche deeply admired Schopenhauer's honesty and his willingness to articulate truths that Schopenhauer knew were displeasing to his contemporaries, but Nietzsche also classified Schopenhauer's fascination with weird, abnormal, and paranormal phenomena among the "vices and excesses" found in his philosophy, such as "the nonsense about compassion, about how it makes possible the penetration of the *principium individuationis*, how it is the basis of all morality; also such claims as 'dying is the purpose of existence,' and '*a priori* one cannot altogether deny the possibility that magical effects might emanate from one who has died.'"[2] Nietzsche also assailed Schopenhauer's ability to understand moral phenomena by mentioning that Schopenhauer is "one who still honestly believes in illuminations from above, in magic, in ghostly appearances and in the metaphysical ugliness of the toad!"[3] Nietzsche was, perhaps, too *naturwissenschaftlich* to stomach Schopenhauer's forays into the weird. More succinctly, Arthur O. Lovejoy simply mentions Schopenhauer's "queer weakness for occultism."[4]

Something more than a "queer weakness" may well be suggested by a glance at the oddest and lengthiest footnote to the oddest and lengthiest chapter in *On Will in Nature*, "Animal Magnetism and Magic," in which Schopenhauer recalls his experience of a magician.

> In the year 1854, I had the good fortune to see here [Frankfurt] such extraordinary feats of Mr. Regazzoni of Bergamo, in which the immediate, that is, magical, power of his will over others is unmistakable and to the greatest degree astonishing, of the authenticity of which feats none could remain in doubt, except those to whom nature has completely denied all capacity for comprehending pathological conditions; however, there are such subjects, who must be made lawyers, ministers, merchants, or soldiers, but for heaven's sake not doctors, for the result would be fatal, since in medicine diagnosis is the primary thing.—[Regazzoni] could put his somnambulist, who was under his influence, into complete catalepsy; in fact, merely through his will, without gestures, as she walked forward and he stood behind her, he could make her fall, backwards. He could paralyze her, put her in a state of tetanus [*Starrkrampf*], with dilated pupils, completely insensible, and the unmistakable signs of a completely cataleptic condition. He had a lady from the audience play the piano, and then, standing five paces behind her, through his will, with gestures, paralyzed her so she could not play. Then he put her against a column and charmed her so that she could not move from the spot despite the greatest effort.—According to my observation almost all of his tricks can be explained from the fact that he isolates the brain from the spinal column, either completely, whereby all sensible and motor nerves are paralyzed and complete catalepsy occurs, or the paralysis affects only the motor nerves, while sensibility remains, so that her head retains consciousness atop a body apparently dead. Strychnine works in just the same way: it paralyzes only the motor nerves to the point of complete tetanus, leading to death by suffocation; yet it leaves the sensible nerves, hence also the consciousness, undisturbed. Regazzoni does the same through the magical influence of his will.   (WN, 408n [SW4, 102]).

Schopenhauer's credulity might make one pause, but in many ways the entire chapter is incredible. Indeed, his fascination with weird phenomena like animal magnetism, black and white magic, clairvoyance, spirit seeing, and telekinesis makes it easy to wish that he had been more incredulous.[5]

Schopenhauer, however, thought that his beliefs in the paranormal were no wilder than his commitment to idealism, to his thinking that "we carry the world around in our heads," an idea that "surpasses in incredibility all the fairy tales and fables ever invented," something that led him to feel "like Arjuna when Krishna appeared to him in his true divine form with his hundred thousand arms, eyes, mouths, etc." (MR4, 45).[6] Nevertheless, Schopenhauer philosophized from experience, especially privileging his own, and he had experienced animal magnetism and ghosts. He also had a sense of being mildly clairvoyant.[7] He credited a prophetic dream involving the appearance of a youthful friend, who died when Schopenhauer was ten years old, as a warning to flee Berlin in August of 1831, which he did, thereby avoiding the cholera epidemic that has been said to have taken Hegel in November of that year. Shortly after his arrival in Frankfurt am

Main, he experienced what he called a "perfectly clear apparition" involving his living mother and his dead father; which "indicated that I would now outlive my mother who at that time was still alive; my father who was already dead was carrying a light in his hand" (MR4, 62).[8]

Yet Schopenhauer's belief in spirit apparitions and magic was not philosophically idiosyncratic. His hero, Kant, came to ambivalent conclusions about the paranormal in the pre-Critical essay "Dreams of a Spirit-seer, Elucidated by the Dreams of Metaphysics" (1766), concerning the spiritualism of his contemporary, the Swedish theologian and mystic Emanuel Swedenborg.[9] Schopenhauer's nemeses, Johann Fichte, Friedrich Schelling, and G. W. F. Hegel also believed in the paranormal.[10] Fichte and Hegel accepted animal magnetism, and Schelling and Hegel somnambulism, clairvoyance, and ghosts.[11] Schopenhauer, however, would never consider citing the men he called the "three sophists," even though it was his typical practice to cite whomever he could to back his views. But what more deeply provided Schopenhauer with a sense of the legitimacy of magic and paranormal phenomena was their lengthy multicultural histories: "one will be amazed at the tenacity with which humankind has clung to the idea of magic everywhere and at all times...one will conclude that it has a deep basis at least in the nature of the human being, if not in things generally" (WN, 414/111). Indeed, in his "Essay on Spirit-Seeing and Related Issues" from the first volume of *Parerga and Paralipomena*, Schopenhauer does not feel compelled to provide accounts of spirit-seeing, assuming that his readers were well familiar with such accounts, and he took such experiences as a fact for which he would provide a theory. Schopenhauer took pride in the fact that he considered such paranormal phenomena, and he told his friend Julius Frauenstädt that "[his] metaphysics had vindicated" these neglected phenomena.[12] More importantly, however, Schopenhauer also appealed to these phenomena to corroborate his metaphysics. In what way did these phenomena corroborate his metaphysics? Do they, in some sense, actually corroborate his metaphysics? To answer these questions it is necessary to consider his meta-metaphysics.

10.1 AN IMMANENT METAPHYSICS: BETWEEN DOGMATIC OMNISCIENCE AND THE DESPAIR OF THE KANTIAN CRITIQUE

It is not surprising that Schopenhauer would be silent about the nature of metaphysics in his dissertation, since *On the Fourfold Root of the Principle of Sufficient Reason* is a work in what he later would call "*philosophia prima*," an analysis of the "faculty of cognition [*Erkenntnißvermögen*]," its forms, laws, validity, and limitations (PP2, 21 [SW6, 19]). Even in its extensively revised second edition, where there is more metaphysical content, he says nothing about the nature of metaphysics, although, to show his allegiance to Kant, he assiduously replaced the term "metaphysical" with "transcendental."

Nor is it unexpected that he would be silent about metaphysics in his second work, *On Vision and Colors*, given his task of developing a theory of colors, an undertaking he viewed as primarily scientific. Nevertheless, it is extraordinary that Schopenhauer says little about the nature of metaphysics in the first edition of his main work, *The World as Will and Representation*, and, when he does describe the task of metaphysics, he does so obliquely in the context of a discussion of the metaphysically expressive power of music. Paraphrasing Leibniz, Schopenhauer describes music as "an unconscious exercise in metaphysics, in which the mind does not know it is philosophizing," and he says "philosophy is nothing other than a complete and correct repetition and expression of the essence of the world in very general concepts" (WWR1, 292 [SW2, 312]).[13] He contends that music produces in tones what metaphysics does through concepts. Thus, in the first edition of his main work, the task of metaphysics appears to be to conceptually express the essence of the world, which he does by denominating this essence "will." Indeed, such denominating has such a profoundly illuminating cast that there is something magical about it: "But the word *will*...is supposed to unlock the inner most essence of all things in nature for us like a magic spell" (WWR1, 136 [SW2, 133]). In his fourth book, *On Will in Nature*, Schopenhauer remarks that after "a seventeen-year silence," he is publishing again "to provide some of the corroboration that my philosophy has received from unbiased empiricists who, unacquainted with my philosophy, have, at the end point of their method aimed at mere knowledge from experience, discovered just that which my theory has presented as metaphysics by which experience in general is to be explained" (WN, 323 [SW4, 1]). Yet he neither explains nor attempts to justify this novel idea of metaphysics as explaining experience in general.

In the second edition of *The World as Will and Representation*, Schopenhauer first methodically discusses the idea that metaphysics explains "experience in general." He addresses his metaphysics first in the Appendix to the first volume, "Critique of the Kantian Philosophy," and he elaborates on this conception of metaphysics in the important seventeenth chapter of the second volume of his main work, "On the Human Being's Metaphysical Need." Later he casts more light on metaphysics in section 21 of "On Philosophy and Its Method," from the second volume of *Parerga and Paralipomena*.

In the "Critique of the Kantian Philosophy," in a lengthy paragraph added in the second edition of his main book (1844), Schopenhauer confronts Kant's rejection of "dogmatic metaphysics"—the view that we can have knowledge of that which lies beyond the possibility of experience. Schopenhauer understands Kant to be arguing something like the following:

1. Metaphysics is the science that seeks cognition of what is beyond the possibility of experience (things in themselves).
2. Our cognitions of things are either a priori or a posteriori.
3. But what is cognized a priori is found in human reason and applies only to our representations (experiences of things) and does not concern the existence of things beyond our experiences (things in themselves).
4. Therefore, metaphysics can never be based on a priori cognitions. (1, 3)

5. Therefore, metaphysics must be based on a posteriori cognitions. (2, 4)
6. Yet what is beyond the possibility of experience can never be discovered a posteriori, using principles that are derived from inner or outer experience.
7. Therefore metaphysics cannot be based on a posteriori cognitions. (1, 6)
8. Therefore we cannot have cognitions of what is beyond the possibility of experience (things in themselves). (2, 4, 7)
9. Therefore metaphysics is impossible. (1, 8)[14]

Schopenhauer is willing to accept Kant's argument as it stands, as long as proposition 1 is the proper task of metaphysics. However, Schopenhauer will reject 1, and by this propositions 7 and 9 while agreeing with 2–6 and 8.

Schopenhauer argues that Kant's justification for proposition 7 begs the question because he simply presented an "etymological argument from the word 'metaphysics'" for this proposition in the first section of the *Prolegomena to Any Future Metaphysics* by holding that "metaphysics was identical to *a priori* cognition" (WWR1, 454 [SW2, 506]). This allowed Kant, Schopenhauer continues, to reject experience and *a posteriori* cognition as the source of metaphysics without any proof. But, Schopenhauer claims, "the world and our existence are necessarily given to us as a riddle" (WWR1, 454 [SW2, 506]), implying that the task of metaphysics is to solve the riddle of existence,[15] which entailed for Schopenhauer also the rejection of proposition 7, since "we would need a proof that "the material for solving the riddle of the world could not be possibly be contained in the world itself, but instead could only be looked for from outside of the world . . . under the guidance of those forms of which we are *a priori* conscious" (WWR1, 454 [SW2, 507]). Absent such a proof, Schopenhauer contends that the solution to the riddle of the world must result from an understanding of the world itself and that the task of metaphysics is to understand the world "from the ground up," using the main sources of knowledge, "both outer and inner experience" (WWR1, 455 [SW2, 507]). By connecting outer and inner experience in the right sort of way, he continues, you solve the puzzle of existence without, however, attaining "a complete and self-sufficient explanation of its [the world's] existence . . . that does away with all further problems" (WWR1, 455 [SW, 507]).

To help his readers better understand his view of metaphysics, Schopenhauer refers them to the seventeenth chapter of the second volume of *The World as Will and Representation*, "On the Human Being's Metaphysical Need" (*Über das metaphysische Bedürfniß des Menschen*), where he provides his most robust discussion of metaphysics. Here he rejects proposition 1 by radically redefining metaphysics. It is no longer a science that attempts to know that which lies beyond the bounds of all possible experience; rather, metaphysics is "the science of experience in general . . . the correct explanation of experience as a whole" (WWR2$_{[P]}$, 181 [SW3, 201]).[16] Arguing that "the whole of experience is like a cryptograph [*Geheimschrift*], and philosophy is the deciphering of it [*Entzifferung*], the correctness of which is confirmed by the connectedness that appears everywhere" (WWR2$_{[P]}$, 182 [SW3, 202]), Schopenhauer holds that experience is deciphered "if only this whole [of experience] is grasped in sufficient depth, and inner experience is connected to outer, then must it be capable of being *interpreted* [*gedeutet*], *explained* [*ausgelegt*], from itself" (WWR2$_{[P]}$, 182/202).[17] The verification that experience has been grasped in sufficient depth is when, Schopenhauer continues, "It [the deciphering] must spread a uniform light over all appearances of the world, and even bring the most heterogeneous into agreement, so that the contradiction is resolved also between those that contrast the most" (WWR2$_{[P]}$, 184 [SW3, 205]).[18] This remark about bringing into agreement even appearances that "contrast the most" set the stage for his analysis of the paranormal, for such experiences stand in the greatest contrast with "normal" experiences, those experiences theoretically explicable by the sciences.

Schopenhauer, of course, has to show why proposition 7, "Metaphysics cannot be based on *a posteriori* cognitions" is false. He mounts a curious argument against proposition 7, using a series of rhetorical questions.

> But does it not appear downright backwards that one looks away from experience, ignoring its content [*Inhalt*], and that one should simply take and use as material [*Stoff*] empty forms [*Formen*] of which we are a priori conscious, in order to unriddle [*enträthseln*] experience, i.e., the world which alone lies before us? Is it not rather appropriate for the subject that the science of experience in general, and as such, would just draw from experience? Its problem is given to it empirically; why should its solution also not be aided by experience? The task is certainly not the observation of particular experiences, but rather the correct explanation of experience as a whole. Therefore its foundation must certainly be of an empirical kind.
>
> (WWR2$_{[P]}$, 180f [SW2, 200f])

Schopenhauer appears to reject proposition 7 by simply redefining the nature of metaphysics. If metaphysics is the science of experience in general, then it follows that a posteriori and not simply a priori (nonempirical) cognitions would be the material for metaphysics. Indeed, if metaphysics aims at a comprehensive explanation of experience, it would seem absurd to ignore experience, and it would make sense that there has to be an empirical foundation for metaphysics.[19]

Schopenhauer then claims that metaphysics "is knowledge [*Wissen*] drawn from the intuition of the external actual world and from the information about this by the most intimate facts of self-consciousness deposited in direct concepts" (WWR2$_{[P]}$, 183 [SW3, 203]). But if metaphysics has an empirical foundation, it must draw its materials from what John Locke called "the two fountains of knowledge," sensation and reflection,[20] or from what Schopenhauer called, following Kant, the outer and inner senses.[21] Schopenhauer will still retain allegiance to proposition 6 by appealing to Kant: "And although no one can cognize the thing in itself through the veil [*Hülle*] of the forms of intuition, nonetheless everyone carries this within himself, indeed, it is himself [*so trägt anderseits doch Jeder dieses in sich, ja, ist es selbst*]; therefore, it must be in some way accessible in self-consciousness, if only in a conditional way. Thus the bridge on which metaphysics goes beyond experience is nothing other than that very separation of experience into appearance and thing in itself, that in which I have placed Kant's greatest merit" (WWR2$_{[P]}$, 182f [SW3, 203]). By retaining an allegiance to Kant's transcendental idealism, Schopenhauer accepts that the world of experience, the object of the "outer sense," is mere appearance and that a priori knowledge is valid only in reference to experience. Now, however, he tweaks Kant.

> I added [to Kant] that, precisely as appearance, it [the world] is the manifestation of that which appears; and with him [Kant], I call that which appears the thing in itself. Therefore the thing in itself must express its inner nature and character in the world of experience, and it must be possible to interpret these from it, and indeed from the material, not from the mere form, of experience. Accordingly philosophy is nothing but the correct and universal understanding of experience itself, the true interpretation of its meaning and content. This is the metaphysical, i.e., that which is merely clothed in appearance and veiled [*Verhüllte*] in its forms, that which is related to appearance as the thought or idea is to the word.   (WWR2$_{[P]}$, 183f [SW3, 204])

Employing Kant's distinction between appearance and thing in itself as permitting his claim that the thing in itself is that which appears in all appearances, Schopenhauer ties will as thing in itself to appearance, such that it is known only in reference to appearances and that it is not to be considered "as an *ens extramundanum*, but it is always cognized only in its relations [*Verhältnissen*] and references [*Beziehungen*] to appearance itself" (WWR2$_{[P]}$, 183 [SW3, 203]).

As is the case with any experience, Schopenhauer contends, the experience of our will is within the most basic epistemic condition, the subject–object correlation, and that as an object of self-consciousness, the will has a "being-in-itself" different from our experience of it as an object. Moreover since the will is an object of self-consciousness (the inner sense), will is cognized through the a priori form of time, and so it is experienced in "successive individual acts, not as a whole in and by itself" (WWR2$_{[P]}$, 197 [SW3, 220]). For these reasons, Schopenhauer concluded that we do not know the thing-in-itself "naked," but that the will is that in which the thing-in-itself has "to a great extent cast off its veils" (WWR2$_{[P]}$, 197 [SW3, 220]).[22] Because will is still "veiled" and our forms of cognition only apply to appearances, no final solution to the riddle of existence is possible since such a solution would entail that we peek behind the veil, something that would be a new form of cognition, something akin to Schelling's intellectual intuition, which Schopenhauer mocked as the so-called sixth sense of the bat.[23] Human cognitive capacity is such that concerning the thing in itself, concerning the "naked" thing in itself, it would be impossible for us to derive any intuition or sense of it, even "if a being of a higher type came and took all the trouble to teach it to us, we would be thoroughly unable to understand his disclosures" (WWR2$_{[P]}$, 185 [SW3, 206]).[24] Thus, Schopenhauer's acceptance of Kant's propositions 2–4 and 8.

The metaphysical will qualifies as thing-in-itself compared to other appearances because it has only the "veil" of time and it is the content, stuff, kernel, or essence of the more complexly conditioned appearances. As Schopenhauer claimed in *On Will in Nature*, will is the "in-itself" of all representations: "Everything that is known of things only empirically, only a posteriori, is in itself will; in contrast, as far as things are

determinable *a priori*, they belong solely to representation, to the mere appearance"
(WN, 393/86). Hence, will is that which is expressed in appearance. It is that which is
"represented" in "representations" (PP1, 22 [SW5, 21]) and it is that which is expressed in
all representations that are spatially and temporally ordered within a causal matrix, like
the representation of one's own body. Yet, since the experience of will as thing in itself is
conditioned by human cognition, what the thing in itself is in itself is unknown. In this
way, Schopenhauer retains fidelity to proposition 6 in Kant's argument but rejects 1 and
9. Metaphysics does not seek cognition of the thing in itself, which is an impossible task.
His metaphysics does not seek such, but rather it is the science that explains the totality
of experiences, something that is possible.[25] It is also for this reason that Schopenhauer's
metaphysics, which seeks to explain the totality of experiences, is a theory of almost
everything, recognizing the possibility of something eluding theorizing. In this way, he
claimed "my path lies between the earlier dogmatic doctrine of omniscience and the
despair of Kant's critique" (WWR1, 455 [SW2, 507]). By not seeking to transcend the
bounds of experience, Schopenhauer views his metaphysics as fully immanent, as
describing things within the bounds of all possible experience.

10.2 EMPIRICAL CORROBORATIONS
OF THE METAPHYSICS OF WILL

In *On Will in Nature*, Schopenhauer views the corroborations of his philosophy by the
sciences as concerning "the core and principal point of my theory, its metaphysics
proper…that with which we are immediately acquainted and precisely intimate, that
which we find in our innermost selves as will, [is] the only thing in itself, the only truly
real thing, the only original and metaphysical thing in the world where everything else is
only appearance, i.e., mere representation." He continues, in the same passage, "Will
gives power to everything, whatever it may be, the power by means of which it can exist
and give effect" (WN, 324 [SW4, 2]). Citing a remark from one of Kant's pre-Critical
essays concerning the relationship of metaphysics to science, Schopenhauer claims that
his metaphysics of will grounds science by explaining those basic elements at which the
sciences end or are presupposed as givens (e.g., as natural forces, vital forces, and formative drives).[26] Schopenhauer understands the natural sciences as corroborating his
metaphysics, however, by recognizing will at the endpoints of their investigations,
"when in particularly fortunate cases especially clear sighted and observant investiga-
tors in the realm of the natural sciences succeed at casting a stolen glance beyond the
curtain that, as it were, fixes the limits of their science, not just sensing the boundary as
such, but also in a way perceiving even its constitution [*Beschaffenheit*], and in a way
even peering into the realm of metaphysics that lies on the other side of the curtain"
(WN, 326 [SW4, 4]). Consequently, in the first four chapters of *On Will in Nature*,
Schopenhauer works his way through the natural sciences showing cases in which will

was recognized as basic. This strategy is continued in the fifth chapter, "Linguistics," where he highlights languages that attribute a will to natural processes. The sixth chapter, "Animal Magnetism and Magic," continues the same method, citing instances in which practitioners of animal magnetism and magic credit a will as the force behind their arts.

Yet there is something deeper at stake for Schopenhauer when he considers paranormal phenomena. In such phenomena as animal magnetism,[27] clairvoyance, telepathy, extra-sensory perception, ghosts, telekinesis, and magic, Schopenhauer believed that: "we will see will—which I have presented as the thing in itself, as the only real thing in all exist-ence, as the core of nature—achieving through the human individual things not to be explained by causal connection, i.e., by the law of the course of nature, indeed, things that to a certain extent suspend this law and actually exert action at a distance, thus revealing a supernatural, i.e., metaphysical mastery of nature—then I know of no more factual corroboration of my theory that could still be required" (WN, 409 [SW4, 104]).[28]

Consequently, paranormal phenomena serve as a "factual corroboration" of his meta-physics in ways no other phenomena could because not only do such phenomena elude scientific explanation, but from the point of view of the natural sciences, such phenom-ena also are regarded as delusions, illusions, tricks, or frauds because they contradict the laws of nature. So when the good Signor Regazzoni, whom Schopenhauer discusses in that oddest and longest footnote, exerted the magical powers of his will on his assistant, making her tumble, paralyzing her, and putting her into a cataleptic state, and when Regazzoni paralyzed the volunteer from the audience, simply through gestures, thereby preventing her from playing the piano, he breached the separation between individuals, broke the bounds between distinct spatial-temporal individuals, defying all causal laws. He defied the physical connections between things, the so-called *physical nexus*, and he demonstrated that,

> [T]there must be still another [connection], proceeding through the essence in itself of all things, a subterranean connection, so to speak, whereby one point of appear-ance would be able immediately to affect any other by a metaphysical nexus; that therefore it must be possible to affect things from within, instead of from without as is usual, an effect of appearance on appearance, by means of the essence in itself that is one and the same in all appearances; that, just as we act causally as created nature, we would also be capable of acting as creating nature, and for the moment the micro-cosm would assert itself as macrocosm; that the partitions of individuation and sep-aration, no matter how firm, could still occasionally permit a communication, as it were, behind the curtains, or like a secret game under that table   (WN, 415 [SW4, 111])

Will, of course, provides this metaphysical connection.[29] Just as will underlies normal intuitive appearances, it also underlies paranormal appearances in ways that are inexplicable.

It is clear why Schopenhauer would find paranormal phenomena significant for his metaphysics. If there were such phenomena, Schopenhauer's philosophy would appear to have even more explanatory power than the natural sciences since he could claim that his philosophy explains a greater range of experience than the sciences. More profoundly, however, Schopenhauer claims that the confirmation of a correct decipher-ing of experience is that it "must spread a uniform light over all appearances of the world, and even bring the most heterogeneous into agreement, so that the contradiction may be removed also between those that contrast the most" (WWR2$_{[P]}$, 184 [SW3, 205]). Paranormal phenomena provide a profound contradiction to normal phenomena, and, by having a metaphysics that can account for paranormal phenomena, Schopenhauer finds that his metaphysics explains the totality of experiences. Not simply those phe-nomena presupposed by science that are scientifically unexplainable, but also actual phenomena the existence of which are viewed by science as impossible.

Yet it is doubtful that paranormal phenomena are as Schopenhauer viewed them, viz., as phenomena that elude scientific explanation. Take our old friend Signor Regazzoni who, through the magical influences of his will, was able to isolate the frustrated pianist's brain from her spinal column, so that her head retained consciousness atop an appar-ently dead body. It appears that Schopenhauer is guilty here of employing the concept of causality transcendently since one wonders how the idea of magical influence is not some causal notion, suggesting that the magnetizer has tapped into the metaphysical nexus in such a way as to work his individual will on another. (It seems, however, that the good Signor's metaphysical connection was tenuous. When two Frankfurt physi-cians visited him in his apartment a short time after his astonishing performance, they found him incapable of duplicating the feats exhibited in his stage act.[30] Of course, there could have been a metaphysical disconnect in his apartment.)

When it came to ghosts, however, Schopenhauer was more guarded. He thought that his metaphysics could ground animal magnetism, clairvoyance, telepathy, and magic, but ghosts troubled him metaphysically. Consequently, he ended his essay on spirit-seeing by claiming that his philosophy only cast "a weak light" (PP1, 272 [SW5, 328]) on the phenomenon—one insufficient to illuminate the phenomenon in a way that would resolve the millennia-long debate between believers and skeptics. He even suggested that a living person might have vivid reminiscences of a person and wrongly interpret these as communications from the dead. In any case, unlike other paranormal phenom-ena, which were intersubjective and comparable to our intuitions of objects of the outer sense, he concludes his essay by claiming that "spirit-seeing is first and immediately, nothing but a vision in the brain of the spirit seer" (PP1, 272 [SW5, 328]). Although he believed that a living or dying person could affect such a vision, which would be magi-cal, he left it an open question whether a dead person could affect such a vision. He did so with good reason. Whereas his explanation of clairvoyance appealed to a metaphysi-cal connection provided by will, a connection that at some representational level united all existence and was present in everything that was, is, or will be, Schopenhauer was at a loss to use the same explanation for ghosts. Clairvoyants thought through another's brain as their own brain "slept," but the problem is that the dead have no intellect and thus no brain—indeed, nothing "physical" to direct will. More deeply, death annihilated anything that would individualize one dead person from another—each and everything at the level of will is just will.[31]

10.3 PARANORMAL PROBLEMS

Schopenhauer's positing of a nonspatial and nontemporal nexus provided by will seems as if his metaphysics can explain phenomena that violate the laws of space and time, thereby giving his metaphysics an advantage over the natural sciences. However, Schopenhauer's claim that the agency of the magician and clairvoyant functions to produce these phenomena is parasitic on some notion of causality functioning through subterranean channels, as it were, channels beyond the domain in which causality applies. Indeed, such an explanation involves the transcendent employment of the principle of sufficient reason of becoming; its use being beyond the bounds of possible experience and outside the scope of an allegedly immanent philosophy.[32] Moreover, will as an object for the inner sense is still a temporal object for a subject and as such seems incapable of accounting for things seemingly nontemporal. The idea of some metaphysical connection, some nexus uniting all representations, also appears to involve the idea of space. Consequently, since Schopenhauer attempts to develop a metaphysics that mediates between the omniscience of dogmatic metaphysics and the despair of the Kantian critique by saying something about the thing in itself (will is a veiled thing in itself), but not everything (things in themselves are beyond cognition), he is led to walk a fine line between the immanent and the transcendent, a line he cannot help but cross in his analysis of paranormal phenomena. By claiming it is the cognition of one's own will that is the clue to connecting inner with outer experiences, Schopenhauer can only claim that will is the essence of appearances. Moreover, Schopenhauer appears to make will the *Urphänomen* of his philosophy, since will is the basis for explaining all other experiences, and it is inexplicable and irreducible to something more basic. Perhaps that should be philosophically sufficient.

Nevertheless, Schopenhauer could try to defend his position here as he did when confronted with similar problems. For example, when questioned by his friend Johann Becker about how the intelligible character could constitute an extratemporal act of will, and how a person's empirical character could be its appearance, Schopenhauer replied, "I present this not as an objective truth or as an adequate notion of the relation between the thing in itself and appearance; rather, I present it merely as a metaphor and simile, as a figurative expression of the matter ... in order to make the matter comprehensible."[33] If this were to be the case with Schopenhauer's theory of the paranormal, then again, it is difficult to understand how he would be providing an explanation of the totality of experiences since figurative expressions transcend the principle of sufficient reason, the very principle of all explanation. And if such expressions provide some increase to our cognitive stock, it comes at the cost of the goal of Schopenhauer's metaphysics, viz., a comprehensive explanation of the totality of experience. It also cuts against his "epiphilosophy [*Epiphilosophie*]" (WWR2$_{[P]}$, 640 [SW3, 736]), which pledges his commitment to a philosophy that stays within the bounds of experience.

10.4 CONCLUSION

Schopenhauer's focus on the paranormal provides him with a set of phenomena that contradict the standpoint of the natural sciences, and, by showing how his metaphysics can account for these phenomena, he has more evidence to support his claim that his metaphysics explains the totality of experiences. Whereas he held that his metaphysics grounded science by explaining that which was presupposed but not explainable scientifically, it also had the power to explain phenomena that contradicted the best findings of the natural science. It is for reasons like this that he remarked that "animal magnetism…is an incomparably more important appearance than mineral magnetism" (WWR2$_{[P]}$, 179 [SW3, 198]). The latter is explained by the natural sciences, but not the former, which stood in contradiction to normal phenomena. Thus, he claimed that his metaphysics brought "the most heterogeneous [phenomena] into agreement, so that the contradiction is resolved also between those that contrast the most" (WWR2$_{[P]}$, 184 [SW3, 205]).

One can admire Schopenhauer's willingness to explore phenomena that have been generally ignored by philosophers, just as one can appreciate his willingness to speak his truths without regard to their reception by his contemporaries. At the same time, however, one must question his willingness to uncritically accept paranormal phenomena at face value. If there was one thing that Schopenhauer was not, he was not a skeptic. This lack of skepticism sometimes serves him well, such as his pragmatic rejection of theoretical egoism (solipsism).[34] But with the paranormal, it appears to have failed him.[35] Perhaps he should have just left the paranormal as the subject for parapsychologists and ghost hunters, waiting instead for "facts" for which he could then attempt to supply a theory.[36] Or he could have hunted for such like the solid British utilitarian, Henry Sidgwick, the first president of the Society for Psychical Research, founded in 1882 (London), and the North American pragmatist, William James, the first president of the British Society's counterpart, the American Society for Psychical Research, founded in 1884 (Boston). Better yet, he should have considered different explanations for why belief in magic and the paranormal is such a persistent feature of the human condition, just as he did for religious beliefs, the truths of which Schopenhauer said were expressed allegorically in a "*sensu allegorico*" (WWR2$_{[P]}$, 166 [SW3, 183]).

ACKNOWLEDGMENTS

I thank my friend and colleague Edward E. Erdmann, who assisted with some of the translations, edited, and read an earlier version of the paper, "The World as Weird: Schopenhauer's Use of Odd Phenomena to Corroborate His Metaphysics," at the workshop on the works of Schopenhauer, held at the University of Texas at San Antonio, November 6, 2013.

NOTES

1. WWR1, 575 (SW7, 99).

2. *Die Fröhliche Wissenschaft*, [*The Gay Science*], section 99, "Schopenhauer's Followers," Friedrich Nietzsche, *Samtliche Werke: Kritische Studenausgabe, Vol. 3*, edited by Giorgio Colli and Mazzino Montinari (München:Deutscher Taschenbuch Verlag, 1980), 454. The first passage that Nietzsche places in quotation marks, "das Sterben ist eigentlich der Zweck des Daseins," appears to be a paraphrase of WWR2$_{[P]}$, 637 (SW3, 732), where Schopenhauer writes, "Das Sterben ist allerdings als der eigentliche Zweck des Lebens anzusehen." The second quoted material is from PP1, 268 (SW5, 324). For the way in which Schopenhauer's view of compassion can be viewed as a form of clairvoyance, see my "Compassion as Moral Clairvoyance: The Core of the Poodle," *Schopenhauer - Jahrbuch* 93 (2012), 19–29.

3. Friedrich Nietzsche, *Morgenröte: Gedanken über die moralischen Vorurteile* [*Daybreak: Thoughts on Moral Prejudices*], section 142, Nietzsche, *Sämtliche Werke, Vol. 3*, 136. In one of his later manuscripts, Schopenhauer observed: "the fearful aversion, which many people have for toads and which must rest not on a physical or an aesthetic, but on a metaphysical basis. In this connection, we have still to reflect that from time immemorial toads have been used for the arts of magic" (MR4, 384).

4. Arthur O. Lovejoy, "Schopenhauer as an Evolutionist," *Mind* 21 (1911), 116.

5. With the exception of "magic," I will follow Heather Wolffram, who describes "animal magnetism" or "Mesmerism" as "a system of therapeutics based on the idea that ill health is a result of imbalances of magnetic fluids within the body, which a mesmerist can redistribute by means of magnetic strokes. In some patients the application of Mesmerism leads to a state of somnambulism." She defines "somnambulism," as "a state of sleep, or half-waking trance, spontaneously or artificially induced—i.e., through Mesmerism or hypnosis—in which complex intellectual tasks can be carried out and in which paranormal abilities such as clairvoyance and telepathy are sometimes exhibited"; "clairvoyance" as "the faculty of perceiving events in the future and beyond normal sensory contact"; "telekinesis" as "the ability to move objects at a distance by mental or other non-physical means"; and "telepathy" as "the communication of thoughts and ideas by means other than the known senses"; see her *The Stepchildren of Science: Psychical Research and Parapsychology in Germany, c. 1870–1939* (Amsterdam/New York: Rodopi, 2009), 5–6. Schopenhauer defined something as "…*magical*, whereby we denote something which, without being a *natural force*, and consequently without having the limits of a natural force, nevertheless exercises over nature a power which is therefore inexhaustible, infinite and eternal, that is to say outside of time…." (MR1, 205). Black magic is practiced for harmful ends, according to Schopenhauer, whereas white magic is practiced for salutary ends.

6. Schopenhauer here is referring to the *Bhagavad Gita*.

7. See PP1, 268 (SW5, 324) for Schopenhauer's account of his clairvoyance.

8. Schopenhauer's posthumous library contained more than a hundred books on paranormal phenomenon; see *Randschriften zu Büchern* in HN5 (287–318).

9. In "Essay on Spirit-Seeing and Related Themes," Schopenhauer refers to Kant's essay, accepting the claim that Kant had demonstrated the failure of spiritualist explanations of spirit apparitions. In a commitment that Schopenhauer saw as faithful to Kant, Schopenhauer calls his explanation "idealistic" (PP1, 200 [SW5, 243]). Schopenhauer

viewed "spiritualism" as a form of substance dualism, holding that the subject of cognition is an "immaterial substance," whereas the object of cognition is a material substance. He contrasted this with materialism, which holds that both subject and object are material substances (see WWR2$_{[P]}$, 13 [SW3, 16]).

10. See Diethard Sawicki's excellent study, *Leben mit den Toten: Geisterglauben und die Entstehung des Spiritismus in Deutschland 1770–1900* (Paderborn, München, Wien, Zürich: Ferdinand Schöningh, 2002).

11. For Fichte and animal magnetism, and Schelling and magnetism, somnambulism, and clairvoyance, see, respectively, Sawicki, *Leben mit den Toten*, 141 and 146–49; for Hegel, see *Hegel's Philosophy of Mind*, translated by William Wallace (Oxford: Clarendon Press, 1971), 4–7, 27, 68, 101, 103, and 109; and Stefan Andriopoulos, *Ghostly Apparitions: German Idealism, the Gothic Novel, and Optical Media* (New York: Zone Books, 2013), 49–71.

12. *Arthur Schopenhauer: Gespräche*, edited by Arthur Hübscher (Stuttgart-Bad Cannstatt; Friedrich Frommann Verlag Günther Holzboog, 1971), 127. Schopenhauer was referring specifically to his work on the metaphysics of sexual love and spirit-seeing (*Geistersehn*), both of which he recognizes as including claims that transcend the bounds of all possible experience. In addition to Sawicki, see, for example, Wolffram, *The Stepchildren of Science*, 46–48. For a thorough account of Schopenhauer's work on occult phenomena in the context of the second half of the nineteenth century, see Segala, Marco, *I fantasmi, il cervello, l'anima Schopenhauer, l'occulto e la scienza* (Florence: Leo S. Olschki, 1998).

13. It is not uncommon for Schopenhauer to use the terms "philosophy" and "metaphysics" interchangeably. For example, Schopenhauer writes: "It is true that philosophy has as its object experience; however, not like the other sciences this or that specific experience, but rather experience itself, generally and as such, according to its possibility, its scope [*Gebiete*], its essential content, its inner and outer elements, its form and matter" (PP2, 21 [SW6, 19]).

14. See WWR1, 453–54 (SW2, 505–06).

15. At this point he does not say what this riddle is, assuming that his reader recalls an earlier and somewhat prescient discussion (for our topic) in the second book of *The World as Will and Representation*, where he raised the question of the meaning (*Bedeutung*) of representations; that is, whether the world is nothing more than representation and is, therefore, something akin to either an "insubstantial dream or ghostly phantasm" (WWR1, 123 [SW2, 118]). The quote is from §18, where Schopenhauer articulates a new type of truth, the "*philosophical truth par excellence*," that the body is identical to the will. In his *On the Fourfold Root of the Principle of Sufficient Reason* he recognized four types of truth: logical, empirical, transcendental, and metalogical. He then also claims that "the subject of cognition, appearing as an individual, is given the solution to this riddle: and this solution is will" (WWR1, 124 [SW2,119]). The riddle later assumes a deeply existential tone. It becomes the "ever-disquieting riddle [*stets beunruhigende Räthsel*]" (WWR2$_{[P]}$, 171 [SW2, 189]), by Schopenhauer's connecting the human need for metaphysics to a form of philosophical astonishment prompted by the realization of the ubiquity of suffering and death.

16. The translations from WWR2 are my own.

17. At WWR2$_{[P]}$, 201, Schopenhauer refers to the chapter "Physical Astronomy," from *On Will in Nature*, where he claims to have used inner experience as the key for connecting inner and outer experiences; see WN, 394–400 (SW4, 84–94).

18. David W. Hamlyn views Schopenhauer as employing an "argument to the best explanation" in favor of his metaphysics (i.e., his metaphysics of will yields the best explanation of

experience as a whole). See Hamlyn's "Why Are There Phenomena?" in *Zeit der Ernte: Studien zum Stand der Schopenhauer-Forschung, Festschrit für Arthur Hübscher zum 85. Gerburtstag*, edited by Wolfgang Schirmacher (Stuttgart/Bad Cannstadt: Frommann/ Holzboog, 1982): 343.

19. By basing his metaphysics on experience, Schopenhauer is well aware that he surrenders any claims regarding certainty; see WWR2$_{[P]}$, 181 (SW3, 202). He also holds that we cannot obtain a complete and exhaustive explanation of existence; see WWR1, 455 (SW2, 507).

20. See John Locke, *Essay Concerning Human Understanding, Vol. 1* (New York: Dover, 1959), 122.

21. Schopenhauer will frequently refer to the objects of the outer sense "consciousness of other things" and the inner sense as "self-consciousness"; see, for example, FW, 40 (SW4, 14) and FW, 50 (SW4, 26).

22. In reference to Schopenhauer's claim that the inner experience of will is an experience of the thing-in-itself "under the lightest of veils," Sebastian Schmid raised the obvious question: "Was ist überhaupt ein halb verschleiertes Ding an sich? Schwerlich wird man sich hierunter etwas denken können" [Whatever is a partially veiled thing in itself? It will be difficult to be able to think of anything by this concept], see Schmidt's *Schopenhauer's Willensmetaphysik in ihrem Verhältnis zu neueren Ansichten über den Willen* (Leipzig: 1894), 12.

23. Schopenhauer decries the Post-Kantian philosophers Jacobi, Fichte, Schelling, and Hegel for trying to fashion out of Kant's notion of theoretical reason some oracle with a privileged access to the supersensible; see FR, 116 (SW4, 123) and WWR1, 551 (SW2, 618).

24. For an account of the development of Schopenhauer's view of will as thing in itself in the second edition of *The World as Will and Representation*, see Cartwright, "Two Senses of 'Thing in Itself' in Schopenhauer's Philosophy," *Idealistic Studies* 31, no. 1 (Winter 2001), 34–37.

25. Later, he writes about "metaphysics in the narrower sense," as proceeding from appearances to "*that which appears*, to that which is hidden behind the former, hence *ta meta ta physica* [τὰ μετὰ τὰ φυσικά, that which comes after physic]," (PP2, 21 [SW6, 19]), thereby returning to a somewhat Aristotelian view of metaphysics.; also see the following note.

26. Schopenhauer quotes from one of Kant's pre-Critical works, his first book, the 1746 *Gedanken von der wahren Schätzung der lebendigen Kräfte* [*Thoughts on the True Estimation of the Vital Forces*], §51: "It is apparent that the original sources of the effects of nature must absolutely be the subject of metaphysics" (WN, 325 [SW4, 5]). This remark was added to the second edition of WN (1854).

27. When visiting patients of a well-known advocate and practitioner of animal magnetism, Karl Wolfart, Schopenhauer claimed to have managed to induce a state of somnambulism in a woman simply by looking at her; see Cartwright, *Schopenhauer: A Biography*, Cambridge: Cambridge University Press, 2010), 442–43.

28. In a passage that Schopenhauer would drop from the second edition of his main work, he claimed "I would like to apply to this property [of will's objecthood (*Objektität*)] an unusual and indeterminate word that is in fact badly regarded, but is fitting for a property in respect of which the will as thing in itself is utterly opposed to all things in nature. I would like to call it the magic of the will, for in this concept we are thinking of something that, despite not being any natural force, and consequently not being subordinated to the laws of nature and restricted by them.... [L]ike a magician, it [will] calls into visibility things that for us are of the greatest reality, but that in respect of the will are merely reflections of

its essence.... The use of the word magic is just a thoroughly causal comparison, though, and no more weight should be placed upon it, nor will further use be made of it" (WWR1, 575 [SW7, 99]).

29. In addition, Schopenhauer found a connection between compassion, animal magnetism, and magic, classifying them, along with sexual love, as forms of "Sympathy [*Sympathie*]"; that is, of forms of "The empirical emerging of the metaphysical identity of will through the physical multiplicity of will's appearance" (WWR2$_{[P]}$, 602 [SW3, 691–92]). In this regard he referred to animal magnetism, magic, and compassion as "practical metaphysics," as expressions of what (theoretical) metaphysics describes; see WN, 408 (SW4, 102) and BM, 245 (SW4, 260).

30. See William von "Der Frankfurter Skandal um den Magnetiseur Ragazzoni," *Frankfurter Allgemeine Zeitung*, December 31, 1957, for scandals associated with Ragazzoni's Frankfurt act. Two Frankfurt physicians interviewed Ragazzoni in his apartment and found him incapable of reproducing the feats of his stage act. Hübscher cites Schröder in Arthur Schopenhauer, *Gesammelte Briefe*, edited by Arthur Hübscher (Bonn: Bouvier, 1987), 593.

31. Schopenhauer holds that "Individuality is also inherent in will, insofar as the character is individual; however, this [character] is annihilated [*aufgehoben*] in the denial of will. Thus individuality is inherent in will only in its affirmation and not in its denial" (WWR2$_{[P]}$, 609 [SW2, 700]). Perhaps ghosts are the dead who did not deny will (no wonder that they are troubled!). Ultimately, how deeply the roots of individuality go in the being itself in the world is a question that Schopenhauer holds cannot be answered since it entails an answer that is transcendent; see WWR2$_{[P]}$, 641 (SW3, 736–37). Also see Damir Barbarić, "Der Weg durch das Ding an sich. Schopenhauers Versuch über das Geistersehn," *Schopenhauer-Jahrbuch* 93 (2012), 176.

32. One could argue that Schopenhauer is suggesting that space, time, and causality are also features of will. However, it appears that he has ruled out that possibility; see Sandra Shapshay's "Did Schopenhauer Neglect the 'Neglected Alternative' Objection?" *Archiv für Geschichte der Philosophie* 93.3 (2011): 321–48.

33. Schopenhauer, *Gesammelte Briefe*, 217; Schopenhauer to Becker, September 21, 1844. This sort of reply falls short of calling his analysis of paranormal phenomena a "metaphysical fantasy," as he called his analysis of the belief in "special providence, or else in the supernatural guidance of events in the course of an individual's life... and is even found, firmly and unshakably, in thinking minds averse to all superstition" (PP1, 177 [SW5, 213]). Of course the title of this essay from which this quote was taken tells it all: "Transcendent Speculation on the Apparent Deliberateness in the Fate of the Individual." Schopenhauer also claimed that some of his work on the metaphysics of sexual love involved transcendent claims (see WWR2$_{[P]}$, 533 [SW3, 609]). Sandra Shapshay claims that Schopenhauer's designation of the thing in itself as "will" is a metonymical identification (see her "Poetic Intuition and the Bounds of Sense: Metaphor and Metonymy in Schopenhauer's Philosophy," in *Better Consciousness: Schopenhauer's Philosophy of Value*, edited by Alex Neill and Christopher Janaway [Malden, MA: Wiley-Blackwell, 2009], 58–76, and her Chapter 6 in this volume).

34. See WWR1, 129 (SW2, 125).

35. Gottlieb Florschütz argues that Schopenhauer's account of extrasensory perception as an emanation from a metaphysical will established a philosophical foundation for modern parapsychology long before parapsychology was established as a "science"; see his "Schopenhauer und die Magie: die praktische Metaphysik?" *Schopenhauer- Jahrbuch* 93 (2012), 483.

36. Psychologist Terence Hines observes "Many theories have been proposed by parapsychologists to explain how psi [psychic phenomena] takes place. To skeptics, such theory building seems premature, as the phenomena to be explained by the theories have yet to be demonstrated convincingly"; see his *Pseudoscience and the Paranormal* (New York: Prometheus, 2003), 14.

FURTHER READING

Andriopoulos, Stefan. *Ghostly Apparitions: German Idealism, the Gothic Novel, and Optical Media*. New York: Zone Books, 2013.

Barbarić, Damir. "Der Weg durch das Ding an sich. Schopenhauers Versuch über das Geistersehn." *Schopenhauer- Jahrbuch* 93 (2012): 175–82.

Cartwright, David E. "Compassion as Moral Clairvoyance: The Core of the Poodle." *Schopenhauer Jahrbuch* 93 (2012): 19–29.

Cartwright, David E. *Schopenhauer: A Biography*. Cambridge: Cambridge University Press, 2010.

Cartwright, David E. "Two Senses of 'Thing in Itself' in Schopenhauer's Philosophy." *Idealistic Studies* 31, no. 1 (Winter 2001): 31–53.

Florschütz, Gottlieb. "Schopenhauer und die Magie: die praktische Metaphysik?" *Schopenhauer- Jahrbuch* 93 (2012): 471–84.

Hamlyn, David W. "Why are there Phenomena?" In *Zeit der Ernte: Studien zum Stand der Schopenhauer-Forschung, Festschrit für Arthur Hübscher zum 85. Gerburtstag*, edited by Wolfgang Schirmacher. Stuttgart/Bad Cannstadt: Frommann/Holzboog, 1982, 335–43.

Hegel, Georg Wilhelm Friedrich. *Philosophy of Mind*, translated by William Wallace. Oxford: Clarendon Press, 1971.

Hines, Terence. *Pseudoscience and the Paranormal*. New York: Prometheus, 2003.

Kant, Immanuel. *Gedanken von der wahren Schätzung der lebendigen Kräfte und Beurteilung der Beweise derer sich Herr von Leibniz und andere Mechaniker in dieser Streitsache bedienet haben, nebst einigen vorhergehenden Betrachtungen welche die Kraft der Körper überhaupt betreffen*. Königsberg: Martin Eberhard Dorn, 1746.

Kant, Immanuel. *Prolegomena zu einer jeden künftigen Metaphysic, die als Wissenschaft wird auftreten können*. Riga: F. J. Hartknoch, 1783.

Kant, Immanuel. *Träume eines Geistersehers, erläutert durch Träume der Metaphysik*. Königsberg: Johann Jakob Kanter, 1766.

Locke, John. *Essay Concerning Human Understanding, Vol. 1*. New York: Dover, 1959.

Lovejoy, Arthur O. "Schopenhauer as an Evolutionist." *Mind* 21 (1911): 195–222.

Nietzsche, Friedrich. *Die Fröhliche Wissenschaft*. In *Samtliche Werke: Kritische Studenausgabe*, 3, edited by Giorgio Colli and Mazzino Montinari. München: Deutscher Taschenbuch Verlag, 1980, 320–663.

Nietzsche, Friedrich. *Morgenröte. Gedanken über die moralischen Vorurteile*. In *Samtliche Werke: Kritische Studenausgabe*, 3, edited by Giorgio Colli and Mazzino Montinari. München: Deutscher Taschenbuch Verlag, 1980, 12–312.

Sawicki, Diethard. *Leben mit den Toten: Geisterglauben und die Entstehung des Spiritismus in Deutschland 1770-1900*. Paderborn, München, Wien, Zürich: Ferdinand Schöningh, 2002.

Schmid, Sebastian. *Schopenhauers Willensmetaphysik in ihrem Verhältnis zu neueren Ansichten über den Willen*. Leipzig: NC, 1894.

Schopenhauer, Arthur. *Randschriften zu Büchern, Volume 5 of Arthur Schopenhauer, Der handschriftliche Nachlaß*, edited by Arthur Hübscher. München: Deutscher Taschenbuch Verlag, 1985.

Segala, Marco. *I fantasmi, il cervello, l'anima Schopenhauer, l'occulto e la scienza*. Florence: Leo S. Olschki, 1998.

Shapshay, Sandra. "Did Schopenhauer Neglect the 'Neglected Alternative' Objection?" *Archiv für Geschichte der Philosophie* 93, no. 3 (2011): 321–48.

Shapshay, Sandra. "Poetic Intuition and the Bounds of Sense: Metaphor and Metonymy in Schopenhauer's Philosophy." In *Better Consciousness: Schopenhauer's Philosophy of Value*, edited by Alex Neill and Christopher Janaway. Malden, MA: Wiley-Blackwell, 2009, 58–76.

Wolfram, Heather. *The Stepchildren of Science: Psychical Research and Parapsychology in Germany, c. 1870–1939*. Amsterdam/New York: Rodopi, 2009.

CHAPTER 11

··

THE MYSTERY OF
FREEDOM

··

PILAR LÓPEZ DE SANTA MARÍA

IN 1838, Schopenhauer submitted an essay for a contest that the Royal Norwegian Society of Sciences had established in the previous year, wherein he tried to answer the question of whether it is possible to prove the freedom of human will from self-consciousness. He won the first prize at the beginning of 1839, and, by 1841, had published his paper along with a second essay, "On the Basis of Morality" (*Über die Grundlage der Moral*), although the latter had worse luck with the Royal Danish Society of Sciences, having received no prize in spite of its having been the only essay submitted. The joint publication was entitled *The Two Fundamental Problems of Ethics*, and it was the only monographic work on this subject that he published.

Schopenhauer's first essay, *On the Freedom of the Human Will* (*Über die Freiheit des menschlichen Willens*), takes as its motto and conclusion the phrase *La liberté est un mystère* (freedom is a mystery). He attributed it to Malebranche, though it seems to have been Helvetius who used these words to describe Malebranche's opinion.[1] But the mystery of freedom did not date from either Helvetius or Malebranche; it went back long before. Since the pre-modern age, its troublesome and simultaneously undeniable character had become obvious, raising perplexity in those who reflected upon it. In this way, freedom had to face successively theology, science, and philosophy, coming to occupy an increasingly more exiguous and ethereal place within human consciousness.

The great Greek and Roman thinkers set freedom as the target of their reflections in its individual as well as its social side, and, in this way, they inspired later Christian authors. However, since Saint Augustine (widely quoted in Schopenhauer's work) the major question to discuss was the conflict between human freedom and the truths of faith, especially in relation to the problem of evil. In his fight against the Manichaean, Augustine turned to human freedom to avoid attributing the evil in the world to the Creator. But then he found himself needing to reconcile freedom with the goodness of creation, divine omnipotence, God's prescience, or the need for grace—problems in which he committed his best, providing a solution that would continue to be discussed in the centuries to come.

In Modernity, theology yielded the protagonism to the New Science. This, driven by Galileo's hypothetical-deductive method and the introduction of mathematics into the "book of nature", was striving to present a universe ruled by the strictest necessity. But, at the same time, Modernity witnessed a second, opposing phenomenon: the demand of the struggle for freedom in all spheres of individual, political, and social life. As Rüdiger Safranski says: "That is modernity: a longing for freedom and, simultaneously, an awareness of a necessity of Being shown to us by sciences."[2]

Philosophy could not be oblivious to all this: it remained largely involved with the problems of theology and continued to question the problems that occupied Saint Augustine, especially the "problem of theodicy"—a problem that became acute as a result of the Lisbon earthquake of 1755. On the other hand, modern science exerted a great influence on philosophy, which, still unrecovered from the Renaissance crisis, set knowledge up as its central problem and gave rise to rationalism, which sought to operate *more mathematico* and impose deductive inference as the only method of the knowledge.

With this background, it is not surprising that freedom appears clad with mystery throughout the entire Schopenhauerian treatise. Moreover, bearing in mind that Schopenhauer is the forerunner of contemporary irrationalism, which holds that questions of greater relevance to human life are beyond the reach of reason and dwell in the realm of what, as Wittgenstein would say, cannot be expressed or explained but only shown: namely, the metaphysical meaning of the world. But precisely because of this, it is not surprising that freedom appears not only in Schopenhauer's ethics, but also in the different chapters of his system, from the theory of knowledge to his metaphysics, and from his aesthetics to the denial of will, always accompanied by the same evident and inexplicable character. From this conviction, I will examine the different contexts in which freedom emerges and the different configurations it adopts in a journey that, like that of Schopenhauer's own treatise, begins as it ends: in the mystery of freedom.

The treatise *On the Freedom of the Human Will* (FW) is the center of reference of our examination and will require special attention. From there, we examine the role of freedom in other chapters of the Schopenhauerian system.

11.1 FREEDOM AND THE PRINCIPLE OF SUFFICIENT REASON

On the Freedom of the Human Will addresses the problem of freedom from the standpoint of the theory of knowledge and focuses on developing relationships (or, better, the conflict) between a model of knowledge governed by the principle of sufficient reason (PSR) and the awareness that each one has to be the agent of his or her actions. So it is not surprising that it has as antecedent and as an assumption the dissertation that Schopenhauer wrote as a doctoral thesis and that took the name of *On the Fourfold Root of the Principle of Sufficient Reason*. There Schopenhauer presents the PSR as the law that governs without exception, the linking of all our representations or, in other words, all possible objects for a subject. These representations can be of four kinds: (1) complete empirical representations, (2) abstract representations (concepts), (3) pure intuitions (space and time), and (4) acts of will.

In view of this fourfold division, Schopenhauer establishes the roots upon which this universal principle is based. Despite its different configurations, it retains the same validity and applies with the same necessity: (1) the PSR of becoming (causality), (2) that of knowing, (3) that of being in space and time, and (4) that of wanting or law of motivation. It is precisely this latter law with its corresponding representations (the acts of will) that constitutes the focus of the treatise on freedom.

In fact, the dissertation is more than a merely preliminary foundation: rather, we can say that everything Schopenhauer says about the freedom of human actions is already decided in it. Thus in §49, entitled *Necessity*, it is said: "The principle of sufficient reason in all of its forms is the sole principle and the sole support of any and all necessity.... For *being necessary* can never mean anything other than following from a given ground.... Being necessary and following from a given ground are convertible concepts" (FR, 146). The four types of necessity corresponding to the forms of the principle are listed here, the last of which is "moral necessity, according to which any human being, and even any animal, upon the appearance of a motive, must carry out the only action which is in conformity with his innate and inalterable character" (FR, 147).

From there, *On the Freedom of the Human Will* begins by stating the negative character of the concept of freedom: by this term, we mean only the absence of obstacles. In the case of physical freedom (freedom of actions), this negative character can be translated into a positive one: being free would mean that one can do what one wants; that is, act according to one's will. But this is not the case with moral freedom (that of the will itself), which is the focus here, granted that we would be led to a tautological concept of freedom that would be expressed as "I can want what I want."

Faced with this difficulty, Schopenhauer resorts to the premises set forth in the dissertation to define freedom as "the absence of all *necessity*" and to reproduce his earlier definition of what is necessary as "*that which follows from a given sufficient ground*" (FW$_{[C]}$, 38). Since "the *contingent*[3] will be considered to be the opposite of *necessity*," it follows that "the free, the distinguishing mark of which is absence of necessity, must simply be independent of any cause, whereby the *absolutely contingent* will be defined" (FW$_{[C]}$, 39).

We see, then, that Schopenhauer does not hesitate to immediately link the PSR with necessity, converting sufficient reason into forced reason and then opposing it to free action. But this approach is not new, for it appears—albeit implicitly—already since the beginning of the Modern Age, although it is Schopenhauer who uncovers it unequivocally. Hence, to properly understand the approach of our philosopher it is necessary that we go back to those who preceded him.

The PSR has always operated, in one way or another, not only in philosophy but also in the most elementary reasonings and human actions. But it is from the Modern Age that it acquires a special relevance and is introduced as a guest of honor in philosophy, hand in hand with the rationalists, who affirm it with great emphasis and make it a favorite object of their reflections. The cause of this sudden interest on that principle, which until then had been so neglected because of its obviousness, can be intuited if we consider the double meaning that the term "reason" has in languages such as English, Latin (*ratio*), French (*raison*), and Spanish (*razón*). In fact, it means either the ground or reason for being of something (assimilable in some cases to the cause), or the superior faculty of the person who characterizes it as such. As it is known, in German, these two meanings have two clearly differentiated terms: *Grund* for the first and *Vernunft* for the second.

It is clear that the PSR refers to the first meaning. But the fact that language allows us to designate with the same term two things at first sight so different indicates that between them there is a close kinship. This was especially noticed by rationalists, which is why they made the PSR one of their banners.

Actually, the relationship between the *Grund* and the *Vernunft* constitutes the nucleus of the rationalist postulate of the equivalence of the logical and ontological order, or the identity of the *ordo rerum* and the *ordo idearum*, which can be expressed in the idea of intelligibility or rationality of reality. For the latter is based on the fact that the model of the logical connection of ideas is the same as the ontological connection of phenomena; namely, the model of reason and consequence. The possibility of a rational explanation of reality demands that the course of the real can be reproduced by the order of reason, so that to the logical inference from one idea to another corresponds the causal sequence of phenomena, not being both more than two different versions of the connection between reason and consequence. Thus, the PSR is presented as the guarantor of the rationality of the real, insofar as it is only explicable by reason (*Vernunft*) that for which a reason (*Grund*), that is, a foundation, can be found. In this way, the irrational would be the random, that for which no foundation can be pointed out, and therefore no explanation at all.

But that of rationalism is not any Reason, but just the deductive Reason, the only one that can satisfy the ideal of apodictic and complete knowledge. And that means demanding of PSR much more than what itself contains. If we examine its various formulations (including that of Schopenhauer, which adopts that of Christian Wolff), we see that the only thing that it demands is that everything that happens has "a why" whose relevance is greater than the mere "just because" and is enough to account for what happened. That is to say, every phenomenon has a foundation that explains it, and nothing originates, so to speak, by magic. This is why Leibniz called it, in a letter to Nikolaus Hartsoeker, *le grand principe du pourquoi*.[4]

Thus, the PSR simply endorses the possibility of making an inductive inference from a phenomenon to its raison d'être, from *explicandum* to *explicans*. But that is not enough for the foundation of the certain knowledge that rationalism claims. It is not only a question of explaining *B* as a consequence of *A*; it must be ensured that, given *A*, it will have to be given B and only B. In other words: the certainty of knowledge requires that the inductive inference from the consequence to the ground, the only requirement established by the PSR, becomes a deduction from the ground to the consequence and, therefore, a logical implication. But that means including in the PSR the idea of necessity. So that every sufficient reason is at the same time a determinant or forced reason, and, conversely, no reason that is not determinative will be a sufficient reason nor, ultimately, reason at all.

The scope of all this related to the problem of moral freedom is easy to see: if at first freedom was opposed to necessity, and if the PSR and the rationality attached to it were opposed to chance and irrationality, respectively, now oppositions intersect. When introducing the need in the PSR and in the idea of the rational, both remain faced with freedom and this, in turn, is identified with what is random and totally irrational. The free is now simply what has no reason to be because, if it had, that reason would be determinant. This new approach, which is clearly and bluntly expressed in Schopenhauer's conceptual definitions, confronts several modern thinkers, from Descartes to Kant, with the arduous task of reconciling need and freedom. Only Spinoza and Hume are free of this problem, but for opposed reasons: Spinoza because he inscribes everything in the domain of necessity and reduces freedom to a mere power of understanding, consisting in the knowledge of the necessity that governs us; Hume because he does not need to sacrifice anything to knowledge since knowledge has been sacrificed beforehand.[5]

Descartes seems to avoid as far as possible the problem of freedom, and, on the few occasions when he deals with it, he does so preferentially with respect to the use of understanding and not to moral action. Moreover, his reflections do not go much further than considering the freedom of the will as an obvious fact[6] or conceiving the degrees of freedom in terms of indifference: "The will simply consists in our ability to do or not do something…such that we do not feel we are determined by any external force.…But the indifference I feel when there is no reason pushing me in one direction rather than another is the lowest grade of freedom."[7]

Perhaps because he is a great theorist of the PSR, it is Leibniz who, with the greatest determination, strives to reconcile the principle with free actions. Consistent with his rationalism, he expressly converts sufficient reason into a determining reason while attempting to found a freedom that is not at odds with rationality.

The starting point for this is the rejection of a freedom understood as absolute indetermination: the famous *liberum arbitrium indifferentiae*; this point with which, by the way, Schopenhauer will fully agree. For Leibniz, the freedom of a rational being not only excludes but requires determination, though not any kind of determination, but only that of Reason (*Vernunft*). According to this, free actions are those that have their sufficient and determinant reason (*Grund*) in Reason (*Vernunft*). Freedom is rational determination or, in Leibniz's words, "spontaneity according to Reason." To avoid the need this implies, Leibniz introduces the notion of inclining or predominant reasons which do not compel the will but incline it in a particular direction. With these inclining reasons we return to the previous "weak" version of the PSR, but limited to human actions, while the events of the natural world are still ruled by necessity. Thus, Leibniz seeks to reconcile need and freedom, but the problem shifts to another place: how to justify that duplicity of reasons and different applications of the PSR.

We see how the gnoseological demands of rationalism leave the possibility of freedom in a very precarious situation. Kant, on the other hand, is not willing to give up on the pretensions of scientific knowledge and follows the path of rationalists, albeit using the new resources provided by transcendental idealism. In it, the PSR acquires a validity unknown until then, by means of becoming, no longer a necessary law of the objects but even a condition of them: "Thus the principle of sufficient reason is the ground of possible experience, namely the objective cognition of appearances with regard to their relation in the successive series of time."[8] The law of causality governs without exception or qualification within the scope of all phenomena, including human actions, which could be calculated with the same certainty as the eclipse of the moon or sun on the condition that the empirical character of a person and the motives that act upon that person should be absolutely known.[9]

Kant finds no snag at not making room for freedom in a world governed by necessity because he has another world to locate it in: the intelligible world. This is reflected in the inspired pages of the Third Antinomy,[10] where he explains the possibility of reconciling causality through freedom with the universal law of natural necessity and establishes the famous distinction between the empirical character and the intelligible character that later plays an important role in Schopenhauer's thought. With this Kant solves many of the problems that his predecessors had raised, albeit at the cost of raising new ones.[11]

11.2 From *Operari* to *Esse*

After this brief journey through some predecessors, we find the paradox that is precisely Schopenhauer, the great irrationalist and the outspoken defender of experience, who carries to its ultimate consequences one of the central theses of rationalism (which Rationalists had never done), although he does so by relying on some of the results of his teacher, Kant. Following the line marked by both, Schopenhauer assumes the conception of sufficient reason as forced reason and its opposition to freedom. From there, he maintains that acts of will, like any other phenomena, are subject without exception to the PSR, which in this case appears as a law of motivation and dictates that no act of the will originates without a sufficient reason. Once the motive is given, however, the act of the will occurs in a necessary way. Motivation is defined as "causality that occurs through *cognition*" (FW$_{[C]}$, 59) and supposes a maximum distance and disproportion between cause and effect, but in no way a diminution of the necessity with which the cause acts: "...as little as a ball on a billiard table can be set into movement before it receives a nudge, just so little can a man rise from his chair before a motive draws him away or compels him, but then his arising is as necessary and inevitable as the roll of a ball upon a nudge" (FW$_{[C]}$, 70).

Schopenhauer is thus in a position to respond properly to the question posed by the Royal Society: self-consciousness can do no more than hold on to the statement, "I can do what I will"; it speaks only of the relation of his *doing* to his *willing*. But this is a mere physical freedom, the freedom of doing ($FW_{[C]}$, 52). Only the consciousness of other things is capable of pronouncing on moral freedom (of wanting), and it does it categorically: "You can *do* what you *will*: but in any given moment of your life, you can only *will* one definite thing and absolutely nothing other than this one" ($FW_{[C]}$, 52).

So, I cannot will what I want: my willing is determined by the causes (motives) that are presented at any moment, but not only by them: for, just as the efficacy of causes and stimuli supposes the natural force that manifests itself in each body, so the action of motives has an assumption: character, which is the specially and individually determined nature of the will in each person and configures the receptivity to motives. Schopenhauer characterizes it as individual, empirical, constant, and innate. But this empirical character has as its condition and foundation the intelligible character, that is, the will as thing in itself, which transcends the phenomenon and its forms. And just as Schopenhauer takes from Kant the distinction between empirical and intelligible character, he adopts a scholastic maxim to express the necessity of a person's will: *operari sequitur esse*. Our acts of will are not a first principle but the necessary manifestation of what we are ($FW_{[C]}$, 73ff).

In this way the PSR expels freedom from the scope of the phenomenon and clears the way to natural necessity. But although the answer has been reached, Schopenhauer's treatise does not end here. For he knows that no matter how much freedom is attacked, it remains knocking at the door of our consciousness in the form of a peculiar fact: "This is the perfectly clear and certain feeling of *responsibility* for that which we do, of *accountability* for our actions, resting on the unshakeable certainty that we ourselves are the *doers of our deeds*" ($FW_{[C]}$, 112). It is that fact of consciousness—moral responsibility—that puts us on the track of "*true moral freedom*, which is of a higher sort" ($FW_{[C]}$, 112). As has been said, even when the motive necessarily acts, it does so only under the assumption of character. So the motive would not have been effective and the action would not have occurred if the character in question had been another. Guilt or merit do not really address what we do, but what we are, even though we are only aware of what we are from what we do. And since where responsibility lies freedom must also be located, this not a property of an individual's action, but of the intelligible character that constitutes the individual's essential being. Thus, moral freedom can only exist as transcendental freedom in an intelligible world in which the PSR is not in force.

At this point, we can appreciate that Schopenhauer's posture poses more problems than it solves. To mention only a few, we can first wonder to what extent we can speak of moral imputability where the PSR is no longer valid, for responsibility and with it, freedom, excludes not only the necessary causality, but also the absence of all causality. One is not responsible for what one has been forced into, nor for what has simply happened to one. In other words, responsibility (and with it, freedom) is opposed to necessity, but not to a lesser extent to chance. Schopenhauer intends to resolve this by transferring the imputability of acts to the *esse*, but, as we shall see, it merely increases the problem and turns freedom into pure irrationality.

Furthermore, it is questionable how Schopenhauer articulates the relationship of the empirical to the intelligible character. Thus, on the one hand, we cope with a character that is depicted as individual, empirical, constant, and innate: it is clear that such a character has to belong to the world of experience (and therefore of necessity), thus constituting the phenomenal *esse* of man, which would be the manifestation or objectification of the intelligible character. The problem arises when Schopenhauer speaks of virtue and vice in a clearly moral sense and relates them to the empirical character, attributing to them the same innate nature of this (FW$_{[C]}$, 78). So, how could morality derive from the empirical? Later, when he approaches transcendental freedom, the individual's *esse* is no longer the empirical character, but the intelligible one. This is the true subject to which guilt or merit and, therefore, freedom are imputed. But this intelligible character (and this is where the problem becomes acute) is conceived as different in different individuals.

The ethical difference of characters, to which is dedicated §20 in the second treatise, is one of the pillars of Schopenhauer's ethics: on it is based his rejection of the *liberum arbitrium indifferentiae*, and it explains the great difference that exists in the moral conduct of people. But this difference comes into direct conflict with transcendental idealism insofar as it affects something that transcends the forms of the phenomenon and is therefore alien to the *principium individuationis*; namely, the moral character. Schopenhauer is aware of the problem and has no qualms about confessing it. This can be seen in the Manuscripts of 1833, where he wonders about the root of ethical diversity, concluding by saying: "Perhaps there will come someone behind me to enlighten and clarify that abyss" (MR4, 193–94).

Years later, in the second volume of *Parerga and Paralipomena*, Schopenhauer abounds in the subject to more explicitly recognize the limits of his explanation: "that *individuality* does not rest solely on the *principium individuationis* and so is not through and through mere *phenomenon*, but that it is rooted in the thing-in-itself, the will of the individual; for his character itself is individual. But how far down its roots here go, is one of those questions which I do not undertake to answer" (PP2$_{[P]}$, 227). And presently, after recognizing the "*immeasurable difference of the inborn moral dispositions of individuals*" (PP2$_{[P]}$, 229), he adds to the mystery of freedom that of the ethical difference of characters: "That we are so fundamentally different in this main point is, however, a great problem and indeed a mystery" (PP2$_{[P]}$, 229).

The third problematic point is the attribution of the freedom to the *esse* on the part of Schopenhauer. Two questions immediately arise:

1. If freedom is in the *esse*, should not responsibility fall exclusively on the author of being?
2. According to Schopenhauer, we are and feel responsible for who we are; that is character. But could we really have been others? This question, however, cannot receive a full answer until later, when we refer to the denial of the will.

The first point, however, presents no difficulty to Schopenhauer, who responds with a resounding *yes*: according to the *operari sequitur esse*, we can only be and feel responsible for what we are. But this in turn is only possible insofar as our own being is our work: if we were mere creatures, then guilt and merit for our being and our acts would ultimately have to go back to our Creator, just as, if the clock is malfunctioning, the clockmaker is responsible. Henceforth, the consequence is self-evident: the freedom of the will has as its condition its aseity.

> I freely admit that to think of the moral responsibility of the human will without its aseity exceeds my power of comprehension.... The responsibility falls back on the one ... whose work is the person with such inclinations. For this reason, the person is responsible for his doings only in the case that he himself is his own work, i.e., has aseity.   (FW$_{[C]}$, 96–97)

Thus, we find here a striking paradox from the historical point of view: if until now the existence of a Creator God had been an indispensable foundation of morality, either as a dogma or as a postulate of moral praxis, it now becomes an incompatible assumption with human morality itself. And religion not only becomes unable to ground an ethic, but closes the way.

Freedom has become omnipotence, as the young Schopenhauer's program statement said: "So far, philosophers have made great efforts to teach freedom of will: I, however, will teach the *omnipotence of the will*" (HN1, 239). But, also, the subject of freedom has been transformed: it is evident that the will of which we speak here is no longer the one for whose liberty the Norwegian Academy asked. The creature has become Creator, and being free is not equivalent simply to not being constrained, but to be owner and master of all reality. Here echo the famous words of Friedrich Schlegel: "Man is free whenever he produces or manifests God, and through this he becomes immortal."[12] Freedom ceases to be human freedom to become the property of an absolute being that reminds us of the God of Spinoza. Not in vain does Schopenhauer quote the Dutch thinker to support his conception of freedom as aseity (FW$_{[C]}$, 96). But it is not precisely a God governed by the geometrical order that we are going to find, but a thing in itself ruled by chaos, confusion, and absurdity.

We have thus reached the point where freedom has left the ethical ground to enter into metaphysics. It is no longer acting or wanting what is at stake, but the being of the world, which depends entirely on the will. For here lies precisely its omnipotence: that from it comes, not only its action, but also its world.[13] This way, we are led from the mystery of freedom to the enigma of the world and existence that philosophy seeks to decipher. The question about the human will ends in the will as a thing in itself, the essence and nucleus of all that exists. The freedom of that metaphysical will is simply that it lacks reason, purpose, and target since it is beyond the forms of the phenomenon and the PSR. To that is finally reduced the intelligible freedom: to the irrationality of a thing in itself that is anything but intelligible.

Certainly, the will unveils the enigma of our own essence and that of the world through the inner experience of our own body. But from there, what it offers us is darkness, contradictions, and unreason; not in vain, its freedom and omnipotence coincide with its irrationality. But it offers us even more: because that of the will has nothing to do with the idyllic life of a deity installed in his particular Eden, but with an eternal damnation to dissatisfaction; it is a will that "must live on itself, since nothing exists besides it, and it is a hungry will" (WWR1$_{[P]}$, 154).

We see how freedom shows us its worst face here: it is a will that fights itself through its phenomena, generating all the pain of the world. In its omnipotence, it is incapable even of willing, because its willing is in the end only a mere privation, which, in its irrationality, does not admit questions of any kind because it transcends the domain of PSR, the only one containing reasons and answers. Now the only reason is the absence of reason (WWR2, 640–41). However, things do not end here. For Schopenhauer still presents us a new aspect of freedom: that which passes through knowing.

11.3 FREEDOM THROUGH KNOWLEDGE

We have seen that for Schopenhauer necessity is tied to the domain of theoretical knowledge of the Reason, whereas freedom is linked to the mere absence of reason. The world of phenomena, ruled by the PSR, delimits the "demonstrable fatalism" with respect to nature; this can in turn be completed and surmounted by a "transcendent fatalism" that finds internal planning and need in the lives of individuals (PP1$_{[P]}$, 202–205). Beyond this world, a freedom understood as aseity, irrationality, and lack of foundation prevails. However, in Books III and IV of *The World as Will and Representation*, the Schopenhauerian perspective of the topic gives a radical twist and we are shown a freedom that to a great extent contradicts the theses developed previously—the freedom that passes through knowledge. But, of course, this is not knowing through the PSR, devoted to where, when, and why, but that which refers to the "what" of things and from which philosophy, art, and the liberation of the world are born (WWR1$_{[P]}$, 274). Here we will not speak so much about freedom *of* the will as about freedom *from* the will: in the first case it is the pure subject of knowledge that is freed from the servitude of the will; in the second, it is the will itself that frees itself from its own contradiction thanks to knowledge, arriving at its own self-denial.

In art, in fact, we are shown a cognitive subject—the genius—involuntary but free, because its intelligence has managed to emancipate itself from the servitude of the will. Let us recall that for Schopenhauer knowledge has a secondary nature; the original is the will, which generates knowledge as an instrument and puts it at its service to be provided with motives for its wanting.

However, there are individuals whose cognitive forces exceed the measure necessary for that service, so that they can temporarily cease to fulfill their mission to devote themselves to the pure contemplation of things and to grasp in them their eternal forms:

namely, Platonic Ideas. That is aesthetic experience, and its subject is "the man of genius, whose power of knowledge is, through its excess, withdrawn for a part of his time from the service of his will, dwells on the consideration of life itself, strives to grasp the Idea of each thing, not its relations to other things" (WWR1$_{[P]}$, 188). A man of genius is doubly free, both from the objective and the subjective point of view: genius is free from natural necessity because it contemplates Ideas, which are not subject to the PSR nor to the forms of the object. Genius is also free from the subjective point of view because it has freed itself from the servitude of the will. Anyone who contemplates Ideas is no longer an individual subject, yielding to the pains of existence, but the pure subject of knowledge, the unique eye of the world (WWR1$_{[P]}$, 197–98). And just as before freedom presented its worst face, now we find the opposite: the enjoyment of contemplation not disturbed by the agitations of the will nor touched by the horror of existence. That is why art has something of catharthis in Schopenhauer, since in it the will presents its "friendly face" and allows us to contemplate it and its objectifications, purified of its radical evil.[14]

The freedom provided by art and the knowledge from which it is derived is, as it happens in ethics, as undeniable as it is inexplicable. The contemplation of Ideas and—in the case of music—of the will itself has as irrefutable proof the work of art, which is also the means by which the genius tries to transmit to us, as much as possible, that knowledge given to few. But how the man of genius comes to that state and what that knowledge consists in is something that neither he nor anyone else can account for. Here we are confronted with intuitive knowledge, not with the concept, which is as sterile for art as for ethics; hence, neither genius nor virtue can be taught (WWR1$_{[P]}$, 206, 271). The capture of Platonic Ideas possessed by genius is no exception to the rule that no intuition is communicable. At most, we can approach that uptake according to the measure of our intellectual capacities thanks to the work of art. But that approach will never be complete because only a genius can have ears for the wisdom that the work of art pretends to tell. That is why "the most excellent works of any art, the noblest productions of genius, must eternally remain sealed books to the dull majority of men, and are inaccessible to them. They are separated from them by a wide gulf, just as the society of princes is inaccessible to the common people" (WWR1$_{[P]}$, 234).

The work of art brings together the evidence and the mystery of art: it is proof of the artist's intuition but, at the same time, contains within itself the secret that none of the other humans are capable of deciphering. A similar role is played by moral goodness and asceticism, as they appear in the fourth book of *The World as Will and Representation*. And, analogous to that of art, it is also the source from which both sprout: intuitive knowledge, in which the will reaches full self-consciousness and can achieve self-denial (WWR1$_{[P]}$, 288).

Contemplation, as we have seen, frees the genius both from the PSR and from the servitude of the will. But this release is transient. Full and definitive freedom is only achieved by the practical route, which presents two stages: moral goodness and denial of the will.

If freedom is mysterious in Schopenhauer, no less is it the source and foundation in which he places moral goodness: compassion. It is "the great mystery of ethics" (BM$_{[C]}$,

213, 231, 270), the original phenomenon from which all actions of moral value are born and which, despite its evidence, is absolutely inexplicable. Compassion arises from some knowledge analogous to art, which transcends the forms of the phenomenon. But it is not Ideas that are now captured, but the essential identity of all beings, once man pierces the barriers of individuality and tears the "Veil of Maya." Then the other is not "Not-I", but "I once more" (BM$_{[C]}$, 269), and their pleasure or pain may be reasons for my wanting exactly like mine.

The second fundamental difference with art is that the knowledge reached here does not provide any kind of pleasure; on the contrary, the individual knows and appropriates the pain of all beings and a horror is born in him toward the will that causes it, which in some cases reaches a final liberation namely, the denial of the will.

Now is the time to return to the question that we left in abeyance: could we have been others? If this means that a person is able to choose how he or she wants to be, as some old theories suggest, Schopenhauer's answer is no, since in that case knowledge would have to be prior to the will, when it is just the other way around. For him, on the contrary, the individual:

> "is his own work prior to all knowledge, and knowledge is merely added to illuminate it. Therefore he cannot decide to be this or that; also he cannot become another person, but he *is* once for all, and subsequently knows *what* he is. With those other thinkers, he *wills* what he knows; with me he *knows* what he wills." (WWR1$_{[P]}$, 293)

However, there is something in which the individual is able to choose, at least in some cases: it is choosing between wanting or not wanting. That is what the liberty of *esse* ultimately points to: namely, the possibility of continuing to affirm the will or deny it. The latter is the path of asceticism. Asceticism starts from the same knowledge that gives rise to compassion and goes a step beyond, since it is not confined to seek the good of others, but proposes the direct and intentional denial of the will in the phenomenon of oneself: the body. In it the will, enlightened by knowledge, notices the vanity of its endeavors and, so to speak, "throws in the towel," and opts for the path of nothingness rather than continuing to engage in a wanting that only perpetuates an irremediable absurdity. This is the transition from the freedom of the *voluntas* to the freedom of *noluntas* [non-willing] and the state of the great liberation: because it is the will that frees itself from itself.

This transition from the state of nature to the order of salvation is to Schopenhauer's eyes the only occasion in which freedom manifests itself in the phenomenon (WWR1$_{[P]}$, 288). Although rare, its evidence is, if anything, greater than that of art and morality. To prove it there are numerous cases that appear above all in the asceticism and mystique of Christianity and the great Eastern religions. These conquerors of the world are then left only as pure knowing beings, as the undimmed mirror of the world. Nothing can distress or alarm them any more; nothing can any longer move them (WWR1$_{[P]}$, 390). They have reached the highest wisdom but cannot transmit it because their state is only accessible to their own incommunicable experience (WWR1$_{[P]}$, 410).

The cycle of freedom is thus definitively closed: the mystery of freedom which Schopenhauer echoed in his essay ends up finally revealing itself as identical with the order of salvation and grace—"now we unexpectedly see both coincide into one and can understand in what sense the admirable Malebranche could say: "*La liberté est un mystère*," and he was right. For just what the Christian mystics call the *effect of grace* and the *new birth*, is for us the only direct expression of the *freedom of the will.... Necessity is the kingdom of nature; freedom is the kingdom of grace*" (WWR1$_{[P]}$, 404).

NOTES

1. See Arthur Hübscher, "La liberté est un mystère," *Schopenhauer-Jahrbuch* 45 (1964), 26–30.
2. Rüdiger Safranski, *Schopenhauer and the Wild Years of Philosophy*, translated by Ewald Osers (Cambridge, MA: Harvard University Press, 1991), 309.
3. It should be noted that the German term *zufällig* employed by Schopenhauer means "contingent" or "casual," which has important implications for the concept of freedom that we cannot explore more deeply here.
4. G. W. Leibniz, Letter to Harsoecker, July 12, 1711, in *Die philosophischen Schriften von Gottfried Wilhelm Leibniz*, herausg. von C. J. Gerhardt, III, 529 (Berlin: Weidmann, 1875).
5. Hume is in this sense the counterpoint of rationalism: on the one hand, he shares with the rationalists the opposition between freedom and necessity and the identification of the former with chance, which leads him to deny it and affirm the necessary character of human actions. But, on the other hand, the concept of necessity has radically changed here, and it is no longer a rational implication, but a union of a lively idea and a present impression, which is run by an associative mechanism of imagination. The Humean need is so weak that, far from impeding the freedom of human actions, it manages to suppress fatalism in nature. This is pointed out in the following words of his *Treatise*: "Let no one, therefore, put an invidious construction on my words, by saying simply, that I assert the necessity of human actions, and place them on the same footing with the operations of senseless matter. I do not ascribe to the will that unintelligible necessity, which is suppos'd to lie in matter. But I ascribe to matter, that intelligible quality, call it necessity or not, which the most rigorous orthodoxy does or must allow to belong to the will. I change, therefore, nothing in the receiv'd systems, with regard to the will, but only with regard to material objects" (David Hume, *A Treatise of Human Nature* [Oxford: Clarendon Press, 1789], 410).
6. René Descartes, *Meditations on First Philosophy*, in *The Philosophical Writings of Descartes*, Vol. II, translated by John Cottingham and others (Cambridge: Cambridge University Press, 1984–85), 9.
7. René Descartes, *Principles of Philosophy*, in *The Philosophical Writings of Descartes*, vol. I, p. 40.
8. Immanuel Kant, *Critique of Pure Reason*, translated by Paul Guyer (Cambridge: Cambridge University Press, 1998), 311, B246.
9. See *Critique of Practical Reason*, translated by Mary J. Gregor (Cambridge: Cambridge University Press, 1996), 219.
10. See *Critique of Pure Reason*, 535–36, B 566–67.
11. Among them, and to name someone, how transcendental freedom can be conceived as a special kind of causality (*Critique of Pure Reason*, 485, B 473) when causality is a category of understanding that is only valid in the realm of phenomena.
12. Friedrich Schlegel, *Ideen*, in *Kritische Friedrich-Schlegel-Ausgabe*. Erste Abteilung, Band 2, Hg. v. Ernst Behler (Paderborn, Ferdinand Schöningh, 1967), 29.

13. "In the light of our whole view, the will is not only free, but even almighty; from it comes not only its action, but also its world; and as the will is, so does its action appear, so does its world appear; both are its self-knowledge and nothing more. The will determines itself, and therewith its action and its world also; for besides it there is nothing, and these are the will itself" (WWR1[ₚ], 272).

14. See Pilar López de Santa María, "Art as Catharsis in Arthur Schopenhauer," *Schopenhauer Jahrbuch* 73 (1992), 159–62.

FURTHER READING

Hübscher, Arthur. "La liberté est un mystère." *Schopenhauer-Jahrbuch* 45 (1964): 26–30.

Janaway, Christopher. "Necessity, Responsibility and Character: Schopenhauer on Freedom of the Will." *Kantian Review* 17, no. 3 (November 2012): 431–57.

López de Santa María, Pilar. "Art as Catharsis in Arthur Schopenhauer." *Schopenhauer Jahrbuch* 73 (1992): 159–62.

Safranski, Rüdiger. *Schopenhauer and the Wild Years of Philosophy*. Translated by Ewald Osers. Cambridge, MA: Harvard University Press, 1991.

PART III

AESTHETIC EXPERIENCE, MUSIC, AND THE SUBLIME

CHAPTER 12

....

CLASSICAL BEAUTY AND
THE EXPRESSION OF
PERSONAL CHARACTER
IN SCHOPENHAUER'S
AESTHETICS

....

ROBERT L. WICKS

AMONG the areas in which Arthur Schopenhauer's philosophy has had a substantial cultural impact is aesthetics. His theory of music influenced Richard Wagner especially, and when we recall a movie such as Hitchcock's *Psycho* and remember the screeching violins that accompany the murder-in-the-shower of Janet Leigh's character, Marion Crane—a cinematic screech that has now become iconic—we hear the implicit impact of Schopenhauer and Wagner upon the soundtrack's composer, Bernard Herrmann (1911–1975), as the tension in the violins' sound resembles and reinforces the emotional tension of the brutal scene.

Wagner's music is the grandfather of today's motion picture music, having inspired some of the finest contemporary composers for the cinema, such as John Williams. As an example of its own cinematic appropriateness, Wagner's music appears powerfully in a well-known scene in *Apocalypse Now* (1979), when a set of attacking helicopters blast the "Ride of the Valkyries" (c. 1854) through their loudspeakers to intimidate a targeted village. Inspired by Schopenhauer's theory of music, Wagner influenced future generations of composers in his ability to sustain the flow of emotion in the musical work by constantly deferring the feeling of resolution. Alessandro Pinzani describes this Wagnerian technique well.

> In a sense one could claim that the whole *Tristan and Isolde* is just a single suspension, since the real resolution only occurs as the last chord of the opera. The Tristan chord with which the opera starts contains two dissonances and only one of them is

resolved, while the resolution of the other is prolonged – and this goes on for the whole opera: every resolved chord is followed by an unresolved one, so that the hearer remains at the same time satisfied and unsatisfied and the suspense is maintained until the end.[1]

In contrast to his theory of music, Schopenhauer's theory of beauty has been less influential. This is partly because, unlike his theory of music, it ostensibly accounts for the experience of beauty in reference to entities the reality of which is uncertain: namely, Platonic Ideas. Much nonetheless can be said in favor of Schopenhauer's theory of beauty, for its emphasis on the apprehension of idealized forms captures a significant aspect of how we appreciate natural and artistic beauty. What is more, the experience of apprehending idealized forms permeates Schopenhauer's aesthetics as a whole, including his theory of music.

As is true for most aesthetic theories that appear during the nineteenth century and before, Schopenhauer's aesthetics was not composed as a stand-alone theory. It serves and supplements a larger philosophical project that rests on the following propositions: (1) as far as we can tell, all of reality is nothing more a single, unitary, senseless, driving impulse; (2) the lives of sentient beings are constituted by this impulse and are consequently filled with desire, frustration, and suffering; and (3) the best response to this situation is to adopt attitudes that minimize desire and hence minimize suffering. Schopenhauer refers to this impulse as "will" (hereafter capitalized for clarity). There is only Will, and we humans, along with everything else that exists, are manifestations of this senseless impulse.

The structure of Schopenhauer's metaphysics is pantheistic or, on some interpretations, panentheistic, except that the single being that constitutes everything is not, as would be the case in a pantheistic framework, divine, holy, moral, or intelligent, but rather mindless and well beneath any moral ascriptions. One could call Will demonic, but this would impart too much intelligence and self-conscious immorality, for Will is a dumb and insensitive impulse. Nonetheless, a more appropriate adjective than "pantheistic" for describing Schopenhauer's characterization of ultimate reality would be "pandemonic."

Schopenhauer's metaphysics entails that all individuals come into the world as self-enclosed centers of Will and, as such, find themselves immediately pitted against one another in a perpetual struggle to continue their existence. Since Will constitutes everything, desire and frustration permeate experience, where, for any one desire that is satisfied, there will, so to speak, always be at least ten more that remain unsatisfied. A feeling of futility consequently defines ordinary human existence, as it compares to an intense and relentless itch that, when scratched, only returns to itch with the same intensity after a short period of respite.

Given the nature of Will, Schopenhauer finds it morally repugnant to be constituted by an energy of this kind—one that manifests itself as a world within which each individual feeds upon another and where the whole feeds upon itself, like the mythological serpent that eats its own tail, the ouroboros. The cannibalistic nature of Will appalls him, and he feels disgusted with himself for being constituted by it. He thus seeks to divest himself of his own being, appreciating with some philosophical worry that as he struggles to wash the moral stain of reality from himself, he is metaphysically none other than that very stain.

After reflecting on the accumulated suffering of all sentient beings, Schopenhauer concludes that a world containing such widespread suffering is one whose existence is regrettable and, from a moral standpoint, ought not to be. A significant aspect of his philosophical project, noticeably Buddhistic, accordingly explores ways to diminish suffering, all of which involve minimizing the force of the individual will, which is the force of reality itself. His aesthetic theory primarily serves this tranquillizing purpose as it presents one of the main ways that Will, in its manifestation as self-conscious, morally aware human beings, subdues itself and generates peace of mind.

Upon this background, this chapter interprets Schopenhauer's theory of beauty, which constitutes the bulk of his aesthetics, through his quasi-autonomous theory of music to illuminate some problems involved with the artistic representation of personal character. The main presentation of Schopenhauer's aesthetics and theory of beauty is in Book III of the first volume of *The World as Will and Representation*, which is composed of twenty-two sections (sections 30–52) wherein the last section (52) discusses music separately as an art with unique metaphysical characteristics. This concluding section on music is not a mere appendix, but neither does it reside at the core of Schopenhauer's aesthetics, which centers on the theory of beauty. The theory of music nevertheless illuminates his aesthetics as a whole: when applied to the art of representing the human being, as in painting or sculpture, we will see that it discloses the limits of classical beauty as a representational style. This will become evident in view of a problem we will now consider: Schopenhauer's aesthetics promotes classical beauty, which, when applied to portraiture, expresses a generic ideal of human character, but his conception of the human being as a manifestation of insatiable Will implies that virtually all representations of individual people as beautiful are misrepresentations.

To appreciate this peculiar feature of classical beauty within the context of Schopenhauer's aesthetics, consider the transformation in the appearance of the painting that figures centrally in Oscar Wilde's novel, *The Picture of Dorian Gray* (1890). The painting is portrayed effectively in the 1945 motion picture version of the work, where, as it reflects the experiences of the main character, Dorian Gray, it begins with a beautiful appearance and ends with a horrible one. In the motion picture version, the transformation is represented by two different paintings. When Gray first views the portrait of himself, he is impressed with its beauty but is also saddened: it makes him realize that he will age and degenerate while the painting will remain beautiful in the years to come. His consequent wish is that the painting will age in his place and that he will remain always young, handsome, and attractive. Gray is magically granted his wish, but he soon discovers that the portrait gradually displays not only his age, but his increasingly corrupt character, which he grows to despise.

As seen in the 1945 motion picture, the first of these paintings, by the Portuguese artist, Henrique Medina (1901–1988), classically and beautifully portrays Dorian Gray with an idealized physical appearance as tall, handsome, elegant, wealthy, young, composed, strong, and inspiring, as he was initially. The second, by the American painter, Ivan Albright (1897–1983), presently hanging in the Art Institute of Chicago, more expressionistically portrays Gray in his later condition with a horrifically distorted physical appearance that reveals his corrupt soul. Together, the two paintings juxtapose Gray's attractive outer appearance and his repulsive inner character.

Owing to the tranquility of mind that the apprehension of Platonic forms provides, as well as the metaphysical location of Platonic Ideas in Schopenhauer's metaphysics as standing transcendently above the changes in the spatio-temporal world, Schopenhauer's aesthetics, with its emphasis on the experience of beauty, prima facie directs us toward the beautiful painting of Gray that obscures his corrupt character, rather than toward the distorted, emotionally upsetting painting of Gray that reveals it.

In accord with Schopenhauer's manifest aesthetic preference for beauty as a means to tranquility, his prescription for aesthetic experience directs us to contemplate the beautiful painting, apprehend Gray's idealized human form, much as we would that of a classical Greek statue, appreciate the timeless Platonic form that informs it, achieve a sense of detachment from the ordinary, spatio-temporal world, and experience a consequent peace of mind. The situation, however, is confusing: the kind of truth that is being apprehended and appreciated in this transcendent and detached state of awareness is unclear for the idealized form of Gray's physical appearance does not convey or express Gray's evil character, but instead presents him misleadingly as attractive and respectable.

Since Schopenhauer's philosophical disposition is to advocate truth over illusion, it is important to understand how his aesthetics can accommodate instances where a beautiful portrait of a person, as it generates a transcendent peace of mind in the contemplation of its beauty, simultaneously conveys a false impression of the person's character. The problem is significant in general but is particularly acute in Schopenhauer's aesthetics, for, as we can infer from his characterization of the human condition, almost all beautiful portraits must be counted as misrepresentations since ordinary human experience is marked by frustration, selfishness, disappointment, and disillusionment in a continual striving to satisfy desire. Contrary to how people are in general—and for Schopenhauer worse yet, since their inner character tends to be represented through the repulsive image of Dorian Gray—beautiful portraits, with rare exceptions, misrepresent individuals as having an ideal state of mind, tranquil and at peace with themselves and the world.

Although the main exposition of his aesthetic theory does not convey this impression, Schopenhauer does appreciate how the experience of beauty harbors deception. He states the following, for example, which we can keep in mind to set the scene for the rest of our inquiry: "an optimist tells me to open my eyes and look at the world and see how beautiful it is in the sunshine, with its mountains, valleys, rivers, plants, animals, and so on. But is the world, then, a peep-show [*ein Guckkasten*]? These things are certainly beautiful to behold, but to be them is something quite different" (WWR2$_{[P]}$, 581).

12.1 SCHOPENHAUER'S THEORY
OF BEAUTY

Schopenhauer characterizes the experience of beauty as follows, in a well-known excerpt:

> [R]elinquish[ing] the ordinary way of considering things...we no longer consider the where, the when, the why, and the whither in things, but simply and solely the *what*. Further, we do not let abstract thought, the concepts of reason, take possession of our consciousness, but, instead of all this, devote the whole power of our mind to perception, sink ourselves completely therein, and let our whole consciousness be filled by the calm contemplation of the natural object actually present, whether it be a landscape, a tree, a rock, a crag, a building, or anything else. We *lose* ourselves entirely in this object, to use a pregnant expression; in other words, we forget our individuality, our will, and continue to exist only as pure subject, as clear mirror of the object, so that it is as though the object alone existed without anyone to perceive it, and thus we are no longer able to separate the perceiver from the perception, but the two have become one, since the entire consciousness is filled and occupied by a single image of perception. If, therefore, the object has to such an extent passed out of all relation to something outside it, and the subject has passed out of all relation to the will, what is thus known is no longer the individual thing as such, but the *Idea*, the eternal form, the immediate objectivity of the will at this grade. Thus at the same time, the person who is involved in this perception is no longer an individual, for in such perception the individual has lost himself; he is *pure* will-less, painless, timeless *subject of knowledge*...Now in such contemplation, the particular thing at one stroke becomes the *Idea* of its species, and the perceiving individual becomes the pure *subject of knowing*.   (WWR1$_{[P]}$, 178–79)

Schopenhauer describes here what he believes happens naturally when we are perceptually captivated by a beautiful natural object, as when walking through the forest and seeing an especially attractive flower. His description, however, does not encapsulate his intentions well. If we adhere to his direction and "devote the whole power of our mind to perception, sink ourselves completely therein, and let our whole consciousness be filled by the calm contemplation of the natural object actually present," the probable result would be to attend to the object's perceptual details at a higher level of intensity than usual, such that the object's individuality would become more, rather than less, pronounced. By "losing ourselves" perceptually in the object, a more existential grounding in the "here and now" naturally follows, along with a consequent step away from, rather than toward, a universalizing state of mind.[2] If this is where Schopenhauer's description for the experience of beauty actually leads, it is important to consider what modifications in our aesthetic awareness would be required to generate the kind of experience he has in mind, for he is indeed describing a genuine and specific kind of aesthetic experience.

A way to understand Schopenhauer's account of the experience of beauty more clearly is through Kant's aesthetics. To experience an object's pure beauty, Kant prescribes that we attend exclusively to the object's spatio-temporal form and reflect simply on the configuration's degree of systematicity, introducing no background conception of the kind of object we are judging, and by further disregarding whether or not the object actually exists. Kant maintains that the more systematic the form, the more beautifully it will resonate with our cognitive faculties. It could be a dream image that we are judging aesthetically, with the same resulting feeling of beauty.

In this situation, we are appreciating the object's presentation of intelligent design in reference to its pure configuration. Kant expresses this technically by saying that we apprehend the purposiveness (*Zweckmäßigkeit*) in the object's design without assigning any specific purpose (*Zweck*) to the design or object. We do not apply any defining concepts to the object, but appreciate the sheer intelligibility of its form, left uninterpreted.

This is not Schopenhauer's account of beauty, but he has something similar in mind that relates closely to this Kantian notion of apprehending the "purposiveness without purpose" that an object's design conveys. If we understand Kant's account of pure beauty as involving a teleologically oriented awareness that attends to the sheer "form" of teleology, appreciating merely that the object's form displays a noticeable degree of "designedness," "purposiveness," or "teleological suggestiveness" and make a small modification, then the kind of aesthetic awareness that Schopenhauer is prescribing presents itself.

Akin to the teleologically oriented awareness that Kant describes is another kind of teleologically oriented awareness that operates when we survey a set of forms and imagine, through a process of visual implication, a perfected version of those forms. This is the kind of awareness referred to when it is said that artists present in their imagery a completion or perfected version of what nature only imperfectly presents.[3] It is a process of idealization, where one apprehends a bird on the beach, perhaps with some ruffled feathers and bumps on its beak and legs, and imagines for oneself a more idealized image of the bird. Traditional portraiture is often described along these lines. Hegel gives a clear statement, for example:

> But even the portrait-painter, who has least of all to do with the Ideal of art, must flatter, in the sense that all the externals in shape and expression, in form, colour, features, the purely natural side of imperfect existence, little hairs, pores, little scars, warts, all these he must let go, and grasp and reproduce the subject in his universal character and enduring personality. It is one thing for the artist simply to imitate the face of the sitter, its surface and external form, confronting him in repose, and quite another to be able to portray the true features which express the inmost soul of the subject.[4]

Although the Dorian Gray example renders it questionable that the artistic idealization of a person's physical features typically results in the expression of "the inmost soul of the subject," as Hegel seems to assume, Schopenhauer's account of the perception of beauty rests on this idealizing style of awareness. If we sink ourselves perceptually into the object, attend to it alone, and introduce a process of idealization into our perception, we will apprehend imaginatively a version of the object in its ideal form. If done successfully, it is possible to imagine the object acquiring, one can say, a "shining" quality as we perceive it with an imaginative superimposition of the perfected form that the given, existential form suggests. A traditional portrait painter would have this kind of teleologically oriented awareness as a matter of course, or, as Schopenhauer describes such a person, an artistic genius, who has a natural ability to discern the inherently beautiful form implicit in any given face or object.

> In the true genius this anticipation is accompanied by a high degree of thoughtful intelligence, so that, by recognizing in the individual thing its Idea, he, so to speak, understands nature's half-spoken words. He expresses clearly what she merely stammers. He impresses on the hard marble the beauty of the form which nature failed to achieve in a thousand attempts, and he places it before her, exclaiming as it were, "This is what you desired to say!"   (WWR1$_{[P]}$, 222)

If this style of awareness is projected on every object in the perceptual field, the result will be to perceive the physical world as containing objects wherein each shines forth as an ideal version of itself. This would yield a transfiguration of the commonplace world insofar as each ordinary object would be perceived as having the image of its perfected form superimposed upon it. Such a thoroughly idealized visualization of the physical world can be referred to as a "heavenly," "fairyland," or "wonderland" vision of the world. An artistic genius would live in this kind of satisfying scene, as universal forms present themselves in every surrounding item and at every turn of the glance.

In reference to any given object's form, there are, though, different levels of idealization that can be constructed. One can look at a seagull with its ruffled feathers and imagine that particular seagull as appearing more perfect without the ruffled feathers, idealizing that particular seagull. One can also think more broadly, not about this or that particular seagull, but of "the" seagull, as might be depicted in the archetype or generic anatomical drawing for the bird species. This is the level of idealization Schopenhauer has in mind when he states that, in our aesthetic perception, "the particular thing at one stroke becomes the *Idea* of its species."

The process of idealization is central in this kind of aesthetic, where art's main purpose becomes the depiction of universal types. At a familiar level, an example would be wedding portraits that render individuals as lovingly, beautifully, and perfectly as possible. Such portraits remain focused on the particular individuals and do not extend the process of idealization to the point of rendering a person's more individualistic characteristics indiscernible. At a higher level of idealization are classical Greek statues that come closer to presenting the generic human form in a perfected manner. Standing midway between the wedding portraits and the Greek statues are many Roman sculptural portraits that idealize the individuals but display more of the abstract Greek character.

The limits of this aesthetics of idealized images are clear with respect to portraiture, for it is sufficient to consider in contrast why Rembrandt's self-portraits are so impressive. It is not because he presented himself more attractively, without wrinkles or warts.

He admits imperfections and uses them to reveal a depth of character that escapes rendition by mathematically perfected and polished facial shapes. His concern is not with the portrait's beauty, but with its profundity or expressiveness, appreciating that a more nuanced, truer presentation of character can be achieved by departing from what nature ideally intends in its physical forms.

With this notion of expressiveness in view, we can turn to Schopenhauer's theory of music, which can be applied retrospectively to his account of painting and the visual arts to illuminate some differences that attend utilizing classical beauty as opposed to more expressionistic ways to represent personal character.

12.2 SCHOPENHAUER'S THEORY OF MUSIC

Schopenhauer's theory of music is grounded on his leading metaphysical claim that ultimate reality is a timeless, blind, senseless impulse that is best described as "Will." He maintains that, as far as its appearance to us is concerned, Will manifests itself immediately and *directly* as a set of timeless and tranquil Platonic Ideas and *indirectly* through these Ideas as the violent spatio-temporal world within which we live and die. As we have seen, Schopenhauer describes the experience of beauty in nature and art as the apprehension of Platonic Ideas, accessible through a disinterested, teleologically oriented, idealizing attitude that is directed toward some physical object. The experience of beauty does not bring us into direct contact with ultimate reality, or Will, but into contact with the immediate objectifications of Will, namely, Platonic Ideas.

Music is an art, though, that according to Schopenhauer brings us into closer contact with Will and, by implication, into closer contact with the complexity of emotional life. He characterizes music as a copy of Will and explains this in two complementary ways, one of which draws an analogy to Platonic Ideas and the other of which refers to the structures of the flow of our emotional experience. Before describing these, it will be helpful to add a brief historical remark about Schopenhauer's claim that music is a copy of Will.

It might sound strange or implausible for Schopenhauer to assert that music is a copy of Will, but his view is more traditional than it seems. We can see this by recalling Hegel's definition of beauty as the sensuous appearance of the divine, where he understands "the divine" to be reason. In this definition, Hegel modifies in an abstract and philosophical way the familiar, religiously grounded thought that beauty is the sensuous appearance of God by replacing "God" with "reason." In the same spirit, Schopenhauer's assertion that music is a copy of Will implicitly replaces "God" with "Will." This leads him to assign to music the highest metaphysical status among the fine arts, thereby bringing music into a more intimate relationship to metaphysical truth than those arts whose aesthetic satisfaction rests on the experience of beauty as the apprehension of Platonic Ideas.

Schopenhauer elaborates on the superior significance of music by drawing an analogy between what he understands to be music's fundamental structure and the hierarchy of Platonic Ideas that give shape to the spatio-temporal world. He maintains that the relationship between bass, harmony, and melody in music, as well as the hierarchical relationship of overtones that occur when a bass note is struck, is analogous to the structure of the set of Platonic Ideas that, in their hierarchy, define what has been called the "great chain of being": the bass is analogous to Platonic Ideas of inanimate nature, harmony to Ideas underlying the plant and animal kingdom, and melody to those underlying humans and their activity. In this respect, music embodies the entire world by analogy. Playing music is isomorphic to the full play of Platonic Ideas as they stand as the underlying patterns of the physical world.

It is easy to judge this parallelism between music and Platonic Ideas as too arbitrary to support the view that music is special among the arts. One might, for example, construct analogies to the set of Platonic Ideas using light, asserting that the primary colors are analogous to Platonic Ideas of inanimate nature, secondary colors to those underlying the plant and animal kingdom, and tertiary colors to those underlying humans and their activity. Or, one might compare white light to Will and the various colors to the objectifications of Will.

Schopenhauer maintains in addition, however, that music has a special significance in view of how the structures of individual musical works are isomorphic with the abstract structures of emotional experience, where the latter are understood to be manifestations of Will. The exact nature of the isomorphisms is vague, but he is appreciating how musical patterns of tension and resolution, movement and pause, loudness and softness, etc., resemble the structures of our emotional life, as mentioned at the beginning of this chapter. Since the isomorphisms are abstract, music expresses emotions without representing the specific events that would render the feeling of sadness, for example, painful. Moreover, insofar as music embodies the forms of emotional experience, it allows us to understand the essences of emotion, considered generally as "sadness itself," "joy itself," and so on.

Schopenhauer does not develop the important idea that the expression of emotion in music can involve resemblances to typical behaviors that attend ordinary emotional expression, but this lacuna in his theorizing does not affect the point at hand. We need only appreciate that, for Schopenhauer, music presents a complicated, painless, and essentialistic rendition of the structures of emotional life; brings us closer to ultimate reality as Will and does not involve an experience of beauty as the apprehension of Platonic Ideas.

Music can be harsh, discordant, and expressive of turbulent emotions. It can also be beautiful, and Schopenhauer offers some reflections on this. To explore them, it will help to consider the notion of idealization as it appears in music and in Schopenhauer's aesthetics as a whole, for this bears on how music can be beautiful, even though music does not involve the apprehension of Platonic Ideas, but instead more directly embodies Will.

Despite how beauty is not an aspect of Schopenhauer's definition of music as a copy of Will, a process of idealization—a process at the very basis of beauty—is present that establishes a connection to his theory of beauty as involving the apprehension of Platonic Ideas. First, as noted, Schopenhauer holds that music expresses the essences of emotional life such as "sadness itself" or "joy itself." These are not Platonic Ideas, understood as the natural kinds that underlie the objective structure of the material world, but are rather idealizations of emotional experience. Just as for any individual rose, or starfish, or piece of gold there is a Platonic Idea that would be the ideal rose, ideal starfish, and ideal gold, for any individual experience of sadness, joy, etc., Schopenhauer recognizes idealizations that he calls "sadness itself," "joy itself," etc., that underlie the individual experiences of sadness, joy, and other emotions. It is uncommon, but perhaps not too implausible, to speak of ideal joy, ideal sadness, ideal horror, and so on, despite the vagueness of such notions. A writer, for instance, might aim to have one of the characters in a novel embody ideal horror or ideal sadness. Such idealizations operate in Schopenhauer's theory of music, and they help link the theory of music to his theory of beauty.

There is yet another presence of idealization in music, usually gone unnoticed, that lends more substance to Schopenhauer's claim that music is a copy of Will in its analogy to the set of Platonic Ideas, as well as his appreciation of beauty in music. Schopenhauer does not mention this dimension of idealization, but Kant does. In ordinary life, we are surrounded by noise, chatter, talk, rumblings, and such, all constituted by mixtures of sounds of different tones and qualities, somewhat like mud. Pure tones, as we might hear from a tuning fork, are less common and can be understood as idealizations or perfections of the mixed-up sounds that constitute ordinary life. The sound of a tuning fork compares to light from a laser beam, constituted as it is by waves that are of a single wavelength. Pure colors are similar and are more prevalent in our experience. In their purity, Kant observes that they are beautiful.[5]

If we understand music fundamentally as the harmonious combination of pure sounds (if we exclude ambient noise as a kind of "music," for example), not only can we start to explain the pleasantness in the sound of a flute or a choir of voices, we also can more effectively draw the Schopenhauerian analogy between music and the entire play of Platonic Ideas that Schopenhauer saw as special to music. A work of music constituted by a set of pure sounds in sequence, harmony, and development would, as constituted by pure sounds, each of which compares to an idealized Platonic Idea, be a small world of its own, analogous to the actual set and play of Platonic Ideas that underlie the physical world. A discordant musical piece constituted by pure tones in interaction, as we might find in atonal music, would present abstract structures reminiscent of a tortured world filled with imperfection and more akin to the imperfect spatio-temporal world in which we live but still constituted by pure tones as its elements, each of which is beautiful on its own. A harmonious musical piece, as we might find in Mozart, would present abstract structures reminiscent of a happier, pleasant, and idealized world, not unlike the fairyland-like vision of the world that we described earlier as the apprehension of the physical world as manifesting beauty throughout, through the idealization of each object's shape and color.

Schopenhauer appears to have appreciated this idealized foundation of music in a set of pure tones, for he concludes his discussion of the metaphysics of music in the second volume of *The World as Will and Representation* with the remark that music "so often exalts our minds and seems to speak of worlds different from and better than ours" (WWR2$_{[P]}$, 457). Without elaborating on the point, he adds a footnote that refers to the bliss experienced in yogic meditation that follows from apprehending the highest Atman, or inner self. As we have interpreted it here, the aesthetic experience of music is beautiful for essentially the same reason that the fairyland-like apprehension of the physical world as shining through with Platonic Ideas is beautiful; namely, in that it provides a relief from suffering on a par with how Schopenhauer describes the experience of apprehending "sadness itself" in music is painless and transcendent of the ordinary world of suffering.

It should now be evident that *the idealization of form* is among the leading ideas in Schopenhauer's aesthetics as a whole. It is present in his theory of beauty as the apprehension of Platonic Ideas. It is present in his theory of music insofar as he speaks of quasi-Platonic forms such as "sadness itself" and "joy itself." It is present in his theory of music insofar as pure tones—the tones whose harmonic combinations express human emotion in music—can be conceived of as idealizations of the ordinary sounds in daily experience and as the ground of beauty in music.

To bring these points to bear upon our inquiry regarding the tension between classical beauty and the expression of inner character, it is common knowledge that there can be a mismatch between how a person appears or behaves and how a person feels. Similarly, there can be a mismatch between how a person is artistically portrayed, either as beautiful or not, and how the person's character actually is. With Schopenhauer's theories of beauty and music in mind, we can return to the Dorian Gray example with which we began; namely, where a portrait presents a person as classically beautiful and where the person's character does not match. Let us then consider how some early twentieth-century painting tried to translate onto the canvas the forms associated with the musical expression of emotion.

12.3 Classical Beauty, Expressionist Truth, and the Portrayal of Personal Character

In 1912, Wassily Kandinsky (1866–1944), the well-known Russian painter, member of the Munich avant-garde artistic group, Der Blaue Reiter (The Blue Rider), and father of abstract art, published *Concerning the Spiritual in Art* (*Du Spirituel dans l'art*), where he argued for adopting methods in painting that correspond to methods in musical composition. Applying these methods to his own work and entitling his paintings "compositions," he went far in creating paintings that embody the formal abstractness and nonrepresentational quality of pure music. He was not "painting" music in the sense of constructing a series of visual images that sequentially match the tensions and resolutions in some given musical work in a one-to-one correspondence, as we see in segments of the Disney movie, *Fantasia* (1940). He was trying to create paintings whose formal composition captures—one could say objectifies—the flow of feeling that is characteristic of music. Through the expression of emotion in painting, he aimed to convey the mood or "spiritual vibration" of a given state of mind.

As they express the nuances of human feeling, Kandinsky's paintings are not beautiful in the classical sense. Neither are they unattractive. As abstract, nonrepresentational compositions, they do not achieve their expression of emotion by distorting the shapes of ordinary objects or standard patterns of bodily expression in a departure from classical idealization. His self-contained, well-organized works each present an emotional world of their own through their juxtaposition of abstract forms.

Schopenhauer, living before Kandinsky's time, was in no position to discuss abstract, nonrepresentational painting as in Kandinsky's compositions, so we can ask where Kandinsky's paintings would fit within a Schopenhauerian framework and how they might help us understand those cases where the utilization of classical beauty in the expression of personal character in a more representational, rather than nonobjective framework, becomes significantly misleading.

The suggestion here will be that, in their capacity to convey a wider spectrum of emotion and hence more individualistic expressions of emotion, expressionist paintings help foster an outlook that counterbalances the tendency toward deception that enters into portraits that embody the classical ideal of beauty. The essential claim of this chapter is that such paintings assist in reminding us that classical beauty fundamentally presents an abstract ideal of personal character, rather than references to the characters of actual individuals.

Within the parameters of Schopenhauer's aesthetics, Kandinsky's paintings, like music, would not be presenting Platonic Ideas. Similar to music, they can be regarded as copies of Will, or close correlates of Will, or perhaps even "frozen" Will that present the abstract patterns of emotional experience. That the paintings are static images does not preclude this, since paintings are experienced in time and viewers move their attention across the work in an experience filled with tensions and resolutions that parallel music. The experience is admittedly freer than that of music since there is no rigid determination of which forms one would attend to first, second, third, and so on, as is true for music. In contrast to the classical beauty that paintings can embody through the process of idealization and the respective kind of truth related to the apprehension of Platonic Ideas, Kandinsky's works can be interpreted as presenting abstract patterns of emotional experience and, in terms of Schopenhauer's aesthetics and metaphysics, a copy of Will that is closer to ultimate reality.

As it compares to music, expressionist painting within Schopenhauer's aesthetics consequently has the capacity to express a deeper level of truth than does painting that aims at classical beauty. At first sight, one would not expect this result, given how Schopenhauer devotes the bulk of his aesthetic theory to the experience of beauty as the apprehension of Platonic Ideas. This, however, is significantly because he did not live long enough to experience the early twentieth-century development of abstract painting in work such as Kandinsky's, where the art of painting blends with the art of music. Had he been aware of how painting can be so musical, he might neither have separated music from the rest of the arts as sharply as he did, nor have associated painting almost exclusively with the presentation of beauty.

One need not be an adherent of Schopenhauerian aesthetics, though, to appreciate that classical beauty operates within only a narrow band along the spectrum of emotional possibilities and is not effective in conveying the more angst-ridden kinds of emotional experience that Kierkegaard, for instance, associates with passionate subjective inwardness. Hegel was aware of this limitation when he asserted that, for us moderns, art as such is a thing of the past, identifying the ideal of art with the classical beauty of Greek sculpture. He observed that Christian and later art convey more complicated emotional states and, with this, a more realistic and truthful expression of personal individuality.

This indicates that the development of early twentieth-century abstract art was not, at its root, a reaction to photographic techniques that left artists with nothing more to do with respect to depicting the world accurately. At the end of the eighteenth and beginning of the nineteenth centuries, there emerged more influentially a strong cultural and intellectual interest in understanding unconscious, instinctual energies, individuality, and, consequently, the complex quality of a person's emotional experience. We see this, for instance, in German Romanticism and in the thought of Schopenhauer, Kierkegaard, and Freud.

Accompanying this interest in the unconscious, instinct, and individuality is a more intense sense of existentiality and a corresponding weakening of otherworldly beliefs. This is clear in the history of nineteenth-century philosophy but in the history of art as well; it is evident in how, through the intensification of existentiality and individuality in pictorial expression, the classical ideal in the tradition of neoclassical art gradually lost its transcendent appearance and plausibility after the late 1700s.

The works of Jacques-Louis David (1748–1825) from the late 1700s effectively contain the cool and distant quality characteristic of classical Greek sculpture. Those of Jean-August-Dominique Ingres (1780–1867) from the early 1800s, despite how masterfully they render the physical body, assume a more fleshy appearance, the existentiality of which begins to disrupt their ideality, as in his *La Grande Odalisque* (1814). Later in the century, William-Adolphe Bouguereau (1825–1905) presents classically rendered images, the more fleshy quality of which renders their beauty close to implausible in its inspiration. By the time we reach National Socialist art of the 1930s and 1940s, the portrayal of female nudes has gone a noticeable step beyond Bouguereau in undermining the ideal of classical beauty, for their renditions are close to pornographic. As the ideal of classical beauty became more implausible, the expressionistic style arose to express a stronger sense of individuality through a wider variety of personal feelings, often highlighting suffering, internal disharmony, and ugliness.

An appreciation for the effectiveness of expressionist art in rendering a wider variety of human emotions in contrast to the classical ideal of beauty helps explain what underlies, if subconsciously, the feeling of misguidedness that attends the National Socialist's 1937 highly publicized and attended exhibition of so-called degenerate art that ran in parallel and in contrast to their own "great German art" exhibition of the same year. The degenerate art exhibition featured expressionist works by, among other artists, Marc Chagall, Max Beckmann, Max Ernst, Lionel Feininger, Georg Grosz, Erich Heckel, Wassily Kandinsky, Ernst Ludwig Kirchner, Paul Klee, Oskar Kokoschka, Franz Marc, Piet Mondrian, Emil Nolde, and Karl Schmitt-Rottluff.

Complementing the genre paintings in the nineteenth-century style, the hallways of the great German art exhibition were filled with sculptures—many of which were excellently done—that idealized the human form in the manner of the ancient Greeks. The difference between the two exhibitions in the case of sculpture, at least, was not obviously one of artistic quality, but one of style. These reflections highlight the increasing awareness and appreciation of expressionist art as having the capability to express a wider range of emotions than the classical ideal of beauty.

Where, then, does this leave us with respect to Schopenhauer's aesthetics of classical beauty and the issue of how beautiful portraits tend systematically to misrepresent human character? One way to understand this situation is to observe that classical beauty is ambiguous in its expressiveness. Although in rare instances it can express truly the quality of a person's character, classical beauty primarily presents an abstract ideal of human personality, rendering it no surprise that its actual instantiations are so infrequent.

In this regard, an influential characterization of classical Greek sculpture from Johann Winckelmann (1717–1768) is useful to recall. Winckelmann wrote the following in his essay, "Reflections on the Imitation of Painting and Sculpture of the Greeks" (1755), stated here as it was first translated into English in 1765:

> The last and most eminent characteristic of the Greek works is a noble simplicity and sedate [tranquil] grandeur in gesture and expression. As the bottom of the sea lies peaceful beneath a foaming [raging] surface, a great soul lies sedate beneath the strife of passions in Greek figures.[6]

The image of noble simplicity and tranquil grandeur that overcomes what can sometimes be raging emotion presents an ideal character type, sublime in its combination of tranquility and agitation. Schopenhauer presents a similar ideal as the epitome of painting, somewhat less sublime, more ethereal, and more unattainable, purged of disturbing emotion in its pure beauty. His paradigm images are of the Madonna and Child.

> These presentations are in fact the highest and most admirable achievements of the art of painting, and only the greatest masters of this art succeeded in producing them, in particular Raphael and Correggio, the latter especially in his earlier pictures. Paintings of this kind are really not to be numbered among the historical, for often they do not depict any event or action, but are mere groups of saints with the Saviour himself, often still as a child with his mother, angels, and so on. In their countenances, especially in their eyes, we see the expression, the reflection, of the

most-perfect knowledge, that knowledge namely which is not directed to particular things, but which has fully grasped the Ideas, and hence the whole inner nature of the world and of life.... Here is the summit of all art that has followed the will in its adequate objectivity, namely in the Ideas, through all the grades, from the lowest where it is affected, and its nature is unfolded, by causes, then where it is similarly affected by stimuli, and finally by motives. And now art ends by presenting the free self-abolition of the will through the one great quieter that dawns on it from the most perfect knowledge of its own nature.   (WWR1$_{[P]}$, 232–33)

We started originally with a problem concerning the relationship between beauty and truth in Schopenhauer's aesthetics, where a person of corrupt character is depicted falsely as a beautiful person. It is, of course, difficult to know the exact quality of any person's character, but Schopenhauer's metaphysics implies that almost everyone is frustrated, anguished, disposed toward selfishness, and not faithfully represented by a beautiful portrait. In this respect, the juxtaposition of the two portraits of Dorian Gray is not exceptional, but is instead an intensified version of the standard human condition.

Schopenhauer admits that beauty is misleading in how it covers up suffering, and, in view of his account of the human condition, it is a misleading mode of portraying people as individuals. At the same time, he presents the beautiful Madonna and Child image as expressing the highest level of human character development, as it refers to individuals who presumably do not suffer and who are at peace with themselves. The two assertions are consistent in that the former is true of representations of actual people, whereas the latter is true as an ideal, for rarely do the two coincide.

A subsequent way to navigate between actuality and ideal is self-consciously to *resist* how beautiful portraits naturally mislead our interpretive attitude to refer to the portrayed person's actual character and to attend exclusively instead to the trans-individual ideal that the person's beautiful bodily form suggests. There are no actual individuals referred to in classical Greek sculptures, for example, but the shapes of their bodies and countenances are inspiring. From this perspective, it is beside the point that Dorian Gray has an evil character or that the people pleasingly presented in a wedding portrait actually may be tortured souls. The interest in beauty is best not conceived in connection with a reference to the character quality of the individuals portrayed, but in how a person's bodily contours and shapes convey the thought of an ideal character that is essentially independent of the individuals' actual characters.

Schopenhauer's emphasis on beauty in portraiture can consequently be understood in a classical Platonic way as intending to draw our attention to an ideal of human character that transcends all individuals. This does not imply that there are no people who embody the composure, compassion, and tranquility of character that the ideal of beauty conveys; it is that since there are so few of these saintly individuals, we can assume that most people do not have characters of this kind and that, if they do happen to have such characters, it remains immaterial to appreciating the ideal of beauty that their physical form expresses. When Stendhal wrote that "beauty is no more than the promise of happiness," he appreciated how beauty arouses and directs us toward our dreams for perfection and not to daily reality.[7]

The value of the expressionist style of portrayal resides in its contrasting capacity to refer us well to the actual character qualities of people—finite, often frustrated, fallible, striving, worried, and yearning—and to provide within the realm of artistic representation a more realistic understanding of actual individuals. Insofar as it functions as a reminder not to conceive of beauty as primarily indicative of a person's real character, it counteracts the assumptions that motivated the great German art exhibition, where its advocates presented themselves as embodiments of the ideal of classical beauty, as being peaceful, morally pure, family oriented, and socially dedicated when in fact they were substantially aggressive and murderous.

In this regard, the expressionist style of art that the exhibition of so-called degenerate art condemned stands morally as a conscience to the artistic employment of the classical ideal of beauty, for, despite the existence of saintly people, only when the ideal of beauty is perceived as an ideal, rather than as the possession of an individual or set of individuals, can it serve more universally and effectively as a source of inspiration. This is one of the more important pragmatic implications of Schopenhauer's having highlighted the apprehension of Platonic Ideas in his theory of beauty. Conversely, on the side of being more down-to-earth, it follows that a main reason why ugliness is disturbing is because it tends to display more truth than we are typically disposed to acknowledge.

NOTES

1. Alessandro Pinzani, "How much Schopenhauer is there really in Wagner?" *ethic@* 11, no. 2 (2012), 218.
2. A good example of such a down-to-earth perception is in Jean-Paul Sartre's novel, *Nausea*, where Sartre describes the perception of a tree's root in its full existential and incomprehensible detail.
3. An ancient source of this idea is Aristotle's *Physics*, Book II 199a, 16–17.
4. G. W. F Hegel, *Lectures on Fine Art, Vol. 1*, translated by T. M. Knox (Oxford: Oxford University Press, 1975), 155.
5. Immanuel Kant, *Critique of Judgment*, §14.
6. Johann Winckelmann, *Reflections on the Painting and Sculpture of the Greeks*, translated by Henri Fusseli (London: A. Millar, 1765).
7. "*La beauté n'est que la promesse du Bonheur,*" in *De L'Amour* (1822), ch. 17.

FURTHER READING

Davies, Stephen. *Musical Meaning and Expression*. Ithaca & London: Cornell University Press, 1994.
Freeland, Cynthia. *Portraits and Persons*. Oxford: Oxford University Press, 2010.
Jacquette, Dale, ed. *Schopenhauer, Philosophy and the Arts*. Cambridge: Cambridge University Press, 1996.
Kant, Immanuel. *Critique of Judgment*, translated by J. H. Bernard. London: Macmillan, 1914.
Langer, Susanne K. *Philosophy in a New Key: A Study in the Symbolism of Reason, Rite, and Art*. Cambridge, MA: Harvard University Press, 1942.

CHAPTER 13

THE GENIUS AND THE METAPHYSICS OF THE BEAUTIFUL

MARIA LUCIA MELLO OLIVEIRA CACCIOLA

SCHOPENHAUER presents his aesthetics—in the sense of a knowledge concerning beauty—in the third book of *The World as Will and Representation*, and names it the "metaphysics of the beautiful." In this chapter, we investigate what it means to understand the "doctrine" concerning the beautiful, either natural or artistic, as a "metaphysics."

The way Schopenhauer reflects on the concept of metaphysics is the key to understanding not only his aesthetics, but also his philosophy as a whole, which encompasses his epistemology and moral theory, together with his aesthetics, to constitute the wisdom about what he calls the "world."[1]

Kant's contrasting understanding of metaphysics, the guide to his entire critical project, is the main target of Schopenhauer's criticism. Indeed, what Schopenhauer considers to be Kant's "mistake," as revealed in the first paragraph of the *Prolegomena to Any Future Metaphysic*, following a Platonic inspiration, consists in defining metaphysics as the knowledge of everything that surpasses experience.[2] In his criticism, developed in the "Appendix [*Anhang*]—Criticism of the Kantian Philosophy" of the first volume of *The World as Will and Representation* (WWR1[P], 415–534)[3], Schopenhauer condemns Kant for locating metaphysics beyond the field of experience, and, therefore, for abandoning inner and outer experience, which he believes is its most profitable source. These two kinds of knowledge are united in the body—the precise point from which, for him, all metaphysical knowledge comes. Once Schopenhauer considers experience as the source of metaphysics—a source that Kant despised—his metaphysics becomes immanent. Indeed, he refers to himself an immanent dogmatist in the "Fragments of his History of Philosophy" (PP1[P], 129).

On the other hand, in his "Criticism of the Kantian Philosophy," he does not go as far, stating only that "my path lies midway between the doctrine of omniscience of the earlier dogmatism and the despair of the Kantian Critique" (WWR1$_{[P]}$, 428). The metaphysics of the beautiful, as Schopenhauer sees it, does not refer to something transcendent, where the aesthetic experience could reveal something supersensible, but refers rather to the subject's inner and outer experience concerning the beautiful, describing how it takes place in the subject. For Kant as well, aesthetic experience is subjective, and here Schopenhauer follows Kant, to whom he recognizes the great merit of giving art a "subjective direction" with the feelings of pain and pleasure, instead of explaining it as an object's quality (WWR1$_{[P]}$, 530). In philosophical aesthetics ever since Kant, the beautiful and the sublime have rarely been predicated of an object, but have been understood as states of the subject.

Kant's merit lies in investigating the emotion "in consequence of which we call the object giving rise to it beautiful, in order, if possible, to discover its constituent elements and conditions in our nature" (WWR1$_{[P]}$, 530). Nonetheless, Kant only showed the right path by suggesting the method of this investigation; he did not reach the goal, viz., the objective truth obtained from this subjective feeling.

What Schopenhauer criticizes is precisely this possibility of apprehending the beautiful by means of a judgment, namely, the judgment of taste—a statement or proposition that requires understanding, although in a manner that differs from that knowledge of the objects of possible experience since, in the aesthetic judgment, the concept is indeterminate.[4] Kant missed the mark because he followed his own method of privileging abstraction, placing abstract knowledge at the basis of intuitive knowledge and starting with forms of judgment as keys to the knowledge of our intuitive world. Here, Schopenhauer employs the same criticism he directs toward the *Critique of Pure Reason* because Kant, faithful to the love of symmetry, is reproducing the same architectonic of his first *Critique* in his aesthetic theory.

Kant deals with the beautiful by means of an aesthetic judgment, a judgment that manifests a process in the subject, calling it the judgment of taste (*Geschmacksurteil*)—a poor name choice according to Schopenhauer (WWR1$_{[P]}$, 531). Despite some ingenious solutions, Kant allegedly remains below the dignity of his object, the beautiful, for, by means of this judgment, he seeks to establish universal validity to this subjective process but ends up running the risk of making us think nonetheless that the beautiful is a quality in the object.

According to Schopenhauer, instead of beginning with the immediate feeling of the beautiful, Kant resorts to a judgment, as if the beautiful appeared only with someone else's pronouncement and not in the subject's own intuition. Schopenhauer speculates that, besides his "love for architectonic symmetry" (WWR1$_{[P]}$, 514), the fact that Kant never had any real contact with any significant work of art in the remote city of Königsberg in which he lived might explain why he was more impressed with the judgment regarding the beautiful than with the beautiful itself (WWR1, 529). On this point, a cosmopolitan philosopher such as Schopenhauer, who traveled throughout Europe and lived in cities with important museums and art galleries, such as Berlin, Weimar, Frankfurt, and Dresden, undoubtedly would have the upper hand. It is not without some irony that he shows his admiration for the way Kant, despite that lack, "was able to render a great and permanent service to the philosophical consideration of art and the beautiful" (WWR1$_{[P]}$, 529). But after all, notwithstanding its many insightful observations, Schopenhauer considers Kant's solution to his theory of the beautiful to be simply insufficient. The same clothing from the *Critique of Pure Reason* is forcibly adapted to the whole of his philosophy, which is what we see, for instance, in the judgment of taste's antinomy, where Kant *deduces* the beautiful. And, in order to keep such a symmetry, Kant is forced to create a peculiar faculty of judgment: namely, that of reflecting (*reflektierende*) judgment.

Instead of following the criticism that can be directed at Schopenhauer for not having understood the reach of reflection as a pre-logical instance and the role Kant assigns to the imagination in its interplay with the understanding in the judgment of taste, or, finally, the very specificity of this judgment, we will focus on what Schopenhauer intends by proposing a kind of knowledge—a knowledge through aesthetic experience—that is different from that which is based on the principle of sufficient reason, as presented in the first book of *The World as Will and Representation.*

In Kant's judgment of the beautiful, or judgment of taste, we find no determination by means of a concept, but rather a reflection made by the subject by means of her or his imagination that is coupled to the understanding in a relationship of free play. It seems, however, that Schopenhauer does not really take into account this kind of judgment. He reasons that if the imagination, as *Phantasie*,[5] is present in the experience of the beautiful, then it is not related to the understanding, the source of the possible connection between the phenomena—that is, of causality—for it is a kind of reasoning that, dealing with the mutual conditioning of the phenomena, is unable to focus on something in isolation. The mark of the aesthetic experience as a knowledge distinct from common sense or scientific knowledge, as presented in the first book of *The World as Will and Representation*, however, consists in apprehending the object isolated in front of the subject, free of the chain of conditions imposed by the principle of sufficient reason. This immediate apprehension, stripped of any interest characteristic of all other kinds of knowledge, can only take place in relation to the Platonic Idea, as a universal given in a pre-reflective manner, as a universal *ante rem* (WWR1$_{[P]}$, 263).

With this apprehension of the world, Schopenhauer indicates a special mode of representation—one that is not subjected to the principle of sufficient reason in its four modes.[6] The relationship between a representing subject and a represented object is present but is no longer submitted to causality (i.e., to the condition of "becoming") nor to the concepts coming from the principle of sufficient reason of knowing, nor to the succession in time or simultaneity in space, nor to the law of motivation referred to the will of the subject who would follow, in his or her choice among the representations, the precepts of his or her will or interest. Subject and object are in a unique relationship of mutual reference, isolated from everything else surrounding them. The beautiful is present in this representation that overcomes itself in the encounter of subject and object, where one is no longer facing the other mediated by an interest.

This mode of representation allows the apprehension of what Schopenhauer calls the Platonic Idea, an objectification of the essence as will.

> When the Idea appears, subject and object can no longer be distinguished in it, because the Idea, the adequate objectivity of the will, the real world as representation, arises only when subject and object reciprocally fill and penetrate each other completely. In just the same way the knowing and the known individual, as things-in-themselves, are likewise not different.   (WWR1$_{[P]}$, 180)

The Platonic Idea differs from the concept because it does not arise from a process of abstraction. Unlike concepts, which are universals that are a posteriori abstracted from things, the Platonic Idea precedes the configuration of existing individuals as a universal archetype. As Schopenhauer says, the Platonic Idea is a universal *ante rem*, whereas the concept is a universal *post rem*. The character of universality is thus present in the Idea, allowing us to see the Will as the metaphysical essence of everything. In this sense, the aesthetic apprehension of Platonic Ideas enables a mode of knowledge distinct from the conceptual knowledge: it is not abstract, but intuitive knowledge. It is the only possible objective knowledge, because, despite being originated in the Will, the Idea guarantees that this knowledge is disinterested by creating a different, viz., universal, relation between subject and object. As described in the first book, common sense knowledge (either from the understanding's causality or from the concepts of reason—namely, ordinary language) remains too close to individual subjectivity due to its characteristic interestedness and consequently never truly reaches objectivity.

Since what is at stake here is a criticism of the notions of concept and abstraction, it is worth returning to Kant so we can clearly delineate Schopenhauer's conception of the Platonic Idea, which is formed from his criticism of Kantian speculative reason and its respective notion of system made possible by abstraction (WWR1$_{[P]}$, 452–54).

When Schopenhauer removes from his own concept of reason any precept that is not purely logical, he is reducing it to an operational instance of the combination of concepts. Although he claims in *The Fourfold Root of the Principle of Sufficient Reason* that the characteristic of scientific knowledge is to be systematic, something more than a "mere aggregate of findings" (FR, 9), this systematicity is nonetheless entirely subjective and purely ideal since it is bestowed by the principle of sufficient reason. The criticism of the notion of system, already in germ in his criticism of Kant's Transcendental Analytic, is completed in Schopenhauer's rejection of Kant's Transcendental Dialectic. Indeed, his criticism of the Kantian project spares only the Transcendental Aesthetic and aims at saving, once for all, the dualism between phenomenon and the thing-in-itself so criticized by other post-Kantian philosophies, with the exception of Reinhold[7] (WWR1$_{[P]}$, 452 and 480).

In the "Appendix to the Transcendental Dialectic" in the *Critique of Pure Reason*, Kant establishes as "indispensably necessary" the regulative use of transcendental ideas, consisting in "directing the understanding to a certain aim, toward which all the lines of its rules converge," to a "*focus imaginarius*."[8] According to Kant, these rational ideas confer systematic unity to the empirical knowledge of the understanding, and, since they are not formed from nature, they can guide the research of nature. Schopenhauer opposes such a regulative use, considering that Kant could not "have been serious in making this assertion," for instead of ensuring the scientific progress, he maintains that these transcendental ideas hinder and even destroy all scientific investigation (WWR1$_{[P]}$, 513–14). Thus, the goal of providing a conducting wire to the empirical knowledge by the "systematic unity of reason" actually deviates it from its true source, namely, the intuitive and immediate world: it is as if one prefers the shadows to the objects themselves. And since "our reason can always be concerned only with objects," it is better not to lose them from our sight (WWR1$_{[P]}$, 483).

This is why a critique of reason "by means of antinomies and their solution" is entirely dispensable to Schopenhauer and is easily replaced by a critique of reason that investigates "the relation of abstract knowledge to immediate intuitive knowledge" (WWR1$_{[P]}$, 483). The concept of reason in Schopenhauer's philosophy does not allow any other principles but those that are purely logical. Kant's transcendental principles of reason are not only unacceptable to him, but are also the source of an "unending conflict" to knowledge (WWR1$_{[P]}$, 265). To Schopenhauer, reason cannot produce ideas simply because its main function is neither productive nor creative, but operational. The function of Ideas, both in the philosophy of nature and in the arts—as models or archetypes of individuals, I mean species, in the former case, or as beautiful objects, in the latter—is not provide systematicity to knowledge, but to discover or give way to a new kind of knowledge that, despite coming from the subject, may aspire to objectivity.

One can, as does Victor Goldschmidt, differentiate Schopenhauer's Platonic Ideas from Kant's rational ideas by attributing to the former, in addition to its regulative character, a constitutive aspect, in such a way as to recover the idea of a purpose in nature as well as the idea of final causes.[9] However, I believe this conclusion extrapolates the role of the idea as something that objectivates but is not identified with the Will in its essential aspect. After all, despite its origin in feeling (and not in reason), it remains paradoxically a representation and, as the philosopher states, by the path of representation we can never achieve the will nor the thing-in-itself, only its image (WWR1$_{[P]}$, 502). If reason had a constitutive aspect, it would be that of creating in the subject the condition of receiving the feeling of the beautiful. But this last feeling can only come from the will, being for the representation a mere "occasional cause" for its manifestation, or rather, for the objectification of the Will (WWR1$_{[P]}$, 137).

Schopenhauer's metaphysics of the beautiful is built on the notion of a knowledge of the Platonic Idea, which is peculiar to the genius (*Genius*). To him, the genius is the eye of the world, to whom is given the ability to see it in its truth, in a disinterested view. In what follows, we explore what this pure subject of knowledge involves in Schopenhauer's metaphysics of the beautiful, pinpointing both its similarities and differences vis-à-vis the Kantian conception of genius.

Genius is attributed to the subject in virtue of the special kind of knowledge that, by means of the Platonic Idea, makes the fusion of subject and object possible. Such fusion can only be achieved when the principle of sufficient reason does not function as an intermediary between them. The distinguishing mark of the genius is thereby a disinterested view (i.e., the possibility of dissociating his or her knowledge from the multiplicity of objects that only exist in connection with each other and which constitute the theater of appearances). Liberty and contemplation render it possible to apprehend the Platonic Idea, the objectification of the will itself. That is, one can go beyond the phenomenal world and lift the veil of Maya that obscures the view of things as they are. When the genius unveils the world, however, he or she necessarily cómmunicates to other spectators, although to see what is expressed in the artist's representation—to apprehend the beautiful and the sublime and appreciate the works of art and natural beauty (WWR1$_{[P]}$, §37)—one must also possess this capacity or ability (*Fähigkeit*), even if in a lower and different degree. This saves the genius from solipsism and allows his or her work to convey a rich meaning.

How does Schopenhauer explain the transmission of the knowledge proper to the genius? Since "idea" means to him the possibility of ascending to an objective knowledge, it is precisely this form of objectivity that would allow for communication between the genius, "the eye of the world," and other human beings, for if there were no bridge between him or her and the remainder of people, art would die out with its creator. There would be no aesthetic fruition if the non-geniuses did not possess some degree of genius, which is nothing more than a capacity to apprehend the beautiful, although at a lower level (WWR1$_{[P]}$, 194). The so-called solipsism of the genius is thus softened as long as one recognizes the necessity to show what the world is or could be by means of the work of art. Indeed, art has the power to complete nature where it is not able to do this itself (WWR1$_{[P]}$, 186).

Against this interpretation—one that sees in the metaphysics of the beautiful the same immanence of Schopenhauer's conception of metaphysics, with experience as its source—there are critics who claim a mystical character for Schopenhauer's apprehension of the beautiful and fruition of art. In the pair "Idea-Genius"—that is, in the creation and apprehension of art by the genius by means of the Idea as a Platonic heritage—readers such as Gérard Lebrun anchor their criticism to Schopenhauer by focusing on a sort of "aesthetic enthusiasm." They insist that Schopenhauer characterizes the creative genius as an exceptional and isolated individual, capable of seeing an occult truth that, however, already exists in ordinary knowledge.[10] Lebrun cites the *Anthropology*, where Kant distinguishes between "to find" (*erfinden*) and "to discover" (*entdecken*). According to Kant, art could not discover something already existing, but would find, or better, invent something that is not yet. By resorting to Platonic Ideas, Schopenhauer would have developed a mystical conception of genius, once it is by the knowledge of Ideas that he or she can see beyond the appearances. Here, Lebrun recalls Plato's cave, from where the genius would emerge to contact the real.

Schopenhauer does explicitly mention Plato in *The World as Will and Representation*, but it is important to appreciate how he modulates the notion of Idea that he borrows from the Greek philosopher. To this purpose we should explore the meaning of the contemplation of Ideas in Schopenhauer. What precisely does the Idea reveal in the genius's creation? Is it something preexisting that is found, something already given? Is it something that could hinder the creation or the finding of something new produced by the activity of the genius? When Lebrun states that, in Schopenhauer's hands, the third *Critique* was "deformed" due to an "enthusiastic metaphysics,"[11] he associates

Schopenhauer with Jacobi, who Kant calls the delirious (*Schwärmer*); that is, someone who "employs an intuitive reason (*intuitive Vernunft*)," some sort of divine language that Kant refuses to understand.[12]

I would like to propose a different interpretation: instead of understanding the metaphysics of the beautiful as a perversion of Kant's transcendental philosophy, could we not see it as offering the conditions of possibility to explain the feeling of the beautiful, both in nature and in art, by means of an intuitive path, giving up, once and for all, the framework of logic and abstraction? Here, we can remember Schopenhauer's own criticisms, first to Jacobi, where he rejects "a reason that senses the absolute," and second, in his reference to the philosophy of identity, to Schelling's intuitive reason, capable of achieving the Absolute. Such passages show how Schopenhauer, not unlike Kant, expresses his aversion to all sorts of "mystical reason."

When Kant employs rational ideas in the first *Critique*, he warns about the "excesses" of a mystical deduction of ideas, unduly understood as a means to achieve the supersensible.[13] Heinz Heimsoeth quotes a passage where Kant, with exquisite wit, criticizes Plato with the beautiful image of a free dove that flies in the sky and imagines "to be more successful in an airless space." Likewise, "Plato would have abandoned the sensible and, in the wings of the ideas, thrown himself into the emptiness of pure understanding."[14] Indeed, it is Plato who, in morals, places himself in opposition to the Epicurists who aimed at building a sensible morality from the description of human characteristics and the facts surrounding them. Like Kant, Plato was the first to seek the standard and ideal of all authentically moral behavior in the supersensible and not in the phenomena. In his *Manuscript Remains* (*Nachlaß*), Kant says that Plato builds morality from ideas, not from inclinations (*Neinungen*) or experience.[15] But as he seeks the Idea of morals in God, he is considered a "delirious genius" who exceeds himself in the Ideas. At the same time, though, he might also be seen as a precursor of mysticism once he states that there is no progress of the spirit without imitation of what is already known in a new relation (*neue Beziehung*).[16] With this in mind, the affinity between genius and madness exposed in §36 of *The World as Will and Representation* could be seen as emphasizing precisely the Platonism and the "mysticism" of Schopenhauer's aesthetics and conception of genius. The Platonic genius would be endowed with the Ancient's "mania" as a divine attribute, enabling him free access to the supersensible and authorizing Kant's epithet of "*Schwärmer*" that was also used for Jacobi and Plato. However, Schopenhauer intends to present only "the *purely intellectual ground* of the kinship between genius and madness—a discussion that certainly contributes to explaining the real nature of genius" (WWR1$_{[P]}$, 191–92; emphasis added).

This kinship does not directly refer to an abnormal physiological constitution of the genius or the mad, but to an affective disturbance of memory as the organizing thread of past events and facts. Although the memory (because it presupposes language) obviously refers to the causal and abstract chains, to Schopenhauer, it belongs, after all, to the Will—that which is truly responsible for organizing the occurrence of images. In what sense does this happen? It concerns memories unpleasant to the Will that involve offending or painful facts.

Whenever they appear, the Will pushes them back, hindering such representations to be properly recollected and producing a sort of interruption in their thread, a void or a gap (*eine Lücke*). If this gap is filled with a fictitious content, we have what Schopenhauer defines as madness, a psychological dysfunction. The association with genius comes precisely from the cut in the causal and abstract thread of representations, from the absence of connections established by the principle of sufficient reason necessary to constitute both daily and scientific knowledge based on the objects' interaction. For the genius also employs a kind of knowledge that is strange to the representations connected by the principle of sufficient reason whenever he or she makes the idea of an object stand out; that is, he or she also makes a cut in the thread of representations that is similar to the one we find in madness—hence follows the kinship between genius and madness. Nevertheless, despite the similar affection of memory, Schopenhauer insists in a distinction between a genius and a mad person using some observations that he made in psychiatric hospitals, where he found individuals with sharp intelligences but whose development was hindered precisely by madness (WWR1$_{[P]}$, 190). The intellectual reason for the difference between them lies in the cause of the memory gap: in the genius, it comes from a resistance to ordinary knowledge due to the absence of interest, whereas in the mad person it comes from the refusal in returning to the traumatic event.

In Schopenhauer, the Platonic Idea, as the immediate objectification of the Will, is a condition outside time, space, and causality; it is a place of a unity that comes prior to the multiplicity of space-time representations. This universal configures the field of the different modulations, viz., of the beings of nature as species, of humankind as an intelligible character, and of the work of the genius as universal beauty. This truth is not expressed by an adequacy to something preexisting (because there is absolutely no previous reference), but refers to a form of possible expression. By referring to the imagination (*Phantasie*), necessary not only to the artist, but to the philosopher as well, Schopenhauer states,

> Thus imagination extends the mental horizon of the genius beyond the objects that actually present themselves to his person" not only in quantity, but also in quality, that is, "the actual objects are almost always only very imperfect copies of the Idea that manifests itself in them. Therefore the man of genius requires imagination, in order to see in things not what nature has actually formed, but what she endeavoured to form, yet did not bring about, because of the conflict of her forms with one another. (WWR1$_{[P]}$, 186–87).

Imagination, therefore, expands the circle of vision (*Gesichtskreis*) beyond the objects offered by reality, and its strength becomes "a condition of genius" (WWR1$_{[P]}$, 187). By asking for what is "beyond the objects that actually (*in der Wirklichkeit*) present themselves," we know we will not find there anything more than representations and that this beyond does not point to something supersensible but to the possible contained in the Platonic Idea as a universal *ante rem*. The genius is not a demiurge, replacing the divinity or inspired by it, but is instead the interpreter of the Will, its translator; as the natural forces that express the Ideas, the genius is, as in Kant, a "favorite of nature (*günstlig der Natur*)."[17]

If we respect the immanent character that Schopenhauer gives to his philosophy, it is implausible to interpret his aesthetics or metaphysics of the beautiful as an "enthusiastic metaphysics," exceeding itself by seeking outside of the world and of the will that expresses itself in some exterior reality that would somehow be its truth. The aesthetic feeling offers an image of the world in which the subject sees and fuses him- or herself with the object in the contemplation of the Platonic Idea overcoming the "simple representation (*blosse Vorstellung*)" and its poles, subject and object. It remains a world seen as representation, but one that exposes in a different manner what is given to the subject in the thread of his or her relations. In such conditioned series, we can find an interested knowledge, focused on the individual's survival and obeying a blind impulse from his or her will.

On the other hand, art and its metaphysical knowledge offer the object detached from all individual interests, in a universal dimension provided by the Platonic Idea. The will is not present anymore as an untamed impulse, opening its ways at all costs, but is objectified and stripped of the individual's impetus of satisfaction to keep him or her alive; from now on, the subject is a pure subject of knowledge. For a few moments, this subject withdraws from his or her corporeal needs and plunges into the beautiful with its contemplative fruition. By taking such an attitude toward the world and as the ensurer of a peculiar posture, the beautiful is seen by Schopenhauer as a "quieter of the Will." Thus pacified in its objectification, the Will denies, for a single moment, the will-to-live (WWR1$_{[P]}$, 391).

We should not see here, as Nietzsche, a "will for nothing," but an instantaneous rest of the Will, a rest that enables the manifestation and fruition of beauty in the world. Art is not the imitation of nature, but a creation of what nature misses. The tranquility and the spaceless and timeless point of view offered by the true being, brought to us by the artist and the philosopher, should not be searched for in a hereafter for it is made of the same matter that forms this world. Even in Schopenhauer's hierarchy that privileges those arts carrying less "natural" content—with music being on the apex—I believe their relation is with the world in both points of view, as Will and representation.

The highest of the arts, music, dispenses with representation and is the most diaphanous, made entirely of sounds and employing a minimum of matter, creating something as a world of sound parallel to this one, allowing us to hear directly the voice of the Will. On the opposite extreme, the most material of all the arts, architecture, where weight and resistance struggle, creates several styles in which this conflict is historically manifested. In architecture, Schopenhauer sees the objectification of the lower forces of matter, gravity, and the efforts to overcome it. Thus, weight and rigidity (*Starrheit*), that can also be translated as *stability*, show the discord between these qualities of the matter revealing itself in architectonic constructions. This duality corroborates the *dynamic character* of architecture against a static (or mathematical) view of the buildings: the dynamic effects result from "those fundamental forces of nature, those primary Ideas, those lowest grades of the will's objectivity" (WWR1$_{[P]}$, 214). It is also above form and symmetry because it is the contribution of each part in the stability of the whole that works in facilitating the apprehension of the whole. This is why the regularity of the figures, although contributing to its beauty by manifesting the regularity of space, is not indispensable and has a subordinate value. They depend on the unceasing conflict between weight and rigidity (WWR1$_{[P]}$, 214). The two arts that occupy the extreme opposite poles in this hierarchy, architecture and music, have something in common: namely, their dynamic character and constant activity, even if this happens outside time and space.

Schopenhauer's hierarchy of arts places music in the highest place, followed by poetry and plastic arts, ordered according to the decreasing degree of matter involved. Music is the art par excellence because its material, sound is least attached to any sort of empirical or conceptual manifestation. To explain music, he does not resort to the Ideas as mediators between a plurality of sensible images and the single Will. Given the fluidity of the sound world and despite its specific dissimilarity with the phenomenal world, music expresses directly the essence of things; it manifests the will in a way that is completely adequate as the very world that is within us and in front of us. In music there is no representation whatsoever. Schopenhauer parodies Leibniz in this respect, who sees in music the exercise of arithmetic, claiming that "music is an unconscious exercise in metaphysics" manifesting the will as well as the world (WWR1$_{[P]}$, 264, 256).

Since music no longer represents anything at all—it does not point to any sort of external reference—it is form and content at once: "Its [music's] object is not the representation, in regard to which deception and ridiculousness alone are possible, but [its seriousness is explained from the fact] that this object is directly the will; and this is essentially the most serious of all things, as being that on which all depends" (WWR1$_{[P]}$, 264). Therefore, as seen, it is in music as overcoming of the point of view of the world as representation, and peculiarly, in this art, we find ourselves *almost* on the core of the will were it not for the fact that we are still dealing with a universal language, that of sounds. But by this language of sounds, we transmit feelings not in an individual mode; that is, not a feeling of a determinate pain, or joy or peace, or hate, but pain *itself*, joy *itself*, peace *itself*, and hate *itself*, all in a universal mode.

Schopenhauer keeps the Kantian distinction between the beautiful and the sublime as fit to the genius that expresses itself in art. However, although he preserves the subjective character of both, their meaning is different from Kant's. Schopenhauer describes the beautiful as the pacifying feeling of the pure subject of knowledge while facing the object that, somehow, makes this connection easy in the Platonic Idea produced by the genius. On the other hand, the sublime implies, at the beginning, a hostile relationship between subject and object. To arrive in the feeling of the sublime, the pure subject of knowledge or the genius must tame such hostility and contemplate the object, completely withdrawing him- or herself from the conflict (WWR1$_{[P]}$, 202). The menace must cease, and the feeling of the sublime must rise above the conflict with the will. In tragedy, for instance, the feeling of resignation regarding the fate of the main character prompts us to overcome the impact caused by his or her pain and disgrace. The great intellectual force of the genius tames the will, softening its powerful stimuli: harmoniously and almost effortlessly in the beautiful, conflictingly in the sublime.

In both cases, we see the superiority of the pure subject of knowledge over his or her body and intrepid will achieving a state of contemplation that enables the work of art's calm and quiet fruition. This exceptional victory can be verified in the contemplation of the Platonic Idea, where the intellect ceases to serve the will and takes the higher place. Unlike Kant's third *Critique*, where the idea of reason triumphs over imagination,[18] the triumph here is over the interests connected to the knowledge, both of understanding and reason, involved in the intellectual operations dedicated to the will-to-live. The genius, in turn, at the same time possesses a powerful intellectual force and must concomitantly possess an enormous force of the will, once both will and intellect have the same source and demand a lot from each other. The genius is thus endowed with a strong temperament, and his or her intellect, disentangled from ordinary (pre)occupations, overcomes the sensible impulses, freeing him- or herself to invent or produce a work of art.

Schopenhauer's conception of art as contemplation often gives the impression of creating an abyss between art and world, of cutting off all historical and critical relations.

Yet another interpretation is also possible, according to which this withdrawal from individuals' interest and petty selfishness might mean some sort of nonconformity, deploying a conflicting relationship with the *status quo*. This is how Max Horkheimer reads Schopenhauer's philosophy in general: as refusing all conciliation and rebelling against the injunctions of the surrounding society. The aversion toward the impotence of an "instrumental reason" as the sole kind of possible rational knowledge, unable to provide any truthful meaning to human life, would have taken Schopenhauer to think of an "enlarged reason"[19] or a knowledge that would manifest itself in other cultural domains as art and morals. Schopenhauer's concept of reason, as presented in the *Fourfold Root* and in the first book of *The World as Will and Representation*, is too narrow to encompass what Horkheimer calls objective reason,[20] but the expression of this reason in Schopenhauer's philosophy, by extrapolating the causal relation that explains the becoming and the reason of knowing that connects the abstract representations, is enlarged to fit all the other fields of wisdom, such as art and morals. In the latter, the feeling of compassion prevails, metaphysically grounded in the same essence of each person; namely, the Will. We know that reason in Schopenhauer is necessarily limited, so, if we want to employ Horkheimer's expression, it has to be metaphorically expressing the other kinds of knowledge in addition to the selfish and interested knowledge involved in the representation subsumed to the Will and subordinated to the principle of reason, and committing itself solely to the preservation of life.

We have to regard art as the greater enhancement and the more perfect development of all this, for essentially it achieves just the same thing as is achieved by the visible world itself, only with greater concentration, perfection, intention, and intellectual clarity (*Besonnenheit*).[21] It can therefore, in the full sense of the word, be called the flower of life. If the whole world as representation is only the visibility of the will, then art is the elucidation of this visibility, the *camera obscura* that shows the objects more purely and enables us to survey and comprehend them better. It is the play within the play, the stage on the stage in *Hamlet* (WWR1$_{[P]}$, 266).

ACKNOWLEDGMENTS

Translated from Portuguese by Leonardo André Paes Müller

NOTES

1. This is yet another concept we should investigate regarding its Kantian origin. To Kant, whenever we try to solve what the world is (finite or infinite, simple or composed), we fall into an antinomy because both thesis and antithesis, even if they are proved, cannot refer to the "world-in-itself." In Schopenhauer, who inherited Kant's dualism (phenomenon and thing-in-itself), the question turns around how can we speak about the world as will and representation. As I will try to present in this chapter, it is only by acknowledging both points of view about the world (i.e., a double meaning) that we can speak as philosophers without the risk of falling in antinomies.
2. There are two competing etymologies for the word "metaphysics": (1) what is beyond physics and (2) the book Aristotle wrote after the *Physics*, without any transcendent meaning.
3. The word "representation" translates the German *Vorstellung*, which literally means *to stand before* or *to be in the face of something*. The usual English translation bears an imprecision, for in the original German there is no reference to the prefix "re," which usually means a reference or an unfolding. According to some, it would be better to simply say "presentation," instead of "representation." This is particularly relevant to Schopenhauer's philosophy because this *standing before* refers exclusively to the subject and to nothing beyond this *presenting itself*: object and representation are one and the same regard.
4. Robert Wicks distinguishes Kantian judgments of pure beauty and judgments of the sublime in Kant's third *Critique* as species of aesthetic judgments, where an object is presented with some conceptual activity. This conceptual activity nevertheless is not the same as reflecting cognitive judgments, for the reflection on a given object does not issue in the application of a determinate concept to the object to produce empirical knowledge. See Robert Wicks, *Kant on Judgement* (New York: Routledge, 2007), 95.
5. Schopenhauer seems to prefer the word "*Phantasie*" to express the imagination in his aesthetics, and we can attribute this choice to his desire to highlight the difference in relation to Kant. To the critical philosopher, the *Einbildungskraft* refers to the imagination, either in a subordinate position, as in the first *Critique*, or in a relation of free play, as in the third *Critique*. Another reason for this choice is etymological: *Phantasie* comes from the Greek *phantasia*, that in German corresponds to *Erscheinung*, from the verb *erscheinen*, appearance, to appear. It is only during the Renaissance that the term "phantasy" suffers a twist due to the theory that attributes to it an "almost corporeal spirit," adequate to incorporate itself in nature and to animate the universe, not far from Plotinus's astral body.
6. See FR, §46.
7. See Reinhold's *Letters on the Kantian Philosophy*.
8. Immanuel Kant, *Critique of Pure Reason*, translated by John Miller Dow Meiklejohn (London: Henry G. Bohn, 1855), B672 (Ak III, 427/428).

9. Victor Goldschmidt, "Schopenhauer, lecteur de Lamarck." In *Écrits, vol. 2* (Paris: Vrin, 1954), 207.

10. "L'enthousiasme" esthétique consistera em rétablir le primat de la contemplation et à interpréter l'idée esthétique comme une Idée platonicienne; l'oeuvre d'art sera rendue inséparable de la "conaissance de l'idée", et le génie tenue par um découvreur d'essences— ce qu'il n'est certainement pas, selon Kant" (Gerard Lebrun, *Kant et la fin de la méthaphysique*, Paris: Armand Colin, 1970, 406).

11. "Qu'elle ait été jugée en des critères psychologiques ou gauchie dans le sens d'une métaphysique 'enthousiaste,'" Ibid., 316.

12. See the letter to Hamman, from April 6, 1774 quoted in Lebrun (*Kant et la fin de la méthaphysique*, 408): "Pour moi, pauvre fils de la terre, je n'ai aucune disposition à entendre la langue divine de la raison intuitive...."

13. Heinz Heimsoeth, "Kant und Plato," *Kant Studien* 56, no. 3 (1966), 349.

14. Ibid., 350.

15. "Plato: Moral aus der Idee, nicht den Neinungen oder den Erfahrungen gemäss, auch nicht aus Reflexionsbegriffen. Nur er suchte seine in Gott, oder machte den Begriff von Gott aus diesen Ideen," cited in Heimsoeth, "Kant and Plato," 354. See AK XIX, 177 [No. 6842].

16. See Immanuel Kant, *Reflexion*, 788, XV 340, Ak Ausgabe.

17. Immanuel Kant, *Kritik der Urteilskraft*, Ak Ausgabe V 318.

18. Kant, *Kritik der Urteilskraft*, Ak V, 285, 286.

19. Mauricio Chiarello, *Das lágrimas das coisas. Estudo sobre o conceito de natueza em Max Horkheimer* (Campinas: Editora da Unicamp, 2001), 96 and 26n. Chiarello glosses the radical character of Horkheimer's position in *Reason and Self-preservation* (*Vernunft und Selbsterhaltung*), softened two years later in *Eclipse of Reason*, where he admits an objective reason.

20. Max Horkheimer, "Means and Ends," in *Eclipse of Reason* (Oxford: Oxford University Presss, 1947), 5.

21. I prefer *intellectual clarity* instead of Payne's choice, *intelligence*, as a translation for *Besonnenheit*. It can be understood, in a certain way, as Horkheimer's notion of an "enlarged reason" in *Eclipse of Reason*.

FURTHER READING

Chiarello, Maurício. *Das lágrimas das coisas. Estudo sobre o conceito de natureza em Max Horkheimer*. Campinas, SP: Editora da Unicamp/Fapesp, 2001.

Goldschmidt, Victor. "Schopenhauer, lecteur de Lamarck." *Écrits, Vol. 2*, Paris: Vrin, 1954.

Heimsoeth, Heinz. "Kant und Plato." *Kant Studien*, 56, no. 3 (1966): 349–72.

Horkeimer, Max. *Eclipse of Reason*. Oxford: Oxford University Presss, 1947.

Kant, Immanuel. *Kritik der Urteilskraft*. Akademisches Textausgabe, Band V. Berlin: Walter de Gruyter & Co., 1968.

Lebrun, Gérard. *Kant et la fin de la méthaphisique*. Paris: Armand Colin, 1970.

Wicks, Robert. *Kant on Judgment*. New York: Routledge, 2007.

....

CHAPTER 14

SCHOPENHAUER AND THE PARADOX OF THE SUBLIME

....

BART VANDENABEELE

SCHOPENHAUER offers an intriguing account of the experience of the sublime, one that explores its aesthetic nature in a far richer way than his predecessors by rightfully emphasizing the prominent role of the aesthetic object and the ultimately affirmative character of the pleasurable experience it engenders.[1] Unlike Kant, Schopenhauer's doctrine of the sublime does not appeal to the superiority of human reason over nature to resolve (what I call) the paradox of the sublime (i.e., how it is that we can take aesthetic pleasure in disturbing and overwhelming objects and inhospitable environments). On the contrary, he explores and affirms the ultimately superhuman unity of the world, of which the human being is merely a puny fragment. Exploring this and several other related issues in Schopenhauer's theory will require seeing Schopenhauer's account of the sublime as rather more original, nuanced, and complicated than is often acknowledged.

I focus on Schopenhauer's treatment of the experience of the sublime in nature. On the account I provide, Schopenhauer makes two distinct attempts to resolve the paradox of the sublime, and I argue that, despite its shortcomings, Schopenhauer's second attempt, which has been unjustly neglected in the literature, establishes the sublime as a viable aesthetic concept with profound significance.[2]

14.1 FROM THE BEAUTIFUL TO THE SUBLIME

....

In line with Addison, Burke, and several other British eighteenth-century empiricist philosophers, Schopenhauer develops a psychological theory of the sublime, but he supplements it with important metaphysical insights. Contrary to Kant, for Schopenhauer there is no *transcendental* difference between the beautiful and the sublime. The distinction between both aesthetic experiences is not grounded in transcendental faculties— "understanding" in the beautiful and "reason" in the sublime, respectively—but primarily in empirical and phenomenological features. Schopenhauer's novel thought that the beautiful and the sublime cannot be distinguished as sharply as several of his predecessors thought is of paramount importance in this respect.

One of the most revealing passages in this context is one in which Schopenhauer describes so-called transitions from the experience of the beautiful to the sublime. He actually attaches great importance to these often very subtle transitions. He also specifies that there are "several degrees of the sublime" and that, contrary to Kant, the sublime is not a reflective judgment, but an aesthetic feeling which is "in the main...identical with the feeling of the beautiful" (WWR1$_{[P]}$, 202).

Schopenhauer takes great pains to minimize the distinction between both aesthetic experiences. He insists that "the feeling of the sublime is distinguished from that of the beautiful only by the addition, namely the exaltation beyond the known hostile relation of the contemplated object to the will" (WWR1$_{[P]}$, 202). Their main difference lies in the fact that appreciating beauty is characterized by a fairly smooth transition from ordinary, will-dominated perception into a state of pure, "will-less" perception, whereas the sublime involves a painful *struggle* with that which opposes the will in order to obtain a purely aesthetic state of mind, which allows us to engage with the Idea embodied by the object (see WWR1$_{[P]}$, 201–02).

When we admire the beauty of nature, we easily become absorbed in our tranquil perception of it and "not even a recollection of the will remains" (WWR1$_{[P]}$, 202).[3] Schopenhauer offers several fascinating examples of how the experience of "easy" natural beauty can begin to show traces of sublimity. A first nice example is worth quoting *in extenso*.

> Now if in the depth of winter, when the whole of nature is frozen and stiff, we see the rays of the setting sun reflected by masses of stone, where they illuminate without warming, and are thus favourable only to the purest kind of knowledge, not to the will, then contemplation of the beautiful effect of light on these masses moves us into the state of pure knowing, as all beauty does. Yet here, through the faint recollection of the lack of warmth from those rays, in other words, of the absence of the principle of life, a certain transcending of the interest of the will is required. There is a slight challenge to abide in pure knowledge, to turn away from all willing, and precisely in this way we have a transition from the feeling of the beautiful to that of the sublime. It is the faintest trace of the sublime in the beautiful [*der schwächste Anhauch des Erhabenen am Schönen*], and beauty itself appears here only in a slight degree.   (WWR1$_{[P]}$, 203)

This fascinating description of "der schwächste Anhauch des Erhabenen," which E. F. J. Payne translates as "the faintest trace of the sublime"—the German *Anhauch* actually refers to "breath," as the verb "*anhauchen*" means "to breathe on" (see also WWR1$_{[P]}$, 182).

Translating *Anhauch* with "trace" is too strong, for the example clearly shows that beauty here is rather *tinged with sublimity*, as the air can be tinged with rain. It is as if the faintest touch of the sublime here somehow mildly qualifies the smoothness of the transition from will-driven into will-less, tranquil perception.[4] Schopenhauer explains why this is the case here: because of our awareness of the lack of warmth of the sunrays, some effort is required to overcome our sense of uneasiness and perhaps even worry about the lack of life energy the winter sun is providing, which adds a peculiar thrill to this experience of beauty and makes us shiver slightly at the sight of it. As Schopenhauer puts it: "through the faint recollection"—we will see how crucial the term "recollection" really is in the context of Schopenhauer's theory of the sublime—of the thought that in winter the sunrays are not strong enough to provide much warmth, "a certain transcending of the interest of the will is required." In the German text, "transcending" is "*Erheben*," which is very closely related to "*das Erhabene*" (the sublime).

What distinguishes the mildly sublime experience just mentioned from a pure experience of beauty is that, despite the beauty of the sunlit scene, the faint awareness of the lack of solar energy in winter affects our will negatively. Hence, Schopenhauer argues, a certain elevation is needed somehow to remain in a purely contemplative mood instead of yielding to the negative emotions that are caused by the affection of the will, which slightly tarnishes the purity of our experience of natural beauty. The key difference with "easy beauty" is that here we are aware of a mild challenge to engage the object purely contemplatively, since we somehow realize that when "nature is frozen and stiff," it is not a hospitable environment. We are faintly reminded of our dependence on the energy of the sun to be able to survive in nature *as the will-driven, embodied creature that we are*.

Now, I would like to suggest that this example of an experience of beauty slightly tinged with sublimity—which might be better categorized as an example of terrible beauty rather than sublimity—shows how far removed we already are from a Kantian explanation of the sublime. For Schopenhauer, neither our imagination nor our senses are violently dominated by reason to measure the might of nature, as Kant holds, and there is no mention of what forms the core of Kant's theory: namely, the judgment of (moral) purposiveness, the superiority of practical reason, and the susceptibility to moral feeling. Even if we disregard the *prima facie* difference between their respective approaches (i.e., Kant's being a *transcendental* story and Schopenhauer's a *psychological* account), the gap between the way they aim to resolve the so-called paradox of the sublime—the way they account for how it is that we can actually *enjoy* what is disturbing and overwhelming—is already very wide. For Kant would argue that even mild experiences of the sublime are based on our (perhaps subconscious) acknowledgment of the inadequacy of our imagination to the power of practical reason, whereas Schopenhauer makes it clear from the outset that any reference not only to "that fatal faculty of reason" but also to transcendental imagination is superfluous. On Schopenhauer's account, the pleasure in the sublime is based on the deliverance of knowledge from the service of the will, whereas for Kant reason's dominance delivers the will merely from the influence of inclinations upon it. In Schopenhauer's view, the sublime is a purely aesthetic experience that expresses not our (moral) superiority over nature but the struggle with "our broken will" and thus intensifies awareness of our fragility and nullity in comparison with sublime nature.

Like, for example, Burke and Mendelssohn, but unlike Kant, Schopenhauer attaches particular importance to the *existential* dimensions of the sublime experience. Schopenhauer rightly intimates that the experience of the sublime is based on an existential awareness of ourselves as fragile, puny individuals and our precarious *embodied* engagement with the world.[5] What explains the mildly sublime character of lonely prairies and deserts, for instance, is not so much their limitlessness which the imagination fails to "comprehend" in a single image, but rather the sense that these surroundings are felt to be *existentially* disturbing to finite embodied individuals like ourselves who need objects to strive for in order to *feel alive* and life-enhancing environments in order to survive (see WWR1$_{[P]}$, 203–04).

Schopenhauer argues that whoever is incapable of contemplating such rather uncanny surroundings and whose perception remains in the service of the will, will be "abandoned with shameful ignominy to the emptiness of unoccupied will, to the torture and misery of boredom" (WWR1$_{[P]}$, 203–04) The tinge of the sublime that we experience in such surroundings is grounded in an experience of *contrast*: the contrast between the goals of our willing self and the lack of objects to satisfy it.

The experience of "the sublime in a low degree" can become more intense—the Schopenhauerian sublime is indeed often more a matter of intensification (as in Burke) than of elevation—if we imagine "such a region denuded of plants and showing only bare rocks" (WWR1$_{[P]}$, 204). For then the threat which the surroundings pose to our physical existence becomes far clearer and, suggests Schopenhauer, "the will is at once filled with alarm [*schon geradezu beängstigt*] through the total absence of that which is organic and *necessary for our subsistence* [*zu unserer Subsistenz nötigen*]" (WWR1$_{[P]}$, 204). Here we find a splendid echo of Burke's existential sublime.[6] What really terrifies us is nothing less than our awareness that the surroundings that we perceive are possibly life-threatening since they lack what we need "for our subsistence," for our survival. To be able to contemplate serenely such surroundings, "a more decided emancipation from the interest of the will" is needed, and therefore "the feeling of the sublime distinctly appears" (WWR1$_{[P]}$, 204). Here the feeling of the sublime comes close to an experience of the uncanny, which translates the poignant German term *unheimlich* (literally "unhomely"). The environment Schopenhauer describes is more distinctly sublime because we cannot imagine it to be our home. We feel that we could not survive in an environment that does not offer the necessary means to feed us; this is what causes it to be felt as *unheimlich*. Much more effort is therefore required to be able to persist in the state of pure, "will-less" cognition that is essential to aesthetic contemplation for we feel uneasy in this environment because it is not conducive to our will-to-life, and we are aware that we would not be able to live and survive in it.[7]

The core of the experience of the sublime involves a struggle with our will which is negatively affected by the (real or imagined) hostile character of the object through which "we feel ourselves reduced to nothing…like drops in the ocean, dwindling and dissolving into nothing" (WWR1$_{[P]}$, 205). The sublime, Schopenhauer insists, is indeed a *humbling* experience, but not because (as Kant insists) we feel humbled "by the superiority of the rational vocation of our cognitive powers."[8] Schopenhauer develops a more adequate explanation of the peculiarly humbling effect of the sublime. What is particularly humbling when we are faced with sublime phenomena is that they "oppose our will" and cause *our sense of vulnerability to nature's might to be heightened* (WWR2[P], 433). Schopenhauer's approach thus surpasses Kant's (and several of his predecessors') for being more clearly object-centered.[9] We feel our inability to withstand the tremendous shock that the overwhelming object causes to our self-esteem: we are being made vividly aware of the insignificance and vulnerability of our *existence* as desiring, embodied individuals.[10]

14.2 THE FULL IMPRESSION OF THE SUBLIME AND THE STRUGGLE WITH THE WILL

The problem of why such tremendously shocking and usually (but not necessarily) fearful experiences can actually be sought out, enjoyed, and positively valued has yet to be answered. Why is it that we experience this humbling of our self-esteem *with pleasure*? Schopenhauer is, of course, fully aware that not all frightening experiences are necessarily sublime. What is it that renders terrifying vistas aesthetically pleasing and uplifting?

Schopenhauer offers the following answer. Our being negatively and often painfully affected by the immensity of what we face when we realize, *through feeling*, the destructive threat of the natural forces suggests that we are "helpless against powerful [or, rather, "violent" (*gewaltige*)] nature, dependent, abandoned to chance, a vanishing nothing in the face of stupendous forces" (WWR1[P], 205). *Contra* Burke and Kant, Schopenhauer justly contends that we need not be in a safe place to experience the sublime (see MR2, 321 [HN2, 289]). It is neither necessary (as both Burke and Kant hold) nor sufficient (as Burke holds). Whereas being (or imagining ourselves to be) in a safe place may definitely aid in overcoming the anxiety aroused by a distressing object, feeling too safe might also have the opposite effect of making our awareness of the object's threat too weak actually to experience the danger it might cause, and it would thus also lose its sublime effect.

Hence what procures the ambivalent pleasure of the sublime is not—as Burke supposes—reducible to a sense of moderation of experienced terror by beholding the object from a safe distance.[11] There is indeed a major difference between, for instance, the relief felt on having escaped from a perilous situation and the pleasurable, uplifting feeling of the sublime. For, although we would actually dread confronting a similar dangerous situation again or even thinking about it or remembering it, we will surely gladly revisit a sublime environment in nature and also seek out objects that give rise to a similar sublime feeling. This crucial difference between relief and sublimity is one that

Burke's theory has trouble accommodating. The sublime cannot be reduced to an experience of "uneasiness" or "instability" either, let alone to the recognition of the power of (practical) reason over our imagination and the superiority of our morality above nature, as Kant argues. Quite the contrary.

Schopenhauer rightly holds that "we feel ourselves reduced to nothing," and, "with the state of pure knowing in its peace and self-sufficiency there is mingled, *as a contrast*, a recollection of the dependence and wretchedness of the will" (WWR1$_{[P]}$, 205; 204, emphasis added). By emphasizing that the sublime involves awareness not just of "uneasiness" but of *contrast*, he clearly moves beyond his predecessors' doctrines.[12] Schopenhauer defines an aesthetically sublime experience as one based on the *felt contrast* between our "broken will" and our unmoved contemplation of the cause of this "brokenness" (WWR1$_{[P]}$, 204; see WWR2$_{[P]}$, 433). "In this contrast," Schopenhauer urges, "is to be found the feeling of the sublime" (WWR1$_{[P]}$, 204). Hence, even though we may not be, nor imagine ourselves to be in safety, we are still able to experience the sublime when faced with objects that have a hostile relation to the human will. Again, this manifests itself in "a consciousness, merely felt" that we are both "a vanishing nothing in face of stupendous forces" *and* "the unmoved beholder of this scene" (WWR1$_{[P]}$, 204).

What is, on Schopenhauer's account, then required to experience the sublime is that we do not direct our attention to the hostile relation of the object to *our own will* and do not let "*personal* affliction...gain the upper hand" (WWR1$_{[P]}$, 204, emphasis added; see also WWR1$_{[P]}$, 203; 199; WWR2$_{[P]}$, 372–73). This is of paramount importance. For although Kant maintains that we merely "*present* nature as arousing fear" and "consider an object fearful without being afraid *of* it, if we judge it in such a way that we merely *think* of the case where we might possibly want to put up resistance against it," what is truly at stake in the sublime is not actual safety and mere thinking of something as fearful, but rather being able to mentally withstand considerable levels of real danger and fear. What is at stake is a heightened awareness of human fragility compared to overwhelming nature and the psychological (not moral) *strength* to cope with this. That this is what Schopenhauer, *contra* Kant, considers to be essential to the sublime experience is clear from his insisting that "the individual will" is "actually affected" by the overwhelming object and that the beholder, "although he perceives and acknowledges" the hostile relation of the object "to *his* will which is so pressing...may not direct his attention to this relation to his will" and "consciously turn away from it, forcibly tear himself from *his* will and its relations" (WWR1$_{[P]}$, 201, emphasis added). This gives the lie to those who hold that what really matters in the sublime is overcoming the hostile relation of the object to the *human* will in general instead of to the individual will. For, while taking into account human willing in general obviously plays an important part in the aesthetic experience of tragedy, Schopenhauer does not argue that this forms the core of the experience of the sublime in nature. Schopenhauer rightly argues that real fear is involved in the experience of the sublime and that consciousness of the (individual) will is not lost, even though we may not focus our attention on it. But I see no inconsistency in holding, as Schopenhauer does, that we are both aware of the threat posed to our will and of wresting ourselves from our own will. In the sublime, we raise ourselves above our individual willing, but (unlike what happens in the case of the beautiful) we remain fully aware of the threat posed by the hostile object to our will. Consciousness of the threat to our will has not vanished from consciousness. It is, indeed, essential for the feeling of the sublime. If there were no such awareness, it is hard to see how the ambivalent, "mixed" emotion of the sublime could arise altogether.

14.3 SCHOPENHAUER'S FIRST ATTEMPT TO RESOLVE THE PARADOX OF THE SUBLIME

How does Schopenhauer explain the possibility of aesthetically enjoying that which makes us feel insignificant creatures, abandoned to powerful natural objects that could easily annihilate us? The answer he offers is extremely complicated and not always easy to distil from his dense account. I think he actually provides two different answers but does not sufficiently distinguish between them.

One explicit answer is what I have called elsewhere Schopenhauer's doctrine of "transcendental pride."[13] According to Schopenhauer, when we regard an overwhelming phenomenon as personally threatening or distressing, we may also manage to disregard the *actual* threat and not let *personal* feelings of distress take the upper hand.[14] Hence, Schopenhauer never denies that I may really feel fear for myself, and feeling myself as a vulnerable individual, "as the feeble phenomenon of will...helpless against powerful nature, dependent, abandoned to chance" may even heighten the sublime character of the scene and the fierceness of the concomitant emotion (WWR1$_{[P]}$, 205). But Schopenhauer is fully aware that not all frightening experiences are also necessarily *sublime*, so he needs a clear distinction between them. That is why he stresses the *aesthetic* character of the sublime experience, not only by emphasizing the relational and even correlative quality of it and granting (much more explicitly than Kant) a prominent causal role for the *object* of the aesthetic experience, but also by pointing out that, despite the distress caused by the object, we do "remain in aesthetic contemplation" and "the pure subject of knowing gazes through...this picture of the broken will, and comprehends calmly, unshaken and unconcerned, the Ideas in those very objects that are threatening and terrible to the will" (WWR1$_{[P]}$, 204).

Whereas beautiful objects easily invite us to transcend our will and are very accommodating to tranquil contemplation, sublime objects offer *resistance* (*Widerstand*) to this transition in the beholder from willing individual into pure contemplative subject. From this follows that sublime "exaltation must not only be won with consciousness but also be maintained, and it is therefore accompanied by a constant recollection of the will" (WWR1$_{[P]}$, 202). Rather surprisingly, this seems to suggest that, despite Schopenhauer's earlier remarks on the similar tranquil contemplation both experiences share, the sublime now clearly differs phenomenologically from the beautiful. For now Schopenhauer maintains that sublime exaltation is necessarily accompanied by "a constant recollection of the will" which may obviously disturb the tranquil character of the sublime state of consciousness.

I used to think that this fundamental feature of the sublime undermines the unity of Schopenhauer's doctrine of aesthetic appreciation, which is supposedly based on a Platonic ideal of calm contemplation.[15] Now, I still believe that Schopenhauer should have paid more attention to the peculiar way in which the turbulent character of sublime experiences cannot always be easily reconciled with his outspoken Platonic ideal of tranquil, will-less knowledge of Ideas. Yet it is important to point out that what Schopenhauer identifies here as "will-less" contemplation is not to be identified solely with pure knowledge of Platonic Ideas nor with a resigned, disembodied state through which we may escape from our attachment to the will-to-life. Rather, what unites beauty and sublimity, and what keeps these experiences squarely within the *aesthetic* realm, is that we turn away from the interest of the will not to give up the will-to-life, but to gain insight into what the object essentially is and how it manifests itself in the world of representation. This is particularly obvious when we are faced with the sublime in nature. For then, "we turn away from the interest of the will, *in order to behave in a purely perceptive way*" (WWR2$_{[P]}$, 433, emphasis added). Thus, by engaging with sublime nature, we do not turn away from the will-to-life in order to achieve what Christopher Janaway calls "sublime resignation"[16] but *to remain an aesthetic spectator of the world* (i.e., an unmoved beholder focusing not on our *personal* afflictions and concerns, but transcending our self-centered desires in order to contemplate and admire even those objects that are threatening to the human will). Contemplation is what is required, not resignation: our personal needs and desires are transformed into a disinterested interest for the aesthetic object but have not completely vanished.[17]

Here we arrive at Schopenhauer's idea of so-called transcendental pride, already mentioned. Schopenhauer does not offer a merely negative account of aesthetic pleasure—sublime exaltation is not mere relief from pain. On the contrary, it is through identifying with the eternal subject of pure knowing—that is to say, by being aware that our perception no longer operates in the service of our will—that sublime exaltation is realized to the full. Thus the "full impression of the sublime" is, Schopenhauer suggests, ultimately based on our realizing that "the fearful struggle of nature" is only a "mental picture or representation." By identifying with the pure subject of knowing, we are conscious of being liberated from the thralls of our will and feel exalted since our dependence on the world, suggests Schopenhauer, "is now annulled by its dependence on us" (WWR1$_{[P]}$, 205).

Summarizing, Schopenhauer's first answer, which dominates his account of the sublime, is that we can actually enjoy aesthetically what is really contrary to the interests of our will through sensing that we are not merely a feeble phenomenon of the will but are somehow able to (partly) identify with an unshaken beholder standing, as it were, outside nature.

Schopenhauer's reference to the pure subject of knowing (or cognition, *Erkenntnis*) does not aid much in finding an adequate resolution for the paradox of the sublime. For, although he avoids some of the pitfalls of Kant's transcendental account, there are still a number of weaknesses in Schopenhauer's first resolution to the paradox of the sublime.

First, Schopenhauer does not sufficiently explain how it is that we come to "find ourselves to be" the eternal subject of knowing, with which we are to identify. How does this transition from the will into a state of tranquil contemplation come about in beings like us, who are embodied individuals wholly determined by appetites, needs, and desires? How could a *willing* individual be able to tear itself away from the whims of the will if the latter dominates not only our perception but also our actions, emotions, thoughts, our whole existence—if, in short, "the real self is the will-to-life" (WWR2$_{[P]}$, 606; see WWR2$_{[P]}$, 239)?

Second, Schopenhauer here offers another, albeit impressive, variant of what Tom Cochrane aptly calls the "heroic model" of the sublime.[18] On Schopenhauer's account, we rise above the strivings of the will and enjoy our engagement with a sublime object because it provides an enhanced awareness of our cognitive powers. However, this Kantian-inspired model is flawed for a number of reasons. For, although Schopenhauer avoids Kant's appeal to the indestructible power of reason, he does seem to ground sublime pleasure in the superiority of a pure subject that cannot be annihilated by the threatening object in nature, being itself the epistemic supporter of the representation that gave rise to the affective response in the first place. This is not only counterintuitive; it is also difficult to see why realizing that I am really the subject that is perceiving the sublime object would allow me actually to enjoy the aesthetic qualities *of the object*. The kind of awareness Schopenhauer seems to have in mind is clearly self-centered. This might be a perhaps rather unfortunate remnant of Kant's transcendental account, although Schopenhauer (unlike Kant) refrains from suggesting that it is ultimately the mind that is sublime and not the object in nature. Still, in his first attempt to resolve the paradox of the sublime, Schopenhauer unjustly downplays the aesthetic properties of the object that produce the sublime pleasure in the first place. Furthermore, a sense of (Kantian) self-aggrandizement seems to have taken the place of the earlier, impressive, and far more plausible focus on the threatening, dislocating, and deeply distressing effects that sublime objects have upon us. This "heroic" story also fails to explain why we may actually take *aesthetic* pleasure in them.

Third, the thought that the sublime temporarily lifts us "out of ourselves" does not properly accommodate the phenomenology of the sublime experience for it downplays that we actually sense that we *really are* puny and insignificant in comparison to the sublime object in nature.

Finally, Schopenhauer's "transcendental pride" model fails to explain why sublime objects are appealing and why we are genuinely attracted to such "hostile" objects. Identifying the pleasure of the sublime with an enhanced appreciation of the scope of our cognitive powers does not sufficiently focus on the core of the experience of the sublime, which is to be situated in our *relation* to the overwhelming characteristics of the hurricane, the mountain range, the erupting volcano, and so on. By downplaying the *positive* qualities of the sublime object, Schopenhauer fails to offer an acceptable resolution to the paradox of the sublime. Schopenhauer's explanation does not end here, however, or he offers several crucial and substantial modifications to his Kantian-inspired doctrine that have frequently been downplayed in the literature.[19]

14.4 SCHOPENHAUER'S SECOND ATTEMPT TO RESOLVE THE PARADOX OF THE SUBLIME

Recall that Schopenhauer's first solution focused especially upon the thought that in the sublime we discover the twofold nature of our consciousness and that by feeling oneself as the pure subject of knowing (which is the condition of every possible object of perception), one experiences the pleasurable exaltation which emerges in contemplating sublime objects. The feeling of sublime pleasure is characteristically more *intense* than the feeling of the beautiful since the latter does not involve any conscious awareness or "recollection" of oneself as dependent on the will, whereas the former does. Schopenhauer yet adds a particular twist to his argument by specifying that, although "we feel ourselves reduced to nothing" by the sublime object, at the same time: ... against such a ghost [*Gespenst*] of our own nothingness, against such a lying impossibility, there arises the immediate consciousness that all these worlds exist only in our representation, only as modifications of the eternal subject of knowing. This we find ourselves to be [*als welches wir uns finden*], as soon as we forget individuality; it is the necessary conditional supporter of all worlds and of all periods of time" (WWR1$_{[P]}$, 205).

Although *prima facie* a repetition of his earlier claim that it is by identifying with the pure subject of knowing that we can actually relish in sublime objects, this passage actually offers several novel, significant elements to his earlier endeavour to come up with a resolution to the paradox of the sublime.

First, although he still explicitly refers to the pleasure of discovering that I am the one who actually represents the sublime scene, he significantly adds that the consciousness with which we identify or, rather, "that we find ourselves to be" is the epistemic ground not just of this representation but "of all worlds and of all periods of time." This pure "I" ultimately has genuine metaphysical significance. The "cosmic consciousness" does not primarily refer to myself as the tranquil beholder of the object, but is, Schopenhauer urges, "the necessary supporter of all worlds and all periods of time." So what at first seemed to be, as in Kant, a discovery of the supersensible side of *our* being which *distinguishes us from nature* is now more precisely qualified as "the felt consciousness of what the Upanishads of the Vedas express repeatedly in so many different ways, but most admirably in the saying "*Hae omnes creaturae in totum ego sum, et praeter aliud (ens) non est*" [I am all this creation collectively, and besides me there exists no being]" (WWR1$_{[P]}$, 205). Unlike many commentators who focus exclusively on the Kantian influence, I believe we should not underestimate the importance of this reference to the Indian Upanishads for it shows how Schopenhauer arrives at a position that radically parts ways with Kant's morally orientated doctrine of the sublime and offers a more plausible (albeit merely partially successful) alternative to it.[20]

What Schopenhauer suggests here offers a way out of the anthropocentric and "negative" approach that has dominated the recent literature on the sublime for so long. Schopenhauer adds a metaphysical argument to his explanation that is of the greatest importance as it rightly considers the experience of the sublime to be deeply *affirmative*. For, as Schopenhauer clarifies, the pleasure in the sublime is not based primarily on the recognition of our superiority to nature, as Kant believed. Admittedly, Schopenhauer writes that "the vastness of the world, which previously disturbed our peace of mind, now rests within us," and this might suggest—as it has indeed struck several commentators[21]— that he settles with a "heroic," anthropocentric explanation of the sublime (WWR1$_{[P]}$, 205). Yet, in an extremely revealing passage he specifies the basis of our pleasure in the sublime as follows:

> All this [i.e. that our dependence on nature is now annulled by its dependence on us], however, does not come into reflection at once, but shows itself as a consciousness, merely felt [*als ein nur Gefühltes Bewusstsein*], that in some sense or other ... we are one with the world [*dass man mit der Welt eines ist*], and are therefore not oppressed but exalted by *its* immensity. (WWR1$_{[P]}$, 205; emphasis added)

At least two insights from this important passage are worth considering. First, unlike Kant, Schopenhauer succeeds in properly safeguarding the purely *aesthetic* character of the sublime experience by insisting on the nonrepresentational nature of our consciousness of exaltation. Our exaltation does not come into reflection; it is not propositional, discursive, or bound up with conceptual representation, but (as Schopenhauer insists) "merely felt." It is not based on the thought that I am somehow elevated above my will, but on *feeling* this, that is to say, on a bodily response and an inner affect of sorts.

Second, and perhaps more importantly, the source of sublime pleasure is now clearly situated in our *relation* with the world. There is thus clearly no Kantian "subreption" at all here for we are not elevated primarily by discovering that *we* are somehow epistemically or morally superior to nature. We are not exalted by our own power but, as Schopenhauer argues, "we are one with the world, and are therefore not oppressed but exalted by *its* immensity." Not the immensity of our cognitive powers is what is ultimately judged sublime, as Kant insists; what produces sublime exaltation is *the immensity of nature's powers in which we become absorbed.*

This brings out the third crucial element in Schopenhauer's impressive account. Contrary to his predecessors, Schopenhauer rightly claims that sublime delight is not merely more precarious than pleasure in the beautiful but also more intense and even ecstatic. Schopenhauer radically modifies his Kantian-inspired account of "transcendental pride." For what is ultimately pleasurable in the sublime is not our separation from the world but, rather, as one commentator aptly puts it, "a pleasure in . . . the affirmation of the individual's underlying identity with a greater reality."[22]

Now, although Schopenhauer insists that we remain, at least partly, the "unmoved beholder" of the threatening object and of our feelings of terror and anxiety when faced with it, in contrast with beauty, the source of sublime pleasure cannot be traced back to this disengaged attitude. For, even though Schopenhauer may not sufficiently elaborate this important aspect of the sublime in nature, he does suggest that the felt absorption into and ultimate identity with the core of the world offers an additional basis to the experienced pleasure in the sublime—a basis that is existential and ultimately metaphysical.

Schopenhauer's doctrine therefore surpasses Burke's, Kant's, and many others' in offering a metaphysical and ultimately affirmative basis of the sublime experience, one that is rooted in humanity but also transforms it. For, on Schopenhauer's account (and again *contra* Kant), the sublime reveals not the supersensible power of human reason but the presence of *a superhuman unity beyond good and evil*, which disrupts our perception and evaluation of the phenomenal world. Schopenhauer values nature not merely "for the challenges it presents to us, as something that is difficult for us to face, and against which morality provides the resources needed to cope,"[23] but for its awe-inspiring, superhuman qualities that enable us to realize the nullity and fragility of our existence as individuals as well as the ability to affirm our deep identity with a greater reality, with life as a whole— albeit one that is necessarily mediated by a sense of the struggle with our individual desires, interests, and needs.[24] Faced with overwhelming objects, "we feel reduced to nought in their presence, and yet revel in the pleasure of beholding them" (WWR1$_{[P]}$, 206), and, in my view, this is due to our ability to somehow identify with their awesome aesthetic properties.[25] Taking pleasure in sublime objects and environments is therefore a matter of rejoicing in our *belonging to a larger whole* and being called upon to renounce our everyday self-concern. It is in this sense that the sublime is more akin to an experience of the *sacred* character of the world than to a self-centered admiration of one's (moral) superiority over nature.[26]

Furthermore, Schopenhauer's account also allows us to understand better why the sublime really offers a shock to our self-esteem. By identifying with the core of the world and grasping the insignificant and illusory character of our individual existence, we are able to identify with and find our home in the world—even if only temporarily. The sublime offers a path to identifying with reality as it is in itself, which involves *expanding* our consciousness.

The sublime privileges human beings not because of their rationality, but because they may be the only beings capable of suspending themselves as center of the world and identifying with the true core of the world from which everything (including us) emanates. The self becomes, as it were, a limitless point of view through which the world perceives itself as it really is. We become one with the bottomless emptiness that we essentially are.

14.5 CONCLUSION

Schopenhauer's account parts ways with Kant's and several other philosophers by insisting that a heightened awareness of our manifest fragility in the natural world offers us a unique occasion (perhaps matched only by engaging with profound music) to experience elatedly our ultimate identity with and nonseparateness from the world as a whole.[27] Sublime experience is neither moral nor merely relational; it is (no matter how uneasy it may be) close to being *fusional* since it allows us to become *one*, as it were, with the primal life energy permeating the whole of reality.[28] The sublime is not so much an experience of the indestructability of "humanity in our person," as Kant avers, as an "inhuman" or "superhuman" experience; that is, an experience by which we transcend our typically human concerns and become absorbed by inhuman nature itself. Schopenhauer's complex and ultimately affirmative account of the sublime intimates an aesthetic as well as existential and metaphysical intensity that is absent from other kinds of aesthetic experience. For, although we necessarily remain contemplating subjects when faced with sublime nature, our exalting experience of it offers a unique and particularly energizing way to confront the life-threatening and tragic aspects of the world and its exhilarating, unfathomable, awe-inspiring might.

This may be part of a plausible explanation of why it is that we actually *seek out* sublime objects. If Schopenhauer is right that confronting sublime objects may enable us to affirm our identity with the tremendous primal life energy of reality, then this cannot only inspire, comfort, and delight us but also *revitalize* us powerfully. Then we feel the will's exuberant lust for life and affirm our identity with it. By ultimately lifting the burden of anxiety that overwhelming natural objects cause, the sublime may enable confronting real-life disasters and suffering without denying life or yearning to escape from them. The experience of the sublime in nature may indeed considerably boost our energy levels, enabling us to cope more adequately with the vicissitudes of life instead of fleeing from them or ignoring them. Prefiguring Nietzsche's account of tragedy and the Dionysian, for Schopenhauer, the feeling of the sublime in nature is not ultimately moral but fundamentally existential and life-enhancing for it shows how even the utmost terror can be transformed into a joyful identification with and affirmation of the will-to-life. Schopenhauer's doctrine of the sublime thus offers an impressive, authentic route to appreciating fully the profound import of this type of complex, intense, and ennobling aesthetic experience.

NOTES

1. This chapter contains modified versions of material that appears in chapter 4 of my book *The Sublime in Schopenhauer's Philosophy* (Basingstoke: Palgrave Macmillan, 2015).
2. As said, in this chapter, I focus on the sublime in nature, which forms the core of Schopenhauer's theory of the sublime. For extended discussion of Schopenhauer's view of

the sublime in art, especially tragedy, and its connection with Schopenhauer's ethics, see chapter 6 of *The Sublime in Schopenhauer's Philosophy*. For more on the sublime in art, see Bart Vandenabeele, "Kant, the Mannerist and the Matterist Sublime," *Journal of Aesthetic Education* 49 (2015), 32–49, and Robert Wicks, "Kant on Fine Art: Sublimity Shaped by Beauty," *Journal of Aesthetics and Art Criticism* 53 (1995), 189–93.

3. The thought that in contemplating beauty "not even a recollection of the will remains" will prove to be pivotal in the comparison with the sublime.

4. In the Cambridge edition, "*Anhauch*" is translated as "intimation," which is a bit closer to the original German.

5. I offer a more extensive account of the existential and metaphysical significance of the sublime in the final chapter of *The Sublime in Schopenhauer's Philosophy*.

6. I borrow the term "the existential sublime" from Paul Crowther, *Critical Aesthetics and Postmodernism* (Oxford: Oxford University Press, 1993), chapter 6.

7. Schopenhauer does not insist that we need to be consciously aware of this to be able to experience the sublime, and it would be misguided if he had done so. Feeling uneasy is essential, Schopenhauer justly argues, but not our conscious recognition of the reasons for it. Here I cannot agree with Sandra Shapshay, who argues that Schopenhauer defends a type of, what she calls, "thick sublime" experience and that this type of experience would be more profound for having a cognitive (and often scientific) basis. See Sandra Shapshay, "Contemporary Environmental Aesthetics and the Neglect of the Sublime," *British Journal of Aesthetics* 53 (2013), 181–98. That the thick sublime "involves reflection upon the relationships between humanity and nature more generally" (189) turns the sublime into an overly intellective experience and unjustly undermines its aesthetic credentials. As I have argued in *The Sublime in Schopenhauer's Philosophy*, reflection on humanity and nature can be a valuable consequence of an experience of the sublime, and the sublime may lead to deep metaphysical insights, but these are not (necessarily) part of the aesthetic experience itself.

8. Immanuel Kant, *Critique of Judgment*, translated by Werner Pluhar (Indianapolis, IN: Hacket Publishing Company, 1987), 114.

9. Here and in what follows I take issue with Sophia Vasalou, who argues that, according to Schopenhauer, "the mind [is] the true object of sublimity." See Sophia Vasalou, *Schopenhauer and the Aesthetic Standpoint* (Cambridge: Cambridge University Press, 2013), 7 and *passim*. This seems to me to be a gross distortion of Schopenhauer's highly sophisticated analysis of the experience of the sublime. I would suggest that, despite obvious Kantian remnants in Schopenhauer's account, one important reason that Schopenhauer's doctrine is superior to its predecessor's is that it is more genuinely object-centered.

10. I am indebted to Malcolm Budd, "The Sublime in Nature," in *Kant's Critique of the Power of Judgement: Critical Essays*, edited by Paul Guyer (Lanham: Rowman & Littlefield, 2003), 121–42.

11. See Edmund Burke, *A Philosophical Enquiry into the Origin of Our Ideas of the Sublime and the Beautiful*, edited by J. T. Boulton (New York: Routledge, 2008), 136. See also Emily Brady, *The Sublime in Modern Philosophy: Aesthetics, Ethics, and Nature* (Cambridge: Cambridge University Press, 2013), 156: "As a baseline, actual physical safety from a lightning storm or erupting volcano is crucial for enjoying the spectacle. We could not engage in aesthetic disinterestedness if we were not in some position of safety or the equivalent, where we can give proper attention (e.g., we are not running away)."

12. Alex Neill argues that "uneasiness is the distinguishing mark" of the experience of the sublime. See Alex Neill, "Schopenhauer on Tragedy and the Sublime," in *A Companion to Schopenhauer*, edited by Bart Vandenabeele (Chichester: Wiley-Blackwell), 216 and *passim*. This cannot be right, however, for uneasiness is not sufficient to experiencing the sublime. Experiences of, for instance, ugliness, terrible beauty, and disgust involve uneasiness but are not therefore sublime.

13. The expression "transcendental pride" is Hans Blumenberg's. See Bart Vandenabeele, "Schopenhauer, Nietzsche, and the Aesthetically Sublime," *Journal of Aesthetic Education* 37 (2003), 94, and *The Sublime in Schopenhauer's Philosophy*, 109, 112, 114, 125, 127. See also, e.g., Brady, *The Sublime in Modern Philosophy*, 97; Paul Guyer, "The German Sublime after Kant," in *The Sublime: From Antiquity to the Present*, edited by Timothy M. Costelloe (Cambridge: Cambridge University Press, 2012), 112–14; Dale Jacquette, "Schopenhauer's Metaphysics of Appearance and Will in the Philosophy of Art," in *Schopenhauer, Philosophy, and the Arts*, edited by Dale Jacquette (Cambridge: Cambridge University Press, 1996), 22.

14. Here I differ from Christopher Janaway who argues that "what the sublime demands is that I recognize a situation as threatening or distressing—but without feeling personally threatened or distressed." See Christopher Janaway, "Knowledge and Tranquillity: Schopenhauer on the Value of Art," in *Schopenhauer, Philosophy, and the Arts*, edited by Dale Jacquette (Cambridge: Cambridge University Press, 1996), 56. I see no arguments in Schopenhauer's account to deny the possibility of feeling personally threatened and still being able to experience the sublime. On the contrary, Schopenhauer rightly maintains that "perceiving and acknowledging this hostile relation to *his* will" is essential to the sublime; that "the beholder may not direct his attention to this relation to *his* will"; and that "he may consciously turn away from it, forcibly tear himself from *his* will and its relations ... [!] those very objects terrible to the will" (WWR1$_{[P]}$, 201). Moreover, in his account of tragedy, the "shuddering" quality of our personal engagement in the sublime is developed more fully. I discuss this extensively in chapter 6 of my book *The Sublime in Schopenhauer's Philosophy*.

15. See Bart Vandenabeele, "Schopenhauer and the Objectivity of Art," in *A Companion to Schopenhauer*, edited by Bart Vandenabeele (Chichester: Wiley-Blackwell, 2012), 219–32, and Bart Vandenabeele, "Schopenhauer on Aesthetic Contemplation," in *Arthur Schopenhauer: Die Welt als Wille und Vorstellung*, Klassiker Auslegen, Band 42, edited by Oliver Hallich and Matthias Koßler (Berlin: De Gruyter, 2014), 101–18.

16. Janaway, "Knowledge and Tranquillity," 58.

17. See Bart Vandenabeele, "Beyond the Principle of Sufficient Reason? Schopenhauer's Aesthetic Phenomenology," in *Schopenhauer's Fourfold Root*, edited by Jonathan Head and Dennis Vanden Auweele (New York: Routledge, 2017), 169–74. See also Bart Vandenabeele, "Schopenhauer on the Values of Aesthetic Experience," *Southern Journal of Philosophy* 45, 2007, 565–82; Vandenabeele, "Schopenhauer on Aesthetic Contemplation," 112–16.

18. See Tom Cochrane, "The Emotional Experience of the Sublime," *Canadian Journal of Philosophy* 42 (2012), 134.

19. One notable exception is Paul Guyer, "Pleasure and Knowledge in Schopenhauer's Aesthetics," in *Schopenhauer, Philosophy, and the* Arts, edited by Dale Jacquette (Cambridge: Cambridge University Press, 1996), 109–32. There he rightly emphasizes that the Schopenhauerian sublime is "positively exalting" and offers not merely an escape

from the thralls of willing, since "we are not just relieved from the pain of being" but also experience "a joyful affirmation of our identity with reality" (129). He adds that Schopenhauer offers "no merely negative account of aesthetic pleasure, but a complex and ultimately affirmative account" (129). Unfortunately, he seems to have changed his mind recently and now completely disregards this essential affirmative aspect of Schopenhauer's doctrine of the sublime. While in the former article he still justly stressed the close link between Schopenhauer and Nietzsche, he now asserts that only Kant and Nietzsche offer "affirmative" accounts of the sublime and that, "given Nietzsche's later dismissal of Schopenhauer's aesthetics…, we should not expect him to be drawn to Schopenhauer's account of the sublime." See Guyer, "The German Sublime After Kant," 115. This seems to me to be utterly misguided, for while Nietzsche dismisses Schopenhauer's all too moral interpretation of the effect of tragedy, his treatment in *The Birth of Tragedy* of the Apollonian and Dionysian and his emphasis on transcending individuality and joyfully identifying with the primal unity of reality clearly build on Schopenhauer's affirmative account of the sublime.

20. For an alternative to Schopenhauer's theory of the sublime, see chapter 5 of my *The Sublime in Schopenhauer's Philosophy*.

21. See, most notably, Sandra Shapshay, "Schopenhauer's Transformation of the Kantian Sublime" and "The Problem with the Problem of Tragedy: Schopenhauer's Solution Revisited," *British Journal of Aesthetics* 52 (2012), 17–32; Julian Young, "Death and Transfiguration: Kant, Schopenhauer and Heidegger on the Sublime," *Inquiry* 48 (2005), 131–44.

22. Guyer, "Pleasure and Knowledge in Schopenhauer's Aesthetics," 129.

23. Brady, *The Sublime in Modern Philosophy*, 83. On the same page, she also contends that Kant "is not arguing for a dominion of humans over nature." It depends on what is exactly meant by "dominion" here. Obviously, Kant does not contend that we ought to spoil nature or behave disrespectfully toward it, but he does argue that the sublime manifests a dominion of practical reason over nature, and practical reason is a capacity possessed by human beings—a capacity, which allows us (to speak Kant's idiom) to make use of nature's power to express the infinite superiority of our own rationality. See also Guyer, "The German Sublime after Kant," 112.

24. Interestingly, the "constant struggle" of "saintly people" with their wills parallels the violent struggle with the will in the aesthetically sublime. See WWR1$_{[P]}$, 391. From this does not follow, however, that "we thus have reason to question whether Schopenhauer has really left the rational spontaneity view behind," as Sandra Shapshay nevertheless claims. See Sandra Shapshay, "Schopenhauer's Early *Fourfold Root* and the Ghost of Kantian Freedom," in *Schopenhauer's Fourfold Root*, edited by Jonathan Head and Dennis Vanden Auweele (New York: Routledge, 2017), 91. Schopenhauer does not describe nor defend some kind of (neo-)Kantian rational freedom which comprises liberating reason from the influence of inclinations, but a somehow more radical possibility; namely, of wholly transcending our will-to-life by contemplating the beautiful and the sublime and of abolishing will-to-life altogether through asceticism.

25. I have developed this line of thought in more detail in chapter 5 of *The Sublime in Schopenhauer's Philosophy*.

26. See *The Sublime in Schopenhauer's Philosophy*, 171–76.

27. Schopenhauer's doctrine hence prefigures Nietzsche's account of Dionysian pleasure in tragedy. See Friedrich Nietzsche, *The Birth of Tragedy and Other Writings*, edited by

Raymond Geuss and Ronald Speirs, translated by Ronald Speirs (Cambridge: Cambridge University Press, 1999), especially in *The Birth of Tragedy*, §17, 80–85.

28. Compare with Nietzsche's famous reference to Heraclitus' image of the playing child-god in *The Birth of Tragedy*, §24, 114.

FURTHER READING

Brady, Emily. *The Sublime in Modern Philosophy: Aesthetics, Ethics, and Nature.* Cambridge: Cambridge University Press, 2013.

Budd, Malcolm. "The Sublime in Nature." In *Kant's Critique of the Power of Judgement: Critical Essays*, edited by Paul Guyer. Lanham: Rowman & Littlefield, 2003, 121–42.

Burke, Edmund. *A Philosophical Enquiry into the Origin of Our Ideas of the Sublime and the Beautiful* (1757), edited by J. T. Boulton. New York: Routledge, 2008.

Cochrane, Tom. "The Emotional Experience of the Sublime." *Canadian Journal of Philosophy* 42 (2012): 125–48.

Crowther, Paul. *Critical Aesthetics and Postmodernism.* Oxford: Oxford University Press, 1993.

Guyer, Paul. "Pleasure and Knowledge in Schopenhauer's Aesthetics." In *Schopenhauer, Philosophy, and the Arts*, edited by Dale Jacquette. Cambridge: Cambridge University Press, 1996, 109–32.

Guyer, Paul. "The German Sublime after Kant." In *The Sublime: From Antiquity to the Present*, edited by Timothy M. Costelloe. Cambridge: Cambridge University Press, 2012, 102–17.

Jacquette, Dale. "Schopenhauer's Metaphysics of Appearance and Will in the Philosophy of Art." In *Schopenhauer, Philosophy, and the Arts*, edited by Dale Jacquette. Cambridge: Cambridge University Press, 1996, 1–36.

Janaway, Christopher. "Knowledge and Tranquillity: Schopenhauer on the Value of Art." In *Schopenhauer, Philosophy, and the Arts*, edited by Dale Jacquette. Cambridge: Cambridge University Press, 1996, 39–61.

Neill, Alex. "Schopenhauer on Tragedy and the Sublime." In *A Companion to Schopenhauer*, edited by Bart Vandenabeele. Chichester: Wiley-Blackwell, 2012, 206–18.

Nietzsche, Friedrich. *The Birth of Tragedy and Other Writings*, edited by Raymond Geuss and Ronald Speirs, translated by Ronald Speirs. Cambridge: Cambridge University Press, 1999.

Shapshay, Sandra. "The Problem with the Problem of Tragedy: Schopenhauer's Solution Revisited." *British Journal of Aesthetics* 52 (2012): 17–32.

Shapshay, Sandra. "Contemporary Environmental Aesthetics and the Neglect of the Sublime." *British Journal of Aesthetics* 53 (2013): 181–98.

Shapshay, Sandra. "Schopenhauer's Early *Fourfold Root* and the Ghost of Kantian Freedom." In *Schopenhauer's Fourfold Root*, edited by Jonathan Head and Dennis Vanden Auweele. New York: Routledge, 2017, 80–98.

Vandenabeele, Bart. "Schopenhauer, Nietzsche, and the Aesthetically Sublime." *Journal of Aesthetic Education* 37 (2003): 90–106.

Vandenabeele, Bart. "Schopenhauer on the Values of Aesthetic Experience." *Southern Journal of Philosophy* 45 (2007): 565–82.

Vandenabeele, Bart. "Schopenhauer and the Objectivity of Art." In *A Companion to Schopenhauer*, edited by Bart Vandenabeele. Chichester: Wiley-Blackwell, 2012, 219–32.

Vandenabeele, Bart. "Schopenhauer on Aesthetic Contemplation." In *Arthur Schopenhauer: Die Welt als Wille und Vorstellung*, Klassiker Auslegen, Band 42, edited by Oliver Hallich and Matthias Koβler, Berlin: De Gruyter, 2014, 101–18.

Vandenabeele, Bart. "Kant, the Mannerist and the Matterist Sublime." *Journal of Aesthetic Education* 49 (2015): 32–49.

Vandenabeele, Bart. *The Sublime in Schopenhauer's Philosophy*. Basingstoke: Palgrave Macmillan, 2015.

Vandenabeele, Bart. "Beyond the Principle of Sufficient Reason? Schopenhauer's Aesthetic Phenomenology." In *Schopenhauer's Fourfold Root*, edited by Jonathan Head and Dennis Vanden Auweele. New York: Routledge, 2017, 162–78.

Vasalou, Sophia. *Schopenhauer and the Aesthetic Standpoint: Philosophy as a Practice of the Sublime*. Cambridge: Cambridge University Press, 2013.

Wicks, Robert. "Kant on Fine Art: Sublimity Shaped by Beauty." *Journal of Aesthetics and Art Criticism* 53 (1995): 189–93.

Young, Julian. "Death and Transfiguration: Kant, Schopenhauer and Heidegger on the Sublime." *Inquiry* 48 (2005): 131–44.

CHAPTER 15

SCHOPENHAUER AND THE METAPHYSICS OF MUSIC

PAUL GORDON

One becomes more of a philosopher the more one becomes a musician.

—Nietzsche

OF the four symphonic "movements" that constitute, according to Thomas Mann, *The World as Will and Representation*, this chapter focuses on the rather wordily titled Book III: "The World as Representation Second Aspect: The Representation Independent of the Principle of Sufficient Reason: The Platonic Idea: The Object of Art" and, in particular, on the climactic discussion of music (WWR1$_{[P]}$, 255–67). However, it is impossible to discuss Schopenhauer's view of art in general and music in particular as metaphysical being without first explaining his famous redefinition of Kant's supersensible thing-in itself (*eine Sache an sich*) as Will and his redefinition of the Platonic Idea mentioned prominently in Book III's subtitle.

Schopenhauer referred to his redefinition of the Kantian "thing in-itself" in terms of the Will as his most important idea: "In 1836...I already published the really essential supplement to this book, which contains the most characteristic and important step of my philosophy, namely the transition from the phenomenon to the thing-in-itself, given up by Kant as impossible" (WWR2$_{[P]}$, 191). There are thus two "wills" in Schopenhauer, the more obvious one being the temporal reality of our subjective striving that is governed by the "principle of sufficient reason" as the limited truth of our own immediate needs and concerns. But while this "reality principle" of our constantly striving will only appears to us through the temporally limited experiences of our everyday reality, there is another, original Will that can never know itself as such, for it knows only what it knows objectively at any given moment: "Time is merely the spread-out and piecemeal view that an individual being has of the Ideas. These are outside time, and consequently eternal" (WWR1$_{[P]}$, 176). As Sophia Vasalou notes: "driven by the needs and desires of our embodied existence, what we know is always particular things in particular times and places, and how these affect us or impact on our self-interest. This road, which I must take for work, this tree…Schopenhauer's claim was that this mode of interested knowledge could be overcome."[1]

Here we see that, under special circumstances, it is possible to both be the Will as well as to stand outside it, albeit with the equally necessary caveat that such Platonic Ideas—whether through the representations of philosophy (WWR1, Book I) or art (WWR1, Book III)—stand "outside time" and are consequently eternal, rather than being mere objective "ideas" or lesser works of art that do not really represent the Will since they are trapped within it. In his introduction to a recent volume on Schopenhauer and art, Dale Jacquette notes how aesthetic contemplation provided Schopenhauer with a way of accessing the metaphysical Will while, at the same, allowing us to understand art.

> Aesthetic contemplation induces a silencing of the individual will, without which the intellect cannot be receptive to the Platonic forms embodied in nature and art. This ability Schopenhauer insists is reserved for a gifted minority. To stand enthralled before a magnificent artwork or natural scene is at least briefly to lose oneself, and to enter a state of relative will-less admiration of form, in which the slightest taint of desire or striving disqualifies the experience as truly aesthetic. The artist, then, is first and foremost a knower, someone with a distinctive albeit nonrepresentational imagination-enhanced knowledge of Platonic Ideas acquired by sensory experience of the world as idea.[2]

Given Vasalou's and Jacquette's reference to Platonic Ideas, as well as the subtitle of Book III of *The World as Will and Representation* ("The Representation Independent of the Principle of Sufficient Reason: The Platonic Idea: The Object of Art"), we will now turn to the second question posed earlier concerning Schopenhauer's redefinition of the Platonic Idea as art. Our ordinary view of things, which is governed by the aforementioned principle of sufficient reason, is perfectly "sufficient" for our everyday needs in taking, as it were, "snapshots" that we can then substitute for reality, but such static images do not give us their true nature or underlying Reason (*Vernunft*; Schopenhauer thus redefines Kantian *Verstand* as less "necessary" than Reason's less necessary truths!). Schopenhauer is drawn to Plato's philosophical Ideas as an attempt to replace these merely sufficient truths with necessary ones that *do* represent reality "in itself," but as the "Third Man" argument of Aristotle[3] and others have argued, Plato's Ideas, insofar as they are concepts, are in reality no more necessary than the merely sufficient truths they would replace, and they are certainly not reality "in itself." As Paul Lauxtermann notes, Schopenhauer's version of Plato's "Ideas are not to be conflated with concepts (*Begriffe*). Idea is original unity fallen apart owing to the forms of space and time of our perceptive apprehension (*unitas ante rem*)."[4] This distinction between Ideas as concepts and the Idea as original "oneness" is important in light of Schopenhauer's reference to Ideas as lesser "levels of the objectification of will" that are more evident in, say, the plastic arts, and the Idea as "will itself," which is expressed in music.[5]

Art, the very thing that Plato rejects as merely part of the ever-changing world of appearances, is thereby in a position to solve the "Third Man" difficulty and to represent the very thing-in-itself that Plato's Ideas fail to capture. It is for this reason that Schopenhauer embraces the idea of the Idea while, at the same time, redefining it in the very aesthetic terms that Plato seemingly rejected.

I say "seemingly" because I would like to consider a text where Plato himself redefines the Platonic Idea in terms that prefigure Schopenhauer's and that challenge his so-called rejection of art's importance, metaphysical or otherwise. Diotima's speech in the *Symposium* constitutes the philosophical center of Plato's most formally refined dialogue about love/beauty (beauty is defined as the object of love, and love as the pursuit of beauty), and the philosophical center of that speech is where Diotima—as opposed to Socrates who, according to his mentor, may or may not be capable of understanding this speech—attempts to describe "a beauty whose nature is marvelous indeed" [*ti thaumaston ten phusin kalon*], the absolute truth toward which all lesser forms of knowledge aspire.

> The man who has been guided thus far in the mysteries of love...*will* suddenly (*hapnos*) *have revealed to him...a beauty whose nature is marvelous indeed*...This is the right way of approaching or being initiated into the mysteries of love, to begin with examples of beauty in this world, and using them as steps to ascend continually with that absolute beauty as one's aim, from one instance of physical beauty to two and from two to all, then from physical beauty to moral beauty, and from moral beauty to the beauty of knowledge, until from knowledge of various kinds one arrives at the supreme knowledge whose sole object is that absolute beauty, and knows at last what absolute beauty is, viz., *kai gnô auto teleutôn ho esti kalon*.[6]

Notwithstanding Plato's—as opposed to Diotima's—famous rejection of art, it is there that one "suddenly" finds the highest form of beauty (Diotima insists on this adverbial qualifier) "whose sole object is absolute beauty"—beauty that is absolute, eternal, unchanging, and perfect in itself. For although Diotima makes a point of excluding all *objects* from this realm, be they intellectual or corporeal ("Nor again will this beauty appear to him like the beauty of a face or hands or anything else corporeal"[7]), the art "object" which, as Kant, New Criticism, and others have all argued, is no object at all, perfectly fits Diotima's description of a sphere of absolute ideas (the same, I would argue, as Kant's "aesthetic ideas"). Indeed, Bart Vandenabeele claims that music, in particular, corresponds best to the ultimate, absolute form of beauty Diotima describes: "In his account of the value of music, however, Schopenhauer comes closer to Plato's description of the experience of beauty, since enjoying music is really rejoicing in being part of being itself."[8]

And so, when Schopenhauer insists that Plato's "greatest mistake" was in excluding art from the realm of absolute ideas, and thus from any metaphysical importance, he is, in fact, merely agreeing with Socrates's mentor against her seemingly befuddled student.

But now, what kind of knowledge is it that considers what continues to exist outside and independently of all relations, but which alone is really essential to the world, the true content of its phenomena, that which is subject to no change, and is therefore known with equal truth for all time, in a word, the Ideas that are the immediate and adequate objectivity of the thing-in-itself, of the will? It is art, the work of genius.   (WWR1$_{[P]}$, 184)

Although Schopenhauer does not, in this redefinition of art as the Platonic Idea, refer to the *Symposium*, further evidence of his having been influenced by that particular dialogue is found in his statement that "the transition that is possible, but to be regarded only as an exception, from the common knowledge of particular things to knowledge of the Idea takes place *suddenly* [*plötzlich*], since knowledge tears itself free from the service of the will precisely by the subject's ceasing to be merely individual, and being now a pure will-less subject of knowledge" (WWR1$_{[P]}$, 178). Note, in particular, Schopenhauer's insistence, which repeats Diotima's, that the shift from our ordinary understanding of things under the domination of the principle of sufficient reason to absolute knowledge of Being in-itself occurs "suddenly." In light of Schopenhauer's definition of the ordinarily persistent principle of sufficient reason their—Diotima's and Schopenhauer's—insistence on the "suddenness" of such "knowledge" is important, for, since the aesthetic Idea is not an object (Kant repeatedly insists upon this), it can only appear "suddenly," and, for the same reason, disappear just as quickly.

So, how is it possible to represent something that, in the words of Diotima, is "absolute beauty in its essence, pure and unalloyed"? Schopenhauer states: "It is certain that, if it is possible for us to raise ourselves from knowledge of particular things to that of the Ideas, this can happen only by a change taking place in the subject. Such a change is analogous and corresponds to that great change of the whole nature of the object, and by virtue of it the subject, in so far as it knows an Idea, is no longer individual" (WWR1$_{[P]}$, 176). He goes on to describe this "change taking place in the subject," and thus also in "the whole nature of the object," in terms of the aesthetic *disinterestedness* described by Kant: "If all these [interested] relations were eliminated, the objects also would have disappeared for knowledge " (WWR1$_{[P]}$, 177). Warhol's famous soup can, for example, accomplishes this by taking an ordinary object and completely removing it from its ordinariness, thereby freeing the "object" from any previous recognizable relationship, including that of its own existence.[9] Or, to use Schopenhauer's own example of this new relationship between subject and object,

Now, as a rule, knowledge remains subordinate to the service of the will, as indeed it came into being for this service; in fact, it sprang from the will, so to speak, as the head from the trunk. With the animals, this subjection of knowledge to the will can never be eliminated. With human beings, such elimination appears only as an exception, as will shortly be considered in more detail [viz., in art]. This distinction between man and animal is outwardly expressed by the difference in the relation of head to trunk. In the lower animals both are still deformed; in all, the head is directed to the ground, where the object of the will lie. Even in the higher animals, head and trunk are still far more one than in man, whose head seems *freely* set on to the body, only carried by the body and not serving it. This human superiority is exhibited in the highest degree by the Apollo Belvedere. The head of the god of the Muses, with eyes looking far afield, stands so *freely* on the shoulders that it seems to be wholly delivered from the body, and no longer subject to its cares.

(WWR1$_{[P]}$, 177–8, emphasis added)

This is not said, as readers of Schopenhauer know full well, to the detriment of our animal friends; it merely points to the essential difference between interestedness and the disinterested "contemplation" (also a Kantian notion) that sees nothing in particular but everything in its higher reality—precisely the Idea as opposed to any object, or idea, as such.

Schopenhauer's indebtedness to Kant's groundbreaking (and often misunderstood[10]) notion of aesthetic disinterestedness is often overlooked entirely or, what is worse, given only passing reference by his critics, as is his repeated insistence on "contemplation," which Kant had already defined as the essential mode, or mood, of aesthetic disinterestedness. With regard to the "sudden" appearance of the Idea mentioned earlier, Schopenhauer adds: "Such a subject of knowledge no longer follows relations in accordance with the Principle of Sufficient Reason; on the contrary, it rests in fixed contemplation of the object presented to it out of its connexion with any other, and rises into this" (WWR1$_{[P]}$, 178) and, a page later: "Now in such contemplation, the particular thing at one stroke becomes the Idea of its species, and the perceiving individual becomes the pure subject of knowing." As this is Schopenhauer's explanation of the "aesthetic absolute,"[11] the elevation of the aesthetic "object" to the status of metaphysical Being, it is worth pausing to contemplate this essential idea further.

Both Kant and Schopenhauer describe the proper attunement to art as "contemplation" because it is, so to speak, a state of "intellectual intuition" (*intellektuale Anschauung*) in which the spectator sees or hears the "object" as it really is, not as it is seen or heard by the noncontemplating individual.[12] What is seen or heard in a state of aesthetic contemplation is not the object one is seeing or the sound one is hearing but, rather, a *moment* outside time in which the object is freed from its objectivity and, correspondingly, the subject is freed from her subjectivity. This "exceptional" state resembles thinking, but it is pure thinking rather than thinking about something in particular. It is linked to the absolute "thing-in-itself," the very absolute described by Diotima, because it is necessarily infinite rather than finite or, in Schelling's words, the "infinite finitely displayed."[13] It is thus that Schopenhauer redefines the art "object," the "aesthetic Idea," as the very embodiment of the "eternal, unchanging" Idea described by Diotima:

We may take this opportunity to mention yet another point on which our theory of Ideas differs widely from that of Plato. Thus he teaches (*Republic*, X) that the object which art aims at expressing, the prototype of painting and poetry, is not the Idea, but the individual thing. The whole of our discussion so far maintains the very opposite, and Plato's opinion is the less likely to lead us astray, as it is the source of one of the greatest and best known errors of that great man, namely of his disdain and rejection of art, especially of poetry.   (WWR1$_{[P]}$, 212)

Rather than tempering Schopenhauer's comments I would go even further in pointing to Plato's "error" as largely responsible for a devaluing of art that, despite subsequent arguments that "maintain the very opposite" by Nietzsche, Heidegger, and others, continues to inform—or rather, deform—our understanding not only of art but, indeed, of knowledge itself. When Diotima describes the highest state of Being in surprisingly sensory terms that make of its participant "a god, if that is possible," we may further our understanding of this exceptional state by claiming that, in the experience of fine art in general and music in particular, we experience exactly that. For Schopenhauer himself, this exalted relationship between art, music, and Being is stated in the beautiful conclusion of the second version of Book III, where he states: "Perhaps someone or other might take offence at the fact that music, which indeed often spiritually exalts us to such an extent that we might believe that it speaks of other and better worlds than our own ... really only flatters the will for life ... expressing its satisfaction and gratification. The following passage from the Vedas may serve to still such doubts: 'And *Anandsroup*, which is a form of joy, they [also] call the Great Soul, because wherever there is joy it is part of its joy'" (WWR2$_{[AC]}$, 514).

15.1 THE METAPHYSICS OF MUSIC

We will now attempt to demonstrate the truth of Schopenhauer's view of art in general and music in particular as the "Idea." Although Philip Alperson has argued that Schopenhauer "fails in his main aim—to show that musical experience provides us with a unique kind of revelation,"[14] I hope to show that this "failure" is rather the failure to understand the "unique kind of revelation" that art and music provide. As Alperson himself notes in this quotation from Schopenhauer, it is imperative that we recognize the different sort of "object" with which we are dealing before dismissing it as inadequate in ordinary, objective terms: "These Platonic Ideas lie outside the sphere of knowledge available to us in our normal world of experience. However, they can become an object of knowledge in aesthetic contemplation. In aesthetic contemplation, one steeps oneself in the disinterested perception of an object and the contemplated object passes out of the relations of the principle of sufficient reason to reveal Platonic Ideas."[15]

It is impossible to read these words without realizing the profound agreement between Schopenhauer's view of "aesthetic contemplation" and Kant's, and we would again point to Schopenhauer's inheritance of Kant's important notion (the first

"Moment" of the *Analytic of the Beautiful*) that art has nothing to do with the "interested" object or, indeed, with any object as such, as itself a reason for Schopenhauer's elevation of music. That is to say, precisely because music is the least objective of the arts—indeed, it doesn't really exist insofar as it is always already elsewhere in time—Schopenhauer turns the usual devalorization of music by Aristotle[16] and others on its head. (If, as Nathan Rotenstreich notes, Kant also devalued music, then this is less damning given that "Music, according to Kant, advances from sensations to indefinite ideas while other art advances from definite ideas to sensation."[17]) And yet one must not take Schopenhauer's rankings of the various arts, and his elevation of music, too seriously, for music is merely quantitatively, not qualitatively different from the other arts, which are also nonobjective representations of the metaphysical will: "For, at the moment when, torn from the will, we have given ourselves up to pure, will-less knowing we have stepped into another world, so to speak, where everything that moves our will, and thus violently agitates us, *no longer exists*" (WWR1$_{[P]}$, 197, emphasis added). The Platonic Idea as art "object" is thus both the highest expression of the will and the least will-full because it sees (or hears) *itself* rather than continuing to exist under the sway of a principle of sufficient reason that separates the subject from its object: "Then, as pure subject of knowing, delivered from the miserable self, we become entirely one with those objects" (WWR1$_{[P]}$, 199). In this respect, music is no different from any of the other arts: "we are no longer the individual; that is forgotten; we are only pure subject of knowledge. We are only that one eye of the world" (WWR1$_{[P]}$, 198). As Paul Guyer notes: "This implies, first, that responding to a piece of music need not involve or invoke the individual will of the particular listener."[18]

To the extent that one exists in the world as a separate will-full subject, one is also separate from "that blessedness of will-less perception which spreads so wonderful a charm over the past" (WWR1$_{[P]}$, 198). Schopenhauer's passing reference to a "remembrance of things past" among his examples of aesthetic will-less representation is important for our understanding of his reverence for music because, just as music bears no relation to our will as such but only to its representation, so the past can become a vehicle for such will-less representation provided that it is purged of its own reality. This, one imagines, was the inspiration for Nietzsche's famous statement, made when he was still under the sway of Schopenhauer's influence, that "the world is to be viewed in aesthetic terms" rather than real or moral ones: "Then the world as representation alone remains; the world as will has disappeared" (WWR1$_{[P]}$, 199).

Just as Schopenhauer refers to art as the "blessedness" of a will-less knowing that remembers the past by forgetting it (another notion adopted by Nietzsche), he also refers to sight—or rather light and color—as vehicles of the Idea insofar as they, unlike the other senses (including hearing), are immune from pleasure and pain and, thus, of willing. Pure light and color, as opposed to the objects in which they "inhere," are like the Idea as opposed to the idea: that is, they have nothing to do with the reality that they illuminate for they are illumination as such. Although Schopenhauer's privileging of sight over sound here would seem to contradict his privileging of music over the visual arts later in Book III, it would be better to consider this a reminder that it is what the various arts have in common—namely, their separation from the senses and willing as such—that matters more than what separates them. I would thus strongly disagree with Philip Alperson's contention that "music is not so much at the top of Schopenhauer's hierarchy of the arts (as some commentators say) as beyond it."[19] There is, to be sure, a quantitative difference between the different arts, but as the term itself suggests, there is only one "art."

This leads to a fundamental question with regard to Schopenhauer's privileging of music: How is it that the medium most closely akin to the will, and most closely associated with one of the senses other than the one least associated with the will (sight), is viewed as the highest of the will-less forms of representation? With regard to the essential problem of whether or how music can possibly embody the Will, it is essential to realize that we are not talking about the literal, personal will but, rather, the metaphysical Will that is the ground of the former but different. In other words, it is essential to approach music via the absolute, metaphysical will as a way of "knowing" the latter, rather than to approach music via the will in nonmetaphysical, nonabsolute, personal terms. This is the only way that Schopenhauer's statement that "We could just as well call the world embodied music as embodied Will" (WWR1$_{[P]}$, 262–63) and that, paraphrasing Leibniz, ~~that~~ music is "an unconscious exercise in metaphysics in which the mind does not know it is philosophizing" (WWR1$_{[P]}$, 264) makes sense, as opposed to Israel Knox's view that "Music peals forth the metaphysics of our own being the crescendo, the climax, the crises, the resolutions, of our own striving impetuosity, peace, and the retardations and accelerations, the surging and passivity, the power and silence of things"[20]

Schopenhauer is no mere vitalist. Rather, as the "thing-in-itself," Will is also the supersensible absolute, the Idea that can never be perceived or known as such because it underlies such ideas as the unity between ourselves and the world, before said absolute is divided into subject/object, self/other, etc. Understood thus, all art is music that is, more or less, frozen in time[21]; "more or less" because Schopenhauer ranks the various arts according to their proximity to the pure nonexistent (as such) of music, with architecture the lowest, most material grade: "The common aim of all the arts is the unfolding and elucidation of the Idea expressing itself in the object of every art, of the will objectifying itself at each grade" (252). What painting, for example, gives us "objectively" is really what music gives us less objectively—which is why, in the twentieth century in particular but even earlier, painters have often described their work in musical terms that border on, and even at times become, synesthetic.[22]

Having explained why music represents the will best because it represents the will least objectively, we can understand Schopenhauer when he insists that "In it [music] we do not recognize the copy, the repetition, of any Idea of the inner nature of the world" and yet, on the same page (WWR1$_{[P]}$, 256), that "we must attribute to music a far more serious and profound significance that refers to the innermost being of the world and of our own self." This is because the relation of music to "the innermost being of the world and of our own self"—i.e., the absolute—must remain a mystery, the same and different from the absolute of which it is the closest avatar. Because music is thus both the highest and the lowest of the arts relative to its objectivity and thus comprehensibility

Schopenhauer is forced to admit: "I recognize...that it is essentially impossible to demonstrate this explanation, for it assumed and establishes a relation of music as a representation to that which of its essence can never be representation, and claims to regard music *as the copy of an original that can itself never be directly represented*" (WWR1$_{[P]}$. 257, emphasis added).

He continues: "Therefore music is by no means like the other arts, namely a copy of the Ideas, but a copy of the will itself, the objectivity of which are the Ideas." This is *not* to say that music is the direct expression of our own individual, subjective will. This *is* to say that music is the beginning of the Idea that is then expressed in the other arts and, next, in philosophy. Schopenhauer thereby reverses the usual, Platonic order of things in which the more "frozen," objectified understanding is closest to the absolute (Truth). The difference between these two views is critical, although clarification of the latter, of how music is the "immediate objectification and copy of the whole will as the world itself is" is not readily apparent.

Since, by Schopenhauer's own admission, it is "essentially impossible" to explain literally how music represents the absolute will of the world, "Schopenhauer must decide: either he can stop writing about music altogether or he can continue to write indirectly. He chooses the latter."[23] Schopenhauer thus proffers a famously and explicitly "analogical" explanation that may serve as a catachresis—a necessarily metaphorical explanation of that which cannot be explained literally—of how this works: "However, in my view...Schopenhauer's philosophy of music can be interpreted as a deliberately unfitting, and hence, if successful, a perfectly fitting, monument to the musical art....Like Augustine, but more explicitly like Aquinas, Schopenhauer demonstrates the use to which arguments by analogy...can be put if philosophers are to say anything about that which, in the strictly philosophical terms of rational explanation, cannot be spoken about."[24]

In her insightful recent book on Schopenhauer, Sophia Vasalou argues that Schopenhauer's metaphysics is essentially aesthetic (a standpoint copied by the early Nietzsche) and, as such, cannot be expressed literally: "The appeal of traditional forms of rational persuasion, as already mentioned, was hard to surrender....One may thus pick up on the remarkable note of defeat that Schopenhauer would elsewhere strike when struggling to communicate particular philosophical insights."[25] Indeed, before one dismisses this figurative description in the name of a more literal but nonexistent "explanation," one should also ask oneself: what IS music? What *does* explain the existence of, say, Mozart's Fortieth Symphony in G minor, or Chet Baker's "My Funny Valentine," or Billie Holiday's "Strange Fruit," or Muddy Waters's "Long Distance Call"? Indeed, we have, all of us, listened to music for so long, not only individually but collectively as a species, that we must begin by acknowledging that we don't really understand the thing that we think we most readily understand—the mystery of music. So, let us listen to Schopenhauer despite his own caveat, a caveat that itself serves as a caveat to dismissing such a description.

With all these caveats in mind, I would like to modify Schopenhauer's own figurative description with slightly different ones, keeping in mind that these are not necessarily better figures but merely serve to drive home Schopenhauer's meaning, the "tenor" of his slightly different "vehicle." Instead of speaking of the mass of the earth as the "ground-bass" of our planetary existence from which melody, "high notes" emerge as the beginning of the objectification of the will ("Further, in the whole of the ripienos that produce the harmony, between the bass and the leading voice singing the melody, I recognize the whole gradation of the Ideas in which the will objectifies itself" [WWR1$_{[P]}$, 258]), think of the relation of the folk or blues singer to the instrument that accompanies her or him. The "ground-bass" in that case may be replaced by a guitar, which provides both the bass accompaniment as well as the accompanying chords. Think, for example, of the legendary folk singer, Bob Dylan. As Schopenhauer, Nietzsche, and others have written, the "words" of a song are not the song but only its further objectification, and not a very good one at that, for the song is the words *and* the music together, not one nor the other. Lyrics emerge from the music as both different and the same from the "ground bass" of the music, and, according to Schopenhauer, the melody/lyrics are an expression, not of some objective idea but, rather, of the perfect harmony between the guitar accompaniment (Schopenhauer's "ground-bass") and the melody that emerges from that, and the words that emerge from that.

Although artists themselves know full well that this is a continuum, the more literal-minded spectators often separate these various parts into their constituent elements, never realizing that by doing so they have lost track of the very thing they hope to explain. But, following Schopenhauer's insistence on the connection between such music and the absolute will of the world, one must rather acknowledge the "metaphysical" nature of such music in rejoining us to our origins—hence the importance, everywhere acknowledged since Telemachus first insisted upon it in the *Odyssey*, of "originality" in art.

The same can be said of Mozart's Fortieth Symphony, where the melody emerges out of—"in concert with"—the strings' opening ostinato. The memorable melody might seem to leave the rhythmic opening behind, but that is surely not the case. However, the fact that we think this is the case is important, for it is part of a common pattern of excluding the very "ground-bass" without which the melody, the first objectification of the will, would not exist. This is the "metaphysics of music": the emergence of something out of a "nothing" which is the underlying reality of that something. This differs from but resembles the emergence of thought out of the unconscious, for, in becoming conscious of an idea, as opposed to hearing a melody, we are even more inclined to dismiss the underlying un-conscious and thereby attenuate, or lose altogether, the underlying will which music expresses more fully.

In other words, music is the essence of what in the phenomenal world is mere appearance, although, to the extent to which that phenomenal world appears objectively in a poem or in a painting of seemingly recognizable objects, those other arts can represent that essence less directly. Metaphor, which moves in time if it is a "living," poetic metaphor and thereby eschews any singular objectivity, is a good example of this musical essence of things, which is why, as the founder of New Criticism I. A. Richards once stated that this metaphorical/musical essence is the truth of all important matters like religion, ontology, and of course art itself in all its forms.[26] "As a result of all this," says Schopenhauer, "we can regard the phenomenal world, or nature, and music as two different expressions of the same thing...we could just as well call the world embodied music as embodied will" (WWR1$_{[P]}$, 262–3). The Idea, it turns out, is that music and the phenomenal world only exist to the extent that it express that musical essence.

It is because of this identification of the innermost essence of the world with art in general and music in particular that Schopenhauer states that music expresses "a paradise quite familiar and yet eternally remote" (WWR1$_{[P]}$, 264). Most would doubtless agree that music is the expression of a certain "paradise," but Schopenhauer goes on to describe this paradise as "eternally remote" because it is our world and yet, in reality, not our world at all. For it is the expression not of who we are in reality nor, for that matter, any reality as such, but of who we were before our concept-/consciousness-ridden language grew into our ascendancy as adults (if ascendancy it can be called). In this respect, one encounters further connections between Schopenhauer and Freud (the one philosopher Freud acknowledged as an influence) insofar as Freud, too, identified paradise and all its "golden age" avatars with an infantile "Unconscious" that would later become the model of all art.[27]

In the final pages of Book III, Schopenhauer adds the tantalizing statement that "supposing we succeeded in giving a perfectly accurate and complete explanation of music," such "would also be at once a sufficient repetition and explanation of the world in concepts, or one wholly corresponding thereto, and hence the true philosophy" (WWR1$_{[P]}$, 264). Schopenhauer himself calls this a "paradox," thereby demonstrating that he is fully aware of the contradictory nature of such an explanation "of the world in concepts"; and yet, this leaves open the possibility of such an explanation in other terms, such as those proffered by Nietzsche, Freud, Heidegger, and others. Indeed, a more complete understanding of music such as Schopenhauer describes has begun to appear on the horizon of certain contemporary philosophers, such as Jean-Luc Nancy, whose notion of listening (as opposed to hearing) promises further progress in this regard.[28] In the words of Schopenhauer's student quoted at the beginning of this chapter, "One becomes more of a philosopher the more one becomes a musician."

NOTES

1. Sophia Vasalou, *Schopenhauer and the Aesthetic Standpoint* (Cambridge: Cambridge University Press, 2013), 24.
2. Dale Jacquette, "Schopenhauer's Metaphysics of Appearance and Will in the Philosophy of Art," in *Schopenhauer, Philosophy and the Arts*, edited by Dale Jacquette (Cambridge: Cambridge University Press, 1996), 11.
3. See *Metaphysics* 990b17–1079a13, 1039a2.
4. P. F. Lauxtermann, *Schopenhauer's Broken World-View* (Dordrecht: Kluwer Academic Publishers, 2000), 241.
5. "Because music does not, like all the other arts, depict the Ideas, or levels of the objectification of will, but immediately will itself" (WWR2$_{[AC]}$, 505).

6. *The Symposium*, translated by W. Hamilton (London: Penguin Books, 1951), 93. Note Plato's use of *ti thaumaston*, "something wonderous," which Plato described as the starting point of all philosophy.

7. Ibid., 93.

8. Bart Vandenabeele, *The Sublime in Schopenhauer's Philosophy* (Houndmills, Basingstoke, Hampshire: Palgrave Macmillan, 2015), 150.

9. This is attested to by Warhol's supposed response to someone who declared "I could have done that": "But, you didn't!"

10. For example, see Pierre Bourdieu, *Distinction: A Social Critique of the Judgement of Taste* (Cambridge, MA: Harvard University Press, 1984).

11. See my recent study of *Art as the Absolute: The Relation of Art to Metaphysics in Kant, Fichte, Schelling, Hegel and Schopenhauer* (New York: Bloomsbury, 2015).

12. Schopenhauer's contemptuous rejection of the *term* "intellectual intuition" was an obvious attempt to distance himself from "the period of pseudo-philosophy between Kant and myself" (WWR2$_{[AC]}$, 330) and from the false identification of this notion with any kind of cognition rather than a rejection of the *aesthetic* importance of this idea.

13. *System of Transcendental Idealism* (1800), translated by Peter Heath (Charlottesville: University of Virginia Press, 1978), 225.

14. Philip Alperson, "Schopenhauer and Musical Revelation," *Journal of Aesthetics and Art Criticism* 40 (Winter 1981), 155.

15. Ibid., 156. The author's main thesis is that "Schopenhauer, however, wants to have it both ways: he wants to say that musical revelation is otherwise ineffable and yet he wants to philosophize about it. But in the final analysis, Schopenhauer fails to demonstrate that music reveals or provides insight into a transcendental reality (and does this in a way or to a degree unparalleled by the other arts). Schopenhauer's theory of musical revelation cannot be justifiably maintained" (162).

   Respectfully, the kind of "revelation" that music provides *is* "justifiably maintained" every time we listen. "The claim to revelation is empty" (169) only insofar as all art, like Being itself, is "empty" of the sort of objectivity that, as Kant demonstrates, is completely irrelevant to art.

16. Aristotle, one will recall, ranked music as the next to least important of the six elements of tragedy.

17. Nathan Rotenstreich, "Schopenhauer on Beauty and Ontology," in *Schopenhauer, Philosophy and the Arts*, 152.

18. Paul Guyer, "Pleasure and Knowledge in Schopenhauer's Aesthetics" in *Schopenhauer, Philosophy and the Arts*, 127.

19. Alperson, "Schopenhauer and Musical Revelation," 157.

20. Israel Knox, "Schopenhauer's Aesthetic Theory," in *Schopenhauer—His Philosophical Achievement*, edited by Michael Fox (Sussex: The Harvester Press, 1980), 144.

21. Although Jacquette states that "Schopenhauer renounces Goethe's image of architecture as frozen music" (*Schopenhauer, Philosophy and the Arts*, 19), one won't get very far contradicting Goethe, and even less far in arguing that Schopenhauer (as well as other German artists and intellectuals) contradicted Goethe. The only thing made clear in the passage quoted to demonstrate this "renunciation" is that Schopenhauer viewed architecture, which is the most "useful" and thus unaesthetic of the arts, as a lesser medium. Indeed, in this passage (WWR2$_{[AC]}$, 511), it is clear that architecture as the frozen music reported by Eckermann is good as far as it goes; that is, as an analogy ("a kind of frozen music") which, given Schopenhauer's extensive use of same, is hardly to be rejected as such.

22. Shehira Doss-Davezac ("Schopenhauer according to the Symbolists: The Philosophical Roots of Late Nineteenth-Century French Aesthetic Theory," in *Schopenhauer, Philosophy and the Arts*, 249–76) describes Schopenhauer's enormous influence on Baudelaire and the Symbolists which included, but certainly not limited to, his privileging of music: "The identification of the arts with music rather than with words was to become the leit-motif of Symbolist, Decadent and Synthetist art.... [Symbolist theories] were developed further by Kandinsky and Klee, and later by the Abstract Expressionists, who experimented with painting so as to find how best to express in Schopenhauer's words 'joy and sorrow...to a certain extent in the abstract'" (273). I would also add that Baudelaire and the Symbolists were equally renowned for their interests in synesthesia. I discuss this and similar matters in my book on Synaesthetics: Art as Synaesthesia (New York: Bloomsbury Academic, 2020).

23. Lydia Goehr, "Schopenhauer and the Musicians," *Schopenhauer, Philosophy and the Arts*, 209.

24. Ibid., 201.

25. Vasalou, *Schopenhauer and the Aesthetic Standpoint*, 117.

26. "To this world belongs everything about which civilized man cares most...poetry is a central and typical denizen of this world." I. A. Richards, *Practical Criticism* (New York: Harcourt, Brace Jovanovich, 1929), 5.

27. This psychoanalytical view of art is expressed beautifully in the title as well as the substance of Sarah Kofman's study of Freud, *L'enfance de l'art* (*The Childhood of Art*, New York: Columbia University Press, 1988).

28. Jean-Luc *Nancy, Listening*, translated by Charlotte Mandell (New York: Fordham University Press, 2007).

FURTHER READING

Alperson, Philip. "Schopenhauer and Musical Revelation," *Journal of Aesthetics and Art Criticism*, 40 (Winter 1981): 155–66.

Bourdieu, Pierre. *Distinction: A Social Critique of the Judgement of Taste*. Cambridge: Harvard University Press, 1984.

Gordon, Paul. *Art as the Absolute: The Relation of Art to Metaphysics in Kant, Fichte, Schelling, Hegel and Schopenhauer*. New York: Bloomsbury, 2015.

Jacquette, Dale, ed. *Schopenhauer, Philosophy and the Arts*. Cambridge: Cambridge University Press, 1996.

Israel Knox, "Schopenhauer's Aesthetic Theory." In *Schopenhauer: His Philosophical Achievement*, edited by Michael Fox (Sussex: Harvester Press, 1980), 132–46.

Lauxtermann, P. F. *Schopenhauer's Broken World-View*. Dordrecht: Kluwer Academic Publishers, 2000.

Vandenabeele, Bart. *The Sublime in Schopenhauer's Philosophy*. Houndmills, Basingstoke, Hampshire: Palgrave Macmillan, 2015.

Vasalou, Sophia. *Schopenhauer and the Aesthetic Standpoint*. Cambridge: Cambridge University Press, 2013.

PART IV

HUMAN MEANING, POLITICS, AND MORALITY

CHAPTER 16

··

THE MORAL MEANING
OF THE WORLD

··

CHRISTOPHER JANAWAY

It is easy to come away from Schopenhauer's works with the impression that he regards existence as meaningless. After all, he writes,

> It is truly unbelievable how vacuously and meaninglessly [*Bedeutungsleer*] (viewed from the outside) and how dismally and insensibly (viewed from the inside) life flows away for the vast majority of human beings. It is a feeble yearning and a torment, a dream-like whirl through the four ages of life through to death, accompanied by a series of trivial thoughts. They are like mechanical clocks that are wound up and go without knowing why; whenever someone is begotten and born, the clock of human life is wound again so it can play the same hurdy-gurdy that has already been played countless times, movement by movement, beat by beat, with insignificant [*unbedeutenden*] variations.   (WWR1, 348)

The idea here is that each life, when viewed from a distance, abstracting from its particular goals and projects, comes and goes without apparent meaning and that, even from within each person's own life, no meaning is discerned because we do not really know why we go on living (Schopenhauer says of every human being "when asked why he wills in general, or why in general he wills to exist, he would not have an answer and in fact the question would make no sense to him" [WWR1, 188]). Moreover, all of this is not just a subjective impression, in Schopenhauer's view: as he emphatically states in chapter 46 of the second volume of *The World as Will and Representation*, human life genuinely has the property of *Nichtigkeit*—nothingness, vanity (in the sense of being in vain). The will, which is our essence, achieves no final satisfaction that amounts to real happiness, and no amount of transitory satisfaction compensates for the suffering to which any individual being (as a manifestation of the will) is inevitably subject. Worse still, it is not just that each petty individual life is in vain. The *whole* of existence shares the same emptiness. For the whole world is this aimless will. It has no positive value and is rather to be lamented than rejoiced over. Schopenhauer even states that, given the nature of our existence, it would have been better not to have existed: "A mature weighing of the matter yields the result that complete non-being [*das gänzliche Nichtseyn*] would be preferable to an existence [*Daseyn*] like ours" (PP2, 242).[1] So is not existence, the existence of the whole world, meaningless for Schopenhauer? The answer, perhaps surprisingly, is No.

We may have a tendency to group meaninglessness together with pessimism and presence of meaning together with optimism, or at least with the absence of pessimism. Surely the pessimist will be the one who finds *no* meaning in the world? But this is emphatically not the case for Schopenhauer. For one thing, he asserts that the world *must* have a meaning, on pain of failing to satisfy a fundamental human need. And furthermore, as I shall argue, he sees pessimism precisely as the key to the world's *having* such a meaning. In what follows we shall consider how Schopenhauer arrives at this position and whether he succeeds in expounding a coherent meaning for the world.

16.1 THE NEED FOR MEANING

First, we find Schopenhauer claiming that there must be what he calls a moral meaning to the world. In a rather dramatic passage in *Parerga and Paralipomena*, he writes,

> That the world has a mere physical but no moral significance [*Bedeutung*] is the greatest, most ruinous and fundamental error, the real perversity of the mind and in a basic sense it is certainly that which faith has personified as the antichrist.... Yet as certain as the feeling of a moral significance of the world and of life is, still clarifying it and unravelling the contradiction between it and the course of the world is so difficult that it was left to me to explain the true, only genuine and pure foundation of morality, which is therefore everywhere and always effective, along with the goal to which it leads.   (PP2, 183–84)

There are many points of note here. First, the significance (or meaning) of the world is "moral" and can be understood by grasping the "foundation of morality." Second, there is also a goal, end, or aim (*Ziel*) to which morality leads. Third, the moral meaning of the world stands *in contradiction to* the "course" of the world (*dem Laufe der Welt*)—the course, that is, of the very same world. The world runs on in a way that counters its own meaning. Fourth, the fundamental error of finding no moral significance or meaning is equated with "the antichrist," showing that Schopenhauer regards his view of the world's meaning as continuous with a view found in Christianity.

In another passage Schopenhauer calls the meaning in question "metaphysical" or "transcendent": "everyone bears within himself the conviction, however vaguely, that the world does not have merely a physical meaning but instead something like a metaphysical one, and even that with respect to such meaning our individual actions... are actually of transcendent significance" (PP2, 239). It may be true that some or all of us have this kind of conviction. Why, though, is the conviction correct? Why would it be such a drastic mistake to think otherwise? Schopenhauer's answer is that all humans have a constitutive need for metaphysics. He spells out this foundational thought in a chapter of the second volume of *The World as Will and Representation*, entitled "On Humanity's Metaphysical Need." The human being is a "metaphysical animal" and, by nature, seeks a kind of interpretation of reality that "claims to go beyond the possibility of experience, which is to say beyond nature or the given appearance of things, in order to disclose that which in some sense or other conditions appearance; or in common parlance, about what is hidden behind nature and makes it possible" (WWR2, 173). Metaphysics takes two distinct forms, philosophy and religion. Philosophy's concern is with truth in the literal sense (*sensu proprio*), which religion can never provide. The positive use of religion, however, is to provide truth in the allegorical sense (*sensu allegorico*), thus satisfying the metaphysical need for the benefit of the great mass of people who are not capable of philosophy.[2]

As we saw with his reference to the "antichrist," Schopenhauer is in an important respect on the same side as religion, and specifically of Christianity. There is a tradition of interpretation that strongly emphasizes this continuity. For instance, Paul Deussen, Schopenhauer's early twentieth-century follower (and founder of the Schopenhauer-Gesellschaft) called him *philosophus christianissimus*—the most Christian philosopher.[3] While Schopenhauer rejects any conception of a personal God and any notion of the world's being created out of nothing,[4] and while he shares the common view that the advance of science in the nineteenth century has caused a decline in religious belief and will eventually make it redundant, he does not accept that an exclusively naturalistic, scientific account of the world is satisfactory. Schopenhauer explains that a mere *physics*, or philosophy of nature, will always be inadequate because it gives us understanding of a mere surface, of appearance, whereas "*metaphysics* aims beyond appearance itself to that which appears" (WWR2, 187); in other words, the thing in itself. Despite this talk of what is "beyond" and "hidden behind" nature, Schopenhauer also insists that his metaphysics is immanent in that "it never breaks entirely free of experience but rather remains nothing more than an interpretation and analysis of experience" and "never speaks of the thing in itself other than in its relation to appearance" (WWR2, 192). He claims that his metaphysics is rooted in and gives an interpretation or "deciphering" of what is given in inner and outer experience (WWR2, 192). So his metaphysics of the thing in itself could be called a unifying and sense-making account of the world as we experience it.[5]

In Schopenhauer's view, then, to think that there are only naturalistic truths about reality is to deprive ourselves of an in-built human need. If there were no metaphysics at all, neither religious nor philosophical, then what Schopenhauer calls the mere "course of the world," one thing succeeding another in physical reality, one human individual arising, striving, suffering, and perishing, only to be succeeded by countless others, must indeed remain fundamentally meaningless and fundamentally unsatisfying. But if we land ourselves in that position we are in serious error, in Schopenhauer's view.

There must be some purpose beyond the world. In another passage he explains that the fundamental error of finding no meaning may be perpetrated by those who regard the world as an end in itself, or its own purpose (*Selbstzweck*). Some rival views to his own, namely pantheism and "mere fatalism," *cannot* assign the world a *moralische Bedeutung* precisely because "in assuming the latter the world always manifests itself as a means to a higher purpose" (PP2, 94).[6] If it were a *Selbstzweck*, it could not signify or point to any purpose beyond itself, and that would negate the possibility of the kind of meaning for which we have need. So, in other words, if the world has a moral meaning, then the world is a means to a higher purpose. And if we fail to assign it a higher purpose, we fail to find moral meaning and remain caught in the pernicious error. We will avoid that error only if we accept that the world should be viewed as a means to a higher purpose.

But what exactly is the higher purpose? Schopenhauer's programmatic statement already contains within it something of a conundrum because of its dual form, linking the elucidation of the all-important meaning both to a "foundation of morality" and to a "goal to which it leads." Independently of the question of how this goal is to be characterized, a potential problem of interpretation seems to open up. Is the meaning-giving goal something distinct, beyond morality, to which morality merely "leads"? And, if so, does the meaning of the world lie in the foundation of morality as such, or in the further goal, or somehow in both? Before squarely addressing this question, a preliminary task will be to explore these two notions in turn.

16.2 THE FOUNDATION OF MORALITY

Schopenhauer's foundation of morality is presented most clearly in the final chapter of the essay *On the Basis of Morals*. In the preceding chapter of the essay (chapter 3), Schopenhauer has argued that compassion is the sole basis of moral action and that what characterizes the compassionate agent is "making less of a distinction... between himself and others" (BM, 249). In the final chapter he turns to the related questions of metaphysics and meaning. He states that the ethical significance (*ethische Bedeutsamkeit*) of human actions must be metaphysical and that "the final summit in which the meaning of existence [*Bedeutung des Daseyns*] culminates must be the ethical [*das Ethische*]" (BM, 245). In the remainder of the chapter the issue of metaphysical meaning is addressed through the claim that the genuine moral agent, who acts out of compassion toward others, is seeing the world aright because the ultimate truth is that individuation is an illusion. Each human being is not really distinct from the All, and the foundation of morality is its being based in cognition of this truth.

This at least gives us a clear sense in which the "moral meaning" of the world stands in contradiction to the course of the world. This world as manifest to us empirically is inescapably individuated: we find ourselves as individuals separated by the forms of space and time, which Schopenhauer always refers to as the principle of individuation (*principium individuationis*). As empirically separate individuals, we each have a built-in drive to promote and satisfy one particular individual's natural needs and desires and a propensity to regard the individual as the center of the world. In Schopenhauer's famous image,

> Just as a captain sits in a boat, trusting the weak little vessel as the raging, boundless sea raises up and casts down howling cliffs of waves; so the human individual sits calmly in a world full of sorrow, supported by and trusting in the *principium individuationis*, which is how the individual cognizes things as appearance.   (WWR1, 379)

Morality taps into a deeper meaning because it shows us that the *principium individuationis* is not to be trusted. It intimates that individuals are less separate than they appear and, ultimately, not separate at all. Yet, at the same time, we cannot lightly throw off our sense of individuality and its associated egoism, which is endemic in every individual (animal as well as human) because it is "linked... with his innermost core and essence, and indeed is properly identical with it" (BM, 190). Thus egoism, and the outlook that assumes the individual as important and real, will inevitably continue to determine the course of the world despite its allegedly erroneous construal of ultimate reality.

There might be different ways of interpreting Schopenhauer's notion of "seeing through the *principium individuationis*" (WWR1, 405). Taken at its most literal, it would mean ceasing to believe that individuals are real and explicitly assenting to a metaphysics of the One. In the essay *On the Basis of Morals*, Schopenhauer is not overconcerned to discriminate between versions of this broad metaphysical position. He invokes the Vedas and Upaniṣads with their doctrine that *ātman* is *brahman*, then a whole host of parallel theories, including the Eleatics, Neo-Platonism, Sufism, Spinoza, and even Schelling (BM, 251–52). So, in order to "see through individuation," one need not believe specifically that the world is will. Action with moral worth is not tightly dependent for its foundation on the literal truth of Schopenhauer's own metaphysics: his is just one version of the required position.

But if moral agency merely reflects the illusoriness of individuation rather than requiring theoretical adherence to a metaphysical doctrine, we might also canvass another reading of "seeing through" that makes it an even looser notion. We ordinarily say that someone "sees through" something when they are not deceived as to its worth. Metaphysics aside, for the ordinary, straightforward agent, *trusting in* the principle of individuation presumably means locating supreme *value* in one's own individual existence and in satisfying the desires that pertain to it. *Not* trusting in the principle of individuation would correspondingly signify one's not finding privileged value there, not regarding the individual and its ends as mattering any more than all other parts of reality. Being able to adopt that evaluative attitude as an agent is arguably more central to the foundation of morality for Schopenhauer than adopting any metaphysical *belief*. For Schopenhauer holds that "moral excellence stands higher than all theoretical wisdom" (BM, 253), so that, in acting out of compassion, the ordinary agent already embodies the insight that sees through the principle of individuation. While there is no doubt that Schopenhauer holds the metaphysics of nonindividuation as true, the ordinary person who, in acting morally, ceases to trust in the *principium individuationis* need have no explicit cognition of this truth.

The point remains, however, that the true significance of moral action for Schopenhauer is its tracking of the alleged metaphysical truth. The moral agent is acting and apprehending others in line with the kind of metaphysics that Schopenhauer holds true and may be said to have an incipient distrust of individuation as such. We are now in a position to elucidate Schopenhauer's claims that "with respect to [moral] meaning our individual actions…are actually of transcendent significance" (PP2, 239) and that "the ethical significance of actions must be at the same time a metaphysical one" (BM, 245). Any action of genuine compassion reveals to the agent, at an intuitive, pre-theoretical level, that she relates to the world as a whole in a manner entirely different from the way appearance naturally suggests. The agent is not truly distinct from the world and therefore not distinct from other individuals. So this kind of human action has a higher moral or ethical significance because, in implicitly displacing value from its apparent center— that isolated individual afloat in an alien world—it reveals a truth about the world as a whole and the self's relation to it.

16.3 THE FINAL GOAL

Now recall once again that, when promoting his claim that there must be a moral meaning or significance to the world, Schopenhauer mentions not only the foundation of morality, but also the "the goal to which it leads" (PP2, 184). Much evidence suggests that the goal, end, or purpose to which Schopenhauer alludes is the negation of the will, the cessation of desire. He says, for example: "it is pain and suffering that work towards the true goal [*den wahren Zweck*] of life, the turning of the will away from it" (WWR2, 651). Some of Schopenhauer's most famous and most eloquent passages are devoted to this topic.

> We can gather…how blissful life must be for someone whose will is…calmed forever, indeed extinguished entirely except for the last glowing spark that sustains the body and is extinguished along with it. Such a person who, after many bitter struggles with his own nature, has ultimately prevailed completely, remains as only a pure, cognizing being, as an untarnished mirror of the world. Nothing can worry him anymore, nothing more can excite him, because he has cut all the thousands of threads of willing that keep us bound to the world and which, in the form of desires, fears, envy and anger, drag us back and forth amid constant pain. He gazes back calmly and smiles back at the phantasm of this world that was once able to move and torment his mind as well, but now stands before him as indifferently as chess pieces after the game is over, looking like discarded masks the morning after Carnival, although their forms taunted and disturbed us the night before. (WWR1, 417)

[W]e might figuratively call the complete self-abolition and negation of the will, the true absence of will, the only thing that can staunch and appease the impulses of the will forever, the only thing that can give everlasting contentment, the only thing that can redeem the world...—we might call this the absolute good, the *summum bonum*. We can look upon it as the one radical cure for the disease against which all other goods—such as fulfilled wishes and achieved happiness—are only palliatives, only anodynes.   (WWR1, 389)[7]

If "all other goods" are inferior to the self-abolition and negation of the will, where does this leave the value of morality? The notion that there is a higher value to which morality merely "leads" suggests what has been called an "instrumental" interpretation of the value of morality: the view that morality is ultimately valuable just in so far as it facilitates or prepares the way for the turning, or self-abolition, of the will and an eventual state of will-lessness.[8] Such an interpretation is supported by many passages. Schopenhauer says that the moral virtues of justice and loving kindness "encourage self-denial, and thus the negation of the will to life" (WWR2, 621). And in a letter of November 20, 1844, to Johann August Becker, he makes these explicit remarks:

> You ask: *for whom* moral actions have value?—For *him* that performs them....*Now as to what this value of moral action ultimately rests on*—...the value that such actions have for the one who performs them himself is a transcendent value, inasmuch as it lies in their leading him towards the sole path of salvation, i.e. deliverance from this world of being born, suffering and dying....So this contains the really *final elucidation* concerning the value [*Werth*] of morality, which value is not itself something absolutely final [*ein absolut Letztes*], but rather a step towards it.
>
> (GB, 220, my translation)

The notion of "final value" chimes with a number of passages in which he describes the apparently totally will-less state of motivational withdrawal from the world as the "final goal" of existence.[9] Though there is a good in an agent's alleviating or preventing suffering solely for the sake of the would-be sufferer, the "final value" accrues to the agent, who is thereby placed upon the path to salvation or revealed to be already upon it. My acting morally is then ultimately, and more importantly, good for me, in Schopenhauer's view.

16.4 A COHERENT MEANING?

It was suggested earlier that, by linking the putative meaning of the world both to the "foundation of morality" and to a distinct "goal," Schopenhauer may make it harder to understand how it is that just one single meaning is at stake. Now that we have seen that the goal, purpose, or end is the negation of the will, the difficulty seems to assume a more specific form. First, if the meaning we must seek (on pain of pernicious error) lies in this final state toward which morality is only a step or means, why is it to be called a "moral" meaning? If the meaning lies beyond morality and consists in having one's will turned away from the world, and from any action that intervenes in the world, then what is "moral" about it? To see the acuteness of this difficulty, consider the following points. If we take him literally at his word, Schopenhauer thinks that the ultimate state of salvation or deliverance is one of "true absence of will [*wahre Willenslosigkeit*]" (WWR1, 389). By contrast, the moral agent, in acting out of compassion, "wills someone else's well-being" (BM, 201). To be moral is to *will* a specified end; to be delivered from the world is to *cease* willing. It may be that Schopenhauer's talk of *total* will-lessness, or absence of all desires, is hyperbolic. After all, it is the naturally occurring desires of the "will to life" that must crucially be lost: that is to say, self-regarding desires centered upon the individual's pleasure and well-being and desires for acts that propagate the species. Schopenhauer says that "it...amounts to the same thing if, instead of simply saying 'the will,' we say 'the will to life'" (WWR1, 301). So perhaps some supremely selfless, ascetic desires will after all remain in someone in whom self-abolition of the will has occurred. At the very least, one has to desire to remain in that state.[10] However, the way in which Schopenhauer repeatedly characterizes the will-less state must cause us to wonder whether the supposed moral meaning of the world is to be found through indifference not only to self, but to the world, other beings included (as seems implied in "He gazes back calmly at the phantasm of this world that...now stands before him as indifferently as chess pieces after the game is over" [WWR1, 417]), or whether it is to be found through engagement *in* the world on behalf of other beings from whom one no longer feels separated.

A parallel tension is apparent if we consider Schopenhauer's views about suffering. If I am a supremely moral person, the suffering of others is precisely what motivates me: Schopenhauer defines willing the well-being of others in terms of preventing or alleviating their suffering (see BM, 202–19). On the other hand, he argues that suffering can benefit an individual: its occurrence can, if of sufficient magnitude, bring about the redemptive state in which the will negates itself (see WWR1, 424). "The fastest animal to carry you to perfection is suffering" says Schopenhauer in the words of Meister Eckhart (WWR2, 649). There is no contradiction in finding value both in freedom from suffering and in a redemptive deliverance from willing brought about through suffering, but it is nonetheless hard to see how these two values can coalesce in a way that helps to "clarify" that "moral significance of world and life" that Schopenhauer claims to have revealed. Does meaning reside in our identifying with (and indeed feeling[11]) the pain of others in a way that motivates us to remove it, or in acquiescing in pain as something that enables us to renounce our care for individual well-being? If morality per se genuinely furnishes some meaning and answers the metaphysical need (as *On the Basis of Morals* implied), are we not now going to be faced with two "meanings," one residing in the possibility of unselfish willing toward others, reflecting our essential nondistinction from them, the other residing in a redemptive absence of all willing and rejection of the world?[12]

Schopenhauer appears to see no problem here: he consistently treats the value of morality as continuous with that of the self-negation of the will. A prime instance of this can be seen in his interpretation of Christianity. He states that "Christianity is closest to us; its ethics...lead not only to the highest degree of loving kindness but also to renunciation" (WWR1, 413). For example, he praises the simplest early form of Christianity, which consists in the moral doctrines of the New Testament, "love of our neighbour as ourselves; beneficence; repayment of hatred with love and good deeds; patience; gentleness; the tolerance of all possible insults without resistance; abstinence in eating for the suppression of desire; resistance to the sex drive" (WWR1, 413), but does not regard this as Christianity in its fullest form. "In more developed Christianity, we see the *ascetic* seed coming into full blossom through the writings of the Christian saints and mystics" (WWR1, 413). Mysticism reaches "consciousness of the identity of one's own being with that of all things" (WWR2, 628) and is thereby the proper culmination of the ascetic self-denial that begins in New Testament morality. The initial seed and the final efflorescence are in a sense one and the same. Their uniting feature is the rejection of the individual self.

The chief difference between religions, for Schopenhauer, lies in whether they are optimistic or pessimistic.[13] What Christianity gets right, at least allegorically, in Schopenhauer's view, is its pessimism: "The nucleus and heart of Christianity are the doctrines of the Fall, original sin, the wickedness of our natural state and the corruption of natural mankind, connected with the intercession and reconciliation through the redeemer, in which one shares through faith in him. Thus, however, all of this reveals itself as pessimism" (PP2, 349). The "great fundamental truth" is thus "the need for redemption from an existence given over to suffering and death, and our ability to attain this redemption through negation of the will, that is, by assuming a decisive stand in opposition to nature" (WWR2, 644). By nature we are "fallen" into a world that is no good, a world that really ought not to be. We need salvation from it, and that salvation must come in the turn away from the individual self. Schopenhauer particularly approves of the passage in the mystical *Theologia Germanica* which states that Adam "was lost, or fell...because of his claiming something for his own, and because of his I, Mine, Me, and the like."[14] Losing the "I" is the route to salvation.

From this reading of Christianity we can see that the Schopenhauerian foundation of morality, which weakens the grip of our individuated nature upon us, is really of a piece with the final goal of self-negation in will-lessness. What, then, is the "moral meaning" of the world that both enable us to find? It is arguably as follows. The essential nature of the world into which we are "fallen," and the essential nature of ourselves as individuated parts of that world, is will. But this is not a merely descriptive truth for Schopenhauer. The world as will does not just exist, but rather points beyond itself to a higher purpose. The world reveals to us that it ought not to exist and indicates that its higher purpose is to turn us away from itself by liberating us from the "I" that the world tricks us into thinking we are. Those who remain unenlightened as to this purpose and cling to the principle of individuation are condemned to the vacuous and meaningless round of striving and suffering. It is the pessimist who finds the meaning of the world and the path to salvation.

16.5. Epilogue: Nietzsche on Schopenhauer, Meaning, and Christianity

In his assessment of Schopenhauer in his book, *The Gay Science*, Nietzsche asserts correctly[15] that Schopenhauer is an "admitted and uncompromising atheist."[16] As such Schopenhauer deserves credit, in Nietzsche's view, for being in tune with his times. While other German philosophers supposedly could not let go of the legacy of theism (Hegel is charged with a "grandiose attempt to persuade us of the divinity of existence"), the "ungodliness of existence" goes without saying for Schopenhauer. As a result, Nietzsche continues: "...looking at nature as if it were proof of the goodness and care of a god; interpreting history in honour of some divine reason, as a continual testimony of a moral world order and ultimate moral purposes; interpreting one's own experiences as pious people have long interpreted theirs, as if everything were providential, a hint, designed and ordained for the sake of salvation of the soul—that is *over* now."[17]

But it is then precisely the issue of meaning that Schopenhauer's work throws up for his contemporaries and immediate successors.

> As we thus reject the Christian interpretation and condemn its "meaning" [*Sinn*] as counterfeit, *Schopenhauer's* question immediately comes at us in a terrible way: *Does existence have any meaning at all?*...What Schopenhauer himself said in answer to this question was...a mere compromise, a remaining and staying stuck in precisely those Christian–ascetic moral perspectives, *faith in which had been dismissed* along with faith in God.[18]

In this analysis there is the implied threat is that, upon abandoning theism, we shall be faced with a disturbing absence of meaning. At first sight we may suspect that Nietzsche is attributing a no-meaning view to Schopenhauer himself. But that is not so. Schopenhauer's answer, as Nietzsche makes clear, is rather to uphold a meaning for existence—namely, a "Christian–ascetic moral" meaning. Thus Nietzsche in effect locates two distinct meanings juxtaposed within Christianity, or within Christianity as Schopenhauer interprets it. We may call them the Theistic Meaning and the Ascetic Meaning. According to the first, existence is good because the all-wise, all-benevolent creator made it so. Schopenhauer repeatedly mocks this view, which he encapsulates in the Septuagint's formula πάντα καλὰ λίαν ("everything was very good").[19] Interpreting the world in that way involves the kinds of optimistic attitude Nietzsche mentions: "Looking at nature as if it were proof of the goodness and care of a god; interpreting history...as a continual testimony of a moral world order and ultimate moral purposes" and so on. *That* meaning is now "over" for Schopenhauer and for European intellectual life in general. However, Schopenhauer finds—also in Christianity—another, opposed "meaning": existence is lamentable, something that ought not to be, and the true end or purpose of life is found in a turn away from the world into the peace of total will-lessness and loss of the individual self.

Nietzsche's analysis seems highly accurate. He recognizes that in abandoning theism and optimism, Schopenhauer has not abandoned certain Christian values. For Nietzsche, this is a criticism: he sees Schopenhauer as "stuck" with Christian values. One reason for this verdict relates to the conservative nature of Schopenhauer's most funda-mental assumption: that there must be moral meaning delivered up by metaphysics. It is an assumption Nietzsche himself rejects, as he says in his retrospective preface to *The Birth of Tragedy*: "Here, perhaps for the first time, a pessimism 'beyond good and evil' announces itself, here is put into words and formulations that 'perversity of mind' which Schopenhauer never tired of bombarding (before it had actually emerged) with his most wrathful imprecations and thunderbolts."[20] The distinctive phrase "perversity of mind" (*Perversität der Gesinnung*) is exactly that used by Schopenhauer in the passage from *Parerga and Paralipomena* quoted earlier, referring to the view that the world lacks a moral meaning. Nietzsche embraces this, the so-called antichrist: the world has no moral meaning.

But Nietzsche makes a deeper point: the whole idea that there must be a meaning that answers to a "metaphysical need" exists only as an outdated inheritance from Christianity: "The metaphysical need is not the origin of religion, as Schopenhauer has it, but only a *late offshoot* of it. Under the rule of religious ideas, one has got used to the idea of 'another world (behind, below, above)' and feels an unpleasant emptiness and deprivation at the annihilation of religious delusions—and from this feeling grows 'another world,' but this time only a metaphysical and not a religious one."[21] Schopenhauer's equation of the alleged perverse error with "the antichrist" is sympto-matic of this delayed influence of Christianity. It is as though the illegitimacy of ques-tioning the priority of the metaphysical need rests upon its conflicting with Christianity's most basic premise. A different kind of atheism, one with which we are more familiar since Nietzsche, would have no place for metaphysics in Schopenhauer's sense, no prej-udice in favor of a "meaning" or "significance" of the kind he seeks. Then the so-called metaphysical need would dwindle to a mere psychological dissatisfaction, felt by some during a particular historical period when the demise of theism is under way. But Schopenhauer, still in the midst of that demise, is seemingly unable to rid himself of the quest for a substitute metaphysics to ensure the kind of meaning Christianity had seemed to provide.

NOTES

1. Variations of this thought occur at WWR1, 350; WWR2, 482, 523, 591–92; PP1, 273; PP2, 19, 259–60. In the 1870s and 1880s, this was recognized as the heart of philosophical pessi-mism. See Olga Plümacher, *Der Pessimismus in Vergangenheit und Gegenwart: Geschichtliches und Kritisches* (Heidelberg: Georg Weiss, 1888), 1: "Modern philosophical pessimism, first presented by Arthur Schopenhauer as an indispensable part of a complete philosophical system…means the axiological judgement: *the sum of displeasure outweighs the sum of*

pleasure: consequently the non-being of the world would be better than its being" (my translation). See also Frederick Beiser, *After Hegel: German Philosophy 1840–1900* (Princeton, NJ: Princeton University Press, 2014), 160, 218–19; Beiser, *Weltschmerz: Pessimism in German Philosophy 1860–1900* (Oxford: Oxford University Press, 2016), 182–85; Tobias Dahlquist, *Nietzsche and the Philosophy of Pessimism: A Study of Nietzsche's Relation to the Pessimistic Tradition: Schopenhauer, Hartmann, Leopardi* (Uppsala: Uppsala Studies in History of Ideas, 2007), 37, 222.

2. This is brought out clearly in the dialogue "On religion" between Philalethes and Demopheles, PP2, 292–324.

3. See Paul Deussen "Schopenhauer und die Religion," *Schopenhauer-Jahrbuch* 4 (1915): 8–15. Hans Vaihinger also wrote: "no recent philosopher has penetrated so deeply into the essence of Christianity, and so warmly defended its core, as Schopenhauer" (*Nietzsche als Philosoph*, Berlin: Reuther and Reichard, 1902, 64). On German theorizing about Schopenhauer as a Christian thinker, see Matthias Koßler, *Empirische Ethik und christliche Moral* (Würzburg: Königshausen and Neumann, 1999), 11–20.

4. See, e.g., PP1, 111–15.

5. For a discussion of the immanence of Schopenhauer's metaphysics of the thing in itself and of insufficient recognition of it by earlier commentators (including the present author), see Beiser, *Weltschmerz*, 28.

6. "Purpose" here is *Zweck*. I shall assume for present purposes that Schopenhauer uses *Zweck* and *Ziel* more or less interchangeably.

7. On the question of why this is only figuratively, not literally the *summum bonum*, or highest good, for Schopenhauer, see Christopher Janaway, "What's So Good About Negation of the Will? Schopenhauer and the Problem of the *Summum Bonum*," *Journal of the History of Philosophy* 54 (2016), 649–69.

8. For a recent treatment of this issue, see Sandra Shapshay and Tristan Ferrell, "Compassion or Resignation: That is the Question of Schopenhauer's Ethics," *Enrahonar: Quaderns de Filosofia* 55 (2015), 51–69. While Schopenhauer views morality and the will's self-renunciation as continuous, with the former being a step to the latter, Shapshay and Ferrell suggest that there is a grand-scale contradiction in Schopenhauer's position and that moral compassion and renunciation should rather be viewed as "two independent, mutually antagonistic ethical ideals" (54) jostling within his system.

9. See, e.g., WWR2, 508, 623; PP2, 279.

10. See WWR1, 418: "Thus we also see people who have succeeded at some point in negating the will bend all their might to hold to this path by wresting renunciations of every sort from themselves, by adopting a difficult, penitent way of life and seeking out everything they find unpleasant: anything in order to subdue the will that will always strive anew."

11. See BM, 200.

12. For more on this central dichotomy, see Shapshay and Ferrell, "Compassion or Resignation."

13. See PP2, 349. On criteria for the optimism/pessimism distinction, see Dennis Vanden Auweele, "Schopenhauer on Religious Pessimism," *International Journal of the Philosophy of Religion* 78 (2015), 53–71.

14. *Theologia Germanica*, trans. Susanna Winkworth (London: Stuart and Watkins, 1966), 37–38. See WWR2, 628.

15. For support for this assessment, see Christopher Janaway, "Schopenhauer's Christian Perspectives," in *The Palgrave Schopenhauer Handbook*, edited by Sandra Shapshay (London: Palgrave Macmillan, 2017), 351–72.

16. Friedrich Nietzsche, *The Gay Science*, translated by Josefine Nauckhoff (Cambridge: Cambridge University Press, 2001), 219 (from Section 357; translation modified).

17. Ibid.

18. Ibid., 219–20.

19. See, e.g., PP2, 271, 279, 342–43.

20. Friedrich Nietzsche, *The Birth of Tragedy*, translated by Ronald Speirs (Cambridge: Cambridge University Press, 1999), 8. (Section 5 of the preface, "Attempt at a Self-Criticism," translation modified.)

21. Nietzsche, *The Gay Science*, 131 (Section 151).

FURTHER READING

Beiser, Frederick. *After Hegel: German Philosophy 1840–1900*. Princeton, NJ: Princeton University Press, 2014.

Beiser, Frederick. *Weltschmerz: Pessimism in German Philosophy 1860–1900*. Oxford: Oxford University Press, 2016.

Dahlquist, Tobias. *Nietzsche and the Philosophy of Pessimism: A Study of Nietzsche's Relation to the Pessimistic Tradition: Schopenhauer, Hartmann, Leopardi*. Uppsala: Uppsala Studies in History of Ideas, 2007.

Deussen, Paul. "Schopenhauer und die Religion." *Schopenhauer-Jahrbuch* 4 (1915): 8–15.

Janaway, Christopher. "Schopenhauer's Christian Perspectives." In *The Palgrave Schopenhauer Handbook*, edited by Sandra Shapshay. London: Palgrave Macmillan, 2017, 351–72.

Janaway, Christopher. "What's So Good About Negation of the Will? Schopenhauer and the Problem of the *Summum Bonum*." *Journal of the History of Philosophy* 54 (2016): 649–69.

Koßler, Matthias. *Empirische Ethik und christliche Moral*. Würzburg: Königshausen and Neumann, 1999.

Nietzsche, Friedrich. *The Birth of Tragedy*, translated by Ronald Speirs. Cambridge: Cambridge University Press, 1999.

Nietzsche, Friedrich. *The Gay Science*, translated by Josefine Nauckhoff. Cambridge: Cambridge University Press, 2001.

Plümacher, Olga. *Der Pessimismus in Vergangenheit und Gegenwart: Geschichtliches und Kritisches*. Heidelberg: Georg Weiss, 1888.

Shapshay, Sandra, and Tristan Ferrell. "Compassion or Resignation: *That* is the Question of Schopenhauer's Ethics." *Enrahonar: Quaderns de Filosofia* 55 (2015): 51–69.

Theologia Germanica, translated by Susanna Winkworth. London: Stuart and Watkins, 1966.

Vaihinger, Hans. *Nietzsche als Philosoph*. Berlin: Reuther and Reichard, 1902.

Vanden Auweele, Dennis. "Schopenhauer on Religious Pessimism." *International Journal of the Philosophy of Religion* 78 (2015): 53–71.

CHAPTER 17

SCHOPENHAUER'S PESSIMISM IN CONTEXT

MARK MIGOTTI

If one measures thoughts by their power, the stupidity of the Will is Schopenhauer's greatest thought....No one would give the name "God" to something stupid.

—Nietzsche, 1875[1]

The only thing that keeps me from killing myself is the will to live.

—Ben Wanderhope in Peter DeVries's novel *The Blood of the Lamb*, 1961[2]

IN this chapter, I examine Schopenhauer's pessimism from three angles: a philological, a theological, and a practical-epistemological. In the first section, I bring to light the essential interconnectedness of philosophical optimism and theism, thus preparing the ground for the themes I develop in Section 17.2. In Section 17.3, I turn to the question of suicide and investigate Schopenhauer's response to an obvious challenge to his daunting view: "If you're such a pessimist, why don't you kill yourself?" Although I will not argue the point explicitly, I believe that the enduring importance of Schopenhauer's pessimism is better captured by his answer to this question than by his views on the well-worn subjects of suffering and happiness, pleasures and pains, and so on.

I also believe that what mattered to Schopenhauer still matters to us, and I suspect that we have yet to develop substantially better answers than his or those of his theistic opponents to the questions that make investigation into philosophical optimism and philosophical pessimism worthwhile. But I do not support this suspicion directly either.

17.1 PHILOLOGY AND PHILOSOPHY

As Christopher Janaway observes, although Schopenhauer's system "incorporated an extremely negative evaluation of ordinary human life from the start," he didn't "initially use the term 'pessimism' to describe it."[3] But neither Janaway, nor any other Schopenhauer scholar I know of,[4] has taken this to be of more than incidental significance. In fact, the history of the words "pessimism" and "optimism" as terms of philosophical art has much to teach us about Schopenhauer's reasons for thinking that pessimism was true, important, and severely underrepresented in mainstream Western philosophy.

A familiar joke asks: What's the difference between an optimist and a pessimist? And it answers, They both think this is the best of all possible worlds. We get the joke, but no one before the middle of the nineteenth century could have; no one before then would have found the joke intelligible because the crucial words hadn't yet acquired the senses necessary for understanding it. Surprisingly (to me anyway), the now familiar uses of "optimistic" and "pessimistic" to mean "upbeat" and "downbeat" are latecomers to the field.[5] "Optimism" and "pessimism" began as technical terms in philosophy, with the second achieving currency long after the first. Philosophical pessimism—which, as we will see begins as Schopenhauerian pessimism—is an inherently reactive phenomenon; it arose in opposition to an established tradition of philosophical optimism.[6]

In 1710, Leibniz had coined the term "optimum" on the model of "maximum" and "minimum."[7] In 1737, the author of an article in the *Mémoires pour l'Histoire des Sciences et des Beaux-Arts* described Leibniz's "system of the optimum," the theory that this is the best of all possible worlds, in a single word: "*optimisme*." Some twenty years later, Voltaire's *Candide*, subtitled "*sur l'Optimisme*," was an instant hit; and, in 1762, just three years after its publication, the *Academie Française* officially granted "*optimisme*" entry into the French language. The *Oxford English Dictionary*'s (OED) first citation for "optimism" in English is a straight borrowing from the French: the word is spelled "Optimisme," with a capital "O" and an "e" on the end, and occurs in a discussion of *Candide* by Bishop Warburton.[8] The OED's first entry for "optimism," spelled as it has come to be spelled in English, is from 1782.

In the 1760s, writing in the same publication that had ushered "*optimisme*" into print,[9] Jesuits hostile to Voltaire took to accusing him of "*pessimisme*."[10] Unlike *optimisme*, however, this coinage didn't stick. By "*pessimisme*" the anti-Voltairian Jesuits of the eighteenth century meant something unappealing (but not in any specific way) that could be plausibly foisted on the anti-Jesuit Voltaire. Once polemics between Jesuits and Voltairians abated, the term disappeared, not to be revived for another century, and it was Schopenhauer who revived it, beginning in 1844 with a sprinkling of occurrences in the second volume of WWR. In the wake of the "pessimism controversy"[11] of the later nineteenth century, instigated by the surge of interest in Schopenhauer's work after his death in 1860, the *Academie* gave its blessing to "*pessimisme*"[12] in 1878, a hundred and twenty-six years after it had done the same for "*optimisme*." The OED reports that "pessimism" emerged in English in the 1870s "as a term for the doctrine associated with Schopenhauer and those philosophers influenced by him."

If we mark the original, Leibnizian sense of "*optimisme*" typographically (in English) as OPTIMISM, it becomes analytically true that to believe that this is the best of all possible worlds is to believe something OPTIMISTIC. But it is a serious question what bearing OPTIMISM has on being optimistic in anything like the current understanding of such an attitude. Our joke reveals that this being the best of all possible worlds can be read *either* as an enthusiastic commendation of what is *or* as a rueful commentary on the limits of what's possible. If this world is the best of a bad lot, that's cold comfort, not cause for celebration.

But Leibniz would have found it silly, or worse, to think that the best of all possible worlds could be the best of a bad lot. God chooses from all possible worlds, and if, *per impossibile,* the full set of eligible worlds didn't include a single one that was good—good enough to be made actual—He would have elected not to actualize anything. Since God *didn't* elect not to actualize any world, but instead to actualize this world, to believe that this is the best of all possible worlds is arguably to believe something reassuring. With God in the picture, OPTIMISM acquires an optimistic cast.

Schopenhauer describes Leibniz as "the founder of systematic optimism" (WWR2$_{[P]}$, §46)[13] and, at one unfortunate point, goes so far as to argue that his OPTIMISM has things exactly backward—that this is in fact the *worst* of all possible worlds. By "possible," Schopenhauer avers, we must mean "not what we may picture in our imagination, but what can actually exist and last." Leibniz would presumably agree. You cannot refute OPTIMISM by simply *imagining* a better world than this one, and you cannot refute Schopenhauer's rebuttal by simply *imagining* a world that is worse. And, continues Schopenhauer, when we note how delicate the complex balance of forces is that holds this world together, and how deep and ramifying seemingly insignificant changes can be, we should conclude that putative alterations for the worse aren't possible: to try to make this or that worse than it presently is would spell the end of the world altogether.

As Christopher Janaway justly remarks, Schopenhauer's reasoning here is "very far from convincing."[14] That the conditions for the continuation of the world are "sparingly and scantily given" does not mean that they couldn't be changed to result in a world a little bit worse than this one. A turn for the worse, however small, is a turn for the worse. And if Schopenhauer, who is a determinist about the empirical world, thinks that this is the *only* world consistent with laws and materials capable of existing in a stable condition for an appreciable period of time, the contrast between worst and best is eliminated.

What's more interesting, and stranger, about Schopenhauer's ill-advised attempt to turn the tables on Leibniz is the way he concludes it with a thoroughly garbled "proof" of his thesis. "The fossils of entirely different kinds of animal species which formerly inhabited the planet," he writes, "afford us…records of worlds whose continuance was no longer possible and which were in consequence somewhat worse than the worst of possible worlds." Unless we understand "the worst of possible worlds" as the worst of *presently* possible worlds, this is nonsense. And if it isn't nonsense, then Schopenhauer's argument undermines itself. For while dinosaurs may not presently be possible, they once were possible, and the delicate balance of forces that held their world together is still holding our world together. As Schopenhauer knows perfectly well, when the world of the Mesozoic era unraveled, the world itself did not vanish. So, on his own showing, what follows the collapse of one world may be a marginally better world.

As the somewhat tortured phrasing of the previous few sentences makes plain, we need to ask what makes two global conglomerations of things different *worlds*, rather than different states or parts or time slices of the *same* world. And we need to know how we are to compare and order distinct worlds in respect of goodness. Leibniz's theism makes his OPTIMISM optimistic in crucial part by giving a measure of intelligibility to the idea that, before any of them is made actual, the totality of possible worlds could be ranked in order of relative goodness. Leibniz's God takes the part of a judge in a literary competition: candidates—novels or, in God's case, worlds—are inspected and a prize is awarded to the one judged best.[15] In the case of possible worlds, the prize takes the form of actualization, being promoted from a merely possible world to *the*, actual, world.

If you do not think that the universe is here by divine choice, you cannot think that it owes its existence to being plucked from a realm of the merely possible and given the stamp of actuality. And if there was no choice involved in the matter, it's hard to see the point of questions about whether our universe is better than any of the others that might have been, but never were and never will be. One intelligible thing that might be meant by a quasi-Leibnizian OPTIMISM in a world without God requires us to shift from comparing possible worlds to one another to comparing possible states of this world to one another. But the thesis that our world is presently in the best condition it can ever possibly be in is surely no more plausible than the claim that it could never be in a worse condition: at any given moment, the world is susceptible both to improvement and deterioration in any number of respects.

Against this background, Schopenhauer's argument that the world was once worse than the worst of all possible worlds can be seen to be not just garbled, but perverse. Not only does the argument's conclusion undermine its own major premise, but the whole exercise distracts us from the key issues. Schopenhauerian pessimists deny that "the being of this world is justified through itself, and so should be lauded and prized" (WWR2, §17); they think that this world is fundamentally flawed, so that no possible improvements could "justify" its existence.[16] In some sense of "fundamental," it is virtually tautologous that no possible changes to the world can make a difference to its *fundamental* character. So Schopenhauer can grant that the world may improve (or deteriorate) in insignificant respects, but he is entitled to ask why that should matter to anybody. The question is whether, in essential, crucial respects, the world is worthy of appreciation and admiration and whether, in consequence, the lives human beings can live in it can be made worthy of commendation and endorsement.[17]

17.2 GOD AND WORLD

"At bottom," Schopenhauer writes, "optimism is the unwarranted self-praise of the real author [*Urheber*] of the world, the will-to-live, which complacently mirrors itself in its work" (WWR2$_{[P]}$, 584). To get the point, we need to distinguish the optimistic self-*praise* of the will-to-live from its natural self-*affirmation*. All living organisms affirm their lives through and in living them. In useful terms not available to Schopenhauer, living is a homeostatic process aimed at maintaining a "dynamically stable state" by means of "internal regulatory processes that tend to counteract any disturbance of the stability by external forces or influences."[18] In lay terms, beings that live cling to life, ward off threats to their lives, and so forth. In Schopenhauer's terms, to live is to will life, and to will life is to affirm it.

While everything that lives affirms *its* life by exercising its natural powers and striving to maintain them, animals that reproduce sexually also affirm life by eagerly generating more of it. In living, organisms affirm *their lives*; in reproducing sexually, they affirm *life itself* (or at least that of their species), and we are no exception.[19] In us, as in the rest of the living world, an inarticulate affirmation of life "lives in [the] veins as a power without understanding,"[20] to borrow an apt phrase of George Eliot's. But, unlike the rest of the animal kingdom, we can also think, understand, and inquire, and this makes it possible to for us think well of life (philosophical optimism) or ill of it (philosophical pessimism).

But the Schopenhauerian will-to-live cannot think, understand, or speak, much less inquire. So when, in systems of optimistic philosophy, the will-to-live praises itself—an undertaking that must be carried out in articulate terms—it can only do so through us. Nevertheless, in optimistic schemes of thought, Schopenhauer says, the will-to-live praises *itself*, and we need to know what he can mean by this. What he has in mind, I suggest, is a contrast between our praising and esteeming the *source* of our existence and our praising and esteeming *ourselves*. I may be down enough on myself to have lost all inclination or ability to think well of my*self*. But I may still think, optimistically (in a sense that nicely bridges the technical-philosophical and the everyday), that it's worth soldiering on. Things may improve, and, if they do, I may think better of my situation. I may regain my ability to adopt hopeful views and take adversity in stride; I may chalk up the unpleasantness that so perturbed me to instructive experience.

In Schopenhauer's view, a mere determination to soldier on in the face of blank despair isn't necessarily a sign of philosophical optimism; what matters is the rationale behind it. Animals that cannot speak or reason will fight against the longest of odds to survive—out of instinct, without deliberation. Human animals can behave similarly. Most of the time when we need to work hard to keep going, we do not ask whether it's worth the effort. But we can also keep going for a reason, and if our reason for refusing to be beaten into submission is merely the prospect of things getting better, we are nonetheless showing optimistic colors.[21]

The second epigraph to this paper juxtaposes an implicitly invoked importunate sea of troubles that might drive the speaker to end them by ending himself to an explicitly registered indomitable will to live that keeps him from doing this. To understand this idea optimistically the recognition that the only thing stopping you from killing yourself is the will-to-live must provoke a sigh of relief, make you happy to have had the helping hand, pleased that the will to live has prevented you from giving in to regrettable inclinations. It may be possible to believe that you *ought* to commit suicide, but find yourself unable to do it because of your will to live. In such a case you would be suffering from akrasia: the inclinations you regret would be those that are keeping you alive, not those that motivate you to stop living.

In Schopenhauer's pessimistic opinion, no one who is wise to the ways of the will-to-live, who knows that the world is nothing more than the will to live in objectified form,[22] could be grateful to it for anything. And, as interpreters of Schopenhauer's pessimism, we need to distinguish the "to" from the "for." Because it has no intelligence, the Schopenhauerian will-to-live cannot be the addressee of an attitude such as gratitude. In terms of my first epigraph, to be grateful to the will to live is surreptitiously to turn it into something divine. Only someone who believes that God is the real author of the world can be grateful to anyone for its existence. Given what Schopenhauer thinks the will-to-live is—a blind urge without consciousness or reason—it makes no more sense to be grateful to *it* than it does to be grateful to the Big Bang or Mount Everest. But we can be grateful *for* things in full awareness of there being no one and nothing to thank for them. We can be grateful that things have turned out as we had hoped they would, that the sun shone on our picnic, or the roulette ball landed in the right spot, even when it was happenstance or natural necessity that brought about the desired result.

According to Schopenhauer, only someone already inclined to philosophical optimism will find it tempting to believe in God. Optimism, he says, is a necessary condition of "theism proper" (*eigentichlen Theismus*) (PP2$_{[P]}$, 378), reminding us that theism was a necessary condition of making Leibnizian OPTIMISM an optimistic doctrine in our familiar sense of the term. Schopenhauer's taking care to say that optimism is a necessary condition, specifically, of *genuine* theism suggests that he would not count some worldviews ordinarily taken to be theistic as the genuine article. He argues that "polytheism" is a contradiction in terms (i.e., that if there is *a* God, there is at most one).[23] In effect, by "genuine theism" Schopenhauer means belief in the God of the Hebrew Bible and/or the so-called "God of the philosophers," for example, God as understood by Descartes or Leibniz.[24]

If optimism is required for (genuine) theism, theism must be sufficient for optimism. In general, philosophical optimism is a theoretical *rationalization* of our natural disposition to affirm life willy-nilly. In theistic optimism in particular, the blind will-to-live that actually motivates us to live on and relish and promote life gets itself (mis)taken for an intelligent being. God, we might say is a mask or guise (a dis-guise) behind which the Schopenhauerian will manages to praise itself with (as believers hope) a good intellectual conscience.

Reflection on the account of the creation of the universe in the first chapter of the Book of Genesis throws the connection Schopenhauer sees between theism and the self-praise of the author of the world into relief. In the familiar story of those eventful six days "in the beginning," the fact that God thinks well of his unprecedented handiwork is heavily underscored. "In the beginning, God said 'Let there be light,' and there was light; And God saw the light, that it was good"; and when the work of creation is done, "God saw everything that he had made, and, behold, it was very good."[25] The Book of Genesis doesn't tell us what it was about the world that God beheld that called forth his approving comments, whether, in admiring his Creation, the Lord God basks in his own reflected goodness and praises himself, or whether instead he appreciates the inherent goodness of what he has brought into existence, or both.

Wherever the goodness comes from, if the Genesis account is true, both God and the world are good. According to Schopenhauer, the worldview of the Hebrew Bible is decidedly optimistic, but that of the Christian Gospels is thoroughly pessimistic. So while Judaism is an internally consistent religion, Christianity is fractured, awkwardly caught between an optimistic metaphysics and a pessimistic ethics. Insofar as Christians profess adherence to what they call the Old Testament, they must believe in the Creation story of Genesis, with its God who is supremely good creating a world that is also (somehow) good. But insofar as they believe in the Saviour of the *New* Testament, Schopenhauer argues, Christians must believe that life is a painful burden from which we need to be saved and the world a temporary structure due to come to a welcome end—and this is pessimism.

Christian apologists have tried to smooth over these issues by distinguishing between the world before the Fall and the life that was given to Adam, which were good, and the ruined condition into which we and the world have fallen thanks to Original Sin. From Schopenhauer's perspective, this only means that Christians must strive to be grateful to God both for his having created the world and for having providing deliverance from it. And this is not really a coherent combination of attitudes: if we need to be delivered from it, the world cannot be good, and if it is good, we do not need to be delivered from it.[26]

17.3 YOU AND YOUR LIFE

People who believe in God can have a reason quite different from Ben Wanderhope's not to take their own lives. As we've seen, someone who is fed up with his lot yet recognizes within himself a surd will to put up with it nonetheless is not necessarily a philosophical optimist; that depends on his reaction to this recognition. Unlike someone who, optimist or not, carries on living because he cannot overcome the will to live, a theistic optimist typically thinks that suicide is to be shunned because it is contrary to God's commandment, "the Everlasting," as Hamlet puts it, "[having] set his canon against self-slaughter"[27]—perhaps because it was He who gave us life.

A genuinely theistic reason for rejecting suicide must be an optimistic reason, and there can be no optimistic grounds for committing suicide. "Why not?" you may ask; "Isn't it possible to believe that life and the world are fundamentally good, but also think that people may fall into circumstances in which dying as soon as possible, by your own hand if necessary, is preferable to continuing to live?" It may be possible to combine these views; however, it will not be optimism that motivates someone to end his life (or seek ways to have it ended for him), but beliefs about his circumstances and prospects. The point is not that no one who is a philosophical optimist can, on pain of logical inconsistency, endorse suicide under certain conditions, but rather that the endorsement will take some explaining: we will need to know how a good world can give rise to circumstances that make suicide desirable, what such circumstances might be, etc.

When a Christian finds himself tempted to end it all but refrains from doing so on the grounds that this would conflict with his faith, we cannot, from Schopenhauer's perspective, automatically know whether his reasons for living on betoken philosophical optimism; it depends on how clear he is about his own faith. Christians who choose to live on because they believe that God forbids suicide may do so *either* because they are crypto-theists who do not appreciate the pessimistic core of their own creed, *or* because they do appreciate that core but express themselves in a misleading theistic idiom.[28] If Christian doctrine is inherently confused, so are people who try to adhere to it.

And what goes for Christians goes (*mutatis mutandis*) for the rest of us. Because of our long-ingrained habit of affirming it, we are predisposed when we consider the matter to think that life is a very good thing; it seems "only natural" to do so. The hard question is whether the joys and satisfactions of living can make the game worth the candle: optimists say, "yes"; pessimists, "no." A further question is how a pessimistic "no" to the alleged goodness of life and the world could be manifested in action: What would a pessimistic ethics look like? Mightn't the most effective and honest way to put pessimistic theory into practice be to kill yourself, to show your disdain for life by discarding it? If life really is "a business that doesn't cover its costs" (WWR2$_{[P]}$, 574), why not cut your losses? Because, Schopenhauer would say, it is deeply immoral to do so; not, however, for reasons familiar to mainstream Western, optimistic thinking.

Schopenhauer first presented his pessimistic grounds for eschewing suicide in WWR1, §69. Twenty-five years later, in WWR2, he did not deem the subject worthy of the expanded commentary he gave to other elements of his philosophy. Ten years after that, however, he included a short essay on the topic in PP, the argument of which bears closely on our present concerns. "On Suicide" is mostly a diatribe against legal prohibitions against suicide, a characteristically acerbic attack on the idea that to kill yourself is to murder yourself, to carry out an unlawful killing.[29] Schopenhauer observes that such prohibitions are an idiosyncratic feature of theistic cultures: "So far as I can see," he writes, "it is only the monotheistic religions...whose adherents regard killing yourself as a crime."

Monotheistic denunciations of suicide are "all the more remarkable, as nowhere in the Old or the New Testament do we find a prohibition against suicide, or even a decided disapproval of it" (PP2$_{[P]}$, 306).[30] In consequence, "the teachers of religious doctrine have to base their condemnation of it on their own philosophical grounds," for the patent weaknesses of which they try to compensate by pious expressions of disgust. Given that neither scripture nor the philosophical arguments of proponents of scripture supports either a legal or a moral prohibition against suicide, Schopenhauer conjectures that what motivates rabbis, priests, ministers etc., to insist so fervently on both is that "the voluntary giving up of life is a poor compliment to the one who said 'everything is very good'...once again it would be the obligatory optimism of these religions which denounces the killing of oneself in order not to be denounced by it" (PP2, 279).

The optimism of monotheistic thinking is "obligatory" both because monotheism entails optimism and because it gives rise to conceptions of ethics organized around the concept of moral obligation. Anticipating an influential argument of Elizabeth

Anscombe's by a hundred years, Schopenhauer sees the moral history of the West as marked by a decisive shift from a eudaimonist conception of ethics, signally exemplified by Aristotle, to a juridico-deontic conception, according to which "an ethics in legislator-imperative form is the only one possible" (BM, 125).[31] In his essay on the basis of morality, Schopenhauer identifies this assumption as the "*proton pseudos*" (first error or false step) of Kant's ethical philosophy, but the point is not restricted to anything specifically Kantian. Kant's false step is also mainstream modern moral philosophy's false step: it is the assumption that being ethical is mainly a matter of fulfilling your moral obligations,[32] where the problem lies in the very idea of a moral obligation. For his part, Schopenhauer "recognise[s] no other origin for the introduction of the concept *law, prescription, command* into ethics than one that is foreign to philosophy, namely, the Mosaic Decalogue" (BM, 53–54).[33] Theism, then, leads both to philosophical optimism and to an understanding of morality in quasi-legal terms, as a system of injunctions and prohibitions enforced not by the police and the courts, but (in the next world) by God Himself[34] and (in this world) by individual conscience.

In any meaningful sense of the phrase then, you are, in Schopenhauer's opinion, "at liberty" to end your life before nature ends it for you. But this doesn't mean that nothing of moral value hangs on whether you do. As mentioned earlier, Schopenhauer is convinced that killing yourself is deeply immoral: by which I take him to mean, not only very immoral, but also immoral for deep, metaphysical reasons. But the only standpoint from which the immorality of suicide can be made evident, he tells us, is "much higher than that which European moral philosophers have ever occupied [and if] we descend from that very high point, there is no longer any valid moral reason for condemning suicide" (PP2$_{[P]}$, 309).

If theistic optimists inveigh against suicide because it contravenes God's will, atheistic Schopenhauerian pessimists do so because it testifies to a callous disregard for anyone but yourself, and this brings back into view the distinction between life as such and your life in particular. As long as you are sane, you will not think that the end of your life spells the end of life itself. But it is *life* that the philosophical pessimist holds in disregard, and this is why killing your*self* cannot be a way of putting pessimistic philosophical theory into practice. Once we recognize this, we have to ask what possibly could do this job. As we've seen, Schopenhauer thinks that in sexually reproducing animals the affirmation of life itself, as distinct from the affirmation of the life of a particular organism, is revealed in the intensity of the desire, not just to live, but to reproduce. But it is hard to see how an analogous distinction could be drawn with respect to denying life. Maybe you do, in a way, "deny" *your* life when you end it voluntarily, but what could you possibly do to deny life itself? Killing other people will not do the job: your victims will likely die affirming life as fervently as they ever did.

From a biological point of view, death by suicide is just one among many cases of untimely death, brought about not by the natural course of events but by something untoward; whether you fall off a cliff despite your best efforts to be careful or throw yourself off it deliberately, you end up dying not of natural causes, but of the impact of your fall. From an ethical perspective, however, the two cases are very different—on anybody's account, presumably, but especially on Schopenhauer's. From Schopenhauer's perspective, suicide born of misery testifies to the self-frustrating character of the will-to-live in a uniquely pathetic and revealing way. For, while there can be no optimistic grounds for committing suicide, the will-to-live can, improbably enough, provoke people to end their lives rather than prolong them.

All living organisms affirm life by affirming *their* lives; but in much of the animal kingdom, the life of one organism can only be maintained and affirmed at the expense of others. To some extent nature *is* "red in tooth and claw." Moreover, from the point of view of an individual animal, death marks the end of what it has affirmed from birth. In its individual embodiments, the will-to-live strives ceaselessly to avert an inevitable outcome.[35]

Unlike other animals, we humans can devote ourselves to more than our own survival or that of our kin, and we can do this because we can think and inquire. In Schopenhauer's terms, our ability to think is a consequence of the (scarcely comprehensible) fact that the will-to-live has managed to generate organs of thought; in and of itself, the will-to-live has no inkling of what it is or does, but through us it can generate ideas about this. Moreover, each of us knows that he will not survive indefinitely. And this makes the project of simply prolonging our days inherently problematic. Just as we can *keep on* living for a reason, as opposed to unthinkingly, so, too, we can *live* for a reason. We can distinguish merely extending our days from enjoying them, merely living from living well or flourishing, and we can take survival as such to be worthwhile only as a necessary condition of flourishing. For its part, living well can be regarded as its own reward, in no need of a further "reason for."

Things that live can flourish but can also merely subsist; they can thrive or barely survive. In both philosophy and ordinary life, it is common to construe human flourishing in terms of human happiness, and, if we do this, we will need to decide how to respond if we become miserable with no prospect of improvement. In such a circumstance, we may think it better not to live at all than to live miserably. If, believing ourselves to be insurmountably miserable, we act on this maxim, it would seem that the will-to-live has failed to do its job; it hasn't kept us from killing ourselves. *Au contraire*, Schopenhauer argues, in such circumstances it is precisely the will-to-live that has driven us *to* suicide.

How can the will to live motivate the voluntary end of one of its animal embodiments? By reproducing within an individual organism the familiar relationship between predator and prey, killer and killed. Someone who kills himself is both perpetrator and victim of homicide, and (sometimes) his reason for killing himself is that he sees no way to live well. But this doesn't mean that he stops *wanting* to live well, wishing he could live well, or thinking that others are living well. He may still think well of human life or think that he thinks well of it; it is just that he is no longer willing to live it in his own person. As Schopenhauer puts it, someone who kills himself to end his misery "wills life, and is dissatisfied merely with the conditions under which it has come to him" (WWR1$_{[P]}$, 398); it is his ongoing desire to live well that motivates a preference for not living at all if the only way to live on is to live very badly. People driven by misery to end their misery by ending their lives don't necessarily give up on life; they give up only on their *own* life, the one that has led to such unbearable suffering.

The moral standpoint that reveals why, in Schopenhauer's opinion, it is wrong to kill yourself depends in crucial part on the value of compassion. While putting an end to my life may put an end to all further suffering of mine, it may increase your suffering greatly, and I may know this. If, under such circumstances, I choose not to keep going, I show myself to be unwilling to give the same weight to your suffering as I do to mine. So far, it may seem, so familiar: whenever someone's killing themselves would lead to a net increase in suffering, for example, it will be morally criticizable on utilitarian grounds. By the same token, however, from a utilitarian standpoint, if my committing suicide would lead to a net decrease in suffering, it would be meritorious of me to undertake it. Schopenhauer couldn't disagree more profoundly.

In the ordinary course of events, selfish behavior aims to benefit the one behaving selfishly: I scant you to benefit me. When, knowing that my suicide will cause you pain, I kill myself anyway, your suffering is real, but my "benefit" is Pickwickian. What causes you to suffer and me to stop suffering is the cessation of all further benefits (or harms) for me. In Schopenhauer's view, a suicide born of misery demonstrates that there are no limits to peoples' capacity to refuse to acknowledge any claim of the well-being of others on their actions and decisions: as long as *I* don't have to be, the suicide says, nothing else matters.

Whereas utilitarian moral thinking, like the moral thinking of the ancient Stoics, will condone suicide under certain circumstances, Schopenhauer denies that it is ever morally acceptable to kill yourself,[36] and in this he resembles his theistic optimist opponents more closely than he might care to admit. Nobody chooses to be born, and nobody can choose not to die, not to be mortal. But when a human being chooses to die at a time of his own appointing, he does something analogous to arrogating to himself a divine privilege; he does to himself what God in the sixth chapter of the Book of Genesis would have done to his creation had he really "blotted out" all living things instead of sparing Noah and the animals in his ark. It is the hubris implicit in the very idea of suicide that makes carrying out the act so singularly appalling to Schopenhauer.

* * *

When a recent commentator tells us that Schopenhauer's pessimism is rooted in "a rediscovery of the problem of evil,"[37] he gestures at something important but gets it backward. The (traditional) problem of evil is tied to theism: it is the problem of how an all-good, all-knowing, all-powerful being could allow any evil at all, and that problem makes no sense if responsibility for whatever evil there is cannot possibly be assigned to such an entity. Schopenhauer's problem is the inverse of the traditional problem of evil: it is the problem of how a blind, ignorant will-to-live can give rise to anything good— and his pessimistic answer is that it cannot.

Schopenhauer's reasons for thinking that the will-to-live cannot produce a world worthy of our good opinion are beyond the scope of this chapter. As I intimated at the outset, I hope here only to have established that his reasons for thinking such reasons are needed are philosophically significant. Granted that the world does not care about us, or anything else, is its fundamental character nevertheless conducive to our well-being and/or that of some of our fellow creatures? Or does it merely permit some of its creatures to flourish some of the time? If so, how many, and how much of the time? And why is it so hard to figure out what the well-being of human creatures consists in? What's the connection between the nature of the world and the nature of human flourishing? To work through Schopenhauer's pessimism carefully and sympathetically is to realize how hard and how worthwhile these questions are, and how regularly they are brushed aside or swept under the carpet in present day philosophical debates.

ACKNOWLEDGMENTS

I owe Susan Haack more than the usual debt of gratitude for her patient help with untold drafts of this chapter; without the improvements prompted by her, my ideas would not have taken their proper shape. I am grateful also to Noa Latham, Brian Copeland, and Andrew Payne for helpful comments and encouragement. My debt to Chris Janaway is evident in the footnotes, and I thank him especially for sending me his not yet published piece on Schopenhauer's Christian perspectives.

NOTES

1. An unpublished note from 1875, in *Sämtliche Werke: Kritische Studienausgabe*, edited by Giorgio Colli and Mazzino Montinari (Berlin/New York: Walter DeGruyter, 1967–1977), 8.46.
2. Peter DeVries, *The Blood of the Lamb* (University of Chicago Press, 2005), 118.
3. "Schopenhauer's Pessimism," in *The Cambridge Companion to Schopenhauer*, edited by Christopher Janaway (Cambridge: Cambridge University Press, 1999), 319.
4. Myself included, in "Schopenhauer's Pessimism and the Unconditioned Good," *Journal of the History of Philosophy* 33 (1995), 645.
5. The earliest OED citation for "optimism" in the sense of "hopefulness and confidence about the future;...a tendency to take a favourable or hopeful view" is from 1859, about a hundred years after the word entered the language in its technical philosophical sense. Remarkably, the same time lag is found in the exemplary quotations for pessimism: the earliest citation that isn't connected to the Schopenhauerian context in which the term was introduced is from 1967!
6. A survey of his use of "optimism," "pessimism," and their cognates reveals that Schopenhauer takes pessimism to be first and foremost anti-optimism. Occurrences of "optimism" (in its different grammatical forms) outnumber those of "pessimism" by a factor of five to one.
7. That is, the formation of a count noun (maximum, minimum, optimum) from a superlative adjective ("*maximus*," *minimus*," "*optimus*").
8. Warburton writes in a letter to Richard Hurd, July 8, 1759, that "the professed design [of Voltaire's book] is to ridicule the Optimisme, not of Pope, but of Leibnitz" (Richard Hurd and William Warburton, *Letters from a Late Eminent Prelate to One of His Friends*, 2nd edition [London: T. Cadell and W. Davies, Strand, 1809], 289).
9. Commonly known as the *Journal de Trevoux*, the name of the town in which it was published.

10. Joshua Foa Dienstag, *Pessimism: Philosophy, Ethic, Spirit* (Princeton, NJ: Princeton University Press, 2006), 9; Dienstag thanks M. Aurelian Demars for this fascinating piece of history.

11. As Frederick Beiser calls it, in *After Hegel: German Philosophy 1840–1900* (Princeton NJ: Princeton University Press, 2014), ch. five, 158–215.

12. Dienstag, *Pessimism*, 9.

13. Quotations from Schopenhauer in the next three paragraphs are to this section of WWR2.

14. Christopher Janaway, "Schopenhauer's Pessimism," in *The Cambridge Companion to Schopenhauer*, edited by Christopher Janaway (Cambridge: Cambridge University Press, 1999), 322.

15. In a paper of 1689 entitled, "On Freedom," Leibniz writes that "many stories, especially those which are called 'romances' are possible, even if they do not find a place in this series of the universe which God has chosen" (*Gottfried Wilhelm Leibniz: Philosophical Papers and Letters*, edited by Leroy E. Loemker [New York/Dordrecht: D. Reidel, 1970]), 263–66. I owe this reference to Yual Chiek.

16. The scare quotation marks around "justify" are meant to prompt the question, what, outside of a theistic context, it could it mean to justify the existence of the world.

17. And this, for present purposes, is my answer to the question what, apart from its being created by God, could justify the existence of the world: if the world is conducive to human beings (and at least some other animals) leading worthwhile lives, its existence is justified; but otherwise not.

18. Excerpted from the OED definition for "homeostasis."

19. What seduces us into life, Schopenhauer writes, "can be…seen in the longing looks of two lovers; it is the purest expression of the will-to-live in its affirmation" (WWR2$_{[P]}$, §45). What Schopenhauer would say about plants that reproduce sexually is a good question, but not one I will address in this chapter.

20. *Daniel Deronda* (Harmondsworth: Penguin Books, 1995 [1876]), 536.

21. This sort of thinking is well conveyed in lyrics to Burt Bachrach's "Raindrops Keep Falling on My Head" from *Butch Cassidy and the Sundance Kid* (1969) when the singer/narrator insists that no amount of adversity the world may be able to throw at him can beat him down since happiness is sure to cross his path soon enough.

22. Strictly speaking, Schopenhauer's world as representation is objectified will-to-live in its entirety, in both its animate and its inanimate parts. To account for the evident fact that some things exist that are not alive, Schopenhauer must give his metaphysics a vitalist twist of an unorthodox sort: he must hold that all existence is infused with the impulse to live (i.e., to exist in a heightened form).

23. "The polytheism of the ancients," he writes, "is something utterly distinct from the mere plural of monotheism" (PP2$_{[P]}$, 362).

24. Among philosophers Schopenhauer's restriction of theism, properly so-called, to monotheism—and his tacit assumption that if there were a God, then God would have to be supremely powerful, knowledgeable, and righteous—are far from idiosyncratic. Leibniz's arguments for this world's being the best of all possible worlds make no sense without these assumptions. Conceiving of God (singular) as a rational chooser able to actualize or not actualize a given world, Leibniz can reason that the world God actualized, our world, is the *uniquely* best world on the grounds that (a) rational choice is inherently optimizing, and (b) if two or more worlds were equally good, and superior to all the rest, God would be in the situation of Buridan's ass and would recognize this, and so would not actualize any world at all.

25. King James translation, Genesis 1:4,31.

26. Schopenhauer's critique of Christianity opens up an interesting perspective on the major religions of the East and the West. Because he takes theism to be resolutely and unequivocally optimistic, and takes the Hebrew Bible to be resolutely and unequivocally theistic, Schopenhauer is driven to conjecture that "the New Testament must somehow be of Indian origin" (PP2$_{[P]}$, 380), in which case it would have roots in the same intellectual soil that produced the pessimistic doctrines of ancient Hinduism and Buddhism. In world-historical terms, Schopenhauer's Christianity is a misbegotten child of the pessimism of the atheistic East (the hosts of Hindu deities not qualifying as gods, and Buddhist teachings taken to be avowedly atheist) and the optimism of the monotheistic West. For a searching discussion of Schopenhauer's understanding of Christianity and references to further literature on the topic, see Janaway, "Schopenhauer's Christian Perspectives," in *The Palgrave Schopenhauer Handbook*, edited by Sandra Shapshay (London: Palgrave Macmillan, 2017), 351–72.

27. *Hamlet*, I ii, 132–33.

28. In a recent discussion of Schopenhauer on salvation and "the apophatic," Andrew King, à propos Schopenhauer's affinity for the writings of the German Christian mystic Meister Eckhart, asks ("poignantly" as Janaway aptly puts it): "Is Eckhart a crypto-atheist, or Schopenhauer a crypto-Christian?" ("Philosophy and Salvation: the Apophatic in the Thought of Arthur Schopenhauer," *Modern Theology* 24 [2005], 253–74). According to Schopenhauer, to understand pessimism, theism, and Christianity correctly is to see that the answer to both of King's questions is a resounding "Yes," with the proviso, perhaps, that it would be more accurate to call Christians crypto-Schopenhauerians than the reverse.

29. The German "*Selbstmord*" builds the unlawfulness of suicide into the very word for the act, "*selbst*" meaning "self," and "*mord*" meaning "murder."

30. Since Schopenhauer leaves the Koran out of it, we can take "monotheistic religion" here to be tantamount to what has come to be called "Judeo-Christianity."

31. The shift from an aspirational ethics, ethics as about what you would do best to strive for, to an imperatival ethics, ethics as about what you are morally required to do, is described by Anscombe as a matter of "the ordinary ... terms 'should,' 'needs,' 'ought,' 'must' ... [acquiring] a special [specifically moral] sense by being equated in the relevant contexts to 'is obliged to,' or 'is bound' or 'is required to,' in the sense in which one can be obliged or bound by law, or something can be required by law" ("Modern Moral Philosophy," in *Collected Philosophical Papers, Volume III: Ethics, Religion, and Politics*, [Minneapolis: University of Minnesota Press, 1981/1958]), 30.

32. This assumption is common to what is arguably the present-day mainstream both of consequentialist and deontological moral theory—camps that are routinely assumed to differ profoundly on how moral obligations are to be established. The two factions agree, however, on the preeminence of obligation as a guiding concept in ethical thinking.

33. Anscombe also thinks that Christianity—which, she says, in sharp contrast to Schopenhauer and without mentioning him, "derives its ethical notions from the Torah" (30)—played a crucial role in the shift in Western philosophy from eudaimonistic ethics to imperatival ethics.

34. This is, of course, a distinctly Christian way of putting it. Schopenhauer takes the fact that the Hebrew Bible contains little to nothing about an afterlife to be evidence of its candid, worldly optimism. The God of Abraham, Isaac, and Jacob rewards the faithful of Israel with prosperity in the here and now, not supernal bliss in an alleged hereafter.

35. Insofar as the sexual drive just is the drive to reproduce, an animal that manages to procreate has not lost everything that it affirmed. Nevertheless, when it dies, it loses the precondition of its affirming anything at all.
36. More precisely, he denies that it is ever morally acceptable to kill yourself in order to end your own unhappiness.
37. Frederick Beiser, *Weltschmerz: Pessimism in German Philosophy 1860–1900* (Oxford: Oxford University Press, 2016).

FURTHER READING

Beiser, Frederick. *Weltschmerz: Pessimism in German Philosophy 1860–1900*. Oxford: Oxford University Press, 2016.

Dienstag, Joshua Foa. *Pessimism: Philosophy, Ethic, Spirit*, Princeton, NJ: Princeton University Press, 2006.

Janaway, Christopher. "Schopenhauer's Pessimism." In *The Cambridge Companion to Schopenhauer*, edited by Christopher Janaway. Cambridge: Cambridge University Press, 1999, 318–43.

Janaway, Christopher. "What's So Good About Negation of the Will? Schopenhauer and the Problem of the *Summum Bonum*." *Journal of the History of Philosophy* 54, no. 4 (2016): 649–70.

Janaway, Christopher. "Schopenhauer's Christian Perspectives." In *The Palgrave Schopenhauer Handbook*, edited by Sandra Shapshay. London: Palgrave Macmillan, 2017, 351–72.

Migotti, Mark. "Schopenhauer's Pessimism and the Unconditioned Good." *Journal of the History of Philosophy* 33 (1995).

CHAPTER 18

SCHOPENHAUER'S MORAL PHILOSOPHY

Responding to Senselessness

ROBERT GUAY

MORAL philosophy always comes with a tension between its traditionalist and its revisionist strands. Without its traditionalism, it risks losing any grasp on its subject matter: since the field is not as world-responsive as one might hope, identifying a continuous object of inquiry can require staying close to what has already been said. Without its revisionism, moral philosophy has little to say. For Schopenhauer, the tension between these two strands is particularly intense. Consistent with tradition, he claims to articulate the underlying, universal core of morality. This has often been obscurely expressed or confounded in the attempts to link it to its ground, but his own expression of the content of morality is something that "all teachers of morality" (BM, 140) and "all ethical theorists" (BM, 139) have already agreed upon. At the same time, however, he sweeps aside deontology and eudaimonism and replaces them with resignation and quietism; since there is nothing worthwhile in phenomenal existence, morality must ultimately refer to its metaphysical ground rather than to particular human concerns. Schopenhauer, furthermore, forswears the strategies that have been typically adopted to resolve this tension between consensus and innovation: he does not try to show that the traditional answers have covertly appealed to a highest good, fundamental principle, or hidden source of authority. Tradition has instead groped unsteadily toward the truth but has failed to recognize that morality depends on something chaotic and groundless outside of itself.

In this chapter, then, I will examine how Schopenhauer manages this tension not by surveying the whole of his moral philosophy, but by offering a reconstruction of a central philosophical problematic. For Schopenhauer, the basic considerations that run through human life are empty, our existence is worthless and incapable of furnishing satisfaction, and philosophy is powerless to ameliorate or mitigate this in any way. Indeed, philosophy is unsuited even to articulate a demand for improvement, let alone effect change. All this raises a question of how there can be any moral philosophy at all. The kinds of considerations in terms of which we might understand the demands of morality—welfare, the first-person standpoint, agency, perfection—are senseless and unreal. In fact, metaphysical insight reveals that the very idea of a prescriptive morality is impossible. The problem for Schopenhauer is that, on one hand, offering a genuine philosophical account of morality requires identifying it from a "higher metaphysical-ethical standpoint" (PP1$_{[P]}$, 3),[1] while having anything informative to say about the proper structuring of human activity or the practice of virtue requires an appeal to "morality in the narrower sense" (WWR2$_{[P]}$, 589).[2] Yet the narrow sense of morality may be so distant from its metaphysical ground that it is hard to see how it could be connected.

What this chapter focuses on, then, is how moral philosophy, in establishing such a connection, is possible at all. My discussion will neglect many facets of Schopenhauer's moral philosophy, such as his treatments of virtue, responsibility, compassion, character, motivation, and holiness. In general, I have little to say about either the specific *content* or the psychological mechanisms involved in morality. There is a good Schopenhauerian reason for this neglect, however: nothing in its phenomenal manifestation intrinsically matters anyway. Neglecting the particulars also allows for more focus on the overall issue: how there can be an individual standpoint from which morality is compelling or important in some way. The possibility of a moral philosophy depends, minimally, on the coherence of an individual standpoint from which moral concerns can be recognized. And for an individual standpoint to be possible, there must be some way in which some end, reason, or consideration matters. The difficulty, then, is understanding how moral concern can be taken seriously when nothing seems to have the importance to sustain it.

All of this is particular to Schopenhauer, of course, but it also bears a resemblance to a common problem in moral philosophy. Moral philosophy often includes a demand to prioritize others' interests, incorporate others' ends into one's own, act on reasons that one does not have, or simply adopt an alien standpoint, whether someone else's or an impersonal one. Indeed, the mark of a distinctively moral perspective might be precisely that one's natural standpoint is altered, disrupted, or obliterated. We can thus look at Schopenhauer's treatment of this issue as his extreme approach to a familiar problem: how to make sense of a moral standpoint that is at once mandatory and at the same time no one's standpoint at all. If we look at his project in this way, then his aim is for metaphysics to clarify whether there can be any such standpoint and, in so doing, to purify morality's essential content so that its significance can be properly appreciated.

Schopenhauer's solution, I argue, is that morality consists in the appropriate kind of responsiveness to the metaphysical truth about existence. He distinguishes between the *sense* of ethical practices and their *meaning* and claims that ethical practices, like all human affairs, are senseless; there is, accordingly, no way to pursue them well or poorly as practices. They do have an ethical significance, however: they can exhibit metaphysical insight into the ultimate unreality of individual existence. Morality is thus the appropriate form of responsiveness to the intrinsic senselessness of existence; ethical practice is expressive of theoretical insight rather than meaningful on its own terms, according to its surface description. This solution, then, does not involve the recognition of a normative constraint, the observance of a moral law, or any kind of rational or strategic pursuit. There is nothing that one could do that would make sense on its own terms, but actions and character can be assessed from a theoretical standpoint as expressions of the correct attitude toward the unavailability of any sensible pursuit. This is practical insofar as it needs to be sustained in one's phenomenal existence; it points to a redemptive hope but, in itself, does not try to accomplish anything.

In Section 18.2, I clarify the nature of the problem that Schopenhauer addresses by identifying some of the obstacles that Schopenhauer faces in articulating a moral philosophy. Section 18.3 presents my reconstruction of Schopenhauer's position, and Section 18.4 offers, in conclusion, some reservations about the success of his solution.

18.1 OBSTACLES TO A MORAL PHILOSOPHY

The aim of this section is to explicate the nature of the challenge that Schopenhauer gave himself in articulating a moral philosophy that meets the requirements on what an adequate moral philosophy must be. To this end, it helps first to identify the requirements and how they inform, for Schopenhauer, the contents of morality.

We can take Schopenhauer to be setting three main requirements on any adequate moral philosophy. These requirements are overlapping and yet in some tension with each other, but they nevertheless serve to define the subject matter for him. First, moral philosophy must be *realistic* in the sense of accounting for how human agents' behavior is in fact motivated. Moral philosophy cannot depend on attributing to persons the extraordinary ability to exempt themselves from the causal order of things or to act on the basis of motives or norms that are otherwise unexemplified in the natural world. Moral philosophy, rather, starts from "empirical" (BM, 189) methods and moves to "clarifying and explaining ways of acting among human beings...and tracing them back to their ultimate ground" (BM, 189). "Real life" (BM, 181) shows that action is effected by nonrational, unreflective impulses that stem from fixed traits of character, so morality must acknowledge this. Second, moral philosophy must be *metaphysical*. The demands of morality are necessary, unconditional, and unchanging, and the only way of accounting for such demands must accordingly "reject any empirical basis" (BM, 133). Morality refers to human experience, but it must be grounded in "the ultimate and true revelation concerning the inner essence of the entirety of things" (BM, 116). The third requirement on moral philosophy is that it must identify something *distinctive* about moral action. Moral action is not a species of ordinary human behavior that happens to be unusually praiseworthy or valuable. Moral action, rather, stems from a *sui generis* impulse that, although potentially available in everyone, is utterly discontinuous from ordinary human behavior and incentivizes all and only moral behavior.

In light of these requirements on moral philosophy, Schopenhauer offers a metaphysical basis of morality that determines its basic content. The metaphysics of morality fits neatly within Schopenhauer's more comprehensive view, but we can isolate elements as centrally important for their moral implications. The most basic is that the very distinction between subjects and objects is an illusion. This dichotomy is the "general form . . . under which any representation is possible or even conceivable" (WWR1$_{[P]}$, 23). Without it, there can be no representation of anything by a subject; accordingly, this dichotomy pertains to the nature of representation rather than to how the world is in itself. Subjectivity allows us to represent a world of things but does not itself belong among what is real. We can therefore dismiss concerns that appear from the first-person standpoint, such as ones about well-being or the realization of ends. We can, furthermore, dismiss concerns about the distinctness or integrity of individuals. Another basic metaphysical claim is that actions follow from necessity, without the involvement of reason. Schopenhauer writes, "every individual action follows with strict necessity from the effect of a motive on character" (WWR1$_{[P]}$, 138). We cannot, therefore, base moral assessments on ascriptions of responsibility that depend on the choice or distinctive intervention of the agent. Furthermore, since reason is motivationally ineffective, morality cannot be a matter of recognizing or acting on rational demands; it simply is not possible to do so. In fact, acting on the basis of any kind of imperative is impossible, so moral philosophy must work by "describing not prescribing" (WWR1$_{[P]}$, 297). Also bearing moral implications is Schopenhauer's very general metaphysical claim that the "inner essence of things" (WWR1$_{[P]}$, 121), as *will*, is aimless, ceaseless, inarticulable striving that can never be fulfilled or satisfied. The world in itself is chaos and flux, and this is alien to all human concerns.

This is perhaps not the most promising metaphysical picture on which to build a moral philosophy, but Schopenhauer insists that it not only produces an ethics, but also furnishes a "foundation for the universally recognized requirements of morals" (BM, 121). The unreality of the individual standpoint, the vanity of the human pursuit of ends, and the senseless chaos of existence grounds, first of all, the so-called *neminem laede* as the "basic proposition" (BM, 139) of morality: "harm no one; rather, help everyone to the extent that you can" (BM, 140 *inter alia*). Every other moral principle, Schopenhauer claims, is based on this one. Moral action, furthermore, is motivated by *compassion* (BM, 200 *et passim*). Through immediate participation in others' suffering, natural egoism is overcome and purely moral action can take place. Compassion, that is, provides the specific incentive peculiar to morality. And this overcoming of egoism produces two cardinal virtues: freely willed justice and disinterested loving kindness (BM, 186).

There are some oddities in this picture of morality that are worth pointing out. In general, it is hard to make sense of the importance of these considerations, both in and of themselves and in relation to each other. The *neminem laede* is puzzling right away: it has an imperative form and thus appears to be a prescription for action, contrary to Schopenhauer's claims about the impossibility of prescriptions. It seems, furthermore, to have two desiderata that could come into conflict: causing harm might be necessary to help as much as possible. Schopenhauer does insist elsewhere on the priority of not causing harm (BM, 203), but it is not clear why this should be or how there can be restrictions on actions at all. We can also wonder about whether "helping" and "harming" means producing a suitable result or simply acting from the right motivation or the proper virtue. The virtues, too, are puzzling. They seem superfluous as loci of moral value if incentives and actions can be valuable; it is not clear, in any case, what it means for them to have "*genuine moral worth*" (BM, 189) or in what sense they could be valuable. It is likely possible to clarify all of these issues and furnish constructive accounts that specify, in greater detail, just what the demands of morality are. Schopenhauer, however, seems curiously uninterested in doing so, although that is part of the picture, too: the ineffectiveness of human agency, the unimportance of worldly concerns, and the unalterability of human character render it relatively unimportant precisely how morality is specified.

Even at the level of detail at which Schopenhauer presents his account of morality, however, the account remains generally problematic. Schopenhauer is advocating an altruistic—or unegoistic—morality based on metaphysical claims about agency and personhood: once the status of individual subjectivity is identified, then the content of morality follows. But how this could be so is puzzling. If Schopenhauer were making the case that one's own desires ought to be weighted less, that the distinction between my desires and those of others is less important, or that others' interests should play a greater role in my own concerns, then that would support other-regarding considerations and dispositions. But Schopenhauer's position seems to be that no one's interests have any weight, and no one acts on the basis of ends that they set or reasons that they recognize. In that case, it is hard to see how any moral standpoint could be supported. Others' interests are discounted as much as one's own, and the very idea of adopting any particular policy of action is discarded. One *could* respond altruistically in light of the global insignificance of human ends and the lack of relevant distinctions between persons. But that response seems just as arbitrary as wanton impulsiveness, complete inaction, indifferent aggressiveness, or any other course of action. Nothing about others' interests or one's own capacities supports it.

We can analyze this in terms of three specific puzzles that a Schopenhauerian moral philosophy would need to resolve. First, what is the point of being compassionate if human well-being does not in general matter? If metaphysics were to tell us that others' ends are equally important or that an impersonal good is important, then compassion might seem appropriate, but if no one's ends are important, why should "human action" be "of direct concern to everyone" (WWR1$_{[P]}$, 297)? Since the individual standpoint lacks "genuine reality" (WWR1$_{[P]}$, 303), then it becomes unclear how not only the egoism of the individual, but also the altruism of the individual could matter. Compassion and the terms of morality generally only make sense as such if the interests of persons matter to someone. If all the sources of importance are ultimately empty, then morality as a subject matter seems to disappear.

Before moving to the second puzzle, it is worth pointing out that there is a short answer to it. This answer is that altruism and compassion represent a denial of the "will to life" (WWR1$_{[P]}$, 368 *inter alia*), whereas nonmoral dispositions and behavior affirm it. That is, our phenomenal activity does not carry any weight by itself, but only because of how it situates itself relative to something of metaphysical significance. This, then, is the correct form of Schopenhauer's answer: it suggests that compassion and suffering are not intrinsically important but indicate something else that does matter. The problem here is just that this, by itself, explains little. There could be a private psychological difference between denying and affirming the will to life, but it is hard to see how such a psychological difference could count as bearing such a significance. From an appropriately higher standpoint, compassion itself fails to make sense: if the distinction between persons is unreal, then nothing could count as taking on another's woes or another's ends. We take for granted the phenomenal significance of compassion, but this phenomenal significance does not fit with Schopenhauer's view of the metaphysics of individuation. The gap between how things seem from an individual's standpoint and what really counts as significant is great and as yet unbridged.

The second puzzle for a Schopenhauerian moral philosophy is how the terms of morality can preserve their meaning if all events—in particular, all human actions—follow from necessity. Schopenhauer insists further that "the innermost essence of the man" (WWR1$_{[P]}$, 29f) is unalterable, that accordingly philosophy cannot produce virtuous persons, and that constant suffering is ineliminable from life. In this condition, it seems, moral philosophy cannot accomplish much. One can still assess what is necessary, and Schopenhauer sometimes does leave room for reflection to lead persons to better dispositions. But if character is unalterable and actions can neither realize worthwhile ends nor be freely chosen, then it is unclear how much "ethical content" (WWR1$_{[P]}$, 388) there could be. The terms of morality would not seem to pick out anything distinctive in the unalterable course of events. That is, even if they could pick out particular states or events, it is hard to see in what sense they would be more important than waves breaking or breezes blowing.

The third puzzle is that it remains unclear in what sense we can speak of a moral philosophy at all if "all philosophy is always theoretical" (WWR1$_{[P]}$, 271). A moral philosophy from a purely theoretical standpoint would be a descriptive or explanatory enterprise, or explaining what people believe or how they formed their beliefs, or perhaps reconstructing how moral discourse could have the sense that it does. To some extent, Schopenhauer is indeed advocating such a descriptive enterprise. But he also expresses favored moral views; it is important to his position that he is not only reporting on views that exist, but explaining the availability of views *for us*, that we can and should meaningfully adopt. And he uses his descriptive (or "contemplative") enterprise to dismiss so much moral philosophy that there is little left to explain or describe. He not only describes, but also intervenes in existing moral views to dismiss their prescriptive enterprises as senseless. If he is genuinely dismissing all prescriptions as much as philosophically impossible, then there is not much left for moral philosophy to be about.

18.2 SOLUTIONS

There are many possible ways to resolve these puzzles. I do not claim to have Schopenhauer's unique solution. He invoked so many different potentially countervailing considerations that multiple solutions are possible; each, however, involves some hermeneutic and logical costs and benefits. In the rest of this section, I outline some general approaches to offering a solution and then present my preferred solution.

The nature of the problem is that the various elements of moral philosophy seem to make sense in terms of each other, but Schopenhauer seems to take all of them away. For example, one can understand actions in terms of reasons and ends, character in terms of responsiveness to (correct) reasons, ends in terms of what persons value, and prescriptions in terms of any of these elements that are in some way required. But if the elements lack their ordinary meaning, then all of them risk being empty. One basic form of a solution, then, is to identify some term as preserving its meaning and centrally important and then to explain the rest of morality in terms of it. There are at least three options to privilege and then structure moral philosophy around: the inner attitude of *compassion*, *virtue* of character, and the *alleviation of suffering*. And one could also settle on nothingness and read Schopenhauer as, despite his words, abandoning ethics.

One possibility, then, is to take an altruistic "inner disposition"[3] as primary; the moral value of actions would depend on emerging from this disposition, and virtue would be a tendency to act in according with this disposition. This raises questions, I think, about how clearly any such disposition could be connected with the other considerations that Schopenhauer invokes: how reliably it would help or avoid harming others, whether it would track with the sense of justice or loving kindness, and whether it would consistently serve as the basis for action. The bigger cost, however, is that it leaves inexplicable why this inner disposition is so important or valuable or even coherent; there is nothing in terms of which to explain what makes it good. Any disposition or attitude is itself merely phenomenal, and it responds to phenomenal things and has at best a tenuous causal connection to behavior that does not achieve anything worthwhile. Nothing that it is, does, or brings about is intrinsically important, so building moral philosophy around it seems stipulative.

Similarly, if we take the enterprise of Schopenhauer's moral philosophy to be a "descriptive virtue ethics,"[4] then that gives up the project of explaining how the central elements are valuable. It might promise to describe how ethical practice is indeed structured around considerations of virtuous character and how Schopenhauer's moral philosophy is best understood in this way, but it will not explain why a virtue ethics would matter more than any other ethics. The very idea of a descriptive enterprise ensures that. More promising, perhaps, is an ethics built around the idea that "suffering will diminish"[5] if we adopt a Stoic worldly wisdom and restrain our desires. The core idea that suffering is bad and should be minimized is a plausible one, but, even here, there remains a difficulty in seeing how it could be important in such a way as to produce a particular moral response. On one hand, we need to see why a response to suffering should be compulsory; on the other hand, we need to see why other considerations might not be overriding. Otherwise the alleviation of suffering might be an incidental (and contingent) effect of morality, rather than its core. Finally, one could abandon the idea that any of this matters; morality could simply be the form that denial of the will happens to take. Here, however, we would be giving up on explaining why the path to oblivion takes just that form. In this case, furthermore, there is not much left for moral philosophy to say when it recommends sinking into oblivion to no one in particular.

In each of these cases, of course, there is a fuller answer that can be developed. For every question of why some action, attitude, or virtue counts as important, an appeal can be made that purports to explain it in terms of some more basic consideration. Some of these considerations, moreover, might help us to understand how morality might fit within *someone's* standpoint and cohere with their motivations. What I suggest, however, is that all such solutions neglect the radicality of Schopenhauer's views of phenomenal experience; they take our ethical practices to make sense, in some way, on their own terms, when in fact they do not. Moral philosophy, for Schopenhauer, involves responding to the senselessness of human existence rather than trying to make sense of it in even a partial, local way.

There are two general kinds of significance for Schopenhauer. One is *Bedeutung*, which appears frequently in his writings and can be translated as "meaning": it comes with a correlative notion of *Gehalt*, or content. This notion of significance operates primarily by a thing referring to something outside of itself. Significance in this sense is a "bridge" (BM 123), and its content is that to which it connects. In the case of empirical concepts, for example, their significance is the perceptual representations to which they are related. There is an immediate relationship between signifier and signified. The other kind of significance is one that Schopenhauer mentions rarely, perhaps because there is little point in doing so. This kind of significance is that of *sense*.[6] Sense is what makes for the intelligibility of how discursively articulated content is *presented*, rather than depending on that to which it refers. This kind of significance, then, must be articulable, rationally responsive, and in accordance with rule-governed interpretive practices. We make sense of content by fitting signifiers into general standards of interpretation, or at least by figuring out how they engage with other signifiers and with our interpretative abilities.

As Schopenhauer repeatedly insists, "the human way of acting has a *meaning* [*Bedeutung*]" (BM, 123). Indeed, it has an "ethical meaning" (BM, 116) and it has a "metaphysical" (BM, 127) meaning; together these facts about human behavior make moral philosophy possible. In human activity, we have available to us a direct, felt acquaintance with something entirely outside of our phenomenal experience. By virtue of this kind of meaningfulness, our activity acquires "an interest that engages our entire being" (WWR1$_{[P]}$, 119). In sum, human activity is important because its meaning connects us to something outside of itself; it sustains ethical interest because its content concerns the ultimate standing of our own nature.

But there is no *sense* in human activity, at least not within the proper sphere of moral philosophy. There is no hope in trying to make sense of it, to sort out its categories rationally and articulate why they matter. Nothing that you could possibly do or feel matters as such, but only in relation to its *Bedeutung*. We see this, for example, here, although it is presented in the context of a more specific issue: "That *ought* has any sense [*Sinn*] and meaning [*Bedeutung*] at all only in relation to a threatened punishment or promised reward…once those conditions are thought away, the concept of ought remains empty of sense" (BM, 128). Ought claims, like commanding in general, only make sense to us when they are backed by rewards or sanctions that engage with our motivational dispositions; then, but not before, we can understand them in terms of their empirical meaning—their reference to incentives and the prospect of altered behavior. This cannot support any ethical interest: the sense that this provides is that of providing a hypothetical path to moving us in some way or another.

Commands are just threats or promises, and threats and promises are at best motivational features of the world, like any other incentive we might encounter in nature. If we were to try to make sense of commands that amount to more than threats or promises, they are "simply impossible to think of" (BM, 128); indeed, they would be a "contradiction in terms" (BM, 128). The very idea of a moral imperative is not only wrong, but utterly empty of sense: when we speak of such things, we fail to say anything at all. We perhaps conflate something that has empirical significance with morality, which has metaphysical significance, and think it possible to say something substantial. And this is the form of human activity in general. It has an empirical sense, in terms of responsiveness to stimuli according to set dispositions. But the terms by which we act and feel are otherwise empty.

Moral philosophy, then, is not about carrying out activities or cultivating dispositions that are important on their own terms. It does not accomplish anything that matters or respect important norms. Our ethical practices, rather, have a metaphysical significance: morality as traditionally conceived, in particular in its anti-egoism, corresponds to a metaphysical insight into the nonreality of individuals. Morality is thereby the appropriate kind of responsiveness to the senselessness of human existence. It is not a rational or strategic pursuit, but an expression of the correct attitude toward the unavailability of any sensible pursuit. The point of morality is to manifest insight into the nature of reality, not properly to *do* anything. This is a practical enterprise only because the appreciation of metaphysical truth needs to be sustained through otherwise incomprehensible unegoistic action. This can convey a wisdom that might otherwise be inexpressible.

On the reading that I am proposing, Schopenhauer frames his moral philosophy around the ultimate vanity of human pursuits. The question that he wishes to answer, then, is what could be worth doing, or what must be done, when nothing makes any sense; even our ability to ascribe actions to agents or a point of view to a moral subject is in doubt. The answer that he gives is that the appropriate response is not, *per impossibile*, to do anything significant, but to make one's own activity manifest knowledge. Schopenhauer has something like a teleological argument for this, oddly enough.

He writes, "*cognition* [*das Erkennen*], together with the movement upon motives which it makes possible, is the fundamental *characteristic of animal life*" (WWR1$_{[P]}$, 42). What is fitting for us in our animal lives is cognition. The movements that accompany cognition are the incidental byproducts of its interaction with motivations; we act in a cognition-laden way. "The truly philosophical way of looking at the world," furthermore, provides a cognition that leads to "that state of mind which alone leads to true holiness and redemption from the world" (WWR1$_{[P]}$, 300). Our lives aim at cognition, and cognition does not aim at meaningful activity but produces activity that aims at redemption from the world.

Even if we take up this line of thought, however, and understand morality to be a way of manifesting metaphysical knowledge, then the question still needs to be addressed as to why compassion is the proper form that this takes. After all, it might seem as if metaphysical insight could be manifested in a variety of different ways or that no expression could count as privileged. Schopenhauer provides three sets of justifications, however, for the appropriateness of compassion.

First, through compassion we focus on suffering because suffering is something that we all, universally, dislike. A basic feature of human nature is that avoiding suffering (and seeking pleasure) is our most basic incentive and criterion of well-being: "the happiness of any given life is to be measured not by its joys and pleasures, but by the absence of sorrow and suffering" (PP2$_{[P]}$, 293). So, this justification runs, compassion is the appropriate response to the senselessness of existence because alleviating it is the sole thing that everyone would agree on, and this, in turn, is a way of acknowledging the lack of distinction between persons. Compassion does not require a commitment to anything beyond avoiding suffering, which relates to the "innermost core and essence" (BM, 190) of all. It is uncontroversial, and thus the sort of phenomenon that does not need any deeper ground to be privileged. This form of justification is still mysterious, however. Not only does it not provide an explanation for why compassion—concern for others' suffering—should matter to anyone, it also concedes that no explanation could be forthcoming. It appeals to the lack of any ground in privileging compassion, but some such ground would still be needed to support that privilege.

Schopenhauer's second line of justification is that compassion is the only form of our connection to others. "Immediate sympathy towards the other," he writes, "is restricted to his *suffering*" (BM, 202). Compassion, then, is the way in which we extend our awareness outside of ourselves to take account of and indeed experience others' pain. This justification of compassion as a form of responsiveness is that it brings about an enlarged appreciation of the unity of all things. In compassion, "the not-I to a certain extent become[s] the I" (BM, 201), and we gain insight into this. This insight must be limited, however, since it preserves the distinction between persons. We feel suffering *as someone else's* in compassion, and this, of course, requires treating someone as a separate individual. Schopenhauer writes, "it remains clear and present to us at every single moment that he is the sufferer, not *us*: and it is precisely *in his* person, not in ours, that we feel the pain, to our distress. We suffer *with* him, thus *in* him: we feel his pain as *his* and do not imagine that it is ours" (BM, 203).

The third justification is similar to the previous one. Instead of *connecting* us to others, however, this justification obliterates the distinction between self and others. The point is no longer that we feel for others' pain, but that we no longer experience pain as belonging to anyone in particular once "the barrier between I and not-I is removed" (BM, 218). In this way, compassion constitutes a recognition of the illusoriness of the *principium individuationis*. In compassion, that is, we appreciate and even experience a metaphysical truth that is otherwise inaccessible in empirical consciousness, viz., that the distinction between persons is unreal. In this way compassion constitutes the most appropriate response to the senselessness of existence.

For just this reason, however, it is no longer truly compassion, at least in any ordinary sense. Compassion normally requires preserving some distinction between persons: one feels and cares about another's suffering. What is distinctive about compassion as metaphysical expression, however, is that pain and others' perspectives do not truly matter except as a form of truthfulness; they are vehicles for greater enlightenment.

18.3 CONCLUSION

On my reading, Schopenhauer's moral philosophy is about identifying the appropriate form of responsiveness to the lack of any practical standards of appropriateness. The conditions of our existence do not allow us to make sense of any activity as meaningful on its own terms, so the best that we can do is to think of our lives as a way of orienting ourselves to metaphysical truth; a theoretical solution is the best response to the lack of a practical solution. This unegoistic form of orientation both expresses metaphysical insight and corresponds to the self-denying content of morality as it is traditionally understood.

There are a number of virtues of this account: it preserves Schopenhauer's insistences that moral philosophy is a theoretical enterprise and that all human endeavor is in vain, for example. Still, like any reading of Schopenhauer's moral philosophy, it has its drawbacks. The main interpretive drawback is that it renders trivial nearly everything that Schopenhauer says about the concrete practice of morality. He devotes considerable effort to explicating various elements of morality and relating them to traditional thought and metaphysics. On my reading, none of this particularly matters. Unegoistic morality, in general, expresses metaphysical insight, and whether such expression succeeds or fails, there is little one can do to refine that message. Moral philosophy can do little to inform practice, offers little hope of success, and cannot engage with anyone's concerns. It cannot appeal to the reasons, ends, or ideals that might make sense within someone's individual perspective.

As moral philosophy, the biggest drawback is that it preserves at most a shell of a conventional sense of morality. In any conventional moral philosophy, it matters, deeply, to someone, what one does, or how one does it, or what it achieves, or what one becomes as a person. Although this might conceivably be to its advantage, none of these can be important in any familiar way in Schopenhauer's moral thought. Compassion is not an expression of care for another individual, but a way of moving outside of all individual perspective altogether. As a result, the stance of moral philosophy itself remains sense-less. It provides a point of access to a reality that we have little purchase on, but it does not give us reasons to act upon in the familiar, phenomenal world. It does not show us how to care about ourselves and the things around us or make some way of life seem less arbitrary. It functions more like a promise that, once complete metaphysical insight comes, none of those concerns will be troubling any more.

NOTES

1. This is quoted in David Cartwright, "Schopenhauer's Narrower Sense of Morality," in *The Cambridge Companion to Schopenhauer*, edited by Christopher Janaway (New York: Cambridge University Press, 1999), 252.
2. Ibid., 253.
3. Patrick Gardiner, *Schopenhauer* (Baltimore, MD: Penguin Books, 1960), 260. I found this suggestion in Gardiner, but his views are much more complex than the schematic views that I am putting forward here. Here and in the rest of this paragraph, I am solely trying to set out broad possibilities of interpretation, not reckon with scholars' views in their entirety. Some of these views might not fit well in my categories. For example, Christopher Janaway, in *Schopenhauer: A Very Short Introduction* (New York: Oxford University Press, 2002), privileges compassion as the center of Schopenhauer's moral philosophy but ends up with a view similar to my own.
4. Cartwright, "Schopenhauer's Narrower Sense of Morality," 263. Please see the qualification in the previous note.
5. Robert Wicks, *Schopenhauer* (Malden, MA: Blackwell Publishing, 2008), 92. The same qualifications apply here as in the previous notes.
6. "*Sinn*" usually and very often refers to the senses and sensuous experience; only rarely does Schopenhauer use *Sinn* to refer to a semantic notion.

FURTHER READING

Cartwright, David. "Schopenhauer's Compassion and Nietzsche's Pity." *Schopenhauer Jahrbuch* 69 (1988): 557–67.

Cartwright, David. "Schopenhauer's Narrower Sense of Morality." In *The Cambridge Companion to Schopenhauer*, edited by Christopher Janaway. New York: Cambridge University Press, 1999, 252–92.

Cooper, David E. "Self and Morality in Schopenhauer and Nietzsche." In *Willing and Nothingness: Schopenhauer as Nietzsche's Educator*, edited by Christopher Janaway. New York: Oxford University Press, 1988, 196–216.

Gardiner, Patrick. *Schopenhauer*. Baltimore, MD: Penguin Books, 1960.

Janaway, Christopher. *Schopenhauer: A Very Short Introduction*. New York: Oxford University Press, 2002.

Schopenhauer, Arthur. "Prize Essay on the Basis of Morals." In *The Two Fundamental Problems of Ethics*, translated by Christopher Janaway. New York: Cambridge University Press, 2009.

Wicks, Robert, *Schopenhauer*. Malden, MA: Blackwell Publishing, 2008.

Young, Julian, *Schopenhauer*. New York: Routledge, 2005.

CHAPTER 19

....

SCHOPENHAUER ON LAW
AND JUSTICE

....

RAYMOND B. MARCIN

ALTHOUGH Schopenhauer would certainly agree with the notion that laws should be just rather than unjust, "law" and "justice" are really two quite separate topics in his theoretical understanding. Schopenhauer's theory of *law* is practical and pragmatic. It yields concepts of law and legal responsibility that are distinctly behaviorist in tone, and modern scholarship in the area of legal pragmatism, law-and-economics, and public-choice theory suggests a trend in the direction of behaviorism.[1] Schopenhauer's theory of *justice*, on the other hand, is genuinely ontological. It focuses on the fundamental nature of being itself.

In the legal literature of the past and present, the concept of justice has almost always been examined from an epistemological vantage point.[2] Seldom have we seen, outside the natural law tradition, an ontological examination of justice, and that is exactly what Schopenhauer gives us. With its ontological basis, including its focus on the inter-identity of all beings, Schopenhauer's theory of justice bridges a gap that has long existed between Western and Eastern approaches to philosophy.[3] Some modern and contemporary jurisprudential movements (e.g., civic-republican and communitarian jurisprudence) may be taking up the chord struck by Schopenhauer as they have of late taken an interest in the concept of "community." And the idea of "community" in its most basic and most literal sense is at the heart of Schopenhauer's definition of justice. Schopenhauer's approach to law and justice is, of course, dictated by the dualist world that he posits in the title and throughout the content of his two-volume magnum opus, *The World as Will and Representation*.

19.1 SCHOPENHAUER ON LAW

....

"Law" in Schopenhauer's thought simply refers to the various rules and regulations imposed by governments on the governed. It addresses the problems associated with the everyday world that we experience around us—the world of phenomena—the world as presented (or re-presented) to us by the structure of our perceiving instrument, the self-conscious mind. The ideal government, Schopenhauer recognizes, would be one that produces "beings whose nature permits them generally to sacrifice their own good to that of the public" (WWR1$_{[P]}$, 343). But reality intrudes—reality in the form of the implications that inhabit Schopenhauer's dualist worldview of "will" and "re-presentation."

The fact that there is such a vast difference, in Schopenhauer's thought, between the world as it appears and the world as it really is—between the world as appearance and the world as thing-in-itself—between the world as re-presented to us by the structure of our perceiving instrument and the underlying world as "will"—creates a strange and difficult situation. The underlying world as thing-in-itself *affirms* itself. Affirming itself is the existential task of the "will." Viewed from the world of appearances, the self-affirming activity of the "will" is subject to time, space, causality, and plurality—all the limitations and conditions imposed by the structure of the perceiving mind. But the "will" itself is timeless, space-less, cause-less, and un-individuated. In our everyday view, however, from our vantage point in the world of appearances, the "will" manifests itself in the time, space, causality, and plurality that condition our experience of phenomena. Most importantly, when the "will" affirms itself in the world of appearances, it does so as an *individuated* act of self-affirmation. In Schopenhauer's thought, *plurality* is one of the conditions imposed by the structure of the perceiving mind, and, as such, plurality applies only to the world of appearance, not to the world as thing-in-itself (i.e., the world as "will"). Since, at the deep-down level of true reality, all is an un-individuated "will," the *entire* "will" exists in each apparently individual entity.[4] This situation naturally leads to an *egoism* that Schopenhauer posits as the all-pervasive original motivation in human beings. Self-affirmation in the plant and animal world appears in the all too familiar "law of the jungle," with predator affirming itself at the expense of prey. At the human level, it assumes moral proportions in phenomena ranging from selfish behavior all the way to Thomas Hobbes's *bellum omnium contra omnes*.[5]

In the individuated self-affirmation that the "will" imposes on us, Schopenhauer sees not only the source of the "egoism"—so well described in Hobbes's *bellum omnium contra omnes*—but also the source of "wrong."

> [S]ince the will manifests that *self-affirmation* of one's own body in innumerable individuals beside one another, in one individual, by virtue of the egoism peculiar to all, it very easily goes beyond this affirmation to the *denial* of the same will appearing in another individual.... This breaking through the boundary of another's affirmation of will has at all times been distinctly recognized, and its concept has been denoted by the word *wrong* [*Unrecht*].   (WWR1$_{[P]}$, 334)

"Wrong" is, in Schopenhauer's thought, such an inexorably prevalent result of the individuated self-affirmation that the "will" imposes on the human condition that it (i.e., "wrong") is the norm and "right" is the exception, or, as Schopenhauer himself words it, "the concept of *wrong* is the original and positive; the opposite concept of *right* is the derivative and negative....The concept of *right* contains merely the negation of wrong" (WWR1$_{[P]}$, 339).

Schopenhauer's dualism yields some interesting conclusions for contemporary jurisprudential theorists. At the phenomenal (i.e., world-as-representation) level—the level of everyday life—Schopenhauer is one with the legal economists and public-choice theorists who inhabit today's law-and-economics movement. A theory of law should be behaviorist.[6] Schopenhauer found the essence of the behaviorist credo in Seneca's *Laws*: "No sensible person punishes because a wrong has been done, but in order that a wrong may not be done" (WWR1$_{[P]}$, 349). Law must operate to cure the ills that beset us at the phenomenal level, where individuated self-interest reigns supreme.

But the obvious cure for those ills of all-prevalent egoism is altruism (*other*-interest as opposed to a self-interest), and altruism obviously cannot be mandated or legislated.[7] The only thing that can be legislated is a mandated course of conduct whose results would be the same as those that would ensue if people *were* altruistically *other*-interested. The law, in Schopenhauer's thought, can only affect behavior and cannot effect a change in will and disposition. Schopenhauer's words: "will and disposition, merely as such, do not concern the State at all; the *deed* alone does so (whether it be merely attempted or carried out), on account of its correlative, namely the *suffering* of the other party. Thus for the State the deed, the occurrence, is the only real thing....If the State attains its object completely, it will produce the same phenomenon as if perfect justice of disposition everywhere prevailed (WWR1$_{[P]}$, 344–45).

Because of the egoism inherent in the individuated self-interest, there is a societal need for "law." Altruism can neither be expected nor legislated.

> The State is set up on the correct assumption that pure morality, i.e., right conduct from moral grounds, is not to be expected; otherwise it itself [i.e., the State] would be superfluous. Thus the State, aiming at well-being, is by no means directed against egoism, but only against the injurious consequences of egoism arising out of the plurality of egoistic individuals, reciprocally affecting them, and disturbing their well-being.   (WWR1$_{[P]}$, 345)

At first glance, the mischievous gremlin of "egoism," so prevalent in Schopenhauer's theory of law, seems to derail this apparently optimistic view of the State. The State itself, in Schopenhauer's thought, is indeed infected with egoism: "[I]t is precisely from egoism that [the State] has sprung, and it exists merely to serve it. This egoism well understands itself, proceeds methodically, and goes from the one-sided to the universal point of view, and thus by summation is the common egoism of all" (WWR1$_{[P]}$, 345).

How can a State, "sprung" from egoism and existing "merely to serve" egoism (albeit from "the universal point of view"), "produce the same phenomenon as if perfect justice of disposition everywhere prevailed"?[8] Has Schopenhauer contradicted himself?

The solution to the apparent contradiction lies in an understanding of what happens when egoism "goes from the one-sided to the universal point of view" (WWR1$_{[P]}$, 345). From the *universal* point of view, the State "is...directed...against the injurious consequences of egoism arising out of the plurality of egoistic individuals, reciprocally affecting them, and disturbing their well-being" (WWR1$_{[P]}$, 345). Just as each individual human being's egoism is often at war with the egoism of every other individual human being in its incessant efforts to affirm itself and advance its individual well-being (Thomas Hobbes's *bellum omnium contra omnes*), so, too, the State ("by summation...the common egoism of all" [WWR1$_{[P]}$, 345]), in its incessant efforts to affirm and advance "the common egoism of all," is similarly often at war with other egoisms (i.e., the individual egoisms of the chaotic gaggle of individual self-interested human beings). Affirming and advancing "the common egoism of all" somehow results in societal well-being, according to Schopenhauer.

In this context, some may see an echo of the thought of the great eighteenth-century economist Adam Smith, a central figure in the scholarship generated by the law-and-economics movement.[9] Smith wrote famously of an "invisible hand," whereby somehow the apparent chaos of individuals acting in their own often-conflicting individual self-interests results in the general betterment of society. He held to such a theory not only in his economics treatise, *The Wealth of Nations*, but also in his work on ethics, his *Theory of Moral Sentiments*.[10] Although Schopenhauer never mentioned Adam Smith in his *magnum opus*, one cannot help surmising that, in his doctrine on the State, Schopenhauer may have made Adam Smith's "invisible hand" to some extent "visible"—or at least he gave a reasoned explanation of an ontological basis behind Adam Smith's "invisible hand."

19.2 SCHOPENHAUER ON JUSTICE

In all that happens or indeed can happen to the individual, justice is always done to it.[11]

Schopenhauer's theory of *law*, directed as it is to behavior alone (i.e., the deed rather than the disposition or motive), may seem somewhat superficial to some of us today. If so, his theory of *justice* more than makes up for any perceived superficiality—it delves deeply into the very essence of the human psyche.

Schopenhauer's theory of *justice*, as his theory on *law*, draws initially on his doctrine of the affirmation of the will-to-live.[12] At the human level, the affirmation of the will-to-live, as we have seen, assumes its worst moral proportions in Hobbes's *bellum omnium contra omnes*. Its exercise in that context is usually regarded by individuals in possession of common sense as socially inappropriate, even morally wrong. As we have also seen, Schopenhauer's theory of *law* addresses the damaging aspects of the conflicting and chaotic exercises of the will-to-live at the individual human level—but only the damaging aspects. Schopenhauer's theory of *law*, as we have seen, is behaviorist. Beyond its preventative and deterrent features, law does not address the *cause* of the conflicting and chaotic exercises of the will-to-live at the individual human level—that is, the cause that lies deeply embedded in the human psyche. One recalls Schopenhauer's words.

> [W]ill and disposition, merely as such, do not concern the State at all; the *deed* alone does so (whether it be merely attempted or carried out), on account of its correlative, namely the *suffering* of the other party. Thus for the State the deed, the occurrence, is the only real thing.   (WWR1$_{[P]}$, 344).

Schopenhauer's theory of *justice* addresses the cause; that is, the perceived need for an altruistic element to offset the prevalence of the egoistic element in the human psyche. Addressing, as it does, the cause of the suffering brought about by excesses of the activity of the will-to-live at the phenomenal level, Schopenhauer's theory of *justice* deals directly and intensely with what philosophy and theology refer to as the age-old "Problem of Evil."[13]

In most systems of ethics and moral theology, the Problem of Evil is a stumbling block, or even an embarrassment, but not in Schopenhauer's system. And the solution to the Problem of Evil lies at the very heart of his metaphysics.[14] Most systems of ethics either founder or else wallow in circumlocutions when they confront the fact of the existence of evil in the world and try to reconcile it with either an all-good God or with the supposed essential goodness of human nature.[15] The problem is impossible to avoid, and any system of ethics or moral theology must confront it. The conventional explanation, remarkably consistent over the centuries and across many cultures, posits a judgment after death in which the oppressor receives his or her "comeuppance" and the oppressed receives his or her reward. In contemporary times, that explanation seems not to be wearing well, and a century and a half ago it ill-suited Schopenhauer, who quoted Euripides to impugn it.

> Do you think that crimes ascend to the gods on wings, and then someone has to record them there on the tablet of Jove, and that Jove looks at them and pronounces judgement on men? The whole of heaven would not be great enough to contain the sins of men, were Jove to record them all, nor would he to review them and assign to each his punishment. No! the punishment is already there, if only you will see it.
> (WWR2$_{[P]}$, 351)[16]

Schopenhauer's solution to the Problem of Evil is presaged quite clearly in his metaphysics. Recall that for Schopenhauer the true reality, the thing-in-itself, of everything is "will"; and the timeless, spaceless, and causeless "will" is un-individuated. That is, there is a basic, very real, unity among all existence. We are more than our brother's keeper. In the most basic ontological sense, we *are* our brother. Schopenhauer applies all this to the Problem of Evil.

> [T]he difference between the inflicter of suffering and he who must endure it is only phenomenon, and does not concern the thing-in-itself which is the will that lives in both. Deceived by the knowledge bound to its service, the will here fails to recognize

itself; seeking enhanced well-being in *one* of its phenomena, it produces great suffering in *another*. Thus in the fierceness and intensity of its desire it buries its teeth in its own flesh, not knowing that it always injures only itself, revealing in this form through the medium of individuation the conflict with itself which it bears in its inner nature. Tormentor and tormented are one. The former is mistaken in thinking that he does not share the torment, the latter in thinking he does not share the guilt.   (WWR1$_{[P]}$, 354)

At the deep-down level of true reality, according to Schopenhauer, tormentor and tormented are one and the same—the "will." If the tormented shares the guilt, Schopenhauer is quite correct in reaching the otherwise cryptic conclusion that "in all that happens or indeed can happen to the individual, justice is always done to it" (WWR1$_{[P]}$, 351). This is Schopenhauer's doctrine of eternal justice. It is the "will" feeding on itself.

19.3 THE VIRTUE OF JUSTICE

Can individual human beings, steeped as they are in the Problem of Evil, rescue themselves? Or are they condemned inexorably to struggle in the *bellum omnium contra omnes*? It may seem anomalous to find in the teachings of the great Philosopher of Pessimism[17] a doctrine of salvation from the torments of life, but it is there in his teachings on the virtue of justice. Indeed, Schopenhauer called justice "the first and fundamentally essential cardinal virtue."[18]

A slight digression: a century or so after Schopenhauer, Mohandas K. Gandhi, the sainted Mahatma of India, also wrote about the Problem of Evil, which he discussed in terms of "*himsa*," a Sanskrit word carrying the connotation of violent harm or killing.

We are helpless mortals caught in the conflagration of *himsa*. The saying that life lives on life has a deep meaning....Man cannot for a moment live without consciously or unconsciously committing outward *himsa*....[B]ecause underlying *ahimsa* (*i.e.*, nonviolence) is the unity of all life, the error of one cannot but affect all, and hence man cannot be wholly free from *himsa*.[19]

It is well known that Gandhi's understanding of *himsa* (i.e., violence) led him to a doctrine of *ahimsa* (i.e., nonviolence) and through that to a positive and remarkable state of holiness and wholeness. Gandhi clearly viewed the "conflagration of *himsa*" as something to be striven against. One cannot envision Gandhi choosing the term "eternal justice" to express the "conflagration of *himsa*," but Schopenhauer did use the term "eternal justice," and in doing so was suggesting that an understanding of what Schopenhauer calls eternal justice "is something to be sought and even embraced, something that can lead to *virtue*:...[E]ternal justice will be grasped and comprehended only by the man who rises above that knowledge which proceeds on the guiding line of the principle of sufficient reason and is bound to individual things....Moreover, it is this man alone who, by dint of the same knowledge, can understand the true nature of virtue...although for the practice of virtue this knowledge in the abstract is by no means required" (WWR1[P], 354).

How does "grasping and comprehending" eternal justice lead to an understanding of the true nature of virtue? Schopenhauer explained, and in doing so, he touched upon the underpinning of Gandhi's *ahimsa*—the metaphysical identity of all being.

> [T]he most fundamental of all our errors is that, with reference to one another, we are not-I. On the other hand, to be just, noble, and benevolent is nothing but to translate my metaphysics into actions. To say that time and space are mere forms of our knowledge, not determinations of things-in-themselves, is the same as saying that the teaching of metempsychosis, namely that "one day you will be born again as the man whom you now injure, and will suffer the same injury," is identical with the frequently mentioned formula of the Brahmans, *Tat tvam asi*, "This thou art." *All genuine virtue proceeds from the immediate and* intuitive *knowledge of the metaphysical identity of all being.* (WWR2[P], 600–01, emphasis added)

It must be admitted that at this point Schopenhauer leaves conventional Western philosophical concepts behind. Up to a point he expresses himself as a philosopher using the vocabulary and the methodology of philosophy. But how can he describe a non-abstract, non-reasoned-to kind of knowledge in the vocabulary and methodology of philosophy? Here Schopenhauer calls upon myth and symbol.[20]

> [T]hat great fundamental truth contained in Christianity as well as in Brahmanism and Buddhism, the need for salvation from an existence given up to suffering and death, and its attainability through the denial of the will, hence by a decided opposition to nature, is beyond all comparison the most important truth there can be.
>
> ...But in order to understand the truth itself contained in this myth, we must regard human beings not merely in time as entities independent of one another, but must comprehend the (Platonic) Idea of man....Now if we keep in view the Idea of man, we see that the Fall of Adam represents man's finite, animal, sinful nature, in respect of which he is just a being abandoned to limitation, sin, suffering, and death. On the other hand, the conduct, teaching, and death of Jesus Christ represent the eternal, supernatural side, the freedom, the salvation of man. Now, as such and *potentiâ*, every person is Adam as well as Jesus, according as he comprehends himself, and his will thereupon determines him. (WWR2[P], 628)

It is startling when we read Schopenhauer's statement that "every person is Adam as well as Jesus" (even if the statement is qualified by the Latin adverb *potentiâ*, meaning "virtually"). But if time, space, causality, plurality, and individuation are mere impositions of the structure of the perceiving mind and are not attributes of true reality (and this is precisely the claim of Schopenhauer's entire metaphysical theory), then, "*potentiâ*," every individual is, at that deep level of true reality, every other individual. There is an identity between Adam and each of us, between Jesus and each of us, and between Jesus and Adam.[21] The source of the startling nature of the comment, therefore, lies not in its being inconsistent with anything Schopenhauer had said previously (it is quite consistent), but rather in its implications. If true, Schopenhauer's statement at once solves two great theological enigmas: the doctrine of the inherited responsibility for original sin and the doctrine of the mystical body of Christ. Anyone raised in the Christian tradition will recall the difficulties that theologians have had in explaining how it is that each of us is saddled with the responsibility for the original sin of Adam, difficulties so obvious that they moved the monk Pelagius in the fourth century to deny the doctrine and to found a heresy that was still being addressed a thousand years later at the Council of Trent.[22] In Schopenhauer's thought, each of us *is* Adam, and the justice of holding each of us responsible for Adam's sin exists at the level of what Schopenhauer refers to as "eternal justice."[23] At the level of deep reality, we are more than our brother's keeper—we *are* our brother. We *are* our neighbor. We *are* our enemy. Schopenhauer indeed startles and unnerves us—not so much because he *attacks* what Christians believe as because he somehow seems to *defend* it so much better than Christians themselves have been able to defend it.[24]

But this metaphysical interidentity among us all is just that: metaphysical. It exists only at the deep level of true reality, a level that is all but foreclosed to our organs of perception. We must of necessity—a necessity imposed by the very structure of our perceiving minds—function at the level of phenomena, within the constraints of time, space, causality, plurality, and individuation, behind Brahmanism's Veil of Mâyâ.[25] But there are occasional breakthroughs. At times the breeze of the Platonic Idea sweeps the veil aside momentarily and we get a glimpse of the unity of subject and object in aesthetics. And, at times, in our relations with one another, we have another glimpse at the deep level of true reality. Aesthetics is often linked with ethics, and the two are not unconnected in Schopenhauer's thought. Just as, in aesthetics, one can reach the level of the Platonic Idea and see through, as it were, the delusional separation of subject and object, so too, in ethics, one can also see through the delusion of plurality. The vehicle? Sympathy (or Compassion): "[S]*ympathy or compassion*...is...the basis of justice and philanthropy, *caritas*" (WWR2$_{[P]}$, 601–02).[26]

Sympathy or compassion—the words are synonymous, one from the Greek, the other from the Latin, and both meaning "feeling with"—is the basis of the virtue of justice. But sympathy or compassion, in Schopenhauer's thought, is not confined to the occasional emotional tear drawn from ardent theatergoers. It has an ontological basis in the human psyche itself.

> [T]he world as thing-in-itself, the identity of all beings, justice, righteousness, philanthropy, denial of the will-to-live, spring from *one* root.... [M]oral virtues spring from of that identity of all beings; this, however, lies not in the phenomenon, but in the thing-in-itself, in the root of all beings.   (WWR2$_{[P]}$, 610)

19.4 JUSTICE AND THE DENIAL
OF THE WILL-TO-LIVE

The immediately preceding quote introduces us to an essential element in Schopenhauer's theory of justice as a virtue: his curiously named doctrine of the denial of the will-to-live. Perhaps because Schopenhauer leaves conventional Western philosophical concepts behind in dealing with his understanding of the underpinning of the virtue of justice and enters the world of myth and symbol, some commentators seem to have rejected his doctrine of the denial of the will-to-live almost out of hand.[27]

Because of the way in which it manifests itself in the world of appearances; that is, the world as re-presented to us through the structures of our perceiving mind (time, space, causality, plurality, etc.), the "will" which, at the human level, Schopenhauer refers to as the "will-to-live,"[28] is involved in a delusion. Despite the countless individuals who inhabit the world, the will-to-live is un-individuated and is present, whole and entire, in each individual. Moreover, it seeks to affirm itself in this delusional milieu, often at the expense of itself.

This delusional milieu in which the will finds itself is not unknown in the cultural traditions that have developed over the years. Schopenhauer sees it in both Christianity and Hinduism. In Christianity, this delusion takes the form of the doctrine of Original Sin. Quoting the poet Calderon who wrote " [M]an's greatest offence is that he has been born," Schopenhauer concludes that "[i]n that verse Calderon has merely expressed the Christian dogma of original sin" (WWR1$_{[P]}$, 355). In Brahmanism, Schopenhauer found this delusional milieu in the doctrine of the Veil of Mâyâ: "...[T]he ancient wisdom of the Indians declares that "it is Mâyâ, the veil of deception, which covers the eyes of mortals, and causes them to see a world of which one cannot say either that it is or that it is not" (WWR1$_{[P]}$, 8). "[I]t is...individuation that keeps the will-to-live in error as to its own true nature; it is the Mâyâ of Brahmanism" (WWR2[P], 601).

Both religious traditions, of course, provide a solution for the human being's predicament, and both employ the same word when they discuss their solutions: salvation. But the word "salvation" on the lips of the average Christian means something quite different from what it means on the lips of a Brahman. Christian salvation traditionally accommodates and preserves the individuality of the saved person. Hindu salvation does not. In fact, in Hindu philosophy (carried over into and developed more fully in Buddhism) existence itself is transcended in the state known as *nirvāṇa* (a Sanskrit word that is somewhat paradoxically but correctly translated as both "enlightenment" and "extinction").[29]

In its final analysis, Schopenhauer's "salvation" is much closer to the Hindu/Buddhist than to the traditional Christian understanding, although he couches it more often than not in Christian terminology.[30] Salvation, for Schopenhauer, lies in the denial of the will-to-live, but this should not be understood superficially. Thinking simplistically, it would seem that the clearest and most direct route to salvation, in Schopenhauer's mind, would be suicide. Suicide seems at first glance to involve a denial of the will-to-live. But Schopenhauer very clearly held to the contrary. Suicide, according to Schopenhauer, involves an affirmance and not a denial of the will-to-live.

> The suicide wills life, and is dissatisfied merely with the conditions on which it has come to him. Therefore, he gives up by no means the will-to-live, but merely life, since he destroys the individual phenomenon.... [S]uicide...is a quite futile and foolish act, for the thing-in-itself remains unaffected by it.... [I]t is also the master-piece of Maya as the most blatant expression of the contradiction of the will-to-live with itself.   (WWR1$_{[P]}$, 398–99)

True salvation (i.e., true denial of the will-to-live) involves the "will" *itself* doing something about the "veil of Mâyâ." It is not simply a matter of the "saved" individual choosing to ignore the delusion involved in the apparent plurality of things in the world. In Schopenhauer's thought the individual human being has no free will and therefore cannot make such a choice. The only thing that has "free will" in Schopenhauer's scheme of things is the will itself, as thing-in-itself.

> [I]f the will-to-live exists, it cannot, as that which alone is metaphysical or the thing-in-itself, be broken by any force, but that force can only destroy its phenomenon in such a place and at such a time. The will itself cannot be abolished by anything except *knowledge*. Therefore the only path to salvation is that the will should appear freely and without hindrance, in order that it can *recognize or know* its own inner nature in this phenomenon. Only in consequence of this knowledge can the will abolish itself and thus end the suffering that is inseparable from its phenomenon.
> (WWR1$_{[P]}$, 400, emphasis in original)

Since, in the usual course of the world, the will is constantly involved in affirming itself in individual phenomena, most often at the expense of itself in other individual phe-nomena, the will is constantly sinking its teeth into its own flesh. The alternative to this unpleasant state of affairs is for the will to deny itself—not for the individual human being to deny the will, but for the will itself to deny itself, to become quiescent, to cease its aimless striving. This event—the will denying itself—can occur in the context of a human being's life, and, when it does, something not unlike the Buddhist *nirvāṇa*—something transcendent and inexplicable—occurs.

> [W]hat remains after the complete abolition of the will is, for all who are still full of the will, assuredly nothing. But also conversely, to those in whom the will has turned and denied itself, this very real world of ours with all its suns and galaxies, is—nothing.
> (WWR1$_{[P]}$, 411–12)

There is a point to human existence, according to Schopenhauer. True, the will is aimless. And true, "existence is certainly to be regarded as an error or mistake"

(WWR2$_{[P]}$, 605). But there is a point, or an aim, of our existence, and, as Schopenhauer characteristically words it, it seems to be a trivial, negative point or aim.

> [N]othing else can be stated as the aim of our existence except the knowledge that it would be better for us not to exist. This…is the most important of all truths.
>
> (WWR2$_{[P]}$, 605)

If indeed this is "the most important of all truths," then we should, perhaps, analyze it carefully. The "aim of our existence" is "knowledge"—knowledge of a particular type. Our task in life is to acquire the knowledge that would enable us to conclude "that it would be better for us not to exist." What kind of knowledge would enable us to draw that strange conclusion? The knowledge that the will-to-live, our very being-in-itself, is "involved in a delusion" (WWR2$_{[P]}$, 606). But, of course, it can't stop there. That kind of knowledge might lead to some sort of doctrine of ethical suicide, and Schopenhauer condemns suicide.[31] It is, rather, knowledge such that the will *itself* can freely recognize the delusion in which it is involved, and can freely choose to abolish itself. It is not an abstract, reasoned-to kind of knowledge; it is intuitive and finds its expression in experience.[32]

In a way, it is difficult to see in Schopenhauer's doctrine of the denial of the will-to-live, something that is very close to the profound religious conversion that lies at the heart of born-again Evangelical Christianity. Schopenhauer was an avowed atheist. But it is perhaps more difficult to ignore Schopenhauer's own ultimate elucidation of his doctrine, steeped at its conclusion in born-again Evangelical terminology.

> [W]hen the *principium individuationis* is seen through, when the Ideas, and indeed the inner nature of the thing-in-itself, are immediately recognized as the same will in all, and the result of this knowledge is a universal quieter of willing, then the individual motives become ineffective, because the kind of knowledge that corresponds to them is obscured and pushed into the background by knowledge of quite a different kind. Therefore, the character can never partially change, but must, with the consistency of a law of nature, realize in the particular individual the will whose phenomenon it is in general and as a whole. But this whole, the character itself, can be entirely eliminated by the above-mentioned change of knowledge.… [I]t is…that which in the Christian Church is very appropriately called *new birth* or *regeneration*, and the knowledge from which it springs, the *effect of divine grace*.
>
> (WWR1$_{[P]}$, 403, emphasis in original)

19.5 SCHOPENHAUER'S LAW AND JUSTICE IN CONTEMPORARY JURISPRUDENCE

The implications of Schopenhauer's theory of justice for contemporary jurisprudential thought are as sweeping as they are profound. Contemporary jurisprudential thought, plagued as it is by polar inconsistencies in its views of humanness itself and without a metaphysical grounding for its tenets and propositions has been drifting back toward early twentieth-century forms of philosophical pragmatism.[33]

On the one hand, legal economists and public-choice theorists sometimes see the human being as nothing more or less than "an egoistic, rational, utility maximizer."[34] On the other hand, contemporary civic republicans and other communitarians see the human being as an entity fully capable of an altruistic cooperative solidarity.[35] Both views cannot be true, yet both views command responsible adherents, leading some, like John Rawls and Adam Smith long before him, to strive for a melding of the two seemingly inconsistent views,[36] with problematic success in each case.

Schopenhauer's theory of justice accommodates both views of humankind with ease. At the phenomenal level, the level at which we live our daily lives, the human being *is* an egoistic, rational utility maximizer, wallowing in the chaos of self-interest which permeates the affirmation of the will-to-live. And yet, according to Schopenhauer, that level of phenomenal reality is but an illusion. Deep down at the unfathomable level of the noumenal, the human being is different. At the noumenal level, the human being *is* a oneness, a unity that goes even beyond "comm-unity," beyond social siblinghood, a unity of all-encompassing identity.

The legal economists and public-choice theorists sense the phenomenal level of everyday reality. The civic republicans and other communitarians sense the noumenal level of eternal reality. Each grasps reality at a level which is incomplete, and contemporary jurisprudence has come to sense that fact; that is, that neither the communitarians nor the economists have successfully taken the measure of humankind. Hence the attraction of philosophical pragmatism with its skeptical attitude towards truth, wherein "the ideas of truth and falsehood, in their full development, appertain exclusively to the experiential method of setting opinion."[37]

It is an interesting fact that contemporary quantum physicists tell us that there are two levels of reality, or two "worlds" inhabited by us—a Newtonian world at the level of perception in which we are ruled by the principle of cause and effect, discreteness, and the arrow of time—and a quantum world at the unobservable level of bare existence in which all is one and one is all, and one and all are driven by the angst of tendency and probability.[38] Schopenhauer, as we have seen, tells us the very same thing in the context of his theory of justice. We inhabit two worlds—a legal world at the everyday level of phenomena in which we rule and are ruled by responsibilities, duties, rights, and entitlements, all controlling for what would otherwise be the law of the jungle—and a noumenal world at the unfathomable level of true reality in which the law of the jungle can be understood as an inexorable demand of eternal justice, the inevitable result of the "will" feeding on itself.

Schopenhauer's only answer to the duality between the phenomenal world of law and the noumenal world of justice was his advocacy of the denial of the will-to-live. He saw the denial of the will-to-live as the only way of reaching the otherwise unreachable and incorporating into one's consciousness that fundamental truth about human existence.

It may be that the civic republicans and other communitarian theorists of today are trying, consciously or unconsciously, to do exactly that: that is, to touch the noumenal unity which lies at the deepest level of human existence, to free us from the individual self-interested utility maximization of the old "Adam" nature and bring us to the new spiritual *aion* of enlightenment and incorporation into the "Christ" nature. The civic republicans and other communitarians *do* seem to want to lead us *from* a present age or *aion* characterized by something unpleasant—an unsatisfying centering on isolating and divisive individual and group self-interests—to a new salvational age or *aion* characterized by something that has been missing—a productive spirit of solidarity and a recognition of a unifying interidentity among all of humankind. If so, Schopenhauer, for all his crusty misanthropy, may have something to contribute to their quest, for Schopenhauer's doctrine of the denial of the will to live is a look at salvation from the vantage point of the unsaved.

Whether Schopenhauer himself was "saved" is a matter between him and the God in Whom he disbelieved, but some might argue that his personal views and his crass social commentaries cast doubt on the matter. But Schopenhauer had a ready answer for those who would identify his personal and social views as sexist and anti-Semitic[39] and his many outbursts against those with whom he disagreed as peevish, petty, and malicious. Schopenhauer seemed to recognize his personal vulnerability on many a moral score when he wrote, in his *magnum opus*:

> It is . . . just as little necessary for the saint to be a philosopher as for the philosopher to be a saint; just as it is not necessary for a perfectly beautiful person to be a great sculptor, or for a great sculptor to be himself a beautiful person. In general, it is a strange demand on a moralist that he should commend no other virtue than that which he himself possesses.   (WWR1$_{[P]}$, 383)

Schopenhauer's decidedly salvational theory of justice is not the effort of a Gautama Siddhartha or a Christian mystic to explain what he or she has seen on the other side of enlightenment or salvation. It is the affirmation of someone who has *not been* there that something *is* there, something ineffable, yet real—something that may just be worth the quest.

Notes

1. See, e.g., Richard A. Posner, *The Problems of Jurisprudence* (Cambridge, MA: Harvard University Press, 1990), 169–84.
2. The seminal and somewhat question-begging definition of "justice" is that of Ulpian: *Honeste vivere, alterium non laedere, suum cuique tribuere*—"To live honestly, to cheat no one, and to give each his due." T. Cooper, *The Institutes of Justinian* (Philadelphia: P. Byrne, 1812), § III, at 6. Beyond that Roman principle of giving everyone his due, most attempts at defining "justice" have been content-based and have included notions of equality and rationality. See 365–67 in Raymond B. Marcin, "Justice and Love," *Catholic University Law Review*, 33 (1984), 363–91. Insofar as "justice" has occasionally been treated ontologically, it

seems to have simply been recognized as having an almost unassailable claim of absoluteness attached to it, to the point where at least one commentator has observed, with perhaps only slight exaggeration, that "[a]ll wars have been fought by all parties in the name of justice, and the same is true of the political conflict between social classes." Alf Ross, *On Law and Justice* (Berkeley: University of California Press, 1959), 269.

3. See, e.g., Marcin, "Justice and Love," 363–91 (tracing the concept of justice from positivist and Rawlsian Western models to the Gandhian concepts of *ahimsa* and *Satyagraha*).

4. Schopenhauer's words:

[T]he will will everywhere manifest itself in the plurality of individuals. This plurality, however, does not concern the will as thing-in-itself, but only its phenomena. The will is present, whole and undivided, in each of these, and perceives around it the innumerably repeated image of its own inner being; but this inner nature itself, and hence what is actually real, it finds immediately only in its inner self (WWR1$_{[P]}$, 331–32).

5. "War of all against all." See Thomas Hobbes, *Leviathan* (1651), edited by Richard Tuck (Cambridge: Cambridge University Press, 1991), 149. Schopenhauer heartily endorsed Hobbes's thesis (see WWR1$_{[P]}$, 333).

6. On behaviorism in the context of law, see Posner, *Problems of Jurisprudence*, 169–96. In Posner's view, "Behaviorism is the only practical working assumption for law, and its dangers have been exaggerated."

7. See, e.g., Marcin, "Justice and Love," 363–91.

8. See text at WWR1$_{[P]}$, 345.

9. See, for example, *Adam Smith and the Philosophy of Law and Economics*, edited by Robin Paul Malloy and Jerry Evensky (Dordrecht, The Netherlands: Kluwer Academic Publishers, 1994), and Jerry Evensky, *Adam Smith's Moral Philosophy: A Historical and Contemporary Perspective on Markets, Law, Ethics, and Culture* (Cambridge: Cambridge University Press, 2007).

10. See Adam Smith, *An Inquiry Into the Nature and Causes of the Wealth of Nations*, vol. 1, bk. 4, ch. 2 (1776), 9, Liberty Classics ed. (Indianapolis: Oxford University Press, 1976), 456; and *The Theory of Moral Sentiments*, part IV, ch. 1 (1759), 10, Liberty Classics ed., (Indianapolis: Oxford University Press, 1976), 184–85.

11. The quoted passage is Schopenhauer's doctrine of "eternal justice." See WWR1$_{[P]}$, 351 and the later discussion on eternal justice in this chapter.

12. On the expression "will-to-live" in Schopenhauer's thought—the "will" as the thing-in-itself of all reality is something like tendency or probability. There is no clear word for it because it is a transcendent concept. Schopenhauer calls it endless, aimless, limitless striving. In that sense, it is a tendency without an aim other than that of eternal becoming or flux. The "will" as re-presented to the perceiving mind of the human being, however, is seen as a will-to-live. The perceiving mind cannot understand an aimless tendency and so it separates will into two thoughts. In reality, the tendency *is* the existence. The perceiving mind, however, records it as a tendency *to* exist. Hence, at the human level, a will-to-live. See WWR1$_{[P]}$, 162–65, 275; and WWR2$_{[P]}$, 349–60.

13. Schopenhauer recognizes it in our common, everyday experience that "sees the wicked man, after misdeeds and cruelties of every kind, live a life of pleasure and quit the world undisturbed. It sees the oppressed person drag out to the end a life full of suffering without the appearance of an avenger or vindicator" (WWR2$_{[P]}$, 353–54).

14. See WWR2$_{[P]}$, 643.

15. For Schopenhauer's account of the circumlocutions that Christian theologians go through in their effort to reconcile the problem of evil with a supposedly all-good God, see his essay on Scotus Erigena (PP1$_{[P]}$, 61–64).

16. The quoted language is from Euripides, *Apud Stobaeus*, Eclog., I, c. 4.

17. See, for example, Frederick Copleston, SJ, *Arthur Schopenhauer: Philosopher of Pessimism* (Andover, Hants, UK: Burns, Oates & Washbourne, 1946).

18. For a survey account of Schopenhauer's teachings on the virtue of justice, see BM$_{[P]}$, 148–62. The quoted language appears on page 162.

19. Mohandas K. Gandhi, *An Autobiography: The Story of My Experiments With Truth* (first published in 1927 and 1929 in the Gujarati language), translated by Mahadev Desai (Boston: Beacon Press, 1957), 349.

20. The importance of myth and symbol to psychology and metaphysics has since been widely recognized, especially in the writings of Carl Jung. See, for example, Carl G. Jung, *Symbols of Transformation*, translated by R. F. C. Hull (Princeton, NJ: Princeton University Press, 1967); and *The Archetypes and the Collective Unconscious*, translated by R. F. C. Hull (Princeton, NJ: Princeton University Press, 1968); Carl G. Jung and Carl Kerenyi, *Essays on a Science of Mythology*, translated by R. F. C. Hull (Princeton, NJ: Princeton University Press, 1949); and James N. Powell, *The Tao of Symbols* (New York: Quill, 1982). Jung himself was strongly influenced by the writings of Schopenhauer. See Carl G. Jung, *Memories, Dreams, Reflections*, translated by R. and C. Winston (New York: Random House, 1963), 69–72. Both Jung and Schopenhauer saw Jesus Christ as the symbol or embodiment or personification of the goal of human existence; for Jung, the "Self" archetype; for Schopenhauer, the denial of the will-to-live. See Jung, at 279 and WWR1$_{[P]}$ at 405.

21. Not incidentally, the strong connection between the phenomenon of Jesus and the phenomenon of Adam is recognized by Paul in his Epistle to the Romans 5:14.

22. See John Hardon, SJ, *The Catholic Catechism: A Contemporary Catechism of the Teachings of the Catholic Church* (Collegeville, MN: Liturgical Press, 1975), 99.

23. For Schopenhauer's treatment of Adam, original sin, and the Savior, see WWR1, 580.

24. The clarity with which much (though obviously not all) of Schopenhauer's thought fits the Christian mold has alarmed Frederick Copleston, SJ, who felt it necessary to admonish his Christian readers, through several pages of his monograph on Schopenhauer, that the philosopher should not be read as a Christian apologist. Frederick Copleston, SJ, *Arthur Schopenhauer: Philosopher of Pessimism* (Andover, Hants, UK: Burns, Oates & Washbourne, 1946), 209–12.

25. On Brahmanism's Veil of Mâyâ in Schopenhauer's thought, see Indu Sarin's essay, "Schopenhauer's Concept of Will and the Veil of Mâyâ," in *Schopenhauer and Indian Philosophy: A Dialogue Between India and Germany*, edited by Arait Barua (New Delhi: Northern Book Centre, 2008), 138–50; and Douglas L. Berger, *"The Veil of Mâyâ": Schopenhauer's System and Early Indian Thought* (Binghamton, NY: Global Academic Publishing, 2004).

26. See also BM$_{[P]}$, 162.

27. See, for example, Bryan Magee, *The Philosophy of Schopenhauer*, revised edition (Oxford: Clarendon Press, 1983), 242–43.

28. See note 12 *supra*.

29. See Heinrich Zimmer, *Philosophies of India*, edited by J. Campbell (Princeton, NJ: Princeton University Press, 1951), 183, 448, 478–480, 666.

30. Schopenhauer writes: "The doctrine of original sin (affirmation of the will) and of salvation (denial of the will) is really the great truth which constitutes the kernel of Christianity.... Accordingly, we should interpret Jesus Christ always in the universal, as the symbol of personification of the denial of the will-to-live" (WWR1$_{[P]}$, 405).

31. See PP2$_{[P]}$, 306–12, where Schopenhauer discounts all but one of the moral arguments against suicide. "The only valid moral reason against suicide...lies in the fact that suicide is opposed to the attainment of the highest moral goal since it substitutes for the real salvation from this world of woe and misery one that is merely apparent" (PP2$_{[P]}$, 309).

32. See WWR1$_{[P]}$, 301, 383–84.

33. See, for example, Posner, *Problems of Jurisprudence*; Steven J. Burton, *An Introduction to Law and Legal Reasoning* (Boston: Little, Brown, 1995); Stephen M. McJohn, "On Uberty: Legal Reasoning by Analogy and Peirce's Theory of Abduction," *Willamette Law Review* 29 (1993), 191; Daniel C. K. Chow, "A Pragmatic Model of Law," *Washington Law Review* 67 (1992), 755; Dennis M. Patterson, "Law's Pragmatism: Law as Practice and Narrative," *Virginia Law Review* 76 (1990), 937 and "Symposium on the Renaissance of Pragmatism in American Legal Thought," *Southern California Law Review* 63 (1990), 1753; and Steven D. Smith, "The Pursuit of Pragmatism," *Yale Law Journal* 100 (1990), 409.

34. Dennis Mueller, *Public Choice II* (Cambridge: Cambridge University Press, 1989).

35. See, for example, Michael Sandel, *Liberalism and the Limits of Justice* (Cambridge: Cambridge University Press, 1982); Kathleen M. Sullivan, "The Republican Civic Tradition: Rainbow Republicanism," *Yale Law Journal* 97 (1988), 1713; and Robert Cover, "Nomos and Narrative," *Harvard Law Review* 97 (1983), 4.

36. John Rawls's "veil of ignorance" device (see John Rawls, *A Theory of Justice* (Cambridge, MA: Harvard University Press, 1971) can be seen as a melding of the two views of human-kind, starting as it does from a premise of self-interest but yielding communitarian results. See Marcin, "Justice and Love," 372–78. Adam Smith's device for melding the two views was the "invisible hand" whereby somehow the result of individuals acting in their own self-interests is social betterment. See Adam Smith, *An Inquiry Into the Nature and Causes of the Wealth of Nations*, vol. 1, bk. 4 ch. 2, p. 9 (1776) Liberty Classics ed. (Indianapolis: Oxford University Press, 1976), 456; and *The Theory of Moral Sentiments*, Part IV, ch. 1, p. 10 (1759) Liberty Classics ed. (Indianapolis: Oxford University Press, 1976), 184–85.

37. Justus Buchler, ed., *Philosophical Writings of Peirce* (New York: Dover Publications, 1955), 37.

38. See Raymond B. Marcin, *In Search of Schopenhauer's Cat: Arthur Schopenhauer's Quantum-Mystical Theory of Justice* (Washington, DC: Catholic University of America Press, 2006).

39. For Schopenhauer's views on women, see PP2, Chapter XXVII. For Schopenhauer's views on Judaism and Jewish people, see the essay in this volume by Jacob Golomb.

FURTHER READING

Barua, Arati, ed. *Schopenhauer and Indian Philosophy: A Dialogue Between India and Germany*. New Delhi: Northern Book Centre, 2008.

Berger, Douglas L. *"The Veil of Mâyâ": Schopenhauer's System and Early Indian Thought*. Binghamton, NY: Global Academic Publishing, 2004.

Bridgwater, W. P. *Arthur Schopenhauer's English Schooling*. New York: Routledge, 1988.

Buchler, Justus, ed. *Philosophical Writings of Peirce*. New York: Dover Publications, 1955.

Burton, Steven J. *An Introduction to Law and Legal Reasoning*. Boston: Little, Brown, 1995.

Chow, Daniel C. K. "A Pragmatic Model of Law." *Washington Law Review* 67 (1992): 755.

Cooper, Thomas. *The Institutes of Justinian*. Philadelphia: P. Byrne, 1812.

Copleston, Frederick,. SJ. *Arthur Schopenhauer: Philosopher of Pessimism*. Andover, Hants, UK: Burns, Oates & Washbourne, 1946.

Cover, Robert. "Nomos and Narrative." *Harvard Law Review* 97 (1983): 4.

Evensky, Jerry. *Adam Smith's Moral Philosophy: A Historical and Contemporary Perspective on Markets, Law, Ethics, and Culture*. Cambridge: Cambridge University Press, 2007.

Gandhi, Mohandas K. *An Autobiography: The Story of My Experiments with Truth* (first published in 1927 and 1929 in the Gujarati language), translated by Mahadev Desai. Boston: Beacon Press, 1957.

Hardon, John, SJ *The Catholic Catechism: A Contemporary Catechism of the Teachings of the Catholic Church*. Collegeville, MN: Liturgical Press, 1975.

Hobbes, Thomas. *Leviathan* (1651), edited by Richard Tuck. Cambridge: Cambridge University Press, 1991.

Jung, Carl G., and Carl Kerenyi. *Essays on a Science of Mythology*, translated by R. F. C. Hull. Princeton, NJ: Princeton University Press, 1949.

Jung, Carl G. *Memories, Dreams, Reflections*, translated by R. and C. Winston. New York: Random House, 1963.

Jung, Carl G. *Symbols of Transformation*, translated by R. F. C. Hull. Princeton, NJ: Princeton University Press, 1967.

Jung, Carl G. *The Archetypes and the Collective Unconscious*, translated by R. F. C. Hull. Princeton, NJ: Princeton University Press, 1968.

Magee, Bryan. *The Philosophy of Schopenhauer*. Oxford: Clarendon Press, 1983.

Malloy, Robin Paul, and Jerry Evensky eds. *Adam Smith and the Philosophy of Law and Economics*. Dordrecht, The Netherlands: Kluwer Academic Publishers, 1994.

Marcin, Raymond B. *In Search of Schopenhauer's Cat: Arthur Schopenhauer's Quantum-Mystical Theory of Justice*. Washington, DC: Catholic University of America Press, 2006.

Marcin, Raymond B. "Justice and Love." 33, Catholic *University Law Review* 33 (1984): 363–91.

McJohn, Stephen M. "On Uberty: Legal Reasoning by Analogy and Peirce's Theory of Abduction." *Willamette Law Review* 29 (1993): 191–35.

Mueller, Dennis. *Public Choice 1I*. Cambridge: Cambridge University Press, 1989.

Patterson, Dennis M. "Law's Pragmatism: Law as Practice and Narrative." *Virginia Law Review* 76 (1990): 937–98.

Posner, Richard A. *The Problems of Jurisprudence*. Cambridge, MA: Harvard University Press, 1990.

Powell, James N. *The Tao of Symbols*. New York: Quill, 1982.

Rawls, John. *A Theory of Justice*. Cambridge, MA: Harvard University Press, 1971.

Ross, Alf. *On Law and Justice*. Berkeley: University of California Press, 1959.

Sandel, Michael. *Liberalism and the Limits of Justice*. Cambridge: Cambridge University Press, 1982.

Smith, Adam. *An Inquiry Into the Nature and Causes of the Wealth of Nations* (1776). Liberty Classics edition. Indianapolis: Oxford University Press, 1976.

Smith, Adam. *The Theory of Moral Sentiments* (1759). Liberty Classics edition, Indianapolis: Oxford University Press, 1976.

Smith, Steven D. "The Pursuit of Pragmatism." *Yale Law Journal* 100, no. 2 (1990): 409–49.

Sullivan, Kathleen M., "The Republican Civic Tradition: Rainbow Republicanism." *Yale Law Journal* 97, no. 8 (1988): 1713–24.

Zimmer, Heinrich, *Philosophies of India*, edited by J. Campbell. Princeton, NJ: Princeton University Press, 1951.

CHAPTER 20

....

SCHOPENHAUER, BUDDHISM, AND COMPASSION

....

RICHARD REILLY

WHILE Arthur Schopenhauer's magnum opus, *The World as Will and Representation* (1818), coheres with Indian thought, it primarily has its genesis in Schopenhauer's reflections on Kant's seminal work. However, much in Schopenhauer's writings on ethics appears to be working out of basic Buddhist principles.[1] In his masterful, comprehensive study, Stephen Cross details the ways Schopenhauer encountered Indian thought, and he demonstrates how both Hindu and Buddhist views bear "a systematic rather than casual resemblance to Schopenhauer's doctrine of the will."[2] The focus of this chapter is Schopenhauer's *On The Basis of Morality* (1841), one of the most engaging and inspiring contributions in the history of ethics. I first spell out Schopenhauer's conception of compassion. Second, I indicate how this conception reflects central insights of Mahayana Buddhism. I then present the Schopenhaurerian case, contra Kant, for compassion as the basis of moral value. Last, I consider the extent to which Schopenhauer recognized in Buddhist thought a path to transcend the all-pervasive suffering of ordinary existence.

20.1 COMPASSION

....

To frame our discussion, consider this case of a member of a Dutch citizen's resistance organization during the Second World War, who nevertheless saved the life of a severely wounded German soldier.

> One day there was an air raid on the German barracks near our house, some five kilometers away. My husband happened to be there....A German soldier came

running out with his head practically destroyed. He was bleeding heavily and obviously in shock. He was running in panic. My husband saw that within minutes he would fall down and bleed to death. So my husband put him on his bicycle— without thinking about it—and brought him to the commandant's house. He put him on the step, rang the bell, waited to see the door open, and left. Later some of our friends and people who were hiding with us heard about it and said: "You are a traitor because you helped the enemy." My husband replied: "No, the moment the man was badly wounded, he was not an enemy any more but simply a human being in need.... We just helped human beings who were in need."[3]

While compassion is a cardinal virtue in both Indian and Chinese cultures and is certainly at the forefront of Jesus's teachings, it was of little note in Western philosophy until the eighteenth century. Aristotle treats the notion of "pity" [*eleos*] in his works on rhetoric and poetics, but not as a disposition of moral conduct. Rather, it is an unpleasant feeling at the sight of undeserved suffering that may or may not lead to helpful behavior. More notably, for Aristotle, the orator and the tragic poet might arouse pity for pragmatic or aesthetic purposes, typically in persons not in a position to be motivated to relieve undeserved or tragic suffering.[4]

Major thinkers of the eighteenth century provided accounts of sympathy and fellow-feeling as the basis of altruistic motivation. For instance, David Hume based altruistic motivation toward strangers on two factors: an imaginative understanding of another's suffering that combines with the benevolence one feels toward loved ones.[5] Adam Smith's account is more direct: an "imaginative projection" into the suffering person's situation itself is sufficient to generate the fellow-feeling of sympathy for another's sorrow.

> By the imagination we place ourselves in his situation, we conceive ourselves enduring all the same torments, we enter as it were into his body, and become in some measure the person with him, and thus form some idea of his sensations....His agonies, when they are thus brought home to ourselves, when we have thus adopted and made them our own, begin at last to affect us, and we then tremble and shudder at the thought of what he feels.[6]

However, Smith leaves us without an account of how sympathy motivates altruistic *conduct* and with puzzlement over how one might enter into another's body, become in some measure that person, and form some idea of his sensations.

Schopenhauer credits Rousseau, "undoubtedly the greatest moralist of modern times" (BM$_{[P]}$, 183), for introducing the virtue of compassion into European thought. An often-recited passage in *Èmile* (Bk. 1V) is quoted in *On The Basis of Morality*:

> In fact, how can we let ourselves be moved to pity unless by transporting ourselves outside ourselves and identifying ourselves with the suffering animal, by quitting, so to speak, our own being in order to assume his? Here we suffer only to the extent that we think he suffers; it is not in ourselves but in him that we suffer.   (BM$_{[P]}$, 184–86)

Rousseau's view has four distinguishing features: (a) Compassion often does extend to animals and others quite unlike us or our loved ones. Schopenhauer, a champion of animal welfare, even proclaims, "Compassion for animals is intimately associated with goodness of character, and it may be confidently asserted that he who is cruel to animals cannot be a good man" (BM$_{[P]}$, 179); (b) contra Hume, we can identify directly with the suffering other, without transferring to that other the sentiment of benevolence for loved ones; (c) we can sympathetically suffer with another "to the extent that we think he suffers," without notions of entering into the other's body "to form some idea of his sensations," which is how Adam Smith and others explain the "fellow-feeling" of sharing in another's sorrow; (d) the human capacity for genuine sympathy can be cultivated—hence, Rousseau attaches importance to providing youth with occasions to experience deeply the sufferings of others. Yet what distinguishes compassion from sympathy as fellow-feeling is that compassion signifies motive and conduct to relieve suffering. Rousseau offers no explanation of how compassion *directly motivates* altruistic conduct.

Arthur Schopenhauer, among Western theorists, was the first to provide an account of altruistic conduct being directly motivated by the suffering (distress, woe) of another.

> But now how is it possible for a suffering which is not *mine* and does not touch *me* to become just as directly a motive as my own normally does, and to move me to action? As I have said, only by the fact that although it is given to me merely as something external, merely by means of external intuitive perception or knowledge, I nevertheless *feel it with him, feel it as my own*, and yet not *within me*, but *in another person....* But this presupposes that to a certain extent I have identified with the other man, and in consequence the barrier between ego and non-ego is for the moment abolished; only then do the other man's affairs, his needs, distress, and suffering, directly become my own....I share the suffering *in him*, in spite of the fact his skin does not enclose my nerves. Only in this way can *his* woe, *his* distress, become a motive *for me*; otherwise it can be absolutely only my own. I repeat that this *occurrence is mysterious*, for it is something our faculty of reason can give no direct account of, and its grounds cannot be discovered on the path of experience. And yet it happens everyday; everyone has often experienced it within himself... even to the most hard-hearted and selfish it is not unknown.   (BM$_{[P]}$, 165–66)

Schopenhauer begins by asking "how is it possible for a suffering which is not *mine* and does not touch *me* to become just as directly a motive as my own normally does, and to move me to action?" David Cartwright, an important commentator on Schopenhauer's ethics, provides this analytical model of Schopenhauer's conception of compassion:

A has compassion for B, if and only if;
(i)   A and B are sentient creatures
(ii)   A apprehends that B is, or will be, suffering
(iii) A participates immediately in B's suffering
(iv)   A feels grief or sorrow for B
(v)   A desires B's well-being because B is, or will be, suffering

(vi) A is moved to do X for B, where X is some action aimed at relieving B's suffering (philanthropy), or A is moved not to do Y, where Y is an action A has planned to perform which would cause B's suffering (justice).[7]

Clearly, this model provides a non-egoistic account of altruistic conduct, immune from Nietzschean criticisms of "pity" marked by self-centeredness and contemptuousness.[8] However, since Schopenhauer admits that it remains mysterious how another's woe might be an immediate motive for me, Cartwright contends:

> His model of compassion is sound if we reformulate the third condition in the following way: (iii)* A participates imaginatively in B's suffering. This reformulation of the third condition removes the need to explain the agent's participation in another's mental state metaphysically. The agent participates in the other's mental state by imagining how he or she would feel in the other's situation, or how he or she would feel in this situation if the agent had the recipient's history, personality temperament, etc.[9]

Cartwright's amendment is precisely not where we should go. A psychological explanation involving the participation in (or sharing of) another's felt sensations or mental states is neither required nor possible.

Yes, the compassionate person does share in the other's suffering (distress, sorrow, woe plight), but this does not *require* one to participate in and/or make inferences from another's *mental state*; it only requires us to *fully apprehend* the other's *situation*. After all, often a sentient creature is suffering from injury, illness, or distress and is not in sorrow or experiencing any other type of pain. Think of the person who takes a fall (or suffers a drug overdose or has been severely beaten) and is rendered unconscious; or the mother's young child with a serious infection needing immediate care, but who "feels fine"; or the pet cat that is found quietly listless though consciously aware. Might not one be moved out of compassion for each of these beings who are suffering from illness or injury, even though they are not experiencing sorrowful or painful mental states to be shared?

Max Scheler, in *The Nature of Sympathy*, credits Schopenhauer for "recognizing that commiseration is an 'immediate' participation in the woes of others, and does not depend on inference or on any artificial mode of 'projecting' oneself into the other person's situation."[10] As he keenly observed, it is neither necessary nor possible to get into another's skin, as it were, in order to share in another's suffering.

> Hence an identical sorrow may be keenly felt (though in one's own individual fashion), but never an identical sensation of pain, for here there are always two separate sensations. Again, one may see the same shade of red as another person (without actually reducing the color to wave-motions), or hear the same sound of C. But the aural and ocular sensations involved are accessible only to the possessor of the organs in question.[11]

Charles Taylor also largely follows Schopenhauer in arguing that one's compassionate responsiveness to others is as direct as one's responsiveness to one's own distress. As there normally is no inferential reasoning that mediates my awareness of my own distress and my being motivated to lessen my distress, Taylor reasons that compassion or sympathy is a "primitive response to the suffering of another."[12] Here "primitive" carries a threefold meaning: genuinely compassionate responses are not mediated by reasons (or even the thought that another's suffering is a good reason to act); rather, in their spontaneity, they expresses a constitutive element in our conception of human nature; and, they cannot be explained empirically in terms of more fundamental categories or facts about human beings.

Importantly, Schopenhauer's account reflects the understanding of compassion found in several diverse cultures. His Holiness the Fourteenth Dalai Lama reports:

> When I speak of basic human feeling...I refer to the capacity we all have to empathize with one another, which in Tibetan we call *shen dug ngal wa la mi sö pa*. Translated literally this means "the inability to bear the sight of another's suffering"...it is one of our most significant characteristics. It is what causes us...to recoil at the sight of harm done to another, to suffer when confronted with others' suffering.[13]

Similar notions in Chinese culture are "empathic/heart-felt pain" (*xin-teng*) and "unbearing mind" (*bu ren zhi xin*), which, according to Mencius, express the intimate connections between ourselves and other beings.[14] The comparable notion in Christian culture is "mercy."

> As Augustine says...*mercy is heartfelt sympathy for another's distress, impelling us to succor him if we can.* For mercy takes its name *misericordia* from denoting a man's compassionate heart (*miserum cor*), at the sight of another's unhappiness [distress].[15]

How do we explain the compassionate heart's "inability to bear the sight of another's suffering" and so being "impelled" to assist him? Section 20.2 lays the groundwork for Schopenhauer's "metaphysical explanation" of the direct motivation characteristic of compassion, which is again addressed in Section 20.4.

20.2 WISDOM AND COMPASSION IN MAHAYANA BUDDHISM AND IN SCHOPENHAUER

Schopenhauer was profoundly influenced by the early discourses of Buddha Shakyamuni, especially on dependent origination and on the Four Noble Truths, as well as by later Mahayana teachings, including the *Madhyamaka* (Middle Way) and the

Prajnaparamita (Perfection of Wisdom) views associated with Nagarjuna (second century CE) and Shantideva (eighth century CE). Schopenhauer notes: "with me alone ethics has a sure foundation, and is completely worked out in agreement with the sublime and profound religions [of] Brahmanism, Buddhism, and Christianity" (WWR2$_{[P]}$, 643). I shall use Shantideva's famous *Bodhicaryāvatāra* (*The Way of the Bodhisattva*) to provide a clear Buddhist basis for Schopenhauer's conception of compassion and for how this underlies his ethics more generally.

In the Mahayana, the spiritual ideal is the *bodhisattva*, one who embodies universal compassion: that is, the aspiration to liberate all beings from suffering cyclic existence (*samsara*) and who aims to live multiple lifetimes for the benefit of suffering beings. Prior to being fully actualized, this aspiration is known as intentional *bodhicitta* ("awakened/enlightened mind"). In *The Way of the Bodhisattva*, Shantideva provides guidance on how one should train in the *paramitas*, the ego-transcending virtues, in order to put intentional *bodhicitta* into practice. The final two virtues considered are Meditation and Wisdom. The Meditation chapter, with which we will be dealing, aims to cultivate universal compassion. Wisdom is the full realization of the true nature of reality, the attainment of which renders one spontaneously compassionate in all circumstances. Absolute *bodhicitta*, we may say, is the wisdom that manifests as compassion.

The three crucial elements of compassion are (a) A apprehends that B is, or will be, suffering; (b) A participates immediately in B's suffering; and (c) A is moved to relieve or prevent B from suffering. What I will show is that Shantideva provides an account of how (a)–(c) are *conceptually* connected and that Schopenhauer's "metaphysical explanation" of compassion mirrors this account.

Let us start with the meanings and connections between (a) and (b). First, what is the "reality" to be apprehended when I apprehend another?

> Strive at first to meditate
> Upon the sameness of yourself and others.
> In joy and sorrow all are equal.
> Thus be guardian of all, as of yourself. (8.90)[16]
> The hand and other limbs are many and distinct.
> But all are one—one body to be kept and guarded.
> Likewise, different beings in their joys and sorrows,
> Are, like me, all one in wanting happiness. (8.91)
> Hands and other limbs
> Are thought of as the members of a body,
> Shall we not consider others likewise—
> Limbs and members of a living whole? (8.114)

Here we have an application of the *Madhymaka* view of *shunyata* ("emptiness"). Although we might designate "the hand and other limbs" as having independent existence, in fact they arise interdependently upon causes and conditions, which, in turn, have dependently arisen. Obviously, "my" limbs, organs, and other physical components comprise "my body." Yet, while "my body" can be conventionally designated as an object, it, too, is empty of inherent reality since it has arisen and is sustained by a myriad of causes and conditions. All designated objects are empty of inherent, self-same existence; they are constantly changing, impermanent manifestations of a larger network of causes and conditions, which is similarly empty of inherent existence. So, while I can designate myself and the other as separate beings, this obscures the truth of our interdependent origination.

Second, what does it mean to apprehend another's suffering? As I might see the other as not distinct from me, I might see the other's suffering as not distinct from my own.

> My pain does not in fact afflict
> Or cause discomfort to another's body.
> Through clinging to my "I," this suffering is mine.
> And, being mine, is very hard to bear. (8.92)
> And other beings' pain
> I do not feel, and yet
> Because I take them for my own
> Their suffering is likewise hard to bear. (8.93)

Why is my bodily pain hard for me to bear? Because I designate/identify the painful body as mine (me), I take the suffering to be mine, and, not wishing to suffer, the suffering is hard to bear. While I cannot feel the others' pains, with an awakened heart-mind that desires all beings to be free from suffering, I take the others' pains as my own; in which case, not wishing suffering, the others' sufferings are hard to bear.

From (a) and (b), (c) follows. If we, *not wishing suffering but desiring well-being*, take another's suffering as our own, we are immediately moved to protect or relieve another from suffering; or, as Schopenhauer expresses it, the other's suffering becomes just as directly a motive as my own normally does and so moves me to action.

> The pain felt in my foot is not my hand's,
> So why, in fact, does one protect the other? (8.99)
> And therefore I'll dispel the pain of others,
> For it is simply pain, just as my own.
> And others I will aid and benefit,
> For they are living beings, just like me. (8.94)

Shantideva's themes are reflected in the following excerpt from a lengthy paragraph central to Schopenhauer's metaphysical explanation of compassion:

> If it is one and the same essence that manifests in all living beings, then ... it would be the metaphysical basis of ethics and consist in *one* individual's again recognizing in *another* his own self, his own inner nature.... Whoever is morally noble reveals by his actions the deepest knowledge, the highest wisdom.   (BM$_{[P]}$, 209)

It is this knowledge that "bursts forth as compassion on which all genuine, i.e., disinterested, virtue therefore depends and whose real expression is every good deed" (BM$_{[P]}$, 210).

Elsewhere, Schopenhauer puts it this way: "Accordingly, sympathy is to be defined as the empirical appearance of the will's metaphysical identity, through the physical multiplicity of its phenomena" (WWR2$_{[P]}$, 602).

Why is every genuinely compassionate act "mysterious?" Precisely because the compassionate person sees himself in all others, and such mystical consciousness is outside the domain of self-will and the principle of sufficient reason. We will return to this theme in Section 20.4.

20.3 COMPASSION AS THE BASIS OF MORAL VALUE

Thomas Aquinas offers as the first precept of the moral law: *good is to be done and ensued and evil is to be avoided.*"[17] In Zen Buddhism, one encounters as "pure precepts": "Do not create/cause evil" and "Practice [Do] all that is good."[18] The challenge for the ethical theorist is to explain what moral "good" and "evil" are, and, accordingly, what distinguishes morally right and morally wrong conduct.[19]

Schopenhauer intends his account of morality to be descriptive, grounded in the facts of human nature, rather than prescriptive.

> There are generally only three fundamental incentives of human actions, and all possible motives operate solely through their stimulation:
>
> a) Egoism: this desires one's own weal...
> b) Malice: this desires another's woe...
> c) Compassion: this desires another's weal...
>
> Every human action must be attributable to one of these incentives, although two can also act in combination. Now as we have assumed that actions of moral worth are given facts, they too must result from one of these fundamental incentives.
>
> (BM$_{[P]}$, 145)

Schopenhauer claims that all acts of moral worth have compassion as their sole incentive: actions that include a malicious motive are evil, and egoistic conduct (that does not include malice) is neither morally good nor evil. Generally, Schopenhauer sees morality as requiring an empirical motivation that "unbidden" can "overcome the opposing and immensely strong motives of egoism" (BM$_{[P]}$, 75). Egoism is one's interest in what benefits oneself; compassion is one's interest in what benefits others: they each move us in proportion to the strength of the interests we take in ourselves and in others.

Schopenhauer identifies as the supreme principle of ethics: *Neminem laede; imo omnes, quantum potes, juva*—"Injure no one; on the contrary, help every one as much as you can" (BM$_{[P]}$, 147). "Injure no one" is identified as the fundamental principle of justice, and since its meaning is wholly negative it can be practiced simultaneously by all. "Help every one as much as you can" references the virtue of loving-kindness (philanthropy). For Schopenhauer, justice and loving-kindness are the two cardinal virtues (from which all others can be derived) and are rooted in compassion as "two clearly separate degrees wherein another's suffering can directly become my motive" (BM$_{[P]}$, 148).

The root meaning of "justice" is to give each person his or her due. Schopenhauer argues that it is the general sense of an individual's *refraining* from injustice that constitutes "giving others their due." He states: "Contrary to appearance, the negative meaning of justice is established even in the trite definition, 'Give to each his own.' If a man has his own, there is no need to give it to him; and so the meaning is, 'Take from no one what is his own'" (BM$_{[P]}$, 153). Presumably, to take what is another's own is to cause harm or injury, so refraining from such conduct is justice.

The principle of justice, in turn, grounds the notions of right and wrong conduct: "The concepts *wrong* and *right* are synonymous with doing harm [causing injury] and not doing harm,[20] and to the latter belongs also the warding off of injury" (BM$_{[P]}$, 154). Stated examples of "warding off of injury" include one's defending oneself against an intended injustice and one's failure to fulfill duties of care, whether contractual or natural, as parents have for children (BM$_{[P]}$, 156–57). In such cases, it seems, the negligent failure to ward off preventable injury is seen as a contributing cause of harm and so as injustice and hence wrong.

Acts of loving-kindness primarily aim to *relieve* need, suffering, and distress that have occurred, and, we might presume, they also include preventing injuries from occurring in situations where one does not have a duty of care to do so. The odd result, in any case, is that compassionate acts of loving-kindness have moral value but are not morally "right" because they do not constitute "justice," and, nonmalicious failures to perform such acts are not morally "wrong" or "unjust." Schopenhauer's position, then, is that we "owe" others justice but not loving-kindness. Accordingly, the priest and the Levite who passed by the battered traveler (*Luke*, 10:30–36) did not act unjustly or wrongly if we presume that they were acting egoistically and without malice.

In *Friendship, Altruism, and Morality* (1980), Lawrence Blum argues that since the Kantian ethical framework can neither defeat nor accommodate the moral value of altruism, morality has no unified nature. Such bifurcation arises if, following Kant, reason can provide a categorical basis of action that might oppose Schopenhaurerian justice and loving-kindness.

Immanuel Kant's well-known view on ethical duties in *The Metaphysics of Morals* distinguishes between "perfect" and "narrow" duties of justice on the one hand and "imperfect" and "wide" duties of virtue on the other. Examples of the former are the duties not to steal, to keep one's promises, and to repay one's debts; examples of the latter are duties to develop one's talents, duties of gratitude and friendship, and duties to help others in need. Perfect/narrow duties are wholly determinate: it is clear precisely what is to be done, when, how, and for whom; failure to fulfill such duties merits contempt, moral censure.

Imperfect/wide duties do not specify morally required behavior on any given occasion; it is up to the agent to embody or to express such virtues, but how this is carried out is a matter of discretion. In particular, "To be beneficent, that is, to promote according to one's means the happiness of others in need, without hoping of something in return, is everyone's duty."[21] Failure to act beneficently on any given occasion, however, does not merit moral contempt since it does not inherently constitute a transgression of one's duty to others. With this Schopenhauer agrees. On the other hand, for Kant, one is never justified in willingly failing to fulfill a perfect duty; hence, acting "beneficently" in lieu of fulfilling a determinate obligation to another is never morally worthy. Here, Schopenhauer disagrees.

Schopenhauer's ethical viewpoint is that our moral nature is not bifurcated since compassion is the basis of all moral value. *Moral evil* is the intentionality to cause injury or harm and *moral good* is the intentionality to preserve (protect, relieve) beings from injury of harm. Since acting compassionately is always morally good, what Kant takes to be a perfect duty (e.g., that one ought to return what one borrows or keep one's promises) is hypothetical: if one's sole motive in returning what one borrows or in keeping a promise is to bring the recipient (or others) benefit rather than harm, then doing so has moral value; however, if doing so were to intentionally cause the recipient (or others) significant harm, then doing so is morally wrong (see $BM_{[P]}$, 88–94).

To generalize, one may take the traditional Buddhist precepts of right action—for example, refrain destroying life (killing), refrain from taking what is not given (stealing), and refrain from verbal transgressions (e.g., lying), which are akin to Kantian perfect ethical duties—as helpful *reminders* of what kinds of acts *generally* cause harm and so generally are to be avoided, while, in specific situations, compassion may justifiably motivate one to act contrawise.[22] The challenge, then, is to show how Schopenhauer's view can *rationally* accommodate "the demands of duty" and so defeat Kant's position that "perfect duties" are categorical in such a way that they cannot be overridden by acts of compassion.

W. D. Ross suggested that my *prima facie* duties, including the duty of "not injuring others" as well as "duties of beneficence," are grounded on *claims on me*. Says Ross, "It would be quite natural to say, 'a person to whom I have made a promise has a claim on me,' and also, 'a person whose distress I could relieve (at the cost of breaking the promise) has a claim on me.'"[23] In coming upon the battered traveler in dire need, a compassionate person's apprehension of the traveler's suffering directly motivates altruistic behavior, on Schopenhauer's view. Alternatively, in the language of duty, we might say that the claim upon the passerby made by another's suffering engenders a *prima facie* duty of beneficence to aid the battered traveler at hand, assuming that she is able to render assistance and not thereby (intentionally) cause serious harm to another.

Suppose our Good Samaritan promised her spouse that she would return by three o'clock for their afternoon walk. Must her duty to keep her promises override her duty of beneficence to the battered traveler? In failing to provide assistance, would she not fail to respect the humanity of the victim? Reasoning from the Golden Rule, the Good Samaritan may think, "I would wish/accept another's breaking a routine promise to me to help someone in dire need, and, so I will treat my spouse in this circumstance as I would wish/accept being treated." It might even be argued that a maxim of the sort "I shall keep all promises except in circumstances when not doing so does not cause significant harm and is urgently necessary to the well-being of another" can be willed to be a universal law. So acting compassionately can, in standard case scenarios, be accommodated by a universalizable maxim of what one ought to do even when it conflicts with the fulfillment of a Kantian "perfect duty." Still, in so far as acts of loving-kindness are not "owed" and cannot be commanded, they are supererogatory, merciful acts of moral value.

It is of interest to note that what compassion motivates certainly might be justifiable. Justification, giving justifying reasons, explains why some conduct is appropriate (e.g., has moral value). Indeed, Schopenhauer indicates that, empirically, the recipient of compassionate assistance *experiences* the goodness of the act and the moral goodness of the agent (BM$_{[P]}$, 174). Compassion as an agent's motivation for acting and justification as that act's external rationale often are equal measures of the same act—the first indicating the good intended by the agent and the second indicating the good done for the recipient.

20.4 A PATH OUT OF SUFFERING?

Christopher Janaway notes: "Schopenhauer looks around the world and finds it full of suffering—frustration, tedium, pain, and misery."[24]

> [T]he will finds itself as an individual in an endless and boundless world, among innumerable individuals, all striving, suffering, erring…its desires are unlimited, its claims inexhaustible, and every satisfied desire gives birth to a new one. No possible satisfaction in the world could suffice to still its craving, set a final goal to its demands.   (WWR2$_{[P]}$, 573)

In Janaway's perspicacious phrase, the individual's suffering is "ineliminably present." The will is the individual's *never-ending striving* to protect and promote its existence (and its species); therefore, will is invariably suffering since one strives only to eliminate dissatisfaction.

Schopenhauer's account of suffering is remarkably similar to Buddha Shakyamuni's discourse on the Four Noble Truths.

> Now this, *bhikkhus* [monastics], is the noble truth of suffering: birth is suffering, aging is suffering, illness is suffering, death is suffering; union with what is displeasing is suffering, separation from what is pleasing is suffering, not to get what one wants is suffering; in brief, the five aggregates subject to clinging are suffering. Now this, *bhikkhus*, is the noble truth of the origin of suffering: It is this craving which leads to renewed existence, accompanied by delight and lust, seeking delight here and there; that is craving for sensual pleasures, craving for existence, craving for extermination.[25]

When it is said, "in brief, the five aggregates subject to clinging are suffering," reference is made to the constituents of "self-identity"—bodily form/senses, feelings (positive, negative or neutral) about what one senses, perceptions (cognitions of what is experienced), mental formations (including volitions that move us to accomplish ends or goals, in response to what one believes and experiences), and consciousness (awareness) that underlies and integrates the constituents to form a sense of self or ego-identity. The cravings (and aversions) that give rise to suffering are generated by self-clinging. The ego-self is dominated by what Schopenhauer deems "will-to-live" and what the Buddhist calls the "eight ordinary (worldly) concerns": gain and loss, pleasure and pain, praise and criticism, fame and infamy. This is the life of pervasive suffering.

The source of suffering, then, is our sense of self as separate and distinct from other selves and entities that we experience.

> This conception that underlies egoism is, empirically considered, strictly justified. According to experience, the difference between my own person and another's appears to be absolute. The difference in space that separates me from him, separates me also from his weal and woe (BM$_{[P]}$, 205).

We empirically experience ourselves individuated in space and time. Moreover, the phenomena I perceive as a subject of experience, *my* representations, are themselves manifestations of will-to-live. "The act of will, from which the world springs, is our own" (WWR2$_{[P]}$, 646).

For both Schopenhauer and for Buddhists, the key to overcoming suffering is the cessation of the grasping and striving that characterize us as individuals separate from other beings and phenomena which, consequently, are seen as sources of desire and fear. Transcending dualistic, self-other awareness occurs for those capable of contemplation and/or compassion, as we see in Schopenhauer's description of the person of "good character" (i.e., the compassionate person) who

> lives in an external world that is homogeneous with his own true being. The others are not a non-ego for him, but an 'I once more.' His fundamental relation to everyone is, therefore, friendly; he feels himself akin to all beings... The results of this are the deep inward peace and that confident, calm, and contented mood by virtue of which everyone is happy when he is near at hand.   (BM$_{[P]}$, 211–12)

While most people naturally experience episodes of contemplation and compassion, their will-to-live comes to the fore again and again. Schopenhauer's consequent pessimism is largely due to his thinking that persons' empirical characters are inborn and mainly unalterable; hence, the sufferings inherent in the will-to-live are as endless as they are pervasive. Rousseau, as we noted, thought it important to expose youths to the suffering of others in order to cultivate compassion. The Buddhist view basically agrees with Schopenhauer's stance that compassion is a something known to all human beings, as well as Rousseau's view that the extent of its activation is a matter of nurture as well as nature. Indeed, meditation is the "mind-training" that enables one to glimpse, to nurture, and to actualize (more) fully one's "Buddha nature."

Interestingly, Schopenhauer did entertain the notion that one has the choice of "whether to be *reason* or *better consciousness*" (MR1, 23)—a point emphasized by Cross.

> [T]his is the *only* freedom of choice we have, for within the sphere of empirical con-sciousness our actions are held by Schopenhauer to be fully determined. If we iden-tify with the empirical consciousness, we remain an individual human being, the subject of consciousness undergoing suffering and death; but if we identify with the better consciousness, then *genius*…will appear in the place of theoretical reason and virtuous action in the place of practical reason or instinct.[26]

Identification with the "better" [aka "mystical"] consciousness requires the denial of the will-to-live. Schopenhauer indicates that such renunciation takes three related forms.

> Quietism, i.e., the giving up of all willing, asceticism, i.e., intentional mortification of one's own will,[27] and mysticism, i.e., consciousness of the identity one's own inner being with that of all things, or with the kernel of the world, stand in closest connec-tion, so that whoever professes one of them is gradually led to the acceptance of the others, even against his intention.   (WWR2$_{[P]}$, 613)

Not only are these three forms of renunciation intimately connected, but Schopenhauer discusses them in the contexts of multiple spiritual traditions—Christian, Hindu, and Buddhist, primarily—which have differing understandings of mystical attainment.

First, consider Schopenhauer's vivid description of the fruit of the denial of the will, with reference to the French Quietist, Madam Guyon.

> How blessed must be the life of a man whose will is silenced not for a few moments, as in the enjoyment of the beautiful, but forever.…Nothing can distress or alarm him anymore; nothing can any longer move him; for he has cut all the thousand threads of willing which hold us bound to the world, and which as craving, fear, envy, and anger drag us here and there in constant pain.…From these consider-ations we can learn to understand what Madam Guyon means when, towards the end of her *Autobiography*, she often expresses herself thus [sic.]: 'Everything is indif-ferent to me; I cannot will anything more; often I do not know whether I exist or not.'   (WWR2$_{[P]}$, 392–93)

So, wherein is the blessedness? Is it simply in the absence of distress and of "the thousand threads of willing?" Robert Wicks calls this "desireless tranquility."[28] Indeed, Schopenhauer understands the import of the fundamental Eastern insight that "evil" is the suffering of injury or harm and "good" is the absence of such suffering (BM$_{[P]}$, 146). On the Buddhist view, this "good" has positive, experiential qualities—tranquility, clear understanding, joyfulness, and compassion. Absent privation, one's humanity, one's being, flourishes. Wicks points out that some Upanishadic and Christian Quietists advocate the denial of will "for the sake of allowing infinite and sacred content to enter freely into one's awareness."[29] Schopenhauer, being an atheist and denying a transcendent "thing-in-itself" is prone to go instead in the direction of Buddhism, claims Wicks, "which values the experience of desireless tranquility without any metaphysical complications."[30]

As discussed, Buddhists see ignorance of the true nature of self and phenomena as empty of inherent existence as the root of suffering, cyclic existence (*samsara*). In short, seeing oneself as an independent, self-existent ego in a world of other independent beings *is* suffering, is *samsara*. On the Buddhist view, *nirvana* is the extinction of the ego-self, of what Schopenhauer calls "the will-to-live":

> ...to die willingly, to die gladly, to die cheerfully, is the prerogative of the resigned, of him who gives up and denies the will-to-live. For he alone wished to die *actually* and not merely *apparently*, and consequently needs and desires no continuance of his person. He willingly gives up the existence that we know; what comes to him instead of it is in our eyes *nothing*, because our existence in reference to that one is *nothing*. The Buddhist faith calls this existence *Nirvana*, that is to say, extinction.
>
> (WWR2$_{[P]}$, 508)

This passage concludes a paragraph that states "death is the great opportunity [to] no longer to be I" (WWR2$_{[P]}$, 507). Nevertheless, spiritual masters can "no longer to be I" while very much alive, as Schopenhauer acknowledges. Chögyam Trungpa observes,

> If we give up the watcher, then we have nothing left for which to survive, nothing left for which to continue.... That aloneness is freedom, fundamental freedom. That aloneness is described as the marriage of *shunyata* and wisdom in which your perception of aloneness suggests the needlessness of dualistic occupation. It is also described as the marriage of *shunyata* and compassion in which aloneness inspires compassionate action in living situations.... Ultimate asceticism becomes part of your basic nature.[31]

Now, it might appear that compassionate motivation and action require a dualistic, "self-other" perspective. But this is not how awakened Buddhists see it. Rather, as one understands the emptiness and primordially pure nature of self, so, too, one sees the emptiness and primordially pure nature of others. As one is liberated from the appearances of one's own suffering, one is no longer weighed down by the appearances of the suffering of others.

> Ho! In the state of same taste, the great self-realization,
> Deluded beings appear without existing; however,
> By the blessings of great secret means,
> I will place everyone in primordial wisdom-space.[32]

While "compassion in action" may indeed address the appearances of suffering, it also might (begin to) free individuals from the dualistic delusion that appearances distinguish and define them and others.

Is *nirvana* just "nothing" in *our* ordinary eyes? When another's ego-self is extinguished, what "remains" for *us* to experience?

> The great masters give you all the space you need. When you are in the master's presence, confusion vanishes and there is simple space to dwell in....Manifesting space...everything becomes magical. Even if the master has nothing to say...you leave feeing pacified and content because the master has just shared with you a glimpse of this infinite space.[33]

Schopenhauer's basic insight is that, in addition to egocentric motivation characteristic of the will-to-live and empirical consciousness, there are saintly presence and altruistic conduct that manifest the unconditioned consciousness of the mystic. The witness and teachings of legendary mystics, in turn, profoundly transform disciples and the community more generally.

Often Schopenhauer identifies this higher consciousness by reference to substantive, eternalist Hindu terms, such as "Self" [*atman*]," "One," and "Unity." When *On the Basis of Morality* was written (1839–40), European translations of the *Bhagavad-Gita* and the *Upanishads* had appeared, but an acquaintance with Mahayana Buddhism would not be expected. Therein, Schopenhauer refers to the Upanishadic phrase "*tat tvam asi*" (this art thou) as "the standing expression" for the knowledge that "my true inner being exists in every living thing (BM$_{[P]}$, 210)," that "others are not a non-ego, but 'an I once more'" (BM$_{[P]}$, 211). Such expressions, however, quickly give rise to metaphysical complications since they provoke ontological speculations on "my true inner being."

Since, elsewhere, Schopenhauer declares, "If I wished to take the results of my philosophy as the standard of truth, I should have to concede to Buddhism pre-eminence over the others" (WWR2$_{[P]}$, 169), we may take note on how Buddhism represents "mystical consciousness" without Upanishadic ontological commitments. From the Middle Way perspective of *shunyata*, what appear as "multiple selves" are not "one" or "identical," but "same" qualitatively in that they similarly arise dependently and are expressions of "emptiness"; that is, of the energy (cf. Schopenhauer's "will-force") that manifests as appearances to consciousness. Pure awareness (*rigpa*), on this view, is the awareness of "emptiness" (aka "dependent origination") as the ineffable energy that manifests as ever-changing selves and phenomena, a wondrous display.[34]

20.5 CONCLUSION

Where Buddhism and Schopenhauer part ways is on whether mystical consciousness is *inherently* compassionate. Schopenhauer tended to follow Hegel's lead in viewing moral consciousness, aesthetic (contemplative) consciousness, and mystical (religious) consciousness as distinct (though sometimes overlapping) and successively higher forms of human potential. Accordingly, religious consciousness has no inherent connection with compassion, as exemplified by the benign indifference of Madam Guyon.

On the Buddhist view, enlightenment manifests as joyous compassion as represented by Shakyamuni Buddha. It is absolute bodhicitta—the full awakening of the bodhisattvas, as we read in the *Laṅkāvatāra Sūtra*.

> Before they had attained realization of Noble Wisdom they had been influenced by the self-interests of egoism, but after they attain realization they will find themselves reacting spontaneously to the impulses of a great and compassionate heart endowed with skillful and boundless means and sincerely and wholly devoted to the emancipation of all beings.[35]

When asked, "Has the Blessed One a body?," Shakyamuni Buddha replied: "The three bodies of the *Tathagata* are these: the pure nature is the *dharmakaya* [truth body], pure meditation absorption is the *sambhogakaya* [luminous, bliss body], and pure conduct is the *nirmanakaya* [manifest body] of all buddhas."[36] In a familiar Tibetan-Buddhist idiom, Sogyal Rinpoche observes,

> When we looked at the nature of mind, we saw that it had these three aspects: its empty, sky-like essence, its radiant luminous nature, and its unobstructed, all-pervasive, compassionate energy, which are all simultaneously present and interpenetrating as one within Rigpa.[37]

Schopenhauer did not embrace the Buddhist view on how enlightenment signifies the thorough integration of contemplative consciousness, moral consciousness, and mystical consciousness. Nevertheless, Schopenhauer's understanding of compassion and how its possibility is best explained mirrors the Mahayana Buddhist view. More than any other major Western theorist, it is Schopenhauer who best understands the meaning of compassion, its centrality to ethical thought and conduct, and its importance for understanding the nature and potential of the human person.

NOTES

1. Bhikkhu Ñāṇajivako, *Schopenhauer and Buddhism* (Kandy, Sri Lanka: The Buddhist Publication Society, 1970).
2. Stephen Cross, *Schopenhauer's Encounter with Indian Thought: Representation and Will and their Indian Parallels* (Honolulu: University of Hawai'i Press, 2013), 172.
3. Charles Taylor, "Sympathy," *The Journal of Ethics* 3 (1999), 74–75.
4. For an extended account of how "compassion" as understood by Schopenhauer is quite unlike Aristotelian "pity" and the "felt sympathy" of British moralists, see Reilly (2008, ch. 2).
5. See David Hume, *A Treatise of Human Nature*, Bk. II–II, Sections VII–IX.
6. Adam Smith, *The Theory of the Moral Sentiments* (New Rochelle, NY: Arlington House, 1969), 3–4.
7. David E. Cartwright, "Compassion," in *Zeit der Ernte: Studien zum Stand der Schopenhauer-Forschung, Festschrift für Arthur Hübscher zum Geburtstag* (1982), 63.
8. See David E. Cartwright, "Schopenhauer's Compassion and Nietzsche's Pity," *Schopenhauer-Jahrbuch*, 69 (1988), 557–67.

9. David E. Cartwright, "Compassion," 67–68.
10. Max Scheler, *The Nature of Sympathy*, translated by Peter Heath (London: Routledge & Kegan Paul, 1954), 51.
11. Scheler, *The Nature of Sympathy*, 255.
12. Taylor, "Sympathy," n15.
13. His Holiness the Dalai Lama (aka Tenzin Gyatso), *Ethics for a New Millennium* (New York: Riverhead Books [Penguin Putnam], 1999), 64.
14. Louise Sundararajan, *Understanding Emotion in Chinese Culture: Thinking Through Psychology* (New York/Cham, Switzerland: Springer International Publishing, 2015), 84f.
15. Thomas Aquinas, *Summa Theologica*, translated by the Fathers of the English Dominican Province (London: Burns, Oates & Washbourne, Ltd., 1920), I–II, Q. 94, Art. 2.
16. As Schopenhauer's understanding of Mahayana Buddhism largely stems from Tibetan Buddhism, I rely on a translation of the *Bodhicharyvatara* from the Tibetan text: Shantideva, *The Way of the Bodhisattva* translated by the Padmakara Translation Group (Boston/London: Shambhala Publications, 1997). References to this work are by chapter and verse.
17. Thomas Aquinas, *Summa Theologica*, translated by the Fathers of the English Dominican Province (London: Burns, Oates & Washbourne, Ltd, 1920), I–II, Q. 94, Art. 2.
18. John Daido Loorie, *The Heart of Being: Moral and Ethical Teachings of Zen Buddhism* (Rutland, VT: Charles E. Tuttle Co, 1996), 50–74.
19. This section reworks material in Reilly (2008, Ch. III).
20. Similarly, Shakyamuni Buddha's articulations of "right action" and "right speech" in his discourse on the Noble Eightfold Path indicate that right conduct is to refrain from wrong conduct; that is, causing others harm (Bodhi, 2000, 1528).
21. Immanuel Kant, "The Metaphysics of Morals," in *Immanuel Kant: Practical Philosophy*, translated and edited by Mary J. Gregor (Cambridge: Cambridge University Press, 1996), 572.
22. This is worked out in some detail in Reilly (2008, Ch. IV).
23. W. D. Ross, 1988. *The Right and the Good* (Indianapolis/Cambridge: Hackett Publishing Co., 1988), 20.
24. Christopher Janaway, *Schopenhauer: A Very Short Introduction* (Oxford/New York: Oxford University Press, 2002), 104.
25. Bhikku Bodhi, trans., *Saccasamyutta*, 11, in *The Connected Discourses of the Buddha: A Translation of the Samyutta Nikāya* (Boston: Wisdom Publications, 2000) 1844.
26. Cross, *Schopenhauer's Encounter with Indian Thought*, 201. Peter Abelson cautions: "holiness, though seeming to spring from an insight, is also something that simply happens—being an act of the only free agent in the whole of reality: the motiveless Real itself" (Peter Abelson, "Schopenhauer and Buddhism," *Philosophy East & West* 43 [1993], 270).
27. Kenneth Hutton (2014) claims that Schopenhauer's "self-mortification" is incompatible with Buddha Shakyamuni's teachings. However, his case rests on an equivocation. The Buddha famously renounced mortification of the body. While Schopenhauer does make positive references to ascetic practices of bodily mortification, he understands that extreme asceticism is neither an accepted Buddhist practice nor necessary for the denial or mortification of self-will (WWR2$_{[P]}$, 607–08).
28. Robert Wicks, *Schopenhauer* (Malden, MA/Oxford: Blackwell Publishing, 2008), 132–35
29. Ibid., 134.
30. Ibid., 135.

31. Chögyam Trungpa Rinpoche, *The Myth of Freedom and the Way of Meditation* (Boulder, CO: Shambhala Publications, 1976), 150–51.

32. This is the *bodhicitta* mantra of the Pema Sangthig Ngöndro. *Sangha Prayer Book* (Hong Kong: Wencheng Gongzhu International Foundation, n.d.), 71.

33. Shyalpa Tenzin Rinpoche, *Living Fully: Finding Joy in Every Breath* (Novato, CA: New World Library, 2012), 246.

34. The Yogacara School supplements the Madhyamaka (Middle Way) view by postulating the *ālaya-vijñāna* ("store-house consciousness") doctrine in order to account for karma over multiple lifetimes being the basis of self and empirical consciousness. While Cross argues (*Schopenhauer's Encounter with Indian Thought*, ch. 12–13) that this doctrine fits Schopenhauer's views on the arising and constancy of the empirical world, it raises "metaphysical complications" unless what is designated by this doctrine, as with any concept, is seen as "empty" of real existence.

35. This passage from the *Laṅkāvatāra Sūtra* (3 *LKS*, 105–06) appears in Ronald Fussell (2008, 10).

36. Buddha, *Trikāyasūtra* (*The Sutra on the Three Bodies*), Buddhavacana Translation Group. Online: http://read.84000.co/translation/UT22084-068-017.html

37. Sogyal Rinpoche, *The Tibetan Book of Living and Dying*, edited by Patrick Gaffney and Andrew Harvey (New York: Harper Collins Publishers, 1994), 345.

Further Reading

Abelson, Peter. "Schopenhauer and Buddhism." *Philosophy East & West* 43 (1993): 255–78.

Bodhi, Bhikku, trans., *The Connected Discourses of the Buddha: A Translation of the Samyutta Nikāya*). Boston: Wisdom Publications, 2000.

Cartwright, David E. "Compassion." *Zeit der Emte; Studien zim Stand Schopenhauer-Forschung; Festscrift feur Arthur Hübscher zum 85. Geburtstag*, ed. Wolfgang Schirmacher (Struttgart-Bad Cannstatt: Frommann-Holzboog, 1982), 60–69.

Cartwright, David E. "Schopenhauer's Compassion and Nietzsche's Pity." *Schopenhauer-Jahrbuch* 69 (1988): 557–67.

Chodron, Pema. *No Time to Lose: A Timely Guide to the Way of the Bodhisattva*. Boston: Shambhala Publications, 2005.

Cross, Stephen. *Schopenhauer's Encounter with Indian Thought: Representation and Will and their Indian Parallels*. Honolulu: University of Hawai'i Press, 2013.

Dalai Lama (aka Tenzin Gyatso). *A Flash of Lightning in the Dark of Night: A Guide to the Bodhisattva's Way of Life*. Boston: Shambhala Publications, 1994.

Dalai Lama (aka Tenzin Gyatso). *How to Practice: The Way to a Meaningful Life*, translated and edited by Jeffrey Hopkins. New York/London: Simon & Schuster (Pocket Books), 2002.

Dalai Lama (aka Tenzin Gyatso). *Essence of the Heart Sutra*. Boston: Wisdom Publications, 2005.

Fischer, Norman. *Training in Compassion: Zen Teachings on the Practice of Lojong*. Boston/London: Shambhala Publications, 2012.

Fussell, Ronald. 2008. *The Nature and Purpose of the Ascetic Ideal*. Kandy, Sri Lanka: The Buddhist Publication Society, online edition: https://www.scribd.com/document/37730513/The-Nature-and-Purpose-of-the-Ascetic-Ideal

Hanh, Thich Nhat. *The Heart of Understanding: Commentaries on the Prajnaparamita Heart Sutra*. Berkeley, CA: Parallax Press, 2009.

Hopkins, Jeffrey. *Meditations on Emptiness*, revised edition. Boston: Wisdom Publications, 1996.

Hutton, Kenneth. *Ethics in Schopenhauer and Buddhism*. PhD thesis, University of Glasgow. 2009. Online: http://encore.lib.gla.ac.uk/iii/encore/record/C__Rb2671166

Hutton, Kenneth. "Compassion in Schopenhauer and Śāntideva." *Journal of Buddhist Ethics* 21 (2014): http://blogs.dickinson.edu/buddhistethics/files/2014/12/Hutton-Schopenhauer.pdf

Janaway, Christopher. *Schopenhauer: A Very Short Introduction*. Oxford and New York: Oxford University Press, 2002.

Ñāṇājīvako, Bhikkhu. *Schopenhauer and Buddhism*. Kandy, Sri Lanka: The Buddhist Publication Society, 1970.

Neill, Alex, and Christopher Janaway, eds. *Better Consciousness: Schopenhauer's Philosophy of Value*. Malden, MA/Oxford: Wiley-Blackwell, 2009.

Reilly, Richard. *Ethics of Compassion: Bridging Ethical Theory and Religious Moral Discourse*. Lanham, MD: Rowman & Littlefield Publishers, 2008.

Scheler, Max. *The Nature of Sympathy*, translated by Peter Heath. London: Routledge & Kegan Paul, 1954.

Shantideva. *The Way of the Bodhisattva*, translated by the Padmakara Translation Group. Boston/London: Shambhala Publications, 1997.

Taylor, Charles. "Sympathy." *The Journal of Ethics* 3 (1999): 73–87.

Wicks, Robert. *Schopenhauer*. Malden, MA/Oxford: Blackwell Publishing, 2008.

CHAPTER 21

SCHOPENHAUER AND CONFUCIAN THINKERS ON COMPASSION

DOUGLAS L. BERGER

IN hindsight, it is something of an irony that nineteenth-century philosopher Arthur Schopenhauer, given his rather cursory familiarity with the classical Chinese tradition, took special notice of the twelfth-century Confucian master Zhu Xi. It was after all merely one sentence, summarizing a thin mid-1820s translation of a Zhu essay, that inspired Schopenhauer to suspect that the Song Dynasty Confucian exegete entertained a metaphysical worldview that was remarkably similar to his own. At the time he wrote of this suspicion in the mid-1830s, it was precisely metaphysical resonances between his own system and ideas from a broad range of other thinkers that he actively sought. And it is most doubtful that, when understood in its own context, the cosmology that we find in Zhu Xi's works can at all be reconciled with Schopenhauer's famous metaphysics of will. However, it is in the realm of ethical theory, and most notably the theory of human compassion, that Schopenhauer's and Zhu's thought come closest together. This closeness does not necessarily lie in the details of their respective conceptions of compassion, but in their general inclinations to see in compassion something revealing about the metaphysics of human existence.

This chapter explores how Schopenhauer and Zhu Xi, though surely in variant ways, ground the feeling of compassion in deeper metaphysical structures of human character or personhood. We begin with a brief review of Schopenhauer's familiarity with classical Chinese thought as of the 1830s, when he first happens upon the ideas of Zhu that intrigue him. We then articulate how Schopenhauer's formulation of compassion fits into his typological depiction of the human character and thus what the relationship is between compassion and the metaphysical ground of human existence: namely, the will. At this point, we will turn to a few important works of Zhu Xi to understand how he hermeneutically reworks the depiction of compassion found in the fourth-century BCE philosopher Mencius to demonstrate how compassion lies within the natural constitution of human existence. Though their overarching metaphysical frameworks are then literally worlds apart, both Schopenhauer and Zhu find compassion to be not just a human feeling or emotion, but a key to understanding the natural foundations of human existence. And yet, even in the context of this apparent general agreement, there emerges an incredible difference between the thinkers, a difference that makes Schopenhauer the famed pessimist about human existence and Zhu a staunch, and typical, Confucian optimist.

21.1 METAPHYSICAL INTRIGUE: SCHOPENHAUER AND ZHU XI

Schopenhauer's essay, "Sinology," originally penned for his 1836 work *On the Will in Nature* and slightly updated for the 1842 edition of the same work, dwells a great deal on the classical Confucian notion of 天, *tian* or "heaven." The chapter rehearses both Schopenhauer's general contrast between predominant forms of theism in the major Western religious heritages stemming from the Middle East and more abstract conceptions of the divine to be found in both Indian and Chinese traditions, most notably Buddhism. When focusing on Chinese thought, he relies on a wide range of then-recent Orientalist scholarship, though much of it, ironically, was produced by men with pronounced missionary interests in China, to demonstrate that this idea does not have the theological connotations of "God" in the religious traditions familiar to the West. Though this identification of *tian* with God had been promulgated by seventeenth- and eighteenth-century Jesuit missionaries serving in the early Qing Dynasty imperial court, Schopenhauer quotes Upham's 1829 *History of the Doctrine of Buddhism* as well as works by two East India Company employees in Guangdong, Robert Morrison's *Chinese Dictionary* and a tract by George Thomas Staunton, to debunk it (SW3, 311–12 [WN, 436]). In this refutation, Schopenhauer relies most heavily on Morrison's definitions, which parse *tian* as having the double meaning of the visible "sky" and the invisible "metaphysical principle of nature" (SW3, 312 [WN, 437]).[1] Toward the end of the essay, particularly to elaborate on the latter of Morrison's alternative definitions, Schopenhauer turns to a brief article from one of his favorite journals.

The article appeared in 1826, in volume 22 of the *Asiatic Journal and Monthly Miscellany*, which was published by the East India Company. It was entitled "Chinese Theory of Creation" and written by John Bruce, who was educated at the University of Edinburgh and was at the time "Historiographer of the East India Company." The paper was actually quite damning, lamenting the supposed vagueness of the notion of *tian* in classical Chinese literature, both in terms of its lexical meaning and in the so-called incoherence of ways in which it was used to describe both male and female deities, the order of *yin* and *yang*, the "principle" of natural order, and the sky above. It was probably the degree to which the essay relied on Morrison's dictionary, as well as the very vagueness of the idea of *tian* the author roundly condemned, that appealed to Schopenhauer. There are in Bruce's essay numerous references to Morrison's dictionary and a few quotations from an unnamed text authored by "Choo-foo-tze" or Zhu Xi that Schopenhauer in turn quotes in full, in both the English original and his own German translation in his chapter on "Sinology." The Morrison reference appeals to one lexical denotation of *tian* as "great," while the quote from Zhu runs: "to affirm that heaven has a man (i.e., a sapient being) there to judge and determine crimes should not by any means be said; nor on the other hand must it be affirmed that there is nothing at all to exercise a supreme control over these things" (SW3, 313 [WN, 436]). Such suggestive but unde-tailed passages easily sparked Schopenhauer's imagination, particularly insofar as this representation of *tian* was distinguished from a straightforward theistic interpretation, an interpretation for which Schopenhauer roundly denounced scholars with Christian missionary interests in China (SW3, 311 [WN, 431]).

It is the last passages that Schopenhauer cites from the Bruce essay that entice him the most. The passages read,

> The same author being asked about the heart of heaven, whether it is intelligent or not, answer'd [sic]: it must not be said that the mind of nature is unintelligent, but it does not resemble the cognitions of man…
>
> According to one of their authorities, *Teen* [sic]) is call'd ruler or sovereign (*choo*), from the idea of the supreme control, and another expresses himself thus: 'had heaven (*Teen* [sic]) no designing mind, then it must happen, that the cow might bring forth a horse, and on the peach-tree be reduced to the blossom of the pear.'
>
> On the other hand it is said, that the mind of Heaven is deducible from what is the Will of mankind.   (SW3, 313–14 [WN, 438])

Schopenhauer cites these paragraphs contiguously with foregoing quotations that were overtly from Zhu Xi's works, and it is apparent in his commentary that he takes them all to originate from Zhu's philosophy (SW3, 314 [WN, 438]). A look at the original essay by Bruce, however, reveals that this is not the case. In fact, a "Dr. Milne," more specifically William Milne, who, with Morrison, was one of the first active and successful nineteenth-century missionaries in China, is citing the material in the second paragraph just quoted, and, just after, the identification of the "mind of Heaven" with the "Will of mankind" was Bruce's own characterization of Milne's references. Schopenhauer then is simply mistaken about the equivocation of *tian* with the human will being a central tenet of Zhu Xi's thought on the mere basis of his reading of the cited passages, not to mention due to the lack of such an equivalence in Zhu's own Confucian system.

Nonetheless, the very suggestion that ancient Chinese thinkers could have deduced some great metaphysical identification between the basic nature of the cos-mos and will compels Schopenhauer to assure his readers that he did not derive his own metaphysics from those ancients. Not only, Schopenhauer is at pains to point out, does he not know the Chinese language, which precludes him from direct access to original texts, but he came to discover philosophical works on Chinese thought, and specifically Zhi Xi, in the 1820s and 1830s, long after his system was formulated (SW3, 314 [WN, 438]). He also realizes that the connection between his own ideas and what he takes to be Zhu's are tenuous, and he ends his essay with the mere hope that a future British scholar will be able to clarify the matter with more rigorous work on the classical Chinese texts.

In any event, what fascinates Schopenhauer about ancient Chinese thought, and where he suspects it may have some resonance with his own, lies in what he takes to be its basic metaphysics. The ambiguities surrounding the fundamental conception of *tian*, including its supposed elision of any reference to a divine personage, its relationship with the apparently but not inherently rational order of the cosmos, and a mysterious deep connection to the human will collectively draw Schopenhauer strongly. Schopenhauer, perhaps somewhat mysteriously, does not explore the question of how such a penetrating metaphysical insight could have occurred to the Confucian master Zhu Xi in light of the fact that he believes the early teachings of Confucius amounted to little more than a "predominantly political moral philosophy, general and rife with truisms, without a metaphysics to support it," much of which was "faded and boring" (SW3, 306 [WN, 432]). A seeker after Chinese systems of metaphysics, Schopenhauer asserts, must look to Daoist and Buddhist thought, especially given that the latter, in his estimation, was by far the most widespread Chinese religion in his time. Schopenhauer does describe Zhu as "the most famous of all Chinese scholars, because he incorporated and systematized the entire collective wisdom of the ancients" (SW3, 312 [WN, 438]). But beyond this comment, he does not reflect on why the most non-metaphysical of Chinese traditions in his view, Confucianism, could have produced a scholar like Zhu, whose metaphysics may have been so much like his own.

However, even the most cursory readings of the respective philosophies of Schopenhauer and Zhu would easily reveal that their conceptions of the natural order are not compatible. Schopenhauer sees the world through what John Atwell once called a "double-aspect essentialism," as representation (*Vorstellung*), in terms of the appearance and law-governed interaction of the objects of knowledge, and as will, in terms of the "nearest and clearest" manifestation of force or impulsion to exist as the thing-in-itself.[2] For his part, Zhu's programmatic and basic cosmological distinction between 理 *li*, the "coherence" or "pattern" of nature as a whole and 氣 *qi*, the "vital vapor" or "psychophysical stuff" that is the most elemental kind of matter, would place a sort of rational order at the root of all things and anything associated with willing in the derivative realm of *qi*.[3] However, Schopenhauer did not know enough about classical Chinese thought to realize that Zhu Xi makes the most important subtle qualification of his distinction between nature's "coherence" and its "psychophysical stuff" in the realm of ethics, specifically with regard to the feelings and principles that govern human conduct. Zhu's qualifications in this context appear to bring his general conception of personhood closer to Schopenhauer's, at least insofar as they both end up seeing the feeling of compassion as revealing some deep metaphysical structures of the specifically human character. We will spend the remainder of this chapter exploring these possible similarities of general philosophical framework between Schopenhauer and Zhu. But in the midst of these similarities is revealed a conspicuous axiological gulf between them, one that concerns what they each believed human nature was capable of.

21.2 SCHOPENHAUER ON COMPASSION AND THE ESSENCE OF CHARACTER

Though the attention paid by scholars to compassion as the pinnacle of ethical conduct in Schopenhauer's system has been entirely appropriate, it is just as important to remember what role compassion plays in his theory of the human character. Ultimately, for Schopenhauer, seeing the world through the eyes of a compassionate person can unlock one of the mysteries to the universe; it provides a kind of temporary window into the illusory nature of individuality. But for all its inspiring features, Schopenhauerian compassion also reveals the implacable ethical limitations within which individual human beings are bound.

As he himself reports, Schopenhauer was a great admirer of the distinction found in Kant's moral thought between the "empirical character" and "intelligible character." In Schopenhauer's estimation, this distinction accurately delineates those portions of our actions that are determined with law-like necessity by the empirical character and those portions that ensue from the really free moral agent, namely the intelligible character (WWR1$_{[P]}$, 422). However, Schopenhauer formulates the details of this distinction quite differently from Kant. Unlike the latter, Schopenhauer did not think the intelligible character had anything to do with the autonomous rational determination of universal ethical duties but was instead a form of will which served as the basis of each unique person's character, each person's particular and basic set of desires. Schopenhauer takes the empirical character to be the actions of the physical body of each person, which behave according to a host of causal determinations, while the intelligible character is a direct manifestation of each individual person's will, which becomes instantiated by the natural will as a whole (WWR1$_{[P]}$, 289–90). This, of course, begs the question of how that part of us which is truly free of all causal determination, the will in our intelligible character, can influence the most causally determined aspect of our existence, the body. Schopenhauer's answer to this question, which was first formulated in a pre-metaphysical context in his 1813 dissertation *On the Fourfold Root of the Principle of Sufficient Reason* but tailored to his metaphysics of will later, is that "motives" are the mediums through which the empirical character is directed by the intelligible character.

Motives on Schopenhauer's view are desired ends of specific actions that are represented by and known to the intellect. The intellect, that is, presents possible ends of alternative actions in concrete circumstances to the intelligible character (WWR1$_{[P]}$, 291). But it is the intelligible character, fixed for each individual and outside the categories of all change—namely space, time, and causality—that determines which motive will compel the empirical character to act (WWR1$_{[P]}$, 292). Though this theory of human ethical agency has been heavily criticized by Schopenhauer's contemporaries and successive generations of philosophers and commentators, this notion of motives as determined by the intelligible character for the empirical character is how he conceived of "the union of freedom and necessity" in human action. It explains for Schopenhauer how our physical bodies can be thoroughly causally determined, as are all other representations, and yet how we may be free moral agents responsible for our deeds (WWR1$_{[P]}$, 297).

In the famous 1840 essay *On the Basis of Morality*, which, despite being the only entry in a Danish Royal Society essay contest, was not rewarded the prize, Schopenhauer takes up explicitly and in detail the most general basic motives that may affect the character. The first is malice, which actively seeks the suffering of others and operates according to an "axiom" of action which runs: "injure all if it brings you any advantage" (BM$_{[P]}$, 136). The second is egoism, which directs the person to secure their own happiness regardless of the consequences to others and operates according to the axiom: "help no one; on the contrary, injure all if it brings you any advantage" (BM$_{[P]}$, 92; 136). The third and only genuinely praiseworthy motive from an ethical standpoint is compassion, which seeks the happiness of others and follows the axiom: "injure no one; on the contrary, help everyone as much as you can" (BM$_{[P]}$, 69). Corresponding to these motives are four different moral or anti-moral kinds of intelligible character, and thus four different "types" of person who are susceptible to those motives. A "wicked" character or person is motivated by malice, which, due to the privations of his own will or the beholding of others' pleasure, seeks intentionally to inflict cruelty on others (WWR1$_{[P]}$, 362–63). A "bad" character or person is always inclined to seek his own advantage, either with disregard for the well-being of others or with intent to harm them if this would lead to his own advantage (WWR1$_{[P]}$, 362). A "just" character or person is compelled by a sort of weak egoism, which motivates him to seek his own and his loved ones' well-being but within the bounds of the law and with no consciously intended harm to others (WWR1$_{[P]}$, 370–71). Finally, there is the "good" person, who makes no hard and fast distinctions between his own well-being and the well-being of others and who therefore actively seeks to help others (WWR1$_{[P]}$, 370–73). On the one hand, then, compassion is for Schopenhauer a motive, an end or purpose of action that is represented by the intellect to the intelligible character of each person, but the only type of person who can act on the basis of this motive is a "good" one, one who sees the relationship between individuals in a certain way. In this respect, compassion as an ethical motive for action reveals something about the deep structure of an individual human being's moral character when he or she is prompted to action by it.

There is another and generally more celebrated respect in which Schopenhauer believed compassion was a metaphysically significant type of human incentive. This has to do with how a person motivated by compassion uniquely "sees" the world and, particularly, how she understands the relationship between individuals. The basic forms of representation in Schopenhauer's estimation—space, time, and causality—present not only objects in our environment as individuated and heterogeneous, but also make specific persons with whom we relate, and we ourselves, appear to us as individuated and heterogeneous also. But, for most of us, because the principles of representation depict individual persons as heterogeneous and because we can only have a direct and immediate experience of our own will and not the willing of others, we also appear to ourselves as more valuable, more important, axiologically more significant, than others; we take our own interests most seriously and predominantly seek our own ends.

This "practical egoism" is an extension of "theoretical egoism," the epistemological or metaphysical conclusion that only I must exist since all other representations in my experience are only indirect representations "for" me, while I alone am directly aware of my own will ($BM_{[P]}$, 131–32). In stark contrast, the compassionate person sees in the suffering other a being whose essential nature, willing, is the same willing that lies at the core of their own being and therefore beholds the other as just as much in need of relief, comfort, and happiness as themselves. The good person is, on the basis of this insight that partially and temporarily abrogates the separateness between individuals artificially constructed by representation, compelled by the motive of compassion.

Schopenhauer frequently invokes the vocabulary of classical Indian texts like the *Bhagavad Gītā* and commentaries on the *Upaniṣads* by calling the represented separateness between individuals "the veil of *māyā*" or "illusion," and he argues that the compassionate person, in breaking through this separation and seeing all beings as manifestations of a unitary will, possesses not merely the most admirable of human virtues, but the correct metaphysical knowledge of the nature of the world.

> If plurality and separateness belong only to the phenomenon, and it is one and the same essence that manifests itself in all living things, than that conception which abolishes the difference between ego and non-ego is not erroneous, but on the contrary, the opposite conception must be. We find also that this latter conception is described be the Hindus as *Māyā*, i.e. illusion, deception, phantasm, mirage. It is the former conception that we found to be the basis of the phenomenon of compassion; in fact compassion is the proper expression of that view. Accordingly, it would be the metaphysical basis of ethics and consist in one individual's again recognizing in another his own self, his own true inner nature.   ($BM_{[P]}$, 209)

Contrary to how his position is portrayed by many commentators, Schopenhauer is quite careful in his discussion in *On the Basis of Morality* not to suggest that the compassionate individual completely negates the distinction between herself, her own feelings and aims, and those of another; he insists that the compassionate person makes "less of a distinction" between self and other, for beholding another's suffering makes one aware of a metaphysical and not a phenomenal unity with the other, and this is accomplished by "recognition" and "immediately, without reason or argument" ($WWR1_{[P]}$, 272–73). Although then we often experience compassion as a feeling, a sentiment of pity and a sense of the pain of another person, what is really communicated by compassion is a kind of insight, a form of knowledge that makes the easing of another's suffering just as important to me as the easing of my own—in other words, a Schopenhauerian motive. But that motive can only compel a person with a certain kind of fixed intelligible character, that of a "good" person, to act at its behest, for it will not inspire the "wicked," "bad," or even "just" person to action.

We will return to this notion of the fixed moral character in the concluding section. What is important at the moment is to underline the two respects in which Schopenhauer believed that compassion provided a key to fundamental metaphysical realizations. In the first respect, Schopenhauer thought that human conduct reveals fundamental things about an individual's ineligible character, their personal essence, and, in the case of compassionate acts, we could find all the evidence we need of an essentially good human being. In the second respect, compassion as a motive represents to the character not only purposes of specific actions to relieve the suffering of others, but also an insight into the true nature of the world as a whole as unitary will rather than the ultimately illusory separateness of individual beings. Though Schopenhauer may have been mistaken in his suspicion that the Song Dynasty Confucian exegetical master Zhu Xi was a forerunner of his metaphysics, he may have been quite interested to learn that Zhu also believed that compassion offers us clues about the deepest nature of persons.

21.3 ZHU XI ON COMPASSION AS A CLUE TO NATURE

Zhu Xi 朱熹 (1130–1200) was at the forefront of the Song Dynasty reforms to the Confucian Civil Service Examination system, as well as the inheritor and foremost advocate of the philosophical "School of Coherence" (理學 *li xue*). His elevation of and commentaries on the "Four Books" of the *Analects, Mencius, Great Learning,* and *Maintaining Equilibrium,* along with the time-honored classic books of the ancient Zhou Dynasty as paramount for Confucian scholarship established his thought, with few interruptions, as canonical for the next seven hundred years of academic training in China. Inspired by several eleventh-century philosophical predecessors, Zhu formulates a distinction between the physical, animate, and in some beings conscious matter (氣 *qi*) that resides in the world and the "coherence," "patterns," or "order" (理 *li*) according to which these things are designed and interact. To illustrate this relationship between *qi* and *li,* Zhu invokes various analogies, for example, that between a physical building and the design according to which it was constructed, or the physical seeing of eyes and the structures that enable them to have their visual capacities.[4] The distinction between physical matter and natural coherence pervades everything, which means that it does not merely characterize nonliving phenomena but also the affective, cognitive, and moral lives of human beings.

In both the ancient and medieval Confucian worldview, the heart-mind (心 *xin*) is a physical, bodily organ, and, as such, its sensuous, emotional, and reflective states are varying states of its matter (氣 *qi*). When the heart-mind's matter is turbulent or opaque, the person is subject to all kinds of turmoil, agitation, confusion, and incomprehension, whereas when the heart-mind's *qi* is tranquil, transparent, and clear, the person may attain heightened levels of self-mastery, attentive responsiveness, and intelligence. These two possible basic modes of awareness, occluded by turbulent upset of its matter and illuminated when its *qi* has been calmed, are often referred to by Zhu as the "merely human heart-mind" (人心 *ren xin*) and the "heart-mind of the way" (道心 *dao xin*).[5] All people, regardless of their status or lot, may become subject to both of these modalities, but when the heart-mind is captivated by desires and upset, its ability to understand the natural order and moral ideals is severely diminished. So ongoing forms of practice and even disciplines of learning must be pursued in order to train the heart-mind to remain pure and translucent.

A fascinating and crucial feature of Zhu Xi's thought depicts a tranquil and lucid heart-mind as one that has achieved a certain equilibrium or harmony between the host of its inherent feelings (情 *qing*). For the heart-mind, as the preferred standard translation of 心 *xin* reflects, is not merely an organ of cognition, but one of feelings. In this analysis, Zhu follows an early second-century BCE Confucian text, the *Zhong Yong* or *Maintaining Equilibrium*, in seeing the nature or natural disposition (性 *xing*) of the human heart-mind as being in a state of balance between all its possible emotions. It is by restoring and maintaining that state that one can guard oneself against the perils of the frenetic uproars of the heart-mind's *qi*. But of all the possible emotions that can shatter the balance of feelings, desires (欲 *yu*) are not only the most dangerous, but also the most unnatural, for, Zhu argues that, contra Buddhist insistences, we are not born with desires but only acquire them with life experience.[6]

So certain kinds of intense feelings, particularly those feelings that are associated with impulses to acquire and possess certain things or other persons, must be quelled or calmed. However, the moral virtues most prized by Confucian thinkers are also manifested as feelings, and these feelings must be cultivated such that they may be felt and expressed in measures that are appropriate to the demands of circumstance. One of the most vital of these moral emotions is compassion or "inner pity" (惻隱 *ceyin*). Compassion, for Zhu, reveals something to us about the inherent moral nature, or moral coherence (理 *li*) of human beings.

One of the earliest significant works on Confucian moral thought was the fourth-to third-century BCE text, *Mencius* (or *Mengzi*) which, though it had languished in Confucian scholarship for centuries, was raised by Zhu Xi's educational curriculum to the status of a classic required for study. In one of the early books of *Mencius*, after the argument is given that the spontaneous pity one feels upon seeing an unsuspecting toddler about to fall into a well is proof of inborn human moral goodness, the text asserts,

惻隱之心, 仁之端也; 羞惡之心, 義之端也; 辭讓之心, 禮之端也; 是非之心, 智之端也

.人之有是四端也, 猶其有四體也. 有是四端而自謂不能者, 自賊者也, 謂其君 不能,

賊其君者也。凡有四端於我者, 知皆擴而充之矣, 若火之始然, 泉之始達. 苟能充之,

足以保四海; 苟不充之, 不足以事父母.

The feeling of compassion is the sprout of benevolence. The feeling of disdain is the sprout of righteousness. The feeling of deference is the sprout of propriety.

The feeling of approval and disapproval is the sprout of wisdom. People having these four sprouts is like their having four limbs.

To have these four sprouts, yet to claim that one is incapable (of virtue) is to steal from oneself. To say that one's ruler is incapable is to steal from one's ruler.

In general, having these four sprouts within oneself, if one knows how to fill them all out, it will be like a fire starting up, a spring breaking through! If one can merely fill them out, they will be sufficient to care for all within the Four Seas. If one fails to fill them out, they will be insufficient to care for one's parents.[7]

The *Mencius* claims here that feelings such as compassion, disdain, deference, and the capacity to approve and disapprove are feelings, or emotions of the heart (心 *xin*). In their turn, these feelings are said to be the "beginnings" (端 *duan*), a homophone of the word "sprouts" used in the preceding translation, of the moral virtues. Specifically, compassion is said to be the beginning or sprout of the highest of all virtues prized by Confucians, 仁 *ren*, the ability to care for others and ensure that all one's relationships in life flourish. There is nothing in this passage from the *Mencius* to indicate that it is anything but the feelings of compassion, disdain, deference, and approval and disapproval that are themselves the origins or roots of moral conduct. However, in Zhu Xi's explication of this passage in his commentary on the *Mencius*, these feelings are not themselves the beginnings of virtue but are the signs of virtue inherent not in the physical stuff of the human heart-mind, but in its indwelling coherence or order (理 *li*).

惻隱, 羞惡, 辭讓, 是非, 情也. 仁, 義, 禮, 智, 性也. 心, 統性情者也.
端, 緒也. 因其情之發, 而性之本然可得而見, 猶有物在中而緒見于外也.

Inner compassion, shame and revulsion, deference and approval and disapproval, these are emotions (情 *qing*). Loving care, rightness, ritual propriety and wisdom, these are nature (性 *xing*). The heart-mind is that which unifies nature and emotions.

The extremities (端 *duan*), these are visible feelings (緒 *xu*). Because it manifests (發 *fa*) in emotions, the root (本 *ben*) of nature can become visible. It is like things (物 *wu*) that are found within (在中 *zai zhong*) but their traces (緒 *xu*) are visible on the outside.[8]

Zhu here performs a hermeneutic play on the term 端 *duan*, which in the original text clearly means "beginnings," and he capitalizes on another of its possible meanings, "extremities" or "end points." If the feeling (情 *qing*) of compassion is an end-point, then instead of being the root of virtue itself, it is but a trace, a visible clue (緒 *xu*) to something that lies deeper than it. The virtues like loving care (仁 *ren*) are not then outgrowths of human feelings like compassion, but are the underlying nature (性 *xing*) that constitutes the moral possibilities of being human, and those possibilities lie in the natural coherence of the general human design, as it were. That is to say, once again, that feelings are not the beginnings of virtue, but merely the evidence that virtue is there. It is virtue that is at the root (本 *ben*) of human feelings and not the other way round. The *Mencius*, as well as every other Confucian classic, is reinterpreted by Zhu to be arguing that compassion and other prized emotions, though they certainly help bring about the highest moral aims of human conduct, are clues to the natural pattern (天理 *tian li*) of human existence. But because it is the natural coherence of all human life that serves as the basis for virtues, in principle, all human beings, with the right nurturing, education, and training, can become morally perfect. And on these grounds, Zhu can embrace the faith of all his Confucian predecessors in the ability of every person in the street to become a sage.

21.4 METAPHYSICS AND OUTLOOK

From our preceding examinations, it should be clear that, contrary to Schopenhauer's intrigued suspicions, there is little or no ground for believing that there is any kind of deep correspondence between his metaphysical system and the cosmology of Zhu Xi. For one thing, the line of text from the *Asiatic Journal* that captured Schopenhauer's special attention was not even a direct quote from any of Zhu's writings but instead a characterization of its author, the Orientalist John Bruce, of some quotations he had found in the scholarship of William Milne. Furthermore, Schopenhauer places all of human rationality and natural order in the realm of "representation" (*Vorstellung*) and willing as closest to the thing-in-itself of all beings. Zhu, on the contrary, decidedly considered willing, and especially willing in the form of human desires (欲 *yu*), to be a movement of psychophysical energy (氣 *qi*), while the actions and interactions of the universe were grounded in a metaphysically primary order or coherence (理 *li*). In a general and formal, though important, sense, their systems of metaphysics are inverses of one another, with correspondingly different axiological estimations of the roles of willing and rationality in human life and conduct.

Nonetheless, though again in a general and formal sense, there might be found some significant agreement between the Song Dynasty Chinese exegete and nineteenth-century German philosopher with regard to the nature of compassion. While both would attest that compassion is experienced as an intense feeling for the suffering and misfortune of others, it also reveals something metaphysically fundamental about the human character and even nature as a whole. For Schopenhauer, compassion is in a strictly technical sense a motive of conduct, a possible overarching purposiveness of human action which follows a moral maxim that demands we help others. This maxim is in turn based on a metaphysical insight that the apparent separateness between individuals is only a construction of representational knowledge and that, in fact, all individuals, being alike manifestations of will, are of equal value. This is all to say that, for Schopenhauer, compassion is the most praiseworthy ethical motive precisely because it sees the essential nature of the world, a unitary willing, rightly, and comports people in their conduct toward others on the basis of that truth.

For Zhu Xi, particularly given his reinterpretation of classical Confucian texts like the *Mencius*, compassion is the highest moral feeling because it is a manifestation of the highest virtue, 仁 *ren*, or loving care, that human beings are capable of. And the reason human beings are capable of this highest virtue is because it is inherent in their nature (性 *xing*), it is a possibility of feeling and conduct that constitutes that natural patterns (天理 *tian li*) of human beings. For both thinkers, then, compassion is not merely an emotion of interest to human psychology or anthropology, but it is incipient in the deepest recesses of the natural order as a whole. It is, of course, a futile gesture to hypothesize about such things, but it is at least possible that Schopenhauer, had he known enough about Zhu's system to recognize this similarity, may have been even more excited about it than the vague connection he conjured up when reading second- and third-hand characterizations of Chinese thought by nineteenth-century Orientalists.

And yet, this general resonance between Schopenhauer's and Zhu Xi's thought is bounded by an even more important disagreement. As we have seen, Schopenhauer did not believe that compassion was a motive that appealed to every human being, or even could. At least from within the confines of his systematic philosophy, Schopenhauer persistently argued that compassion could only serve as a motive of action for those with morally good intelligible characters. Those with other kinds of types of intelligible character, certainly not malicious or "bad" characters and not even "just" characters, could not be moved to consistently act to achieve compassionate ends. And, on an even more dire note, Schopenhauer was convinced that the intelligible character, being an "act of will outside time," was forever fixed and unchangeable (WWR1$_{[P]}$, 289–90; 294).

While there are passages where Schopenhauer admits that even "bad" persons can have a "presentiment," that all people are manifestations of one will and that, by hurting others, they are only hurting themselves, that "presentiment" was too weakly received by the "bad" character to transform a "bad" person's conduct (WWR1$_{[P]}$, 365). It is for this reason that Schopenhauer constantly repeated the maxim of the ancients that "virtue cannot be taught" and that he maintained that, were it possible for all of a person's motives and the entirety of their empirical character to be known, that person's actions could be predicted with the same accuracy as eclipses of the sun (WWR1$_{[P]}$, 292). Indeed, perhaps the most deeply pessimistic feature of Schopenhauer's thought, even beyond the abstract metaphysical certainty he always gives voice to that it would have been better had the world never existed, is the fact that he did not believe that human beings could ethically change or grow, but only learn more about what kinds of character they possessed. The intelligible character of each person can only be "destroyed" or "negated" by ultimate mystical experience, on Schopenhauer's view, and thus his formulation of the great "denial of the will to live." Compassion then, for as beautiful and true a moral virtue as it is, cannot change anyone; it only serves as evidence of a uniquely and even rarely "good" individual.

This pessimism was quite removed from the worldview of the Confucian advocate Zhu Xi. For him, not only does the human species as a whole exhibit more moral potential than other animal species due to its possession of relatively rarified 氣 *qi*, but within each human being resides the entire gamut of moral possibilities that are embedded in the deep structure (理 *li*) of personhood. This means that, with the appropriate degrees of diligence and constant practice, every human being can increasingly perfect themselves. And since the height of moral virtue, 仁 *ren*, is a possibility of that deep structure, the feeling of compassion, when experienced and rightly cultivated, can make sages of us all. Though Schopenhauer—again, had he been more fully informed about Zhu's thought—may have held this degree of Confucian "optimism" about human potential to have been naïve and even contemptible, we can imagine how compassion in Zhu's framework can play a more universally ennobling role than it is permitted to have in Schopenhauer's philosophy.

NOTES

1. Unless otherwise indicated, all translations from German or Chinese into English in this essay are my own.
2. John E. Atwell, *Schopenhauer on the Character of the World: The Metaphysics of Will* (Berkeley, University of California Press, 1995), 21–25.
3. In rendering *li* as "coherence" or "pattern" rather than as the till-then predominant "principle," I follow Willard Peterson, "Another Look at *Li*," *Bulletin of Song and Yuan Studies* 18 (1986), 13–32.
4. Zhu Xi, *Learning to be a Sage: Selections from the Conversations of Master Zhu, Arranged Topically*, translated by Patrick Gardiner (Berkeley: University of California Press, 1990), 92; 130, 140.
5. Ibid., 144–45.
6. Ibid., 181.
7. Mengzi, *The Essential Mengzi: Selected Passages with Traditional Commentary*, translated by Bryan van Norden (Indianapolis, Hackett Publishing Company, 2008), 46–47.
8. Zhu Xi, *Zhuzi Yu Lei*, edited by Qingde Li (Beijing, Zhonghua Shu Chu, 1986), *Mengzi Ji Zhu*, 2A6.

FURTHER READING

Atwell, John E. *Schopenhauer on the Character of the World: The Metaphysics of Will*. Berkeley: University of California Press, 1995.

Gardiner, Patrick. *Learning to be a Sage: Selections from the Conversations of Master Zhu, Arranged Topically*. Berkeley: University of California Press, 1990.

Mengzi. *The Essential Mengzi: Selected Passages with Traditional Commentary*, translated by Bryan van Norden. Indianapolis: Hackett Publishing Company, 2008.

Peterson, Willard. "Another Look at *Li*." *Bulletin of Song and Yuan Studies* 18 (1986): 13–32.

Zhu Xi. *Zhuzi Yu Lei*, edited by Qingde Li. Beijing: Zhonghua Shu Chu, 1986.

PART V

RELIGION AND SCHOPENHAUER'S PHILOSOPHY

CHAPTER 22

....

SCHOPENHAUER AND
THE *DIAMOND-SŪTRA*

....

CHRISTOPHER RYAN

IN the closing section (§71) of *The World as Will and Representation*, Schopenhauer turned to consider the condition of the saintly ascetic, in whom the will has asserted its original freedom and denied itself. To elucidate this enigmatic state, Schopenhauer drew a contrast between an absolute nothing (*nihil negativum*) and a relative nothing (*nihil privativum*) (WWR1, 436). The latter he summarily dismissed as "not even conceivable," in accordance with his habitual disdain for phrases that affix adjectives such as "absolute" and "unconditioned" to otherwise meaningful concepts. This is because his main purpose in the section was to set in opposition the incommensurable perspectives included within the concept of a *nihil privativum*, or relative nothing. On the one hand, there is the nothing (*Nichts*) of the saint's internal state, and particularly his consciousness which, in the absence of the will's striving, perceives no distinctions between phenomena, even between his own body and external objects, so "cannot really be called cognition, because it no longer has the form of subject and object." On the other, there is the vanity or nothingness (*Nichtigkeit*) of the aims and activities of a consciousness shot through with insatiable will, pursuing a variety of particular external objects to satisfy its empty subjectivity, but receiving only suffering for its efforts. Schopenhauer recognized that, for most of his readers, the nothing of the saint's condition is likely to appear menacing and fearful, but he explained this as simply a reflex and "expression of the fact that we will life so much, and are nothing other than this will and know nothing other than it" (WWR1, 438). For, from the antithetical perspective of the saint, the "being" for which we strive appears as "nothing," so that he looks back upon the objects and values of our lives with an abhorrence equal to that with which we regard his mode of life:

> ...for everyone who is still filled with the will, what remains after it is completely abolished is certainly nothing. But conversely, for those in whom the will has turned and negated itself, this world of ours which is so very real with all its suns and galaxies is—nothing. (WWR1, 439)

This is the point at which Schopenhauer closed his first systematic articulation of his single thought—with nothing (*Nichts*). If Schopenhauer had hoped that this final word might have clarified his conception of the point of termination of his philosophy, and thereby the condition and consciousness of the saint, then debates in the secondary literature suggest that he failed. One might issue the rejoinder that the attempt itself was foolhardy, since—as he observed elsewhere—"the more that is thought *under* a concept, the less is thought *in* it," so that "the most universal concept, e.g. being (i.e. the infinitive of the copula) is practically no more than a word" (WWR2, 70). But if being—arrived at through negation of concrete perceptual content—provides no purchase for thought, how much more so does its opposite, nothing?

The debate in the secondary literature is not confined to the semantic issue of the meaning or possible referent of the word "nothing," nor is it limited to Schopenhauer's conception of the soteriological condition and consciousness of the saint. The nature of the nothing realized by the saint in the absence of willing raises issues concerning the ontological status of the will itself, in addition to the propriety of Schopenhauer's pretensions to objective knowledge of Kant's thing-in-itself.

Two broad positions can be found in the literature concerning Schopenhauer's metaphysics of will and soteriology of its negation, both of which relate their interpretations to Schopenhauer's concept of nothing. On the one side are commentators such as D. W. Hamlyn and Robert Wicks, who take Schopenhauer at his word when he says that the will is the thing-in-itself and the ascetic's salvation its negation.[1] This interpretation considers the opposition between the incommensurable perspectives contained in the concept of a *nihil privativum* as central to Schopenhauer's point in §71. Since will as thing-in-itself is the original reality, the soteriological nothing of the saint denotes "a condition of liberation from desire that reveals no new worlds or higher dimensions, but that provides a detached, liberated, and tranquil outlook on life"[2] and hence a negative state that is nevertheless desirable because "by comparison with the misery of our lot it is nothingness that provides the only clear contrast and the only release."[3]

On the other side are commentators who take the contrast between a *nihil negativum* and a *nihil privativum* as the key to interpreting §71, with Schopenhauer's dismissal of an absolute nothing denoting his denial of a purely negative condition of salvation, and his concept of relative nothing an apophatic disavowal of the applicability of our linguistic and conceptual forms to the positive reality allegedly attained by the saint. Julian Young and John Atwell have developed versions of this reading, supporting it by qualifying Schopenhauer's claim that the will is thing-in-itself, which—the argument goes—he could not have meant literally, insofar as it illegitimately transports Kant's thing-in-itself into the phenomenon, making it an object for a subject. Young maintains that the will is not the thing-in-itself, but an intermediary object of metaphysical investigation that lies between perceptual appearance and unknowable thing-in-itself.[4] Atwell contends that there are two implicit accounts of the thing-in-itself in Schopenhauer's philosophy— one knowable as object, expressing itself as will in the phenomenon, and another that transcends subject-object cognition, describable only through negations, such as "ultimate reality…noumenon…or, to say it best, unconditioned being."[5] Young in particular argues that a transcendent thing-in-itself apart from will is presupposed by Schopenhauer's soteriology, for "the possibility of salvation *demands* that a metaphysical account of the world as Will should not be an account of the world in itself,"[6] and that one of Schopenhauer's key arguments for this position is "the 'relativity of nothingness' argument."[7] As such, Schopenhauer's closing reflections on nothing is not an ontological descriptor on the order of being (*ordo essendi*), but only a negation on the order of knowledge (*ordo cognoscendi*), so that when Schopenhauer "says that the saintly ascetic achieves, ultimately, salvation (*Erlösung*), there is some positive state or condition which he believes the term to designate."[8]

These two opposed commentarial stances can and do marshal a variety of quotes from Schopenhauer's published works, notebooks, and letters in support of their contrary interpretations. Schopenhauer's dominant position is that the will is Kant's thing-in-itself, so that once we remove the subject-object form of representation, what is left over "can be nothing other than *will*, which is therefore the true *thing in itself*" (WWR1, 187). However, alongside these unequivocal statements there are some tentative qualifications of this position, which concede at least *the possibility* of a distinction between knowable will and unknowable thing-in-itself, such as that "the thing-in-itself (which we cognize most directly in willing) may have—entirely outside of any possible appearance—determinations, properties, and ways of being that entirely elude our grasp or cognition, but which would remain as the essence of the thing in itself even when . . . this has freely annulled itself as *will*" (WWR2, 209).[9]

Such quotations pose a genuine difficulty for any exposition of Schopenhauer's philosophy that strives to present it as a coherent, atemporal, and seamless whole, in accordance with Schopenhauer's own characterization of his system as the unfolding of a "single thought" (WWR1, 5). As a result, commentators are confronted with a choice concerning which quotations to prioritize, while limiting the force or relevance of others to the overall presentation of Schopenhauer's philosophy.

The debate concerning whether unknowable being or literal nothingness is attained by Schopenhauer's saint in whom the will has turned and denied itself, recalls a comparable debate that absorbed academic Buddhology in the nineteenth century, concerning whether key Buddhist concepts, such as *nirvāṇa*, *śunyatā*,[10] and *prajñāpāramitā*,[11] denote extinction or entry into a higher mode of existence signposted through negations.[12] It is significant, therefore, that in 1860—forty-two years after Schopenhauer brought the first statement of his system to a close with the word "nothing"—he annotated a handwritten footnote to the effect that "[t]his is precisely the Pradschna-Paramita [*prajñāpāramitā*] of the Buddhists, the 'beyond of all knowledge', i.e. the point where subject and object are no more. (See I. J. Schmidt, *Ueber das Mahajana und Pradschna-Paramita*)" (WWR1, 439).

Schopenhauer's citation is to a treatise published in 1840 by the Russian-based Buddhologist, Isaak Jacob Schmidt.[13] Schmidt's work was a translation of a Mahāyāna scripture known as the *Diamond-Sūtra*, accompanied by Schmidt's exposition of the key teachings of Mahāyāna Buddhism. Schopenhauer's reference to Schmidt's publication provides a clue to the aforementioned equivocations found in his work concerning the status of the will and what is at stake in its denial. This is because Schmidt's publications indicate that his position on the controversy over Buddhist soteriology was that *nirvāṇa* and *prajñāpāramitā* constitute a transition into the "beyond of wisdom [*Jenseits der Weisheit*]," and hence reunion with the "incomprehensible and fathomless fullness of the immaterial, simple abstraction of the divine being."[14] Or, in Schopenhauerian language, reabsorption into the inner nature of the thing-in-itself.

Schopenhauer associated the "nothing" that terminated his first work with Schmidt's positive and transcendent account of Buddhist soteriology for a reason, one that becomes clearer when the negative reviews and subsequent neglect to which his system was exposed after 1818 are taken into account, alongside his exposure to mystical religious literature between 1818 and 1860. It is the thesis of this chapter that the inconsistent statements concerning the status of the will and its denial found in Schopenhauer's works are best unraveled diachronically rather than synchronically, because Schopenhauer surreptitiously modified the connotation of key concepts such as "will" and "nothing" between 1818 and 1860. His tendency to juxtapose confident reassertions of the central proposition of his *Willensmetaphysik* with subtle qualifications in later works, as well as the footnote to Schmidt's treatise appended to the word "nothing" in 1860, are unifying techniques of his authorship, employed to sustain the conviction that his philosophy was based on a single thought, in relation to which his works were the empirical-temporal unfolding of its unified transcendental character. However, it is highly unlikely that Schopenhauer's understanding of his key concepts, developed over four decades, remained stable. If, instead, we carry over an insight from Nietzsche's genealogical method, we might regard the words "will" and "nothing" as the stable element, whose meaning is unstable and subject to mutation so that, by 1860, they contain not just "one meaning but a whole synthesis of meanings," insofar as "only something which has no history can be defined."[15]

The thesis that Schopenhauer's growing encounter with literature on Buddhism relates to the "shift in his thinking concerning the nature of the thing-in-itself" has been previously articulated by Moira Nicholls.[16] However, whereas Nicholls regards the relation as one of influence, this chapter develops the view that Schopenhauer's reading of the work of Schmidt, and especially the latter's treatise on *prajñāpāramitā*, provided a way out of difficulties concerning the relation between metaphysical will and soteriological nothing highlighted in critical reviews of the first volume of his chief work.

The next section of this chapter develops an interpretation of Schopenhauer's conception of relative nothing in 1818, using only quotes from the first volume of *The World as Will and Representation* to elucidate his meaning at that time. In the following section, Schmidt's translation of the *Diamond-Sūtra* and commentary on Mahāyāna will be analyzed, with particular reference to the positively transcendent account of *prajñāpāramitā* that he imported into the *Sūtra*. The fourth section of the chapter will trace the steps and developments in Schopenhauer's *Willensmetaphysik* and soteriology that followed on from his initial statement in 1818, which led up to his appropriation of Schmidt's apophatic account of Buddhist soteriology in the footnote of 1860.

22.1 SCHOPENHAUER ON ABSOLUTE AND RELATIVE NOTHING: 1818

If the closing section of the first edition of *The World as Will and Representation* is interpreted using only materials from that time period, then there is no indication that the concept of relative nothing (*nihil privativum*) is an indirect affirmation of the saint's entry into a positive reality that exceeds our linguistic and conceptual categories. Indeed, Schopenhauer positively excluded such an idea. He unequivocally stated that "[o]nly nothing remains before us" (WWR1, 438), and counseled his readers not to bypass or "evade" (*umgehn*) it with "myths and meaningless words [*Mythen und bedeutungsleere Worte*] as the Indians do, words such as 're-absorption into the primal spirit' [*den Urgeist*[17]], or the *Nirvāṇa* of the Buddhists" (WWR1, 439).

This comment clearly signifies that Schopenhauer at this stage regarded any suggestion of mystical reabsorption or equivocal negation (*nirvāṇa*) as mere evasive fig leaves for the saint's attainment of a negative state, despite Schopenhauer's nascent admiration for other aspects of Indian thought at this stage. Urs App has argued the contrary, contending that Schopenhauer's comment is "very positive," and "is usually completely misunderstood as a critique of *nirvāṇa* and Buddhism."[18] However, rather surprisingly, App's argument turns solely on the circumstance that Isaak Schmidt used the word *bedeutungsleer* to expound the Mahāyāna critique of all names and forms, including *nirvāṇa*, in a work published in 1843, from which App argues back to Schopenhauer's supposed identical use in 1818. But App's argument assumes that Schopenhauer possessed a level of sophisticated knowledge of Mahāyāna's negative dialectic unknown to any European in 1818, and also ignores the force of Schopenhauer's contention that Buddhists use *nirvāṇa* to "evade" (*umgehn*) "the dark impression of that nothing that hovers behind all virtue and holiness as the final goal" (WWR1, 439). Schopenhauer's reference is clearly dismissive, and indicates that, at this stage, mystical reports of the soteriological condition were not a respectable source.

Instead, Schopenhauer's conception of the nothing of the saint was worked out in relation to European philosophers, specifically Kant and Plato. He cited Kant as the origin for the contrast between an absolute nothing (*nihil negativum*) and a relative nothing (*nihil privativum*): Kant defined the former as an "[e]mpty object without concept," which coheres with Schopenhauer's comment that it is "not even conceivable," for it "would be nothing in every respect" and hence self-cancelling (WWR1, 436). Nothing in every respect suggests that, were there an absolute nothing, there would never have been a world at all, and hence no will and no representation to wonder at—just nothingness for eternity. By contrast, Kant defined a *nihil privativum* as an "[e]mpty object of a concept,"[19] and hence the concept of an absence or void. By itself a void has no content, so can only be thought indirectly, through the relation of thinking away, absenting, or emptying out that in relation to which it is nothing—namely, the will as thing-in-itself, along with its mirror, the world as representation.

Schopenhauer also referenced Plato's *Sophist* in §71 (WWR1, 437), a dialogue concerned with how to say or think what is not, the solution to which was given in the Form of Otherness or Difference (το ἕτερον). The section of the dialogue to which Schopenhauer referred has the Eleatic Stranger outlining how the parts of Difference pervade all other Forms, allowing each one to remain itself, by virtue of not being, or being different from, all the others. However, Difference itself has no specific nature and so cannot be thought independently, apart from not being, or being different from, all other Forms. Since non-being is Difference, it is not therefore the contrary of being, for that would be absolute nothing; instead, non-being is a relative nothing that can be brought into discourse because it is *different from* being, "and necessarily, because it is different from *that which is*, it clearly can be *what is not*."[20]

In sum, Schopenhauer's line of thought in §71 might be compared to the response that Silenus gave to King Midas's question concerning the best life:[21] Schopenhauer's concept of relative nothing would correspond to dying very soon and absolute nothing to never having been born at all, a condition that is—insofar as we have heard those words—"not even conceivable," because "nothing in every respect" (WWR1, 436). Both indicate a negation or absence, one absolutely without a preceding condition of existence—and hence inconceivably—and the other relative to the existence that both King Midas and the reader of *The World as Will and Representation* are currently enduring, whose negation gives it content for our understanding.

It seems, therefore, that Schopenhauer's dismissal of the concept of absolute nothing proceeded from assumptions that also prompted his dismissal of the concept of absolute good, for just as "every good is essentially relative: because its essence is to exist only in relation to a desiring will" (WWR1, 389), so every nothing is essentially relative, because its essence is related to and assumes a recently extinguished will. Saintly mystics may resort to positive phrases when celebrating their liberation from willing, such as "ecstasy, rapture, enlightenment, unity with God" (WWRI, 438), but these will be as empty of content as exclamations of happiness, contentment, and satisfaction of willing, which are similarly "of a negative rather than positive nature" (WWR1, 346). Schopenhauer would not, therefore, have taken mystical phrases as reliable reports from the beyond, insofar as the experiences and actions of a saint "do not come from abstract cognition, but from an intuitively grasped, direct cognition of the world and its essence, and he filters this through some dogma only to satisfy his reason" (WWR1, 410). The saint thereby has no other language in which to express his phenomenological experience of negative liberation from willing, or relative nothing, than the abstract myths and meaningless words made available by his religious and cultural tradition. These will often consist of transcendent terms denoting union with some positive object or supernatural reality, but the terms that Schopenhauer himself used to describe the nature of the saint were psychological and hence ontologically neutral, such as the "peace [*Friede*] that is higher than all reason...that completely calm sea of the mind [*Meeresstille des Gemüths*], that profound tranquillity [*tiefe Ruhe*], imperturbable confidence and cheerfulness [*unerschütterliche Zuversicht und Heiterkeit*]" (WWR1, 438). On this reading, the intuitive content of ascetic wisdom converges with what was, for Hamlet, the abstract knowledge that "our condition is so miserable that complete non-being would be decidedly preferable" (WWR1, 350).

This, at least, is how Schopenhauer understood the concept of relative nothing in 1818; in his published works from 1844, it undergoes a subtle shift. In the supplementary essays that accompanied the second volume of 1844, Schopenhauer posited an "essence of the thing-in-itself" that might be left over (*übrig bleiben*) after the abolition of the will. For "cognition" this state appears as "an empty nothingness", but if "the will were simply and absolutely the thing in itself, then this nothingness would be *absolute*, instead of which it expressly proves precisely here to be a *relative* nothingness" (WWR2, 209). It seems, therefore, that absolute nothing is no longer an empty object without concept, "not even conceivable," but a possible state of simple non-existence, *were* the will the thing-in-itself without remainder; in other words, the condition that, I have argued, was denoted by relative nothing in 1818. By contrast, the 1844 passage states that the self-abolition of the will is a nothingness only for "cognition", and hence relative to our intellects.

Schopenhauer often juxtaposed this possibility of an "essence of the thing in itself", inaccessible to our intellects, with Buddhist concepts such as *nirvāṇa* (WWR2, 576; 624) and *prajñāpāramitā*. In the supplementary collection of essays of 1844 he remarked that "in the essence in itself of all things, to which time and space and therefore plurality as well must be foreign, there can be no cognition", and in 1860 annotated to this a handwritten note to the effect that "Buddhism describes this as *Prajñāpāramitā*, i.e. what is beyond all cognition",[22] citing Schmidt's translation of the *Diamond-Sūtra* as his source for this claim (WWR2, 288). This is the same treatise cited at the close of his chief work of 1818, to which we now turn, to see what light it can throw on the development of Schopenhauer's concepts of "will" and "nothing" between 1818 and 1860.

22.2 SCHOPENHAUER AND SCHMIDT'S *DIAMOND-SŪTRA*

Isaak Jakob Schmidt (1779–1847) originally learned Tibetan and Mongolian as a Moravian Missionary to Kalmyks, but from the mid-1820s he began to publish translations of and commentaries on Mongolian and Tibetan Buddhist scriptures. Although isolated from the main activities of European Buddhology centered in Paris, Schmidt's work was noticed by Eugène Burnouf, who had instigated the *nirvāṇa* controversy in 1844 by defining the term as "complete annihilation."[23] To establish his interpretation, Burnouf questioned the fidelity to the original Sanskrit of the Tibetan manuscript from which Schmidt translated his *Diamond-Sūtra*, in order to dispute the accuracy of Schmidt's rendition of *nirvāṇa* as a transcendent location, or "region free from misery."[24]

Schopenhauer first encountered Schmidt's scholarship in 1830, when he read and took notes from Schmidt's 1829 *History of the Eastern Mongols* (MR4, 47–48).

Schopenhauer recommended this work (alongside two by other authors) in the footnote covering recent Buddhist scholarship in the first, 1836, edition of *On Will in Nature*.[25] Citations to Schmidt's publications became a regular feature in Schopenhauer's works thereafter, occasionally accompanied by tributes, such as that Schmidt is "an admirable scholar whom I firmly believe to be the most thoroughly knowledgeable expert on Buddhism in Europe" (FR, 118). In the expanded version of the footnote that appeared in the second edition of *On Will in Nature* in 1854, Schopenhauer recommended three more books by Schmidt, in addition to the lectures on Buddhism that Schmidt had delivered to the Academy of St. Petersburg between 1829 and 1832, and published in its proceedings (WN, 432–33n).

One text by Schmidt not mentioned by Schopenhauer in the footnote of 1854 was the treatise on *prajñāpāramitā* and translation of the *Diamond-Sūtra*, published in the Academy's proceedings of 1840. It is not completely clear when Schopenhauer might have first *read* the text, but it is safe to assume that it was late. Urs App has usefully recorded that Schopenhauer's personal copy indicates that he received it from the Librarian at the St. Petersburg Academy in 1860.[26] This accords with the absence of any notes to the text in Schopenhauer's *Nachlass* and only two references in his published works, both late and handwritten (WWR1, 439; WWR2, 288). These references indicate that the main idea that Schopenhauer carried over from Schmidt's treatise was the notion of an "essence in itself of all things" that transcends the division into subject and object, and is therefore "beyond all cognition" (WWR2, 288). It would be implausible to maintain, given Schopenhauer's late encounter with the treatise, that he *derived* this idea from Schmidt's work. However, his citations signify that his encounter with it merged with and confirmed key trends in his later thought, specifically that of the nothing that characterizes the condition of the ascetic.

Schmidt's treatise is a compound of elements: it reproduces the Tibetan text of his manuscript of the *Diamond-Sūtra*, followed by a German translation; there is also a translation of a Tibetan primer summarizing Buddhist doctrine, along with Schmidt's own general exposition of Mahāyāna religious philosophy. Schmidt's account of Mahāyāna is not rigorously derived from his translation of the *Diamond-Sūtra*, for the latter's account of *prajñāpāramitā* does not support Schmidt's gloss that it consists of the view that "only the greater unity outside of the borders of nature, in which every ego disappears, this Beyond all Knowledge [*prajñāpāramitā*], is to be accepted as true and unmistakable being."[27] The *Sūtra* itself makes no reference to true being beyond nature, but confines itself to applying a deconstructive logic to all phenomena, followed by an affirmation of their conventional existence. Shigenori Nagatomo describes this procedure as a "logic of not," which he formalizes as "A is not A, therefore it is A." This may, *prima facie*, appear to be a nonsensical statement, but as Nagatomo contends, "to understand it properly… one must read it by effecting a perspectival shift to a non-dualistic, non-egological stance. Only then can one see that it is not contradictory, and hence that it is not nonsensical."[28]

The non-dual, "non-egological stance" to which Nagatomo refers is the Buddhist teaching that subjects and objects are empty (*śūnya*) of an inherent, self-defining nature (*svabhāva*).[29] The first part of the *Sūtra's* logic—A is not A—negates the common view that the objects of sense are self-grounding substances or Selves, negation of which is the ultimate truth (*paramārtha-satya*). The second part—therefore it is A—affirms the existence of subjects and objects on the level of conventional truth (*samvṛti-satya*), as empty assemblages of changing elements, which is the perspective that the Bodhisattva must assume toward them in order to fulfill his vow to "liberate all of these aggregates from misery without remainder."[30] The Bodhisattva entertains both perspectives simultaneously, taking his stance on the field of emptiness, beyond subject and object, in which phenomena are indistinguishable and hence non-dual, while recognizing on a conventional level that these aggregates experience themselves as suffering beings in need of deliverance. In Schmidt's translation, the Buddha teaches his disciple Rabdschor (Skt. Subhūti) "that which is called living beings, Deshinschegpa [Skt. *Tathāgata*] has declared as non-beings [A is not A]; this is why they are called 'the living beings [therefore it is A].'"[31] The Bodhisattvas' ability to move between the ultimate perspective of emptiness and the conventional truth of suffering aggregates parallels, to an extent, Schopenhauer's 1818 conception of two states of nothing that are relative to one another—one vain, the other nothing, as outlined in the previous section.

It is nevertheless a tribute to Schmidt's conscientiousness that the *Sūtra's* studied avoidance of transcendent speculation comes across even in his German translation, but his exposition of the main principles of Mahāyāna tends to steer his readers toward a specific interpretation of the *Sūtra's* enigmatic dialectic. One might be tempted to argue that Schmidt projected his Christian presuppositions onto a non-theistic text when he remarked that, for Buddhists, "the fullness of the godhead resides in the beyond of human knowledge."[32] This, however, would be unfair, for as with any religious tradition, Buddhism as a living practice does not fully inhere within its scriptures: these are always interpreted within the context of a commentarial tradition that takes its bearings from the metaphysical assumptions of a particular school. As Paul Williams notes,

> Buddhist texts were intended as no more than mnemonic devices, scaffolding, the framework for textual exposition by a teacher in terms of his own experience and also the tradition, the lineage transmission from his teachers, traced back to the Buddha himself, or to *a* Buddha, or to some other form of authorized spiritual revelation. This approach to, and treatment of, the sacred text in Buddhism is not only of historical interest. In traditional Mahāyāna cultures, particularly among the Tibetans, these texts are still used and studied in the age-old way. The scholar who would write a study of Buddhist practice or even doctrine without bearing this in mind is like an art historian who would study architecture by ignoring the building and looking only at the bricks![33]

The lineage from which Schmidt obtained his manuscript of the *Diamond-Sūtra* was Tibetan Vajrayāna, a school that posits an innate, non-dual Buddha-nature in all beings, so that *prajñāpāramitā* constitutes the realization that one has been, always already, enlightened. Its philosophical underpinnings were derived from the Indian Mahāyāna school known variously as *Yogācāra*, *Cittamātra* (Mind-Only), or *Vijñānavāda* (The Way of Consciousness), which developed its doctrines in response to the emptiness (*śūnyatā*) school of Madhyamaka. The Yogācārins concurred with Madhyamaka that objects and subjects of experience are void or empty of self-nature, but objected that the theater in which phenomena arise and pass away must have inherent existence. They identified this with the non-dual consciousness experienced in yogic trance, in which there is merely a flow of phenomena, with no awareness of a self or subject within the flow that might be opposed to an object. This they named the *param-ālaya*, or "abode beyond," which when corrupted appears as the *ālaya-vijñāna*, or storehouse consciousness, in which resides the seeds that ripen as karmic fruits and perpetuate the round of *saṃsāra*. *Prajñāpāramitā*, the condition beyond all knowledge, occurs when the mind realizes that phenomena are nothing but mental constructs, which thereby effects a return to "the ultimate source of mind or consciousness, which is in itself empty of all natures and features."[34]

The metaphysics of Yogācāra pervades Schmidt's commentary on the *Diamond-Sūtra*, although it ought to be emphasized that, for Tibetan Vajrayāna, the Buddha-Nature is a monist principle or "*immanent presence* in reality,"[35] rather than a transcendent abstraction. This does not come across in Schmidt's fairly gnostic and dualist account of Mahāyāna, according to which Buddhas and Bodhisattvas are docetic appearances of a "hidden godhead," appearing in physical nature to liberate "spirits captured within the bonds of matter."[36] Schmidt maintained that the "idea that threads the system [Mahāyāna] together cohesively" is that "the indwelling spirit [*Geist*] of matter does not belong to the living organism, but to the godhead hidden in abstraction, because like this, it is eternal, immaterial and immutable in essence, and is thus willingly assimilated into and absorbed by it, as a related and constituent part."[37] This sounds very much like the mythic and meaningless notion of reabsorption into the primal spirit, which Schopenhauer in 1818 regarded as an evasion of "that nothing that hovers behind all virtue and holiness as the final goal" (WWR1, 439).

The treatise nevertheless indicates that Schopenhauer and Schmidt were in agreement on the origin and nature of religion, for Schmidt similarly traced religions to something akin to Schopenhauer's metaphysical need, stating that it is "not sufficient for the human mind to remain within the authorized limits of its intuition; the feeling of its overly narrow margin drives [*treibt*] it over these limits."[38] And, like Schopenhauer, Schmidt regarded Buddhism as one of the foremost attempts to satisfy this drive (WWR2, 178), commenting that "among the many philosophical systems, from grey antiquity up to our days, all owe their existence to mental efforts of which Buddhism occupies the first place."[39] However, whereas Schopenhauer regarded monotheism as a minority (FR, 118) and dispensable faith (WWR2, 170–71), and located metaphysical need in wonder and distress (WWR2, 180), Schmidt traced the quest for metaphysical meaning to the universal question, "what and where is god?"[40]

It is likely that Schopenhauer would have taken Schmidt's suggestion that Buddhism was motivated by an alleged universal quest for god with a grain of salt, for he habitually distinguished Buddhists from other mystics who "mean *nirvāṇa* by the name God" and thereby "relate more than they could know, which the *Buddhists* do not do; hence their *Nirvāṇa* is merely a relative nothing" (PP2, 94). Indeed, Schopenhauer often referred to Schmidt's works in support of his view that Buddhism was atheistic, insofar as "[t]he writings of the Buddhists lack any positive indication of a supreme being as the principle of creation" (FR, 119). This suggests that, for Schopenhauer, a necessary condition of monotheism was a doctrine of creation out of nothing, which Schmidt consistently emphasized was absent from Buddhism. In his treatise on the *Diamond-Sūtra*, Schmidt noted that the "creation of worlds and their different regions is not at all regarded as an act of the highest divine essence," but proceeds or emanates (*ausgang*) "from the fragmentation of mind [*Geistheit*]" into a plurality of individual egos on contact with matter. And whereas Schopenhauer stressed that monotheism proper was obliged to regard creation as a gift, "πάντα καλὰ λίαν" (PP2, 271), Schmidt observed that "according to the main teaching of Buddhism, in the connection between spirit and matter that issues in creation, there lies only disaster and ruin."[41]

Schmidt's Yogācāra-inspired account of the world's emanation from fragmented mind would possibly have struck Schopenhauer as a religious and hence *sensu allegorico* version of his theory that the world as representation arises when "the *one* eye of the world that gazes out from all cognizing creatures" carves up the thing-in-itself in accordance with the principle of sufficient reason (WWR1, 221). For, central to Schmidt's exposition of Mahāyāna was that the world of sense-experience, and everything conditioned by "materialistic-consequent reason," is "empty [*leer*] and void [*nichtig*]."[42] The same claim is stated in poetic fashion in Schmidt's translation of the *Sūtra*, when the Buddha describes objects of sense using imagery that resonates with Schopenhauer's own figurative descriptions of the phenomenon.

> Consider all things and any accumulation (issuing from essence) like the covering of the stars, like a lamp, like an optical illusion (word-jugglery), like the thaw, like a water-bubble, like a dream, like a weather-light (lightning-flash), like the clouds![43]

However, the subtle balance between two opposed but relative states—one painful but vain (*Nichtigkeit*) and the other painless but nothing (*Nichts*)—that characterized Schopenhauer's conception of nothing in 1818, contrasts with Schmidt's presentation of Mahāyāna's opposition between the "apparent being of the forms and shapes of the world of appearance (phenomena)" and the "true immutable being" that lies beyond subject and object in *prajñāpāramitā*.[44] Schmidt would thereby have been instrumental in confirming the validity of Schopenhauer's post-1818 conviction that the condition of the saint or Bodhisattva is a relative nothing in an epistemological sense, insofar as the ascetic passes "into the incomprehensible and fathomless fullness of the immaterial, simple abstraction of the divine being."[45]

22.3 SCHOPENHAUER ON ABSOLUTE AND RELATIVE NOTHING: POST-1818

Although it cannot be claimed that Schmidt's *Diamond-Sūtra* influenced Schopenhauer's intellectual development, his 1860 citation to Schmidt's treatise on *prajñāpāramitā* at the close of his first work indicates the direction in which Schopenhauer had been revising his key concepts after 1818. This project of revision evidently began early, in response to the few reviews of his chief work, but especially that by Johann Friedrich Herbart published in 1820.[46] Herbart was the first to articulate a set of objections to Schopenhauer's system that have since become standard in the literature: concerning the inconsistency of Schopenhauer's self-identification as a Kantian, who nevertheless assumes to know the thing-in-itself;[47] and the problem of understanding how the original freedom of the will can break into the order of determined phenomenal causes.[48] Both objections relate to the compatibility between Schopenhauer's concepts of "will" and "nothing."

Schopenhauer's *Nachlass* evidences his immediate concern with these criticisms: in a note from late 1820 he considered the idea, later aired publicly in 1844 (WWR2, 209), that the will merely appears as thing-in-itself in the phenomenon, but may have other aspects unknowable to us (MR3, 41). This line of thought became clearer in a note from 1829, where it is tied into the soteriological concept of nothing that closed his first work.

> I have, of course, declared this will to be the thing-in-itself, yet not absolutely, but only in so far as the thing-in-itself is to be named after its most immediate phenomenal appearance and accordingly the extreme boundary-stone of our knowledge is to be found in the will. When subsequently I represent this will as abolishing itself, then here I have expressly stated that the nothing that is left for us is only a relative and not an absolute nothing. From this it is obvious enough that that which abolishes itself as will must yet have another existence wholly inaccessible to our knowledge, and this would then be simply the existence of the thing-in-itself.   (MR3, 595)

Schopenhauer's further ruminations on these themes did not appear in his next publication, *On Will in Nature* of 1836, which contained no new elaboration of his metaphysics, but a motley assemblage of alleged empirical confirmations of it. These new developments made their first appearance in 1844, in the second edition of *The World as Will and Representation*, accompanied by supplementary essays larger than the original work. The expanded material also indicated the extent of Schopenhauer's engagement with mystical religious literature between 1818 and 1844, including Schmidt's works on Buddhism. The work contains the aforementioned qualifications of his original statement that the will is the thing-in-itself, and what occurs in its denial. Schopenhauer still made a point of the immanence of his philosophy, which "sticks to the facts of outer and inner experience, as they are accessible to everyone" (WWR2, 657), so that his soteriology can only positively indicate "what is denied, surrendered" and hence "needs...to describe as *nothing* what is thereby gained or grasped" (WWR2, 627). One might contend that the suggestion that there is a something to be "gained and grasped" after the will's abolition is already straying beyond facts accessible to everyone, but Schopenhauer goes further by adding the consolation that

> ... this still does not mean that it is absolutely nothing, that it has to be nothing from every possible perspective and in every possible sense; but only that we are restricted to a wholly negative cognition of it, due very probably to the restrictions of our standpoint. —But this is precisely where the mystic proceeds positively; from this point onwards, nothing remains but mysticism." (WWR2, 627)

This recognition of mysticism does not amount to a literal validation of its propositions, since the intuitions of mystics are grounded in individual rather than common experience, and their statements impossible, insofar as they aim to pass beyond wisdom or knowledge and express the inexpressible (WWR2, 626): as such, mystical propositions will still be "myths and meaningless words" (WWR1, 439). However, the quote above concedes a positive proceeding to the mystical quest that was absent in 1818, and moreover indicates how Schopenhauer's soteriological concept of nothing surreptitiously moved its focus from the opposed perspectives denoted by a *nihil privativum*, to the epistemological contrast between an absolute and relative nothing.

The possibility that there may be an unknowable entity prior to the will soon began to appear in Schopenhauer's works as *philosophical knowledge*, without reference to mysticism. In his last work of 1851, *Parerga and Paralipomena*, he maintained against "certain silly objections" that "the *negation of the will to life* in no way signifies the annihilation of a substance," and posited a prior, transcendent subject for which willing and not-willing are equal options, and which is consequently therefore "not annihilated by one or the other act" (PP2, 281).

Although these qualifications of his originally bold claim that the will is the thing-in-itself, and its negation nothing, enabled Schopenhauer to bypass the objections of critics and find in mysticism an independent confirmation of his soteriology, they unintentionally produced an imbalance in the explanatory power of his philosophy. This is because, as Schopenhauer often pointed out, the strength of his original statement resided in its ability to acknowledge the reality of evil and suffering without resorting to Ptolemaic epicycles, such as evil as non-being, the will's indifferent freedom, or a historical Fall of a Primal Man. By contrast, almost all other systems have optimistically but naïvely deduced the world of finite squalor from an infinite principle of perfection and plenitude. But, having done so, they have been immediately confronted by

> ... the question of the origin of evil, of the monstrous, nameless evil, of the horrible, heart-rending misery in the world, and to settle such a costly account they become dumb or have nothing but words—empty, sonorous words. In contrast, if the existence of evil is already woven together with that of the world in the foundation of a system, then it need not fear this spectre, just as a vaccinated child need not fear

smallpox. But this is the case if freedom is placed in the "being" [*esse*] instead of the "acting" [*operari*] and then from freedom proceed wickedness, evil, and the world.

(WN, 444)

But if the will does not possess original aseity, but is merely thing-in-itself in relation to appearance, and beyond all knowledge there is an inscrutable subject, originally indifferent to willing and not-willing, whence evil and suffering? The wickedness, evil and suffering of willing seem to have been relegated to the status of contingent effects of this subject's action or *operari*, as opposed to proceeding from the *esse* of the world. This transcendent subject definitely lacks the "inner conflict with itself" that characterized the will as thing-in-itself of the first volume (WWR1, 381), and that so readily accounted for the war of all against all observed in the phenomenon. By seeking to iron out contradictions in one part of his system, Schopenhauer's late reinterpretation of his concepts of will and nothing opened up a gap elsewhere.

22.4 CONCLUSION

One might regard the conceptual and explanatory problems that this chapter has traced from Schopenhauer's early statement in 1818 up to his closing modification in 1860 as insoluble, and perhaps inherent in the very project of combining a positive metaphysic with a soteriology. This is because a metaphysic that traces the world to an original pristine principle faces the difficulty of explaining why we need to be saved. Christianity has struggled with Adam's Fall from the goodness of his original nature into Original Sin, just as Yogācāra has struggled to explain how the original, non-dual *param-ālaya* manifested itself as a world of subject-object cognition and conventionally suffering beings. Even Schmidt observed in relation to Buddhism that the "gap in the system, the open question, concerns the infinite fragmentation of a multiplicity of minds or one mind into the forms of matter: from whence did this multiplicity or fragmentation *originally* arise?"[49] The *Laṅkāvatāra-Sūtra*, deeply influenced by Yogācāra, attempted to seal this gap by likening the *param-ālaya* to an ocean with still depths, and *saṃsāra* to waves moving on its surface, "stirred uninterruptedly by the wind of objectivity."[50] However, if the original mind is the still ocean, and the waves the round of *saṃsāra*, what is the wind? It appears to be an external element, so that Yogācāra's attempt to establish a positive monism to match its soteriology, passes over into a dualism.

But if Christianity and Yogācāra failed to explain why we need to be saved, Schopenhauer's early statement of his system suffered from the opposite problem—of explaining how we might be saved, given that the essence of self and world is omnipotent will. This is the weak point on which Herbart focused in his review, and which has recently motivated more recent qualifications of the status of the will by Young and Atwell. In response to Herbart's criticisms, Schopenhauer subtly modified his key concepts "will" and "nothing", drawing the former into the background and foregrounding the latter, now taken as merely a negation of our modes of cognition. But by so doing, he introduced a dissonance elsewhere in his system concerning evil, of which he seemed to remain oblivious. These movements back and forth recall Schopenhauer's own, early, critical commentary on the history of Christian theodicy, spinning "in an endless circle by trying to bring these things into harmony, i.e. to solve the arithmetical problem that never works out but whose remainder appears sometimes here, sometimes there, after it has been hidden elsewhere" (WWR1, 434n.).

NOTES

1. D. W. Hamlyn, *Schopenhauer* (London: Routledge & Kegan Paul, 1980), 92–102; 149–55. Robert Wicks, *Schopenhauer's "The World as Will and Representation" – A Reader's Guide* (London & New York: Continuum, 2011), 80; 142–46.
2. Wicks, *Schopenhauer's "The World as Will and Representation,"* 143.
3. Hamlyn, *Schopenhauer*, 155.
4. Julian Young, *Willing and Unwilling: A Study in the Philosophy of Arthur Schopenhauer* (Dordrecht: Martinus Nijhoff, 1987), 31–32.
5. J. E. Atwell, *Schopenhauer on the Character of the World: The Metaphysics of Will* (Berkeley/Los Angeles: University of California Press, 1995), 126.
6. Young, *Willing and Unwilling*, 34.
7. Ibid., 131.
8. Ibid., 130.
9. This passage is reiterated in WWR2 (1844) from Schopenhauer's manuscript notes (see MR3, 40–41 [HN,36]) written down no later than 1821. See later discussion.
10. A Sanskrit term usually translated as "emptiness."
11. A Sanskrit term often translated as "perfection of wisdom," but the original is closer to Schmidt's "beyond all knowledge": a more accurate translation might be "wisdom [*prajñā*] gone beyond [*pāramitā*]."
12. For a comprehensive account of what has become known as the *nirvāṇa* controversy in nineteenth-century European scholarship on Buddhism, see Guy Richard Welbon, *The Buddhist Nirvāṇa and its Western Interpreters* (Chicago: University of Chicago Press, 1968).
13. Isaak Jacob Schmidt, "Über das Mahâjâna und Pradschnâ-Pâramita der Bauddhen," in *Mémoires de l'Académie Impériale des Sciences de St. Pétersbourg*, VI:4 (St. Petersburg: l'Académie Impériale des Sciences, 1840), 123–228.
14. Ibid., 224. Translations from Schmidt's works are the author's own.
15. Friedrich Nietzsche, *On the Genealogy of Morality*, translated by Carol Diethe (Cambridge: Cambridge University Press, 2006), II.13, 53.
16. Moira Nicholls, "The Influences of Eastern Thought on Schopenhauer's Doctrine of the Thing-in-Itself", in *The Cambridge Companion to Schopenhauer*, edited by Christopher Janaway (Cambridge: Cambridge University Press, 1999), 194.
17. The term used in the 1818 and 1844 editions of the first volume, replaced by *Brahma* only in the third of 1859 (see the editorial comment in WWR1, 590).
18. Urs App, "The Tibet of the Philosophers: Kant, Hegel, Schopenhauer," in *Images of Tibet in the 19th and 20th Centuries*, edited by Monica Esposito (Paris: EFEO, 2008), 57n.214.
19. Immanuel Kant, *Critique of Pure Reason*, A292/B348, translated by Paul Guyer and Allen Wood (Cambridge: Cambridge University Press, 1998), 383.

20. Plato, *Sophist*, 259a-b, translated by Nicholas P. White, in *Plato: Complete Works*, edited by J. M. Cooper (Indianapolis/Cambridge: Hackett Publishing Company, 1997), 282.

21. See Friedrich Nietzsche, *The Birth of Tragedy* (1872), §3.

22. See the editorial comment in WWR2, 671. '

23. Eugène Burnouf, *Introduction to the History of Indian Buddhism*, translated by Katia Buffetrille and Donald S. Lopez Jr. (Chicago/London: The University of Chicago Press, 2010), 146.

24. Ibid., 539; Schmidt, "Über das Mahâjâna und Pradschnâ-Pâramita der Bauddhen," 187.

25. For the original footnote from 1836, see FR 458.

26. See Urs App, "Schopenhauers Begegnung mit dem Buddhismus," *Schopenhauer-Jahrbuch* 79 (1998), 51.

27. Schmidt, "Über das Mahâjâna und Pradschnâ-Pâramita der Bauddhen," 213.

28. Shigenori Nagatomo, "The Logic of the *Diamond Sūtra*: A is not A, therefore it is A," *Asian Philosophy* 10, no. 3 (2000), 213.

29. Although it is a unique feature of the *Diamond-Sūtra* that it is the only scripture in the voluminous Mahāyāna literature on *prajñāpāramitā* that contains no explicit discourse on emptiness (*śūnyatā*), and never even mentions the term.

30. Schmidt, "Über das Mahâjâna und Pradschnâ-Pâramita der Bauddhen," 187.

31. Ibid., 206.

32. Ibid., 223.

33. Paul Williams, *Mahāyāna Buddhism: The Doctrinal Foundations* (London and New York: Routledge, 1989), 38.

34. Stephen J. Laumakis, *An Introduction to Buddhist Philosophy* (Cambridge: Cambridge University Press, 2008), 243.

35. Douglas Duckworth, "Tibetan Mahāyāna and Vajrayāna", in *A Companion to Buddhist Philosophy*, edited by Steven M. Emmanuel (Chichester: Wiley Blackwell, 2013), 104.

36. Schmidt, "Über das Mahâjâna und Pradschnâ-Pâramita der Bauddhen," 222.

37. Ibid., 225.

38. Ibid., 222.

39. Ibid., 223.

40. Ibid., 222.

41. Ibid., 124.

42. Ibid., 220. A phrase that recalls Schopenhauer's principle of sufficient reason and the essential relativity of its objects.

43. Ibid., 212.

44. Ibid., 220.

45. Ibid., 224.

46. Johann Friedrich Herbart, *Rezension der Welt als Wille und Vorstellung*, in *Hermes oder Kritisches Jahrbuch der Literatur*. Drittes Stück für das Jahr 1820, Nr. 7, 131–47. Reprinted in *Jahrbuch der Schopenhauer-Gesellschft* 6 (1917), 89–117.

47. *Jahrbuch* reprint, 109.

48. Ibid., 113.

49. Schmidt, "Über das Mahâjâna und Pradschnâ-Pâramita der Bauddhen," 226.

50. *The Laṅkāvatāra-Sūtra: A Mahāyāna Text*, translated by D. T. Suzuki (London: George Routledge & Sons Ltd., 1932), 40.

FURTHER READING

App, Urs. "The Tibet of the Philosophers: Kant, Hegel, Schopenhauer." In *Images of Tibet in the 19th and 20th Centuries*, edited by Monica Esposito. Paris: EFEO, 2008, 5–60.

Duckworth, Douglas. "Tibetan Mahāyāna and Vajrayāna." In *A Companion to Buddhist Philosophy*, edited by Steven M. Emmanuel. Chichester: Wiley Blackwell, 2013, 99–109.

Laumakis, Stephen J. *An Introduction to Buddhist Philosophy*. Cambridge: Cambridge University Press, 2008.

Nagatomo, Shigenori. "The Logic of the *Diamond Sūtra*: A is not A, therefore it is A." *Asian Philosophy* 10, no. 3 (2000): 213–244.

Nicholls, Moira. "The Influences of Eastern Thought on Schopenhauer's Doctrine of the Thing-in-Itself." In *The Cambridge Companion to Schopenhauer*, edited by Christopher Janaway. Cambridge: Cambridge University Press, 1999, 171–212.

Schmidt, Isaak Jacob. "Über das Mahâjâna und Pradschnâ-Pâramita der Bauddhen." In *Mémoires de l'Académie Impériale des Sciences de St. Pétersbourg*, VI:4. St. Petersburg: l'Académie Impériale des Sciences, 1840, 123–228.

Welbon, Guy Richard. *The Buddhist Nirvāṇa and its Western Interpreters*. Chicago: The University of Chicago Press, 1968.

Williams, Paul. *Mahāyāna Buddhism: The Doctrinal Foundations*. London/New York: Routledge, 1989.

CHAPTER 23

....

SCHOPENHAUER AND
HINDU THOUGHT

....

R. RAJ SINGH

SCHOPENHAUER's philosophy shows a remarkable connection with Hindu and Buddhist thought systems. Through his rigorous studies of Eastern philosophy and religious texts available in his times, he became increasingly appreciative of the relevance of Indian thought for philosophy in general. Indeed, he was one of the first European philosophers to show a consistent appreciation of the role of Indian thought, and he endeavored to incorporate many of its concepts into his own system.

Despite the indisputable evidence of the influence of Hindu and Buddhist thought on Schopenhauer's philosophy and his creative amalgamation of Western and Eastern concepts within his own metaphysical system, the study of these influences has received only a scanty and casual attention from the various Schopenhauer scholars of our times. This neglect of the Eastern dimension of this thinker's work has also resulted in several misunderstandings of his basic standpoints and has greatly contributed to some extreme assessments of his pessimistic outlook. A lack of study of his Eastern sources makes Schopenhauer more pessimistic and outlandish than he actually might be.

This chapter begins with a brief account of Schopenhauer's connections with Eastern thought in his early and later writings.[1] We also take stock of the remarkably different approach that Schopenhauer had toward the role of Indian thought in European philosophy and consider why his approach toward Eastern philosophy is different from that of other German thinkers of his times who also had an abiding interest in Indian thought (some of whom became full-fledged Indologists). The Romantic thinkers like J. G. Herder (1744–1803), Friedrich Schlegel (1772–1829) and his brother Wilhelm Schlegel (1767–1845), as well as G. W. F. Hegel (1770–1831) and F. W. J. Schelling (1775–1854) were some of the leading figures in German philosophy who wrote about Indian thought approvingly or critically in their own original manners.

Second, after a brief history of Schopenhauer's engagement with Indian thought and a brief inquiry regarding his distinctive approach toward it, we will focus on the content of his actual treatment of Hindu thought within his works. Without going into the futile controversies on whether he preferred Buddhism over Hinduism and how he supposedly modified his standpoints in the light of his advanced studies of Eastern materials in his later works, we will concentrate on the issue of how his philosophical work reflects and treats some of the critical concepts and outlooks of various Hindu thought systems. This is not to deny or minimize the deep impact of Buddhism on his thought. A study of Schopenhauer's connections with Buddhist thought is equally valuable for a fuller understanding of his philosophical standpoints.

Third, some issues will be raised and pursued concerning Schopenhauer's interpretations of Indian thought as well as the role played by the Eastern ways of thinking in his own thought system. Some of the major problems to be discussed are (a) Did Schopenhauer know the fundamentals of Vedanta and Buddhism deeply and comprehensively enough prior to the publication of the first edition of *The World as Will and Representation* (1818) in order for us to conclude that these Eastern philosophies influenced the first enunciation of his metaphysical system? (b) If Schopenhauer's study of the Eastern texts available in Europe grew gradually through his career, what impact did this renewed scholarship had on his later works? (c) Was Schopenhauer's exposition of Vedantic and Buddhist thought comprehensive enough or reasonable enough for his day and age, given that the translated texts were still far fewer and more limited than today? (d) Did Schopenhauer misuse Eastern concepts to serve his own standpoints in philosophy, in particular, to revalidate his pessimistic worldview? (e) Since the relation between Schopenhauer's philosophy in Indian thought is still an uncharted territory in the current secondary literature, what kinds of misinterpretations of this thinker's concepts and standpoints have taken place typically among the modern scholars of his work?

23.1 SCHOPENHAUER AND GERMAN INDOLOGY

To understand Schopenhauer's connection with Indian thought, it is important to examine the growing interest in India and Indian thought that is discernible among the German thinkers of the late eighteenth and early nineteenth centuries. This spadework in the field of Indology provided a fertile ground for the growth of Schopenhauer's own passion for Indian thought. As early as in 1813, he attended the lectures of Friedrich Majer (1771–1818) and responded to them in his intellectual diary. Majer was himself influenced by J. G. Herder, who had overseen some German translations of Indian texts appearing in English, French, and Latin, as Wilhelm Halbfass informs us in his scholarly study, *India and Europe*.[2] The motivation regarding self-criticism—criticisms of Christianity along with the issues of common origins of mankind—characterized the romantic awareness of India and the Orient. Herder was a pioneer of the Romantic Movement in general, but was particularly responsible for popularizing the awareness of India within the Romantic Movement. Herder was impressed with the idea that

Oriental thought had its own, autonomous structures in the Oriental world and represented Europe's childhood. He described the core of Hindu thought as follows: "the idea of one Being in and behind all that there is, the idea of the unity of all things in the absolute, in God."[3]

Herder was, however, critical of the impact of the caste system on the free evolution of the arts and of the myth of metempsychosis, which, in his view, promoted compassion for all living things but lessened sympathy with the sufferings of fellow human beings. Thus he recognized the preeminence of Christianity over India and the Orient since only Christianity was "the religion of purest humanity." Nevertheless, "India became the focal point of an enthusiastic interest, occasionally bordering on fanaticism, within the German Romantic movement. Many authors developed detailed opinions about Indian thought more or less independently of one another, including Schelling, Novalis, Görres, Cruzer, Goethe, Claudius, and, more than any of the others, the Schlegel Brothers. Majer served as a catalyst through the translations he made, and…also helped in shaping Schopenhauer's interest in India."[4]

G. W. F. Hegel (1770–1831) and F. W. J. Schelling (1775–1854) were other significant figures among Schopenhauer's contemporaries who made their original philosophical analysis of Indian thought. Hegel and Schelling were fellow students and roommates at the University of Tübingen and were close friends, until a doctrinal split happened between them. Hegel's forays into Indian thought did not evoke any interest or approval from Indological scholars. In the words of Helmuth von Glasenapp, "Hegel was a bookman, living in a world of abstractions speculations.…He was the prototype of a westerner, who saw western thought as the measure of all things.…Therefore, whatever he knew to say about the Indian world, turned out to be very insufficient, and the result was a caricature."[5]

Hegel, as a critic of the Romantic movement, was also committed to an irreversible direction of history and necessarily judged the past from the standpoint of the present. All antiquity had to be a state of infancy in contrast to the present matured state of the spirit of world history that has accomplished greater richness and complexity. Unlike the Romantics, he did not engage in the glorifications of origins and early stages. The orient might be the *Morganland* (morningland) of early origins and childhood, but the West cannot and need not return to it, says Hegel in his *Philosophy of World History* as well as in his *The History of Philosophy*. Hegel was not an Indologist like the Schlegel brothers; he had no knowledge of Sanskrit and relied on translations of the Indian texts. Although he read some of the latest secondary literature on Indian thought (e.g., by the likes of H. Th. Colebrooke and P. Buchanan), he did not gain detailed knowledge of the six classical systems of Hindu thought such as Samkhya and Nayaya. His basis for the study of Indian thought was Vedanta in general (i.e., selections from the Vedas and Upanishads and through study of the *Bhagvadgita*). He wrote almost 100 pages in review of W. Von Humboldt's essay on the *Bhagvadgita*.[6] He also maintained that the "Orient is the beginning.…The way of the *Weltgeist* (world spirit) leads from East to the West. The Occident supersedes the Orient."[7]

For Hegel, Indian philosophy is inseparable from religion, and Hinduism is the prototype of the "religion of substance," lacking in transcendence. Pure substance means indeterminate being-in-itself, which is exactly what Hegel finds in the Indian conception of *Brahman*: it is formless, indeterminate, unspeakable, and unthinkable. An attempt to describe or think it will lead away from it. Although the Indian mind has thus found its way to the One and the universal, which Hegel considers as the true ground of religion and philosophy, he also believes that Indian thought has not found its way back to the concrete particularity of the world.[8]

Schopenhauer's contemptuous remarks on Hegel and Hegel's philosophy are well known, and his imbalanced invectives against Hegel constitute one of his low points. He described Hegel as "a crude charlatan" and his philosophy as a "confused empty verbiage."[9] Such harsh words were certainly spoken out of a personal dislike as well as due to clear-cut doctrinal differences, for Schopenhauer's philosophy is remarkably free of any acknowledgment of historicality and his metaphysical system is supposedly equally applicable to all periods of history. Historical and cultural differences do not affect the validity of the connection between the human entity and the will-to-live. In Hegel, however, the historical evolution of the world-spirit (*Weltgeist*) is an important factor, and, according to him, modern Western philosophy is a matured version of all ancient philosophies including ancient Indian philosophy, which has failed in producing its own matured stage as it continues to function as a bunch of eternal verities. Thus he refers to Indian thought as constituting the childhood of the world-spirit, whereas the modern Western philosophy represents its full maturity. Oriental thought remains at a static and petrified state, whereas modern Western thought supersedes the Orient through a useful, new, more developed, and comprehensive stage.

There is no such Hegelian conception in Schopenhauer's view of Indian thought. He does not regard it as an infantile version of modernity but approaches it as a fully comparable storehouse of ancient wisdom whose ideas are still applicable and valuable in discovering the true nature of the will-to-live. It may also be noted that Hegel primarily relied on Indian sources pertaining to Vedanta (i.e., the insights of Vedas and Upanishads). He does not comment on the six philosophical systems of Hinduism, regarding which he learned only at the end of his career. He also had hardly any familiarity with or commentary on Buddhism. In this respect Schopenhauer, being eighteen years younger than Hegel, had more access to the sources of the six systems and also of Buddhism which exercised a major influence on his thought.

F. W. J. Schelling (1775–1854), who was initially a good friend of Hegel and later a vehement critic of Hegelianism, offered an analysis of Indian thought in his *Philosophy of Mythology* (1842). In this book, Schelling has extensive sections on India and other Eastern traditions, although his analyses are done from a critical standpoint. He, however, shows a clear-cut commitment to Christian revelation.[10] Schelling developed the idea of the world as a falling off (*Abfall*) from the Absolute and calls the Absolute the only reality and finite things as lacking in reality, somewhat like the Vedantic notion of the world as *maya*. He refers to the etymological connection between *maya* and *magia* (or magic) as well as with *Macht* (power and *Moglichkeit* or potentiality). He also calls Vedanta as "nothing but the most exalted Idealism or spiritualism." However, Schelling found in the Upanishads "a very unsatisfactory reading" because in them "a positive explanation of the supreme unity is not found anywhere." Halbfass remarks that Schelling's response to Indian thought is not that of a neutral scholar, but just like Hegel's, "a philosophically and theologically committed response."[11] Schelling is clearly fascinated with *Advaita Vedanta*, which he calls the Indian system of absolute identity, "the highest point to which idealism could rise without proper revelation."[12] Thus, we may notice that Schopenhauer was more of a neutral scholar without any theological commitments to Christian revelation or monotheism. The Upanishads to him were the "most elevating reading" and not unsatisfactory due to their lack of monotheism, as they were for Schelling.

23.2 SCHOPENHAUER AND INDIAN THOUGHT

Schopenhauer's numerous references and elucidations of Indian thought in the three editions of *The World as Will and Representation* and in his later works show a unique harmony between a modern system of Western philosophy and ancient Eastern thought. Indeed the way some Indian philosophical concepts are incorporated in Schopenhauer's own work shows a deep-seated conviction that various philosophies of the world, both ancient and modern, are outcomes of the same human quest to fathom the perennial issues of being, existence, world, and reality. It also shows that Schopenhauer himself was continually searching for Eastern terms comparable to his own basic concepts such as the will-to-live, denial-of-the-will, *principium individuationis*, etc. perhaps without success of finding the exact equivalents. However, the process of such comparisons seems to have delivered its own rewards and contributed to the originality of his system.

Whether Schopenhauer freely adopted the Indian concepts in his writings or used them to reauthenticate his already developed concepts of the will-to-live and its denial, one thing is certain: no other Western philosopher had studied, elucidated, and incorporated into his own system Indian philosophies as vigorously as he did. He did not subscribe to the usual notion that Indian philosophy is inseparable from religion, the kind of view held by Hegel, but seems to regard the philosophies of the world as one body of knowledge in which the systems of Hindu thought and Buddhism hold their distinctive place. It was a remarkably bold step by a Western philosopher in his day and age, when Eastern philosophies were still barely known and their texts were inadequately translated. Although Schopenhauer recognizes the loftiness of the New Testament Christianity in providing a thoughtful worldview, he never regarded Vedanta and Buddhism as inferior or less-developed in contrast to a supposed superior and fully matured status of the Christian worldview—a tendency that is clearly visible in the writings of several Indologists and Indian philosophy scholars of the times, including Schlegel, Schelling, and Hegel.

With respect to the connection of Schopenhauer's philosophy with Eastern thought, a question is bound to arise. Do Vedanta and Buddhism really contain the elements of pessimism and extreme asceticism that Schopenhauer's philosophy seems to uphold at first sight? How exactly did he match his own concepts with the classical notions of Indian thought such as *brahman, atman, samsara, maya, trsna, upadana,* etc.? Were Schopenhauer's interpretations of Indian thought good enough, even for his age? Did he twist, turn, and simplify perennial Indian concepts to match his own terms and preoccupations? Some of these and similar questions are posed and analyzed by Wilhelm Halbfass in his *India and Europe.*

Halbfass points out that responding to these questions is not an easy matter. In view of Schopenhauer's own ongoing quest to match his own concepts with Indian ideas and the search for exact equivalents—a quest that is recorded in his handwritten intellectual diaries compiled in *Handschriftlichen Nachlass* and his letters compiled in *Gesammelte Briefe,* as well as in his writings—the issue is complex. It will be neither fair nor justified to equate the all-important notion of will-to-live to one of the seemingly similar Indian concepts such as *brahman, maya, trsna,* and *upadana.* "How his knowledge of the Indian material was related to the genesis of Schopenhauer's own system is a question which cannot be answered with complete clarity and certainty; his own explicit remarks, in any case, do not provide a sufficient basis for answering it."[13] Halbfass is referring to Schopenhauer's own frustration in discovering an equivalent Indian concept for the will-to-live and his many declarations concerning the issue.

Halbfass also points out that Schopenhauer considered the concept of *maya* as comparable to his notion of *principium individuations* (WWR1$_{[P]}$, 378). Schopenhauer also believed that basically "the sages of all times have always said the same" (PP1$_{[P]}$, 314) and that "Buddha, Eckhardt and I all teach essentially the same" (HN, IX, 89). Schopenhauer found the Buddhist concept of *upadana* (attachment) comparable to the will-to-live (HN, XV, 46).

We turn now from Schopenhauer's own search for Indian concepts parallel to the will-to-live to the speculations of his interpreters who simplistically equate the will to *brahman, atman, maya, trsna, upadana,* etc., and complicate the issue even more. However, we must take into account that Schopenhauer's concept of the will-to-live was not produced merely in response to Indian philosophy, but primarily to counter certain tendencies that had emerged in Western philosophy of his times, as Halbfass explains:

> Schopenhauer's doctrine of the will implies a critique of the European tradition of representational and rational thinking, of calculation and planning...he continued a critique of some of the most fundamental pre-suppositions of the Judeo-Christian tradition such as the notion of a personal God, the uniqueness of the human individual, and the meaning of history.[14]

This implies that while Indian concepts did influence Schopenhauer's thinking, they were not used to build his own system. Reactions to various developments in the European philosophy of his times, including to the historicism of Hegel, Judeo-Christian dogmas, and rationalism, were the main initial impetus behind the writing of WWR. Indian philosophy especially played a part offering examples of an alternative way of thinking, one that seems to match Schopenhauer's own approach to reality. The will-to-live seeks to correct the well-established Western assumptions regarding the idea of personal God, the supremacy of the rational and the dismissal of the instinct, and the virtues of the heart. Indeed, the Vedantic notions of *maya*, *mamta* (mine-ness), *moha* (attachment), and *aham* (ego) all contain some characteristics of the will-to-live, as do the Buddhist notions of *trsna* (craving) and *upadana* (attachment). However, it would be wrong to equate the will to the Vedantic notion of *brahman*. This characterization of the divine Being as everlasting, pure consciousness and bliss (*sat-chitta-ananda*) is certainly not comparable to the blind, irrational urge to live. Also the concept of the denial of the will-to-live touches on a metaphysical dualism, extreme asceticism, and a pessimistic rejection of the world that is contrary to the spirit of Vedanta and Buddhism.

Did Schopenhauer shift his philosophical standpoint in the light of his growing knowledge of Vedanta and Buddhism after 1818? Moira Nicholls in her article the "Influences of Eastern Thought on Schopenhauer's Doctrine of the Thing-in Itself,"[15] offers some useful information about Schopenhauer's citations of Eastern thought, even though her thesis about the shifts in Schopenhauer's philosophical position after the first publication of WWR (1818) is unconvincing. She notes that Volume I of WWR (1818) contains about 80 references to Buddhist thought, five of which are added in later editions (1844) and (1859) of that volume. By comparison, in Volume II, first published in 1844 (when a second edition of Volume I was also published), there are at least thirty references to Buddhism. References to Hindu thought in Volume I number over fifty, seven of which are added in later editions, and in Volume II there are more than fifty-five references to Hinduism. She states that

> ...while these figures are only approximate, they indicate a marked rise in Schopenhauer's knowledge and interest in Buddhist thought from 1818 on, and strong and consistent interest in Hindu thought from 1813 until his death in 1860...(This) indicate(s) that Schopenhauer had an abiding interest in Eastern philosophy, and that he was keen to demonstrate parallels between his own doctrines and these of the east.[16]

So far Nicholls's assertions are factually true. We should keep in mind, however, that a statistical analysis can only reveal a part of the truth and can very easily lead us astray. Her subsequent conclusions are, unfortunately, seriously flawed.

> Three identifiable ships in Schopenhauer's doctrine of the thing-in-itself occur between the publications of the first Volume of WWR in 1818 in his later works. The first shift concerns the knowability of thing-in-itself, the second...(its) nature, the third...is an explicit attempt to assimilate his own doctrine...with Eastern doctrines.

> Schopenhauer asserts numerous times throughout his work that the thing-in-itself is will or will-to-live, and he claims that we know this through direct intuition in self-consciousness...However...in his later works...he seems to withdraw the claim that in self-consciousness we are aware of the will, suggesting indeed that in self-consciousness we are aware of no more than our phenomenal willings.[17]

The second shift (occurs when he) introduces the idea that thing-in-itself has multiple aspects, only one of which is will. Other aspects of the objects of awareness of such persons as mystics, saints and ascetics, who have denied the will...[18]

(Regarding the third shift)...I have identified six passages in which Schopenhauer asserts that the thing-in-itself can be described as will, but only in a metaphorical sense...(as) similar views are expressed in eastern thought.[19]

In response to Nicholls's speculation, it may be said emphatically that there are no such shifts in Schopenhauer's doctrine of the will which he identifies as the thing-in-itself, for which his enhanced knowledge of Eastern thought or anything else is responsible. Nothing is clearer than the fact that Being of all beings is named will-to-live by Schopenhauer. This thing-in-itself (a Kantian term) was never claimed by him to be entirely unknown or entirely and precisely known in human consciousness. If further attempts are made by the thinker to compare the will with *brahman, nirvana*, or, more specifically, to *maya* or *trsna*, this by no means indicates a shift in Schopenhauer's basic doctrine of the will.

It is well-known that, despite dismal sales, Schopenhauer regarded WWR as the ultimate and complete metaphysical system to which all his later works required no amendments or changes. He calls the contents of WWR2 (1844) merely "supplements" in concordance with the already existing four books of the original, to which only further explications and examples can be added but no conceptual changes to it are ever necessary. His later works, other than WWR, are also, from his point of view, further elaborations of his original metaphysical masterpiece. Nicholls's assertion that in later works Schopenhauer "seems to withdraw the claim that in self-consciousness we are aware of the will" is very doubtful. Not only is such a withdrawal uncharacteristic of Schopenhauer's consistent pride in his fundamental work, but such a claim also shows a misunderstanding of his basic definition of the will. The Being of beings is named after its most excellent species: namely, human will.

However, one is not clearly aware of the will being the source of one's needs, wants, and urges, but knows the will's existence only vaguely or fuzzily. Human beings nonetheless do have the possibility of knowing the will's operations and machinations when knowledge, which usually plays a second fiddle to the will, surmounts the will and inspires the subject to deny the will. The ascetics, mystics, and saints from Western as well as Eastern traditions seem to be practitioners of the denial of the will, provided we ignore their various dogmatic beliefs and religious commitments. Thus the will is never missing from self-consciousness but is seldom known with all its implications. Schopenhauer never shifted or changed this account of the will. As far as Nicholls's reference to another shift of will being known "only in a metaphorical sense" supposedly due to the thinker's advanced readings of Eastern thought, we may again assert that no such shift occurred in the later works.

Although Schopenhauer made use of the biographical or the hagiographical materials concerning the saints and the ascetics of the theistic (Christian, Hindu) as well as atheistic (Buddhist, Jain) religious traditions, he did so without losing sight of his own secular metaphysical system. That is why he warns the reader in Book IV of WWR that the religious dogmas and superstitions of these saints must be disregarded. A denier of the will-to-live knows the will full well (i.e., better than a normal person and not just "metaphorically"), although anyone will find it difficult to know the thing-in-itself precisely or completely, according to Schopenhauer. This position he never changed.

Another extensive study of Schopenhauer's Eastern sources was done by Bikkhu Nanajivako, who is a practicing Buddhist monk in Sri Lanka, in his book *Studies in Comparative Philosophy*.[20] This book provides some useful data and insights on Schopenhauer's connection with Indian philosophy in general and Buddhism in particular. Nanajivako begins with a critique of the Eurocentric interpretations of Schopenhauer's thoughts and demonstrates through numerous citations the central role of Indian thought in it. The bulk of the book is devoted exclusively to Schopenhauer's references to Buddhism, and the author clearly de-emphasizes the role of Vedanta in his highly favored treatment of Buddhism and puts forward the thesis that, although "fragmentary," Upanishads were initially a significant influence on Schopenhauer; he grew out of "mutually discordant" Hindu systems and, in his more mature years, opted for the more "methodical and cohesive" Buddhist philosophy. Thus Nanajivako focuses on Schopenhauer's comments on Buddhism, sprinkled throughout his early and later works. In fact, all the statements of Schopenhauer on Buddhism are reproduced, making these approximately one hundred pages a useful research tool.

An open-minded reader, however, will not find much credibility for Nanajivako's thesis for there is no evidence that Schopenhauer ever lost his admiration for Vedanta and allied Hindu systems. Nor did he ever show in his writings an overwhelming preference for Buddhism over Hinduism. It is true, though, that in his essay on death in WWR2 he praises the Buddhist notion of rebirth as better than the theories of metempsychosis in ancient Greek and Hindu thought: "We find this doctrine in its subtlest form coming nearest to truth in Buddhism" (WWR2$_{[P]}$, 504). Perhaps Buddhist theory of rebirth comes nearest to Schopenhauer's own theory of the indestructibility of the will that, according to him, lives on in the species rather than in individuals.

Sporadic observations of this kind should nonetheless not lead us to conclude that Schopenhauer preferred Buddhism over Vedanta on the whole in his later phase. For, in the same essay on death, he has this to say: "the conviction here described and arising directly out of the apprehension of nature must have been extremely lively in those sublime authors of the Upanishads of the Vedas, who can scarcely be conceived as mere human beings" (WWR2$_{[P]}$, 475). Schopenhauer admires and cites the *Bhagvadgita* as well as the Buddha in the same work, composed in the later years of his career.

Nanajivako correctly points out that Schopenhauer, like Goethe and Schelling, had attended Frederich Majer's lectures in Oriental thought in 1813. In March of 1814, he obtained a copy of the Upanishads from the Weimar library.[21] In the notes made by Schopenhauer in his diaries (HN) in the next two years, there are further reflections on *maya*. These earliest references may suffice to show how deep the first impact of Indian thought was on Schopenhauer at the very time when the idea of his system was beginning to germinate in his mind. However, Nanajivako's thesis that Schopenhauer grew out of his initial fascination with Vedanta and Hinduism and regarded Buddhism as the most worthwhile philosophy is unconvincing. Why would anyone consider Schopenhauer as dismissive of Vedanta when, as late as in 1851, he pays the following tribute to the Anquetil-Duperron translation of the Upanishads: "(It is) the most edifying reading, with the exception of the original text that could be possible in this world; it has been the solace of my life and will be the solace of my death" (PP2$_{[P]}$, 397).

Nanajivako draws some further misleading conclusions, such as the following: "at later stages it can be seen how *this expansion of the Vedic* idea of *maya* subsided and ... was taken over by more explicitly Buddhist connotation of *samsara*." Nanajivako's attempts to claim *samsara* as an exclusively Buddhist notion is quite strange. *Samsara* is a perennial concept of the Indian tradition, which is a colloquial term for the "world." This term is connected with the myth of reincarnation and is older than the Buddhist faith itself. Thus, in Schopenhauer's thought, there is no such thing as a break with Vedanta and full endorsement of Buddhism for there was no abatement of his admiration of Eastern concepts from Vedanta.

However, Schopenhauer's own interpretation of Buddhism is somewhat slanted toward pessimism, and he does not show adequate attention to detail in his reading of the four noble truths. He focuses on the term (*dukkha*) in these truths, the literal meaning of which is suffering or pain, but the more philosophical meaning (namely, existential un-satisfactoriness) is not fully present in Schopenhauer's interpretation. Consider how in the ancient Buddhist *sutras* (discourses), the standard statement of the first noble (aryan) truth is as follows: "now this o monks, is a noble truths of *dukkha* ; birth is *dukkha*, old age is *dukkha*, sickness is *dukkha*, sorrow, lamentation dejection and despair are *dukkha*. Contact with unpleasant things is *dukkha*, not getting what one wants is *dukkha*. In short, five *skandhas* of grasping are *dukkha*."[22] Now the repeated use of the term *dukkha*, if taken in its literal meaning, may create the impression that the Buddha took a gloomy view of human existence and maintained that "all life is suffering," and this would also create the impression of Buddhism as a pessimistic philosophy which turns a blind eye toward possible happiness and the glorious potentials of human existence. But when we recognize that the Buddha took pains to mention some specific occasions of inevitable suffering, the accusation of pessimism is no longer accurate. We should add to the fact that next three noble truths offer a diagnosis, as well as a remedy out of *dukkha*; thus, it is not fair to call it pessimistic on the whole.

Nevertheless, the supposed pessimism and asceticism combined with seeming rejection of *samsara* (worldliness) may be the main attractions that drew Schopenhauer to Buddhism. He seems to oversimplify the four noble truths in WWR2$_{[P]}$.

[In Buddhism] ... all improvement, conversion and salvation to be hoped from this world of suffering, from this Samsara, proceed from knowledge of the four fundamental truths: (1) *dolor* [suffering], (2) *doloris ortus* [origin of suffering], (3) *dolris inferitus* [cessation of suffering], (4) *Octoparite via ad doloris sedation* [eightfold path to the ceasing of suffering ....

> ...Christianity belongs to the ancient true and sublime faith of mankind. The faith
> stands in contrast to the false, shallow and pernicious optimism that manifests itself
> in Greek paganism, Judaism and Islam.   (WWR2$_{[P]}$, 623)

Thus Schopenhauer admires Buddhism, Hinduism, and Christianity for their supposed
rejection of pernicious optimism that prevails in the Old Testament and Islam. At the
same time he oversimplifies the noble truths, especially the first one. He describes the
essence of the first noble truth in one word, namely, *dolor*, suffering. The question arises
that if the Buddha wanted to say that all human existence is nothing but suffering, why
he didn't say so. It would have been easy to say that "life is suffering," and then skip the
remaining descriptions of the specific occasions of suffering. Buddhists, however, believe
that the Buddha's account was realistic rather than pessimistic,[23] for the noble truths
identify a cause of *dukkha*, namely, *trsna* (craving), and assert that this cause can be
"removed without a remainder." They also prescribe the eightfold path that will remove
suffering. Thus, Schopenhauer chooses to overlook the hopeful spirit of the second, third,
and fourth noble truths. The sermon of the Buddha, which contains a statement of four
truths, begins with an admonition of the Buddha to the five former disciples.

> These two extremes, O monks, are not to be practiced by one who has gone forth from
> *samsara*. . . . That conjoined with passions . . . and that conjoined with self-torture. . . .
> Avoiding these extremes, the *Tathagata* (Buddha) has gained the knowledge of the
> middle way, which gives sight and knowledge and tends to claim, to insight enlight-
> enment, Nirvana.[24]

Thus neither the thoughtless pursuit of passions nor other extreme of asceticism and
mounting self-torture can deliver a higher thoughtful life and/or the glimpses of truth.
Thus Buddhism does not advocate either pessimism or asceticism or the denials of the
will in its extreme form.

23.3 SOME HASTY CRITIQUES
OF SCHOPENHAUER

Schopenhauer is not exactly an admired figure in the history of modern philosophy. The
tag of being a committed pessimist is too readily applied to him. However, the reasons
for his pessimism are often oversimplified and the extent of his pessimism is unduly
exaggerated because many of his concepts and standpoints are misunderstood. Many
such misunderstandings are rooted in a lack of appreciation of his connections with
Eastern thought. A lack of even a basic familiarity with Vedanta and Buddhism on the
part of many of his modern critics has driven them to draw some hasty conclusions not
only about Schopenhauer's thought but also about his personality. The fundamental
positions of this thinker regarding the sufferings and the undesirable status in this world

and the concepts of eternal justice, death, and salvation are often misunderstood in the secondary literature. This is so because an assessment of similar concepts in Vedanta and Buddhism is seldom carried out, and the roots of the seemingly discordant notions of Schopenhauer's system are seldom traced in Eastern thought. This is not to say that Schopenhauer simply borrowed these concepts from Eastern thought, nor is it an attempt to exaggerate the role of Eastern influences on Schopenhauer. But an assessment of similar notions in Eastern thought helps us to understand the original way of thinking that Schopenhauer had. Many of Schopenhauer's modern interpreters have misunderstood or oversimplified this thinker's fundamental positions on the status of this world, human existence, and suffering, or the Eastern dimension of his thought.

One of the most bewildering aspects of Schopenhauer's thought for many of his interpreters has been his apparent disdain of the world, human existence, and human nature. His condemnation of individualism, an all-important Western value, as well as his focus on suffering and overlooking of the possibilities of happiness are viewed as quite anomalous. Thus the labels of extreme pessimism, absurdity, perversity, and hypocrisy are applied to Schopenhauer by some well-established scholars. Schopenhauer is widely known as a pessimistic thinker, and he himself is never shy of calling optimism a pernicious philosophy and of rejecting the notion that ours is the best of all possible worlds. Nevertheless the current secondary literature often judges him as more pessimistic than he is and caricatures both his life and work as odd, eccentric, and puzzling. Statements such as these have raised many eyebrows: "To desire immortality for the individual is to perpetuate an error forever, for at bottom every individuality is really only a special error, a false step, something that it would be better should not be, in fact, something from which it is the real purpose of life to bring us back" (WWR2$_{[P]}$, 492). These are the kinds of assertions that are often so difficult for many Schopenhauer scholars to accept at face value. They usually attribute such convictions to his pessimism or begin to see contradictions in his standpoints. For example, Michael Fox in his article "*Schopenhauer on Death, Suicide and Self-Renunciation*" frustratingly remarks that

> The doctrine of palingenesis as promulgated by Schopenhauer is indeed difficult to comprehend and there is more than one lacuna in his account....After all Schopenhauer makes the perverse claim that for mankind it would have been better not to have come into being and to exist; life is just a disturbing interruption of the blissful non-existence. Schopenhauer's doctrine of self-renunciation must be examined independently of his entirely perverse and absurd position....That man is guilty and inexpugnably sinful, not because of his deeds but merely because he exists.[25]

In a similarly unsympathetic and literal reading of Schopenhauer's statement "we are at bottom something that ought not to be" (WWR 2$_{[P]}$, 507), David Cartwright writes, "We suffer and die because we deserve it. The world is perfectly retributive. We deserve what we receive because we are guilty. We are guilty because we exist. Schopenhauer's logic is now as clear as it is unconvincing."[26]

A misunderstanding of Schopenhauer's analysis of *samsara* consistent with his reading of Vedanta and Buddhism, a failure to distinguish between "excessive worldliness" and the "world as such," and a refusal to take seriously the wisdom behind the myth of reincarnation (a living belief of two-thirds of humanity) has driven many interpreters of Schopenhauer to extreme judgments of not only this man's philosophy but of the man himself. For example, Bryan Magee in his *Philosophy of Schopenhauer* writes

> In the light of the present day knowledge there can be little doubt that Schopenhauer's despairing view of the world, above all, his conviction of terribleness of existence as such, were in some degree neurotic manifestations which had roots in his relation-ship with his mother.... If actions speak louder than words, his life as he in fact lives it... tells us of a man in whom protean pleasures are being experienced side by side with mountainous frustration, misanthropy and desolate miseries of neurosis.[27]

Although John Atwell does not offer an adequate analysis of Schopenhauer's connec-tions with Eastern thought in his book, *Schopenhauer: The Human Character*, he offers an important rejoinder to scholars who advocate selective reading of Schopenhauer and wish to rub out some sections, usually those aligning with Eastern worldviews, from Schopenhauer's writings. Atwell cautions that passages deemed as "absurd," "perverse," and "unconvincing" from Western perspectives cannot simply be disregarded.

> Now if the doctrine of eternal justice is "absurd" or "perverse," then it is not so in itself, but only because Schopenhauer's entire metaphysical thesis—the world as will—is absurd or perverse; for the doctrine of eternal justice follows with strict necessity from the metaphysical thesis.... Consequently one cannot logically accept the metaphysical thesis or even regard it as plausible or worthwhile or insightful (as critics often suggest) and then reject the doctrine of eternal justice or regard it as nonsense (as the very same critics often do).[28]

Atwell correctly identifies the tendency to show irritation with some parts of Schopenhauer's writing by his modern critics. It is to be noticed that the passages and the concepts taken to task are frequently those that emanate from Schopenhauer's affinities with Indian thought, which is an area of knowledge that these critics have not adequately taken into account. Thus often some fundamental rationales, presuppositions, and concepts of Schopenhauer are cast aside due to critics' unfamiliarity with Eastern thought.

In response to these hasty and severe critiques, we must assert that there is nothing absurd or perverse about Schopenhauer's appreciation of the Vedantic and Buddhist standpoint that continued life of *samsara* (attachment to the worldliness) is not some-thing to be celebrated for otherwise the higher life of detachment and seeking of salvation will be rendered meaningless. The bliss of *moksha* (salvation, freedom) must be con-trasted with the vulgarity of *samsaric* existence or what Schopenhauer calls the life of a philistine. This is necessary to inspire oneself toward a higher life of detachment; that is, a life of denial of the will. The portrayal of *nirvana* as a release from the cycle of rebirth is a mythological exposition of the philosophical standpoint that *samsara* or worldliness ought not to be valued in a philosophical lifestyle. To desire perpetuation of one's individuality is to give in to mine-ness (*mamta*) and *moha* (attachment). It is tantamount to saying yes to *samsara*, which is neither philosophically desirable nor praiseworthy. Schopenhauer's statement that "at bottom every individuality is a special error, a false step, something that it would be better not to be" (WWR 2$_{[P]}$, 491–92) is consistent with the Vedanta message that to take the ego (*aham*) as real is to dismiss one's larger self (*atman*). All individualities and diversity are superficial and in contrast to One-ness of *brahman*. Agreeing with Vedanta, Schopenhauer maintains that the real purpose of human life is to bring ourselves back from the individuality-based, vulgar living which continues to affirm the seemingly rational pursuits of the irrational urges of the will-to-live, that produce *samsara* for us. In essence, Schopenhauer is revalidating Vedanta as well as what Socrates said: "it is not just living that counts but living well."

23.4 SCHOPENHAUER AND VEDANTA

Schopenhauer, like other contemporary Indologists, studied the texts of Vedanta at first and came to learn about Buddhism a few years later as Buddhist literature became available in Europe. However he was far more advanced than Hegel whose commentaries on Indian thought were based exclusively on Vedanta texts and who had little or no knowledge of Buddhism. Schopenhauer, however, read everything that was being published on the subject in Europe and developed a deep interest in Buddhism. Regarding the rapid advancement of Indian studies in Europe during his lifetime, Schopenhauer says the following in a footnote in a later edition of WWR: "In the last forty years Indian literature has grown so much in Europe, that if I now wished to complete this note to the first edition, it would fill several pages" (WWR1$_{[P]}$, 388n).

Even though Schopenhauer's knowledge of Hindu thought came to him much earlier than that of Buddhism and his respect for it never diminished throughout his life, he developed an equal degree of respect for Buddhism as well. As quoted by Halbfass, the following autobiographical remarks make it clear that his knowledge of Vedanta came to him before the literature on Buddhism even became available in Europe: "On the whole the harmony (of Buddhism) with my teachings is wonderful, all the more so because I wrote the first volume (of WWR) between 1814 and 1818 it did not nor could have known all that."[29]

"Nor, could have known all that" (about Buddhism) indicates that not much was available in print about Buddhism between 1814 and 1818. But the following remarks in his Diary (1816) show his admission that he was already exposed to Hindu thought, perhaps after attending Friedrich Majer's lectures (1813) prior to the writing period of the first volume of WWR: "By the way, I admit that I do not believe that my doctrine could have ever been formulated before the Upanishads, Plato and Kant were able to able to cast their light spontaneously onto a human mind" (MR1, 467).

However, the fact that Schopenhauer's exposure to Hindu thought was earlier than that of Buddhist thought should not lead us to the conclusion that he preferred one over the other or that he revised his doctrinal positions in any way due to his subsequent studies of Buddhism. It is evident to any careful reader of his later works that he often quoted from these two Eastern traditions together and in the same breath.

Schopenhauer maintained a life-long admiration and deep interest in Vedanta. This is evident in his numerous references to the Vedic concepts and doctrines throughout his early and later works. However, this does not mean that his perceptive and creative accounts of Vedic thought were always comprehensive as well as indisputable in their interpretations. Schopenhauer's validations of atheism, asceticism, and, above all, pessimism are obviously in discord with the spirit of Vedanta. That is why it will be most objectionable to compare his concept of the will-to-live with either *brahman* or *atman*. It may be more comparable to *maya*. Although *brahman* is described as beyond everything while being within everything, neutral and indifferent, it is also called *sat-chitta-ananda* (everlasting, pure consciousness, blissful). Thus atheism and pessimism are ruled out by Vedanta.

According to the popular views, Hinduism became explicitly theistic and devotional in the post-Upanishadic period in which the epics and the *Bhagvadgita* were written. *Bhagvadgita*, a favorite text of Schopenhauer, was frequently quoted in his writings. Although Schopenhauer correctly celebrates the contributions of Hindu and Buddhist ascetics such as *sadhus, samanas, munis,* and *rishis* for their remarkably other-worldly lifestyles of the denial of the will-to-live, it is still hard to say whether Hinduism recommends the extreme asceticism of the kind described by Schopenhauer as the prototype of the denial of the will. For the pursuit of *dharma* is not a simple matter of affirmation and denial in various shades and schools of Hinduism. It is not merely a decision to deny or stifle worldliness or *maya*. The Vedantic tradition includes in itself the practice of *bhakti* (devotion, love) which is to be combined with action (*karma*) and knowledge of the divine (*jnana*) according to the *Bhagvadgita*. In other words, the way of *bhakti* is not exactly the path of asceticism but perhaps an alternative to asceticism, a spontaneous embracing of the other-worldly in this world, an invitation to higher love in this life. The work of the bhakti-saints that appeared in India as part of the southern (sixth century onward) and northern (thirteenth century onward) *bhakti* movements of Hindu revivalism show a personal and passionate longing to identify with the object of devotion (*ish*). The role and the superiority of the way of *bhakti* is very succinctly outlined in the following words of the sixteenth-century *bhakti* saint Eknath (1548–1608):

> Though one restrains the senses, yet they are not restrained. Though one renounces sensual desires, yet they are not renounced. Again and again they return to torment one. For that reason "the flame of *hari-bhakti* was lit by Veda." There is no need to suppress the senses, desire of sensual pleasure ceases of itself. So mighty is the power that lies in *hari-bhakti*.

> The senses that *yogis* suppress, *bhakias* devote to the worship of *bhagvat* (Blessed-One, Lord), offer to *bhagvat*. Yogis suffer in the flesh...the followers of *bhakti* become forever emancipated. Though he has no knowledge of the Vedas, still by one

so ignorant may the real *atman* be apprehended. The condition of *brahman* may easily be attained and realized.

Women, *sudras* (lower castes) and all the others...can be borne by the power of *sraddha* (faith) and *bhakti* to the other shore (of the ocean of *samsara*).[30]

It is obvious that Schopenhauer paid hardly any attention to *bhakti* as an important aspect of Hinduism, although he does quote from the *Kural,* which is an important text of the Southern *Bhakti* movement in the Tamil language: "The passion of the mind directed outwards and that of the I directed inwards, should cease." He cites this quote to compare it with a saying of Madame de Guyon in German theology: "In true love, there remains neither I nor me, mine...and the like" (WWR2$_{[P]}$, 613). In the next line Schopenhauer quotes the Buddha: "My disciples reject the idea that I am this or this is mine." For the lack of analysis of *bhakti,* neither Schopenhauer nor other early nineteenth-century Indologists can hardly be blamed. Hinduism of the intellectual variety alone or various treatments of *jnana* (knowledge) alone were offered in Europe of those times. By and large, *bhakti,* which is what makes Indian philosophies "living philosophies" or guidelines to higher living, are given hardly any importance even today. Most Western and Eastern scholars continue to offer intellectualized systems of Hindu thought in Western terminology, although some translations of the work of *bhakti* masters has appeared in recent times. Obviously such accounts of the practice of *bhakti* were not available to Schopenhauer, although he was able to capture the essence of Hinduism in his own original fashion.

In the fourth book of WWR, Schopenhauer, while discussing the denial of the will-to-live, finds much to admire about Christian mystics and ascetics as well as about the saints, ascetics, and monks of Hinduism and Buddhism.

We cannot sufficiently wonder at the harmony we find...(between) a Christian penitent or saint and that of an Indian. In spite of such fundamentally different dogmas, customs and circumstances, the endeavor and the inner life of both are absolutely the same....The Christian mystics and the teachers of the Vedanta philosophy agree in regarding all outward works and religious practices as superfluous for the man who has attained perfection.   (WWR1$_{[P]}$, 389)

Schopenhauer's remarks indicate that the field of religion can also offer much by way of philosophical insight and guidelines for philosophical life, provided the different religious dogmas, rituals, and customs are set aside and what is common to practitioners of the denial of the will-to-live from Western and Eastern religions is studied carefully. Being a secular-minded and atheistic philosopher, unlike Hegel and Schelling, what he admired in Hindu thought was the notion of *brahman*, which cannot simply be equated with that of God, and also the fact that Buddhism remains free of the obsession with God. Thus he was not merely admiring the Indian systems of thought but was also trying to free the philosophical investigations of modern Europe from its hidden agendas

based on monotheistic Christian ideology and the concept of God. Thus his opposition
to Hegel and Hegelianism was not merely a personal dislike but rooted on doctrinal differences. He was also trying to correct the assumptions of Indologists like Schlegel
brothers and Schelling.

> It was necessary to find out whether the ancient and non-European notions especially
> those of Hindustan, and many of the oldest Greek philosophers, actually arrived at
> those concepts, or whether only we, by translating *Brahma* (*brahman*) of the Hindus
> and the *Tien* (*Tao*) of the Chinese quite falsely as "God" charitably ascribe such con-
> cepts to them,... whether it is not the case that theism proper is to be found only in the
> Jewish religion and the two religions that have sprung from it.   (WWR1$_{[P]}$, 486)

Schopenhauer was sharp enough to foresee that the work of the Indologists, gratifying
and complementary as it was to the Indian scholars, also did a great harm to the study of
Indian philosophies and religions by providing some foundational interpretations that
were based on Christian and theistic presuppositions. An example of this is some classical
interpretations of the *Bhagvadgita*, which was hailed as the first theistic work of Hindu
thought because its connections with Vedic and Upanishadic thought was dismissed in
view of its supposedly theistic message. Due to the same line of thinking, the concept of
bhakti (the soul of love, religious or secular) was simplistically understood as "worship
of God," and its origins were traced in the *Bhagvadgita* rather than the Vedas, where it
actually began. It is amazing to see that, in the early nineteenth century, Schopenhauer
was free from such theistic dogmas and largely recognized Hindu thought independently from Western presuppositions.

   In connection with the relative existence of things governed by sufficient reason,
Schopenhauer offers one of the most lucid definitions of *maya*, which reminds us of the
way *maya* was defined by Sankara,[31] eighth-century Hindu philosopher.

> "It is *maya* the veil of deception, which covers the eyes of the mortals and causes
> them to see a world of which one cannot say either it is or that it is not, for it is like
> a dream, like the sunshine on the sand...or like the piece of rope on the ground
> which (one) regards as the snake" (These similes are repeatedly found in innumera-
> ble passages of the *Vedas* and *Puranas*). But what all this meant...is nothing else
> but...the world as representation subordinated to the principle of sufficient reason.
>   (WWR1$_{[P]}$, 8)

This is an example of how Schopenhauer often found parallels for his own concepts in
the doctrines of Vedanta. In the fourth book of WWR, Schopenhauer devotes almost
two pages to comparing his concept of eternal justice, the "vivid knowledge (which) will
always remain inaccessible to the majority of men," with Vedanta and the allied myth of
reincarnation (WWR1$_{[P]}$, 355–56). He explains that the great truth *tat tvam asi* (that
thou art) "was translated into the way of knowledge following the principle of sufficient
reason....This way of knowledge is indeed quite incapable of assimilating that

truth... yet in the form of a myth, it received a substitute" (WWR1$_{[P]}$, 355). Schopenhauer highlights the importance of the myth of rebirth in Hinduism. This myth serves as a guide to conduct by making clear the ethical significance of human conduct through a figurative description.

> Never has a myth been, and never will be, more closely associated with a philosoph-ical truth accessible to so few, than this very ancient teaching of the noblest and oldest of peoples.... We, on the contrary, now send to the *Brahmans* English clergy-men and evangelical linen-weavers.... But this is just the same as if we fired a bullet at a cliff.... The ancient wisdom of the human race will not be supplanted by the events in Galilee. On the contrary, Indian wisdom flows back to Europe, and will produce a fundamental change in our knowledge and thought.   (WWR2$_{[P]}$, 357)

Schopenhauer repeatedly wonders why Hindus were so resistant to the attempts made by the foreign missionaries to convert them in his *Parerga and Paralipomena*. In this major work, which finally made him famous throughout Europe in the last decade of his life, he seems to regard the efforts of the missionaries as futile (PP2$_{[P]}$, 223, 225, 328). The book is a collection of essays and random thoughts on a variety of subjects written in a popular format, where Schopenhauer shows a grasp of the world of Hinduism by interpreting its philosophies, religious texts, and mythologies. In this regard, he does not miss the role of Hinduism as a unique worldview and a way of life. He looks at Hindu mythology as a mirror of Hindu thought as his studies of the primary and secondary texts gave him a unique expertise. He found its concepts of Vedanta, along with those of the six classical systems, as valuable ways of thinking about the grounds of reality. His own slant to reality is often unmistakable, as in the following analysis of Hindu trinity (*Trimurti*):

> Vedas also teach no God creator but a world-soul called *brahma* (*brahman*) in the center. *Brahma* sprung from the navel of Vishnu with the four faces and as part of the Trimutri, is only a popular personification of *Brahma* (*Brahman*) in the extremely transparent Indian mythology. He obviously represents the generation (of beings)...just as Vishnu does their acme, and Shiva their destruction and extinc-tion. Moreover, his production of the world is a sinful act, just as is the world incar-nation of *Brahma*.   (PP1$_{[P]}$, 127)

The last sentence shows Schopenhauer's pessimistic bias. The production of the world by *Brahman* is not described as a sinful act, nor is the world on the whole a sinful rein-carnation of *Brahman* according to Hindu scriptures. As explained by *Sankara,* the world was created as a sport (*leela*), it is a playful act of *Brahman* the Being of beings that is not lacking in anything, before or after the supposed creation of the world.

There are numerous quotes in the two volumes of PP regarding the philosophical issues related to the meaning of death. Schopenhauer brings home the idea that birth, life, and death have to be considered as interconnected. The following remarks regarding life and death and growing old are indicative of his ability to express profound thoughts in a simple metaphor:

> Human life cannot really be called either long or short as it is at bottom the standard whereby we measure all other length of time. In the Upanishad...the normal dura-tion of human life is stated to be a hundred years. I think this is correct because I have noticed that only those who have passed their nineteenth year...die without any illness. The older we grow, the smaller human affairs seem to be, one and all....The vanity and emptiness of the whole stands out.   (PP1$_{[P]}$,495)

The remark that human life is the standard measure of all other temporal durations shows an understanding of time as existential reality, similarly to Heidegger's existential theory of time, which is opposed to Aristotle's notion of time as a series of nows. It is so difficult for the human entity to view life as either too short or too long. We assume these general characterizations alternatively depending on our own judgment of the way life strikes us.

   The insights from the Upanishads play a central role in the culmination of Schopenhauer's system. The identification of one's individuality with all and all others is an insight of the Upanishads that he quotes numerous times in his later works.

> The readers of my Ethics know that with me the foundation of morality rests ulti-mately on the truth which has its expression in the Veda and Vedanta in the estab-lished mystical formula *tat tvam asi* (that thou art) which is stated with reference to every living thing, whether man or animal, is then called the *Mahavakya* or Great Word.   (PP2$_{[P]}$, 219)

Thus, Hindu thought remained an enduring influence on Schopenhauer since his first introduction to it in the time period of the composition of his chief work. Even though he learned about Buddhism and about the various systems of Hindu thought in later years, his respect for the Upanishadic Hindu thought stayed with him to the end of his time. He had great regard for Indian philosophy. He was also interested in the mytholo-gies and broad outlooks of the Hindu people as well as in the art, music, and literary works of that tradition. No wonder that Hindu thought lies underneath the foundations of his system in a special and creative way.

NOTES

1. Some citations and other materials in this essay are taken from my books, *Death, Contemplation and Schopenhauer* (Aldershot, UK: Ashgate, 2007) and *Schopenhauer: A Guide for the Perplexed* (London: Continuum, 2010). However, all materials are revised and supplemented with extensive new analyses.
2. Wilhelm Halbfass, *India and Europe: An Essay in Understanding* (Albany: State University of New York Press, 1988).
3. Ibid., 70.
4. Ibid., 73.

5. Ibid., 84.
6. Ibid., 86.
7. Ibid., 88.
8. Ibid., 89.
9. Ibid., 106.
10. Ibid., 100.
11. Ibid., 102.
12. Ibid.
13. Ibid., 107.
14. Ibid., 120.
15. Moira Nicholls, "The Influences of Eastern Thought on Schopenhauer's Doctrine of the Thing-in-itself," in *Cambridge Companion to Schopenhauer*, edited by Christopher Janaway (Cambridge: Cambridge University Press, 1999), 176.
16. Ibid., 177.
17. Ibid., 171–72.
18. Ibid., 173.
19. Ibid., 174.
20. Bhikku Nanajivako, *Studies in Comparative Philosophy* (Columbo: Lakehouse Publishers, 1983).
21. See Urs App, "Schopenhauer's Initial Encounter with Indian Thought, *Schopenhauer-Jahrbuch* 87 (2006), 35–78, at 41.
22. Samyutta-nikaya, in *A Sourcebook in Indian Philosophy*, edited by S. Radhakrishnan and C. Moore (Princeton, NJ: Princeton University Press 1973), 274.
23. Walpola Rahula, *What the Buddha Taught* (New York: Grove Press, 1959), 16–28.
24. Samyutta-nikaya, *A Sourcebook in Indian Philosophy,* 274.
25. Michael Fox, "Schopenhauer on Death, Suicide and Self-renunciation," in *Schopenhauer: His Philosophical Achievement*, edited by Michael Fox (New York: Barnes and Noble Books, 1980), 161.
26. David Cartwright, "Schopenhauer on Suffering, Death, Guilt and Consolations of Metaphysics," in *Schopenhauer: New Essays in Honor of his 200th Birthday*, edited by Eric Van der Luft (Lewiston, NY: Edwin Mellon Press, 1988).
27. Bryan Magee, *The Philosophy of Schopenhauer* (Oxford: Clarendon Press, 1997), 13; 260.
28. John E. Atwell, *Schopenhauer: The Human Character* (Philadelphia, PA: Temple University Press, 1990), 195.
29. Halbfass, *India and Europe*, 107.
30. Nicole Macnicol, *Indian Theism* (Delhi: Munshilal Manoharlal, 1915), 270. Also see my book *Bhakti and Philosophy* (Lanham, MD: Lexington Books, 2006).
31. Sankara defined *maya* as that which is neither real nor unreal nor real-unreal.

FURTHER READING

App, Urs. "Schopenhauer's Initial Encounter with Indian Thought." *Schopenhauer-Jahrbuch* 87 (2006): 35–78.
Cartwright, David. "Schopenhauer on Suffering, Death, Guilt and Consolations of Metaphysics." In *Schopenhauer: New Essays in Honor of his 200th Birthday,* edited by Eric Van der Luft. Lewiston, NY: Edwin Mellon Press, 1988.

Fox, Michael. "Schopenhauer on Death, Suicide and Self-renunciation." In *Schopenhauer: His Philosophical Achievement*, edited by Michael Fox. New York: Barnes and Noble Books, 1980.

Halbfass, Wilhelm. *India and Europe: An Essay in Understanding*. Albany: State University of New York Press, 1988.

Macnicol, Nicole. *Indian Theism*. Delhi: Munshilal Manoharlal, 1915.

Nanajivako, Bhikku. *Studies in Comparative Philosophy*. Columbo: Lakehouse Publishers, 1983.

Nicholls, Moira. "The Influences of Eastern Thought on Schopenhauer's Doctrine of the Thing-in-itself." In *Cambridge Companion to Schopenhauer*, edited by Christopher Janaway. Cambridge: Cambridge University Press, 1999.

Rahula, Walpola. *What the Buddha Taught*. New York: Grove Press, 1959.

Singh, R. Raj. *Bhakti and Philosophy*. Lanham, MD: Lexington Books, 2006.

Singh, R. Raj. *Death, Contemplation and Schopenhauer*. Aldershot, UK: Ashgate, 2007.

Singh, R. Raj. *Schopenhauer: A Guide for the Perplexed*. London: Continuum, 2010.

CHAPTER 24

SCHOPENHAUER AND CHRISTIANITY

GERARD MANNION[†]

CONTRARY to many textbook assumptions over the years, Schopenhauer's relationship with religion and especially Christianity was much more ambivalent and, in several respects, even paradoxical in character than is often assumed, and his thought cannot be adequately nor even accurately explained through the interpretive lens of atheism.[1] Despite his critiques of the faith, Schopenhauer even received a conventional Christian burial, with the traditional German Evangelical service read at his graveside on September 26, 1860.[2]

Schopenhauer's philosophical system works toward a pinnacle, one that he, himself, stated was its entire point and most important part. He terms this section of his *magnum opus* (*The World as Will and Representation*), the "Doctrine of Salvation." Given this, it is therefore important for anyone seeking a better understanding of Schopenhauer to engage with what he had to say about religion and to appreciate the influence religion had on him personally and on his writings. As a dialogue partner for his philosophy, Christianity clearly emerges as among the three most influential religions for Schopenhauer's thought, alongside Hinduism and Buddhism.[3] Arthur Hübscher suggests that the main theme which he took away from his studies in these Asian religions was the idea of "universality,"[4] something which he found also in romanticism and what he termed "true Christianity." So, in a sense, he was also something of a syncretist and, as another biographer stated, "[Schopenhauer] maintains that the spirit of true religion is everywhere the same...."[5] While all three religions played more than a simply confirmatory role in Schopenhauer's thought, whether consciously or otherwise, a case can be made that Christianity was the religion that exerted the greatest influence on Schopenhauer, if by influence is also included his interaction with and critique of Christianity and Christian theology; that is, through carefully engaging this faith as a dialogue partner, Schopenhauer honed many of his most important ideas.

24.1 SCHOPENHAUER THE
INTERPRETER OF RELIGION

Indeed, Schopenhauer, being fascinated by religion in general, delved deeply into the history, traditions, doctrines and theological interpretations of Christianity from the earliest times of that faith and from multiple differing contexts of the Christian world. Likewise, he was fascinated by accounts of religious communities and institutions, as well as by religious customs, practices, and rituals. He understood that no single religion—least of all Christianity—is uniform in story or character and compared and contrasted not only *between* differing faiths but equally *within* them, too—both synchronically and diachronically. Much Christian art engrossed him, and, on his many travels, he was also captivated by the Christian sites he visited, while his encyclopedic reading transported him to innumerable other religious times, places, and communities upon which his pen recorded so very many insightful and incisive (alongside occasionally acerbic) reflections. His notebooks are littered with entries on religious matters, and Christianity looms large from the very beginnings of these. We can also find references to and discussions of religion and Christianity, from doctrine to practices, throughout his published works from his doctoral dissertation down to his popular essays. And this nowhere more so than throughout both the main pages, as well as the minutiae of the exhaustive footnotes, in his *magnum opus*, *The World as Will and Representation*.

From his student days, he undoubtedly ceased to be a conventional believer and practitioner of the Christian faith into which he was born and at least nominally raised, becoming ever more willing to turn his sharp critical analysis toward religion itself (particularly coming to challenge certain doctrines and practices on the grounds of reason and experience alike). Yet he was anything but a Richard Dawkins-like proponent of doing away with religion and denouncing it as being pernicious per se, seeking to replace it with a purely scientific, rationalistic, and materialistic explanation for the world and every aspect of human existence alike.[6] Rather, when Schopenhauer turned his attention toward religion and especially to Christianity, he sought to understand, interpret, and explain what he could clearly see was a force both for much good, truth, and enlightenment in the world, as well as being something that sometimes stood in the way of greater human fulfillment and understanding for a wide variety of reasons.

Indeed, rather than rejecting religion and Christianity outright (his more patronizing comparisons between religion or faith and philosophy notwithstanding), Schopenhauer should be viewed as among the more significant of modern thinkers who sought to offer a critical and comparative *interpretation* of religion.[7]

Schopenhauer's own interpretation of religion was less rigidly systematic but employed many differing methods that would later become familiar in the wider interpretation of religion—in many respects well ahead of his time.[8] And he influenced numerous subsequent approaches to the study of religion, both consciously and unconsciously (e.g., Emile Durkheim [Schopenhauer particularly influenced his classic text the *Elementary Forms of the Religious Life*,[9]] and Max Weber).

And, despite his epistolary admission that some aspects of his philosophy stood in contradiction to some of the "Judeo-Christian dogmas,"[10] Christian thought helped shape many of Schopenhauer's most important writings. Furthermore, through exploring how Schopenhauer's thought relates to religious thought, long-standing conundrums with regard to the coherence of his philosophical system can be considered in a new light. Indeed, in the same letter he states that the fourth and final book of *The World as Will and Representation* offers a moral philosophy "that agrees exactly with genuine Christianity."[11]

24.2 A LIFE-LONG STUDENT OF CHRISTIANITY: SCHOPENHAUER'S PERSONAL AND INTELLECTUAL RELATIONSHIP WITH CHRISTIANITY AND CHRISTIAN THOUGHT

Schopenhauer's Hamburg schooling exposed him to the moralistic influences of German Pietism, itself influenced by German mysticism. And, despite his protests at having to endure the too numerous Anglican services at the Wimbledon English boarding school to which his parents sent him as a teenager, Schopenhauer was far from indifferent to religion per se and especially not to the intellectual study of Christianity. As a young man, the simple (yet critical) Christian faith articulated in the writings of Matthias Claudius (1740–1815) were particularly important to him,[12] and he was also attracted by the mystical-devotional character of Catholicism on a visit to Ghent Cathedral in 1803— an attraction which was to remain with him throughout his life and work.[13]

However both the death (presumed by suicide) of his father as well as his travels throughout Europe would profoundly shake whatever degree of Christian faith he had. Schopenhauer later remarked that his belief in the traditional notion of a creator-God was being questioned as early as the age of eighteen for he had become increasingly troubled by what he found and saw in the world, and, like many a young person, the existence of evil and suffering greatly distressed his talented mind. And, like many in his era, familiar interpretations of the doctrinal assurances from religion were no longer providing him with sufficient confidence that all shall be well. And yet that young man would also include in his notebook his realization that "If we take out of life the few moments of religion, art and pure love, what is left except a number of trivial thoughts?" (MR1, 9).[14]

As a student in Berlin, even had he wished to, Schopenhauer would have found it difficult to escape Christianity and Christian theology, for both continued to hold great sway in the German university system and society of the time. This influence was still especially significant even among professors of philosophy. But, in any case, it is clear from his student notebooks that he had no wish to escape from engaging such things, scribbling away furiously, even if already his observations display the critical assessment of specific doctrines that he would later develop at greater length.

Schopenhauer continued to attend church until the age of twenty-four. He came to reject religion in the form of a system of dogmas in 1812, coming to the conclusion that one could not begin from eternal truths when the possibility of the comprehension of such truths was a problem in itself.

For Schopenhauer, the concept of God gradually became an increasingly empty husk until he declared he was abandoning the use of the concept and term, also in 1812, stating he could not bear tolerance of a "hollow name" which served to allow one to live a customary routine more comfortably.[15] It was also in 1812 that he attended the polymath Friedrich Schleiermacher's (1768–1834) lectures on the "History of Philosophy in the Christian Era,"[16] for whose work he retained a respect that he rarely granted to other theologians of the era—despite a number of critical and occasionally caustic remarks in his notebooks and published writings alike. He shared with Schleiermacher the belief that religion's most irreducible element is not to be found in dogmas and precepts, although he disagreed with the conclusions Schleiermacher came to with regard to what was at the heart of religion (the latter's famed "feeling of absolute dependence"). In response to Schleiermacher's arguments concerning the mutual dependence of theology and philosophy—the latter suggesting that one could not be a philosopher unless one was religious—Schopenhauer asserted the exact opposite, "No one who is religious will become a philosopher. He does not need it. No one who is a philosopher is in a true sense religious. He walks free of the leash, precariously but free" (MR2, 243). For the young Schopenhauer, philosophy and religious faith were, to some extent, now being viewed as being mutually exclusive. Hübscher notes that this realization coincided with his abandoning the use of the term "God."[17]

Yet all of this goes to demonstrate just how much attention was being given to religion in his own studies, thought, and writings. And as the "God" of the institutional Christianity of his own times, it was gradually supplanted by his own hybrid doctrine of the "better consciousness" (or "higher consciousness," in German, *besseres Bewußtsein*)[18]—an idea that had come to him the previous year and that would continue to preoccupy his thoughts, holding a central place in his philosophy for the remainder of his life. It is a notion that further epitomized Schopenhauer's ambivalence toward religion. The rich cultural diversity to which the young philosopher was exposed meant that it was natural for him, as a student in Berlin, to immerse himself in the Romantic tradition. Thus it was that, as his concept of God faded from the orthodox notion and he rejected formalized doctrinal interpretations, so also was there an increase in his concentration on inner experience. In the year that marked the end of his usage of the word "God" as a meaningful concept, he described this consciousness in the following manner:

> This consciousness lies beyond all experience and thus beyond all reason, both theoretical and practical (instinct). It is not concerned with reason except that,

by virtue of its mysterious connexion with this in one individual, it meets with experience, and here for the individual there then arises the choice whether he will be *reason* or *better consciousness*.[19]   (MR1, 23)

Even at this early stage of his career, this passage introduces ideas that would remain crucial to his philosophy for the rest of his life. Later in his notebooks, he would also call the better consciousness, the "Peace of God" (MR1, 114). The increasingly ambiguous nature of Schopenhauer's relationship with religion is particularly indicated by further remarks from 1813:

> Gradually, especially during the time of Scholasticism and later, *God*, has been dressed in all kinds of qualities; but enlightenment has forced him to take them off again, one garment after another, and one would like to take them all off, were there not the scruple that the results of this might then be that there were only garments with nothing in them. Now there are two garments that cannot be taken off, in other words two inseparable qualities of God, namely *personality* and *causality*. These must always be found in the concept God and are the most necessary characteristics. As soon as we remove these, we may well be able to speak of God, but we can no longer have any conception of him. But I say that in this temporal and sensuous world of our understanding there are indeed personality and causality, in fact they are even necessary. However, the better consciousness in me lifts me into a world where there is no longer personality and causality or subject and object. My hope and belief is that this better (supersensuous and extratemporal) consciousness will become my only one, and for that reason I hope that it is no God. But if anyone wants to use the expression *God* symbolically for that better consciousness itself or for much that we are unable to separate and to name, so let it be, yet not among philosophers I should have thought.   (MR1, 44)

Here Schopenhauer alludes to the analogical and mythical elements of religious doctrine, upon which several theologians of his era focused a great deal—as would Schopenhauer, himself.[20] He also demonstrates that, already, his reading had familiarized him with the mystical *via negativa*, a method in which he would increasingly take refuge.

While, at times, Schopenhauer's interpretation of religion may well have been questionable (as in parts of his analysis of the concept of God), he nonetheless (and in many places) went to great lengths to study and critique traditional theological ideas. He became especially critical of what he perceived to be the overtly optimistic and anthropomorphic theological tendencies prevalent in his time, and he would frequently write cutting remarks dismissing such theologies.

Often when Schopenhauer spoke of "religion," he largely had in mind Christianity. In particular, he found much to criticize with certain forms of theism, and it is important to note that he did not equate theism and religion as one and the same thing: "religion is related to theism as the genus to a single species" (FR$_{[P]}$, 187).

Given all this, alongside his adaptation of transcendental idealism and views concerning the principle of sufficient reason, the younger Schopenhauer became especially critical of natural theology (i.e., attempts to reason directly from things of the world to significant and specific truths about the divine), especially, because (he believed) it seeks to make a causal connection between the world and God in a manner which breaches that very principle.[21] Along with Kant's rejection of the proofs for God's existence (he argued that just because Kant had closed off any way of knowing God by starting with the world, this was no excuse for beginning with God as something known and given) (WWR2$_{[P]}$, 350), he also expressed his admiration for David Hume's *Natural History of Religion* and also his *Dialogues Concerning Natural Religion.*[22]

Schopenhauer would give special attention to critiquing the most typical and well-known philosophical arguments for the existence of God—an undertaking that would preoccupy much of his thought and writing for some years to come. Schopenhauer's particular refutation of such arguments is aimed at notions which see God as an explanatory hypothesis for the world in a logical sense.[23] Indeed, his sharpest critiques of religion in general were aimed toward its functioning and value as an explanatory hypothesis for the world in comparison to his own system.

This can be seen, in particular, in his doctoral thesis,[24] which concerned explanatory hypotheses in general. Schopenhauer deemed *theism* to be such a hypothesis, albeit a flawed one.[25] His main problem appeared to be with the causal linkage between God, understood as creator, and the world. He believed that many aspects of traditional theism breached the "rules" of the principle of sufficient reason and so were found wanting. Hence he rejected the cosmological proof for the existence of God by arguing that causality only applies to the phenomenal world and could have no meaning above/beyond it (WWR2$_{[P]}$, 43, FR, 53, 58, 62): one cannot proceed from the world as totality to God as its sufficient reason or cause.[26]

Schopenhauer also rejected the *teleological* argument for God's existence,[27] both according to his interpretation of the principle of sufficient reason and because the sheer volume of suffering and evil in the world challenges any notion that there lies within the world a purpose, the author of which is a supremely good, all-powerful God. On such grounds Schopenhauer rejected Leibniz's systematic optimism.[28] Such musings on the problem of evil and suffering in the world, of course, heavily influenced the formulation of that part of his own explanatory hypothesis for which he became best known, viz., the metaphysics of the will.

Schopenhauer equally dismissed the ontological proof for God's existence. In his notes from Schleiermacher's lectures, following his statement of Anselm's famous definition of God as the inherent idea of a perfect being—that than which nothing greater can be conceived (from his *Proslogion*[29]).

> (Anselm, Archbishop of Canterbury). "Every man has within himself the idea of an absolute and supremely perfect being; if an object corresponds to this idea, it is God, but if no object corresponds to it, then the concept is deprived of reality and therefore of perfection." (MR2, 244)

Schopenhauer added the following, demonstrating the degree to which he was grappling with the *concept* of God:

> The *concept* of course, but not what is represented in the concept; this remains represented as perfect and hence as existing (real), but always only *represented*.

> I admit that if you represent it perfectly, you really represent it, but in this way you
> never go beyond representing.   (MR2, 244)

Schopenhauer here points toward the inadequacy of human knowledge concerning
questions about what is beyond the conditions of the possibility of such knowledge.
However, while the concept of God may have lost favor with Schopenhauer by the time
he wrote this, he also seems to have been suggesting that what Christianity uses the term
"God" to refer to is not deprived of reality or perfection despite the shortcomings of the
ontological argument itself. Schopenhauer, for the most part, would try to exercise philosophical humility with regard to speculations concerning such questions. And, in later
years, he would sum up his theological grappling with the concept by remarking that "As
soon as anyone speaks of *God*, I do not know *what* he is talking about" (MR4, 368).

Schopenhauer would likewise criticize Descartes's version of the ontological argument for confusing the notion of a *cause* with that of a *ground* or *reason of knowledge*.
Schopenhauer believes the notion that the concept of a supremely perfect being already
contains the existence of such a being as a given is a prime example of the confusion
between a cause and a ground of knowledge. And what Descartes offers is actually a
ground of knowledge (a reason) for why his God needs no explanatory cause to exist.[30]
Overall, Schopenhauer's refutation of the ontological proof rested on its failure to draw
on anything from experience.

In such critiques, Schopenhauer was questioning claims that the existence of God
and the nature of God's relationship to the world could be logically demonstrated in a
conclusive (rather than, for example, a "probable") manner. Religion, for Schopenhauer,
relied more on revelation and faith.[31]

At times, Schopenhauer's critique could appear to be against caricatures of theology
and doctrine or of the approach to God taken by particular philosophers. Sometimes,
he had not delved especially deeply into the writings or theological theories of which
he was so dismissive. At other times, some of his valid points had already been made by
Christian theologians themselves, long before.[32]

Yet Schopenhauer was also aware of alternative interpretations of the Christian
understanding of God and drew upon and referred to them at varying times throughout
his career. So, for example, although Schopenhauer argued against the validity of the
concept of God because he saw that such a conceptualization could not be made of what
concerned that which is beyond the phenomenal, he would later commend the theology
of Pseudo-Dionysius the Areopagite, from his *Mystical Theology*. Demonstrating that
his reading in Christian theology was becoming ever more extensive and wide-reaching,
he expressed a preference for this type of theology (i.e., mystical, negative, or apophatic
theology), which is discourse concerning what we *cannot* know about God as opposed
to affirmative statements about what we can (albeit also pointing to the limitations of
such a method in his typical Janus-faced fashion).

> ... this [theology] consists merely in the explanation that all the predicates of God
> can be denied, but not one can be affirmed, because he resides above and beyond
> all being and all knowledge, what Dionysius calls *epekeina*, "on yonder side" and

describes as something wholly and entirely inaccessible to our knowledge. This theology is the only true one; but it has no substance at all. Admittedly it says and tells us nothing, and it consists merely in the declaration that it is aware of this and cannot be otherwise.   (MR3, 376)[33]

Indeed, as we shall consider, Schopenhauer would be deeply influenced by the mystical traditions in Christianity and engaged in comparative reflections on analogous traditions in other religions, too.

24.3 SCHOPENHAUER AS BOTH FRIEND AND FOE OF RELIGION

The latter paragraph also displays something of Schopenhauer's "Janus-faced" attitude toward religion. In numerous writings he quite openly exhibited a dualistic attitude toward religion, on the one hand embracing much that it seeks to communicate and represent and, at other times, resorting to crude and simplistic rejections of the very same and of its value. Nowhere is this more evident than in his "Religion: A Dialogue" (PP2$_{[P]}$, 324–60), where he articulates his perception of how religion functions as the "metaphysics of the people"(i.e., because it serves to answer the fundamental questions concerning human existence in a digestible form for "the masses" and must be allowed to continue fulfilling this role). In the *Dialogue*, both speakers represent his own views as reflected elsewhere in his numerous works. There is no victor in the debate; rather they both agree to acknowledge merits in one another's cases and to go on their merry way as friends.

In response to the criticisms levied against religion by the philosophical-minded Philalethes (the "lover of the truth"), Demopheles, the "friend of the people," articulates the allegorical and mythological character of religion—a character that cloaks those "higher truths" which the burdensome existence of most human beings has made it impossible for them to discern. Religion fulfills humanity's deep metaphysical yearning and performs a socially cohesive and morally regulative function (PP2$_{[P]}$, 325).[34] Demopheles further suggests that religious truth is more concerned with moral than with theoretical objectivity, again reflecting Schopenhauer's own views as stated elsewhere.

Possibly the metaphysical element in all religions is false, but in all the moral element it is true. This can be surmised from the fact that in the former they clash with one another, whereas in the latter they agree.   (PP2$_{[P]}$, 340)

However, Schopenhauer did not simply see religion therefore as inferior to philosophy: rather, he was minded to see both the great merits and fault-lines that religion displays because of the manner in which it seeks to explain reality and guide those same masses.

> My philosophy is related to *religions* as is a straight line to several curves running close to it, for it expresses *sensu proprio*[35] and consequently relates directly what they show under disguises and reach in roundabout ways. And indeed *Christianity* follows very distant and strangely meandering paths.   (MR4, 378)[36]

Alongside his critique of Christian doctrines on philosophical grounds of reason and logic, Schopenhauer also argued that it was the corrupt and unsustainable outward forms of religion that he opposed, never the essential character and truths contained beneath them. As Arthur Hübscher, one of the foremost authorities on Schopenhauer, observed, his "indignation was not directed at religion, but at the forms in which it manifested itself."[37] Schopenhauer stated that his attack on the shell of religion was so virulent because he sought to protect the core underneath which he valued, once stating that "There is nothing in which we have to distinguish the kernel from the shell so much as in Christianity. Just because I value this kernel highly, I sometimes treat the shell with little ceremony, yet it is thicker than is often supposed" (WWR2$_{[P]}$, 625). Therefore he would also state that, "If the Christian dogmas ... are taken allegorically, they are a sacred myth, a vehicle for conveying to the people truths that would otherwise be quite beyond their reach" (PP2$_{[P]}$, 363). And again, "Christianity is an allegory that reflects a true idea, but in itself the allegory is not what is true" (PP2$_{[P]}$, 389).

So, variously, at times throughout his career and writings, he would criticize Christian doctrines while at other times he sought to reinterpret them or employ them to help draw a parallel with aspects of his own philosophy. Other times, still, he drew comparisons with doctrines in other faiths (and also with his own philosophy). And in still other and perhaps the most significant places, he borrowed from some of those very doctrines and wider Christian traditions themselves—particularly being influenced by a relatively small yet influential group of Christian thinkers throughout history.[38]

And, despite being inspired by famous critiques of *theism*, Schopenhauer would immerse himself in the Bible (just as in the sacred texts of the other main religions), as well as in the works of great Christian theologians and great thinkers who were decidedly Christian in outlook, for the rest of his life. Such included St. Paul, Augustine of Hippo, mystics such as Pseudo-Dionysius[39] and Meister Eckhart, giants of theology such as Martin Luther, and the Spanish authors he devoured from the mid-1820s onward—such as Félix Lope de Vega y Carpio (1562–1635), Pedro Calderón de la Barca (1600–1681), and Baltasar Gracián y Morales (1601–1658), whom he often called his favorite author. Each of these Spanish authors not only treated multiple religious themes in their works, but had also been Catholic priests at some crucial point in their lives and careers. He likewise closely followed debates in nineteenth-century theology and the supposed challenges to religion coming from science. He admired and yet also found fault with the work of David Friedrich Strauss,[40] and he particularly criticized Ludwig Feuerbach's critique of Christianity[41] (countering the latter by arguing that theology was anthropomorphism, as opposed to anthropology),[42] while he further went on to label Darwin's thought (with which he was not fully familiar) as "downright empiricism."

Schopenhauer's numerous random reflections on Christianity included criticisms of particular churches or traditions. For example, he especially criticized the Church of England for stifling intellectual and social development, as well as for the arrogance and unearned privilege of its ministers.[43] He also roundly condemned the American slave owners who were largely "orthodox and pious Anglicans" (PP2$_{[P]}$, 355f).

One of Schopenhauer's own most sustained and idiosyncratic critiques of Christianity in general is found in his collected observations "On Religion" (PP2$_{[P]}$, 362–94),[44] where, again, elements of Christian doctrine and dogma are further scrutinized and found wanting on many fronts when taken in a literal sense. Schopenhauer perceives absurd inconsistencies across the Old and New Testaments, particularly in relation to the doctrines of predestination and grace. He believes the definitive articulations of what Christianity seeks to communicate through such doctrines is exemplified in the works of Augustine and appropriated by Martin Luther. In part, he appears not to grasp some of the finer nuances of the various differing interpretations of the doctrine of grace. And concerning the implication that "moral qualities are actually" inborn, he makes the bold suggestions that, in Hinduism and Buddhism, the doctrine of metempsychosis seeks to express the same fatalistic view of the world only in a superior fashion (PP2$_{[P]}$, 364–65).[45]

In the same essay, he speaks about how Augustine, thanks to "his rigid systematic mind," was responsible for the "strict dogmatizing of Christianity," also charging him with taking what is at best only hinted at in the bible and turning such hints into rigid doctrines that, in Schopenhauer's day, seem palpably unjust to rationalists (PP2$_{[P]}$, 364–65). However, paradoxically given such criticism (and his own consistent antipathy toward such dogmatism), Schopenhauer expresses sympathy with Augustine's thought and contends that if we take the doctrines allegorically, then some sense can be made of them. He even finds further parallels between Augustine's predestination and Buddhism's Nirvana and Samsara—the latter two being paralleled with the two cities Augustine speaks of in his *City of God* (PP2$_{[P]}$, 368–69).

Schopenhauer also suggests that Christianity is "disadvantaged" as compared to other faiths in that, rather than being "pure doctrine," it is "essentially and mainly a *narrative or history*, a series of events, a complex of the facts, actions and sufferings of individuals; and this very history constitutes the dogma, belief in which leads to salvation." While other faiths may recount something of the lives of their founders (e.g., Buddhism), this does not become central to the doctrine and way of salvation commended—it accompanies rather than being part of it. (PP2$_{[P]}$, 369–71).[46]

Schopenhauer also lays down an ontological indictment of Christianity for its failure to accord rights and decent treatment to non-human animals (in sharp contrast with other faiths, such as Buddhism). He especially lambasts Christianity for its perception that animals exist to serve and fulfill humans, for which, as with other aspects, he (unflatteringly) blames Christianity's appropriation of Jewish ideas (PP2$_{[P]}$, 370–71).[47]

Here, as elsewhere—as we shall see—Schopenhauer distills the essence of Christianity down to renunciation of this world as the path to salvation, conveniently paralleling his own doctrine of salvation. He does so in a section contrasting the Old and New Testaments of the Christian Bible (he believes the latter reinterprets, even rectifies the former)[48] and engages in sometimes fanciful, sometimes thought-provoking speculation that the teaching of the New Testament must owe something to Indian thought—even the teachings of Christ—and he draws various parallels with Buddhist and Hindu thought (PP2$_{[P]}$, 380–83). Schopenhauer evens asserts that an understanding of these other two religions is necessary "for a thorough understanding of Christianity" (PP2$_{[P]}$, 381).

The more fanciful comparisons aside, there are some interesting comparative theological observations concerning the relationship of Christianity to Buddhism and Hinduism trying to get out, just as other parts of his work contain several such interesting comparisons. Yet his negative comparisons with Judaism are obviously all too often far wide of the mark and questionable.

Schopenhauer does demonstrate some familiarity with the biblical and theological scholarship of the day here, as elsewhere, yet in parts, some of his engagement with that scholarship is surface-level and again demonstrates a lack of nuanced depth.[49] So, for example, he appears to show knowledge of that biblical scholarship in stating that "in general our [sic.] gospels are based on something original or at any rate on a fragment from the time and associations of Jesus himself..." (PP2$_{[P]}$, 384).[50] He demonstrates an engagement with Hermann Reimarus (1694–1768) and also discusses, here mostly with approval, the contemporary interpretation of Christianity by David Friedrich Strauss (PP2$_{[P]}$, 384–86) as being largely mythical in character, with subsequent elaborations and embellishments by later followers of Jesus.

Yet, at the same time, he demonstrates the limitations of his knowledge of Christian origins when he states that "all we really know of Jesus is the passage in Tacitus (*Annals.,* lib. Xv, c. 44)" (PP2$_{[P]}$, 386).[51] Furthermore, in the subsequent section on "Sects," not for the first or last time in his writings, he interprets certain parallels with (and so confirmation of) some of his own key thoughts in some of these theological interpretations. There he also restates his preference for the Augustinian doctrine of original sin over and against Pelagianism,[52] yet he demonstrates a lack of nuanced knowledge of all three subject matters with regards to such debates. The same can be said with remarks that follow concerning the "Greek Church" as well as the Reformation and post-Reformation debates that those earlier theological disputes about grace, original sin, and free will—particularly with regard to Pelagianism—fed into.

Schopenhauer therefore charges Orthodoxy and post-Tridentine Catholicism with veering toward Pelagianism while, in contrast, Luther is praised, so it appears, for being both Augustinian and more "mystical" in his leanings, as is Calvin. He even speaks of Jansenism as holding what could be conceived as "the most genuine form of Christianity," whereas the Jesuits are "semi-Pelagian." In each case he is dealing in erroneous caricatures that lack historical as well as theological nuance (PP2$_{[P]}$, 386–87). Yet, as elsewhere, he deals in such binary oppositional thinking because it helps him demonstrate, he believes, the validity of his own key ideas.[53]

24.4 WHERE CHRISTIANITY MOST INFLUENCED SCHOPENHAUER'S THOUGHT

All in all, while Schopenhauer fell away from organized religion in his twenties, religious and especially mystical ideas were to remain integral to the development of his thought for the rest of his years, and he would never cease to speculate about the very same questions with which theology is concerned.[54]

Indeed, if Schopenhauer's primary arguments against dogmatic theology and elements of natural theology rested on what he perceives to be their failed attempts at providing an explanatory hypothesis for the world and reality, when it came to the ethical and mystical elements of religion, Schopenhauer's attitude was very different. As Thomas Bailey Saunders, one of his early translators remarked, "however little he may have been in sympathy with the supernatural element, he owed much to the moral doctrines of Christianity and of Buddhism, between which he traced great resemblance."[55]

Schopenhauer made clear that the *denial* of the will constituted the pinnacle of his thought because it is the key to salvation. Over the centuries, for explanatory purposes, such a truth has been variously expressed and passed on via the mythical language of religions. Here we find the most significant parallel between religious ideas and practices and his own moral philosophy that Schopenhauer acknowledges. He acknowledges how the major religions of the world share with him the intention to interpret human existence and to commend a pathway of freedom away from suffering.

> Therefore that great fundamental truth contained in Christianity as well as in Bramanism and Buddhism, the need for salvation from an existence given up to suffering and death, and its attainability through the denial of the will, hence by a decided opposition to nature, is beyond all comparison the most important truth there can be.   (WWR2$_{[P]}$, 628)

Schopenhauer saw this doctrine most vividly in Buddhist teachings and especially in ascetic forms of Christianity—our only hope of salvation is to be free from this "driving," insatiable will that underlies existence. So virtue, holiness, and morality guided by compassion constitute the road to salvation which culminates in that transcendent "peace that is higher than all reason" (WWR1$_{[P]}$, 411), whereby one may break free from ceaseless willing. Through the practice of compassion we see through the principle of individuation and come to appreciate the unity of reality and our oneness with others. Schopenhauer reflected that this was the true meaning behind the Christian commandment to love one's neighbor as oneself (MR3, 6).[56] Indeed, he stated that his ethical writings were in full accord with Christian Doctrines (WWR1$_{[P]}$, 408), which he saw as sharing that similar emphasis on renunciation with his own philosophy.

Schopenhauer even praised Christianity in particular, among religions "in the west," for the virtue and path of salvation it teaches: "In morals, the teachings of *caritas*, gentleness, love of one's enemy, resignation, and denial of one's own will, are exclusively its own, in the West of course" (PP2$_{[P]}$, 363). And further on, "Renunciation in this world and the direction of our hopes to a better are the spirit of Christianity. But the way to such a world is opened by reconciliation, i.e., by salvation from our world and its ways" (PP2$_{[P]}$, 381). And later still, he writes, "original sin and salvation constitute the essence of Christianity" (PP2$_{[P]}$, 389).[57]

According to Schopenhauer, moral truths help reveal the essence of the world (PP2$_{[P]}$, 201), and, in his ethical system, he identifies egoism as the prime "antimoral incentive." His own basis of morality, *Mitleid*—best translated into English as "compassion"—is a virtue central to Christianity just as it is to the other major world religions. His own moral principle, although not acknowledged, is taken from Augustine's *City of God*: "*Neminem laede, imo omnes, quantum potes, juva*"—"Injure no one; on the contrary, help everyone as much as you can" (BM$_{[P]}$, 69).[58] For Schopenhauer, the virtuous person possesses a "deeper" knowledge of reality *and* such knowledge inspires virtuous conduct (BM$_{[P]}$, 40–41).

In relation to his own articulation of the denial of the will-to-live, Schopenhauer was especially apt to draw parallels with specific religious doctrines and to employ them to explain his thought in the figurative ways he claimed were common to religion, despite claiming that his own philosophy captured the "truth" concerning humanity and the possibility of salvation without recourse to mythical elements.[59] He drew particular doctrinal parallels with Christianity's key tenets here.

Schopenhauer argued that we cannot arrive at the state where we deny the will by "intention or design" for it is the state whereupon we enter into freedom, saying that it was thus that the denial of the will arises "from the innermost relation of knowing and willing in man" (WWR1$_{[P]}$, 404). Hence this has the effect that the denial of the will appears to come from "without" the person, and, in this sense, he feels that this stilling of the will is bound up with the freedom of the human will and so likens it to the Christian doctrine of grace because a change in the "inner being" of the individual comes about, with the individual no longer willing what he or she willed so fervently before:

> For this reason, the Church calls the consequence of the effect of grace *new birth* or *regeneration*. For what she calls the *natural man*, to whom she denies all capacity for good, is that very will-to-live that must be denied if salvation is to be attained from an existence like ours. Behind our existence lies something else that becomes accessible to us only by our shaking off the world.   (WWR1$_{[P]}$, 404–05)

And thus Schopenhauer interprets the doctrine of salvation through Christ as being analogous to the doctrines of the affirmation and denial of the will. In Adam's fall, one sees the finite, animal, and sinful side of human nature ("the Idea of man in its unity," WWR1$_{[P]}$, 405), a limited form of existence from which follows suffering and, ultimately, death. But in Jesus Christ, one sees an exemplary teacher whose death is seen to represent humanity's eternal and supernatural side.[60] Christ both expresses and effects the freedom and salvation of human nature.

...the Christian teaching symbolises *grace*, the *denial of the will*, *salvation*, in the God become man.... The doctrine of original sin (affirmation of the will) and of salvation (denial of the will) is really the great truth which constitutes the kernel of Christianity, while the rest is in the main only clothing and covering, or something accessory. Accordingly, we should interpret Jesus Christ always in the universal, as the symbol or personification of the denial of the will-to-live, but not in the individual, whether according to his mythical history in the Gospels, or according to the probably true history lying at the root thereof. For neither the one nor the other will easily satisfy us entirely. It is merely the vehicle of that first interpretation for the people, who always demanded something founded on fact. That Christianity has recently forgotten its true significance, and has degenerated into shallow optimism, does not concern us here.   (WWR1$_{[P]}$, 405)[61]

In addition to illustrating the transcendental-anthropological elements of Schopenhauer's understanding of salvation, Schopenhauer here, again, echoes aspects of the German theological tradition of his time which sought to discern "the" *essence* of Christianity. Thus he could, in parts of his writings, be said to have been seeking to provide a "demythologized" account of Christianity: "Christianity is generally of an entirely allegorical character; for that which in things profane is called allegory, is in religions styled 'mystery'" (PP2$_{[P]}$, 363).[62] He also states that all humans have the potential to be both Adam and Christ (WWR2$_{[P]}$, 628).[63]

Indeed, Schopenhauer's own philosophy can essentially be seen as a way of transcendence that leads toward a *moral* interpretation of reality, just as many religious belief systems do. Schopenhauer would even write, in 1853, that some parts of the fourth book of *The World as Will and Representation*—that is to say the *ethical* part—could in some sense be regarded as having been dictated by the "holy Ghost" (MR4, 306).[64] Schopenhauer outlines the pinnacle of salvation thus, drawing, it appears, from St. Paul in his Letter to the Philippians (Phil. 4:7):[65]

...we turn now our glance from our own needy and perplexed nature to those who have overcome the world, in whom the will, having reached complete self-knowledge, has found itself again in everything and then freely denied itself, and who then merely wait to see the last trace of the will vanish with the body that is animated by that trace. Then, instead of the restless pressure and effort; instant of that constant transition from desire to apprehension and from joy to sorrow; the life-dream of the man who wills, we see a *peace that is higher than all reason.* That ocean-like calmness of the sprit, that deep tranquillity, that unshakeable calmness and serenity whose mere reflection in the countenance, as depicted by Raphael and Correggio, is a complete and certain gospel. Only knowledge remains, the will has vanished.   (WWR1$_{[P]}$, 411)[66]

And while this pinnacle of Schopenhauer's ethical system and philosophy may, famously, at the end of WWR1 be described as "nothing," it is not a *nihilistic* understanding of the "beyond" that Schopenhauer is striving to describe. It is merely an acknowledgment of the limitations of human reasoning: "[W]e see all religions at their highest point end in mysticism and mysteries, that is to say, in darkness and veiled obscurity" (WWR2$_{[P]}$, 610). Schopenhauer's system, then, intentionally ends in mystery.

24.5 Discerning the *Comet Tail*: Schopenhauer's Dependence on Religious Thought, the *Via Negativa*, and a "Godless Religion"?

Schopenhauer argued that this highest point of his teaching must necessarily be *negative* in character because it concerns what is "beyond" the describable. Therefore this further necessitated that he follow the approach of mysticism.[67] In his notebooks, Schopenhauer defined mysticism as "the free expression of direct metaphysical knowledge with a contempt for all the very strong objections of the faculty of reason," observing further how in Christian theology this was interpreted in terms of the doctrine of union with God (MR3, 377&n.). In WWR2 he describes the mystical element in religion as the highest element because it transcends the bounds of knowledge and has to deal in negations in order to be comprehensible at all (WWR2$_{[P]}$, 610–11).[68]

Above all, Schopenhauer took from mysticism the notion of the need to transform self in order to overcome the misery of the world; the need, in effect, to "escape" from, to transcend this world. The abnegation of the egoistic self and the doctrine of "overcoming the world" are the central purposes of Schopenhauer's ethical-soteriological thought in particular, and, indeed, his philosophy in general.[69]

Indeed, mysticism is among the most telling of all religious influences on Schopenhauer's system, something which he searched for and found in each of the aforementioned three faiths and in others besides, with mystical traditions from Christianity proving especially influential on his thought.[70] Common mystical concepts of human illumination and purification from selfishness, rising to contemplation of "eternal truths," can be seen running constantly throughout Schopenhauer's work. This is a theme common in many Christian monastic and spiritual traditions and is known as the "ladder of perfection" (or "Jacob's ladder"). His ethical-soteriological thought is also comparable to mystical notions of deification and the soul's path into the eternal God beyond conceptualization.

The German mystic, Jacob Böhme (1575–1624), was a life-long influence, as was the aforementioned Mathias Claudius, who inspired Schopenhauer's discussion of conversion in WWR1 with a story concerning "catholic transcendental change" (i.e., transformation, WWR1$_{[P]}$, 394). And to this list we can add further eclectic influences, including such works as the Hindu *Upanishads*, the *Enneads* of Plotinus (c. 204/5–270), the aforementioned Pseudo-Dionysius, the Irish philosopher John Scottus Eriugena (815–877), the Sufi traditions of Islam, and, especially, the Dominican friar, Meister Eckhart (c.1260–c.1328) (WWR2$_{[P]}$, 612). The majority of these mystical influences were from Christianity, while Plotinus's ideas influenced a wide range of Christian works and helped shape the character of much Christian theology, both East and West alike. Schopenhauer thus followed the mystics "beyond," so to speak, adopting a mantra from Eckhart that man "seek not God outside himself" (WWR2$_{[P]}$, 612).[71]

Later in his career, upon further immersing himself in the writings of Meister Eckhart, he expressed his admiration for the latter's recognition of the allegorical nature of theological language and especially the fact that Eckhart was "forever squabbling with God" (MR4, 387).

As with other Christian doctrines, Schopenhauer identified the approach found in such mystical writers with his own doctrine of the denial of the will-to-live and even suggested that the similarity of his own thought with such approaches was the reason why "Protestant universities" viewed his philosophy as a stumbling block and accordingly suppressed it (WWR2$_{[P]}$, 615).[72] Schopenhauer also argued that the doctrine of the denial of the will-to-live can be seen in various different forms throughout the history of Christianity, although he believes that Meister Eckhart gave the doctrine "the most perfect explanation" of all (WWR1$_{[P]}$, 387). Indeed, he went on to conclude that Buddha and Eckhart, along with himself, all taught the same thing, only in necessarily different forms (WWR1$_{[P]}$, 387–88).

Schopenhauer ultimately saw morality as something that is *essentially* "mysterious" (i.e., bound up with the "nature" of ultimate reality) and so truly virtuous and disinterested acts are mysterious actions. Thus morality is "…practical mysticism insofar as it ultimately springs from the same knowledge that constitutes the essence of all mysticism proper" (BM$_{[P]}$, 212). Ultimately Schopenhauer proclaims that the phenomenon of compassion (*Mitleid*) and its attendant realization of our metaphysical unity with the other constitutes *das große Mysterium der Ethik* (BM$_{[P]}$, 144).[73]

But here Schopenhauer's thought culminates in a paradox. He argued that philosophy has the onerous task of trying to express in a more direct fashion the truth that is held in common among most of the world's major religions. His own attempt, then, was articulated through his moral philosophy and the soteriological conclusions to his system. But whether or not, in the final analysis, such was actually more a direct form expression is open to question. Schopenhauer claimed to want to retain discourse concerning the mystical without much of the theological "baggage" that he viewed as either mythological or erroneous metaphysics.[74] Likewise, he spoke of the need for independence from "mythical" religious explanations and transcendent hypostases of the truth of ethics: "The task before us is philosophical and we must therefore entirely disregard all solutions to the problem that are conditioned by religions" (BM$_{[P]}$, 138).[75] But Schopenhauer violated both stated rules on numerous occasions and could not have done otherwise given the nature of his own system, its core principles, and the difficult tasks he set himself in philosophy. He even (and somewhat contradictorily, given his other statements on the allegorical nature of religion contrasted with the purer philosophical approach) asserts that it is "immaterial" whether the doctrine of the denial of the will "proceeds from a theistic or from an atheistic religion" (WWR1$_{[P]}$, 385).

Schopenhauer was also blatantly selective in what he chose to "borrow" from religion and what he chose to criticize. He freely drew on writings from religious sources, yet focused more on what is in accord with his own theories, largely overlooking the religious context and relevance of such writings. Furthermore, he ultimately proves to be as guilty as Kant in requiring theological ideas to provide coherence for his own ethical theory.

One key question, then, is how much Schopenhauer truly found religious doctrines and writings to be *in accord* with his own views or how much his extensive reading both from these religions and from philosophers whose own views were greatly shaped by such religions can be said to have been the actual inspiration of and basis for his own theories, as well as how much they influenced the development of those theories in particular directions.

In relation to this question, one of the key reasons why Nietzsche criticized and reacted against Schopenhauer so forcefully was that he believed Schopenhauer was not only unable to free himself from the taint of religion and theology, but also that it continued to permeate his thought:

> Because philosophers have frequently philosophized within a religious tradition, or at least under the inherited power of the celebrated "metaphysical need," they have achieved hypotheses which have in fact been very similar to Jewish or Christian or Indian religious dogmas, similar, that is to say, in the way children are usually similar to their mothers, except that in this case the fathers were not aware of this fact of motherhood....Every philosophy that exhibits a gleaming religious comet-tail in the darkness of its ultimate conclusions thereby casts suspicion on everything in it that is presented as science: all of that, too, is presumably likewise religion, even if it is dressed up as science.[76]

Not only did Nietzsche rail against Schopenhauer's ethics per se, embracing the title of *The Antichrist,* in his work of the same name, along with the attendant naturalistic worldview that Schopenhauer directly condemned, just as every major religion condemns it (as the latter approvingly asserted),[77] but he also criticized Schopenhauer's affinity to Christian morals and especially his conception of *Mitleid.*[78] In particular, Nietzsche's "enemy" was the theological mindset which he believed had corrupted much German philosophy, "I make war on this theologian instinct: I have found traces of it everywhere. Whoever has theologian blood in his veins has a wrong and dishonest attitude towards all things from the very first."[79]

Iris Murdoch once declared that *The World as Will and Representation* should be seen as a "religious book," the central concern of which is ethical.[80] While Bernard Bykhovsky concluded that, when one begins with examining Schopenhauer's rejection of the traditional theistic explanatory hypotheses yet goes on to examine parallels between Schopenhauer's thought and religious belief systems, the results can be surprising, going so far as to label Schopenhauer's philosophy a "Godless religion."

> Such is the reverse side of Schopenhauer's "a-theism," the facade of which turns out to be not genuine atheism, disbelief, but a godless religion, the mystical cult of Non-being. It replaces the "other" world with the anti-world, the original sin with the will to life, the bliss of paradise with the will to non-willing, the Apocalypse with nothing.[81]

There is ample further evidence that Schopenhauer saw certain parallels between his thought and religious systems, and even that certain followers of Schopenhauer regarded his system as a surrogate "faith." Wilhelm von Gwinner, who was also his executor, notes in his *Life of Schopenhauer* how the philosopher, near death, took delight in the fact that "…his seemingly irreligious teachings 'had the impact of a religion,' filling the void created by the loss of faith and giving rise to inward reassurance and satisfaction."[82] While, in 1890, another early biographer would assert that

> …to others still, the dogma of Schopenhauer commended itself as "the religion of the religionless"—a new rock for the faith in the supernatural which had lost all hold on its ancient supports of tradition, and been driven by scientific criticism of its belief in miracle and legend, yet still craved for something more sustaining than matter and force, and other misty abstractions. For those who can read between the lines, or decipher the palimpsest on which Schopenhauer's doctrines are inscribed, much of the old faith lives disguised in the new; they know that God is not as man, and His thoughts far unlike human; when they hear the attributes and faculties of the Will they remember that names are but "sound and smoke, encoding the blaze of heavenly light," and in the message of pessimism and asceticism they can hear the eternal voice of wisdom, from India to Egypt, from Palestine to Greece, proclaiming vanity of vanities behind and the kingdom of heaven within.[83]

Given such judgments and the preceding questions and concerns, as well as our considerations throughout the foregoing, it can be concluded that any engagement with Schopenhauer's relationship with Christianity and Christian thought can prove illuminating for understanding multiple aspects of his philosophy in general.

Notes

1. As Robert A. Gonzales observed, "…the dominant line of thinking has been, of course, to consider Schopenhauer's philosophy as a classic form of atheism. The works of Safranski, Schmidt, Hasse, Hollingdale, McGill, Hübscher, Vecchiotti et al. interpret Schopenhauer in this manner" (*An Approach to the Sacred in the Thought of Schopenhauer* [San Francisco: Mellen Research University Press, 1992], xiii). See also Walter Kaufmann: "…he was the first major European philosopher to make a point of atheism" ("Schopenhauer" in *The Concise Encyclopedia of Western Philosophy and Philosophers*, edited by J. O. Urmson and J. Rée [London: Unwin, 1989], 294) and Bryan Magee: "[Schopenhauer] was the first major Western philosopher to be openly and explicitly atheist" (*The Great Philosophers*, edited by Bryan Magee [London: BBC Books, 1987], 213).
2. See Helen Zimmern, *Schopenhauer—His Life and His Philosophy* (London: Longmans, Green & Co., 1876), 136–37.
3. Schopenhauer is seen by many commentators as being among the earliest of Western philosophers to be well-versed in "Eastern" religious thought. At times, he afforded Buddhism a "special pre-eminence" in relation to his philosophy (e.g., WWR2$_{[P]}$, 169) and even referred to himself as a Buddhist in his later years; see Cartwright, *Schopenhauer: A Biography* (Cambridge: Cambridge University Press, 2010), 273–74. He would also write highly critical annotations in translations of the sacred texts of these religions which employed Western theological concepts in place of truly accurate terms and concepts; see Cartwright, *Schopenhauer*, 270.

4. See Arthur Hübscher, *The Philosophy of Schopenhauer in its Intellectual Context: Thinker Against the Tide*, translated by J. T. Baer and D. E. Cartwright (Lampeter: Edwin Mellen, 1989), 64 ff.

5. Zimmern, *Schopenhauer*, 212.

6. Admittedly, there are bombastic or sweeping passages where Schopenhauer seems to speak of religion eventually dying out to be supplanted by philosophy; for example, where he says that knowledge will continue to grow to the extent that "the myths that constitute the skeleton of Christianity shrink so that faith can no longer cling to them," and he states that humanity will outgrow religion and, possibly anticipating the "death of God" discourse to come in philosophy and theology later: "We see religion in its death-agony cling to morality for which it would like to pass itself off as the mother; but this will not do at all!" (PP2$_{[P]}$, 392), and also "All religion is antagonistic to culture" (PP2$_{[P]}$, 394). But such passages are contradicted by many other parts of his writings where he affirms the truth-conveying character of religion. Note that even in that former passage it is the mythical "skeleton" of Christianity rather than its essence he is speaking about.

7. For a more detailed treatment of several aspects of Schopenhauer in relation to religion, including Christianity, see Gerard Mannion, *Schopenhauer, Religion and Morality* (Aldershot: Ashgate, 2003) and also Gerard Mannion, "A 'Godless' Road to Redemption: Comparing the Moral Visions of Arthur Schopenhauer and Iris Murdoch" (*Schopenhauer-Jahrbuch* 91 [September, 2010], 135–62).

8. Many thinkers would follow after him, developing and employing various differing methods and approaches to interpreting and explaining religion, from the philosophical and theological to the hermeneutical and social scientific, including anthropological. Some approaches to religion particularly explored the sacred texts of faiths, some looked at the differing types of religious organization and community life (e.g., church and sect). Some focused on ritual, on linguistic analysis and interpretation, and some on specific aspects of a faith, such as comparative approaches to mystical traditions and practices or the approach to morality and ethics within and between religions. It could be said that Schopenhauer engaged in a form of each of these approaches to varying degrees.

9. See Stjepan G. Mestrovic, "Reappraising Durkheim's *Elementary Forms of the Religious Life* in the Context of Schopenhauer's Philosophy" in *Journal for the Scientific Study of Religion* 28, no. 3 (1989).

10. See his youthful Letter to the publisher F. A. Brockhaus (April 3, 1818) (GB, 31).

11. GB, 31; See Cartwright, *Schopenhauer*, 286.

12. Claudius remained important for him throughout his life—indeed could be said to have become more so in his later years. See, e.g., Cartwright, *Schopenhauer*, 29–30; and Rüdiger Safranski *Schopenhauer and the Wild Years of Philosophy*, translated by E. Osers (Cambridge, MA: Harvard University Press, 1991), esp. 57–63.

13. Schopenhauer would later tour Italy, including the Vatican's religious sites and museums.

14. Such "religious longings" would not leave him, as opposed to an unquestioning acceptance of traditional doctrinal interpretations, as a further notebook entry from that time indicates, "All philosophy and all the consolation it affords go to show that there is a spiritual world and that in it we are separated from all the phenomena of the external world and from an exalted seat can view these with the greatest calm and unconcern, although that part of us, belonging to the corporeal world, is still pulled and swung around so much in it" (MR1, 8). Such convictions would remain with Schopenhauer for the rest of his days, and, even at this young age, they pointed toward the direction in which his philosophy would develop.

15. Hübscher, *Philosophy of Schopenhauer*, 16.

16. Which followed the same line of argument as his great work of 1799, *On Religion: Speeches to its Cultured Despisers*—a work that sought to bridge the faith and reason divide in an era when religion was coming under constant attack from rationalist thinkers.

17. Hübscher, *Philosophy of Schopenhauer*, 13. It is also no coincidence that the Orientalist, Friedrich Majer, introduced him to "Eastern thought" in the winter of 1813, the year after Schopenhauer had dispensed with the word "God" as a meaningful term in the shaping of his own explanatory hypothesis, being supplanted by the notion of the "better consciousness."

18. See MR1, 23, MR 1, 23 ff; 111–14; 147–49). For a range of commentaries, see *Better Consciousness: Schopenhauer's Philosophy of Value*, edited by Alex Neill and Christopher Janaway (Oxford: Wiley-Blackwell, 2009).

19. He continues, "If he wants to be *reason*, then as theoretical reason he will be a Philistine and as practical reason a scoundrel. If he wants to be *better consciousness*, then we positively cannot say anything more about him, for what we say lies in the province of reason. Therefore we can only say what happens in this sphere, and in this way speak only negatively of the better consciousness. Thus *reason* then undergoes a disturbance; as *theoretical* reason we see it supplanted and in its place *genius*, as *practical* we see it supplanted and in its place *virtue*. —*The better consciousness* is neither practical nor theoretical, for these are merely divisions of reason…." (MR1, 23–24). See also MR1, 111–14; 147–49, as well as Hübscher's discussion of this term in *Philosophy of Schopenhauer*, 29 ff.

20. For example, David F. Strauss and Ludwig Feuerbach. The older Schopenhauer was familiar with the work of both. See later discussion.

21. He would not realize, of course, that, ultimately, his own system, particularly his ethics and doctrine of salvation, could be considered to have followed a similar path.

22. See WWR1$_{[P]}$, 510–11. Schopenhauer offered to translate both philosophers, respectively, into English and German (neither offer was accepted by the publisher).

23. Note, however, that although Schopenhauer examines such arguments for the existence of God in some detail, his refutation of such logical defenses for theism does not hold valid for many of the classical interpretations of the Christian doctrine of God.

24. And its subsequent expanded publication, FR.

25. In another writing, stating that "Just as polytheism is the personification of the individual parts and forces of nature, so is monotheism that of the whole of nature, at one stroke" ("On Theism" [PP2$_{[P]}$, 377]). Today, one might speak as much of a "grand narrative" as of an explanatory hypothesis.

26. On such premises, Schopenhauer also rejected the tenets of absolute idealism which merely turned God into the absolute—giving the "battered" concept of God (as he perceived it) a new and dignified, academically "respectable" air (here he especially had Hegel and his followers in his critical sights).

27. See, for example, WN$_{[P]}$, passim; WWR1$_{[P]}$, 523; WWR2$_{[P]}$, 581.

28. See, for example, PP2$_{[P]}$, 291–385, WWR1$_{[P]}$, 325, 394–5; WWR2$_{[P]}$, 513, 579–83.

29. Anselm, in his *Proslogion*, defined God as "that than which nothing greater can be conceived." He asserted that, because something which exists in actuality is greater than something that is simply just conceived in the mind, as God is that than which nothing greater can be conceived, it therefore demonstrates that God must exist. If God did not exist, God would not be the greatest conceivable thing of all.

30. René Descartes "Responsio ad secundas objectioptions" in *Meditationes de prima philosophia*, axioma I (originally published in 1641) quoted in FR$_{[P]}$, 13–14. (See *Oeuvres des Descartes*, edited by Charles Adam and Paul Tannery [Paris: Cerf, 1904], vol. VII, 164–65.)

31. Although Schopenhauer's own eventual theories concerning the noumenal can also be interpreted as requiring "faith," as well.

32. For example, writing in 1852, he stated that, "The *world* is not made, for, as Ocellus of Lucania says, it has been from all eternity, namely because *time* is conditioned by beings that know, consequently by the *world*, just as the *world* is by *time*. The world is not possible without time, just as time is not possible without world. These two are therefore inseparable, and it is as little possible even merely to conceive a time wherein there was no world at all as to think of a world that would exist at no time at all" (MR4, 359 [emphasis in original]). This echoes Augustine of Hippo's dismissal of the question "what was God doing before he created the world" in Chapter XI of his *Confessions*. Many of the classic expositions of the Christian understanding of God do not seek to define the relationship between God and the world in purely and crudely temporal terms. Schopenhauer engaged with and was influenced by much of Augustine's thought, so perhaps their similarities on this subject should not be seen as merely coincidental.

33. Of course, this would not rule out discourse concerning a *doctrine* of God (as opposed to detailed conception of God) and what that entails, for a doctrine of God could be held through the *Via Negativa* and hence the notion of a God who could not be definitively conceptualized. In fact, this is what much classical Christian theology entails—as demonstrated in a pre-eminent fashion by the works of Thomas Aquinas, who was himself heavily influenced by Pseudo-Dionysius.

34. See also WWR2$_{[P]}$, 164 ff.

35. I.e., in a proper sense.

36. See also PP2$_{[P]}$, 363.

37. Hübscher, *Philosophy of Schopenhauer*, 9. See note 6.

38. His relevance to the theodicy debates, his philosophy as a counter to overtly optimistic philosophical systems such as Hegel's, and his relevance to the whole issue of demythologizing are all further areas of contact with Christian thought. Furthermore, his interpretation of religion aids comparative analysis of diverse faiths.

39. As we have seen earlier.

40. Strauss was most famous for his *Das Leben Jesu: kritisch bearbeitet*, published in two volumes between 1835 and 1836 (translated from the fourth German edition in 1846 by George Eliot as *The Life of Jesus Critically Examined*).

41. Feuerbach was most famous for his 1841 work, *Das Wesen des Christentums* (translated in 1854 by George Eliot as *The Essence of Christianity*).

42. Hübscher, *Philosophy of Schopenhauer*, 22.

43. Cartwright, *Schopenhauer*, 57–61. See also PP1$_{[P]}$, 269f and PP2$_{[P]}$, 16, 355f.

44. This follows, and should not be confused with, his *dialogue* on religion.

45. Although he does believe that Christianity, in the sixth century, through the doctrine of purgatory, adopted something analogous to the idea of metempsychosis, he also believed that what the latter entailed was a truth accepted by most of the human race with the exception of Jewish theism, with its emphasis on creation *ex nihilo* (PP2$_{[P]}$, 365–66).

46. Schopenhauer is unconvincing on Buddhism here. See also PP2$_{[P]}$, 393–94, where he again feels that Christianity is hampered by being grounded on a single event and person, viz., Jesus Christ, whereas Buddhism sees the need for many Buddhas in an ongoing fashion.

47. Because of its attitude toward animals, alone it seems, Christianity's morality is refused the title of holding "the most perfect morality. It really has a serious and fundamental imperfection in that it restricts its precepts to man and leaves the whole of the animal world without any rights" (PP2$_{[P]}$, 371).

48. Schopenhauer is particularly critical of the Jewish sense of creation *ex nihilo* and of what he perceives to be the unjustified optimism of the Old Testament worldview. Cartwright's biography (542–43) sums up the various viewpoints on Schopenhauer's relationship with Judaism succinctly in concluding that while he was critical of Judaism (as, we have here seen, he was of so much of religion in general, as well as of numerous aspects of particular religions), he was rarely ever critical of Jewish people, whether in general or of individuals; indeed, there are many specific Jewish figures for whom he expresses great admiration and who were close acquaintances. For Cartwright, his criticism of Judaism was an intellectual rejection of the religion as an explanatory system in a fashion after his antipathy towards Hegel's philosophical system. See also chapter 25 in this volume by Jacob Golomb.

49. One interesting suggestion from him appears to preempt the theory of cognitive dissonance being applied to the earliest Christians that would become popular in the late twentieth century (PP2$_{[P]}$, 384).

50. Which he concludes precisely because of the eschatological pronouncements of Jesus.

51. In other words, there are other non-Christian historical sources that attest to the existence of Jesus of Nazareth and the movement to which his teachings gave rise.

52. In which he sees affinities with some of the "optimistic" elements he criticizes in Judaism.

53. In the following section, he repeats his preference for Augustine and Luther, as well as statements he has made in many places, about the true character of Christianity being pessimism (the doctrines of the Fall and Original Sin helping to demonstrate this for him), and he opposes (what he deems to be true) Christianity (which he again states must have had Hindu/Buddhist roots) to the optimism of rationalism, which he equates both to Pelagianism and Judaism alike. He recognizes that the Fall, since it is present in the Hebrew Bible, might challenge that assessment, but he dismisses this as the one exception and states that it "remains unused like an *hors d'oeuvre* until Christianity again takes it up as its only suitable point of contact" (PP2$_{[P]}$, 388).

54. As indicated, his "departure" from any reliance on an overt religious explanatory hypothesis nonetheless did not extend to his ceasing to study carefully and utilizing the ideas from several religious traditions, including Christianity. Indeed, he ends up offering something which is analogously similar to such religious explanatory and guiding metaphysical systems.

55. Thomas Bailey Saunders, "Prefatory Note" in Arthur Schopenhauer, *Religion: A Dialogue and Other Essays*, translated by Thomas Bailey Saunders (London: Swan Sonnenschein, 1889), vii.

56. *Agape*, of course, holds especial connotations for the earliest Christians and so therefore down through reinterpretations of Christian doctrine throughout subsequent church history. See also WWR1$_{[P]}$, 376.

57. The same, of course, could be figuratively said to be the essence of the "religion" of Schopenhauer.

58. See Augustine's *City of God*, bk. XIX, 14. While Schopenhauer does not acknowledge Augustine's use of the same formula, he does quote from the *City of God*, bk XIX, 3 earlier at BM$_{[P]}$, 45. This suggests that some debt to Augustine is highly likely.

59. See WWR2$_{[P]}$, 628 f.

60. See WWR1$_{[P]}$, 329. Note certain similarities with Paul Tillich's Christological understanding of the "new being." It is not insignificant that Tillich was influenced by existentialism—a movement wherein many of the main thinkers were influenced by Schopenhauer.

61. See also, WWR2$_{[P]}$, 604–05. Schopenhauer also sides with the Docetists, WWR1$_{[P]}$, 405, concerning the illusory nature of Christ's human body.

62. See also the study by Robert A. Gonzales, "Schopenhauer's Demythologisation of Christian Asceticism," *Auslegung* 9 (1982), 5–49.

63. See also, WWR2$_{[P]}$, 553, where Schopenhauer interprets the story of the adulterous woman (Jn 7:53–8:11) to mean that Jesus is assuming the same guilt in each member of the crowd. Schopenhauer goes on to draw parallels with the doctrine of the Trinity and his own fundamental doctrine (but qualified it as a mere *"lusus ingenii,"* a playful fancy) (WWR2$_{[P]}$, 629).

64. Notwithstanding his dismissal of the notion of revelation in PP2$_{[P]}$, 361. Richard Taylor has argued that Schopenhauer's ethics is where "the inspiration from religion is most obvious" (Richard Taylor, "Arthur Schopenhauer" in *Nineteenth Century Religious Thought in the West*, 3 vols., edited by Ninian Smart, John, Clayton, Patrick and Steven T. Katz [Cambridge, Cambridge University Press, 1985], vol. 1, 170).

65. "And the peace of God, which passes all understanding, will keep your hearts and your minds in Christ Jesus."

66. My emphasis. In German, the parallel with Paul's phrase is even more striking: Schopenhauer's wording being "jener Friede, der *höher ist als alle Vernunft,"* and in Paul the phrase is "Und der Friede Gottes, welcher *höher ist denn alle Vernunft,* bewahre eure Herzen und Sinne in Christo Jesu!" Schopenhauer then describes this state as "ein ganzes und sicheres Evangelium ist: nur die Erkenntniß ist geblieben, der Wille ist verschwunden" (i.e., "a complete and certain gospel. Only knowledge remains, the will has vanished"). He also discusses this peaceful state of mind in WWR1$_{[P]}$, 86, 89, 205, 212, 219, 250, 261, 303, 319, 335, 398, 411, 519; WWR2$_{[P]}$, 233, 370.

67. MR3, 377. He often conflated differing traditions under the title of mysticism, stating that the latter should be accepted "generally as true."

68. See also WWR1$_{[P]}$, 249, 404, 486f and also §68, where Schopenhauer demonstrates his tendency to conflate elements of mysticism with asceticism in relation to the prevailing (if sometimes latent) presence of the idea of "better consciousness" in his thought.

69. See Hübscher, *Philosophy of Schopenhauer*, 32–33. Schopenhauer particularly valued those aspects of quietism and asceticism in religious mysticism which went against what he perceived to be the overt optimism of the European philosophy of his time.

70. This also relates to Schopenhauer's reasoning for dispensing with the word "God" and the aforementioned entry in his notebook that no other theology should ultimately be applied other than that of Pseudo-Dionysius the Areopagite because what the word "God" represents resides above and beyond all knowledge (MR3, 376).

71. Referring to the Pffeifer edition of Eckhart's works, Vol. 1, 626, Hübscher's biography observes that wherever Schopenhauer came across notions of rapture, illumination, and union with God, he instantly warmed to them (Hübscher, *Philosophy of Schopenhauer*, 63).

72. See also WN$_{[P]}$, 143.

73. See also BM$_{[P]}$, 212.

74. As best exemplified by the character Philalethes in Schopenhauer's dialogue "On Religion" (see earlier discussion). Furthermore, Schopenhauer acknowledged that his emphasis on the empirical was something different from the approach found in mysticism, while he nonetheless commended mysticism as an "excellent supplement" to his philosophy and as a positive addition to his own more negative reasoning (MR3, 378).

75. He also sought to define a moral theory free from "bad" religious elements—thus rejecting a *theistic* (divine command) justification for morality because, he argued, such reduces ethics to egoism (we seek a reward or fear punishment): "how could I talk of unselfishness where I am enticed by reward or deterred by threatened punishment," BM$_{[P]}$, 137; see also PP2$_{[P]}$, 219.

76. Friedrich Nietzsche, *Human All Too Human*, translated by R. J. Hollingdale (Cambridge: Cambridge University Press, 1996), §110, 62.

77. "That the world has only a physical and not a moral significance is a fundamental error, one that is the greatest and most pernicious, the real *perversity* of mind. At bottom, it is that which faith has personified as antichrist. Nevertheless, and in spite of all religions which one and all assert the contrary and try to establish this in their own mythical way, that fundamental error never dies out entirely, but from time to time raises its head afresh until universal indignation forces it once more to conceal itself" (PP2$_{[P]}$, 201). See also WN$_{[P]}$, 3, 139–40.

78. See the discussion of Nietzsche's criticisms here in Gerard Mannion, "Mitleid, Metaphysics and Morality: Interpreting Schopenhauer's Ethics" in *Schopenhauer Jahrbuch* 83 (2002), 87–117, and in an extended form in Mannion, *Schopenhauer, Religion and Morality*, ch. 6.

79. Friedrich Nietzsche. *The Antichrist*, translated by R. Hollingdale (Harmondsworth: Penguin, 1990), §9; see also §§7–8. Ironically, Schopenhauer also condemns his philosophical contemporaries for their refusal to let go of theology; e.g., WN$_{[P]}$, 23.

80. Iris Murdoch, *Metaphysics as A Guide to Morals* (Harmondsworth: Penguin, 1992), 72.

81. Bernard Bykhovsky, *Schopenhauer and the Ground of Existence* (Amsterdam: B. R. Gruner, 1984), 174.

82. Wilhelm von Gwinner. *Schopenhauer's Leben* (Leipzig: F. A. Brockhaus, 1878), 615. The full passage is "…und am meisten freute es ihn, wenn er stets neue Beweise erhielt, dass seine scheinbar irreligiösen Lehren "als Religion anschlugen", und den leergewordenen Platz des verlorenen Glaubens ausfüllend, zur Quelle innerster Beruhigung und Befriedigung wurden."

83. William Wallace, *Life of Arthur Schopenhauer* (London: Walter Scott, 1890), 203.

FURTHER READING

Bykhovsky, Bernard. *Schopenhauer and the Ground of Existence*, translated by P. Moran. Amsterdam: B. R. Gruner, 1984.

Copleston, Frederick. *Arthur Schopenhauer: Philosopher of Pessimism*, 2nd edition. London: Search Press, 1975.

Gonzales, Robert A. *An Approach to the Sacred in the Thought of Schopenhauer*. San Francisco: Mellen Research University Press, 1992.

Mannion, Gerard. *Schopenhauer, Religion and Morality*. Aldershot: Ashgate, 2003.

Mannion, Gerard. "A 'Godless' Road to Redemption: Comparing the Moral Visions of Arthur Schopenhauer and Iris Murdoch." *Schopenhauer-Jahrbuch* 91 (September, 2010): 135–62.

Salter, William Mackenzie. "Schopenhauer's Contact with Theology." *Harvard Theological Review* 4, no. 3 (1911): 271–310.

CHAPTER 25

....

THE INSCRUTABLE RIDDLE OF SCHOPENHAUER'S RELATIONS TO JEWS AND TO JUDAISM

....

JACOB GOLOMB

CAN we apply to Schopenhauer the definition of a German philo-Semite as an anti-Semite who happens to love Jews? This chapter will try to answer this query or at least to uncover the necessary material for readers to reach their own conclusion.[1] Robert Wicks reports that, from 1833 until his death on 1860, "Schopenhauer's apartment in central Frankfurt was about three minutes walking distance from the Jewish quarter and about the same distance from the main cathedral in the old city."[2] This information is significant for this chapter since one of its main theses is that Schopenhauer's metaphysical "distance" from Judaism was by far longer than the physical one. I will suggest some reasons for this claim after documenting in text what I call here Schopenhauer's "metaphysical anti-Judaism." Is it just a sheer coincidence that almost the first reference to Jewish issues in Schopenhauer's published writings (in his 1813 dissertation) was not so much to Jews (as persons) but to the "realistic fundamental view of Judaism" (FR, 36)?[3]

I prefer to use the term "metaphysical anti-Judaism" because its proximate alternative, "metaphysical anti-Semitism" is misleading since if we speak about metaphysics we should bear in mind essentialism and introduce—as Schopenhauer indeed has done—some notion of human essence qua humans. And if one of his basic contentions is that human essence is "the will"[4] which is common to all humans, then how can he—from the strictly philosophical point of view—regard Jewish essence (in distinction to its cultural manifestations like religion or prevailing ethos) as being in some way inferior to all other sentient species?

Moreover, the term "metaphysical anti-Judaism" didactically distinguishes his more abstract and theoretical attitude about Jewish religion at large (subsumed in the present chapter under the wider terms "Judaism" or "Theism") from his more personal sentiments he might have for or against contemporary Jews as living individuals, who in their everyday struggle for survival in a hostile milieu exhibited what Schopenhauer called "will-to-life."[5] Despite his close vicinity to the Jewish ghetto in Frankfurt am Main and his possible daily encounters with Jews (also during his early extensive travels around Europe that brought him to cities with large Jewish populations such as Prague and Vienna[6]), we can hardly find in his writings personal vicious utterances against them.

The most pertinent question in this discussion is: Does he see the contemporary Jews as negative and contaminating elements in his society who must be restrained and denied of any political rights? As we will see, the answer is definitely *no*. But if anti-Semitism is judged solely by negative *private* feelings, prevalent stereotypes, certain betraying slips of the tongue or the pen, then such inclinations are indeed present in Schopenhauer's *oeuvre*.

In a wider philosophical context one may notice that Schopenhauer's evaluation of Judaism differs essentially from those of his predecessors such as Kant, Hegel, Fichte, and Schelling, who interpreted Christianity as the culmination of the development of religion. This approach changes fundamentally in Schopenhauer, whose criticism is aimed at the theological presuppositions of Christianity and more so of Judaism: namely, their unreserved theism. Theism amounts to a dualistic position that claims the cause of our world is its divine supervisor and protector who coexists outside the world itself and is intelligent, possessing consciousness, purpose, and will.[7] In *The World as Will and Representation* and also in his later *Parerga and Paralipomena*, Schopenhauer clearly prefers atheism. We should recall in this context that Buddha was not God and hence Schopenhauer, the atheist and metaphysician of the "Blind Will," felt closer to this doctrine and estranged from Judaism. "Revelation," the "God as the personal ruler and creator of the world who made everything good occurs solely in the Jewish faith and the two doctrines of faith derived from it." In contradistinction, "Buddhism...is decidedly and expressly atheistic"[8] (FR, 118) and hence more compatible with Schopenhauer's metaphysics of the Will. Admittedly, when God as the sole creator reigns absolutely, there is no more room for a monistic, autonomous Will. These considerations lie behind the main thesis of this chapter: *Theism is the foremost target of Schopenhauer; Judaism is its first historical and cultural manifestation: hence it becomes his chief enemy.*

This thesis might also explain Schopenhauer's attraction to Spinoza's "so-called God" who is the immanent, timeless, and a-historic "one and only substance" (MR1, 208).[9] Schopenhauer adored Spinoza for his anti-theistic proximity to his own system. He identified himself intimately with Spinoza, so much so that he regarded himself as his heir and follower.

> *My system* is related to *Spinoza* as the new Testament is to the Old.—For what the Old Testament has in common with the New is the same God-Creator, likewise with me as with Spinoza the world exists through itself and out of itself.[10]   (MR3, 263)

This statement reveals his metaphysical inspiration, namely "Spinoza" who "could not ignore the Jews" (MR3, 263). But Schopenhauer could ignore the fact that Spinoza was a Jew because, in his eyes, what is of the utmost importance is not your blood, heritage, or nation but your philosophy. Schopenhauer's overall warm feelings toward Spinoza reminds us of the dictum: "the enemy of my enemy is my friend"; that is, the enemy of any theism (of Jewish, Christian, or Muslim versions) is a thinker, like Spinoza, who propagates a worldview of sheer immanency, atheism, anti-teleology, and strict determinism. Hence Schopenhauer tends to identify himself with Spinoza and frequently compares himself to him even in minor details.[11]

Spinoza's atheism, overt optimism, and vitalism stood in opposition to Schopenhauer's pessimism and thanatotic world view. Still these differences rather attracted him to Spinoza as well as to Jewish people in general. Moreover, it stands to reason that one of the genuine reasons for his attraction to Spinoza stems from the fact that he constructed such a diametrically opposed metaphysics to that of Hegel—the archenemy of Schopenhauer. Spinoza's anti-historical and anti-teleological approach, frozen in a geometrical icicle and timeless system, was closer to Schopenhauer's views despite the above-mentioned differences and made him his favorite thinker.[12]

Schopenhauer hated Hegel as a philosopher and equally as a person. Witness his vicious *ad hominem* attacks against him that were more vicious than anything he had ever expressed regarding the Jews or even Judaism. Notable among them are such passages from 1836 where Schopenhauer refers to Hegel as to "that shameless nonsense-monger" who "has the audacity to promote the most monstrous notions" and has a "little bird brain" (WN, 314).[13]

Schopenhauer was aware that Hegel saw Judaism as a religion inferior to Christianity. He probably also knew of young Hegel's feelings (like those of Schopenhauer himself) that Judaism stands in opposition to his (i.e., Hegel's) metaphysical principles.[14] This, however, did not endear him to Hegel since his anti-Judaism was more moderate than that of Hegel. On a personal level, Jews were never regarded by him as hostile or threatening to his self-esteem (as did the widespread popularity of Hegel).

Furthermore, we ought to remember that, in Schopenhauer's times, two dominating factors conducive in fostering anti-Semitic feelings in Europe were not dominant then as in other periods. I refer here to fanatical religious Christian feelings that gave rise to religious anti-Semitism and to extreme nationalism that saw in national patriotism the highest value and treated Jewish populations as alien to its national aspirations. Both these extreme attitudes were strange to Schopenhauer, who regarded Buddhism (and not Christianity) as being the most valuable faith and was quite moderate in his patriotic feelings, having been born in the free city of Danzig and having spent most of his childhood and youth in a cosmopolitan *Hansa* Hamburg known for its widely spread multiculturalism.

Schopenhauer did not hate Judaism but rather respected it as the arch-enemy of his own philosophy.[15] Moreover, in his eyes there is a moral dimension to our life that depends on our ability to liberate our will from the will itself. Such liberation takes place mainly in mysticism and asceticism. The first one has its due place in Buddhism and the second one also in Christianity. Judaism is not an ascetic religion and its ancient Hebrew great biblical heroes and prophets were far from exhibiting patterns of sainthood. Hence Schopenhauer perceived it as inferior to Christianity.

In contrast to Judaism, Schopenhauer saw in "*Christianity* proper"[16] an ascetic resignation and self-denial in the face of a world that contains only suffering. The pessimistic and world-denying religions (such as Christianity and Brahmanism) find themselves in opposition to the "shallow or wicked" Judaism with its "optimistic rationalism" that follows from Jewish monotheism. There is a disagreement among scholars whether Schopenhauer's pessimism had close links (Janaway, 1999) or not (Magee, 1983: 13–14) with his central metaphysical tenets. Here I will argue that his negative views on Judaism are closely related to his metaphysic of *The World as Will and Representation*.

Now, if Schopenhauer's criticism of Jewish religion stems from his metaphysics, it evidently is not a direct expression of some personal anti-Semitic grudges that he might or might not nurture toward Jews in general. As a contemporary analogy, one might say that not every criticism of the present policy of the Israeli government (some of it shared also by the present writer) is necessarily an expression of anti-Semitism or self-hatred[17] of the present Israeli secular Jews—as some of the ultra-nationalist and religious Israeli fanatics claim it to be.

*   *   *

To distinguish didactically between Schopenhauer's metaphysical anti-Judaism and his personal (if any) one, I present his various writings in chronological order to trace any difference in nuances and shifts of emphasizes in his relations to Judaism in general and to Jews in particular. My exposition here uses two different approaches:

a. The *diachronic* approach that will analyze Schopenhauer's utterances on Jews and Judaism as scattered in his metaphysic of *The World as Will and Representation* published between 1818 and 1819. It will also refer to his views on Christianity, Spinoza, and religion at large.

b. The *synchronic, rhetorical* (in distinction to metaphysical) approach that will deal with his nonsystematic and more *anthropological* writings. Here I will emphasize his view on contemporary Jews. These Jews were joined by common religion and persecution, and lived in the "dirty and stinky" ghettoes.[18] The most relevant text here will be the two volumes of *Parerga and Paralipomena*.

However, to be able to check whether Schopenhauer was anti-Semite before the development of his metaphysical system, I will first look at his *Nachlass*; namely, to the more personal and intimate pieces of diaries and autobiographical sketches of his journeys around Europe and his sporadic notes. But before analyzing the relevant texts, I would like to mention two cardinal points:

First: In the vast scholarly literature on Schopenhauer it is hard to find any extensive discussion of his relation to Judaism and to Jews[19] despite the numerous remarks about them in his writings. Was it a kind of self-imposed censorship or the quite understandable result of the reluctance of his more acclaimed interpreters to deal—in the aftermath of the Holocaust (*Shoah*)—with such a delicate issue as his possible anti-Semitic attitude? Thus I will try to fill this lacuna in Schopenhauer's scholarship that refrained from dwelling into this sensitive topic that has become even more painful after the genocide of European Jewry—especially after it has become known that Hitler, as a soldier during the First World War, carried the works of Schopenhauer in his backpack and referred to him several times in *Mein Kampf*. In *Hitler's Table Talk*, he also mentions him saying: "In our part of the world, the Jews would have immediately eliminated Schopenhauer, Nietzsche, and Kant. If the Bolsheviks had dominion over us for two hundred years, what works of our past would be handed on to posterity? Our great men would fall into oblivion, or else they'd be presented to future generations as criminals and bandits."[20]

Second: There is no reason to think that Schopenhauer could read Hebrew Scriptures in the original. However, it was not the main reason for his quite selective readings of the Hebrew literature. He read the ancient Greeks quite voraciously and hence used extensively the Greek translation of the Hebrew Bible called *Septuagint* (the full title is literally: "The Translation of the Seventy") of which he had a very high opinion and found quite reliable.[21] Belonging to different schools, the seventy-two Jewish scholars undertook around 270 BCE in Egypt this mission that secured the global dissemination of Jewish ethics and tradition. Despite the many flaws and incorrect translations of Hebrew into Greek, but not any viable alternative, we can absolve Schopenhauer for using exclusively this translation.

25.1 AUTOBIOGRAPHICAL *REMAINS* WITH A SPECIAL REFERENCE TO RELIGION AND TO *LETTERS*

25.1.1 Religion

Schopenhauer viewed Judaism in terms of a monotheistic "father" religion from which Christianity and Islam were derived. He did not perceive Judaism as it is popularly regarded today—namely, as a historical and cultural reservoir of moral values and ethos—as an accumulated heritage and life-experiences that stretches over more than four thousand years. He did not relate to it as to a perpetually evolving faith that established different schools (e.g., the Rabbinical vs. the Hassidic trends, the Kabbalistic-Mystical vs. the Rationalistic etc.) in the same way as he distinguished between different denominations in Christianity (especially the Catholic vs. the Protestant Churches). Though being an atheist who did not subscribe officially to any particular faith,

Schopenhauer expressed a keen interest in various religions. He tried to forge strong kinship between philosophy and religion, holding that different religions, like various philosophies, attempt to address the human need for metaphysics.[22] In his eyes, philosophy and religion share the same essential dogma about existence after death: namely, eternal life. He claimed that religion is a "metaphysics for the people" and thought that

> [t]he fundamental difference between various religions is to be found in the question whether they are optimism or pessimism, certainly not whether they are monotheism, polytheism...pantheism, or atheism (like Buddhism). For this reason, the Old and New Testaments are diametrically opposed and their amalgamation forms a queer centaur. The Old Testament is optimism, the New pessimism.   (PP2$_{[P]}$, 388)

For Schopenhauer, "optimism" is disparaging term because he thought that "earthly happiness is destined to be frustrated, or recognized as an illusion. The grounds for this lie deep in the very nature of things" (WWR2$_{[P]}$, 573). Hence, Jewish craving for earthly happiness and material prosperity is anti-metaphysical in its nature, in contrast to the Christian emphasis on misery and sorrow in life. Furthermore, Schopenhauer claimed that "optimistic" religions such as Judaism and Islam affirm earthly existence and see the world as praiseworthy and commendable and as justified by itself. In contrast, the "pessimistic" religions view the world as something that ought not to be, and, since they seem to correspond to Schopenhauer's central metaphysical dogmas, they express the genuine truth. He believed that Buddhism and "genuine" Christianity figuratively express the same truths as his philosophy—in diametrical contrast to Judaism which is essentially anti-Schopenhauerian at its very core.

At the point of what Schopenhauer calls the shallow optimism of Judaism we can locate one of the many inconsistencies of his attitude toward Judaism and Jews. I refer to the fact that one of the major differences between Judaism, on one hand, and Christianity and Islam, on the other, is that the religious Jews do not believe that indeed the Messiah had already arrived on Earth and that it is how the world looks when the Messiah reigns.[23] This stance has pessimistic undertones because it disagrees with optimistic Islam and Christianity who believe in salvation under the auspices of God Almighty or his representatives, namely Jesus or Mohammed. Had Schopenhauer paid sufficient attention to the conclusions of his metaphysical pessimism, he would realize that actually the Jews were closer to his teachings than other creeds. Could Job (*Iyov*) of the Hebrew Bible reject Schopenhauer's pessimistic insight that "if a God has made this world, then I would not like to be the God; its misery and distress would break my heart" (MR3, 63)/[24]

Generally, when it comes to face-to-face confrontation between his metaphysical worldview and Christian theology, he does not spare Christianity his decisive criticism. From his strictly metaphysical perspective Judaism and Christianity are both severely criticized.

The following satirical description of Jews in Amsterdam by Schopenhauer could be easily drawn by Spinoza himself. This actually is one of the first instances in Schopenhauer's writings where he mentions Jews (not as private individuals per se but as people involved in a religious rituals in the Great Synagogue of Amsterdam where, in 1656, Spinoza was publicly excommunicated).

> While the rabbi, with head thrown back and mouth opened enormously wide, was making an eternally long *roulade*, the whole congregation were talking as if at the corn exchange. As soon as the priest had finished they all sang the same verse after him, from their Hebrew books....[25]

Sharper critical statements on Jewish rituals can be found in Spinoza's *oeuvre*, for example in his 1670 *Tractatus Theologico-Politicus*,[26] but nobody dared call him anti-Semitic. Thus Safranski is right in referring to this quoted passage as one that "is not a case of malicious anti-Semitism, for Arthur treated Protestant community singing with the same disrespect."[27] Of course the question remains open about what would be regarded as a "malicious anti-Semitism" in Schopenhauer's case and whether he indeed crossed the line, sometimes thin, between a malicious anti-Semitism and a metaphysical anti-Theism.

In any case, we may regard this unfortunate utterance of the young Schopenhauer as one of the first instances of his general anti-theist viewpoint. Furthermore, not being able to read Hebrew and not versed in Jewish history and theology, Schopenhauer's impression of the Jewish-Hebrew theological or holy writings came to him mainly from second-hand sources, and his occasional encounters with the living species of this faith were not the most reliable sources for getting an intimate acquaintance with its lore. Thus certain distortions or inaccuracies were not altogether of his own making but of many anti-Semitic and hostile to Judaism writers and Christian theologians of his times.

25.1.2 Early Manuscripts (1804–1818)

One of the earliest known references to Jews is found in a lampoon Schopenhauer wrote about one of his schoolmasters at the Gotha gymnasium. The relevant part of this ironic lampoon (on his teacher Christian Ferdinand Schulze) reads as follows:

> The pulpit's ornament, the master's desk's delight,
> The town's storyteller and the lodge's spokesman,
> A perfect Christian, *Perfect Jew* and pagan...
> The flower and crown of all great spirits,
> Who has thousands of friends—and drops their names.[28]

In these ironical lines Schopenhauer puts Christians, Jews, and pagans on the same par. As religious attitudes they are all equal in his eyes, and it seems that he does not believe that it is actually possible to become a "perfect" Christian,[29] a perfect Jew, or a perfect pagan. This is an *ad hominem* lampoon against a concrete figure who is not Jewish, and evidently it is not directed against any other denominations, races, or creeds. However it discloses certain hidden religious sentiments. To speak of a perfect

Christian or a Jew means that you have implicit idea as to what should be regarded as a genuine religious stance.

This impression—one that somewhat mitigates the conventional view of Schopenhauer as a staunch atheist—is justified further by his admission at the age of sixteen that "If we take out of life the few moments of religion, art and pure love, what is left except a number of trivial thoughts?" (MR1, 9). One page after this confession, Schopenhauer speaks about "the Kingdom of God" (MR1, 10).[30] When he refers to *De Republica* of Plato he introduces a kind of Spinozistic view claiming that "the Ideas are realities existing in God" (MR1, 11). An extreme atheist would refrain from using such religious terms.

This is also evident from his statement: "religion, work of genius, was given to all ages, and races as their salvation" (MR1, 19). This naturally includes the Semitic Jews and hence it appears that (at least at age of twenty-two) Schopenhauer was far from holding anti-Judaist prejudices—or at least he was not a kind of anti-Semitic thinker on account of religious reasons. These early attitudes square well with his later intensive preoccupation with world religions and with his view that saw fruitful connections between philosophy and religion. In a spirit of Spinoza, Schopenhauer claims that religion is a "metaphysic for the people" that uses myths and allegories to make life comfortable, and its "truth" is suitable to the level of a limited comprehension of the common "bipeds" that are unable to perceive abstract philosophical truth. Because of his theistic sentiments he never pronounced the fatal statement as did Nietzsche, that "God is Dead."

This fact is highly relevant since not nature nor number of gods is what distinguishes various creeds, but the existential and strictly practical effects that those various faiths exert upon their believers. Schopenhauer later argued that the fundamental contrast between religions is not whether they are monotheistic (Judaism, Christianity, Islam) or polytheistic (paganism) or even lack any God, like Buddhism. The major difference is whether they are *optimistic* and hedonistic (that characterized the polytheism of the Greeks and Romans and the monotheism of Judaism and Islam) or *pessimistic* and ascetic (Hinduism, Buddhism, and "genuine" Christianity). On this account, Judaism has no proper place in Schopenhauer's world outlook, not necessarily because of any personal anti-Semitic under- or overtones but because it squarely negates his most fundamental and metaphysical dogmas that had been developed by him virtually from the time that he began writing.

Alongside this evolving anti-Judaism (and anti-Islamism and anti-paganism), it becomes clear why Jews or Judaism are seldom mentioned in his *Nachlass*. At this early stage of his career, Jews were never high on his list—he did not pay any serious attention to them as he did pay, for example, to Christian creed and to the early theologians of the Church. This is plainly documented also in the Second Volume of his *Manuscript Remains* that contains Schopenhauer's marginal notes and transcripts of lectures written down in the universities of Göttingen (1809–1811) and Berlin (1811–1813). Most of them refer to extensive passages from "*Novum Testamentum*" (MR1, 455–59). No references to "*Die Bücher des Alten Testaments*" are found there but only two sporadic and insignificant remarks on Samson and David.

Thus, in the *Manuscript Remains*, it is hard to find any significant references to Jews or to their religion and almost no citations from the Hebrew Bible. Actually, one of those exceptions reveals Schopenhauer's unfamiliarity with the Hebrew Holy Scriptures.[31] There is no sufficient indication that Schopenhauer was well versed in Hebrew language, and the few occasions where he uses Hebrew words (like e.g., "the rare Hebrew names and titles of God, such as *Adonai* and the like" (WN, 417) are not convincing evidences to a proper mastery of Hebrew; he could easily have picked them up from any of the theological German, Latin, or Greek treatises that he read so voraciously. In contrast, we find ample quotation from *Das Neue Testament*, Shakespeare, Goethe, and from classical Greek and Roman authors. This by itself is not a conclusive ground for regarding him as an anti-Semite since many vicious anti-Semites theologians in Schopenhauer's times such as Ernest Renan[32] and David Strauss,[33] who, despite their familiarity with the Hebrew Bible, were malicious enemies of Jews and Judaism. We should remember that not every Christian automatically becomes, by virtue of his faith, an anti-Semite.

At this point it is worthwhile to recall Nietzsche's attitude toward "every great philosophy" which in his eyes "has been the personal confession of its author and a kind of involuntary and unconscious memoir; also that the moral (or immoral) intentions in every philosophy constituted the real germ of life from which the whole plant had grown."[34] Schopenhauer, who, like Nietzsche, relegated our rationality to second place and also (like Nietzsche) spoke about our mental unconscious processes would gladly adopt this statement, especially since he had already confessed in Berlin of 1813 that his "work expands and the parts grow together slowly and by degrees like a child in the womb, I do not know which was the first and which was the last to come into existence" (MR1, 59). Thus what is clear is that were we to ask Schopenhauer what came first—his anti-Jewish views or his metaphysics—he would not know how to answer it. So how can we?

In his *Early Manuscript Remains*, however, we do find certain "theoretical" seeds for Schopenhauer's later anti-Judaism, disguised under his preference for Christianity, though later on he developed a more ambivalent attitude toward this faith as well. Thus, for example, when he speaks about the doctrine of "*Providence*" which in his eyes "looks after earthly welfare of the virtuous and protects them," he claims that it "is to the highest degree absurd, wrong and utterly opposed to true insight" (MR1, 73). But the dogma of a Divine Providence was widely disseminated in Judaism but less so in Christianity. Since Schopenhauer was quite aware of it, he concludes this remark with a decision "to examine whether *Providence* is a pure doctrine of Christianity" (MR1, 73). One year later he claims that it is not only "quite absurd" but actually "contrary to the spirit of Christianity" (MR1, 197) or, to be more exact, to *his* conception of true Christianity. Here we can already sense the seeds for his metaphysical *anti-Judaism*. As a dogmatic thinker, Schopenhauer's general tactic was to regard any Christian ideas of the New Testament that were compatible with his metaphysic, as being derived from Indian philosophy through the Egyptian priests who supposedly educated Jesus. Consequently, any motif he found in the Christian Bible (like the Divine Providence) that opposed his philosophy was automatically relegated to the Hebrew Bible. However, such a rejection could hardly be regarded as an act of anti-Semitism as, for similar reasons, he later considered Protestantism to be a degenerate form of Christianity because, like Judaism, it negated its "true nature" by defying asceticism, celibacy, and suffering.[35]

Another reference to Jews in *Early Manuscript Remains* appears in his approval of the passage quoted by him from Philip Melanchthon (1497–1560), a German Lutheran reformer and a collaborator of Luther. In his *Augsburg Confession* (1530), while discussing the idea of sin and grace, Melanchthon claims that

> ... the gospel of grace was repeated again and again in the whole of scripture, after it was first given to Adam and then to the Patriarchs, and then elucidated by the Prophets and finally preached by Christ among the Jews and spread by the Apostles in the whole world.   (MR1, 94)

It appears that the young Schopenhauer did not distinguish between the Judeo and Christian traditions regarding sin and grace, and he did not accuse Jews (as did Nietzsche, e.g., in *The Antichrist*, §25) for inventing the notion of sin and guilt feelings. Nonetheless, unlike the overwhelming preference Nietzsche had for the Hebrew Bible over the Christian Testament, Schopenhauer prefers the second. This preference is also revealed in his quote from Matthew 22:39: "Thou shalt love thy neighbor as thyself" (MR1, 342n), which incidentally, completely ignores the first historical appearance of this maxim in Leviticus (Vayikra) 19:18. This is not by any means a symptom of an anti-Semite suppression of Hebrew Bible, or of its utter ignorance, but should be regarded as pointing to the quite natural fact that Schopenhauer felt himself much more at home with Christian literature than with Jewish lore, thus rendering some of his later statements on various aspects of Jewish religion somewhat prejudiced or dogmatic because he barely knew them. But he personally knew quite well, as his letters to them disclose, some prominent, acculturated German Jews. Did he nurture against them any anti-Semitic feelings?

25.1.3 Letters of an Anti-Semite?

Not as charged. Let us look closely into some of them. The testimony from Schopenhauer's letters, especially those of the more intimate nature, carry a special weight since in them he was free to write anything he felt or thought without being hampered by any kind of censorship or public opinion. These letters hardly express negative sentiments or personal grudges against Jews that it is possible to suppose on account of his overall metaphysical anti-Judaism.

Schopenhauer, the philosopher and the private man, knew how to separate his theoretical and intellectual antipathies (which he confessed in his letter to his friend David Asher[36]) from his personal feelings. He refers in this letter to Asher's publication on "Gebirol" and concludes: "I find all Hebraism and Islamism truly objectionable."[37] In this intensive correspondence between the acculturated German Jew (Asher) and

Schopenhauer, the latter conveys, in intimate terms, his warm feelings toward the first that go far beyond sheer mutual respect.[38]

Several times in these letters, as well as in his *Nachlass*, he refers to different persons as to "a couple of Jewish Doctors,"[39] or to "the old Jews."[40] In one letter to his cousin he expresses certain empathy for the miserable fate of Jews in Prussia: "I know the Speciers: they are Jews; and after the recent Prussian persecution of Jews this nation does not desire to acquire any land property there"(GB, 175).[41]

The reappearing references to "Juden" (Jews) is in itself no proof of any anti-Semitic feelings on the part of Schopenhauer or a sign of negative labeling since, in his other letters, he also names people by their nationality or creed.[42]

A slightly different matter is when Schopenhauer mentions Jews or Judaism in a polemical context that deals with his philosophy and its opponents. In these cases it is difficult to draw a clear line between personal versus theoretical anti-Semitism, and it is quite hard to distinguish between legitimate and illegitimate usages of such nicknames as "*Judenjunge*." When he refers to an anonymous "local *Judenjunge*" (GB, 346) does he hint here to the rather anti-Semitic cry "Jew boy" being equivalent to the notorious "nigger"?[43]

In a letter to Julius Frauenstädt (from July 11, 1848), he complains that students were saturated by "Jewish theism and optimism" and "make a big deal of it and of the philosophy of the Jewish God" ("*der Judengott*" [GB, 232]). This can hardly be regarded as an anti-Semitic note since it appears in a wider context of abstract and theoretical polemics. This is true also of his letter from January 28, 1849, to his friend, where he complains that: "you come from Hegel and bring along with you Pantheism and Optimism which are related to my things as pork ham to the Jewish wedding."[44] Here we have another evidence of Schopenhauer's familiarity with Jewish customs,[45] but even this should be hardly regarded as a derogatory remark—perhaps against Hegel, but not against Jews as such.

However the most convincing passage that discredits any sweeping attempt to brand Schopenhauer as a plain anti-Semite is found in a letter to Julius Frauenstädt. There, Schopenhauer complains quite irritably that

> ...to no avail I wrote you that the thing-in-itself [*das Ding an sich*] cannot be found in cloud-cuckoo-land [*Wolkenkukusheim*] where the Jewish God [*Judengott*] sits but in things of this world....I want to tell you what is the thing in itself: it is the well-known *absolute* [*Absolutum*; emphasis in original], also the hidden cosmological proof on which the Jewish God rides [*verkappte kosmologische Beweis, auf dem der Judengott reite*].[46]

He continues: "and it is the case like that of King David who danced and sung before the Ark of Covenant, entirely glorious."[47] This letter ends with a dramatic poem:

> Es ist der Herr von Absolut!—
> Das heißt es ist der alte Jud.

Comparing the absolute, namely the thing-in-itself, to the "old Jew" means to hold Jews in a quite high esteem indeed. The most fundamental principle of Schopenhauer's metaphysics is identical in his eyes with the *Judengott* or *alte Jud*. Thus what I call here his anti-Judaism must be taken with a grain of salt. At this point we approach the most inscrutable and ironic aspect of this entire topic.

25.2 THE METAPHYSICAL APPROACH: WWR1 AND WWR2

We have seen that in his early *Nachlass*, Schopenhauer regarded Judaism and Christianity as equal and usually contrasted both to Indian philosophy. However, after delineating his own system, Schopenhauer counterposed Judaism to Christianity and discriminated between the *positive* (in his eyes) features of Christian creed which, not surprisingly, fit his own metaphysics, and the *negative* aspects of it which were the primitive and redundant residuals of the "Old Testament." When he discusses the notion of "immortality"— that supposedly Christian doctrine adopted from Indian faith—he speculates that

> New Testament Christianity has such a doctrine, because it is Indian in spirit, and therefore, more than probably, Indian in origin, although only indirectly, through Egypt. Such a doctrine, however, is as little suited to the Jewish stem on which that Indian wisdom had to be grafted in the Holy Land.   (WWR2$_{[P]}$, 488)[48]

When he contemplates certain positive aspects of the Hebrew Bible he does not fail to inform his (mainly Protestant) readers that "The myth of the Fall or man...is probably, like the whole of Judaism, borrowed from the *Zend Avesta: Bundahish*, 15." He continues,

> This idea is the only thing in the Old Testament to which I can concede a metaphysical, although only allegorical truth; indeed it is this alone that reconciles me to the Old Testament.... New Testament Christianity, the ethical spirit of which is that of Brahmanism and Buddhism, and which is therefore very foreign to the otherwise optimistic spirit of the Old Testament, has also, extremely wisely started from that very myth; in fact, without this, it would not have found one single point of connexion with Judaism.[49]   (WWR2$_{[P]}$, 580)

To give some credulity to his wild speculation about the formative impact of Indian thought on the New Testament, he refers his readers, here and elsewhere, to detailed and ample references in Indian writings. But none of it is offered from Jewish and, for that matter, from Christian holy writings or other texts. His failure to provide the reader with some hard-core historical or textual evidences for this kind of speculation indicates that on this issue he was prompted more by his wishful thinking and personal religious prejudices than by any empirical data. He uses this peculiar tactic also in reference to other ideas that he "grafted" into his metaphysics from Indian thought, using his notions of the "genuine Christianity" or a "Christian kernel," among other reasons, to enlist support from his Christian readers to his philosophy. These ideas, in addition to "the myth of the Fall" and Original Sin, are the sinister and miserable nature of human existence, the lack of "the freedom of the will" (WWR2$_{[P]}$, 488), etc.

The ideas Schopenhauer employed in his metaphysics that were taken from Indian philosophies, he filtered through early Christian thought, whereas other Christian ideals that he rejected were reduced in his eyes to the status of being merely illegitimate residuals of Judaism, which at the bottom line was and remained the highly respected arch-enemy of his metaphysics. However, while all this is true, it does not amount to any anti-Semitic feelings he might or might not have entertained in his everyday life.

Before continuing, we should pay attention to the fact that, just as in his *Nachlass*, letters, and diaries, here, too, we seldom find any vicious anti-Semitic remarks. The only minor exception is his half-anti-Semitic note where he equates his metaphysics of the Will with the "Crucified Savior" as opposed to "Jehovah" (WWR2$_{[P]}$, 645). Then he exclaims:

> My ethical teaching agrees with the Christian completely and in its highest tendencies, and no less with that of Brahmanism and Buddhism. Spinoza, on the other hand, could not get rid of the Jews: A smelling bottle long retains the smell of that which filled it.[50]   (WWR2$_{[P]}$, 645)

Then Schopenhauer mitigates this uncharacteristic onslaught against Spinoza by declaring that "in spite of all this, Spinoza remains a very great man." And despite this quite anti-Semitic tone, the relevant question that arises on reading this passage is whether it indicates a calculated tactic to endear himself to Christian readers or whether it is a genuine expression of anti-Semitic feelings he might have nurtured. On the background of *Parerga and Paralipomena* and its anthropological frame of reference that allowed him to present such popularly vicious anti-Semitic stereotypes as "Jewish stench,"[51] the answer, I am afraid, tends to be: guilty as charged! Later we will see that, in opposition to his metaphysics, in his more anthropological writings his negative views on *Jews* qua persons and less on *Judaism* as such won the upper hand. Then one can see how gradually his metaphysical anti-Judaism is replaced by an ordinary anti-Semitism that was shared by many of the German "bipeds." And again: the quite Machiavellian speculation that his awareness of the widely spread anti-Semitic sentiments among his contemporaneous Germans induced him to employ them opportunistically in his late writing is not an excuse. On the contrary: cynical (as opposed to innate or religious) anti-Semitism is not an alibi—it is even worse than that.

However, in his major metaphysical work, Schopenhauer overcomes petty personal or religious anti-Semitism. A good case in point is the fact that his attraction to Spinoza continued all his life, as his numerous references to him testify. Actually, and quite surprisingly, the fact is that, in these two volumes, Schopenhauer refers to Spinoza at least twice as many times as to Jesus Christ, despite highly eulogizing the latter as "the greatest poetical truth ... who stands before us with perfect virtue, holiness, and sublimity, yet in a state of supreme suffering" (WWR1$_{[P]}$, 91). Spinoza also gets from this cranky thinker quite a few compliments. Evidently, Schopenhauer's metaphysics helped him to overcome racial and biological racism and religious anti-Semitism. It is consequently difficult to accuse him of pure and simple anti-Semitism. But do we really need to put stigmatic labels on such great thinkers as Arthur Schopenhauer and reduce them to mere slogans and catchwords?

* * *

To arrive at a better understanding of Schopenhauer's tactics, I will use Hegel's dialectical approach as an analogy. Undoubtedly, Schopenhauer would flatly reject such comparison, but, for didactic purposes, I will employ it here, especially the notion of *Aufhebung*, which is the hub of Hegel's dialectics, viz., the intellectual process where different elements of a certain doctrine or faith are abolished, others preserved, and still others elevated to a higher plane of discourse or conduct. This method is implicitly delineated in the following passage:

> The true spirit and kernel of Christianity, as of Brahmanism and Buddhism is the knowledge of the vanity of all earthly happiness, complete contempt for it, and the turning away to an existence of quite a different, indeed an opposite kind. This is the spirit and purpose of Christianity ... but it is not, as they imagine, monotheism. Therefore, atheistic Buddhism is much more closely akin to Christianity than are optimistic Judaism and its variety, Islam.   (WWR2$_{[P]}$, 444)

We cannot find here any traces of anti-Semitic sentiments (especially as many Islam believers are not Semites), but we can easily discern here the operation of Schopenhauer's tactic. He starts with the thesis of Indian atheistic and pessimistic thought and contrasts it with what he believes is its diametrically opposed antithesis, namely, Judaism and its theistic, optimistic, and vitalistic creed. Then he employs a kind of *Aufhebung* (sublimation) and forges an original synthesis which is a "true Christianity" purified of most of its genuinely Jewish elements (the act of *cancellation*) that preserves some of Judaism's elements such as the "myth of the Fall" to which he adds most of the Indian basic components (pessimism, anti-theism, immortality, etc.). This purified "true Christianity" becomes then, on the second and elevated plane of discourse, Schopenhauer's metaphysics or philosophy of the monistic Will and "the denial of the will-to-life" (WWR1$_{[P]}$, 387).

This (almost Hegelian, though anti-teleological and anti-rationalist) scheme approximates the philosophical-existentialist profile of Schopenhauer. Out of his deeply religious sentiments (but not of any anti-Semitic feelings) he attempted to replace the Hebrew Bible and Judaism with the "Indian" New Testament. Then he tried to reform the latter, not by Lutheran revolution, but by his metaphysics of the Will as the only monistic, atheistic, and mono-willing valid worldview. In this far-reaching project, the significance of Judaism becomes clearly a decisive factor. This is so since, in this highly speculative frame, Judaism plays the role of being the necessary dialectical first stage to be overcome (*aufgehoben*) by "Indian Christianity" that will preserve such Jewish elements that could be elevated to the next level (i.e., Schopenhauer's metaphysics; see WWR1$_{[P]}$, 405 etc.). The replacement of a Jewish and Christian personal and purposeful creative God with an absolute blind and impersonal Will was possible not solely through an Indian atheistic stance and non-affirmation of life but also due to its stark antitheses: namely, Judaism. Schopenhauer, overall an honest and a quite reflective thinker, realized this and hence the strong ambivalent feelings that he nurtures for Jewish creed without deteriorating these feelings into sheer personal anti-Semitism. In any case, he found himself in a very precarious situation: he could not do without Judaism because it is the necessary and real starting-point of the first thesis of his dialectics of the Will, but he could not stomach it because of his metaphysical prejudices and dogmas. Being intellectually dependent on Judaism was not his cup of tea; hence his attempt to foster an "Indian" revolution of Christianity that was mainly aimed against Judaism—and after its "cleansing" (I am perfectly aware of the menacing connotations of this term) to use it in his ungodly and post-Christian metaphysics.

His ambivalent feelings toward Judaism find their concrete expression in his claim that the historical role of Jewish people was much more important than their present status whose history

> ... is the history of a small, isolated, capricious, hierarchical (i.e., ruled by false notions), obscure people, like the Jews, despised by the great contemporary nations of the East and of the West ... whose former culture was to serve mainly as the basis of our own.   (WWR1$_{[P]}$, 232)

Clearly, in Schopenhauer's eyes, Jews "are really bad Christians" (WWR2$_{[P]}$, 444), like the "Hegelians" (WWR2$_{[P]}$, 443) and unlike his philosophy, which is conceived in the "true spirit and kernel of Christianity," namely in spirit of "Buddhism" (WWR2$_{[P]}$, 444). Thus, Schopenhauer is convinced that by implanting Indian thought into Christianity he elevates it to highest level possible (i.e., to that of his own metaphysics), which should be regarded from his perspective as a philosophical exegesis of the "true Christianity." From this point of view, his exposition resembles a Hegelian dialectical "philosophy of history" (WWR2$_{[P]}$, 443) of the Absolute with the crucial difference being that in his metaphysics it is the history of the Godless principle working and progressing in history proper without any rational or reasonable telos or *Geist*, like the "unmoved Mover" of Aristotle in his last two books of *Physics*.

To summarize Schopenhauer's views on the Hebrew Bible, we might say that he reflects upon it through three theoretical perspectives: (1) that of the New Testament, (2) from that of the writings of "Brahmanism and Buddhism," and, finally, (3) from his own original metaphysics of Will. However, the actual and de facto order is exactly the opposite: from (3) he moves to (2) and then to (1). Thus we can now understand why he claims that "Pelagianism" (a religious doctrine that denies original sin and believes in the freedom of the will) "or present-day rationalism ... reduces Christianity to Judaism" (WWR2$_{[P]}$, 605). The old "*Geistig*" [Ghost] enemy of Schopenhauer is finally uncovered beneath his convoluted exegeses: it is actually the old "bad Hegel" more than Judaism that he fights all his life[52]; perhaps he even develops his entire philosophy to overcome his formidable intellectual opponent. All these above-mentioned motives uncover fascinating dichotomies and alliances in Schopenhauer's thought: Hegel's theism with that of Judaism opposes Buddhism and Schopenhauer's and Kantian anti-theistic approaches. Hence, when he refers to his most admired philosopher, he exclaims: "Kant ... in all seriousness, has in philosophy put an end to Jewish theism" (PP1$_{[P]}$, 171).

25.3 THE ANTHROPOLOGICAL APPROACH: *PARERGA AND PARALIPOMENA*, VOLUMES 1 AND 2

Despite the fact that in his "Preface" to *Parerga and Paralipomena* (from December 1850) Schopenhauer refers to these "additional writings" as "subsidiary" and less "important" than his "systematic works,"[53] he nevertheless repeats his main ideas as they appeared in WWR1 and WW2. As far as his views on Judaism and Jews go, we can find here slight modifications to and elaborations on his former attitude. We should recall that one of the main purposes of this collection was to attract his readers' attention to the second edition of WWR (in 1844), and that to attract attention you need to express your messages populistically and bluntly. Hence, in regard to Jewish issues, Schopenhauer is much less reserved or restrained than he appeared to be in his more systematic publications. Is it only a rhetorical tactic, or is it an expression of his genuine feelings? Readers have to reach their own conclusion in view of the following exposition. Nonetheless, one cannot fail to notice that here the tone is definitely more militant, although the principal meaning of his ideas and distinctions remains the same, as, for example, his recurrent contraposition between "the basic idea of Brahmanism and Buddhism and of true Christianity" and the "optimistic, Jewish-Protestant rationalism" (PP1$_{[P]}$, 35). The tone indeed becomes more impatient, grumpy, and loud, but this seldom deteriorates into a vicious and aggressive anti-Semitic personal onslaught.

However, even at this late stage Schopenhauer retains high respect toward Judaism *as religion*. Since it managed so successfully to taint Christianity with its theistic ideas, Schopenhauer wishes to purify Europe from it and cleanse Christianity from the damage it inflicted upon this faith. Such a formidable enemy indeed must be feared and respected because one cannot fear things or ideas that have caused almost no damage and hence are quite negligible. This rhetoric, of course, was *not* intended by Schopenhauer to urge Europeans to exterminate Jews, but, in a historic and wider perspective, it proved to be a very dangerous game.

The great peril Judaism caused the Christian nations echoes in Schopenhauer's descriptions of "our Judaized West" (PP2$_{[P]}$, 222) and in his "hope that one day even Europe will be purified of all Jewish mythology" (PP2$_{[P]}$, 226). Evidently he did not read

Heine's ominous prophesy that "where they have burned books, they will end in burning human beings."[54] Thus, he "deplores" the fact that, as he puts it: "This religion has become the basis of the prevailing religion in Europe; for it is a religion without any metaphysical tendency...entirely immanent and furnishes nothing but mere war-cry in the struggle with other nations" (PP1$_{[P]}$, 126n). Following this verdict, Schopenhauer commits the invalid move from speaking about Judaism (as a specific religion of Jewish people who "are the chosen people of their *God*") to speak on "Jewish race," which is an altogether different biological and not cultural category. Then he summarizes, rather admiringly, the "catastrophic" and historical impacts of this Judaism.

> When I observe that the present nations of Europe to a certain extent regard them-selves as the heirs to that chosen people of God, I cannot conceal my regret. On the other hand, Judaism cannot be denied the reputation of being the only really monotheistic religion on earth; for no other religion can boast of an objective God, creator of heaven and earth.   (PP1$_{[P]}$, 126)

This mixture of damnation and admiration, of utter rejection and sincere appreciation of Judaism makes Schopenhauer's attitude deeply ambivalent and inscrutable.

The extent of the damage indicates the enormous power that causes it. From this point of view, Judaism scores quite well in Schopenhauer's book but it also scores highly on account of it being imperishable in contrast to other ancient superpowers. Since its preservation shows a high degree of will-to-life, Schopenhauer cannot but implicitly admire it and its people.

> The religion of the Greeks and Romans, those world-powers, has perished. The reli-gion of the contemptible little Jewish race, on the other hand, has been preserved.
> (PP2$_{[P]}$, 393)

Nonetheless, Schopenhauer cannot forgive Jewish people for their despicable treatment of animals and their view of animals as "something manufactured for man's use" (PP2$_{[P]}$, 371). Hence his final verdict and solution: "The unconscionable treatment of animals must be stopped in Europe. The Jewish view of the animal world must, on account of its immorality, be expelled from Europe" (PP2$_{[P]}$, 377). He maintains that this attitude must be erased from Europe, not for its theistic religion or other elements of faith, but on account of its maltreatment of animals. Still, it is a very far cry from Nietzsche's famous and spontaneous exclamation:

> What a blessing a Jew is among Germans![55]

Finally I will present here two most problematic passages—"problematic" as far as the defense of Schopenhauer against the charge of anti-Semitism is concerned. All these statements are found in his *Parerga and Paralipomena* whose anthropological and anti-systematic manner made it easier for the aging Arthur to vent his prejudices uncritically and quite wildly.

1. The first and the most disturbing description is inserted by Schopenhauer in context with his discussion of Spinoza's "pantheism," which in his eyes is "essentially and necessarily optimism" (PP1$_{[P]}$, 73). Then he refers to several chapters of Genesis and states that here the readers are "overcome by the *foetor judaicus*." The translator, Eric F. J. Payne, evidently tried to weaken this unsettling impression and brought this expression in the original Latin. On the other hand, the conscientious editor of the second English edition of PP, Christopher Janaway, translates: "the 'Jewish stench'" (PP1, 69; PP2, 338) and does not hesitate to provide in a footnote the Latin term *foetor judaicus*, stating, correctly, that it is a "medieval anti-Semitic concept" (PP1, 69n). In any case, *foetor judaicus* or "stench" or even "odor" does not smell better!

Especially not in Schopenhauer's nose, since he regards "Judaism" as "the sole purely monotheistic religion" (PP1, 116) whose derivatives are Christianity and Islam, and hence it becomes *eo ipso* his unrelenting enemy and the most ideal type of a religion that preaches an antithetical learning to those of Indian philosophies and to that of Schopenhauer. He does not like its "theistic" smell and is even cross at Spinoza, whom otherwise he regarded quite favorably. The question, of course, should be raised whether this popular anti-Semitic expression was used by Schopenhauer as the price he had to pay for attracting his mostly anti-Semitic readers to his writings, or if it was a genuine expression of his sentiments. Who can fathom what was deeply hidden in such a complicated nature as that of Arthur Schopenhauer?

This enigma becomes even more inscrutable when we read in his "Dialogue on Religion" (in PP2) traces of certain empathy with the persecuted Jews and an unambiguous condemnation of the

> ... atrocities brought forth by religions, especially the Christian and the Mohammedan, and the misery they have brought upon the world! Think of the fanaticism, of the endless persecutions, of the cruel expulsion and extermination of the Moors and Jews from Spain.[56]   (PP2, 320)

However, one page later, he admonishes his readers: "let us also not forget the chosen people of God who, after stealing the golden and silver vessels loaned to them by their old, trusting friends in Egypt, at the express and special command of Jehovah now made their murderous and plundering raid on the Promised Land" (PP2, 321).

On account of such (and other) passages I am obliged to grant Schopenhauer a certain benefit of the doubt—at least as far as his ambivalent attitude toward Jews and Judaism is concerned. Surely Schopenhauer would not deny the occurrence of the Jewish Holocaust and would condemn it strongly with all the rhetorical power of his German language. And, to paraphrase a witty English saying that "Everybody is innocent—Until proven Irish," I would say that in Schopenhauer's eyes: "Everybody (including himself) is guilty of anti-Semitism—Until proven a philo-Semite!"

2. The most exciting and no less problematic passage regarding this entire issue is found in the same dialogue "On Religion" in an extensive footnote that Schopenhauer appended to his version of the Exodus of Jews from Pharaoh's Egypt. This time he

mobilized for his case the renowned authority of one of the most famous historian of antiquity: Tacitus and his *Histories*. To impress upon the reader an air of credibility, Schopenhauer quotes from Tacitus (not after slightly distorting his text), and the only alibi for this infamous segment is that he downgraded it to a footnote implying thereby that this is not the most crucial passage of his views on Jews and Judaism. Nonetheless, most descendants of the Jewish people will find it still quite offensive.

> Tacitus (*Histories*, Book V, ch. 2) and Justinus (Book XXXVI, ch. 2) have handed down the historical basis of the Exodus...from which we can infer how matters stand regarding the historical basis of the remaining books of the Old Testament. We see there in the cited passage that the Pharaoh no longer wanted to tolerate the filthy Jewish people in clean Egypt, who had sneaked in afflicted with dirty diseases (scabies) that threatened to be infectious; he therefore had them loaded onto ships and dumped on the Arabian coast. It is accurate that a detachment of Egyptians was sent after them, yet not to bring back the precious fellows...but to recover from them what they had *stolen*; for they had indeed *stolen* golden vessels from the temples—who would have loaned anything to such rabble?...We also see from the two Roman classicists cited how much the Jews were loathed and despised at all times and by all peoples; in part this may stem from the fact that they were the only people on earth who did not ascribe to mankind an existence beyond this life, and therefore they were regarded as cattle, as the dregs of humanity—but as great masters at lying.   (PP2, 321)

It is quite surprising that, in this mixture of theological arguments and falsified "alternative" truths, Schopenhauer, who never believed in the validity of "objective" truth and did not distinguish it from subjectivity proper—when it concurs with his dark prejudices—sided with the historians and based his case against Jews and Judaism on such a shaky ground and documentation. However, in this deconstructive period we know today that historical treatises are not exactly the epitomes of truth and nothing but the truth, especially when it comes to such a mobilized historian as Tacitus who represented in his *Annales* mainly the Roman point of view.[57]

All in all, Schopenhauer's sketchy paraphrases from Tacitus are quite anti-Semitic in their content, tone, and malice. Tacitus, though not the most reliable historian, surely did not hold anti-Semitic grudges and sentiments against the Jews who were not exactly the main foci of his scholarly interests. But let him speak (uninterrupted) for himself and let the reader form his own judgment.

> It is said that the Jews were originally exiles from the island of Crete...[where there] is the famous mountain called Idaei, which was later lengthened into the barbarous form Iudaei...Most authors agree that once during a plague in Egypt which caused bodily disfigurement...the oracle of Ammon told to purge Egypt and transport this race into other lands, since it was hateful to the gods....Moses introduced new religious practices quite opposed to those of all other religions....Whatever their origin, these rites are maintained by their antiquity; the other customs of the Jews are base

and abominable, and owe their persistence to their depravity...the Jews are extremely loyal toward one another, and always ready to show compassion, but toward other people they feel only hate and enmity...as a race, they are prone to lust, they abstain from intercourse with foreign women....They bury the body rather than burn it, thus following the Egyptians custom...the Jews conceive of one god only...and they set no statues in their cities, still less in their temples.

(*Histories*, Book V, 177–83)

Tacitus does not mention Jews being unclean or inflicted by scabies but stresses their "customs" and the religious differences of their creed from those of the Egyptians and other people. In any case, the discrepancies between Tacitus's original and Schopenhauer's paraphrases of it speak for themselves.

∗   ∗   ∗

To answer the question I posed at the beginning of this chapter: Schopenhauer did not hate Jews, but he disliked Judaism. For this reason he had much in common with the present-day secular and enlightened Israelis in Israel, which is not solely a Jewish State but a state populated mainly by Jews. Hence the heated dispute in modern, and mostly secular, Israel is whether it should be a "Jewish State" or a "State of Jews" (as Herzl wanted it to be).[58]

Schopenhauer opposed Judaism because he regarded it as the epitome of *theism*, which in his eyes was the most hateful idea, starkly opposite to what he cherished and applauded in his metaphysics. For this reason he also objected to Hegel's theistic and teleological approach. But, in counterdistinction to Hegel, whom he hated personally as a living (and pompous) person, he did not hold such grudges and sentiments against Jews as living persons and even sympathized with their historical distresses as we have shown. Of one thing we can be sure: *Schopenhauer was less an anti-Semite than he was an anti-Theist who defied all monotheistic religions.* And it is exciting to see how Schopenhauer—the pessimistic misanthrope—wished to eradicate what he thought to be the roots of all evil; that is, the various religions, but not the godless Buddhism, which, under his interpretation, was the most amiable, humanist, and "correct" faith. Hence comes my final verdict on this entire issue: Schopenhauer was not an anti-Semite as charged. His militantly anti-Judaism stance did not make him into a vicious anti-Semitic thinker and person.[59] This being said, however, it would be quite instructive to quote here Nietzsche's confession in the "Preface" to his 1888 composition: *The Case of Wagner.*

What does a philosopher demand of himself first and last? To overcome his time in himself, to become "timeless."... Well, then, I am no less than Wagner, a child of this time; that is, a decadent [and Nietzsche thinks here also of anti-Semitic sentiments]: but I comprehended this, I resisted it. The philosopher in me resisted.[60]

I wonder whether this confession can be equally applied to Schopenhauer and to his enigmatic relations to Jews and Judaism?

NOTES

1. This title is inspired by Nietzsche's confession to Wagner in a letter from May 22, 1869, that "*Ihnen und Schopenhauer danke ich es, wenn ich bis jetzt festgehalten habe an dem germanischen Lebenserst, an einer vertieften Betrachtung dieses so räthselvollen und bedenklichen Dasein*" ("I am thankful to you and to Schopenhauer for my up to now firm adherence to the German seriousness of life, to the deep observation into the inscrutable riddle of one's existence"). My translation from *Friedrich Nietzsche Sämtliche Briefe: Kritische Studienausgabe in 8 Bänden,* edited by Giorgio Colli and Mazzino Montinari, München: de Gruyter, 1986, vol. 3, p. 9 (hereafter KSA). For useful comments and cordial encouragement, I am indebted to the editor of this volume.

2. Robert Wicks, *Schopenhauer* (Oxford: Blackwell, 2008), 10.

3. This reference appears in a context of the dichotomy Schopenhauer used later to draw between the realistic (and optimistic) Judaism and the idealistic (and pessimistic) Buddhism. Here and elsewhere Schopenhauer does not squarely contrast Judaism to Christianity, as e.g., did Hegel, but to Indian religions such as "Brahmanism as well as Buddhism" (FR, 36, 125, 710). See also FR, 124–25, where he refers to the "dogma of *a God–Creator*"…whose "authors and originators" belonged to "that crude and barbarous faith of the Jews". On p. 126, he speaks about the "freedom of the will" as a "crude, crass and abhorrent Jewish dogma."

4. As he admits in an early entry: "the essence-in-itself of man, as of every phenomenon, is the *will*" (MR3, 28 [emphasis in original]).

5. I prefer here the translations of Christopher Janaway, 1999 and 1997, for Schopenhauer's German notion of *Wille zum Leben* over the usual translation as the "will to live" since I agree with him that "what Schopenhauer has in mind is more inclusive, it is a striving not just to live, but also to engender life and to protect offspring" (Christopher Janaway, "Schopenhauer" in *German Philosophers* [Oxford University Press, 1997], 261). Simon May concurs with this view, stating that the term "life" captures better the "desire not merely to persevere [as individuals] but to survive [as people] through my offspring" by acts of procreation (Simon May, "Love as the Urge to Procreate: Schopenhauer," Chapter 13 of his *Love: A History* [New Haven and London: Yale University Press, 2011], 176–187, 274). In MR3 we find textual ground for interpreting "will-to-life" as a will to procreate, e.g., "*the act of procreation,* i.e., the most distinct affirmation of the will-to-live" (MR3, 15 and 17). And see also WWR1$_{[P]}$, 329, where he speaks about sexual impulse as "only" aiming "at the propagation of the race."

6. Read his *Reisebuch* and his *Brieftasche* from September 1818–April 1820, in MR3. We should mention as well the flourishing Jewish community in the city of Hamburg where Schopenhauer spent his early years.

7. Read Schopenhauer's definition that "*Theism*…presupposes that the world is divided into *heaven* and *earth*; on the *latter* human beings run about, in the *former* sits the God who governs them…" and who "not only made the world, but afterwards found it to be excellent" (PP1$_{[P]}$: 51; 62). Read also his section, "On theism" (PP2$_{[P]}$: 339–40) where he opposes it to Kant's *Critique of Pure Reason.*

8. See PP1$_{[P]}$, 127. Later in this dissertation he claims that "Judaism and theism are simply identical; therefore, we stigmatize all people who are not Jews, Christians or Muslims, with the popular term heathens. Muslims and Jews even repudiate Christians for not being pure theists because of the doctrine of the Trinity. For Christianity…has Indian blood in its

veins and thus a constant tendency to rid itself of Judaism" (FR, 120). This is a highly original explanation for religious anti-Semitic sentiments and also an echo of the "stigmatic" prejudices against Judaism that Schopenhauer, the "Indian"-Christian, has developed in his metaphysics.

9. See also FR, 37.

10. See also MR3, 153. The same wording is found also in WWR2$_{[P]}$, 644.

11. Thus he writes: "Spinoza died on 21 February 1677, and I was born on 22 February 1788, and hence exactly 111 years, or 100 plus 1/10 of 100 plus 1/10 of 10 years after his death" (MR3, 263). He insisted many times that Spinoza, like himself, was a great "exception to Jewish theism" (PP1$_{[P]}$, 15). On the other hand, he is sometimes hostile toward Spinoza in a rather intense way, as for example, in PP1$_{[P]}$, 73 (I am indebted for the last citation to Robert Wicks).

12. In this letter to Goethe he quotes a passage from Spinoza's rather esoteric letters which only an expert of his writings can do (GB, 21). See also his letter to Johann August Becker from September 21, 1844 (GB, 218) where he states that "their correspondence reminds him that of Spinoza with Oldenburg and Blyenburg." Spinoza's *Epistolae* were published as part of *Opera posthuma* in Amsterdam 1677. In a letter from March 4, 1857, Schopenhauer refers to Spinoza as to his "spiritual Ancestor" ("*geistigen Vorfahren*," GB, 411).

13. See his letter from December 21, 1829, written in English in the context of his proposal to translate into English central writings of Kant (a project that was rejected): "...we now see a mere swaggerer and charlatan, without a shadow of merit, I mean Hegel, with a compound of bombastic nonsense and positions bordering on madness..." (GB, 117).

14. See Yirmiyahu Yovel. *Dark Riddle: Hegel, Nietzsche, and the Jews* (Oxford: Polity Press, 1998).

15. He even compares his most cherished philosopher, Kant, to Moses who "returned from Mount Sinai to find his people dancing before the golden calf" (WN, 314) as happened to Kant vis-à-vis his "misguided" followers and interpreters (like Hegel, Fichte, etc.).

16. This expression (MR3, 710) and its synonym "the genuine Christianity" is frequently used by Schopenhauer. In one of its first appearances, Schopenhauer draws an interesting dichotomy between "Parsees, Jews and Mohammedans" who "worship a *creator of the world*" and "Hindus, Buddhists...who worship an *overcomer of the world* and in a certain sense a destroyer of the world. In his eyes, "*Christianity* proper", namely of the New Testament belongs to this second class of religions, but on the historical path it is forcibly and absurdly connected and ties to a religion from the first class" (MR3, 710).

17. This appalling mental phenomena was quite common among the acculturated European Jews by the *fin-de-siècle*. See my "Jewish Self-Hatred: Nietzsche, Freud and the Case of Theodor Lessing" in *Leo Baeck Year Book* 50 (2005), 233–45.

18. This actually is the description of the Frankfurt ghetto by one of the editors of the *Encyclopedia Hebraica* (Heb.) 28 (1976), 331. This Ghetto, called in German the "*Frankfurter Judengasse*" ("Jewish Alley") was one of the earliest ghettos and home to Germany's largest Jewish community in early modern times.

19. A notable exception is Robert Wicks's essay, "Schopenhauer and Judaism," in *The Palgrave Schopenhauer Handbook* (2017), 325–49. My essay, although published in this volume at a later date, was written at the same time as his and though we approach this topic in different ways, we fundamentally think alike on this matter.

20. *Hitler's Table Talk*, translated by Norman Cameron and R. H. Stevens, 2nd ed. (London: Weidenfeld & Nicolson, 1973), 89. See the "Introduction" in *Nietzsche, the Godfather of*

Fascism? On the Uses and Abuses of a Philosophy, edited by Jacob Golomb and Robert S. Wistrich (Princeton, NJ: Princeton University Press, 2002), 1–16. On Nietzsche's anti-militaristic stand, see my article: "Will to Power: Does It Lead to the 'Coldest of All Cold Monsters'?" in *The Oxford Handbook of Nietzsche,* edited by Ken Gemes and John Richardson (Oxford: Oxford University Press, 2013), 523–50.

21. Read his admission that "Whoever wants to know without understanding Hebrew what the Old Testament is, must read it in the *Septuagint* as the most accurate, genuine and at the same time most beautiful of all translations; there it has entirely different tone and colour" (PP2$_{[P]}$, 357n).

22. "Temples [Jewish] and churches, pagodas [Buddhism and Brahmanism] and mosques...testify to man's need for metaphysics..." (WWR2$_{[P]}$, 162). He adds quite ironically: "the capacity for metaphysics does not go hand in hand with the need for it" (WWR2$_{[P]}$, 162). Two pages later he claims that certain metaphysics "known under the name of religions" have their credentials outside themselves and were developed "exclusively" by "the great majority of people who are not capable of thinking but only of believing, and are susceptible not to arguments, but only to authority" (WWR2$_{[P]}$,164). From this perspective, then, no religion is better than others but still Christianity, due to its being "formed" by the so-called Indian thought, is in better status than other creeds.

23. Schopenhauer was quite aware of what he calls "the flagrant contradiction between the production of the world by an almighty, infinitely good, and wise being and the dreary and defective state of this same world" and decided that it was exactly the task of the "*Cabalistic* and *Gnostic* philosophies" to eliminate this theological discrepancy (PP1$_{[P]}$, 60). He adds that this contradiction was introduced to Christianity from "Jewish theism, where the Lord not only made the world, but afterward found it to be excellent" (PP1$_{[P]}$, 62). Witness also his sober observation to the effect that the "*Cabalistic...philosophies* [though he did not read the *Zohar,* the foundational work of Jewish mystical thought known as *Kabbalah,* printed in Hebrew in Cremona around 1558]...are attempts to moderate the absurdity of theism...to abolish the glaring contradiction between the creation of the world by an all-powerful, all-wise and all-good being and the sad, dismal and defective nature of this world...[by] introducing the story of the Fall, which is generally the culminating point of Judaism" (MR3, 491–92).

24. Schopenhauer knew about Job's tragic figure and scripture, as follows from his remarks on him in PP2$_{[P]}$, 372 and 525, where in a short homage to him he states, "what declamation on the vanity and emptiness of human existence will make a greater impression than Job's?"

25. Arthur Schopenhauer, *Reisetagebücher aus den Jahren 1803 bis 1804,* edited by Charlotte von Gewinner (Leipzig, 1923), 27. The preceding English translation is found in Rüdiger Safranski, *Schopenhauer and the Wild Years of Philosophy,* translated by Ewald Osers (Cambridge, MA: Harvard University Press, 1989), 43. It is actually a pity that, besides this incident, Safranski does not discuss in more detail Schopenhauer's views on Jews and Judaism, a neglect shared also by many other of his best biographers or commentators.

26. With which Schopenhauer was familiar, as follows from his remark in volume 1 of *Parerga and Paralipomena* in the context of his rejection of Spinoza's "pantheism" since, in his eyes, it "is essentially and necessarily optimism" as is stated "in the sixteen[th] chapter of his *Tractatus Theologico-Politicus*" (PP1$_{[P]}$, 73).

27. Safranski, *Schopenhauer and the Wild Years of Philosophy,* 43.

28. Ibid., 90 (my emphasis).

29. This reminds us of Nietzsche's statement: "in reality there has been only one Christian, and he died on the Cross," *Antichrist*, translated by R. J. Hollingdale (Penguin Books, 1968), 151 (for details, see Golomb, 2000).

30. See also MR1, 16, 18, 523.

31. As, for example, when he attributes to "Moses," Psalm 90:10 (MR1, 80) and the translator [E. F. J. Payne] correctly observes in his footnote that "The reference to Moses is based on error" (MR1, 80).

32. Joseph Ernest Renan (1823–1892) was a French theologian and expert in Semitic languages. His highly controversial book, *La vie de Jésus*, was published in 1863.

33. To whom Schopenhauer explicitly refers in PP2, 346, namely to his renowned book: *Das Leben Jesus, kritische bearbeitet (The Life of Jesus Critically Examined)*, 1835–36.

34. Nietzsche. *Beyond Good and Evil*, translated by Walter Kaufmann (New York: Vintage Books, 1966), 13. On many other significant similarities and contrasts between Nietzsche and Schopenhauer, see Ivan Soll (2013) and the classical research of Georg Simmel, *Schopenhauer and Nietzsche* (from 1907), translated by Helmut Loiskandl, Deena Weinstein, and Michael Weinstein, Amherst: University of Massachusetts Press, 1986.

35. In his eyes the really "true nature of Christianity" is personified in Jesus, whom Schopenhauer admired because "*the Christian Saviour* is a superb figure, full of poetical truth and of the highest significance for…he is in a state of supreme suffering. This forcibly expresses life and the world" (MR1, 248).

36. David Asher (1818–1890), a Leipzig Jewish scholar and teacher of English. He published in Germany several works on Schopenhauer's philosophy around 1876.

37. My translation "*Mir ist alles Hebräische und Islamische eigentlich antipathisch*" in a letter from Frankfurt of July 15, 1857 (GB, 417 and see GB, 422; 425). Solomon ibn Gabirol or Ben Gebirol was an eleventh-century Andalusian-Hebrew poet and Jewish philosopher, but Schopenhauer does not distinguish here between the Jewish-Spanish culture known as the "Golden Age of Jews in Medieval Spain" and the Islamic-Arabic tradition there. He feels the same degree of "antipathy" toward both of them. Also, in his letter writing, he used to regard Judaism on the same par as Islam, thus giving the (right) impression of relating to both religions in the same negative terms. Nonetheless, see his letter to David Asher from November 12, 1856, where he speaks about his wish to contribute a parallel from the *Rigveda* to David Asher's "*hebräischen Funde*" (findings, GB, 405). Thus despite his feelings of animosity toward Hebrew literature, he finds it interesting enough to compare it to the Indian writings he cherished. His ability to distinguish between persons and their religious or intellectual convictions is particularly noticeable in his letter to another (gentile) friend of his whom he thanks for his essay on David Asher in which he rejects that rejects "*dem rein jüdischen, niederträchtigen Optimismus*" ("the pure Jewish, malicious Optimism" [GB, 364]). This he writes despite being quite fond of Asher, the man.

38. Thus, for example, he is concerned about the clinical obstruction Asher has suffered and advises him to walk daily two hours (in any weather), reminding him that: "*la santé avant tout*" ("health is above all" [GB, 421, December 3, 1857]).

39. "*Ein Paar Jüdische Doctoren*"; a letter of June 29, 1854 (GB, 347).

40. "*Den alten Juden*"; in a letter to his loyal friend Julius Frauenstädt (from June 6, 1856 [GB, 392]).

41. A letter to Carl W. Labes from Frankfurt, January 23, 1838. In the original: "*Die* Speciers kenne ich: sie sind Juden: und nach der letzten Judenverfolgung in Preußen wird diese Nation nichts Lust haben, dort Grundbesitz zu acquiren.*"

42. As, for example, when he speaks about the "Catholic students of Theology" and remarks that also the "Bonn Prof. Knoondt is Catholic" (October 3, 1857 [GB, 418]).

43. See Theodor Herzl (the political founder of the Zionist movement) who, out of desperation due to the pervasive anti-Semitic sentiments reigning in *fin-de-siècle* Vienna, called upon his brothers: "The nickname *Judenjungen* has been up to now an insult. Reverse the order and it will become a term of honor: *junge Juden*" (my translation from the Hebrew collection of Herzl's aphorisms from the *fin de siècle* entitled: *Ko Amar Herzl* (*Thus Spoke Herzl*), edited by Herzl's secretary, A. Pollack, and printed in Tel Aviv [In Hebrew, Palestine] in 1940. The quote is from pp. 33–34. For details, see ch. 1 in Golomb, 2004.

44. "*Sie kommen gar vom Hegel, und bringen Pantheismus und Optimismus mit,—die zu meiner Sache passen, wie Schweinskarbonade zur Judenhochzeit*" (GB, 232).

45. Further evidence is found in his 1841 treatise on morality where he mentions a Jew who remembered that he was forbidden to smoke "his pipe at home on the Sabbath" (BM$_{[P]}$, 106; see also 127).

46. A letter from August 21, 1852 (GB, 290–92). On the next page, he explains that: "Meine Philosophie redet nie von Wolkenkukusheim, sondern von *dieser Welt* [emphasis in origin] d.h. sie ist *immanent*, nicht transcendent" (GB, 291).

47. My free translation of "*und sind singen tanzend an ganz glorreich.*" And compare to the similar exclamation in Nietzsche's *Morgenröthe* (*Dawn*) §205, entitled *Vom Volke Israel* about "*Volkes freuen...an dem alte Judengott...und wir Alle, Alle wollen uns mit ihm freuen darf*" (KSA 3: 183).

48. See also his remarks twenty-three years later in BM$_{[P]}$, 178.

49. This actually is a mirror image of Nietzsche's attitude, who, despite being influenced at the beginning of his philosophizing (in *The Birth of Tragedy*) by Schopenhauer's Indian metaphysics, wrote later that: "In the Jewish Old Testament, the book of divine justice there are human beings, things, and speeches in so grand style that Greek and Indian literature have nothing to compare with it." *Beyond Good and Evil*, translated by Walter Kaufmann (New York: Vintage Books. 1966), p. 65.

50. The same accusation of Spinoza is found in MR3, 153; and see the earlier discussion.

51. In German, "*Gestank*": and see later discussion.

52. In PP, this is mostly in an *ad hominem* manner. He associates Hegel's philosophy of religion with "the doctrines which were in part made known to the former little race of the Jews" and blames "the professor of philosophy called Hegel" for "welding" "philosophy and religion into one centaur which they call philosophy of religion" (PP1$_{[P]}$: 142).

53. The first sentence of his "Preface."

54. Quoted by Graham Ward, *True Religion* (Oxford: Blackwell, 2003), 142.

55. Friedrich Nietzsche, *The Will to Power*, translated by Walter Kaufmann (New York: Vintage Books, 1968), 31.

56. See also PP2, 322–23: "Truly, this is the worst side of religions, that the faithful of each one consider everything to be permitted against those of all others and therefore treat them with the most extreme ruthlessness and cruelty; thus the Mohammedians against the Christians Christinas and Hindus; Christian against Hindus, Mohammedians, native American peoples, Negroes, Jews, heretics and so on...it is the monotheistic religions alone that provide us with the spectacle of religious wars, religious persecutions and heretic trials." The situation today (in the first half of the twenty-first century) is not altogether different if we recall the mutual atrocities committed by the Sunnis against the Shi'ah, by Isis against Hezbollah, and so on.

57. Read, for example the following statement: "...that the Jews alone had failed to surrender increased *our* resentment." Tacitus in Five Volumes, *Histories*, edited by E. H. Warmington, translated by Clifford H. Moore, The Loeb Classical Library, Book V (London: William Heinemann/Cambridge: Harvard University Press, 1931), 193 (emphasis added).

58. See note 43.

59. This judgment is also shared by two modern Hebrew writers who were responsible for the Renaissance of Hebrew modern literature: Micha Josef Berdichevski (1865–1921) and Joseph Hayyim Brenner (1881–1921). But this topic deserves an independent research. There is very little literature on Schopenhauer's impact on the awakening of the Hebrew Modern Culture and literature. See M. J. Berdichevski, *Über den Zusammenhang Ethik und Aesthetik*, Berner Studien zur Philosophie und ihrer Geschichtem vol. 9 (Bern, 1897); Jacob Golomb (2004), chs. 3 and 4; Aliza Klausner-Eskol, *The Influence of Nietzsche and of Schopenhauer on M. J. Berdichevski* (Tel Aviv: Dvir, 1954, in Hebrew; especially Part 2); Shmuel Hugo Bergmann, "Arthur Schopenhauer," in his *People and Ways* (Jerusalem: Bialik Institute, 1967, in Hebrew), 118–53.

60. Friedrich Nietzsche, *The Birth of Tragedy and The Case of Wagner*, translated by Walter Kaufmann (New York: Vintage Books, 1967), 155.

FURTHER READING

Engel, Morris S. "Schopenhauer's Impact on Wittgenstein." In *Schopenhauer: His Philosophical Achievement*, edited by Michael Fox. New York: Barnes & Noble Books, 1980, 236–54.

Golomb, Jacob. *Nietzsche's Enticing Psychology of Power*. Ames: Iowa State University Press, 1989; Blackwell Publishing, 2004.

Golomb, Jacob. *In Search of Authenticity from Kierkegaard to Camus*. London/New York: Routledge, 1995.

Golomb, Jacob. "Nietzsche and the Marginal Jews." In *Nietzsche and Jewish Culture*, edited by Jacob Golomb. London/New York: Routledge, 1997, 158–92.

Golomb, Jacob. "Nietzsche's Positive Religion and the Old Testament." In *Nietzsche and the Divine*, edited by John Lippitt and Jim Urpeth. Manchester, UK: Clinamen Press, 2000, 30–56.

Golomb, Jacob. *Nietzsche and Zion*. Ithaca/London: Cornell University Press, 2004.

Golomb, Jacob, and Robert S. Wistrich, eds. "Introduction." In *Nietzsche, the Godfather of Fascism? On the Uses and Abuses of a Philosophy*. Princeton, NJ: Princeton University Press, 2002, 1–16.

Golomb, Jacob. "Jewish Self-Hatred: Nietzsche, Freud and the Case of Theodor Lessing." *Leo Baeck Year Book* 50 (2005): 233–45.

Golomb, Jacob. "Will to Power: Does It Lead to the 'Coldest of All Cold Monsters'?" In *The Oxford Handbook of Nietzsche*, edited by Ken Gemes and John Richardson. Oxford: Oxford University Press, 2013, 523–50.

Hitler, Adolf. *Hitler's Table Talk*, translated by Norman Cameron and R. H. Stevens, 2nd ed. London: Widen & Nicolson, 1973.

Janaway, Christopher. "Schopenhauer." In *German Philosophers*, edited by Roger Scruton. Oxford: Oxford University Press, 1997, 219–336.

Janaway, Christopher. "Schopenhauer's Pessimism." In *The Cambridge Companion to Schopenhauer*, edited by Christopher Janaway. Cambridge: Cambridge University Press, 1999, 318–45.

May, Simon. "Love as the Urge to Procreate: Schopenhauer." In his *Love: A History*, New Haven/London: Yale University Press, 2011, 176–87.

Magee, Bryan. *The Philosophy of Schopenhauer.* Oxford: Oxford University Press, 1983.

Safranski, Rüdiger. *Schopenhauer and the Wild Years of Philosophy*, translated by Ewald Osers. Cambridge, MA: Harvard University Press, 1989.

Soll, Ivan. "Schopenhauer as Nietzsche's 'Great Teacher' and 'Antipode.'" In *The Oxford Handbook of Nietzsche*, edited by Ken Gemes and John Richardson. Oxford: Oxford University Press, 2013, 160–84.

Simmel, Georg. *Schopenhauer and Nietzsche* [1907], translated by Helmut Loiskandl, Deena Weinstein, and Michael Weinstein. Amherst: University of Massachusetts Press, 1986.

Spinoza, Benedict de. *The Ethics.* In *The Chief Works of Benedict de Spinoza*, translated by R. H. M. Elwes. New York: Dover Publications Inc., 1955.

Warmington, E. H. ed. *Tacitus in Five Volumes, Histories*, translated by Clifford H. Moore. The Loeb Classical Library, Book V. London: Heinemann/Cambridge: Harvard University, 1931.

Ward, Graham. *True Religion.* Oxford: Blackwell, 2003.

Wicks, Robert. *Schopenhauer*, Oxford: Blackwell, 2008.

Wicks, Robert. "Schopenhauer and Judaism." In *The Palgrave Schopenhauer Handbook*, edited by Sandra Shapshay. London: Palgrave Macmillan, 2017, 325–49.

Yovel, Yirmiyahu. *Dark Riddle: Hegel, Nietzsche, and the Jews.* Oxford: Polity Press, 1998.

PART VI

SCHOPENHAUER'S
INFLUENCE

CHAPTER 26

POST-SCHOPENHAUERIAN METAPHYSICS

Hartmann, Mainländer, Bahnsen, and Nietzsche

SEBASTIAN GARDNER

As Frederick Beiser observes in his recent, ground-breaking study of the late nineteenth-century pessimism debate, the remarkable influence of Schopenhauer in this period owes a great deal to the crisis of identity which philosophy had suffered in the wake of the collapse of the systematic ambitions of Fichte, Schelling, and Hegel, and the (closely associated) self-emancipation of the empirical sciences.[1] Schopenhauer, though not historically effective in either development, was discovered mid-century to have been profoundly attuned to both—to have seen through the rhetoric of "intellectual intuition" and the Concept, and to have rightly emphasized the conditioning of human reason by nature—and moreover to have worked out an alternative path for philosophy to take in light of the impossibility of rationalizing the world in the manner of German Idealism.

This forms the broad background of the thinkers discussed in this chapter, whose major philosophical writings all appeared within a relatively short period, 1869 to 1888. They are selected not in the first instance because of their contribution to the pessimism question tabled by Schopenhauer, but rather because of their concern with the question of what metaphysics can amount to after Schopenhauer. What unifies Eduard von Hartmann, Philipp Mainländer, Julius Bahnsen, and Friedrich Nietzsche, I will suggest, is (A) their recognition of a fundamental respect in which the system set forth in *The World as Will and Representation* (WWR) is problematic, along with (B) their acceptance of a positive insight which they find in Schopenhauer and which shows the limitations of, and the need to revise, other contemporary schools of philosophy.

The former has to do, not ultimately with the particular content of Schopenhauer's major metaphysical theses, though certainly these are subjected to heavy challenge, but with the *status* of his assertions. If, as Schopenhauer claims, reason reveals its necessary total emptiness in face of metaphysical questions, then what kind of discourse can WWR itself amount to? How can the world be known to *be* will and representation—and to include a transcendental subject, and to involve the mediation of Ideas, and so on—if reason is merely a device for structuring phenomena and cognition merely a means for negotiating desire-satisfaction?[2]

What unites Hartmann *et al* is their refusal to take this difficulty as a reason for turning their backs on the system of WWR. This sets them, as Beiser again emphasizes, at odds with the Neo-Kantian attempt at a fully rational reconstruction of human knowledge.

The positive insight which they find in Schopenhauer has two distinguishable but interconnected parts. (B1) The failure of WWR to reflexively validate itself is a direct consequence of what it correctly gets into philosophical focus. The shortfall in Schopenhauer—as it must seem to Fichte and the later Idealists who had staked every-thing on showing that the System of Philosophy demonstrates its own unique correct-ness, and to Kantians convinced that only absurdity can result from any claim to know the Unconditioned—is precisely the mark of its success. What Schopenhauer grasps, and is duly reflected in the way that WWR leaves the status of its own discourse unaccounted for, is the resistance of content to form, the independence of being from thought, of existence from essence, of the *Daß* from the *Was* of the world. The dualism can be for-mulated in indefinitely many ways, but its proximal origin lies in Kant's famous dichot-omy of intuition and concept: Schopenhauer's insight is that, though superficially the two may be annexed, there is a profound and enveloping sense in which (to put the point in Kantian language) rational conceptual form and nonrational intuitive content remain absolutely alien to one another. Whence Schopenhauer's metaphilosophical problem: How can it be *thought* that there is a single world which is thinkable *as* the one and also *as* the other? Indeed, how, without invoking some common measure, can it be meaningfully *said* of these two things, or world-aspects, that they are "absolutely alien" to one another?

The other, complementary component of Schopenhauer's positive insight is (B2) the immediate connection of the world's cognitive impenetrability with its *wrongness*. The claim here is not, of course, that the world's nonamenability to our comprehension is the *reason* for its seeming alienation from the Good—which would make WWR com-patible with traditional theodicies—but that its epistemic opacity on the one hand and its axiological negativity on the other constitute a single, imponderable state of affairs.

Taking this assessment of Schopenhauer to provide the common starting point of Hartmann and the others involves a degree of rational reconstruction. What I none-theless aim to make plausible is that the *positive* metaphysical and axiological signifi-cance of Schopenhauer's limitations provides a basis for unifying these four thinkers in a more systematic sense than that in which the history of philosophy recognizes a *Schopenhauerschule*.[3]

Since limitations of space will allow no more than a brief and selective sketch of the relevant positions, it will help to give in advance an overview of how, on my account, the various post-Schopenhauerians are differentiated and how each may be taken to repre-sent a different path proceeding from the same point of origin. Taking the problem bequeathed by Schopenhauer to be, as explained, that of expressing the ultimate reality of will and the dualistic limit which is thereby set to philosophical reason, their various solutions may be summarized as follows. (1) Hartmann, Mainländer, and Bahnsen may all be regarded as aiming to reunite, in one way or other, the terms that Schopenhauer sets in opposition, though without, of course, reverting to the monism of the German Idealists or any earlier figure in the history of philosophy.[4] (1a) In Hartmann's case, this involves postulating alongside *Wille* an item on loan from Hegel: *die Idee*, to which Hartmann attributes an equal degree of fundamental metaphysical reality. (1b) Mainländer employs a different strategy: if the problem is that Schopenhauer's single world exists (so to speak) in two separate halves, then the solution is to join them by treating them as distinct but intelligibly related world-stages in a single world-narrative. (1c) Bahnsen's treatment, we will see, is the most systematically penetrating and closely attuned to the metaphilosophical problem facing Schopenhauer. Noncoincidentally, it also poses the greatest difficulties of understanding. It consists, in terms which will require clarification, in transposing into reality the structure of reason described in Schopenhauer's *Fourfold Root* and in *identifying* this structure with the theory of world-as-will. The result is a monism in which the "One" is contradictory. (2) When we come to Nietzsche, there is a fundamental shift: mediating Schopenhauer's dualism by means of theoretical reflection is no longer the aim, and, in this regard, his departure from Schopenhauer is more radical. Yet, in another respect, Nietzsche remains, I will try to show, wholly faithful to Schopenhauer—at least, as Nietzsche understands him. Nietzsche's philosophical project is organized *ab initio* around the thought that, though the need for philosophical reflection has never been greater, Schopenhauer has crossed a line: he has shown that the game of philosophical rationalization and systematic innovation is over and that a new *species* of philosophical discourse must be forged.

The final section of the chapter, which briefly outlines Freud's *Beyond the Pleasure Principle* (1920), may seem unconnected in so far as Freud has not the slightest interest in Schopenhauer's metaphysical difficulties, and the text belongs to another century. I include it nonetheless because, as I hope will become clear, it represents a further chapter in the same systematic story: having handed over all intellectual authority to natural science, Freud rediscovers Schopenhauerian metaphysics, or its equivalent, within nature. The further interest of this is to indicate that, though the vision which animates post-Schopenhauerian metaphysics may have slipped out of historical memory, it remains recognizable in contemporary terms.

26.1 HARTMANN

The concept which figures in the title of Hartmann's *Philosophy of the Unconscious*—first published in 1869, followed by another ten editions in Hartmann's own lifetime—carries almost none of the meaning that we now, after Freud, attach to it. Hartmann's unconscious is not localized in human beings, nor has it any special association with problems of psychological explanation, least of all with the irrational aspects of mental life. Hartmann's theory of the unconscious serves instead as a framework for the large-scale philosophical synthesis of Schopenhauer with Hegel that he proposes. The intention is even-handed: it is to give both parties equal weight in fashioning an original form of monism, one that employs the deficiencies of each allegedly one-sided system as a motive for unifying it with the other. Thus, if Hartmann is right, his system can be justified from two directions, either through a critique of Hegelianism which shows the need for its union with Schopenhauerianism, or vice versa. Hartmann also supposes, and this comprises a further important part of his strategy, that Hegel and Schopenhauer can be seen jointly to form an antinomy: because each has an irrefutable claim to truth, their systems must be viewed as contraries, not as contradictories, and his own philosophy of the unconscious, he claims, provides the (unique) solution to the antinomy.[5]

Purely conceptual reflection on the systems of classical German philosophy is not, however, Hartmann's primary method in *Philosophy of the Unconscious*, which is instead provided—stepping out of the idealist tradition—by reflection on the empirical sciences. Hence the book's subtitle: "Speculative Results According to the Inductive Method of Physical Science."

Hartmann's master argument is abductive in nature and allows itself to be stated in relatively simple terms.[6] The special complexity of living creatures finds its best explanation in the supposition that their structural and functional properties, as we know them from ordinary observation and scientific study, are the product of *volition conjoined with representation*: in other words, organisms are organized as they are because they are *meant* to be thus. If this recalls the traditional argument from design, it is because Hartmann is indeed employing one of its major premises: namely, that life can arise only from intelligence or some approximation thereto. He avoids the traditional theistic conclusion by insisting, first, that the representation (or motive) involved is *unconscious*, and, second, that the act of will which executes the motive (i.e., gives the organism its structure) is not external to it, as a Divine Author would be, but immanent within it. Further reasoning of the same type warrants, Hartmann claims, the hypothesis that the manifold of volitions which comprise the natural world is unified in a single Unconscious, the "All-One."[7]

The bulk of *Philosophy of the Unconscious* applies this form of argument to a vast range of cases drawn from the recent empirical literature, and the work's extraordinary contemporary success owed a great deal to the way in which Hartmann impressed his readers with his knowledgeable scientificity, as if he were following the same robustly empirical route as Darwin but arriving at a deeper, more spiritually intriguing conclusion regarding what is going on in Nature—a conclusion from which, if Hartmann is right, an entire ethical and religious *Weltanschauung* can be extracted. Knowledge of the metaphysical meaning of Nature shows us, he argues, how the Good should be conceived.

Hartmann's departure from Schopenhauer is evident and becomes clearer through comparison of their respective theories of organic life. The original agenda for German philosophical thought on the topic as a whole had been set by Kant's account, in the Third *Critique*, of the problem posed by teleological judgment: (1) living beings are unrecognizable, indeed unthinkable, without employment of the concept of an end; (2) yet no ends can be attributed to Nature, which lacks reason and freedom; (3) to attribute those ends to a divine author would, however, reduce living beings to artifacts, which is inconsistent with our conception of them as bearing their purposiveness within themselves. Now Hartmann, we have just seen, rejects (2) and so, too, does Schopenhauer, but for quite different reasons. Schopenhauer invests Nature with purposivity, but it is independent of reason: its teleological character is treated as a consequence of the objectivating, expressive relation that obtains in general between will and representation, which is emphatically noninstrumental. Hartmann by contrast *does* attribute reason (if not freedom) to Nature: its individual phenomena and their collective order are on his account products of instrumental reasoning. The difference in a nutshell is that representation, in the form of a motive, is for Schopenhauer a mere *phenomenon* of will, an *appearance* belonging to a different ontological order, while for Hartmann will and representation have parity (just as, in ordinary practical reasoning, desires and beliefs combine to yield reasons for action). The component of representation, or belief, must be supplied independently, which is why we must also turn to Hegel.

From this emerges a further important point. Hartmann is no transcendental idealist, and he regards Schopenhauer's commitment to this large portion of the Kantian legacy as a major error. Whatever gap there may be between "appearance" and reality can be bridged, Hartmann believes, by inductive inference. In 1871, Hartmann reinforced his rejection of transcendental idealism by publishing a detailed critique of Kant in which he explicitly affirms our knowledge of the constitution of things in themselves and also repudiates Schopenhauer's assertion of an essential difference between consciousness-of-will and object-consciousness: our acts of will are simply, Hartmann maintains, further objects of cognition.[8] This allows Hartmann to furnish will with exactly the same plain realist epistemology as any other object of knowledge. Schopenhauer's metaphilosophical problems thereupon disappear: if things in themselves demand no special mode of access, and if they exhaust the domain of knowable entities, then no special discourse is required for their philosophical articulation. Hartmann consequently has no need for Schopenhauer's dark but crucial notion of the presence and expression of will in worldly things, nor of a "miracle" of subject/body identity.[9]

Hartmann's theory of organic nature also puts him in a position to make an internal criticism of Schopenhauer calling for Hegelian remedy.[10] Schopenhauer affirms that there are essences in Nature which do not derive from the principle of sufficient reason, and, in order to account for these, Hartmann introduces his theory of Ideas. Now these Ideas must themselves be *objects*, while the subject *for* whom they are objects must be timeless and absolute. Since the relation of Ideas to this absolute subject cannot, according to Schopenhauer's own principle of subject-object correlation, be contingent, they must jointly compose an absolute subject-object. Ideas are furthermore, on Schopenhauer's account, expressions of will, and, as such, they must be defined by ends, without which they would be blind striving (i.e., undifferentiated from mere *Wille*). And since these ends presuppose in turn some ideational content, we again arrive at an ontology in which ideation and volition are equiprimordial.

From all that has been said, Hartmann's metaphysics would seem broadly Aristotelian, and, consequently, to lean strongly in Hegel's direction. How then, it may be asked, can

Hartmann suppose himself to have preserved anything much of Schopenhauer? All he offers, it seems, is the very general notion that, if Hegel is not to fall prey to the standard charge of panlogicism, then he must presuppose some kind of ontological *prima materia*, of which Schopenhauer's *Wille* may be redolent, but which scarcely warrants the specific synthesis he proposes.[11]

The answer lies in Hartmann's cosmological prequel.[12] Though his plain epistemology leaves no riddle to be solved concerning the coming-together of subject and object, the central *explanandum* of post-Kantian idealism, Hartmann is nonetheless able to allow that at the end of the day we face a puzzle. The world is a compound of will and idea. But why should there be any such thing? No a posteriori datum can account for it, since all such data presuppose it. But nor can it be understood a priori, for nothing in the bare concepts of *Idee* and *Wille* implicate one another: far from fitting together as hand and glove, they are as alien to one another as numbers and colors. Hartmann therefore reasserts at this point Schopenhauer's dualism, though in a different formulation. And the only hypothesis available, he argues, is that their intermingling results from an *irrational act*, and since no irrationality can infect the *Idee*, and action is the prerogative of *Wille*, the existence of the world must be due to violence done *by* the latter, *to* the former; that is, to *Wille*'s invasion of *Idee*.[13] In this respect Hartmann grants Schopenhauer the last word over Hegel.

One important historical point should be made concerning the deep indebtedness to Schelling of Hartmann's post-Schopenhauerian *Willensmetaphysik* (this is also true to some extent of Mainländer's and Bahnsen's metaphysics). One part of the debt is carried over from (albeit repudiated by) Schopenhauer himself, who in his early years encountered the identification of the absolute with *Wille* in Schelling's widely read *Treatise on the Essence of Human Freedom* (1809). The other part, which Hartmann explains convincingly and at length, concerns the way in which Schelling's later writings provide a template for the program of conjoining Hegel and Schopenhauer: the cornerstone of Hartmann's synthesis—the notion that philosophy must connect mere rational ideation with actual existence—is the defining theme of Schelling's attempt, beginning in the 1820s, to construct what he called a "positive philosophy" that would sublate, without wholly delegitimating, Hegel's merely "negative" "pure-rational" philosophy.[14] Hartmann's claim is to have fulfilled this ambition in a way that Schelling did not.

26.2 MAINLÄNDER

The ethico-religious philosophy which, I said, Hartmann adds to his metaphysics is something of an afterthought: on the face of it no evolutionary or axiological dynamic is built into the (con)fusion of *Wille* and *Idee* that constitutes the world, which exists in consequence of a pre-mundane metaphysical mistake, and may be regarded with equal justification either as strictly unaccountable (the violation was unreasoned and pointless) or as strictly necessary (it is in the nature of sheer idea-less *Wille* to behave in exactly such a manner). Hartmann introduces nonetheless a dynamic element by arguing that the mistake can be *corrected*: it is our job to disentangle *Idee* from *Wille* and to restore the former to its original quietude; that this is the true collective task of humanity may be inferred from the fact that nature has produced self-conscious beings who are able to achieve insight into nature's own metaphysical grounds.[15] This represents Hartmann's revision of Book IV of WWR1.

Mainländer can be regarded as telling a different story of how the world came to be and as building into its very existence the dynamic, teleological dimension which Hartmann merely tacks on. The latter follows from the former because the pre-mundane source of the world can, according to Mainländer, be reconstructed—subject to certain limitations—in terms of an exercise of *practical reason*, allowing the path of the world's development to be understood as the means to the realization of a pre-mundanely projected end, *contra* Hartmann.

The basic model employed by Mainländer—representing the world as the effect of a choice or decision, and to that extent as inherently purposive—is of course familiar from Leibniz and every other theist, while the evolutionary dimension recalls Schelling. This, along with the fact that Mainländer refers to the ground of the world as God, leads us to ask how Mainländer can acclaim Schopenhauer as a genius who shares with Kant the title of the greatest of all philosophers and describe the "philosophy of redemption" presented in *Die Philosophie der Erlösung* (published in 1876, the year of his suicide) as a development of his thought.[16]

The short answer is that Mainländer differs from Christian theism and from Schellingian panentheism by denying that the world's divine origin is, in any ordinary sense, axiologically affirmative. The precise purpose for which the world was brought into being, according to Mainländer, was God's own self-annihilation. In so far as the world's existence testifies to God's having chosen to relinquish his existence in favor of absolute *Nichts*, Schopenhauer's atheism is vindicated on the new basis that, although the existence of God was once (*contra* Schopenhauer) a metaphysical possibility, indeed an actuality, it is so no longer: God himself has *made atheism true*.

Given our actual beliefs and expectations, this is obviously not good news, but if we make the requisite cognitive adjustments—that is, if we recognize what is required of us in accordance with the world's normative source—then we will be able to find fulfilment (redemption, *Erlösung*) in promoting the end that God has built into our constitution. Since God no longer exists, he can be no lawgiver, but since we enjoy no existence beyond his postmortem legacy, there is nothing else it would make sense for us to attempt to do, as residues of extinguished divinity, than continue along the path to non-being.

Before we come to Mainländer's central argument, one thing that is clearly essential, if this departure from Schopenhauerian orthodoxy is to seem more than an imaginative reverie elicited by WWR, is an account of what underpins the temporal, or quasi-temporal, characterizations indispensable to Mainländer's theory of the God–world relation. Why depict the world as God's *successor*—why accord narrative significance to the relation of God to the world, such that "God exists" was true once upon a time but becomes false in the era of worldhood? The question sharpens when we recall that the relation of

Wille to *Vorstellung* as theorized by Schopenhauer is categorically nontemporal, and though Schopenhauer's treatment of it may be charged with obscurity, this very obscurity is integral to his system. Consequently, from Schopenhauer's own standpoint, Mainländer may be regarded as offering only a mythopoeic representation of the world's double-aspectedness, the dramatic appeal of which is outweighed by its philosophical erroneousness in so far as his restoration of end-directedness to the ground of the world-as-representation—Mainländer's reversion to theism, albeit of a peculiar and original variety—occludes Schopenhauer's key insight that *Wille* is essentially blind.

Light can be thrown on Mainländer's narrativization of the *Wille–Vorstellung* relation and the nature of his disagreement with Schopenhauer by returning to a problem in Kant. In the sections of his Antinomy of Pure Reason which deal with the problem of conceiving an original cause or ground of the world, Kant had argued (in the Theses of the Third and Fourth Antinomies) that we are bound by our reason to postulate a purely intelligible (i.e., nontemporal) ground of its causality and existence. This, Kant shows (in the corresponding Antitheses), generates the problem: To what series do the world and its intelligible ground jointly belong?[17]

Now Mainländer is well aware that God, being eternal, cannot belong to the same time-series as the world.[18] But in his view—which veers back toward Kant's solution while also showing the influence of Schelling[19]—this does not warrant Schopenhauer's minimalist treatment of the relation of the two realms. Just as Kant is prepared in his theory of human freedom to postulate a nontemporal ground (the individual's "intelligible character") of certain effects in time (those that define the individual's "empirical character"), allowing a certain empirical act to be morally imputed to an agent's will—a doctrine which Schopenhauer himself endorses—so Mainländer supposes that a *unitary series* may be postulated to encompass the God–world relation. This series must be described in para-temporal vocabulary and conceived as a process of development or instrumentalization.[20] Mainländer's reply to Schopenhauer is therefore that, if *Wille* and *Vorstellung* are to have anything to do with one another—and if the latter is to be subordinated to the former, as per Schopenhauer's claim that representation has only dependent reality—then we must affirm that the world as representation *follows from* the world-as-will (God) in accordance with some principle which joins them in a single series; without which they float free of one another in a way that makes nonsense of WWR.[21]

Assuming this license for further speculation, how does Mainländer propose to determine what exactly took place, and for what reasons, in the moment of God's world-generation? The difficulty here is considerable, for Mainländer takes every opportunity to tell us that his metaphysics are based on exclusively immanent grounds, to which he claims to adhere more strictly than Schopenhauer.[22] Mainländer's central metaphysical argument falls into two parts.[23]

1. The first tells us that monism is inescapable and is achievable only on the condition that we posit a One which is transcendent, pre-mundane, and defunct. The manifold of worldly entities consists in forces, *Kräfte*, and these must be unified, otherwise they would not necessarily interact. But we can form no concept

of their unity (i.e., of a single *Urkraft*). In order to account for the immanent manifold, therefore, we must allow it a transcendent source in the past. Schopenhauer's omnipresent individuation-indifferent *Wille* is thus supplanted by a vanished One possessed of absolute simple individuality.

2. Second, Mainländer argues that, granted this pre-mundane monism, the conjecture that God has elected to disintegrate into the world for the sake of non-being, is epistemically optimal given the resources available to strictly immanent philosophical reflection; that is, the impossibility of knowing God or his motives *an sich*: all we can (and must) do is extrapolate from the character of the world as we find it, to the character of the transcendent realm, which we cannot know as a thing in itself, but only *as it relates* to the sphere of immanence. Such a metaphysics, which aims to describe the world-related "sphere of efficacy" (*Wirksamkeitssphäre*) of the transcendent realm, can only lay claim to the "as if" (*als ob*) legitimacy of Kant's regulative propositions,[24] yet it offers theoretical satisfaction and tells us all we need for the practical purpose of conducting our lives. Mainländer's specific reasoning for this conclusion is as follows:[25]

(1) God willed (his own) non-being. [God enjoyed absolute freedom—to either be or not be[26]—and cannot have chosen to remain in being or to merely alter his manner of being, else no world would have come into existence.]

(2) God's immediate passage into non-being was impeded by own being. [Had God's will directly achieved its end, then worldless non-being would presently prevail; and since nothing outside God can act on him, only God's own being could have impeded his will.]

(3) It was consequently necessary for God's being to disintegrate into multeity, a world in which each individual being strives to achieve non-being. [Only the *finitization* of God's being will allow the end of non-being to be achieved.]

(4) Individual worldly beings hinder one another's striving and, in so doing, weaken their degree of force (*Kraft*). [A modified Schopenhauerian image of the world as a site of conflict.]

(5) God's entire being underwent transformation into a determinate sum total of forces (a *Kraftsumme*). [Mainländer here endorses Schopenhauer's characterization of the world as a manifold of expressions of *Wille/Kraft*, but differs in conceiving it as a finite totality.]

(6) The world as a whole or universe has one end, non-being, which it will achieve through the continual diminution of the sum of forces which compose it. [In Schopenhauer's terms, by contrast, this an impossibility, not only because all teloi are precluded, but also because the world's fund of *Wille/Kraft* is enduring and inexhaustible.]

(7) Each individual being will be brought in the course of its development, by virtue of the dissipation of its force, to a point where its striving to non-being is fulfilled. [For Schopenhauer, this outcome is possible in principle for enlightened human subjects, but not for the universe at large, as it is for Mainländer by virtue of the very laws of nature, which prescribe its own dissipation.]

In a manner similar to Schopenhauer, Mainländer claims that this metaphysical knowledge encapsulates the true, atheistic meaning of Christianity, freed from dogmatic foundations.[27]

26.3 BAHNSEN

The first volume of Bahnsen's major metaphysical work, *Der Widerspruch im Wissen und Wesen der Welt*, appeared in 1880.[28] The title states openly Bahnsen's principal, Hegelian-sounding thesis: there exists a contradiction within the essence of the world and our knowledge thereof. The originality and ingenuity of Bahnsen's position consists (first) in his use of Schopenhauer to give the Hegelian doctrine that contradictions inhabit the objects of knowledge (and not merely, as Kant maintained, our subjective representations) the exact opposite significance from that which Hegel intended;[29] and (second) in his use of Hegel's concept of dialectic to rework WWR in a way that, if Bahnsen is right, brings to light its true meaning and releases Schopenhauer from the charge of incoherence. As with Hartmann, a melding of Hegel and Schopenhauer therefore takes place in Bahnsen, but on this occasion it lies in the first instance at a metaphilosophical level, and the final product bears little resemblance to Hartmann's flat ontology.[30] What follows is a bare-bones reconstruction of Bahnsen's anti-rationalist monism, beginning with a point about its motivation.

We have seen how Hartmann and Mainländer seek to develop Schopenhauer's thought beyond the bounds of WWR. Also clear is the respect in which their innovations are open to challenge. It would be in order for Schopenhauer to respond as follows: no doubt there are alternative forms of *Willensmetaphysik*, which are no more exposed to the charge of strict logical inconsistency than WWR, but all that they can do, at most, is push back the point at which the possibility of explanation evaporates—thus, in Hartmann's case, we come to a halt with an original, violated duality of *Wille* and *Idee*, and in Mainländer's, with God's ontological self-decision. Such proposals complicate our metaphysical vision without gaining any insight into our situation. Philosophical economy instructs us to reject them in favor of the leaner metaphysics of WWR.

Bahnsen may be interpreted as taking his cue from the issue which has just come into view. If the metaphysics of WWR leave empty space extending beyond and behind the world as representation—which Hartmann and Mainländer not unreasonably suppose needs to be filled, and which otherwise invites the mystical pseudo-completion which Schopenhauer himself was later tempted to approve—then the solution, as long as strict immanence remains the principle of our reflection,[31] must be to relocate the nonrational end-of-explanation discovered by Schopenhauer *within* the world as we know it; that is, to *identify* the absolute surdity of reality exposed in WWR with the very *fabric* of the known world. In this way, instead of hiving off *Wille* and projecting it into the world's background—making it a world-independent substance—we translate *Wille* wholesale into the relational structures that constitute the world lying before us. And these, according to Bahnsen, are all instances of contradiction. The philosophical system that analyzes and exhibits them he calls *Realdialektik*.

What makes this strategy immediately sound so peculiar—in advance of seeing how it might be executed—is the fact that, in the terms of any philosopher willing to endorse our ordinary claims to empirical objectivity, including Kant and Schopenhauer, the relational structures in question simply *are* the embeddedness (whether deep or shallow) of reason in reality, where reason entails conformity to logical principles (i.e., absence of contradiction). Indeed our very capacity to *know* the structures at all implies as much. Thus Kant's transcendental proofs seek to show that synthetic a priori principles are constitutive of appearances and that their associated categories also have thinkable application to whatever reality we cannot know, which again must be noncontradictory; whereas, according to *Fourfold Root*, reason exhausts itself in the various logically ordered, contradiction-free domains of individuated objects-as-representations.

One complaint that cannot be made of Bahnsen is that he is unaware of the peculiarity and difficulty posed by his central metaphysical claim:[32] throughout the work, Bahnsen takes pains to flag the numerous misunderstandings to which it is exposed and emphasizes the need to understand *Realdialektik* not as a doctrine that we might embrace on direct conceptual or logical grounds, nor as a conclusion that we might come to in consequence of the adoption of any particular philosophical method, but rather as a position that we find ourselves backing into, under pressure from the cumulative lesson of the history of philosophy, in particular, from the experience of skepticism, Kant's Antinomies, Hegel, and Schopenhauer, and provoked by the presumption of logic.[33] Also of importance in securing the intelligibility of *Realdialektik* is Bahnsen's claim that its status is that of an *interpretation*, not a would-be explanation, of the world: it presents the world's pervasive meaning, testified by enlightened reflection on its physiognomy.[34] Bahnsen here employs the same type of hermeneutical characterization to which Schopenhauer had recourse in his attempt to explain the system of WWR.

Granted these disclaimers and points of orientation, how may it be held that Reality *is* Contradiction, *Urwiderspruch*, and that this is the philosophically final *truth of things*? The proposition of course makes no sense if contradiction is conceived as consisting in a relation of thoughts or judgements for, so construed, it embodies a category-mistake and fails to assert any content. Bahnsen's claim, however, is that this judgment-centered conception of the nature of contradiction is a misconception, which belongs to the grand illusion of the world's logicality. Properly understood, contradiction is a feature of *will*, which, following Schopenhauer, is what constitutes the Real. More precisely, it comprises the essential *nature* of will *as such*. All will, whether blind and object-less in the manner of Schopenhauer's *Wille* or directed to determinate objects, involves an internal dissonance or reflexive discrepancy which, when articulated in judgement form, amounts to a Yes-and-No: acts of will seek both to preserve themselves (each act of will *wills itself as such*) and to abolish themselves (in realizing their end, if they have one, and if not, then in simply coming to rest).[35]

In terms of the judgment-centered view of contradiction, this conception of *conatus* as self-negating is not a (real) case of (real) contradiction, in the sense that logic precludes, but rather a specific type of structure which either amounts simply to a conflict of forces or may be modeled by talking of pragmatic inconsistency and merely performative contradiction. But, as Bahnsen points out, this is hardly an objection, for what is in dispute is precisely the correct order of philosophical understanding: it is not oversight that leads him to describe the principle of *Realdialektik* as "anti-logical."[36]

The several argumentative paths pursued in *Der Widerspruch im Wissen und Wesen der Welt* consist chiefly in attempts to exhibit the alignment of (i) the contradictory character of will just described with (ii) structural features of objects and phenomena which have long been recognized as philosophically problematic—in particular, to take a topic at the heart of classical German philosophy, self-consciousness, the necessity of which is famously matched by its arguable paradoxicality.[37] Bahnsen cannot of course convert such alignments into logical or strict inferential connections—that is, he cannot show that Contradiction is the *explanation* of self-consciousness or that self-consciousness *gives proof* of the reality of Contradiction—but he can justifiably claim for them, as the instances accumulate, the kind of hermeneutical significance described earlier.

For present purposes it will be most helpful to reconstruct Bahnsen's position in relation to WWR. As noted, the upshot of *Fourfold Root* is to reduce reason to a function which constitutes domains of individuated objects, and since this exhausts its nature, reason cannot rationalize itself (i.e., explain its own production of those domains). What WWR adds to this deflation of reason is the theory that the domains are grounded in unindividuated *Wille*, which is in addition present, or expressed, within their objects. Taken singly, neither *Wille* nor the world of objects exhibits contradiction,[38] but Schopenhauer does accept that contradiction emerges from their *conjunction*: the world bears witness to the contradiction between individuatedness, on the side of *Vorstellung*, and its negation, on that of *Wille*. Contradiction—not as between judgments, but outside them—is therefore affirmed in Schopenhauer's philosophy as the resultant of two independent vectors, the Principle of Sufficient Reason and the will's pre-rational unity.

Now the alternative explored by Bahnsen—employing the same basic philosophical materials and agreeing with Hartmann that Schopenhauer's Kantian subjective idealism obstructs the articulation of his insight—is to suppose that the contradiction which Schopenhauer recognizes as manifest in the constitution of the world is not the product of superimposing the Many on the One, but is rather the single original principle of all things, constituting their *Stoff* and their *Form*. This carries two advantages: it avoids the problems of Schopenhauer's dual-layered Kantian ontology, and, in parallel, it disposes of Schopenhauer's metaphilosophical problem since it can no longer be asked how it is possible for a single world to be thought in two mutually alien ways—the one world is thought in a single, *realdialektischen* way.[39] Again, Schopenhauer's "miracle" is disposed of.[40]

Finally it may be urged that the supersession of WWR by *Realdialektik* was lying in wait all along: Schopenhauer presupposed the ultimate reality of contradiction when he posited a *relation* of alienness between *Wille* and *Vorstellung* for, had they not been implicitly contradictory, they would have formed the rationally transparent hylomorphic unity of Aristotle and Hegel.

26.4 NIETZSCHE

The post-Schopenhauerian school having fallen by the historical wayside, the only figure in the prevailing canon generally regarded as relaying Schopenhauer's influence is Nietzsche. Nietzsche's concept of the will to power is what on the surface may seem to align him directly with the three figures just discussed. However, what this supposed doctrine amounts to is much disputed—whether it amounts to a "theory" at all stands in doubt—and concentration on the relation of *Wille zum Leben* with *Wille zur Macht*, though of interest on its own account,[41] tells us relatively little about the general logic of the Schopenhauer-to-Nietzsche development.[42]

Nietzsche's current high standing owes less to his being regarded as having conserved any substantive theses of Schopenhauer's than to his being viewed as having followed through, in a radical way, the move which was (inadvertently) initiated and part-executed by Schopenhauer from classical German idealism to full post-metaphysicality; in other words, to Nietzsche's having taken a further, necessary step in completing the naturalistic humiliation of reason and the world's disenchantment. Though not false, I will suggest that this is only one part of a complex picture.

The extent of Nietzsche's naturalistic overcoming of his predecessor is shown clearly, it may be suggested, in two places, one at each end of his *œuvre*. The Birth of Tragedy (*BT*; 1872) opens with a bold avowal of Schopenhauerianism, but Nietzsche also seems to allow the entire metaphysical apparatus of WWR to be boiled down to contingent psychological roots: Schopenhauer's doctrine that the world exists as representation and as will is, in effect, recast in terms of our dual psycho-physiological capacities for dream and for ecstasy or intoxication (*Rausch*) and the artistic-cultural forms or experiential styles which result from their respective cultivation.[43] It would be too much to suggest that Nietzsche intends here a Humean *explaining-away* of metaphysical ideas, if only because the notion that the world conceals its own nebulous pre-individuated substrate coheres with the story that Nietzsche himself wants to tell of the meaning of tragedy; but it is clear at any rate that he does not mean to argue *from* any metaphysical truth *to* any aesthetic conclusions—what matters for Nietzsche in *BT* is the consonance of the metaphysics with aesthetic experience, irrespective of the theoretical justification of the former, our de facto "commitment" to which has sufficient proximal, pre-normative support in human psychology.[44]

Second, at the other end of his career, in the Third Essay of *On the Genealogy of Morals* (1887), the work which has come to be regarded as a definitive statement of Nietzsche's mature position, Schopenhauer is singled out as an exemplary modern philosophical representative of the "ascetic ideal"—the psycho-ideational configuration which, on Nietzsche's diagnosis, constitutes the chief precipitant of nihilism in late modernity.[45] Nietzsche thus grants Schopenhauer's internal success in promoting life-denial while, at the same time, exposing his failure to understand why this aim was psychologically necessary for him in the first place and in what way the strategy of life-negation is fraudulent. Also shown, Nietzsche argues, is that, at a fundamental level, Schopenhauer endorses the same ("moral") interpretation of existence against which he pitted himself and that the secularized redemption which he offers in place of Christian theism merely entrenches the existential problem that it was intended to dissolve. From which it follows, most importantly, that at least the *possibility* of life-affirmation—its integrity as a task—remains untouched. If we focus on Nietzsche's late portrait of Schopenhauer in the *Genealogy* we are led, therefore, to view their relation as one of flat opposition.

A more nuanced and accurate picture emerges if we look at what Nietzsche originally took Schopenhauer's philosophical project and achievement to consist in.[46] The title of the third of Nietzsche's *Untimely Meditations*, "Schopenhauer as Educator" (1874), may suggest that Nietzsche intends to treat his subject from an angle that is not squarely philosophical. It becomes clear however that Nietzsche is intensely preoccupied with the question of what *counts* as genuinely philosophical understanding and that he sets no store by the narrow type of critique employed by Hartmann, Mainländer, and Bahnsen. For Nietzsche, philosophical significance is properly determined via questions of edification: the primary question is not whether Schopenhauer's system holds itself together internally in a merely logical manner, but rather what Schopenhauer's thought *expands out into*—what form of life it is capable of supporting.[47] And in order to answer this question, it is also necessary, Nietzsche supposes, that we comprehend the personality of the philosopher expressed in his work. Logical criticism of Schopenhauer's ideas is relocated accordingly in a context of personal appraisal: the virtues that Nietzsche ascribes to Schopenhauer, by dint of which his thought is held to edify us, are determined by how we understand him to have confronted and addressed recognizably philosophical challenges and tasks, these being in turn inseparable from (broadly) ethical matters. Thus Nietzsche contrasts Schopenhauer's success in avoiding the post-Kantian "despair of the truth"—the "gnawing and disintegrating skepticism and relativism" to which Kleist, for example, surrendered—and in having instead advanced to "the heights of tragic contemplation" from which he formed "a picture of life as a whole," a "hieroglyphics of universal life."[48] Again, Schopenhauer is credited by Nietzsche with having recognized, but refused to yield to, the irresolvable tension between fact and value: an achievement registered in his very *act of posing the question* of what life is worth, in which, according to Nietzsche, Schopenhauer affirms both the opposition between Ought and Is and our self-divided constitution.[49]

If it is asked why this kind of approach to Schopenhauer—strikingly similar to Nietzsche's Wagner appreciation[50]—is not too oblique and artwork-orientated to qualify as a properly philosophical appraisal, there are a number of points to be highlighted. The first is that Nietzsche had much earlier (we know from unpublished material from the 1860s) rehearsed for himself in a thorough manner, drawing on contemporary sources, a plethora of logical objections to Schopenhauer's metaphysics and that he also took himself to have found a way to sideline them, itself of Schopenhauerian inspiration.[51] The analytical contradictions in Schopenhauer's system, as Nietzsche details them, arise from his declaration that will *is* the thing in itself. This makes Schopenhauer's philosophy, which is officially immanent, transcendent. But the error is of little real consequence because the Kant-derived idiom that Schopenhauer adopts can be subtracted. This subtraction may be taken a step further by suspending the anthropomorphic character of Schopenhauer's *Wille*—at the cost, to be sure, of abandoning all claim to positive philosophical *knowledge*, but preserving intact what Nietzsche regards as Schopenhauer's crucial insights: namely his demonstration of (i) the absolute inexplicability of individuation and the origin of the intellect in a way that would validate cognition, (ii) the existence of "dark and contradictory elements in the region where individuation ends," and (iii) the necessity of rendering these aporetic discoveries in a semi-figurative form.

Nietzsche's endorsement of this strategy is clear from a letter of 1866, in which he enthuses concerning F. A. Lange's *History of Materialism* (1866), which he believes confirms Schopenhauer's illusionism regarding empirical knowledge and thereby shows there to be scope for a type of supra-cognitive reflection which can validate itself in the manner of a work of art—a type of discourse which he takes Schopenhauer's artwork-like philosophy to exemplify.

> Thus the true essence of things—the thing-in-itself—is not only unknown to us; the concept of it is neither more nor less than the final product of an antithesis which is determined by our organization, an antithesis of which we do not know whether it has any meaning outside our experience or not. Consequently, Lange thinks, one should give the philosophers a free hand as long as they edify us in this sense. Art is free, also in the domain of concepts. Who would refute a phrase by Beethoven, and who would find error in Raphael's *Madonna*?
>
> You see, even with this strictly critical standpoint our Schopenhauer stands firm; he becomes even almost more important to us. If philosophy is art, then even Haym should submit himself to Schopenhauer; if philosophy should edify, I know no more edifying philosopher than our Schopenhauer.[52]

If Beethoven's music is "irrefutable," then a fortiori it lays claim to veracity of some sort, and the same must hold for Schopenhauer's edifying discourse. Now it may of course be asked what, if anything, sustains this aesthetico-aporetic conception of philosophical discourse, as it might be called, but the question is not strictly relevant to the exegetical issue of Nietzsche's Schopenhauer reception. The fact is that Nietzsche committed himself to at a very early point, and never abandoned, the Schopenhauer-inspired *idea* of philosophy as a form of reflection which is (a) categorically committed to the value of truthfulness, (b) axiologically orientated, (c) distinct from and elevated above empirical science, and which (d) by virtue of its supra-empirical status allows itself to be counted as metaphysical *at least* in the sense that it corresponds to what man *experiences* as such: "the truthful man feels that the meaning of his activity is metaphysical."[53]

Whether Nietzsche ever succeeded in rationalizing this complex set of commitments or in showing how we can be cured of our metaphysical need may be doubted, and there is abundant evidence that his thoughts on the matter remained unsettled. *Untimely Meditations* praises Schopenhauer for having "liberated philosophical life," as Kant failed to do, by showing the philosopher how to "unlearn" "pure knowledge" and thereby continue to exist as a human being.[54] In *Human, All Too Human* (1878), belonging to Nietzsche's so-called positivistic phase, when he had ceased to regard approximation to art as a sufficient measure of philosophical correctness and begun to criticize Schopenhauer, Schopenhauer's teachings are said to be only half-heartedly *wissenschaftlich* and thus to show how much further the scientific spirit needs to go. At the same time, the nonscientificity of Schopenhauer's mode of contemplation remains invaluable, for without it we would be unable to see modernity for what it is. This equivocation is repeated in Nietzsche's general remarks on philosophy in this text: it is, on the one hand, "the summit of the entire scientific pyramid," yet it also stands in antagonism to "the individual regions of science," having separated itself from them by posing the question of how knowledge might contribute to human happiness. This has had the malign effect of inhibiting empirical enquiry. But without philosophy's ("involuntary") raising of the question of the value of knowledge, we would remain under the tyranny of logic, which is "by its nature optimism."[55] In a still later work, *The Gay Science* (1882), Schopenhauer's supremacy is restored: among Germans, Schopenhauer alone exhibits an "unconditional and honest atheism," grounded on his apprehension of the "ungodliness of existence," "as something given, palpable, indisputable"; whatever vestigial Christian asceticism may be found in him, Schopenhauer at least grasped this new problem.[56]

What seems an outright condemnation in the late *Genealogy* is to that extent continuous with Nietzsche's early attempt to relieve Schopenhauer's metaphysical idiom of its customary weight-bearing function, fueled by a new appreciation of how much hangs on overcoming all attachment to other-worldliness.

The arc of Nietzsche's development begins with his absorbing Schopenhauer's terms of philosophical reflection, and, if in the final act, Nietzsche seems to turn the tables on him, this results from his having attempted to follow through on the task he originally supposed Schopenhauer to have set: that is, of reconceiving philosophy's relation to *Wissenschaft* once its pretensions to rational necessity have been seen through. And if no clear redefinition of philosophy emerges from Nietzsche's own writings, this may be regarded, in his own terms, as a proper consequence of the fact that, as he puts it, "a few centuries will be needed" before Schopenhauer's great question, "*Does existence have any meaning at all?*," can even be "heard completely and in its full depth."[57]

From this standpoint, to suppose, as do Hartmann, Mainländer, and Bahnsen, that Schopenhauer's substantive axiological question can be answered by salvaging his philosophy *qua* theoretical system is to fail to understand him. In terms of the schema I proposed at the beginning, Nietzsche's resolution of Schopenhauer's metaphilosophical quandary is therefore to give precedence to (B2): the problem of the wrongness of the world—which for Nietzsche means the problem of how *we* are—takes precedence over theoretical reflection.

26.5 Appendix: Freud's Post-Metaphysical Revalidation of Post-Schopenhauerian Metaphysics

The naturalistic commitments heavily on display in Nietzsche are of course generally characteristic of much late nineteenth-century thought, and they are also strongly present in another hugely influential thinker standardly regarded as relaying Schopenhauer's legacy, namely Freud. Freud's doctrinal convergences with Schopenhauer, along with the thorny question of his actual indebtedness to him, have been discussed in many places, but there is one particular text, *Beyond the Pleasure Principle* (BPP), Freud's most speculative work, in which not merely the letter but also the deep spirit of Schopenhauer is manifest.

Toward the end of BPP Freud acknowledges that he has "unwittingly steered" into "the harbour of Schopenhauer's philosophy."[58] What he here admits to be Schopenhauerian is the notion that the necessity of death figures *teleologically* in the constitution of human beings, who are not merely finite in life-span, like all organisms, but also death-*directed*.[59] Though Freud's theory of the death drive, among all of his theoretical proposals, has met with fierce opposition, even (or especially) from those who are otherwise sympathetic to psychoanalytic explanation, the consensus is nonetheless that BPP presents a case to be answered,[60] and its deeply Schopenhauerian character makes it appropriate to conclude this chapter with a rehearsal of Freud's circuitous but fascinating argument—if only to show how, in counterbalance to what is widely regarded as Nietzsche's naturalistic deconstruction of Schopenhauer, it is possible to make one's way back, via scientifically orientated psychological theory, to a standpoint which mirrors Schopenhauerian *Willensmetaphysik*.

Freud does not, of course, regard himself as having the aim of metaphysical recuperation. On the contrary, at each point in BPP where problems of psychological explanation are said to favor a certain hypothesis, Freud turns to current biological literature for verification, and repeatedly he concedes that the answers he seeks are quite possibly reserved for future biological science. Like Hartmann, Freud takes himself to be engaged in scientific extrapolation from empirical data, though without Hartmann's expectation that scientific inference will lead us into metaphysics.

The official *explanandum* of BPP is the well-attested failure of human behavior to accord comprehensively with the supposition that we are motivated by pleasure, if possible within the constraints of reality and if not then at its expense. From this can be inferred the existence of a drive which is independent from, and capable of overriding, the pleasure principle. Freud acknowledges that the data which support its postulation are not conclusive—as was to be expected in light of psychoanalysis's success in showing that what appears to merely befall us against our wishes in fact stems from them—yet he insists that it cannot be disregarded: the fact, which clinical practice puts into sharp focus, is that much of what we do is nonsensical if viewed as directed toward pleasure; we are, as it were, so bad at achieving happiness that it cannot be what we most want, or all that we want.

Having granting himself the assumption of a hedonically indifferent drive, Freud argues that, if it is to explain what (psychoanalysis shows) is specifically needed, then it must be regarded as having as its aim the destruction, decomposition, or disaggregation of its object into its original compositional units (i.e., the "restoration of an earlier state").[61] Now such a drive, Freud notes, appears to conflict directly with the sexual instincts, which are directed toward growth. This naturally leads us into a motivational dualism: on the one hand, we have a death-seeking ego, on the other, a libido which seeks the life of the species. This picture is however unsatisfactory, Freud argues, if only because it fails to explain how the two drives might fuse, as they are observed to do in (for example) sadism and masochism. More generally, the manifest failure of human motivation to form a coherent, Good-seeking whole means that no straightforward motivational monism is credible—Freud dismisses Jung's rival conception of the unconscious as seeking the unitary goal of its own developmental perfection. And yet some way must be found to mediate the dualism to which we have been led.

What must be supposed, Freud argues, is that the sexual instinct *too* seeks the restoration of an earlier state of affairs—namely, a return to a condition of sexual *indistinction*, the desired wholeness of which Aristophanes speaks in Plato's *Symposium*. And this induces us, Freud continues, to reexamine our original assumption that the death drive conflicts with the pleasure principle. Pleasure-seeking, he points out, may be interpreted as yet another form of the very same drive, in so far as it, too, can be regarded as consisting in a discharge of energy in the cause of reducing tension; that is, as an attempt to achieve a null state (as Freud had in fact postulated in his own, pre-psychoanalytic model of the mental apparatus in 1895). And if this is correct, then *all* drive seeks the restoration of an earlier state of the organism; *Trieb* as such is *nothing but* a striving to restore a lost equilibrium.

What is this earlier state? It can only be, Freud argues, the equilibrium of *in*organic existence, "the quiescence of the inorganic world."[62] Achieving this condition can have no truly positive character since it is merely the removal of a disturbance, the negation of life's own negation of the inorganic.[63] The necessity of reverting to the organic does not therefore qualify as an "aim" in the sense that Freud had originally postulated *Ziele* as place-holders for objects,[64] nor can it be said that death is the final target of desire in the sense of being what we *most want* (i.e., what would fulfil or *satisfy* us). The upshot nonetheless is that desiring *as such* has the single end of its own cancellation: this is the inexorable law to which it is subject, which provides desire's sufficient explanation and for which no reason can be given. The resonance with Schopenhauerian metaphysics is evident.

As said, Freud does not regard his theory as having conceptual grounds, but it is fair to observe that the necessity which he believes himself to have uncovered is barely warranted by direct needs of empirical explanation (as he himself comes close to admitting). It may be suggested accordingly that, despite his nominally natural-scientific agenda, the overall trajectory of BPP is determined by a *non*-empirical interest in *ultimate* explanation. In contrast with empirical psychology's standard concentration on particular cognitive competences, Freud's starting point is sheer puzzlement at the *very phenomenon* of human desire and agency, in all of its manifest, humanity-defining incoherence. This is by any measure a philosophical matter. The aim of BPP is to show that, confronted with this great puzzle, there is no alternative to the conception of drive as self-erasing: the explanation of human desire—to put the point in a way that echoes the paradox of Schopenhauer's metaphilosophy and Bahnsen's *Realdialektik*—is that it *has no* ultimate explanation. What Freud may be said to have done, in sum, is to have elaborated Schopenhauer's thesis in light of the a posteriori results of clinical work, which display the multiform negativity of human mental life in ways that Schopenhauer at most guessed at.[65] In propounding the idea that desire as such is groundless and has no other "aim" than its own extinction—that its fundamental character is one of *undoing* rather than creation and that individuation is essentially self-dismantling—BPP reasserts the Schopenhauerian metaphysical vision.

NOTES

1. Frederick Beiser. *Weltschmerz: Pessimism in German Philosophy, 1860–1900* (Oxford: Oxford University Press, 2016), 18–19. As the title indicates, Beiser addresses the broader pessimism debate in all of its dimensions. The present chapter has a narrower focus.

2. See my "Schopenhauer's Metaphilosophy: How to Think a World Without Reason," in *Schopenhauer's Fourfold Root*, edited by Jonathan Head and Dennis Vanden Auweele (London: Routledge, 2017), 11–31.

3. Anglophone literature on which is scarce. Beiser, in *Weltschmerz*, chs. 7, 9 and 10, gives excellent accounts of the metaphysics of Hartmann, Mainländer, and Bahnsen. For recent treatments, see *Schopenhauer und die Schopenhauer-Schule*, edited by Fabio Ciraci, Domenico Fazio, and Matthias Koßler (Würzburg: Königshausen & Neumann, 2009), Abt. II. Susanna Rubinstein, *Eine Trias von Willensmetaphysikern. Populär-philosophische Essays* (Leipzig: Alexander Edelmann, 1896), provides an early appreciative overview of the school.

4. All regard Schopenhauer's employment of transcendental idealism—Kant's distinctions of empirical/transcendental and of appearance/thing-in-itself—as failing to resolve the problem he has brought to light. The realism of each is very different, but none can be said to correspond to that of the natural attitude; rather, they recall the non-commonsensical revisionary realism of Leibniz. In Kant's terms, all three qualify as transcendental realists.

5. Hartmann's Hegel-Schopenhauer synthesis is exposited in many places: see *Philosophy of the Unconscious: Speculative Results According to the Inductive Method of Physical Science*, translated by William Chatterton Coupland (London: Trübner & Co., 1884), 3 vols. [*Philosophie des Unbewussten. Speculative Resultate nach inductiv-naturwissenschaftlicher Methode* (original subtitle, in 1st ed. [Berlin: Carl Duncker, 1869]: *Versuch einer Weltanschauung*)], esp. vol. I, 16–42; vol. I (A), ch. 4, 117–26; vol. II, 55–61; and vol. III, ch. 15, 143–204.

6. See *Philosophy of the Unconscious*, vol. I, Introductory: General Preliminary Observations.

7. Hartmann's balancing act, it has been noted, bears comparison with Leibniz.

8. *Das Ding an sich und seine Beschaffenheit. Kantische Studien zur Erkenntnistheorie und Metaphysik* (Berlin: Carl Duncker, 1871), 29–33.

9. See WWR1$_{[P]}$, 102 and WWR2$_{[P]}$, 497.

10. "Ueber die nothwendige Umbildung der Schopenhauerschen Philosophie," in *Gesammelte philosophische Abhandlangen zur Philosophie des Unbewussten* (Berlin, Carl Dunker, 1872), 57–70, esp. 60–66.

11. "Ueber die nothwendige Umbildung der Hegel'schen Philosophie," in *Gesammelte philosophische Abhandlangen zur Philosophie des Unbewussten* (Berlin, Carl Dunker, 1872), 25–56.

12. *Philosophy of the Unconscious*, vol. III, ch. 14, 120–42.

13. See *Philosophy of the Unconscious*, vol. II, 271–74, and vol. III, 125–27.

14. See *Schelling's Positive Philosophie als Einheit von Hegel und Schopenhauer* (Berlin: O. Loewenstein, 1869) and *Schelling's Philosophisches System* (Leipzig: Hermann Haacke, 1897).

15. See *Philosophy of the Unconscious*, vol. III, ch. 14, 120–42.

16. *Die Philosophie der Erlösung* [vol. I] (Berlin: Theobald Grieben, 1876), viii, 401, 465, 621. What is referred to as volume II of *Die Philosophie der Erlösung. Zwölf philosophische Essays* was published posthumously (Frankfurt am Main: C. Koenitzer, 1886).

17. Which Kant claims to solve in the Solutions to the Third and Fourth Antinomies on the basis of a form of transcendental idealism which, as noted earlier, Mainländer rejects. Mainländer's realism (though described as "genuine transcendental or critical idealism") is asserted in *Die Philosophie der Erlösung*, 23–24 and 40–41: things in themselves are forces and have full, subject-independent empirical reality; "objects" are appearances of things in themselves but do not falsify them; the world is a sum of things in themselves.

18. *Die Philosophie der Erlösung*, 325.

19. Ibid., 465.

20. Of importance here are the remarks on explanation, causality, and development: see Ibid., 25–26.

21. Mainländer has another argument for conjoining God and world, one that turns on his ingenious identification of reason rather than understanding—Kantian *Vernunft*, with all of its associated strong commitments, rather than mere *Verstand*—as the faculty of synthesis: from which it follows that ordinary empirical knowledge requires, and warrants, world-transcendence. Compare Schopenhauer's contraction of the Principle of Sufficient Reason, in *Fourfold Root*, to a purely intra-worldly function.

22. *Die Philosophie der Erlösung*, e.g., 3, 603, 605. Note also Mainländer's avowal of methodological solipsism, 42–43. The Appendix contains detailed critical analysis of Schopenhauer's entire system, the major weaknesses of which (in Mainländer's view) are listed at 604.

23. The core argument can be gleaned from §§24–26 of the first chapter, "Analytik des Erkenntnisvermögens" (27–30), in conjunction with §§1–7 of the final chapter, "Metaphysik" (319–27).

24. Here lies one point of disagreement with Hartmann, who is subjected to extended critique in *Die Philosophie der Erlösung*, vol. II, Essay 12.

25. What follows is a loose paraphrase, with annotation, of the argument laid out formally in *Die Philosophie der Erlösung*, 326–27.

26. The notion that God's freedom precedes his being derives from Schelling, who does not however entertain the possibility that God might will non-being. An early expositor of Schelling noted but dismissed it as nonsensical: Hubert Beckers, *Historisch-kritische Erläuterungen zu Schelling's Abhandlungen* (Munich: Akademie Verlag, 1858), 5.

27. See *Die Philosophie der Erlösung*, vi, 222–23. Concerning Schopenhauer and Christianity, see Christopher Janaway's contribution to the chapter 16 in this volume.

28. *Der Widerspruch im Wissen und Wesen der Welt. Princip und Einzelbewährung der Realdialektik*, 2 vols. (Berlin: Theobald Grieben, 1880–82). Bahnsen's earlier *Beiträge zur*

Charakterologie (Leipzig: J. A. Brockhaus, 1867), a theory of human personality, also took its lead from Schopenhauer.

29. How Hegel really meant it to be understood is of course moot and much discussed. Bahnsen at any rate interprets Hegel as (i) reducing dialectic to a mere *means* by which truth is to be determined, (ii) ultimately subordinating contradiction to *identity*, and (iii) offering a merely *Verbaldialektik*. See *Der Widerspruch im Wissen und Wesen der Welt*, vol. I, 1 and 4–7.

30. Hartmann gives short shrift to the notion of dialectical method: see "Ueber die nothwendige Umbildung der Hegel'schen Philosophie" and the Preface to the second edition of his *Über die dialektische Methode. Historisch-kritische Untersuchungen* (Südharz: Hermann Haacke, 1910).

31. See *Der Widerspruch im Wissen und Wesen der Welt*, vol. I, 94.

32. See Ibid., vol. I, 29, 45–46, 58–66, 92, 103.

33. See Ibid., vol. I, 2–3, 16–26, 29.

34. See Ibid., vol. I, 27–32.

35. See Ibid., vol. I, 47, 51, 53, 54–5.

36. See Ibid., vol. I, 66–72.

37. Roughly the first half of volume II of *Der Widerspruch im Wissen und Wesen der Welt* is devoted to the structural contradictions of selfhood; see esp. 10–21. The second half of volume I, a "Doctrine of Being," locates contradiction in the physical world.

38. I am skipping over complications of Schopenhauer exegesis. Does Schopenhauer suppose there to be an inner antagonism in *Wille*, independently of and prior to its objectification in Ideas and/or in the world-as-representation? If so, Bahnsen is elaborating rather than revising Schopenhauer, but the discussion in WWR1, §§27–29, seems to me (on balance) to suggest not: the decisive issue is whether or not will's *Selbstentzweiung* is anything over and above its "hunger" and "striving," and the evidence for this is faint.

39. There is scope for comparison and contrast of Bahnsen with F. H. Bradley, for whom contradictoriness is also (though for different reasons) world-constitutive, but who, unlike Bahnsen, ultimately sublates relational structure into a contradictionless monism.

40. See *Der Widerspruch im Wissen und Wesen der Welt*, vol. I, 35.

41. See, e.g., Bernard Reginster, *The Affirmation of Life: Nietzsche on Overcoming Nihilism* (Cambridge MA: Harvard University Press, 2008).

42. Similar remarks apply to Nietzsche's conservation of Schopenhauer's thesis of the primacy of will over cognition: determination of belief by will is metaphysically explained and rationally transparent for Schopenhauer, not so for Nietzsche.

43. *The Birth of Tragedy* (1872), §§1–2. Some such deflation is arguably prefigured in Nietzsche's early notes on Schopenhauer: "The will appears: how could it appear? Or to ask differently: where does the apparatus of representation in which the will appears come from?," whence Nietzsche turns directly to Schopenhauer's notion of brain development (*Writings from the Early Notebooks* (1867–1873), edited by Raymond Geuss and Alexander Nehamas, translated by Ladislaus Löb [Cambridge: Cambridge University Press, 2009], 6).

44. I owe this point—that Schopenhauer's metaphysics do matter for *BT*, even though the question of their reality may to some extent be bracketed—to Tom Stern.

45. *On the Genealogy of Morals*, Third Essay, §§5–6.

46. See *Willing and Nothingness: Schopenhauer as Nietzsche's Educator*, edited by Christopher Janaway, especially Janaway's "Schopenhauer as Nietzsche's Educator," 13–36.

47. Thus Nietzsche admits to having found only "a little error" in Schopenhauer: "Schopenhauer as Educator," in *Untimely Meditations* (1873–1876), translated by R. J. Hollingdale, edited by Daniel Breazeale (Cambridge: Cambridge University Press, 1997), 134.

48. Ibid., 140–42.

49. Ibid., 146, 158–59. On Nietzsche's construal—which is highly tendentious and helps to explain how he could have regarded *The Birth of Tragedy* as authentically Schopenhauerian—Schopenhauer regards "heroism" as of supreme value, life-affirmative and life-justifying, indifferent to happiness, and as expressed aesthetically in specific cultural forms (pp. 146, 152–55).

50. The Schopenhauer-Wagner parallel is drawn in "Schopenhauer as Educator," 137.

51. "October 1867–April 1868: On Schopenhauer," in *Writings from the Early Notebooks*, 1–8.

52. To Carl von Gersdorff (end of August 1866), in *Selected Letters of Friedrich Nietzsche*, edited and translated by Christopher Middleton (Indianapolis: Hackett, 1969), 18.

53. "Schopenhauer as Educator," 153.

54. Ibid., 137.

55. *Human, All Too Human* (1878), translated by R. J. Hollingdale (Cambridge: Cambridge University Press, 1996), §§6–7 (14–15), §26 (25–26), §110 (61–63). Indicative of this complexity are the subtle variations in Nietzsche's view of Schopenhauer's proximity to the idealism of Schelling and Hegel: compare *Daybreak* (1881) §190 and §197, *The Gay Science* (1872) §370, *Beyond Good and Evil* (1886) §252, and *The Case of Wagner* (1888) §10.

56. *The Gay Science*, edited by Bernard Williams, translated by Josefine Nauckhoff and Adrian Del Caro (Cambridge: Cambridge University Press, 2001), §357, 219. Nietzsche tells us that his post-Schopenhauerian competitors, Hartmann, Mainländer, and Bahnsen, each in his own way fail to grasp Schopenhauer's problem.

57. *The Gay Science* §357, 219.

58. Freud XVIII, 49–50. References, by volume and page number, are to the *Standard Edition* of Freud's works in 24 volumes, edited by James Strachey (London: Hogarth Press and Institute of Psycho-Analysis, 1953).

59. Freud quotes Schopenhauer's statement that death is the "true result and to that extent the purpose of life" (XVIII, 50). Freud might of course equally have referred to Mainländer. Elsewhere it is instead the ubiquity and force of sexual motivation which leads Freud to associate himself with Schopenhauer: see the Preface to the Fourth Edition of *Three Essays on the Theory of Sexuality* (1905), VII, 134; "A Difficulty in the Path of Psycho-Analysis" (1917), XVII, 143–44; "The Resistances to Psycho-Analysis" (1925), XIX, 218; and *An Autobiographical Study* (1925), XX, 59–60.

60. See Paul Ricœur's penetrating discussion in *Freud and Philosophy: An Essay on Interpretation*, translated by Denis Savage (New Haven, CT: Yale University Press, 1970), 281–338. It will become clear that I do not concur with Ricœur's Goethean reading of Freud's *Naturphilosophie*.

61. Freud XVIII, 37. The conclusion, along with much of the supporting reasoning, is later recapitulated with minor modification in Freud's *New Introductory Lectures* (1933), Lecture 32: XXII, 103–08.

62. Freud XVIII, 62.

63. For the existence of which Freud offers no real explanation. His puzzling suggestion, which is tucked into a footnote and vaguely recalls Hartmann, is that "the riddle of life" might be solved "by supposing that the two instincts [Eros and the death drive] were struggling with each other from the very first" (XVIII, 60n1).

64. See *Instincts and Their Vicissitudes* (1915), XI, 122–23, and *Three Essays on the Theory of Sexuality* (1905), VII, 135–36.

65. But that are continuous with Bahnsen, who describes our innate capacity for taking pleasure in "antithetical negativity" as bearing witness to the truth of *Realdialektik* (*Der Widerspruch im Wissen und Wesen der Welt*, vol. I, 37).

FURTHER READING

Bahnsen, Julius. *Beiträge zur Charakterologie*. Leipzig: J. A. Brockhaus, 1867.

Bahnsen, Julius. *Der Widerspruch im Wissen und Wesen der Welt. Princip und Einzelbewährung der Realdialektik*, 2 vols. Berlin: Theobald Grieben, 1880–1882.

Beckers, Hubert. *Historisch-kritische Erläuterungen zu Schelling's Abhandlungen*. Munich: Akademie Verlag, 1858.

Beiser, Frederick. *Weltschmerz: Pessimism in German Philosophy, 1860–1900*. Oxford: Oxford University Press, 2016.

Ciraci, Fabio, Domenico Fazio, and Matthias Koßler, eds. *Schopenhauer und die Schopenhauer-Schule*, Würzburg: Königshausen & Neumann, 2009.

Freud, Sigmund. *Standard Edition*, edited by James Strachey et al., 24 vols. London: Hogarth Press and Institute of Psycho-Analysis, 1953.

Gardner, Sebastian. "Schopenhauer's Metaphilosophy: How to Think a World Without Reason." In *Schopenhauer's Fourfold Root*, edited by Jonathan Head and Dennis Vanden Auweele. London: Routledge, 2017, 11–31.

Hartmann, Eduard von. *Schelling's Positive Philosophie als Einheit von Hegel und Schopenhauer*. Berlin: O. Loewenstein, 1869.

Hartmann, Eduard von. "Ueber die nothwendige Umbildung der Hegel'schen Philosophie." In *Gesammelte philosophische Abhandlangen zur Philosophie des Unbewussten*. Berlin: Carl Dunker, 1872, 25–56.

Hartmann, Eduard von. "Ueber die nothwendige Umbildung der Schopenhauerschen Philosophie." In *Gesammelte philosophische Abhandlangen zur Philosophie des Unbewussten*. Berlin: Carl Dunker, 1872, 57–70.

Hartmann, Eduard von. *Das Ding an sich und seine Beschaffenheit. Kantische Studien zur Erkenntnistheorie und Metaphysik*. Berlin: Carl Duncker, 1871. 2nd enlarged edition, *Kritische Grundlegung des transcendentalen Realismus*. Berlin: Carl Duncker, 1875.

Hartmann, Eduard von. *Philosophy of the Unconscious: Speculative Results According to the Inductive Method of Physical Science* (1st ed. 1869), 3 vols., translated by William Chatterton Coupland. London: Trübner & Co., 1884. [*Philosophie des Unbewussten. Speculative Resultate nach inductiv-naturwissenschaftlicher Methode* (original subtitle, in 1st ed. (Berlin: Carl Duncker, 1869): *Versuch einer Weltanschauung*).]

Hartmann, Eduard von. *Schelling's philosophisches System*. Leipzig: Hermann Haacke, 1897.

Hartmann, Eduard von. *Über die dialektische Methode. Historisch-kritische Untersuchungen*, 2nd ed. Südharz: Hermann Haacke, 1910.

Janaway, Christopher, ed. *Willing and Nothingness: Schopenhauer as Nietzsche's Educator*. Oxford: Oxford University Press, 1998.

Janaway, Christopher. "Schopenhauer as Nietzsche's Educator." In *Willing and Nothingness: Schopenhauer as Nietzsche's Educator*, edited by Christopher Janaway. Oxford: Oxford University Press, 1998, 13–36.

Mainländer, Philipp. *Die Philosophie der Erlösung, Vol. I*. Berlin: Theobald Grieben, 1876.

Mainländer, Philipp. *Die Philosophie der Erlösung, Vol. II. Zwölf philosophische Essays* [post.]. Frankfurt am Main: C. Koenitzer, 1886.

Nietzsche, Friedrich. *Selected Letters of Friedrich Nietzsche*, edited and translated by Christopher Middleton. Indianapolis: Hackett, 1969.

Nietzsche, Friedrich. *Human, All Too Human* (1878), translated by R. J. Hollingdale. Cambridge: Cambridge University Press, 1996.

Nietzsche, Friedrich. *Untimely Meditations* (1873–1876), translated by R. J. Hollingdale, edited by Daniel Breazeale. Cambridge: Cambridge University Press, 1997.

Nietzsche, Friedrich. *The Gay Science* (1872), edited by Bernard Williams, translated by Josefine Nauckhoff and Adrian Del Caro. Cambridge: Cambridge University Press, 2001.

Nietzsche, Friedrich. *Writings from the Early Notebooks* (1867–1873), edited by Raymond Geuss and Alexander Nehamas, translated by Ladislaus Löb. Cambridge: Cambridge University Press, 2009.

Reginster, Bernard. *The Affirmation of Life: Nietzsche on Overcoming Nihilism*. Cambridge MA: Harvard University Press, 2008.

Ricœur, Paul. *Freud and Philosophy: An Essay on Interpretation*, translated by Denis Savage. New Haven, CT: Yale University Press, 1970.

Rubinstein, Susanna. *Eine Trias von Willensmetaphysikern. Populär-philosophische Essays.* Leipzig: Alexander Edelmann, 1896.

CHAPTER 27

NIETZSCHE'S SCHOPENHAUER

TOM STERN

It is difficult to say anything uncontroversial about Friedrich Nietzsche, but the following is as good a candidate as any: he was both heavily influenced by and highly critical of Schopenhauer's philosophy. Early readers and commentators certainly recognized this. As well they should: Nietzsche's early writings advertised their connection with Schopenhauer, while his later writings assume a knowledge of Schopenhauer in order to attack him, often enough by name. There can be no doubt that, without Schopenhauer, there would have been no Nietzsche: no affirmation of life, no Apollonian and Dionysian as Nietzsche understood them in *The Birth of Tragedy*, no attack on compassion or ascetic values, and no "will to power," to name but a few.

Biographically, an enthusiasm for Schopenhauer's philosophy seems to have been a necessary condition for Nietzsche's friendship with Richard Wagner—the only plausible rival to Schopenhauer as the greatest influence on Nietzsche's thought. But to leave things there would risk obscuring wider influences. Many of Nietzsche's other signifi-cant interlocutors were highly enthusiastic about Schopenhauer, including Erwin Rohde, Paul Deussen, Franz Overbeck, and Jacob Burckhardt. Setting aside his personal relations, Nietzsche's entire productive life occurred under the aegis of the so-called *Pessimismusstreit*—the public argument, which began in earnest with Schopenhauer, about whether life was worth living.[1]

Nietzsche followed this debate closely, and many of his leading ideas are formulated in response to its participants. His close reading of Eugen Dühring, Eduard von Hartmann, Philipp Mainländer, Julius Bahnsen, and many others would have exposed him to developments and criticisms of Schopenhauer.[2] He was also exposed to some (by then) standard criticisms of Schopenhauer's metaphysics, including those which informed his own early sketch, known as "On Schopenhauer," in which he dismisses some of Schopenhauer's central metaphysical claims.[3] This reminds us that Nietzsche's treatment of Schopenhauer is not merely the meeting of two minds, but a response, by Nietzsche, to the philosopher who in large part shaped Nietzsche's intellectual environment. It also reminds us that, like many others involved in the *Pessimismusstreit*, Nietzsche can both be highly critical of Schopenhauer and remain substantially in his debt. In sum, it is hard to think of any corner of Nietzsche's philosophy about which we can say, with any confidence, that it is immune from Schopenhauer's direct or indirect influence, although the present discussion will tentatively consider two candidates in due course.

While all of this is well-established, some myths or conventions about the relationship still persist despite being challenged in the literature. One example is Nietzsche's own description of his 1865 "discovery" of a copy of Schopenhauer's masterpiece in a bookshop operated by his Leipzig landlord, as though he was moved, mysteriously, to pick up a completely unknown author: "I cannot say what demon whispered to me: 'Take this book home with you'... At home I threw myself into the sofa corner with the treasure I had acquired, and began to allow that energetic, sombre genius to work upon me."[4] The description, written two years after the event it describes, has the air of a conversion narrative: the reluctant young man, who (he tells us) is not in the habit of buying books, is seduced into buying Schopenhauer's masterpiece, only to be transformed by a work which, he later wrote, seemed as though it were written just for him.[5] In truth, Nietzsche had certainly heard a great deal about Schopenhauer's philosophy before he bought the book.[6] Again, this serves to remind us of the extent to which Schopenhauer was "in the air." Moreover, autobiographical Schopenhauer conversion narratives, in which a budding young pessimist philosopher accidentally stumbles across the masterpiece, seem to be something of a genre unto themselves in this era: "I went into a bookstore... Schopenhauer? Who was Schopenhauer? I never heard the name..."[7]

Another convention may be helpful for the beginner, but soon begins to dissolve on further inspection: namely, that the early Nietzsche was Schopenhauerian, whereas the late Nietzsche broke with Schopenhauer (or, in some versions, the later Nietzsche broke with metaphysical thinking and turned toward a more scientific outlook). This is useful, insofar as significant changes do indeed occur with the publication of *Human, All too Human*—some of which we will discuss shortly. For example, Nietzsche's tone toward Schopenhauer generally switches from reverential to mocking. But the convention is unhelpful if it suggests that Nietzsche's philosophy was straightforwardly Schopenhauerian before 1878 or plainly anti-Schopenhauerian afterward, and it is especially unhelpful if it suggests that Nietzsche became non-Schopenhauerian (i.e., that he eventually stepped out from under the shade of Schopenhauerian influence). A better way of putting things would be that, like many other contributors to the *Pessimismusstreit*—and that, in large part, is what Nietzsche was, even if his thoughts undoubtedly outlasted and outgrew their immediate context—Nietzsche was maneuvering within a set of ideas, concepts, and intellectual concerns laid out by Schopenhauer and Schopenhauerians. Broadcasting praise or hostility, loudly agreeing or disagreeing on some particular point, dismissing even the *Streit* itself as worthless and its principal protagonists as idiots—none of this should distract us from Schopenhauer's lasting and highly variegated influence.

Our approach to this influence is to begin with one point on which there is apparent disagreement—I have chosen to begin with *Mitleid* (compassion or pity[8])—and to look at Nietzsche's objections to Schopenhauer and at responses which might be available to

Schopenhauer or his defender. As we shall see, these objections and responses in relation to *Mitleid* open up into other areas of their respective philosophical outlooks beyond that narrow focus. By chasing these disputes as they move across different areas of philosophy, we will get a sense of Nietzsche's Schopenhauer and of how Schopenhauer might have viewed his most influential disciple, before ending with some remarks on what might truly set them apart.

27.1 A TEST CASE: "THE NONSENSE ABOUT COMPASSION"[9]

Schopenhauer had placed *Mitleid* at the center of his ethical thought, whereas Nietzsche was its fierce opponent. Schopenhauer argued, simply put, that an action is morally evaluable if and only if it is not egoistic; that non-egoistic actions are evaluable as "good" if and only if they are carried out to increase the welfare of another; and that actions carried out to increase the welfare of another are those which spring from compassion (BM$_{[P]}$, §16). Nietzsche's objections form the starting point of our analysis, which will also consider how Schopenhauer might have responded.

A first objection is what we might call psychological: Nietzsche appears to deny that there is such a thing as *Mitleid*, instead presenting himself as the unmasker of the apparently compassionate one's real motives. Hence *Mitleid* will turn out to be an exercise of power over the pitied one, especially prized where it is the only form of power available,[10] or, similarly, it is a form of the "drive to appropriate,"[11] where compassionate behavior is understood as a species of controlling behavior. Schopenhauer was not unaware of the potential for cynicism about *Mitleid* as the true cause of action, and he tries to nip this objection in the bud: by all means, many apparently moral actions are secretly motivated on selfish grounds, but Schopenhauer denies that this is true of *all* such actions and announces that "all argument with such a man [who insisted that all actions are egoistic] would, therefore, be at an end, and I address myself to those who admit the reality of the matter" (BM$_{[P]}$, 126; see also 128, 131). By Schopenhauer's own admission, he and Nietzsche are simply talking past each other.

Nietzsche attempts a different kind of psychological objection when he suggests that the compassionate one never feels the *same* pain as the sufferer, only a new pain of her own: the sufferer feels his own pain, and the compassionate one feels her own pain.[12] Schopenhauer had needed to tread very carefully in this regard because he had to present, for example, my compassionate moral acts as motivated by a suffering which, one the one hand, was sufficiently "mine" to force me to act and, on the other hand, sufficiently "yours" that I am not being merely selfish by acting to relieve it. This balance led to some contorted phrasing: "although [the suffering of the other] is given to me as something external...I nevertheless *feel it with him, feel it as my own*, and yet not *within me*, but *in another person*" (BM$_{[P]}$, 165; Schopenhauer's emphasis). The phenomenon

Schopenhauer describes is not so much feeling your pain as my own as it is feeling *my* pain as *your* own. Schopenhauer acknowledges that this is at least a very mysterious form of motivation. He can, of course, appeal to the (for him) deeper reality that you and I are one, which might go some way to explaining the phenomenon. But, first of all, Nietzsche would not have agreed on this metaphysical point and, second, even if he had, the status of compassion as a half-way house between individuation and unity—a tear in the nonetheless intact Veil of Maya—*still* remains something of a mystery within Schopenhauer's system. Setting aside more fundamental metaphysical disputes, the central point to take from Nietzsche's criticism would be that Schopenhauer seems to prefer appeals to mystery in his explanations of ethics to Nietzsche's more down-to-earth options (on the theory of compassion as mysterious, see $BM_{[P]}$, 144; 167; cf. D, §142). So far, then, Nietzsche has suggested that the phenomenon of compassion is highly mysterious, which Schopenhauer already acknowledges, and that there is no such thing as compassion, a counter-assertion, the possibility of which Schopenhauer recognizes, but one that he does not think most people are likely to bother with.

A second objection is historical: other cultures, and other philosophers in the Western tradition, do not praise compassionate acts, and indeed being pitied has been experienced as an affront to dignity.[13] The point of this is to challenge the Schopenhauerian presentation of compassion as a trans-historical ethical value, something which is or ought always to be recognized as worthy: "the true, only genuine and pure basis of morality, therefore always and everywhere operative" (SW6 [PP2], §109, my translation). While Schopenhauer clearly recognizes that both moral characteristics and pangs of conscience vary according to culture and character ($BM_{[P]}$, 126–27; SW6 [PP2], §117), in the end, he wants to use the approbation of conscience as a criterion of the moral worth of an action ($BM_{[P]}$, 140), whereas Nietzsche finds it naïve to think that a historically complex phenomenon such as morality could be boiled down to a single motivation such as compassion.[14] For our purposes, we should note Nietzsche's reference to the "purge" theory of tragedy—he claims, following one standard interpretation of Aristotle, that the Greeks used tragedy to purge themselves of pity, a clear recognition of its dangers.[15]

A third kind of objection appeals to the relationship between pity and the value of life. When I pity you and help you, I preserve something (you) which, by nature, ought to be allowed to perish. To have a greater number of pitiful living beings around is to encourage further disgust at life.[16] Here again—as Nietzsche knows—we are not presented with an objection to Schopenhauer on his own terms since Schopenhauer ultimately valued compassion precisely insofar as it pointed in the direction of the negation of life. Nietzsche is not arguing against Schopenhauer, then, but assuming hostility to Schopenhauer on the part of his readership, on a central Schopenhauerian point. We can see a similar effect when we look at an earlier Nietzschean *defense* of pity, as when in a pessimistic culture (Nietzsche speaks of "Indian" culture) pity helps people cope with and take part in life by taking care of each other.[17] Here, pity has become valuable for Nietzsche precisely because it is a spur to keep on living under difficult circumstances.

A fourth objection focuses on the nature of pleasure and pain. Nietzsche sometimes argues that compassionate acts increase the amount of suffering.[18] In GS 338, the commitment to compassion is taken as dependent on an erroneous view (so Nietzsche claims) that great pleasure can be experienced by one who does not experience great suffering. Effectively, Nietzsche is arguing that dampening down suffering via compassionate acts will automatically dampen down pleasure, too. The ethicist who values compassion makes a mistake comparable to that of thinking that one can go downhill all the way on a circular walk, when in fact downhill stretches must be matched by equivalent uphill ones.

Here again, Nietzsche's objection amounts to counter-assertion. Schopenhauer had claimed that pleasure is the absence of pain. If so, to alleviate your pain just is to make your existence more pleasurable (less painful). This controversial claim that pleasure is negative had, as Nietzsche well knew, already been challenged by Hartmann and Dühring (among others) in the intervening years. Pleasure, it was claimed, could certainly be positive, and some pains were a necessary backdrop to the pleasures of life, not to mention that certain privations might be thought pleasurable. Still, one could acknowledge this without holding, as Nietzsche suggests, that *every* reduced pain reduces pleasure or the capacity for pleasure. Schopenhauer had also said, of course, that our greatest pleasures are not as pleasurable as our greatest pains are painful—a claim which can stand independently of whether or not pleasure is negative. If so, one could argue that the absence of all pleasure or pain would be superior, despite the loss of potential for great pleasures, and hence that compassion (as Nietzsche describes it) is worthwhile after all.

As we have seen, some of the disagreements between Schopenhauer and Nietzsche regarding *Mitleid* boil down to assertion and counter-assertion—about the nature of pleasure and pain, about whether there are genuinely compassionate acts, and so on. But they also point toward wider philosophical issues at stake, for example in the question of whether it is true (and, if so, whether it matters) that not all cultures base morality on *Mitleid*. Indeed, each variety of objection—psychological, historical and "life" based—opens up another vista onto Nietzsche's criticisms of (and dependence on) Schopenhauer. We now look to each of these in turn.[19]

27.2 PSYCHOLOGY

Our discussion of Nietzsche's objections to pity saw him trying to make two arguments which, *prima facie*, appear to be in tension with one another. One was that there is no such thing as pity (the psychological objection). The other was that acts of pity are in fact harmful (evident in the pleasure/pain and value-of-life objections). But if there is no such thing as pity, then how can pity be harmful? Nietzsche could always say, as indeed he did, that "pity" is not just one thing (D, §133). But a closer look at how Nietzsche developed Schopenhauerian psychology will help us to see how Nietzsche might have drawn these claims together, even if it also shows us some further problems he faced.

We begin with a simplistic picture of mind, to which Schopenhauer and Nietzsche were both opposed. Since Nietzsche associates this (fairly or not) with Socrates and Plato, I'll call it the "Socratic picture."[20] According to this picture of thought and action, when we choose to do something, (1) we could have chosen otherwise, but (2) prior to acting, we could correctly weigh up our options and (3) act according to which option we thought was right; (4) having acted, our motivations are plain for us to see and to be made available to others so that (5) we can be judged morally based on what we do.

There are many different ways of opposing this view of mind and action, beginning with the apparent appeal to freedom of the will (1). But for our purposes, two particular challenges should be noted. First, there are phenomenological problems: a plausible, confessional description of one's own actions, or a cynical description of the actions of others, could easily reveal multiple cases in which we do not act according to the option we think is best (against [3], see e.g., SW6, §118 [PP2]) and we do not correctly understand our own options and motivations (against [2] and [4][21]). Better, then, would be a model which explained both our apparently Socratic actions and our failures by Socratic standards as part of the same overarching story. The overall suggestion from both philosophers, therefore, is that counter-instances to (2), (3), and (4) should be viewed as *normal*, not aberrant, and that we have privileged a (Socratic) model which only occasionally, if ever, gets it right.[22]

To see why non-Socratic behaviors might be normal, we need to look at the second motivation for criticizing the Socratic picture. This is not phenomenological, but rather what we might call "naturalistic," where this just means treating human beings as animals which are part of the natural world. For both Schopenhauer and Nietzsche, that is, our discursive, reasoning capacities, although unusual and distinctive, must be seen as serving a function for us as animals. Hence, just as dogs have an unusually good sense of smell compared with humans, humans have unusually good mental capacities when compared with dogs. But both mental and olfactory capacities serve animal needs such as survival and procreation. When Schopenhauer carefully describes, for example, how bees and spiders build hives and webs without the slightest (conscious) plan and without past experience, he is laying the groundwork for viewing human behaviors in a similar light (SW3 [WWR2], Chapter 27). The point is not, of course, that our behaviors are identical to those of spiders and bees, but that they are contingent on underlying, non-conscious natural goals—according to Schopenhauer, on the blind intentionality of the Will to reproduce and consume itself, as manifested in nature.

By thinking of humans first and foremost as animal-like and nature-governed, we can explain more than the Socratic model can, succeeding both where it succeeds and where it fails—as, indeed, Schopenhauer and Nietzsche (at least sometimes) thought they could. Schopenhauer's focus on sexual reproduction gives him his most plausible example of a natural force which operates through us, where necessary making use of our intellectual capacities, but where necessary manipulating and overriding them (SW3 [WWR2], ch. 44). It would be very odd, to say the least, if all the other animals reproduced due to the blind forces of nature, but human beings did so because they decided that it was the best option available to them and acted accordingly in a process of reasoning which was completely independent of nature.

Before we turn to Nietzsche, note that one problem for Schopenhauer should already be apparent. In the case of the bee or the spider building a hive or web, there is no conscious plan of action or prior experience, just instinctive action. In the case of the human building a house, there is a conscious plan and, usually, a great deal of prior experience. Presumably, the conscious deliberation and planning in the human case makes *some* difference to the outcome. What is that difference? Why do we have conscious deliberation, if nonconscious deliberation does the job for animals? An obvious answer would be that conscious, rational deliberation leads to better outcomes from "nature's point of view," at least in the human case. But then we are pushed back toward a Socratic model, according to which our deliberations determine the outcome of our actions. If our deliberations are indeed so effective, then how and why does "nature" (or the Will) exercise control over them to make sure humans do as "it" wants? In Schopenhauerian terms, the question would be this: to what extent is the intellect independent from the Will?

Schopenhauer was notoriously evasive on this question.[23] It is easier, and more relevant for our purposes, to say what he wants than to say what he can consistently have. The intellect is a truth-seeking capacity which the Will creates because it is useful for the Will to know the truth about various things in the phenomenal world. But the intellect is (usually) not capable of truth-seeking beyond the uses and requirements of the Will. Hence, truths that are harmful to the Will's purposes are not grasped as such, and palpable falsehoods—for example, that getting what we want will make us happy—are taken as probable or true by the intellect, just when it suits the Will. Hence, for example, the intellect might be good at identifying food (good for the Will), but bad at recognizing that eating never seems to bring the happiness that it promises (the recognition of which would be bad for the Will). Of course, the more the Will is in charge of what the intellect can and cannot discover, the more the intellect seems redundant—hence posing a problem for a naturalistic explanation, which sought to explain the intellect in virtue of its natural function. On the other hand, the more independence the intellect has, the less control can be ascribed to the Will—which is a problem for any analysis, like Schopenhauer's, which appeals to the Will as the general explanation of action.

We see this tension at work in Schopenhauer's careful formulations: "hence [in cases of unrealistic hope] the intellect is bound to do violence to its own nature, which is aimed at truth, since it is compelled, contrary to its own laws, to regard as true things that are neither true nor probable, and often scarcely possible, merely in order to pacify, soothe, and send to sleep for a while the restless and unmanageable will. We clearly see here who is master and who is servant" (WWR2$_{[P]}$, 216). Here, the intellect would normally or by nature grasp some truth, but it is not permitted to do so by the Will—a Will that controls the intellect, but which the intellect can *send to sleep*. In the same sentence, we have (1) the Will as the master which compels the intellect to make a mistake and (2) the intellect as the crafty servant who succeeds in getting the master off its back for a while. In another example, the Will prevents the intellect from noticing one of the possible outcomes of its actions—one which the individual would shy away from, but which the Will wants—so that the person does what the Will wants, risking this unwelcome outcome (SW3 [WWR2], ch. 19). If all options are already available to the Will such that it can blind the intellect to some of them, then what use is the intellect? Its job can hardly be to present the various outcomes to the Will so that the Will can make a choice since the whole point is that the Will already knows how to blind the intellect to some of the relevant outcomes. Of course, Schopenhauer's ultimate goal is not only to account for everyday actions, but also to account for those intellects which are in fact to some degree independent from the Will and hence free to seek truth according to their own truth-seeking nature—the geniuses, whose intellects are so powerful that they have extra capacity to reflect on the world (WWR1, 36; PP2, 50) or the ascetics who act against the interests of the Will (PP2, 337). In such cases, the relevant behavior is no longer such that it can be ascribed to nature's (the Will's) interests.

Nietzsche's criticisms of Schopenhauer's model fall into at least two distinct camps, the first of which is more pronounced in his middle period, the second in his later writings (that is, from about 1886 onward). In the middle period, Nietzsche typically rejects the model of a single, underlying natural "goal" for humans, such as the one set out by Schopenhauer's Will. Instead, we are best understood as a cluster of drives or instincts which fight it out between them at a nonconscious level to determine our actions and, to some extent, our thoughts about those actions. By analogy, it is as though Schopenhauer is monotheistic and Nietzsche (in this middle period) is polytheistic. For Schopenhauer, there is only one Will/drive/"god" that ultimately governs us, and all actions (aside from those of geniuses, ascetics, and so on) can be traced to the aims of this deity. For Nietzsche, on the other hand, there are many drives/"gods" that govern us, and each has its own agenda, so an action cannot necessarily be neatly ascribed to any particular one.[24] It is in this context that some of the remarks about pity can be better understood. For Schopenhauer, it is natural to be egoistic, and genuine acts of compassion, which are not egoistic—rare though they are—therefore operate against the principle of individuation which underlies nature.[25] Nietzsche can argue not only that apparently compassionate acts are not compassionate, but also that there can be, for example, a *drive* for pity (D, §115), so that pitying is satisfying the "egoism," as it were, of one part of me even as it frustrates the desires of some other part. He can say, therefore, that all actions are egoistic (in this subpersonal sense) while also saying that actions which satisfy the pity drive are also generally harmful. The drive-cluster model is sometimes explicitly opposed to Schopenhauer's account of the fixity of character (D, §560), a point about which Nietzsche appears to think Schopenhauer is empirically mistaken.

In the later works, a different strand of criticism becomes prominent. By this point, Nietzsche generally reverts to a "monotheistic" model, according to which one drive or will—notably the "will to power," but he will also speak of "nature" or a personified "Life"—is the single driving force in the organic and sometimes even in the non-organic world. Now the main challenge to Schopenhauer changes and focuses on Schopenhauer's model of ascetic life-denial: Schopenhauer, Nietzsche now argues, was naïve to imagine that there was a realm of human action, aesthetic or ascetic, in which the Will does *not* operate. Instead, from a theoretical point of view, it is more likely that those activities which *look* like they run counter to the interests of "nature" are in fact nature's way of getting what it wants, albeit under peculiar circumstances. We can conceive of this as an abductive argument: for Schopenhauer, a great many actions which appear to have nothing to do with the Will are in fact Will-driven, but there are one or two mysterious behaviors which really do have nothing to do with the Will. Nietzsche's counter is that, according to the simplest or best explanation, these supposedly Will-free actions are, in fact, Will-governed like the rest. This is the overall argument of the third essay of Nietzsche's *On the Genealogy of Morality*: in ascetic behavior, we are willing nothingness (the Will chooses asceticism for its own reasons) and not, as Schopenhauer has it, *not* willing (i.e., genuinely free from the Will). We return to this point when we consider the topic of "life" later.

27.3 HISTORY

As we saw from the discussion of pity, Nietzsche appeals to historical explanations in order to show that Schopenhauer has failed to appreciate the context or significance of some concept. The role of history is generally an important focus for the Schopenhauer–Nietzsche relation. Schopenhauer, recall, treated philosophy as exclusively suprahistorical: it did not deal with concepts or questions which changed over time (SW3 [WWR2], ch. 38). To hold to such a conception of philosophy, of course, one has to hold a corresponding view about the world itself: namely, that its most significant features are constant across the ages. Schopenhauer holds this to an extreme which marks him out both against Kant and Hegel before him and against Nietzsche, after. There is no progress at all, to speak of, and any one historical era is indistinguishable from any other in the central and significant facts of human life: "in truth, the essence of human life, as of nature everywhere, exists complete in every present time, and therefore requires only depth of comprehension in order to be exhaustively known" (WWR2$_{[P]}$, 441).

Nietzsche identifies this feature of Schopenhauer's philosophy early on—that is, while still in his "Schopenhauerian" phase—and he rightly connects it with Schopenhauer's advocacy of life-denying resignation. It is a species of what Nietzsche calls the "suprahistorical vantage point," according to which "the world is complete and reaches its finality at every moment," hence containing "a significance which is always the same."[26] A consequence of this view is that there is no special value to studying history as such: the Persian wars have nothing of importance to tell us that is *different* from what the Punic wars can tell us. Insofar as history is the study of that which is *not* constant over time, for example of the difference between the Persian and the Punic wars, it is therefore necessarily a study of what is insignificant. But a further consequence is that there is no room for genuine improvement or change in the course of human history, hence no room for the sorts of actions or discoveries which could, say, improve the human race. Medical advances, for example, might enable us to live longer, but they will not enable us to live better or more happily.

In fact, one can distinguish two Schopenhauerian thoughts here. First, that the fundamental human situation does not differ significantly across space and time. Second, that there is therefore no point in studying different eras. Given that Nietzsche's first book, *The Birth of Tragedy*, is itself a kind of history, it should be clear that Nietzsche could never wholeheartedly agree. Roughly speaking, Nietzsche's earlier writings agree with the first claim, but disagree with the second. Precisely because the human condition— roughly, the pessimistic scenario painted by Schopenhauer—remains constant, different societies can offer different lessons in how to cope with it. The tragic Greeks faced the same problem, but they faced it tragically, not in the scientific way that we moderns do, at least until the crucial historical intervention of Schopenhauer himself. It is not clear that such a revision would concern Schopenhauer greatly since he himself would admit, after all, that (for example) Jewish, Christian, and various Eastern cultures behaved differently in the face of the sufferings of the world and that some responses (especially Eastern, also Christian) are better than others (Jewish). As long as the first claim holds, Schopenhauer has what he needs—that is, as long as the different ways of coping with the fundamental situation do not, as it were, amount to fundamental differences in the situation itself. In the meditation which discusses Schopenhauer's suprahistoricism, Nietzsche is not contesting that first claim: indeed, the suggestion of the essay, if anything, is that a version of the suprahistorical vantage point is *justified*. But he nonetheless sets suprahistoricism aside because he is interested in using history or, perhaps better, the fact of our having a history, as a means to an end, namely "in the service of life." It can be helpful for "life" if we treat different historical periods as differing in significant ways from one another, even if the underlying condition of human beings remains the same. We take up the theme of "life" under that heading later.

But right at the opening of his middle period—just after the so-called break with Schopenhauer—Nietzsche begins to praise history and to advocate "historical philosophy," which contrasts with the common failing of philosophers: namely, to treat man as he is now as the blueprint for man as he has always been.[27] Here we begin to see the first claim challenged: namely, that human beings face the same fundamental conditions over time. What appear to be our timeless "instincts" might just be recent developments to deal with recent problems, and the philosopher who treated current idiosyncrasies as eternal and fundamental would not see the wood for the trees.

An important dimension of our understanding of Nietzsche's response to Schopenhauer rests on how we interpret this "historical philosophy," especially with regards to what happened next. In his later writings, notably in GM and A, Nietzsche developed histories of morality which look to place him in a completely different tradition from Schopenhauer, who could hardly conceive of himself as doing history at all. On a prominent line of interpretation, historical philosophy (of the kind Nietzsche ultimately practices and advocates) presents our major concepts and values as more or less completely open to change and reinterpretation over time.[28] Where Schopenhauer, recalling Plato, advocates the philosophical study of "being" (that which is always the same) over "becoming" (that which changes) (SW3 [WWR2], ch. 38), Nietzsche turns the tables: *becoming* should be the object of study, whereas *being* is treated with the utmost suspicion.[29] What look like eternal values—compassion or selflessness—will turn out to be historically contingent, and the reasons we adhere to those values will turn out to be accidents of cultural history or psychology rather than any insight into the nature of the good. Their meaning will best be set out by giving a well-informed historical account of how they came to be what they are. In the *Genealogy*, for example, Christianity arises out of a set of (purportedly) historical contingencies which provide local solutions to local problems: that loans can be paid off with the pain of the debtor (which Nietzsche relates to the phenomenon of conscience) or that Indo-European grammar makes it easy to imagine a subject that exists apart from an action (which he relates to free will). In *The Anti-Christ*, Nietzsche describes the origins of the idea of a universally binding morality in a response, among ancient Israelites, to military defeat (AC, §§24–26). The consequence of such an analysis (on this line of interpretation) is that we do not have one clear, consistent set of moral values, but rather an internally variegated and ever-shifting cluster of different interests and traditions which, as it happens, can never be made into a coherent whole.

If we accept such a story about the origins and current nature of conscience, or free will, or the supposed universality of moral values, or even if we come to think that *some* such story is the most plausible, then we have moved far away from Schopenhauer. Whether or not this is the best reading of Nietzsche—and we will find reasons, later, to doubt that it is—the legacy of reading him in this way has taken his influence far beyond any localized response to Schopenhauer, whose writings show little appreciation even of the possibility of historical philosophy of this kind. Here is a Nietzsche who is not merely responding to Schopenhauer, but one who presents a completely different philosophical paradigm, namely, one in which we look towards history to find the shifting meaning and significance of human values and institutions. This Nietzsche looks ahead to Max Weber or Michel Foucault, not backward to Arthur Schopenhauer.

27.4 "Life"

One of Nietzsche's charges against pity, as we saw, was that it is in some sense damaging to "Life." Indeed, it is philosophy's relation to "Life"—here best understood as a personified force akin to "the Will" or "Nature"—which marks Nietzsche's most significant form of dependence on and, in the context of that dependence, departure from Schopenhauer. It will help, to begin with, to recall Schopenhauer's conception of the affirmation and negation of life. As we have seen, the Will operates through us to make us behave in certain ways. Most people behave in accordance with the Will, while some people are able to frustrate its (blind) intentions. The terms "affirmation" and "negation" refer to behavior which either accords or does not accord with what the Will wants: hence, it can be helpful to think of affirmation not as saying "yes" to life (that is, not as holding some conscious belief to the effect that life is good or valuable), but rather as saying "Yes, Ma'am!" or "Affirmative!" to life's (the Will's) orders. To negate life, similarly, is to say "No, Ma'am!" or "I cannot comply!" Once understood in this way, we see that affirmation and negation are not judgments about whether or not the world is good: they are ways of behaving, from which we can see whether the individual in question is doing Life's bidding, typically in terms of survival and reproduction. Simply put, Nietzsche's writings never advocate denial as such, and even the early writings place him more on the affirmative side.

We can see this in *The Birth of Tragedy*. For Schopenhauer, the best tragedy effectively encodes the message that, unavoidably, it would be better not to exist. Correspondingly, the aesthetic experience which accompanies the best tragedies is, in a sense, a partial simulation of what it would be like not to exist, or at least what it would be like not to have the Will governing one's behavior (which is characteristic of all existence in the world as representation). On Nietzsche's early reworking, the best tragedy—which for him, unlike Schopenhauer, is Greek—indeed encodes a pessimistic message of sorts. But its doing so is a strategy *on the part of "Life,"* which *saves* the participants from Schopenhauerian resignation: "art saves [the Greek participant], and through art Life saves him—for itself."[30] Notice that, already, Nietzsche implicitly invokes the abductive argument mentioned earlier: rather than tragedy detaching us from Life (or the Will), tragedy is Life's strategy for controlling us. From an orthodox Schopenhauerian point of view, there is no particular reason why it is good to be encouraged to go on living. Nor is it precisely clear what reason Nietzsche himself has in mind at this stage. The most obvious one, however, is that certain kinds of artistic experience, such as tragedy, far from being disinterested, allow us to participate in the Will's pleasurable release in the creation of the world—a participation which Schopenhauer could not have allowed. Whatever else may have changed in the meantime, note that Nietzsche is still praising a similar function of art in *The Gay Science*, a work of the middle period: there, art is not a means of insight into the most terrible features of existence, but rather a means of coming to terms with those features, indeed of seeing them as good (GS, §107). Because art is (Nietzsche claims) a kind of valuable untruth, it sanctifies other kinds of error which we know we unavoidably make and which would otherwise be sources of shame. Similarly, as we saw, Nietzsche's early history essay admits that Schopenhauer may in some sense be right in his suprahistorical stance toward mankind, but the essay simultaneously rejects that stance, in spite of its likely validity, in favor of those approaches to the past which serve "Life." Even when Nietzsche looks at his most pessimistic, then, he looks set on avoiding ascetic denial of life.

In the middle period, when Nietzsche starts to deny that the question of the value of life has any validity at all—that is, the central question in the *Pessimismusstreit*—he *still* advocates the affirmation of life, now understood as some kind of attitude of approval toward all of the interconnected events of the past. The corresponding thought of welcoming the eternal return of one's life, which Nietzsche in some way intends to place at the center of his affirmative outlook, may well have its roots in Schopenhauer, for whom the affirmer of life *implicitly,* though not explicitly, makes the judgment that every aspect of life is good and longs for its eternal repetition (WWR1, §54). Finally, when—as we have seen—Nietzsche returns to a more Schopenhauerian model in his later writings, according to which a "Will" (to power) operates through all things, he effectively argues that we should aid this Will (or Nature, or Life) in the aims that it sets through us. This is more or less the definition of the affirmation of life in Schopenhauer.

Indeed, looking back over our various discussions of Nietzsche's responses to Schopenhauer, it is striking that a differing attitude toward "Life" in this sense may be said to be in the foreground of each of them. Compassion is valuable for Schopenhauer, in part because it moves us away from life's interests; pity is problematic for Nietzsche for precisely the same reason. History is helpful in showing us that nothing of any significance ever really changes, hence there can be no meaningful progress within life (Schopenhauer); or, in Nietzsche's second *Untimely Meditation*, it is helpful, precisely because, when done right, it is a spur to carry on living. Apparently ascetic behavior is good because it is a denial of life (Schopenhauer); or, it is life-driven and therefore a peculiar and troubling but highly interesting example of how life pursues its own interests (the later Nietzsche).

This later return to a version of the Schopenhauerian "Will" places significant limits on the extent of Nietzsche's historicism, discussed earlier. First, the "nature" or "Life" of Nietzsche's later writings also operates in all people at all times and is not fundamentally subject to historical change as such. Second, this unchanging force provides the ultimate criterion for whether or not Nietzsche approves of some behavior or set of values. Nietzsche, that is, tends to advocate for "natural" behavior, as he understands it.[31]

Consequently, although different historical eras have different systems of values, and although these values develop by means of local solutions to local problems, the overriding criterion of evaluation for these value systems *themselves* is, even in the later Nietzsche, whether or not they are "natural" or "Life-promoting." This places Nietzsche right back in the Schopenhauerian fold, albeit as his direct opponent: for Schopenhauer, the natural is a guide to what is *bad* (PP2, 156a), whereas for Nietzsche, real and good values are natural values (TI "Morality as Anti-Nature"). There are clearly similarities in what they take to be "natural": notably egoistic actions aimed at increasing the power of the individual at the expense of others (PP2, 171), and reproductive sexuality, even if Nietzsche ultimately sees the operating force as a form of power-seeking or exploitation rather than of the Will's need to feed on itself. Nietzsche tends to view the dominance of Christian morality, which, like Schopenhauer, he reads as fundamentally ascetic and life-denying, as a temporary, anti-natural form of evaluation that will (with Nietzsche's help) be flipped back to a natural one after a Judeo-Christian hiatus. This "flipping back" is the central notion of the "revaluation of values" in Nietzsche's later writings.

I said at the start that Nietzsche is best seen as maneuvering within a framework that was established by Schopenhauer. His advocacy of the affirmation of life is the most important feature of his intellectual indebtedness. But what of his argument against Schopenhauer? We saw the outlines of this argument when we looked at his later objection to Schopenhauerian psychology: Nietzsche wants to say that there is no area of action that remains insulated from nature's goals; hence, even apparently anti-natural activity is really nature's way of promoting itself. While this has some plausibility as an argument against Schopenhauer, who ultimately treated ascetic freedom from the will as a kind of mystery, the way that Nietzsche develops his argument leaves him vulnerable to Schopenhauerian counters. Effectively, Nietzsche tells the Schopenhauerian that she is always already doing what Life wants and therefore that, since resistance is useless, she might as well do what nature tells her to do. The problem with this line of attack is that it is unclear how resistance is *possible*, given that the premise of the argument is that Life is always acting through you to achieve its goals. And if resistance is possible—that is to say, if one can act in such a way that Life's goals are frustrated—then there is no particular reason why resistance is *bad*. Hence, with respect to pity, for example, we are left with two unsatisfying options. We can either agree with Nietzsche that taking pity on others is what "Life wants" through us; but in that case Nietzsche is rendered toothless because his criticism was supposed to be that pity is bad because it *frustrates* Life's interests. Or we can agree with Nietzsche (as a reader with modern sensibilities probably would not) that compassionate acts preserve beings that Life would prefer to get rid of; but then we don't have a good account of *why* we should behave as Life prefers. Schopenhauer thinks, of course, that behaving as Life prefers ultimately makes us miserable and that we are better off resisting, even though he does not think that his arguments to that effect will actually persuade many people. Nietzsche sometimes says the opposite: namely, that doing as Life instructs us feels better or is more pleasurable (AC, §11). But, generally, he resists this claim for the sorts of reasons we saw raised against pity in the pleasure/pain disagreement: namely, that pleasure and pain are not separable and therefore that desiring more pleasure and less pain is in some sense contradictory while desiring the absence of pain is code for desiring the absence, altogether, of life.

27.5 Conclusion: Style and Doctrine

As these remarks have tried to illustrate, Nietzsche's specific responses to Schopenhauer on the issues we have examined may best be understood, in general, as bedrock disagreements: Are there truly compassionate actions? Would we be better off without pain? What (if anything) does "Life" or nature or the Will want from us, and ought we to do what it wants? It does not much matter whether we say that Nietzsche is fundamentally opposed to Schopenhauer on these questions or whether we say that Nietzsche is fundamentally Schopenhauerian, precisely because he holds that these questions, within their Schopenhauerian framework, are central to philosophical enquiry. What matters is to see that both are true at once.

Are there no truly significant Nietzschean departures from Schopenhauer, as opposed to maneuvers within a Schopenhauerian framework? One candidate is Nietzsche's "historical philosophy," discussed earlier. But another candidate is the one that strikes the new reader most forcefully and which can nonetheless disappear from the scholarly literature: it is the question of style and philosophical method. Schopenhauer is relentlessly systematic, and his insistence on his philosophy as a "single thought" marks him out in stark contrast to Nietzsche's more playful and less systematic approach. That much is clear. But a real break with Schopenhauer would occur if Nietzsche's new style indicated, or was the product of, a different attitude toward the very activity of philosophy. According to such an attitude, Nietzsche would not see himself, or see philosophy practiced correctly, as ultimately being in the business of clearly setting out and arguing for the doctrines of his that we have considered, such as the will to power.

A direct comparison may be found on the issue of "masked" style. Schopenhauer writes frequently about this (see PP2, ch. 23, "On Authorship and Style"), by which he tends to mean anonymity, imitating others, or the use of obscurity or mannerisms to disguise a lack of intelligence. In a similar vein, he attacks the use of expressing oneself cryptically. Essentially, Schopenhauer's remarks on the mask boil down to the claim that one should clearly state what one thinks and own up to stating it. Consequently, any philosopher who could write, of one of his own works, that "a book such as this is not for reading straight through or reading aloud but for flipping open" (D, §454, translation altered), might be thought to be doing something thoroughly non-Schopenhauerian insofar as it suggests that different readers ought to be confronted with different thoughts. Similarly, any philosopher who could be found implicitly praising obscurity or recommending a "masked" philosophy, according to which one courts misunderstanding and appears to be what one is not (BGE 25[32]) should stand out against Schopenhauer. Such features of Nietzsche's writing, together, perhaps, with his apparent willingness to contradict himself and (*prima facie*) the high degree of skepticism he expresses about the concept of truth and our access to it, have undoubtedly led to a tradition of reading him as though the real value of his philosophy, even by his lights, lies not in specific doctrines, but somewhere else. This might be in a kind of free-spirited, experimental attitude to knowledge and enquiry or in the individual's project of self-creation and development, in which "taking on" or "entertaining" Schopenhauerian and anti-Schopenhauerian philosophical stances plays a part, but for which the ultimate goal does not lie in convincing the reader of the truth of any one of them. The point is not that such ways of reading Nietzsche are justified or unjustified. It is, rather, that the Nietzsche they present us with really does seem a world away from *The World as Will and Representation*: he is not in the same game. If we reject such readings of Nietzsche in favor of a focus on reconstructing his doctrines and theories, we will always find Schopenhauer lurking in there somewhere, and, as I have argued here in relation to at least some philosophical domains, there is no special reason to think that Nietzsche's alternatives are superior.

ACKNOWLEDGMENTS

My thanks to the editor and to Sebastian Gardner for helpful comments on an earlier draft.

Notes

1. Frederick C. Beiser, *Weltschmerz: Pessimism in German Philosophy, 1860–1900* (New York: Oxford University Press, 2016).
2. For what Nietzsche read, and when, see Thomas H. Brobjer, *Nietzsche's Philosophical Context: An Intellectual Biography* (Urbana: University of Illinois Press, 2008).
3. See Friedrich Nietzsche, *Kritische Gesamtausgabe: Werke*, edited by Giorgio Colli and Mazzino Montinari (Berlin: Walter de Gruyter, 1967) (henceforth "KGW," followed by section, volume, and page numbers), I–4, 418–30. The notes are translated in Christopher Janaway, *Willing and Nothingness: Schopenhauer as Nietzsche's Educator* (Oxford: Clarendon Press, 1998), 258–65. For discussion, see *Willing and Nothingness*, 18–19; Sandro Barbera, "Eine Quelle der frühen Schopenhauer-Kritik Nietzsches: Rudolf Hayms Aufsatz 'Arthur Schopenhauer,'" *Nietzsche Studien* 24 (1995): 124–36; Brobjer, *Nietzsche's Philosophical Context*, 28–32.
4. KGW I–4, 513.
5. Friedrich Nietzsche, "Schopenhauer as Educator," in *Untimely Meditations*, edited by Daniel Breazeale, translated by R. J. Hollingdale (Cambridge: Cambridge University Press, 1997), §2.
6. Daniel Blue, *The Making of Friedrich Nietzsche: The Quest for Identity, 1844–1869* (New York: Cambridge University Press, 2016), 216; Brobjer, *Nietzsche's Philosophical Context*, 123.
7. The writer is Philipp Mainländer, quoted in Beiser, *Weltschmerz*, 204. But compare Beiser's account of similar conversions in the case of Frauenstädt (p. 70) and Bahnsen (p. 235).
8. As Cartwright argues, Schopenhauer and Nietzsche use the same German term, *Mitleid*, but Schopenhauer's use is best translated "compassion" whereas Nietzsche's is best translated "pity." In English, these are not synonymous, since "pity" has a negative connotation, a sense of superiority in relation to the pitied one, which "compassion" lacks. See David E. Cartwright, "Schopenhauer's Compassion and Nietzsche's Pity," in *Schopenhauer Jahrbuch* 69 (1988), 557–67.
9. Friedrich Nietzsche, *The Gay Science*, edited by Bernard Williams, translated by Josefine Nauckhoff and Adrian Del Caro (Cambridge: Cambridge University Press, 2001), §99. Henceforth "GS," followed by section number.
10. GS, §13.
11. Ibid., §118.
12. Friedrich Nietzsche, *Daybreak* (Cambridge: Cambridge University Press, 1997), §133. Henceforth "D", followed by section number.
13. D, §134–35; see also Friedrich Nietzsche, *On the Genealogy of Morality*, translated by Carol Diethe (Cambridge: Cambridge University Press, 1997), Preface, §5.
14. See the unpublished note in Friedrich Nietzsche, *Sämtliche Werke: Kritische Studienausgabe*, edited by Giorgio Colli and Mazzino Montinari, 15 vols. (Berlin: Walter de Gruyter, 1988), vol. 12, 160 ("2 [188]"). Henceforth "KSA" followed by volume, page, and fragment number.
15. D, §13. See also Friedrich Nietzsche, *The Anti-Christ*, translated by R. J. Hollingdale (London: Penguin Classics, 1990), §7. Henceforth "AC" followed by section number.
16. AC, §7.
17. D, §136.
18. D, §134; AC, §7.

19. Although I have kept them separate in the initial discussion, I will treat the pleasure/pain disagreement as part of the discussion of the "life-based" objection for reasons which will become clear.

20. I discuss Nietzsche's criticisms of the "Socratic picture" in some detail in Tom Stern, "Against Nietzsche's 'Theory' of the Drives," *Journal of the American Philosophical Association* 1, no. 1 (2015), 121–40.

21. See FW, §15; SW2, §55; SW3, §19. See also SW6 [PP2], §§49–50. For Nietzsche, see D, §119, §129 and, for discussion, Stern, "Against Nietzsche's 'Theory' of the Drives."

22. By "normal" I do not mean statistically more common, but rather that such things are not pathological—they are not to be taken as evidence of the psychological system going wrong.

23. For how this objection was embedded in the reception of Schopenhauer's philosophy, see Frederick C. Beiser, *After Hegel: German Philosophy, 1840–1900* (Princeton, NJ: Princeton University Press, 2014), 171–72.

24. GS, §1 is an exception in that the drive for the preservation of the species is, there, the basic, underlying drive.

25. It is curious to note, therefore, that Schopenhauer also describes *Mitleid* as natural. But his wider claim is that self-preservation at the expense of others is the result of the Will's need to feed on itself.

26. Friedrich Nietzsche, "On the Uses and Disadvantages of History for Life," in *Untimely Meditations*, edited by Daniel Breazeale, translated by R. J. Hollingdale (Cambridge: Cambridge University Press, 1997), 66.

27. Friedrich Nietzsche, *Human, All Too Human*, edited by Richard Schacht, translated by R. J. Hollingdale (Cambridge: Cambridge University Press, 1996), pt. I, sections 1–2.

28. Michel Foucault, "Nietzsche, Genealogy, History," in *Language, Counter-Memory, Practice: Selected Essays and Interviews* (Ithaca, NY: Cornell University Press, 1977), 139–64; Raymond Geuss, "Nietzsche and Genealogy," in *Morality, Culture, and History: Essays on German Philosophy* (Cambridge: Cambridge University Press, 1999), 1–28.

29. Friedrich Nietzsche, *Twilight of the Idols*, translated by R. J. Hollingdale (London: Penguin Classics, 1990), "'Reason' in Philosophy." Henceforth "TI" followed by chapter name and number. See also KSA 13, 212–13 ("11 [73]").

30. Friedrich Nietzsche, *The Birth of Tragedy and Other Writings*, edited by Raymond Geuss and Ronald Speirs, translated by Ronald Speirs (Cambridge: Cambridge University Press, 1999), §7, p. 40, translation altered.

31. See Tom Stern, *Nietzsche's Ethics* (Cambridge: Cambridge University Press, 2020) for a detailed treatment of "Life" in Nietzsche's later ethics.

32. For analysis of this passage in context, see Tom Stern, "Nietzsche, the Mask, and the Problem of the Actor," in *The Philosophy of Theatre, Drama and Acting*, edited by Tom Stern (London: Rowman and Littlefield International, 2017), 67–87.

FURTHER READING

Cartwright, David, E. "Schopenhauer's Compassion and Nietzsche's Pity." *Schopenhauer-Jahrbuch* 69 (1988): 557–567.

Constancio, João. "On Consciousness: Nietzsche's Departure from Schopenhauer." *Nietzsche-Studien* 40 (2011): 1–42.

Dahlkvist, Tobias. *Nietzsche and the Philosophy of Pessimism: A Study of Nietzsche's Relation to the Pessimistic Tradition: Schopenhauer, Hartmann, Leopardi*. Uppsala: Uppsala University Press, 2007.

Gemes, Ken, and Christopher Janaway. "Life-Denial Versus Life-Affirmation: Schopenhauer and Nietzsche on Pessimism and Asceticism." In *A Companion to Schopenhauer*, edited by Bart Vandenabeele. Blackwell, 2012: 280–299.

Janaway, Christopher, ed. *Willing and Nothingness: Schopenhauer as Nietzsche's Educator*. Oxford: Clarendon Press, 1998.

Simmel, Georg. *Schopenhauer and Nietzsche* [1907], translated by Helmut Loiskandl. Champaign: University of Illinois Press, 1991.

Stern, Tom. "Nietzsche's Ethics of Affirmation." In *The New Cambridge Companion to Nietzsche*, edited by Tom Stern. Cambridge: Cambridge University Press, 2019: 351–373.

Soll, Ivan. "Schopenhauer as Nietzsche's 'Great Teacher' and 'Antipode.'" In *The Oxford Handbook of Nietzsche*, edited by John Richardson and Ken Gemes. Oxford University Press, 2013: 160–184.

Wicks, Robert. "Schopenhauer: Nietzsche's Antithesis and Source of Inspiration." In *The New Cambridge Companion to Nietzsche*, edited by Tom Stern. Cambridge: Cambridge University Press, 2019: 72–96.

CHAPTER 28

SCHOPENHAUER AND THE UNCONSCIOUS

STEPHAN ATZERT

A footnote to the term "enlightenment" in the first chapter of Theodor W. Adorno and Max Horkheimer's *Dialectic of Enlightenment*[1] refers to §356 in Arthur Schopenhauer's "Psychological Observations" from the second volume of the *Parerga and Paralipomena*:

> That the lowest of all mental activities is arithmetic is proven by the fact that it is the only one that can also be executed by a machine, just as now in England this kind of calculating machine is already in frequent use for the sake of convenience. —Now however all investigation of the finite and the infinite at bottom amounts to a lot of reckoning. In this spirit we should evaluate the "mathematical profundity" ridiculed by Lichtenberg when he says: "The so-called professional mathematicians, relying on the immaturity of the rest of mankind, have acquired a reputation for profundity that closely resembles that of holiness, which the theologians claim for themselves."
>
> (PP2, 546)

In the context of *Dialectic of Enlightenment*, this reference serves to criticize enlightenment rationality as a mechanical adaptation of thought, its ritual being the mathematical method. Schopenhauer is quoted as one of the original instigators of the unmasking of rationality. Indeed, the insight that humans are not masters of their own selves, often ascribed to Freud, originated with Schopenhauer. Though it is true that Freud defined the realm of the psyche, of the human unconscious, with the help of psychoanalytical terminology, it is also true that he appropriated many of Schopenhauer's observations, differentiations, and conceptual structures, often with shifts of emphasis, mostly without acknowledgment. Freud's appropriation of Schopenhauer's philosophemes has been extensively documented, whether it pertains to psychological repression or to the concepts of Id and Ego, which in Freud's works resemble Schopenhauer's will and intellect, not just in spirit, but to the letter. It is also evident in Freud's understanding of dreams. Condensation and displacement, for example, are Freud's "master craftsmen" of the "dream labor." Due to similarities in the unconscious modes of operation in dreams and jokes, they are fashioned after the concepts of subsumption and displacement from Schopenhauer's "On the Theory of the Ludicrous" (the eighth chapter in the second volume of the *World as Will and Representation*). And just as Freud's *Jokes and Their Relation to the Unconscious* (1905) is modeled on "On the Theory of the Ludicrous," Schopenhauer's "Transcendent Speculation on the Apparent Deliberateness in the Fate of the Individual" from the first volume of *Parerga and Paralipomena* served as a blueprint for Freud's development of the death drive in *Beyond the Pleasure Principle*. Given such a determining influence, Freud became the true heir of Schopenhauer's philosophy of the will.[2]

In this chapter, the gradual emergence of the notion of the unconscious is outlined as it pertains to the tradition that runs from Schopenhauer via Eduard von Hartmann and Philipp Mainländer to Sabina Spielrein and C.G. Jung, and, of course, to Sigmund Freud. In particular, we focus on the popularization of the term, "unconscious," by von Hartmann and on the history of the death drive, which has its precursors not only in Schopenhauer's "Transcendent Speculation on the Apparent Deliberateness in the Fate of the Individual," but also in Mainländer's philosophy.

Despite these historical continuities, Schopenhauer's philosophical concept of the will is not synonymous with the unconscious. Indeed, Schopenhauer uses the term "unconscious" very sparingly. In Paul Deussen's edition of *Schopenhauer's Sämtliche Werke*,[3] which runs to several thousand pages, it occurs eight times as a noun and in thirty-three instances as an adjective. Neither do Schopenhauer's will and intellect quite correspond to the unconscious and the conscious mind: even though the will in humans is spurred into action by conscious motives, the intellect itself is a by-product of the will, which forms the basis of cognition. In addition, Schopenhauer introduces the denial of the will as a third point of reference. It refers to an experience beyond will and intellect, which, according to Schopenhauer, corresponds to the Buddhist nirvana. As will be shown later, this third point of reference reemerges in psychoanalytic theory as the nirvana-principle—a momentum wrenched from the death drive by the life forces. Thus, in the context of Schopenhauer's will, the individual human unconscious is one particular instance of a much wider universal will which, in turn, when negated, is part of an even wider unknown.

Only certain aspects of Schopenhauer's will lend themselves to the concept of an unconscious mind in the human individual, but—significantly—they are the most convincing ones. The second book (of four, contained in the first volume) of *The World as Will and Representation* is full of rich descriptions about the will's all-pervasive nature and numerous passages detailing its role in nature. Yet Schopenhauer insists that these conceptualizations are anthropomorphic projections. Their validity is derived only from the actual epistemological and empirical basis of the will, its immediate manifestation for the individual; that is, the experience of one's own living body. In short, the will has a psychological definition, according to which it is synonymous with body and sensation.[4] In *The World as Will and Representation*, Schopenhauer elevates this intuitive basis of perception to a philosophical truth: "It is an entirely distinctive mode of cognition...it is the connection between a judgement and the relationship an intuitive representation, the body, has to something that is not a representation at all, but is rather entirely different in kind from this: will. I would therefore like to distinguish this truth above all others, and call it *philosophical truth par excellence*" (WWR1, 127). We therefore note at the outset that Schopenhauer's will is tangible, as body, as ordinary physical sensations. Hence Schopenhauer chose the term "will," rather than "force," to emphasize the subjective urge felt from within.

We should also note that Schopenhauer—and only as an act of sound philosophical reasoning—concedes that the individual's cognition of his or her own body as expansive, space-filling, and mobile is the result of a mediation: "...it is an image in my brain, which comes about by means of the senses and understanding" (WWR2$_{[AC]}$, 309). But this is only methodological housekeeping on Schopenhauer's part; never does he argue that the world exists only in one's mind. Rather, mind, with its functions of intellect and reason, depends on the will. Early conceptualizations of the human body as will refer to the activity of the muscles and to pain and pleasure. An emphasis on bodily sensation is present from 1814, where Schopenhauer describes the unity of body and will that becomes clear in strong sensations: "The body, (the physical human) *is nothing other than the will become visible*...From the fact that the body is only the visibility of will, the precise connection between will and body; the reason why all passion, all affect, i.e., all intense willing and not-willing jars and modifies the body so much, can be explained" (HN1, 106 [my translation]). A comparison with the first edition of the *Fourfold Root of the Principle of Sufficient Reason* (1813) shows that, at the time, Schopenhauer ascribes only very strong sensations to the will, still conceiving of physical feelings as a separate category.

Twenty-five years later, in his essay *On the Freedom of the Will* (1839), Schopenhauer gives a thorough account of the psychological foundation of the will—an account that does not simply concern itself with the strongest tempests of passion. It is here that Schopenhauer determines that the will expresses itself indiscriminately in all bodily sensations, whether these rest on sense impressions or on subtle, barely perceptible inner impulses. In *On the Freedom of the Will*, Schopenhauer initially repeats the assertions cited in the preceding passages when he writes that self-consciousness is the consciousness of the will, stating that a human being is "immediately conscious of his [or her] own self...entirely as something that WILLS," and so experiences the will in all of his or her "affects and passions" (FW, 38). In the lines that follow, "feelings of pleasure and displeasure," the "pleasant and painful bodily sensations" and—the next part of the sentence is to be emphasized—"all those countless sensations that lie between these two extremes" are understood as the will experienced in one's own body, as the universal will manifested in the instance of one's own body: that is, they are the foundation of human self-experience (FW, 39). Accordingly, experience, self-consciousness, will, body, and physically experienced sensations are synonyms; comfort and pain are extreme poles of a multifaceted experience that always rests on the unity of sensation, body, and will. In this manner Schopenhauer develops the considerations noted down in 1814. The trinity of sensation, body, and will can be separated conceptually but not experientially.

It therefore forms the psychological foundation of the will on which Schopenhauer's metaphysics is based.

In short, the "philosophical truth" described in 1817 refers to the knowledge of the contingency of every experience on bodily sensations. Bernd Dörflinger describes this significance of the sensations in Schopenhauer's philosophy: "[Bodily sensation], however, ought arguably…be accentuated as particularly significant, because it simultaneously elicits the understanding's causal-presentational interpretation of the world and, with regard to its implying pleasure or displeasure, is relevant to the will. It therefore deserves attention as the mediation-point of both perspectives."[5]

We can see how the will as body and sensations forms what Freud calls the primary system, the pleasure-seeking Id. Sensations, while central to Schopenhauer's exposition of the will, have a lesser role in Freud's metapsychological thought. Freud claimed the sphere of the psyche as his area of expertise but avoided naming a location in the body for the unconscious because he wished to avoid any disputes with the physiologists of the day. In contrast, Schopenhauer maintained that the will—as the seat of the deep unconscious in the individual—can be physically located in the solar plexus (PP2, 242).

Two essays in the *Parerga and Paralipomena* and one chapter in *On the Will in Nature* focus on specific qualities of the unconscious. They are the "Transcendent Speculation on the Apparent Deliberateness in the Fate of the Individual," the "Essay On Spirit Seeing and Everything Connected Therewith," and the chapter, "Animal Magnetism and Magic." The subject of this chapter is hypnosis, with which Schopenhauer had familiarized himself in Berlin in the 1820s under Karl Christian Wolfart, who held a chair for medicine and practiced magnetism. Schopenhauer writes that magnetism is applied metaphysics because it goes beyond space and time, similar to somnambulism and clairvoyance. The "Essay on Spirit Seeing" features an application of the will to explain phantasies, dreams, somnambulism, second sight, clairvoyance, spirit seeing and similar phenomena. These are related insofar as they exhibit a reversal of normal sense stimulation. Together, the solar plexus, the spinal nerves, and the brain form the dream organ. It is the solar plexus, the seat of deep emotions and of an intuitive connection with the species, which stimulates the brain from within.

This chapter shows Schopenhauer to be an original yet critical, even cynical, observer of paranormal phenomena. Yet the "Essay on Spirit Seeing" and the chapter on "Animal Magnetism and Magic" were not as relevant for the development of the idea of the unconscious as the "Transcendent Speculation on the Apparent Deliberateness in the Fate of the Individual." The "Transcendent Speculation" has not received the attention it deserves,[6] partly because philosophical interest in Schopenhauer has centered on *The World as Will and Representation,* and partly because of its obscure title and position outside of Schopenhauer's philosophical system. In it, Schopenhauer develops speculatively the notion of a universal, intelligent, supraindividual unconscious—an unconscious with a purpose related to death. It is instructive to review this essay in some detail, given the importance of its central ideas not only for von Hartmann, Mainländer, and Freud, but also—through Mainländer—for Spielrein and Jung.

The title of the treatise makes clear its speculative nature, and in it Schopenhauer abandons empirical reality in favor of a "metaphysical fantasy"[7] (PP1, 201). This does not imply an uncritical approach: Schopenhauer notes that the assumption of supernatural agency (appearing as intentionality) is nothing but "a product of neediness" (PP1, 201). From the outset, he therefore discounts "that most daring idea"—namely that chance has a purpose. Following these disclaimers, however, he lays out his metaphysical fantasy. Central to his initial line of argument are the notions of demonstrable and transcendent fatalism. Demonstrable fatalism is an aspect of determinism, based on the observation that everything occurs strictly in accordance with the laws of nature. In this sense, everything that occurs is predetermined, even though this is not observable in its entirety due to the multitudes of regular causal interconnections. Demonstrable fatalism does not contain an explanation of the meaning of fate for the individual: it is a stepping stone, an explanatory preamble to the notion of transcendent fatalism.

Transcendent fatalism is a consequence of the experience of unusual situations and circumstances which—on the one hand—noticeably favor the individual, in a moral or inwardly necessary way, but—on the other hand—can only have occurred randomly (PP1, 204). In hindsight it appears as if an external agent had directed the individual by means of those circumstances (PP1, 208). This, Schopenhauer emphasizes, is no imaginary reconstruction of events after the fact; it can be verified by experience. Intellectual projection is incapable of producing the highly specific, individually tailored circumstances in which the inner and the outer interlink "through a unity of the random and the necessary which lies at the bottom of all things" (PP1, 207). Obviously, even the most random event results from necessary causes. As it is not guided by understanding, Schopenhauer argues, it must result from a necessity of a higher order which precedes the possibility of understanding (PP1, 213).

This higher order, the subjective relationship to the individually tailored circumstances, is what Schopenhauer calls transcendent fatalism. He further substantiates his approach by highlighting an analogous phenomenon in the experience of dreaming. The question of agency in dreams supposedly points to the fact that they are staged by the will as the "secret theatre director of the individual's dreams" (PP1, 218). Schopenhauer writes that the dream is produced by the will "from a region, which lies far beyond the imagining consciousness and therefore appears as unyielding fate in the dream" (PP1, 217). The same could be true of the waking state: namely "also that fate which rules over our real life, somehow originates in the final instance from that WILL, which is our own, but which here, where it appears as fate, would work from a region far from the imagination of our consciousness" (PP1, 218). Thus it can be said that the will sets the scene and determines the scope of action, in the dream as in waking reality, where it is taken to be fate. Since the will works from a region beyond the individual's waking consciousness, conflicts occur with the goals set by the individual for herself. The individual may fight doggedly to achieve something but stands no chance against what appears to be destiny. Thus, fate appears to be determined by the will as "our guiding genius ... which comprehends far more than the individual consciousness and therefore, in unrelenting opposition to it, as a coercion from the outside, poses and fixes that which it did not leave to the individual consciousness to find out and did not want to be missed" (PP1, 219f).

While Schopenhauer, in this speculative essay, ascribes to the will an overarching view of the fate of the individual, he does not in the least wish to ascribe providence to the will, at least not one of universal proportions. (Eduard von Hartmann diverges from Schopenhauer on this point.) In his essay, the will is merely responsive to the transitoriness and finiteness of all individuality and ensures that the great truth of impermanence is comprehended by the individual. The specific conditions and events of what appears as fateful guidance ought therefore not to be overvalued: "If we remain with the individual cases, it often seems, that they are concerned with our temporary, momentary wellbeing. But this can, due to its insignificance, imperfection, futility and impermanence not seriously be its final goal: thus we have to search for it in our eternal existence which reaches beyond the individual life" (PP1, 233). For Schopenhauer this means the denial of the will, as it is the intention of the "eternal existence, which goes beyond the individual life" to promote inner renunciation in view of death. Appearing as so-called fate, the will ensures that the individual grasps the denial of the will, which is accomplished mainly by repeated encounters with suffering: "Since happiness and enjoyment work against this purpose, we see in accordance with it misery and suffering woven into every life story to fulfil this purpose, even though to very different degrees" (PP1, 223). From the pedagogical vantage point of the will, death is the eventual reality which lurks behind every experience: "Thus that invisible guidance, reflected only occasionally in twilight, guides us to death, this innermost result and insofar purpose of life" (PP1, 223). Death is not only the purpose of life, but also a participant in life, through the agency of the will, which ensures that the individual has the opportunity to develop the necessary distance to suffering and happiness.[8]

It needs to be remembered that the "Transcendent Speculation" is an application of Schopenhauer's philosophy situated outside of his defensible philosophical system. Its teleology, as Schopenhauer noted, is an apparition, the result of the human need to be part of a meaningful sequence of events, yet the basic fact that life has an intimate relationship to death is of no trivial consequence to the individual.

Two concepts expressed by Schopenhauer in the "Speculation"—namely the notion of an inner teleology inherent in life and the role of death as the basis of life—were developed further in the philosophical systems of Eduard von Hartmann and Philipp Mainländer. Their contributions to the formation of the unconscious and to metapsychological theory is discussed in the next two sections, before we turn to Sigmund Freud who, in 1920, established the death drive to explain why numerous phenomena in psychological life contradict the pleasure principle.

28.1 Eduard von Hartmann

Eduard von Hartmann's main work *The Philosophy of the Unconscious*[9] was a bestseller in Imperial Germany. It contains a mixture of nature study and speculative metaphysics, blended with politically conservative notions of culture and hierarchy. Von Hartmann supported, for example, the widespread view at the time—also held by Schopenhauer—of an evolutionary progress which was not only gradual, but could occasionally progress by sudden leaps. He further proposed that these leaps resulted from the guidance by an unconscious idea toward a higher stage of development. Von Hartmann participated in most, if not all, the debates of his day and developed an extensive body of work over several decades.[10] Written in an accessible style, it demonstrates his impressive capacity for synthesizing philosophical systems, but also for repetition in variations on similar themes. Indeed, von Hartmann even penned a sensible and not entirely self-serving critique of his own theses and published it anonymously in order to gain headway over his critics by directing the debate![11]

Even though his relevance faded with the German Empire, von Hartmann is important for introducing the term "unconscious" to a wider reading public. If Schopenhauer rarely used the term "unconscious" von Hartmann made it his trademark. This implied a reworking of Schopenhauer's will. Von Hartmann's will is not a singular entity; it is split up into many specialized wills.[12] Moreover, von Hartmann introduces the unconscious "idea" to complement the unconscious "will."

> Schopenhauer acknowledges as metaphysical principle only the Will, whilst Idea is, according to him, cerebral in a materialistic sense. . . . The Will, the sole metaphysical principle of Schopenhauer is therefore, of course, an unconscious Will. Thought, on the other hand, which with him is only the phenomenon of a metaphysical principle, and therefore, as thought, not itself metaphysical, can, even where it is unconscious, never be comparable to the unconscious Idea of Schelling, which I myself place by the side of unconscious Will, as metaphysical principle of equal value.[13]

Together they form von Hartmann's unconscious. Incorporating the notion of an unconscious idea enables von Hartmann to posit the teleological nature of the unconscious. While Schelling and Hegel form obvious points of reference for von Hartmann, the similarities between the "Transcendent Speculation" and *The Philosophy of the Unconscious* are striking. Nevertheless, von Hartmann diverges from Schopenhauer's general thesis that the will is blind.

> An opening for the true, absolutely unconscious idea is certainly offered by the system of Schopenhauer, but only at the point where it becomes untrue to itself and self-contradictory, when the Idea, which is originally only another kind of immediate experience of the cerebral intellect, becomes a metaphysical entity preceding and conditioning the real individuation.[14]

Schopenhauer is criticized for remaining true to his claim to immanence and for not making more of Plato's Ideas, a principle from the history of philosophy that Schopenhauer uses merely as a didactic device to describe the diversification arising from the unity of the one will. Von Hartmann assumes that Schopenhauer was not aware of this inconsistency.

> But in this he fails to altogether perceive that the unconscious Will *eo ipso* presupposes an unconscious idea as goal, content, or object of itself, without which it

would be empty, indefinite, and objectless. Accordingly, in the acute and instructive observations on instinct, sexual love, life of the species, etc., the unconscious Will acts precisely as if it were bound up with unconscious idea, without Schopenhauer knowing or admitting it.[15]

We can see here the notion of teleology—which for von Hartmann leads to a higher stage of development, not only in terms of physical complexity, but eventually also of hierarchy in a social Darwinist sense—projected onto the world, whereas Schopenhauer saw the Platonic Ideas as projections rather than formative principles. Schopenhauer reinterprets Platonic Ideas in the sense that the artist does not recognize a Platonic Idea, but creates it, he or she constructs an a priori: "…the poet on the other hand is like the mathematician, who constructs these relations *a priori* in pure intuition" (WWR1, 273). The key phrase "constructed *a priori*" nullifies or at least substantially devalues the concept of a priori. Obviously Schopenhauer intentionally refused to emphasize teleology despite his predilection for metaphysical inferences; it could be said that von Hartmann, in contrast, did not know when to stop.

The difference between von Hartmann and Schopenhauer can also be exemplified with respect to their views on evolution. Schopenhauer, based on the findings of his time, assumed that evolution had concluded and that it had consisted not only of gradual incremental change, but also of developmental leaps. He also had a clear idea of the likely path of development, as is evident from a passage in the manuscript remains: "That from inorganic matter the lowest plants, from the spoiling remains of these the lowest animals, and from these in turn, and step by step, the higher animals have emerged, is the only possible thought" (HN4, 32).

We must also bear in mind that Schopenhauer had not been able to read Darwin's *Origin of Species* before his death. Originally published in 1859, it sold out immediately and Schopenhauer was unable to obtain a copy. But throughout his life Schopenhauer had followed the progress of the natural sciences with great interest, and his ambivalence on this topic is representative of the state of knowledge of his time. Von Hartmann, on the other hand, pits his teleological views against Darwin because he decidedly favors the idea of leaps in development. Leaps of development are a suitable complement to the teleological force of von Hartmann's unconscious as the universal principle inherent in nature, endowed not only with the blind expansive driving thrust of the will but guided by the unconscious idea. In numerous variations on a non-theistic theory of intelligent design, von Hartmann uses expressions like "systematic harmony," the "grand unity of the purposeful context,"[16] of which as "carrier or subject a formative metaphysical drive must be assumed,"[17] the goal of which is "an entirely different kind of perfection than that resulting from mere adaptation."[18] Schopenhauer had identified teleology in the "Transcendent Speculation" as the outcome of human neediness, whereas finality for von Hartmann determines causality.[19] He goes as far as stating: "Whoever wants to maintain that the causal mechanism is in accordance with natural law and necessity, but still disputes teleology, does neither understand themselves nor the meaning of the terms."[20] Here we note the rhetorical flavor of von Hartmann's tendentious exposition; the inversion of causality to mean finality is proof to him, and, in many similar instances, he effortlessly moves between philosophical synthesis, autodidactic nature study, and rhetoric. Of those, nature study, or, more precisely, empirical philosophy of nature developed through metaphysical interpretation, constitutes von Hartmann's enduring legacy.

While von Hartmann's main thesis can well be taken as an extrapolation of the teleological aspect of Schopenhauer's "Transcendent Speculation," he himself was reserved about Schopenhauer as predecessor: "But I am an opponent of Schopenhauer's . . . abstract monism in metaphysics, . . . his unhistorical world view, his wavering and contradicting standpoints on teleology."[21] Despite these qualifications, it has become clear that von Hartmann popularized a particular take on Schopenhauer's will, albeit with new terminology and distinct emphases in his theoretical formations. Nevertheless, many passages in *The Philosophy of the Unconscious* read like excerpts from Schopenhauer's later works, where he referred to the findings of natural science to illustrate the will. Von Hartmann seems to paraphrase Schopenhauer's ideas and to replace the term "will" with the term "unconscious," whether it is in a section entitled "The Unconscious in Instinct" or the "The Unconscious in Mysticism," in an assertion of the unconscious against the psychologists of the time[22] or in the appendix on "The Phenomenology of the Unconscious." But von Hartmann has an ambivalent role in the history of the unconscious because he also elevates teleology to a determining principle—for example, in the chapter, "The Unconscious in History."[23] Still, his interpretative methods were of foremost significance for the next generation of thinkers, including Nietzsche and Freud. In von Hartmann's work, they saw how—through shifts in terminology, the sharpening of minor differences, repeated and slight changes of perspective on a problem until it fit the author's thesis, and, in general, the recasting of multiple systems into idiosyncratic forms—a substantial body of philosophical thought could be contrived and then promoted as original insight. However, at the same time, in the face of an emerging scientific paradigm and von Hartmann's insistence on metaphysical speculation to give coherence to the empirical realm, he increasingly became synonymous with straining the credibility of his theses.

In this context Friedrich Nietzsche ought to be mentioned as one of von Hartmann's competitors. Just like von Hartmann, Nietzsche developed his philosophy in opposition to Schopenhauer's overshadowing influence, but it lacks relevance in terms of the history of the unconscious. Friedrich Nietzsche may have been a cultural critic and an advocate of the shaping of one's life rather than being dominated by an ominous unconscious, but he rejects the concept of an intelligent unconscious in order to be able to emphasize the importance of conditioning.

Noteworthy in the present context is Nietzsche's adaptation of Schopenhauer's "Transcendent Speculation" in a remarkable passage from the *Manuscript Remains* with the title, "Concerning the Origin of our Valuations,"[24] in which he reproduces the main ideas of the "Speculation." The entry ends with suggestive mutterings: "In short, granting that a certain conformity of means to end might be demonstrated in the action of nature, without the assumption of a ruling ego: could not *our* notion of purposes, and our will, etc., be only a *symbolic language* standing for something quite different—that is to say, something not-willing and unconscious?" Whether this "something not-willing and unconscious" refers to von Hartmann's unconscious idea recast as Nietzsche's concept of the *Übermensch* is anyone's guess, but this manuscript entry shows that Nietzsche generated his own variation of Schopenhauerian themes, just as von Hartmann, Mainländer, and Freud had or would. Still, Nietzsche had a limited influence on metapsychological theory—and systematic, historical readings of Nietzsche's works identify a more political thrust to his philosophy (e.g., in his rejection of the values of the French Revolution and his radical affirmation of hierarchy).[25] It is interesting to note, however, that Nietzsche's philosophical reception has been dominated by historically decontextualized readings, whereas von Hartmann is invariably read as the superseded philosopher of late Imperial Germany that he was.

As far as the history of the unconscious is concerned, more recent scholarship highlights the role of Philipp Mainländer, a contemporary of von Hartmann and Nietzsche, whose defining contribution to the structure of the unconscious forms the subject of the next section.

28.2 Philipp Mainländer

Philipp Mainländer's philosophy emphasizes death as the goal of the world and its inhabitants. This central idea had a distinctive influence on the formation of the idea of the death drive, which features in Freud's *Beyond the Pleasure Principle*, published in 1920, after Sabina Spielrein and C. G. Jung had introduced the idea into the canon of psychoanalytical theorems in 1911 and 1912. Unlike von Hartmann, Mainländer did not feel the need to distance himself from Schopenhauer. While he was ready to correct him, as is evident from the appendix, "Critique of the Teachings of Kant and Schopenhauer," to his main work *Philosophy of Salvation* (1876),[26] he also acknowledged his debt to Schopenhauer: "I therefore freely admit that I stand on the shoulders of Kant and Schopenhauer, and that my own philosophy is merely a continuation of each of theirs."[27] Mainländer refutes von Hartmann's addition of unconscious idea to unconscious will.

> Furthermore, my main attack will furthermore be directed against an alteration which Mister von Hartmann has made to Schopenhauer's brilliant system, whereby its foundation has been destroyed. Schopenhauer states quite correctly: "The essential feature of my doctrine, which sets it in opposition to everything prior, is the complete separation of the will from cognition, both of which the philosophers before me considered to be inseparable, or the will to depend on or to be a mere function of the cognition, which was seen as the essence of our intelligent being" (Will in Nature, 19). Now, Mister von Hartmann had nothing more urgent to do than to destroy this magnificent, significant distinction, which had cleared an obstacle from the path of genuine philosophy, and to turn the will into a psychological principle once again. Why? Because Mister von Hartmann is a romantic philosopher. —The only captivating feature of Mister von Hartmann's philosophy is the unconscious. But has he comprehended it more profoundly than Schopenhauer? In no way.[28]

Philipp Mainländer developed his highly original philosophy around what he held to be the reason for the dissipation of the one will into many individual wills: the achievement of annihilation, the ultimate goal of the universe. This proposition may at first glance appear simplistic and unexciting, but Mainländer's original worldview effectively constitutes an application of the concept of entropy, referring to principles that resemble the laws of thermodynamics. Everything in the world, including the individual, aspires to the stasis of non-being and conflict exists only to further this common goal of annihilation through the weakness that results from various struggles. Mainländer elaborates in some detail how this principle dominates all forms of existence. Here we limit ourselves to some of his observations on the differences between plant, animal, and human life.

Mainländer argues that the cyclical life of plants shows the will to life alongside the will to death. Plants strive for absolute death, but cannot obtain it—hence life is the necessary means to death. In the depths of its being, every animal craves annihilation, yet consciously it fears death: its mind is the condition for perceiving a threat to its life. If such a threat is present, but not perceived, the animal stays calm and does not fear death. Mainländer concludes: "Thus, whereas in the plant the will to life stands alongside the will to death, in the animal the will to life stands before the will to death and veils it completely: the means has stepped in before the end. On the surface, therefore, the animal wants life only, it is pure will to life, and it fears death, although, in the depths of its being, death is all it wants."[29] In human beings, the will to death is even more obscured: "In man … the will to death, the drive of his innermost being, is not simply concealed by the will to life, as it is in the animal; rather, it disappears completely in the depths, where it expresses itself, from time to time, only as a deep longing for rest. The will completely loses sight and sense of its end and clings merely to the means."[30]

Thus Mainländer unifies the teleological and thanatological aspects of the "Transcendent Speculation"—that is, of death as purpose and determining principle of individual fate (via the will)—in the will to death. He takes this point still further by postulating this inevitable and final result as liberation from suffering and salvation: "At the core of the entire universe the immanent philosopher sees only the deepest longing for absolute annihilation. For him it is as if he heard, resounding through all the heavenly spheres, the unmistakable cry of: 'Salvation! Salvation! Death to our life!' and the comforting answer: 'You shall all find annihilation and be redeemed.'"[31] In order to turn the will to death into a key to salvation, Mainländer draws on the Buddhist nirvana, which he had encountered in Schopenhauer's main work. Importantly, Schopenhauer interpreted it as a relative nothingness, based on a definition he had read in a chapter on Buddhism by Francis Buchanan in the *Asiatick Researches,* published in 1799. It contains the translation of a discourse from the Burmese. The *sayadaw* (senior Buddhist monk), instructing the king, answers the question about the nature of "*Nieban*" as follows:

A. "When a person is no longer subject to any of the following miseries, namely, to weight [of the body; i.e., birth], old age, disease and death, then he is said to have obtained *Nieban*. No thing, no place, can give us an adequate idea of *Nieban*: we can only say, that to be free from the four abovementioned miseries, and to obtain salvation, is *Nieban*. In the same manner, as when any person labouring under a severe disease, recovers by the assistance of medicine, we say he has obtained health: but if any person wishes to know the manner, or cause of his thus obtaining health, it can only be answered, that to be restored to health signifies no more than to be recovered from disease. In the same manner only can we speak of *Nieban*, and after this manner GODAMA taught."[32]

"*Nieban*" is a negative term only in the sense that "health" is a negative term, denoting the absence of disease. It signifies the absence of birth, old age, disease, and death. In a similar vein, Schopenhauer declares being, as generally understood, to be worthless and nothingness to be in fact the true being: "What is generally accepted as positive, which we call *what is* and whose negation has its most general meaning in the concept we express as *nothing*. . . . If the opposite point of view were possible for us, it would involve reversing the signs and showing that what is being for us is nothing, and what is nothing for us is being. But as long as we are ourselves the will to life, we can only recognize and indicate the last thing negatively" (WWR1, 437). Mainländer takes this one step further and discards relative nothingness in favor of absolute nothingness, thus—in his terms— purifying Schopenhauer's philosophy of baseless points of reference[33] and the Buddha's teaching of the falsifications introduced by hair-splitting disciples.[34] Mainländer's commitment to a philosophy of immanence (i.e., of verifiable empiricism) becomes clear in his description of nirvana in the appendix to his main work, where he establishes his definition, in contrast to Schopenhauer's:.

> *Nirvana* is indeed non-being, absolute annihilation, even though the successors of the Buddha tried hard to establish it as something real in contrast to the world, *sangsara*, and to teach a life in it, the life of the *rahats* [arhants] and Buddhas. *Nirvana* is not supposed to be a place, and yet the blessed are meant to live there; in the death of the liberated ones [i.e., the arhants] every principle of life is supposedly destroyed and yet the *rahats* are supposed to live. . . . The kingdom of heaven after death is, like *nirvana*, non-being; for if one skips over this world and the life in it and speaks of a world which is not this world, and of a life which is not this life—where, then, is there a point of reference?[35]

According to Mainländer, there is no experience of nirvana before death as this would constitute an experience of nothingness in the fullness of life. Yet when he describes salvation through absolute nothingness, he refers to qualities similar to those by which Schopenhauer had described relative nothingness: ". . . beyond the world there is neither a place of peace, nor one of torment, there is only nothingness. Whoever enters this nothingness has neither rest nor movement; as in sleep, he is in no state, but with the important difference that even that does not exist which in sleep is no state: the will is completely annihilated."[36] Elsewhere he describes nothingness as "the happiness of sleep, which in contrast to the waking state, is stateless and felt through reflection. Transposed into eternity, it is absolute death."[37] Mainländer's radical secularization of the notion of nirvana employs deep sleep as an analogy for nothingness, corrective of metaphysical speculation, and transcendent mysteries. Mainländer takes the implication of the "Transcendent Speculation" seriously and works his way back from the speculation to the real world of experience where non-being and death are synonymous. In a parallel development, he secularizes the nirvana and merges it with death. Unfortunately, Schopenhauer had not made explicit the important role of sensations with respect to the nirvana. While he understood them as the basis of the experience of the will for the individual, he did not highlight, or was not aware of, the cessation of sensations resulting from sustained insight into their impermanence as being synonymous with nirvana.[38] Nevertheless, the profound comprehension of the pull toward equilibrium meant that, for Mainländer, the Schopenhauerian triad of will-body-sensation was not just an endless affirmation of the thirst for life, but one with the ultimate goal of complete annihilation. Regarding the individual, this idea is present in Schopenhauer's "Transcendent Speculation on the Apparent Deliberateness in the Fate of the Individual" (and in "On the Wisdom of Life"), but in Mainländer's philosophy it encompasses the entire universe, as the one law of nature. In contrast to the social Darwinism of von Hartmann and Nietzsche, he combined it with a philanthropic outlook, an ethics of solidarity with all living beings based on the inherent unity of suffering.[39]

To date, Mainländer's most prominent influence on posterity lies not in the cosmological proof of entropy, but in the psychological aspect of the will to death. In Mainländer's understanding, the unconscious of the individual is the result of the rift in the will between a lively facade and a death-seeking core. The conscious mind, being enamored of life and the world of experience, exclusively identifies with the will to life. It disowns and represses the will to death so that the will to death is relegated to the unconscious in the psyche of the individual. As Thorsten Lerchner's detailed study shows, this idea was taken up by Sabina Spielrein, who pioneered the transposition of Mainländer's will to death into depth psychology.[40] In 1911, Spielrein presented a paper to the Viennese Psychoanalytical Society, "Destruction as the Cause of Becoming," on the conflict between dissipation and dissolution on the one hand and stability and continuity on the other, both in the psychic life of the individual and the life cycle of the species. She relates it to a basic principle she calls the death instinct and describes it as the actual driver of psychic life. She had come across Mainländer in Elias Metchnikoff's *Studies on the Nature of Man*,[41] where he reviews him as the most consistent of pessimist philosophers. Spielrein's great contribution to psychoanalytic theory, evident in her publications, her notebooks, and her correspondence, lies in questioning the premise of a pleasure-seeking unconscious, full of zest for life, and complementing it with a detailed exposition of the death drive. As their correspondence shows, Spielrein discussed this new perspective with C. G. Jung, who promptly included it in his *Psychology of the Unconscious* in 1912: "The phantasy of the world conflagration, of the cataclysmic end of the world in general, is nothing but a mythological projection of a personal individual will to death."[42] Jung perceives the "individual will for death," however, not as a universal principle, but as a means for interpreting psychotic phantasies.[43] Eight years later Freud takes up the topic in *Beyond the Pleasure Principle*, but he does not seem to have read Mainländer. Instead, he refers to Schopenhauer's "Transcendent Speculation," as will be discussed in the next section.

28.3 SIGMUND FREUD

Schopenhauer interpreted nirvana as relative nothingness, but Mainländer's philosophy culminates in absolute nothingness, even though both appeal to the Buddha's teaching for verification. Freud also uses the term "Nirvana-principle," quoting his student Barbara Low,[44] who coined it to refer to infantile regression (i.e., the desire to return to a prenatal stage in which all needs are met). Freud took up the term, but interpreted it differently. For Freud, it signifies the effect the death drive has on the life force, and in his revision of the ideas expressed in *Beyond the Pleasure Principle* he reaffirms the dominance of the pleasure principle by concluding that the nirvana-principle constitutes a strand of the death drive which had been co-opted by the life forces and thus separated from the death drive.[45]

In *Beyond the Pleasure Principle,* however, Freud explains that the therapeutic practice provided overwhelming evidence against the assumption that the pleasure principle was the only factor in the psyche. Non-neurotic suffering—for example, in traumatized soldiers and the suffering due to fateful events—ran counter to such an assumption. He also observed a compulsion to repeat, or revisit, the traumatic experience, even when it contained no pleasure. Here he stipulated the search for equilibrium as its motive since the return to an equilibrium coincides with the goal of the pleasure principle, which also seeks to reduce stimulus tension through gratification. Freud then draws parallels to the dynamic tension which exists between the organic and the inorganic: "If we may assume as an experience admitting of no exception that everything living dies from causes within itself, and returns to the inorganic, we can only say, '*The goal of all life is death,*' and, casting back, '*The inanimate was there before the animate.*' "[46] Freud introduces the term, "death drive," for this inner dynamic, and he does so with a reference to Schopenhauer: "…thus, without realizing it, we sailed into the harbour of Schopenhauer's philosophy, for whom death is the 'result' and thus the purpose of life and the sexual urge the embodiment of the will to live."[47] Quoting Schopenhauer in this context is less an acknowledgment of intellectual debt to the "Transcendent Speculation" than a convenient means for sidelining Mainländer, Spielrein, and Jung—namely, by going to the source. Nevertheless, a greater degree of difference from Schopenhauer and Mainländer was needed. This is apparent from the intellectual framework Freud establishes: after substantiating the metaphysical idea of an unconscious pull toward death as a powerful principle for life with numerous references to the life sciences of his time (although Freud modified his initial stance later to affirm the supremacy of the pleasure principle as the "guardian of life"), he proceeds to refute the notions of liberation from attachment through insight (Schopenhauer) and of outright salvation through absolute nothingness (Mainländer). Hence Freud's rejection of the idea of perfection, both for individuals and humanity as a whole.

Many of us will also find it hard to abandon our belief that in man himself there dwells an impulse toward perfection, which has brought him to his present heights of intellectual prowess and ethical sublimation, and from which it might be expected that his development into superman will be ensured. But I do not believe in the existence of such an inner impulse, and I see no way of preserving this pleasing illusion. The development of man up to now does not seem to me to need any explanation differing from that of animal development, and the restless striving toward further perfection which may be observed in a minority of human beings is easily explicable as the result of that repression of instinct upon which what is most valuable in human culture is built. The repressed instinct never ceases to strive after its complete satisfaction which would consist in the repetition of a primary experience of satisfaction: all substitution- or reaction-formations and sublimations avail nothing toward relaxing the continual tension; and out of the excess of the satisfaction demanded over that found is born the driving momentum which allows of no abiding in any situation presented to it, but in the poet's words 'urges ever forward, ever unsubdued' (Mephisto in 'Faust', Act I. Faust's study). The path in the other direction, back to complete satisfaction, is as a rule barred by the resistances that maintain the repressions, and thus there remains nothing for it but to proceed in the other, still unobstructed direction, that of development, without, however, any prospect of being able to bring the process to a conclusion or to attain the goal.[48]

In short, Freud states that the goal of nirvana cannot be reached (even though the term persists as an echo of Mainländer's reductive notion of nirvana as absolute nothingness). Similarly, we find the dynamic Mainländer refers to in the statement just quoted; namely, that "the will completely loses sight and sense of its end and clings merely to the means"[49] contained in Freud's observation that "…out of the excess of the satisfaction demanded over that found is born the driving momentum which allows of no abiding in any situation presented to it." Even though Freud does not relate this reflection to the death drive, his essay points toward death as the final point of rest, of equilibrium, and, we may add, of ultimate satisfaction. However, Freud's observation about dissatisfaction as the generator of the driving momentum of life casts light on a passage by Schopenhauer, who writes of the "cheap trick" which brings forth life from death and of death as the repository of life. Schopenhauer wrote about Orcus (the Latin name for Thanatos, the Greek god of death) in the last paragraph of "On the Wisdom of Life":

> Here I cannot take into account *Neptune* (unfortunately so dubbed through thoughtlessness) because I may not call it by its true name which is *Eros*. Otherwise I would show how beginning and end are connected together, namely how Eros is secretly related to death. By virtue of this relation, Orcus…is not only the taker but also the giver, and death the great reservoir of life. Therefore everything comes from Orcus and everything that now has life has already been there—if only we were able to comprehend the cheap trick, by which this happens; then everything would be clear.
> (PP1, 497)

Freud's duality of Eros (used as a synonym for the pleasure principle in *Beyond the Pleasure Principle*) and death drives bears distinct similarities to Schopenhauer's Orcus as the older and greater power in relation to Eros. Here, as elsewhere, Schopenhauer breaks off—in the interest of his claim to be taking an immanent, empirically verifiable approach. But his expression of "death the great reservoir of life" prefigures Freud's statement: "The pleasure-principle seems directly to subserve the death-instincts."[50] Nevertheless, Freud offers us a valuable clue to understanding the "cheap trick" when he emphasizes the dynamic aspects, the friction between death drive and pleasure principle that arises from the discrepancy between the levels of satisfaction demanded and attained, as just quoted.

We note, therefore, that the transformation of Schopenhauer's will into the concept of the unconscious after von Hartmann does not only pertain to the will as the pleasure-seeking Id. It has a complement in the will to death, which originates in equal parts from the "Transcendent Speculation" and from Schopenhauer's interpretation of nirvana as relative nothingness. Mainländer, adamant about basing his philosophy on verifiable human experience, stripped Schopenhauer's relative nothingness of uncommon, difficult aspects while maintaining its transformative force. The latter was in turn renounced by Spielrein, Jung, and Freud in order for it to be compatible with psychoanalytic theory. In a nutshell, Mainländer renounces Schopenhauer's relative nothingness as a preposterous piece of transcendence while Freud rejects the idea of perfection as a form of infantile regression.

In conclusion, it should also be remembered that bodily sensations, which were highly significant for Schopenhauer as the immediate manifestations of the will in the human body, do not feature prominently in this process of transforming the will into the unconscious. The unconscious is associated with dreams, slips of the tongue, body language, unconscious choices, strong or nagging unpleasant feelings, etc., but not explicitly with sensations. Moreover, the unconscious, whether viewed as a mass phenomenon or a highly individualized one, is often referred to in terms of mental content. This is a problematic development because the idea or mental representation successfully obscures the will (i.e., bodily sensation) just as the will to life obscures the death drive. Only if sensations were understood as the basis of life experience could the riddle which the Buddhist nirvana poses be solved without reductionism.

Notes

1. Theodor W. Adorno and Max Horkheimer, *Dialectic of Enlightenment,* translated by Edmund Jephcott (Stanford: Stanford University Press, 2002), 19.
2. The following German language studies are particularly relevant: Becker 1971, Wegner 1991, Zentner 1995, Gödde 1999, Atzert 2005, and, in English, Atzert 2012 (see Further Readings list at the end of this chapter).
3. Arthur Schopenhauer, *Schopenhauers Sämtliche Werke,* edited by Paul Deussen (München: Piper Verlag, 1911). Paul Deussen (1848–1919), Indologist and Professor for Comparative Religion in Kiel, was introduced to Schopenhauer by Friedrich Nietzsche, whom he had met in boarding school. A tireless promoter of Schopenhauer's philosophy—albeit in his own interpretation—he founded the Schopenhauer Society in 1912.
4. Schopenhauer's concept of the will in those terms can be traced back to the first edition of his doctoral thesis, *The Fourfold Root of the Principle of Sufficient Reason,* but the scope of

the will gradually came to include all sensations, whether strong or subtle, during the fourth decade of the nineteenth century. On the psychological concept of will, see Stephan Atzert, "Leib und Willensbegründung bei Schopenhauer," in *Philosophie des Leibes,* edited by Matthias Koßler and Michael Jeske (Würzburg: Königshausen & Neumann, 2012), 59–68. This essay has been incorporated into the present chapter.

5. Bernd Dörflinger, "Schopenhauers Philosophie des Leibes," in *Schopenhauer Jahrbuch* 83 (2002), 43–86, 53. My translation.

6. This is by no means a novel experience for one of Schopenhauer's works. The essay itself was originally published in *Parerga and Paralipomena,* a collection of essays with which Schopenhauer achieved fame in the 1850s, thanks mostly to its final chapter "On the Wisdom of Life," since rediscovered and repackaged as an ever-popular self-help guide.

7. Schopenhauer's "Transcendent Speculation on the Apparent Deliberateness in the Fate of the Individual" was translated by E. F. J. Payne, but most passages here are new translations from the German by Christian Romuss (Brisbane). They are based on *Arthur Schopenhauers Werke in Fünf Bänden,* edited by Ludger Lütkehaus (Frankfurt: Zweitausendeins, 2006).

8. Philipp Mainländer expands this idea into the will to death.

9. Due to inconsistencies between German and English editions, all quotations are my translations from the tenth German edition (in three volumes) of von Hartmann's *Philosophie des Unbewußten* (Leipzig: Verlag von Wilhelm Friedrich, 1889), with the exception of quotations from the first volume where I modified William Coupland's 1884 translation published in London by Trübner & Co. This edition is hereafter abbreviated as PU.

10. For a detailed introduction to von Hartmann and his times, see Frederick Beiser's *Weltschmerz: Pessimism in German Philosophy, 1860–1900* (Oxford University Press 2016), 122–200. For a discussion of von Hartmann's philosophical syncretism in relation to Schopenhauer, see Jean-Claude Wolf's essay, "Eduard von Hartmann als Schopenhauerianer?" in *Schopenhauer und die Schopenhauer-Schule,* edited by Fabio Ciraci, Domenico M. Fazio, and Matthias Koßler (Königshausen und Neumann 2009), 189–229.

11. "Das Unbewusste vom Standpunkt der Physiologie und Descendenztheorie" (PU III, 3–93).

12. PU I, 59. What may seem like a shift in emphasis was the result of the establishment of cell biology and the notion of cells as carriers of life. As a result, von Hartmann, Nietzsche, and Mainländer assume a multitude of wills.

13. PU I, 24.

14. Ibid., 29.

15. Ibid., 25.

16. PU III, 417.

17. Ibid., 418.

18. Ibid., 445.

19. Ibid., 461.

20. Ibid., 470.

21. PU I, Preface, 9.

22. Ibid., 280.

23. Ibid., 327.

24. Friedrich Nietzsche, *Nachgelassene Fragemente,* Band 10, Winter 1883–1884, in *Kritische Studienausgabe,* edited by Giorgio Colli and Mazzino Montinari (Munich/New York: de Gruyter, 1980), 653. Translated by Christian Romuss.

25. Domenico Losurdo, *Nietzsche, der aristokratische Rebell* (Berlin: Argument Verlag/InkriT, 2009).
26. Philipp Mainländer, *Philosophie der Erlösung*, Bd. 1 (1876) und Bd. 2 (1886), abbreviated here as PE. Translated by Christian Romuss (Brisbane), who, at the time of publication of this chapter, is preparing a complete translation of both volumes of *The Philosophy of Salvation*. Note that for Mainländer, salvation does not carry Christian connotations; it refers to release from suffering.
27. PE I, 362.
28. PE II, 537.
29. PE I, 333.
30. Ibid., 334.
31. Ibid., 358.
32. Francis Buchanan, "On the Religion and Literature of the Burmas," *Asiatick Researches* 6 (1799), 266. On the origin of this essay and its reception by Schopenhauer, see Stephan Atzert, "Schopenhauer und seine Quellen: Zum Buddhismusbild in den frühen *Asiatick Researches*," in *Schopenhauer Jahrbuch* 88 (2007), 15–27.
33. PE I, 619.
34. PE II, 107. Mainländer's views are not unusual. Compare Welbon on Caroline A. F. Rhys Davids: "For our purposes I shall single out her principal hypothesis: the Pali Canon, insofar as it presents a coherent system, presents a monk-dominated, institutional Buddhism which is discrepant and degenerate from the original message of Sakayamuni" (Guy Welbon, *The Buddhist Nirvana and Its Western Interpreters*. Chicago: University of Chicago Press, 1968, 241). It is likely that Mainländer, when reading the translations of the Rev. Robert Spence Hardy, applied the principles of the historical-critical approach which the Tübingen school had developed for the Bible.
35. PE I, 619.
36. Ibid., 350.
37. Ibid., 216.
38. For a discussion on the role of sensations in the teachings of the Buddha, see S. Salkin, *A Survey of the Use of the Term Vedanā ("Sensations") in the Pāli Nikāyas* (M.Phil. Dissertation, University of Sydney, 2005). There we read about the liberated meditator: "If he feels a pleasant vedanā, he understands: 'It is impermanent; there is no holding to it; there is no delight in it.' If he feels a painful vedanā, he understands: 'It is impermanent; there is no holding to it; there is no delight in it.' If he feels a neither-painful-nor-pleasant vedanā, he understands: 'It is impermanent; there is no holding to it; there is no delight in it.' If he feels a pleasant vedanā, he feels it detached. If he feels a painful vedanā, he feels it detached. If he feels a neither-painful-nor-pleasant vedanā, he feels it detached" (MN III, 244, in Salkin, 26). And futher: "[He] understands vedanā, and the arising of vedanā, and where they cease, and the path leading to (their) destruction" (SN IV 204, in Salkin, 33). Thus the puzzling riddle, which the nirvana posed to generations of scholars, cannot be resolved by Mainländer's reductionism.
    For a comparison of the role of sensations in Schopenhauer and the teachings of the Buddha, see Stephan Atzert, "Zur Rolle der Körperempfindungen für Schopenhauers Willensbegriff und in den Lehrreden des Buddha (gemäß der Textüberlieferung des Theravada-Buddhimus)," in *Schopenhauer und die Philosophie Indiens*, edited by Matthias Koßler (Wiesbaden: Harassowitz, 2007), 24–38.
39. For an overview of Mainländer's philosophy, see Beiser, 201–28.

40. Thorsten Lerchner, *Mainländer-Reflexionen. Quellen. Kontext. Wirkung* (Würzburg: Königshausen & Neumann, 2016), 87.

41. Elias Metschnikoff, *Studien über die Natur des Menschen* (Leipzig: Veit & Comp, 1904), 248f.

42. C. G. Jung (1912), *Psychology of the Unconscious: A Study of the Transformations and Symbolisms of the Libido, a Contribution to the History of the Evolution of Thought*, translated by B. M. Hinkle (New York: Moffat, Yard, 1916), 481. As Lerchner explains, Jung mentions his intellectual debt to Sabina Spielrein regarding the death drive from the fourth edition onward (Lerchner, 75) and also stated later that his student Spielrein had developed the idea of the death drive, taken up later by Freud (Lerchner, 88).

43. Lerchner, 101.

44. Barbara Low, *Psycho-Analysis. A Brief Account of the Freudian Theory* (New York: Harcourt, Brace and Howe, 1920) 75.

45. Sigmund Freud, "Das ökonomische Problem des Masochismus" (1924), in Sigmund Freud, *Gesammelte Werke* (Frankfurt a.M.: Fischer Taschenbuch Verlag, 1999, Vol. XIII), 373.

46. Sigmund Freud, *Beyond the Pleasure Principle* (1920), translated by C. J. M. Hubback (Vienna: The International Psycho-Analytical Press, 1922), 47.

47. Ibid., 63. I have discussed this influence in greater detail in "Zwei Aufsätze über Leben und Tod: Sigmund Freuds 'Jenseits des Lustprinzips' und Arthur Schopenhauers 'Transscendente Spekulation über die anscheinende Absichtlichkeit im Schicksal des Einzelnen.'" An English synopsis of the main argument can be found in the second case study in "Schopenhauer and Freud," in *A Companion to Schopenhauer*, edited by Bart Vandenabeele (London: Wiley, 2012), 317–32.

48. Freud, *Beyond the Pleasure Principle*, 52.

49. PE I, 334.

50. Freud, *Beyond the Pleasure Principle*, 83.

FURTHER READING

Adorno, Th. W. and Max Horkheimer. *Dialectic of Enlightenment*, translated by Edmund Jephcott. Stanford, CA: Stanford University Press, 2002.

Atzert, Stephan. "Leib und Willensbegründung bei Schopenhauer." In *Philosophie des Leibes*, edited by Matthias Koßler and Michael Jeske. Würzburg: Königshausen & Neumann, 2012, 59–68.

Atzert, Stephan. "Schopenhauer and Freud." In *A Companion to Schopenhauer*, edited by Bart Vandenabeele. London: Wiley, 2012, 317–32.

Atzert, Stephan. "Text als Imagepflege: Selbstbild, Anlehnung und Differenz bei Sigmund Freud." In *Seminar. Special Issue: Image, Body, Text*, edited by Tim Mehigan, 2007, 508–16.

Atzert, Stephan. "Zur Rolle der Körperempfindungen für Schopenhauers Willensbegriff und in den Lehrreden des Buddha (gemäß der Textüberlieferung des Theravada-Buddhimus)." In *Schopenhauer und die Philosophie Indiens*, edited by Matthias Koßler. Wiesbaden: Harassowitz, 2007, 24–38.

Atzert, Stephan. "Schopenhauer und seine Quellen: Zum Buddhismusbild in den frühen *Asiatick Researches*."*Schopenhauer Jahrbuch* 88 (2007): 15–27.

Atzert, Stephan. "Zwei Aufsätze über Leben und Tod: Sigmund Freuds 'Jenseits des Lustprinzips' und Arthur Schopenhauers 'Transscendente Spekulation über die anscheinende Absichtlichkeit im Schicksal des Einzelnen.'" *Schopenhauer Jahrbuch* 86 (2005): 179–94.

Becker, Aloys. "Arthur Schopenhauer - Sigmund Freud. Historische und charakterologische Grundlagen ihrer gemeinsamen Denkstrukturen." *Schopenhauer Jahrbuch* 52 (1971): 114–56.

Beiser, Frederic. *Weltschmerz. Pessimism in German Philosophy, 1860–1900.* New York: Oxford University Press, 2016.

Buchanan, Francis. "On the Religion and Literature of the Burmas." *Asiatick Researches* 6 (1799): 163–308.

Dörflinger, Bernd. "Schopenhauers Philosophie des Leibes." *Schopenhauer Jahrbuch* 83 (2002): 43–86.

Gödde, Günter. *Traditionslinien des Unbewussten.* Tübingen: Edition Diskord, 1999.

Freud, S. *Beyond the Pleasure Principle* (1920), translated by C. J. M. Hubback. Vienna: The International Psycho-Analytical Press, 1922.

Freud, Sigmund. "Das ökonomische Problem des Masochismus" (1924). In *Gesammelte Werke.* Frankfurt a.M.: Fischer Taschenbuch Verlag, 1999.

Jung, C. G. *Psychology of the Unconscious,* translated by B. M. Hinkle. New York: Moffat, Yard, 1916.

Lerchner, Thorsten. *Mainländer-Reflexionen. Quellen. Kontext. Wirkung.* Würzburg: Königshausen & Neumann, 2016.

Losurdo, Domenico. *Nietzsche, der aristokratische Rebell.* Berlin: Argument Verlag/InkriT, 2009.

Low, Barbara. *Psycho-Analysis. A Brief Account of the Freudian Theory.* New York: Harcourt, Brace and Howe, 1920.

Mainländer, Philipp. *Philosophie der Erlösung,* Bd. 1 (1876) and Bd. 2 (1886), edited by Winfried H. Müller-Seyfarth, in *Mainländer im Kontext* (CD-ROM). Berlin: Karsten Worm, InfoSoftWare, 2011.

Metschnikoff, Elias. *Studien über die Natur des Menschen.* Leipzig, Veit & Comp, 1904.

Nietzsche, Friedrich. *Kritische Studienausgabe,* edited by Giorgio Colli and Mazzino Montinari. Munich and New York: de Gruyter, 1980.

Salkin, Sean. *A Survey of the Use of the Term Vedanā ("Sensations") in the Pāli Nikāyas.* M.Phil. Dissertation, University of Sydney, 2005. http://ses.library.usyd.edu.au/bitstream/2123/2075/1/01front.pdf

Von Hartmann, Eduard. *Philosophie des Unbewußten.* 10. Auflage in drei Bänden. Leipzig: Verlag von Wilhelm Friedrich, 1889.

Von Hartmann, Eduard. *Philosophy of the Unconscious,* translated by William Coupland, London: Trübner & Co., 1884.

Wegner, Peter. "Das Unbewusste in Schopenhauers Metaphysik und Freuds Psychoanalyse." Inaugural Dissertation Fachbereich Humanmedizin (PhD diss.), Johann Wolfgang Goethe-Universität, Frankfurt, 1991.

Welbon, Guy. *The Buddhist Nirvana and Its Western Interpreters.* Chicago: University of Chicago Press, 1968.

Wolf, Jean-Claude. "Eduard von Hartmann als Schopenhauerianer?" In *Schopenhauer und die Schopenhauer-Schule,* edited by Fabio Ciraci, Domenico M. Fazio and Matthias Koßler. Würzburg: Königshausen und Neumann, 2009, 189–229.

Zentner, Marcel. *Die Flucht ins Vergessen.* Darmstadt: DVA, 1995.

CHAPTER 29

....

SCHOPENHAUER'S
INFLUENCE ON WAGNER

....

KEVIN C. KARNES AND
ANDREW J. MITCHELL

"I have now become exclusively preoccupied with a man who—albeit only in literary form—has entered my lonely life like a gift from heaven. It is *Arthur Schopenhauer*, the greatest philosopher since *Kant*."[1] With these words, penned in a letter to the composer Franz Liszt in December 1854, Richard Wagner revealed his newfound philosophical obsession, describing the origins of a discovery that would transform his work and life. Over the next few years, he would recount his ever-deepening engagement with Schopenhauerian theory to nearly everyone with whom he felt close. Thanks to the philosopher, he confided in May 1855 to a friend who had helped him flee Dresden for Salzburg, "I am suddenly permitted an insight into the essence of life itself in all its undivided coherency."[2] By June, he seemed to have adopted Schopenhauer's metaphysics as his own. "It is like this," he wrote to Liszt, and proceeded to expound a theory of *will* with no reference to the philosopher's name; "man (like any other animal) is a will to live."[3] By August 1856, he had taken to reinterpreting his own earlier works—going back to *The Flying Dutchman*, which premiered in 1843, more than a decade before he had read the philosopher—as intuitive reflections on Schopenhauerian principles. The Dutchman's journey, he told a conductor-friend, reflects "the high tragedy of renunciation, the well-motivated, ultimately inevitable and uniquely redeeming denial of the will."[4] Four years later, in a letter to the poet (and his hoped-for lover) Mathilde Wesendonck, Wagner remarked that Schopenhauer "shows me to myself, and at the same time shows me the entire world!"[5]

Anyone with even a passing knowledge of Wagner's work will know his operas (or music dramas, as he called them) composed after reading Schopenhauer bear the mark of the philosopher's thought. Wagner's debt in this respect was vividly memorialized by the painter Wilhelm Beckmann with a scene from inside Wagner's Bayreuth home: the composer stands, facing his piano, a portrait of Schopenhauer hanging overhead (Figure 29.1).[6]

FIGURE 29.1 Richard Wagner in seinem Heim Wahnfried (Richard Wagner in his home, Wahnfried); l. to r.: Cosima and Richard Wagner, Franz Liszt, Hans von Wolzogen. Wood engraving, c. 1890, after a painting, 1880, by Wilhelm Beckmann (1852–1942).

Photo: akg-images.

Far more rarely have we acknowledged that Wagner's engagement with Schopenhauer's work, which was nearly constant between 1854 and his death in 1883, was hardly that of an uncritical follower.

In fact, every one of his music dramas newly conceived after his discovery of Schopenhauer—*Tristan und Isolde, Die Meistersinger von Nürnberg,* and *Parsifal*—reveals the composer to have been a highly original and deeply creative interpreter of the philosopher's theses. In one instance, he even claimed to have made an emendation or "correction" (*Berichtigung*) to a fundamental aspect of Schopenhauerian theory.[7] Although Wagner often disparaged or denied his own credentials as a philosopher, his engagement with Schopenhauer was fundamentally philosophical, touching on topics ranging from love and the erotic to aesthetics, ethics, and redemption or salvation. His letters to friends and his published essays document his philosophical explorations, but his principal vehicles for working out his positions were always his music dramas—their texts or libretti. These he penned himself, as well as their musical scores, where he turned to the medium of sound to convey the ideas that helped him find creative and personal bearings during the most productive years of his life.

29.1 *Tristan und Isolde*

When Wagner outlined his "correction" to Schopenhauer's statements on the metaphysics of sexual love, in a diary entry of December 1858, he was deep into work on the score of *Tristan und Isolde*, the libretto of which he had already completed in September of the previous year.[8] In fact, his idea of composing a music drama on the courtly romance of the twelfth-century writer Gottfried von Strassburg had, since the start, gone hand in hand with his discovery of Schopenhauer, as he revealed in his letter to Liszt cited at the start of this chapter. While in the thick of composing the score for his vaunted tetralogy *Der Ring des Nibelungen*, Wagner experienced a fundamental shift in his thinking upon first reading the philosopher's work. That shift, in turn, left him increasingly uninterested in the project that had occupied him since 1848. He found his imagination wandering from the heroes, gods, and politics of the *Ring* and toward a topic with which Schopenhauer himself was deeply concerned: erotic love. (Wagner's burgeoning affection for Wesendonck doubtlessly contributed to his turn as well.) "I expect that I must still complete the Nibelung pieces," he confided to Liszt, "But since I have never in my life enjoyed the true happiness of love, I intend to erect a further monument to this most beautiful of dreams, a monument in which this love will be properly sated from beginning to end: I have planned in my head a *Tristan* and *Isolde*."[9]

What Wagner sought to "correct" was chapter 44 of volume 2 of *The World as Will and Representation*. There, Schopenhauer argued that romantic or erotic love is merely a drive toward procreation, with the animating goal of sustaining the vitality of the species. "The ultimate aim of all love-affairs," Schopenhauer wrote, "is nothing less than the *composition of the next generation*." What individual men and woman feel for each other—"the pathetic and sublime elements of love-affairs," as he described it, "the transcendent element of their ecstasies and pains"—is in fact no more than an "instinctive delusion." It is the emotional experience of the workings of will within the individual, "the will of the species" blindly seeking its own propagation. "That which makes itself known to the individual consciousness as sexual impulse in general," Schopenhauer wrote, "and without direction to a definite individual of the other sex, is in itself, and apart from the phenomenon, simply the will-to-live" (WWR$_{[P]}$, 534–35; 557). He concluded: "the passion of being in love really turns on what is to be produced" (WWR2$_{[P]}$, 537)—namely, *offspring*, members of the next generation, through whom the species assures its survival into the future.

For a figure as preternaturally obsessed with romantic love and the erotic as Wagner, it is unsurprising that Schopenhauer's words would strike him as fundamentally wrong. Recording in his diary that he had "slowly been reading through friend Schopenhauer's principal work once again" in December 1858, he was inspired to hazard an "expansion and, on some points, even a correction of his system." Namely, Wagner sought "to describe a path to salvation [*Heilsweg*] that no philosopher has recognized (particularly not Schopenhauer): a path to the complete quieting [*Beruhigung*] of the will through love, and not through some abstract love of humankind but through actual love, which springs from the ground of sexual love [*Geschlechtsliebe*], i.e., the affection between man and woman."[10] Some three years earlier, in another letter to Liszt, Wagner glimpsed the possibility of "permanent freedom from…shameful servitude" to the will, open to someone who had somehow attained "a total end to individual consciousness." As models, he looked to Brahma and the Buddha, each of whom had "*transform[ed] himself into the world*…by taking upon himself the immense sufferings of the world."[11] This seems to have been along the lines of what Wagner had in mind in December 1858, when he claimed to have found "the possibility of rising, in love, above the striving of individual will." He sensed the possibility of merging one's will (or consciousness) with another's and thus of taking one's sufferings upon oneself, of transforming oneself into another. In such an act, Wagner wrote, "the will of the species [*Gattungs-Wille*] comes to full consciousness, which at that point is necessarily synonymous with its complete stilling."[12]

What Wagner meant in his diary is sketchy. But a similar vision of redemption from suffering, attained through the experience of sexual love, is enacted dramatically in the second act of *Tristan*. The second scene of that act stages an extended dialogue between the two eponymous lovers who recognize the possibility of escape from their tormented lives in the metaphysical merging of their individual beings through the experience of their love.

> Both sing together:
>
> | O sink hernieder, | Descend, |
> | Nacht der Liebe, | oh night of love, |
> | gib Vergessen, | grant oblivion |
> | dass ich lebe; | so that I may live. |
> | nimm mich auf | Take me up |
> | in deinen Schoss, | into your womb, |
> | löse von | release me |
> | der Welt mich los! | from the world! |

As the dialogue unfolds, Tristan imagines freedom from the suffering born of willing— an existence, as he sings, "opposed to deceitful delusion." Together, the lovers pick up this thread, echoing Wagner's words to Liszt on the Buddha "transforming himself into the world":

> | selbst dann | then I myself |
> | bin ich die Welt: | am the world: |
> | Wonne-hehrstes Weben, | a weaving of the most sublime bliss, |
> | Liebe-heiligstes Leben, | a living of the most sacred love. |
> | Niewiedererwachens | Never again to wake: |
> | wahnlos | an undeluded, |
> | hold bewusster Wunsch. | conscious wish. |

At the end, the two characters identify directly their path to redemption from suffering: each losing him- or herself in the other, merging their metaphysical beings through their experience of romantic love and, in that way, quieting the will and its torments within.

So starben wir,	So we might die,
um ungetrennt,	so that together,
ewig einig	eternally one,
ohne End',	without end,
ohn' Erwachen,	without waking,
ohn' Erbangen,	without fearing,
namenlos	nameless,
in Lieb' umfangen,	enfolded in love,
ganz uns selbst gegeben,	given wholly to each other,
der Liebe nur zu leben!	we may live only for love.

After giving voice to their vision of redemption, the pair is discovered in illicit embrace and Tristan is mortally wounded. He dies at the end of Act 3, which concludes with Isolde's famous, aria-like *Liebestod* or "death-in-love," in which she hears echoes of Tristan having transcended the illusions and metaphysical confines of the living world. At the end, she collapses onto Tristan's body, joining him in death, merging her being with his.

The impact of Wagner's encounter with Schopenhauer upon the gestation of *Tristan* was not limited to its libretto. Traces of Schopenhauerian theory can also be detected in aspects of its score. First, we might look to Schopenhauer's remarks on musical structure in Volume 2 of *The World as Will and Representation*. There, the philosopher writes of melodic motion in tonal music, which consists of a continual series of transitions of consonance into dissonance, and back into consonance, over a shifting harmonic foundation. That process, Schopenhauer wrote, is, "metaphysically considered, the copy of the origination of new desires, and then of their satisfaction." Schopenhauer also described the contrapuntal device of the suspension—a delayed resolution of melodic dissonance into consonance—as "clearly an analogue of the satisfaction of the will which is enhanced through delay" (WWR2$_{[P]}$, 455–56). Summing up, he wrote the following of melodic motion in general: "we like to hear in its language the secret history of our will and of all its stirrings and strivings with their many different delays, postponements, hindrances, and afflictions, even in the most sorrowful melodies" (WWR2$_{[P]}$, 451). As many commentators on its score have noted, *Tristan und Isolde* can seem at times to be a five-hour-long sounding of postponed resolution, of delayed satisfaction. The second note of the score (in the prelude) is already a suspension: the pitch F in the key of A minor (only implied at that point), hovering in the air, leaving its listeners guessing. And, the very first chord heard in the work is neither major nor minor but the now-famous "Tristan" chord, a collection of four pitches sounding together in dissonance, as if longing for some uncertain resolution.

His psychologizing interpretations aside, however, Schopenhauer's remarks on melodic motion had been commonplace among musicians for a century before he wrote his book. Far more important with respect to *Tristan* is the priority assigned by Schopenhauerian theory to music itself among the arts. As recently as 1851, Wagner had lambasted the entire genre of opera for having assigned a privileged role to music among its constituent arts—poetry, acting, and set design among them. "A means of expression (music) was made the end," Wagner wrote disparagingly of opera, "while the end of expression (the drama) was made a means."[13] In *The World as Will and Representation*, however, Schopenhauer claimed a position nearly the opposite of Wagner's. He argued that while the other arts are merely representational, "music is as *immediate* an objectification and copy of the whole *will* as the world itself is.... Therefore music is by no means like the other arts, namely, a copy of the Ideas, but a *copy of the will itself*" (WWR1$_{[P]}$, 257). Moreover, whereas Wagner had proposed that every note in an operatic score must be justified as inherently necessary to the unfolding of the drama, Schopenhauer held that "the words are and remain for the music a foreign extra of secondary value, as the effect of the tones is incomparably more powerful" (WWR2$_{[P]}$, 448). He continued: "If [words] are incorporated in the music, therefore, they must of course occupy only an entirely subordinate position, and adapt themselves completely to it" (WWR2$_{[P]}$, 448).

Shortly after reading Schopenhauer, Wagner's views on music in relation to the constituent arts in his music dramas also began to change. In an essay of February 1857 entitled "On Franz Liszt's Symphonic Poems," he made no mention of Schopenhauer. But his remarks on music's necessary primacy, in any context where it is paired with prose or a poetic text (whether in opera, music drama, or Liszt's programmatic works), echo closely those of Schopenhauer, and they mark a decisive turn from the aesthetic position he had boldly proclaimed just a few years before. "Listen now to what I believe," he wrote in his essay on Liszt. "*Music can never, and in no alliance into which it might enter, cease to be the highest, redeeming art*. Its nature is such that what all other arts can only hint at attains in music the most indubitable certainty, becomes the most immediate truth."[14]

This, for some, gets to the heart of Schopenhauer's influence on Wagner as manifested in *Tristan*. In *Das Rheingold* and *Die Walküre*, the two music dramas he had completed before discovering the philosopher's work, Wagner had made use of signifying musical motives (*Leitmotiven*) to help illuminate or support the unfolding of the dramatic action. When the Rhine gold was mentioned by a character onstage, the gold motive was played in the orchestra. In sharp contrast to this, for long stretches of *Tristan*, including the Schopenhauerian dialogue of Act 2, the music *is* the drama. It is the principal—even the only—site at which dramatic action takes place. As Bryan Magee aptly notes of *Tristan*, "There can be no question here in anyone's mind of the various arts being brought together on an equal footing. Stage action? For long periods there is scarcely any. Words? Many are repeated cries of distress, the longing, aching, yearning that are being even more piercingly and agonizingly expressed in the orchestra."[15] Also in contrast to Wagner's earlier works, the drama unfolded in *Tristan und Isolde* is chiefly an *inner* drama, a drama not of monumental thefts, heroic acts, or godly deceptions, but of love and will and longing and metaphysical salvation. For Schopenhauer, music was a sounding reflection of the will itself, the essence of the world. Under the spell of the philosopher, Wagner elevated music to a privileged role in his music dramas. On the topic of love, however, he refused to yield.

29.2 *DIE MEISTERSINGER VON NÜRNBERG*

Schopenhauer's influence on Wagner's next music drama, *Die Meistersinger von Nürnberg*, is also widely noted—especially in the famous *Wahn* monologue of Hans Sachs, where the Meistersinger decries the "madness" of the day while reiterating Schopenhauer's distinction between a world of appearances and reality.[16] But the presence of Schopenhauerian theory in *Die Meistersinger* is more pervasive than this, and it gets to the heart of Wagner's central concern in the music drama as a whole: the nature of musical creativity. To understand this requires working through Schopenhauer's "Essay on Spirit-Seeing" of 1850, alongside Wagner's essay "Beethoven," written twenty years later. Once more, we find that Wagner was not only a reader of Schopenhauerian theory but an original and highly creative interpreter of it. And here again, the libretto and the score of a music drama—*Die Meistersinger*—provided the principal vehicle for elaborating his views.

Wagner's interest in Schopenhauer's "Essay on Spirit-Seeing" lay in the philosopher's statements on dreaming. Dreams, Schopenhauer began in unsurprising fashion, are typically dependent on the condition of sleep, on "the cessation of the normal activity of the brain and senses. Only when such activity is at rest can the dream occur, just as the pictures of a magic lantern can appear only after the lights of the room have been extinguished" ($PP1_{[P]}$, 232). When the mind's activity ceases to be provoked by external stimuli, he wrote, dreams arise from within. From there, Schopenhauer went on to distinguish between, on the one hand, the brain itself, "the *outer* nerve-focus…which is exclusively concerned with the direction of *external* relations" and, on the other, "all the large ganglia which…constitute the *great sympathetic nerve* or *inner* nerve-centre" ($PP1_{[P]}$, 234–35). Normally, we do not perceive the workings of this "sympathetic nerve." Although "it has an indirect and feeble connection with the cerebral system through long, attenuated, and inosculating nerves…the sensorium receives on this path only an extremely feeble and faint echo of the events and movements in the very complicated and active workshop of organic life" ($PP1_{[P]}$, 235). Nor do we usually detect this "echo," though it might have an unconscious influence upon us. In darkness, however, when the outward-directed activity of the brain is suspended, this ganglionic echo is able to cross the threshold of our awareness, "like the candle that begins to shine when the evening twilight comes, or the murmuring of the spring which is heard at night but was rendered inaudible by the noises of the day" ($PP1_{[P]}$, 235). These echoes stimulate the sensory workings of the brain from a direction different from that which prevails in waking life—namely, from *within*. These echoes, for the philosopher, give rise to dreams.

Continuing, Schopenhauer identified all such inner perceptions as the work of the "dream organ" (*Traumorgan*), and he raised the prospect that the dream organ might allow us a different kind of access to reality than that provided by the outwardly directed brain. "There is a state in which we certainly sleep and dream," he wrote, "yet we dream only the reality itself that surrounds us" (PP1$_{[P]}$, 239). He continued,

> We then see our bedroom with everything therein; we become aware of people entering the room; and we know that we are in bed and that everything is correct and in order. And yet we are asleep with our eyes shut; we dream; only what we dream is true and real. It is just as if our skull had then become transparent so that the external world now entered the brain directly and immediately instead of by an indirect path and through the narrow portal of the senses.   (PP1$_{[P]}$, 239)

This "dreaming of reality" (*Wahrträumen*) is, for Schopenhauer, typically a morning dream, observed "only in the early morning as also in the evening sometime after falling asleep" (PP1$_{[P]}$, 240). No longer bound by the limitations of the external sense organs, "the range of the dreamer's vision" in the morning-dreaming state "is somewhat extended so that it goes beyond the bedroom. Thus the curtains or shutters cease to be obstacles to vision and the dreamer then perceives quite distinctly what lies beyond them, the yard, the garden, or the street with the house opposite." In such a state, "perception" occurs not through the eyes or the ears but "through the dream organ" itself (PP1$_{[P]}$, 240–41). What one sees or hears while dreaming does not correlate to outer stimuli. It arises from within, from a hypothetical faculty—the dream organ—turned inward.

Schopenhauer's theory of dreams was not without consequences for his theory of will. While the outer world is subject to the *principium individuationis*, he held, the will lies beyond the *principium individuationis*, and thus no spatial or temporal distinctions apply to it. In sleep, he hypothesized, the ability of the dreamer to experience the sights and sounds of other times and places owes to the fact that the workings of the dream organ also transcend the *principium individuationis*. And this, he believed, meant that the dreamer must somehow tap into the will itself. But Schopenhauer also theorized a *waking* path to such transcendence of the *principium individuationis*, a sleepless path by which to tap into the workings of will itself: namely, that of the *clairvoyant*. The clairvoyant, he held, is a person endowed with the ability to access her inner reserve of will outside of sleep. Only in that way, he reasoned, could the clairvoyant's sighting of past and future events be explained (PP1$_{[P]}$, 263). Schopenhauer accounted for spirit-seeing (or ghost sightings) in a similar fashion, alongside an array of related paranormal phenomena, esumed all of which he presumed true.

The extent to which Schopenhauer's theory of dreams captured Wagner's imagination can be seen throughout *Die Meistersinger*, in which the lessons in composition given by Sachs to his student Walther are studded with the teacher's urging Walther to pay utmost attention to his morning dreams. At root, Sachs's instruction amounts to Wagner's reading of Schopenhauer's dream-theory through the lens of the philosopher's own statements on music as an unmediated sounding of will, as we saw earlier with respect to

Tristan. If the workings of the dream organ enable the dreamer to experience the will directly, and if music is itself an expression of will, then the dream, Wagner reasoned, just might well be the source of musical creativity. This is the essential wisdom that Sachs imparts to Walther in *Die Meistersinger*.

The story revolves around the training Walther receives in preparation for a singing competition, at which he hopes to win the hand of his beloved Eva. Walther's first appearance before Nuremberg's Guild of Meistersingers is an unmitigated disaster, for he performs in a way neither informed by tradition nor grounded in any inner vision, and it is utterly incomprehensible to all who hear him. Help comes when Sachs agrees to give Walther composition lessons in the work's third act. At the start of their first lesson, Walther and Sachs trade remarks that brim with the language of Schopenhauer's essay on spirit seeing. Their conversation begins not with talk about music, but with Walther relating his experience of the night before. "I had a wondrously beautiful dream," he explains. "That bodes well," replies Sachs. "Tell it to me!" Then, Sachs launches into his lesson:

Mein Freund, das grad' ist Dichters Werk,	My friend, it is precisely the poet's task
dass er sein Träumen deut' und merk'.	to interpret and record his dreams.
Glaubt mir, des Menschen wahrster Wahn	Believe me, man's truest madness
wird ihm im Traume aufgetan:	is revealed to him in dreams.
all Dichtkunst und Poeterei	All versifying and poetry
ist nichts als Wahrtraumdeuterei.	is nothing but the interpretation of dreams of reality.

"Tell me your morning dream," Sachs urges (*Erzählt mir euren Morgentraum!*), but his student cannot stop thinking about the traditions established by great singers of the past. "How do I begin according to the rules?" Walther asks. Sachs, however, sets him straight: "You make them up yourself and then follow them," he counsels. "Think of your beautiful dream from this morning." With this, Walther begins to sing, and as he does, Sachs cheers him on: "You've rhymed it so well," he proclaims, "I can't tell the difference between what you've composed and what you've dreamt." Each time Sachs mentions dreams in the lesson, an identical three-chord progression sounds in the orchestra, a progression that is wholly nonfunctional in the tonal context of the work. Scored with heavenly, upward-strumming harps, these statements and their soundings appear as if they are themselves figments heard in a dream, echoes of the nonrational, non–rule-bound source of creativity Sachs describes.[17]

Two years after the premier of *Die Meistersinger*, Wagner returned to its central philosophical question—the nature of musical creativity—in an essay commemorating the centennial of the birth of Ludwig van Beethoven. Regarding Beethoven as the epitome of the creative individual, Wagner elaborated theoretically the Schopenhauer-inflected notion of creativity he had staged in Walther's lessons with Sachs. Only now, Wagner did so in an attempt to explain the source of what he considered Beethoven's incomparably powerful artistic gifts. Adapting Schopenhauer's distinction between the "outer nerve-focus" of the brain and the "inner nerve-center" of the ganglia, Wagner proposed his own map of the composer's psychic landscape. This, he held, is configured between an outward-directed world of vision and an inward-facing world of sound.

> Alongside the world that is visible to us when we are awake and also in dreams, we are aware of another world perceptible only through our sense of hearing, declaring itself through sound—literally, a *sound-world* existing alongside the *light-world*, to which we could say it is related just as dreaming is to wakefulness.... Just as the vivid world of dreams can present itself to us only through a special function of the brain, so too can music enter our consciousness only through a similar brain function.[18]

After this, Wagner summoned Schopenhauer's faculty of the dream organ (*Traumorgan*), which he presented (without citing Schopenhauer on this point) as "an inward-facing function of the brain" that becomes active during sleep. And he adapted Schopenhauer's vision of the clairvoyant—one who transcends the *principium individuationis* by tapping into her inner reserves of will—to explain the function of sleep for the artist.

> Since the dream-organ cannot be roused into action by outer impressions, against which the brain is now locked fast, this rousing must take place through happenings in the inner organism, which our waking consciousness merely feels as vague sensations. It is, however, through this inner life that we are directly allied with the whole of nature, and thus [in dreams] are we brought into a relationship with the essence of things that eludes the forms of outer knowledge (space and time).[19]

Through the medium of the dream organ, Wagner argues, a person comes into contact with the will. Waking from such a transcendent dream, he unleashes a terrible scream, which "we can only regard as the most immediate expressions of the will itself," an utterance incomprehensible to those who hear it.[20] However, Wagner went on to explain, "the dream of deepest sleep *can* be apprehended by waking consciousness" in one particular, exceptional way: namely, "when it is translated into the language of a second, allegorical dream, which immediately precedes our waking." At this point, once again repurposing Schopenhauer (and echoing the lessons of his own Hans Sachs), Wagner introduced the idea of the morning dream (*Morgentraum*), the substance of which, he claimed, can best be communicated in music. "In order to reveal to us an image of its own self, the will creates a second communicative organ, of which one side remains turned toward the inner vision while the other reaches out to the outer world, now reappearing to us as we awaken, through the immediate, sympathetic experience of tone."[21]

   Like Schopenhauer's dreamer or clairvoyant, Wagner's composer is a person who somehow comes into contact with his inner reserves of will. Terrified of that inner vision, the composer awakens with a scream. Sometimes, however, his waking is preceded by another, shallower kind of dreaming, morning-dreaming, in which the will no longer appears directly. Rather, its echoes are "translated" into an allegorical language comprehensible by others in their waking hours. That language, for Wagner, was music, which the composer sounds or inscribes when he wakes. This was the project that the Meistersinger Sachs urged on his student Walther in their composition lessons. And this, for Wagner, was the source of creativity for the historical figure of Beethoven himself.

29.3 PARSIFAL

Wagner's final music drama is often considered his most Schopenhauerian. He himself gave cause for this in claims like this one, from before the inception of the work: "Schopenhauerian philosophy and *Parcival* as the crowning achievement."[22] But as we have seen, Wagner's understanding of Schopenhauer's work often diverges from doctrinaire readings of it, and his engagement with the philosopher's ideas in *Parsifal* is no exception. Yes, *Parsifal* is a music drama dominated by Schopenhauerian themes, particularly those concerning sympathy (*Mitleid*), the nature of which Schopenhauer detailed in his *Prize Essay on the Basis of Morals*. But Wagner evinced an understanding of sympathy that goes well beyond anything Schopenhauer proposed, specifically in regard to animals. He made this clear not only in *Parsifal* but in his "Open Letter to Ernst Weber" against vivisection (1879) and in his seminal essay "Religion and Art" and its several appendices (1880–1881).

In Schopenhauer's *Prize Essay*, widely known to have been an influence on Wagner's thinking in the 1870s and '80s, the philosopher delineated the character of the moral act, and he puzzled over how humans could be capable of it. Moral acts, Schopenhauer argued, contravene against self-centered individuality or "egoism," which he deemed "the principal and fundamental incentive for humans, as for animals." Indeed, he continued, "the moral significance of an action can only lie in its relation to others; only with respect to them can it have moral worth or reprehensibility, and consequently be an action of justice or loving kindness, as well as the opposite of the two" (BM$_{[C]}$, 202).[23] To engage in a moral act, Schopenhauer held, is to acknowledge an identity between oneself and another. Such an action "requires that I be *identified with him* in some way, i.e., that the complete *distinction* between me and the other, upon precisely which my egoism rests, to a certain degree be suspended" (BM$_{[C]}$, 212). While overcoming the distinction between self and other might sound metaphysically difficult, for Schopenhauer it was not. As he explained, the moral action is "quite real and in no way uncommon; it is the everyday phenomenon of *compassion* [*Mitleid*], i.e., the quite immediate *participation*, independent of considerations of any other sort, primarily in the *suffering* of another" (BM$_{[C]}$, 212–13). Compassion, for the philosopher, is thus the true incentive for moral actions. "Only insofar as an action has originated from compassion," he wrote, "does it have moral worth, and anything proceeding from any other motives has none" (BM$_{[C]}$, 213).

Schopenhauer's account of moral actions has two implications for our understanding of *Parsifal*. First, the sense of identification that a sympathetic person feels for another is made possible by an underlying commonality or identity between them. Namely, beneath the spatial and temporal distinctions that seem to separate us as individuals (*the principium individuationis*), there is the one underlying will. We are capable of sympathy because underneath all determination, metaphysically we are all one and the same: we are will. Second, given this metaphysical identity, the kind of identification of self and another that he described—the kind of sympathy he envisioned—must extend to animals as well. Indeed, in his *Prize Essay* Schopenhauer argued that "compassion for animals is so closely associated with goodness of character that one may confidently assert that whoever is cruel to animals could not be a good person" (BM$_{[C]}$, 242). He praised the English for being "the first among whom the law to protect animals from cruel treatment had been taken quite seriously," and he lauded the establishment of the Society for the Prevention of Cruelty to Animals in London in 1824 (BM$_{[C]}$, 242–43).

Yet while Schopenhauer's sympathies for animals went further than those of Descartes, Leibniz, Wolff, or Kant, they only went so far. Continuing, he made this clear:

> That compassion for animals must not go so far that, like the Brahmans, we would have to give up animals as food, rests on the fact that in nature the capacity for suffering keeps pace with intelligence, on account of which by abstaining from animals as food, humans, especially in the north, would suffer more than would the animal through a quick and even unforeseen death, which perhaps should be alleviated even more by means of chloroform. In contrast, without animals as food, the human race would never be able to exist in the north.   (BM$_{[C]}$, 245)

For Schopenhauer, the proliferation of humans in northern regions took precedence over the suffering of animals or their use as food. He justified this in part with recourse to a quantitative view of suffering.

> Goodness of heart consists in the deeply felt, universal compassion for all living beings, but primarily for the human[,] because responsiveness to suffering keeps in step with increase in intelligence; hence, humans' countless intellectual and physical sufferings have a much stronger claim to compassion than the pain of animals, which is only physical and, thus, less acute.   (BM$_{[C]}$, 253)

In short, humanity's capacity for suffering is greater than that of any animal. For this reason, one person's sympathy for another must supersede his sympathies for other species.

That Wagner borrowed freely and adapted creatively from Schopenhauer in *Parsifal* is made clear in his treatment of a central topic in the music drama: the Eucharist, the moment in the Catholic Mass when bread and wine become the body and blood of Christ. Put simply, the central problem of *Parsifal* is the failure of the Eucharist, and the solution to that problem is the instantiation of a renewed, successful one. Indeed, Wagner's staging of the Eucharist in the work makes *Parsifal* into something more than a music drama. It was, for the composer, a *Bühnenweihfestspiel*, a "festival-stage consecration play." In Wagner's work, the renewal of the Eucharist is left to the character of Parsifal, "the pure fool" (*der reine Tor*), who saves the church by foregoing his egoism (or self-centered individuality) in an embrace of universal sympathy (*Mitleid*). In the Catholic Mass, the miracle of the Eucharist is a literal transformation, or rather a "transubstantiation." As established by the Council of Trent in 1551, "in the august sacrament of the holy Eucharist, after the consecration of the bread and wine, our Lord Jesus Christ, true God and man, is truly, really, and substantially contained under the species of those sensible things."[24] The Council is explicit in stating that the transubstantiation is not to be understood symbolically, but literally. Wagner shared this literal understanding of the transubstantiation, as his staging of a failed Eucharist in Act I of *Parsifal* makes plain.

Wein und Brot des letzten Mahles	Bread and wine of the Last Supper
wandelt' einst der Herr des Grales	the lord of the grail once transformed
durch des Mitleids Liebesmacht	through the loving power of sympathy
in das Blut, das er vergoss,	into the blood that He shed,
in den Leib, den dar er bracht'.	into the body that he broke.

Taken literally, as enacted here, the ritual of the Eucharist raises the issue of eating meat, even if (especially if?) that meat is human flesh. In his writings of the time, Wagner regarded eating meat as a principal cause of what he considered the degeneration of the human race. As he explained in his vivisection letter, "a curse" was called down on us through "the enjoyment of animal food."[25] In short, the eating of meat entails one being living off the death of another. It initiates a frenzy of destruction and cruelty which, in Wagner's "Religion and Art," culminates in human cannibalism and our acclimation to atrocity. "Then, falling ever lower, human blood and corpses appear the only worthy food for the world-conqueror," he wrote.

> The Feast of Thyestes would have been impossible among the Indians. But the human imagination could entertain such horrifying images, since the murder of animals and humans had become something common. And why should the phantasy of the civilized modern human recoil in horror from such pictures, when it has accustomed itself to the sight of a Parisian slaughterhouse in its early-morning activities?[26]

For Wagner, eating the flesh of animals had corrupted the blood of humanity. This view led him, in the appendices to "Religion and Art," to sympathize with the French racial theorist Arthur de Gobineau, who likewise diagnosed such blood corruption, though for him it stemmed exclusively from racial mixing, from which Wagner also recoiled. Wagner's corrective to such corruption was, surprisingly, to ingest the blood of Christ. "For the most divine purification to flourish, the lowest races may be permitted the enjoyment of the blood of Jesus, as He demonstrated symbolically in the only genuine sacrament of the Christian religion. This antidote would accordingly be set against the decay of the races through their mixing. Perhaps this world has brought forth breathing life only in order to serve that order of salvation [*Heilsordnung*]."[27] As Wagner saw it, ingesting the flesh and blood of Christ can assuage the corruption of humanity brought about in part by eating the flesh and blood of animals. But just how, precisely, could it do this?

To Wagner's mind, partaking of Christ's body is permissible—indeed, transformative—because His flesh and blood is knowingly and freely given. It is sacrificed for our well-being in the ultimate act of sympathy. "In the blood of the savior," he wrote on this point, "we now must recognize the epitome of consciously willed suffering itself, which as divine sympathy [*Mitleiden*] pours through the entire human species and is its originary source."[28] For Wagner, the act of sympathy that motivated Christ's sacrifice is key to understanding the Savior's teaching—a teaching intended not only to be known theoretically but to be enacted practically. Indeed, he believed, such enactment is the crux of Christianity itself. "Its founder was not wise, but divine," Wagner wrote. "His teaching was the deed of free-willed suffering; to believe in him meant to emulate him."[29] In "Religion and Art," to emulate Christ was to act with sympathy at its most self-sacrificing and profound.

On this point, Wagner parted ways with his philosophical idol. Turning directly to Schopenhauer's own invective against eating meat, Wagner expressed skepticism about the philosopher's allowance for such a practice in rugged, northern climes.

> That originally it must have been hunger alone which drove humans to murder animals and feed on their flesh and blood—that the necessity of this did not arise simply due to their transposition into colder climates, as held by those who regard eating meat as a duty of self-preservation in the northern regions—is proven by the obvious fact that there exist great peoples who nourish themselves with fruit or exclusively with vegetables, yet who lose nothing of their power and endurance, even in coarser climates. We see this in the extremely long lifespans of Russian peasants, and also in the Japanese, who attain nourishment only from fruits, yet who are renowned for the most valorous temper and keenest understanding in war.[30]

It was, Wagner explains, not hunger per se but a deranged and rabid sense of mastery over the world that motivated humanity's eating of animals. It was "the human beast of prey [*das menschliche Raubtier*], having made itself master of the peaceful world."[31] He continued along pragmatic lines: if the north is inhospitable, Wagner argued, we simply should not live there. He called instead for "a more reasonable distribution of the population of the earth upon its surface," to be achieved through mass emigration.

> Even assuming that eating meat were indispensable in northern climates, what would keep us from conducting a rationally directed migration of peoples into such lands of our globe that, as is proclaimed of the South American peninsula, are in a condition to nourish the contemporary population of all parts of the world by virtue of their abundant productivity?[32]

Redistributing the human species across the southern continents would bring political benefits as well, Wagner claimed. Namely, it would calm the bellicose tendencies of the species.

> [T]here is nothing bleaker today than to survey all the human clans [*Geschlechter*] whose tribes wandered westward from their Central Asian homeland, and to realize that civilization and religion were not enough to occasion them to distribute

themselves over the favorable climates of the earth. If they had done so, most of the grievances and hindrances to the free and sound development of peaceable community conditions would have disappeared, simply by leaving the barren wastelands where most of them have long resided.[33]

Wagner's notion of sympathy, outlined in "Religion and Art," was far more expansive than Schopenhauer's notion of "human love" (*Menschenliebe*). It extended to all animals unconditionally, and it precluded the aggressive imposition of any living being upon another. The only flesh to be eaten, for Wagner, was flesh that is willingly given. This is the conception of sympathy enacted dramatically in *Parsifal*, encapsulated in the renewal of the Eucharist between the first the final acts.

The opera begins with the eponymous character killing a swan in sport. Witnessing the act, Gurnemanz asks, "Are you now conscious of your misdeed? Speak, boy—are you aware of your grievous guilt?" The answer, of course, is *no*. At this point in his life, Parsifal has no sympathy for animals, and, in this respect, he merely lives in accord with the society of which he is a part. Indeed, the knights of the Grail Brotherhood live without sympathy for living beings of any sort—a fact reflected in their administration of the Eucharist, which lacks the body of Christ. As a result, their Eucharist repeatedly fails, and the Brotherhood and its members have decayed physically and spiritually as a result. As Gurnemanz laments,

Die heil'ge Speisung bleibt uns nun versagt,	Divine sustenance is now denied us,
gemeine Atzung muss uns nähren;	and common food must sustain us;
darob versiegte unsrer Helden Kraft.	thus, our heroes' strength is exhausted.

By the end of the music drama, however, Parsifal comes to see the error of his ways. Indeed, his sympathy now extends not only to animals but to everything that lives, even plants. With this, he attains at last the ability to effect the transubstantiation of the Savior's flesh and blood in the Eucharist, which not only restores the vitality of the Brotherhood but redeems the world itself. The close of *Parsifal* depicts this transformed view of the world. Observing the joyful sense of community that even flowers experience in the radiance of his all-encompassing love, Parsifal exclaims:

Wie dünkt mich doch die Aue heut so schön!	How beautiful the meadow seems today!
Wohl traf ich Wunderblumen an, die bis zum Haupte süchtig mich umrankten;	I recall the wondrous flowers well, which once tried to twine themselves around me to my head,
doch sah ich nie so mild und zart die Halme, Blüten und Blumen, noch duftet' all' so kindisch hold, und sprach so lieblich traut zu mir.	but I never saw such tender and delicate grasses, blossoms and flowers, which all smelled so lovely and fresh, and spoke to me with such tender familiarity.

Hearing this, Gurnemanz explains that what Parsifal experiences owes to *sympathy*.

Des Sünders Reuetränen sind es	It is the tears of remorse wept by sinners
die heut mit heil'gem Tau	that have, today, sprinkled field and plain
beträufet Flur und Au':	with holy dew,
der liess sie so gedeihen.	which thereby consecrates them.
Nun freut sich alle Kreatur	Today all living things rejoice
auf des Erlösers holder Spur,	in God's dear grace
will sein Gebet ihm weihen.	and wish to praise Him in prayer.
...	
Das dankt dann alle Kreatur,	All creatures now show gratitude,
was all' da blüht und bald erstirbt,	all that flourishes and will soon pass,
da die entsündigte Natur	for Nature is renewed,
heut ihren Unschuldstag erwirbt.	and has gained its day of innocence.

Parsifal's sympathy for all living things allows all creatures to show their sympathy for him and each other as well, such that every living thing joins together in gratitude, in a renewal of nature as such. Having learned sympathy for all living things, beginning with animals, Parsifal restores the Eucharist and redeems the world as a whole.

* * *

In the annals of Western Classical music, Wagner's fascination with Schopenhauer is unique. No other composer evinced such broad-ranging and enduring dedication to the ideas of a single philosopher, and no other musician sought so diligently to revise and critique a philosopher's writings through the media of his or her own creative work. "Suit your philosophy to your needs," Wagner urged a friend in 1856, just as he was starting to understand his own compositions in Schopenhauerian terms, and his counsel comported precisely with his understanding of philosophy itself.[34] It did not comprise a body of texts to be read and simply accepted or rejected. Rather, it consisted of a vital exchange of ideas between individuals, ideas that evolve over the course of readings and in relation to lived experience. When deeply in love, Wagner found what he believed to be an unrecognized Schopenhauerian path to redemption from suffering in his experience of the erotic. When trying to fathom the source of artistic creativity, he located what he considered an important key in Schopenhauer's theory of dreams and clairvoyance. When pondering Christian doctrine and human sympathy, he found clarity in his critical reading of the philosopher's allowance for eating meat. In all of these cases, Wagner's philosophical engagements informed his creation of some of the great operatic works of the Western canon. Neither *Tristan*, nor *Meistersinger*, nor *Parsifal* would have been possible without Schopenhauer. But in the end, the philosophy they record is distinctly Wagnerian. It is Wagner's working with ideas in sound.

NOTES

1. *Selected Letters of Richard Wagner*, edited and translated by Stewart Spencer and Barry Millington (New York and London: W. W. Norton, 1987), 323.

2. Letter to Jakob Sulzer of May 10 or 12, 1855, in *Selected Letters*, 338.

3. Letter to Liszt of June 7, 1855, in *Selected Letters*, 344.

4. Letter to August Röckel, in *Selected Letters*, 357.

5. Letter of July 22, 1860, in *Richard Wagner an Mathilde Wesendonk* [sic]. *Tagebuchblätter und Briefe 1853–1871*, edited by Wolfgang Golther (Leipzig: Breitkopf und Härtel, 1922), 283.

6. His audience consists of Cosima Wagner, Franz Liszt, and Hans von Wolzogen. Today, the portrait of Schopenhauer hangs in the museum directly behind Wagner's piano bench. For a recent assessment of Wagner's indebtedness, see Julian Young, "Schopenhauer," in *The Cambridge Wagner Encyclopedia*, edited by Nicholas Vazsonyi (Cambridge: Cambridge University Press, 2013), 519–24.

7. Entry in Wagner's "Venice Diary" of December 1, 1858, in *Richard Wagner an Mathilde Wesendonk*, 130.

8. See Wagner's letter to Wesendonck of September 18, 1858, where he wrote: "A year ago today I completed the Tristan poem, and brought you the final act"; *Richard Wagner an Mathilde Wesendonk*, 96.

9. *Selected Letters*, 324 (emphasis in original).

10. *Richard Wagner and Mathilde Wesendonk*, 130.

11. Letter of June 7, 1855, in *Selected Letters*, 346 (emphasis in original).

12. *Richard Wagner and Mathilde Wesendonk*, 131.

13. Wagner, *Oper und Drama*, in *Gesammelte Schriften und Dichtungen* (Leipzig: E. W. Fritzsch, 1888), 3:282.

14. Wagner, "Über Franz Liszt's symphonische Dichtungen," in *Gesammelte Schriften*, 5:247 (emphasis in original).

15. Magee, *The Tristan Chord: Wagner and Philosophy* (New York: Henry Holt, 2000), 210–11. See also Eric Chafe, *The Tragic and the Ecstatic: The Musical Revolution of Wagner's Tristan und Isolde* (Oxford/New York: Oxford University Press, 2005).

16. See, for instance, Magee, *The Tristan Chord*, 242–55; and Lucy Beckett, "Sachs and Schopenhauer," in *Richard Wagner: Die Meistersinger von Nürnberg*, edited by John Hamilton Warrack (Cambridge: Cambridge University Press, 1994), 62–82.

17. For a music-theoretical explication of these passages, see Kevin C. Karnes, "Wagner, Klimt, and the Metaphysics of Creativity in *fin-de-siècle* Vienna," *Journal of the American Musicological Society* 62 (2009), 671–74.

18. Wagner, "Beethoven," in *Gesammelte Schriften*, 9:87.

19. Ibid.

20. Ibid., 9:88.

21. Ibid., 9:92 (emphasis added).

22. Cosima Wagner, *Die Tagebücher, 1869–1883*, edited by Martin Gregor-Dellin and Dietrich Mack (Munich: Piper, 1982), diary entry for June 10, 1875.

23. The "loving kindness" of this passage is a somewhat euphemistic rendering of *Menschenliebe*.

24. *The Canons and Decrees of the Sacred and Ecumenical Council of Trent*, edited and translated by J. Waterworth (London: Dolman, 1848), session 13, ch. 1.

25. Wagner, "Offenes Schreiben an Herrn Ernst von Weber, Verfasser der Schrift: 'Die Folterkammern der Wissenschaft,'" in *Gesammelte Schriften*, 10:201.
26. Wagner, "Religion und Kunst," in *Gesammelte Schriften*, 10:227.
27. Wagner, "Heldenthum und Christenthum," in *Gesammelte Schriften*, 10:283.
28. Ibid., 10:281.
29. Wagner, "Religion und Kunst," 213.
30. Ibid., 237–38.
31. Ibid., 238.
32. Ibid., 246; 242.
33. Wagner, "Heldenthum und Christenthum," 284.
34. Letter to Röckel of August 23, 1856, in *Selected Letters*, 359.

FURTHER READING

Beckett, Lucy. "Sachs and Schopenhauer." In *Richard Wagner: Die Meistersinger von Nürnberg*, edited by John Hamilton Warrack. Cambridge: Cambridge University Press, 1994, 62–82.

Chafe, Eric. *The Tragic and the Ecstatic: The Musical Revolution of Wagner's Tristan und Isolde*. Oxford/New York: Oxford University Press, 2005.

Karnes, Kevin C. "Wagner, Klimt, and the Metaphysics of Creativity in *fin-de-siècle* Vienna." *Journal of the American Musicological Society* 62 (2009): 671–74.

Magee, Bryan. *The Tristan Chord: Wagner and Philosophy*. New York: Henry Holt, 2000.

Wagner, Cosima. *Die Tagebücher, 1869–1883*, edited by Martin Gregor-Dellin and Dietrich Mack. Munich: Piper, 1982.

Wagner, Richard. *Gesammelte Schriften und Dichtungen*. 10 vols. Leipzig: E. W. Fritzsch, 1888.

Wagner, Richard. *Richard Wagner an Mathilde Wesendonk* [sic]. *Tagebuchblätter und Briefe 1853–1871*, edited by Wolfgang Golther. Leipzig: Breitkopf und Härtel, 1922.

Wagner, Richard. *Selected Letters of Richard Wagner*, edited and translated by Stewart Spencer and Barry Millington. New York/London: W.W. Norton, 1987.

Young, Julian. "Schopenhauer." In *The Cambridge Wagner Encyclopedia*, edited by Nicholas Vazsonyi. Cambridge: Cambridge University Press, 2013, 510–24.

CHAPTER 30

SCHOPENHAUER'S
FIN DE SIÈCLE
RECEPTION IN AUSTRIA

PAUL BISHOP

30.1 HISTORICAL AND INTELLECTUAL BACKGROUND

THE period of Austrian history known as the *fin de siècle* can be said to have begun with the post-revolutionary world that effectively brought the *Biedermeier* or *Vormärz* period to its end. The Revolutions of 1848 which began (hence the term *Vormärz*) in March of that year represented both nationalist and liberal resistance to the conservative policies of Metternich that had implemented the systematic censorship of a police state.

The Austro-Prussian War of 1866 resulted in the Dual Monarchy, established to consolidate the position of the Emperor Franz Joseph I. He presided over a period characterized by the twin growth of nationalism and liberalism that saw economic expansion and a flourishing of culture, earning it the title of the *Belle Époque*. Under the reign of Franz Joseph, the monumental construction of the Ringstraße began in Vienna (completed in 1865). The resignation of several artists from their national association saw the founding of a movement that came to be known as the Vienna Secession, represented by such famous names as Gustav Klimt, Oskar Kokoschka, and Egon Schiele, and the development of a new aesthetic. In architecture, this new aesthetic was represented by Otto Wagner and Joseph Maria Olbrich (who designed the Secession's Building in Vienna, built to house exhibitions of these break-away artists). In terms of music, the age of late Romanticism represented by Johann Strauss, not to mention Franz Schubert and Ludwig van Beethoven, gave way to a new avant-garde aesthetic that became increasingly radical—the ultra late Romanticism of Gustav Mahler and Anton Bruckner, and then the modernism of the Second Viennese School (Arnold Schoenberg, Anton Webern, Alban Berg).

Yet not all was well: a major stock market crash induced the Panic of 1873, a financial crisis that provoked the Long Depression, plunging Austria, Europe, and the world into economic recession for a decade. And as the expression *fin de siècle* implies, the beginning of a new world inevitably involves the end of an old one, and the rapid social and political change of the years left opposing options open: the optimistic belief in progress and a more differentiated, pessimistic appraisal. For this second option, various European thinkers were available as spokesmen: Bénédict Morel (1809–1873) and Max Nordau (1849–1923) with their respective theories of *dégénérescence* or *Entartung*, for instance, or Philip Mainländer (1841–1876) and his *Philosophy of Redemption* (1876, 1886) that proclaimed "the insight that non-being is better than being" to be the supreme moral principle.[1] The godfather of all pessimistic systems is usually considered to be Arthur Schopenhauer, but is it valid to apply the term "pessimism" to him?

Schopenhauer briefly considers the question of whether his philosophy is pessimistic in *The World as Will and Representation* (WWR1), but he rejects the charge because his system "starts from the universal and is conducted *a priori*" (WWR1$_{[P]}$, 324). While maintaining that "*all life is suffering*" (WWR1$_{[P]}$, 310), he concedes in volume 2 that an anecdote told by a traveler to Java of how a squirrel is drawn, as if by magic, by a snake right into its jaws serves "as an argument for *pessimism*" (WWR2$_{[P]}$, 356). In WWR2, §17, he notes that "the *fundamental difference* of all religions" is not whether they are monotheistic, polytheistic, pantheistic, or atheistic, but "whether they are optimistic or pessimistic," defining these terms to mean "whether they present the existence of this world as justified by itself" or "as something which can be conceived only as the consequence of our guilt"—and hence "really ought not to be" (WWR2$_{[P]}$, 170). At the same time, whether Schopenhauer's system is ultimately pessimistic or not must surely remain in doubt[2] for it does appear to offer some form of redemption—through art.

The philosophical outlook of Austria of the *fin de siècle* was not naturally inclined to Schopenhauer, given his credentials as a philosophical Idealist. The essentially anti-Idealist, anti-Kantian tone of Catholic southern Europe's philosophical temperament was set by Bernard Bolzano (1781–1848), a Prague philosopher known as the Bohemian Leibniz. Trained in the Leibniz-Wolff school of philosophy, Bolzano rejected Kant's transcendental philosophy and Hegel's Idealism alike, even if one of his main works, *Wissenschaftslehre* (1837), recalled the title of a very different work by Fichte. In its focus on the relationship of language, thought, and logic, Bolzano's embrace of philosophical Realism and rejection of transcendental philosophy and Idealism reflects, in the view of Peter Kampitz, a fundamental characteristic of Austrian philosophizing.[3] And yet, as David S. Luft has argued, not only did Kant and his successors eventually come to dominate the intellectual scene in Austria, but Schopenhauer had "certain affinities" with the Austrian worldview: namely, Schopenhauer's anti-Hegelianism and anti-historicism; his "static and ahistorical" view; and his overall outlook was congenial to "the ethic of resignation and quietism" that actually underlay Austrian philosophical optimism.[4] From 1860 onward, Schopenhauer was a palpable influence in the cultural life of *fin de siècle* Austria.

At the beginning of their study of *fin de siècle* Austria entitled *Wittgenstein's Vienna* (1973), Allan Janik and Stephen Toulmin point out that the origins of twelve-tone music, modern architecture, legal and logical positivism, nonrepresentational painting, and psychoanalysis not only coincided with each other but also with a revival of interest in Kierkegaard—and Schopenhauer.[5] One anecdote serves to illustrate this intriguing interconnection of intellectual developments: a shared interest in Kantian philosophy that prompted Gustav Mahler to present the conductor Bruno Walter with the collected works of Schopenhauer as a Christmas gift.

30.2 MUSIC

In fact there is a good reason to argue that music served as a conduit for the increasingly lively engagement with Schopenhauer in intellectual, artistic, and literary circles in Austria in general and Vienna in particular, and this is perhaps not surprising given the significance of music within Schopenhauer's philosophy as offering an aesthetic means of direct access to the metaphysical will (see WWR1, §52). In this respect the major protagonist should be seen as Richard Wagner (1813–1883), on the composition of whose *Ring* cycle of operas the discussion of tragedy in Schopenhauer's WWR1, §51, exercised a strong influence—and one that served as a corrective to the optimistic deification of humankind found in Ludwig Feuerbach (1804–1872).[6] As Wagner himself wrote, "For those seeking in philosophy their justification for political and social agitation on behalf of the so-called 'free individual,' there was no sustenance whatever here, where what was demanded was the absolute renunciation of all such methods of satisfying the claims of the human personality....From now on this book never left me entirely through the years, and by the summer of [1854?] I had already gone through it for the fourth time."[7] Although not an Austrian, Wagner's significance lies in his musical propagation of Schopenhauerian thinking, including (and especially) in Vienna.

In *The Gay Science* (§99), Nietzsche listed the chief doctrines of Schopenhauer that he regarded as influential in the nineteenth century, especially on Wagner,[8] and, in *The Case of Wagner* (§4), he colorfully characterized the change in philosophical tone that takes place in *The Ring* in the course of *Siegfried* as follows: "What happened? A misfortune. The ship struck a reef; Wagner was stuck. The reef was Schopenhauer's philosophy; Wagner was stranded on a *contrary* world view....So he translated the *Ring* into Schopenhauer's terms. Everything goes wrong, everything perishes, the new world is as bad as the old: the *nothing*, the Indian Circe beckons."[9] At the same time, it is worth noting that Schopenhauer himself ignored Wagner's attempts at contact, including an invitation to Zurich and involvement with a proposal to create a chair in Schopenhauerian philosophy at Zurich University; indeed, he did not even like *The Ring*, as Wagner later discovered to his immense disappointment.[10] The chief aspect of Schopenhauer's philosophy on which Nietzsche here focuses, its alleged pessimism, was obviously one of the key characteristics of his influence in *fin de siècle* Austria, together with his emphasis on the cognitive value of aesthetic experience (i.e., the power of art)—although which of these is the more significant remains debatable.

30.3 FREUD AND PSYCHOANALYSIS

One of the great movements to emerge from *fin de siècle* Vienna was psychoanalysis, although its founder, Sigmund Freud (1856–1939), seems to have been keen to downplay the significance Schopenhauer may have had for his theories. For Thomas Mann (1875–1955), however, the significance of Schopenhauer for psychoanalysis was obvious: "Schopenhauer, as a psychologist of the will, is the father of all modern psychology: from him there runs, via the psychological radicalism of Nietzsche, a straight line to Freud and to those who developed his depth psychology and applied it to the humanities." Mann declared this in an essay of 1938, adding that "Nietzsche's anti-intellectualism and anti-Socratism is nothing other than a philosophical affirmation and glorification of Schopenhauer's discovery of the primacy of the will, his pessimistic insight into the secondary and subservient relation of the intellect to the will."[11]

Indeed, one of Freud's predecessors, Richard Krafft-Ebing (1840–1902), had used first Schiller, then Schopenhauer as his starting-point in his Foreword to the first edition of *Psychopathia sexualis* (1886), noting that Schopenhauer (in WWR2, ch. 44) had considered it surprising that love—"a matter that generally plays so important a part in the life of man"—has hitherto "been almost entirely disregarded by philosophers, and lies before us as a raw and untreated material," with the exceptions of Plato, Rousseau, and Kant (WWR2$_{[P]}$, 532).[12] While Krafft-Ebing agreed with the analysis attributed to Schopenhauer that, "as a result of senile dementia, the abnormally excited and perverse instinct may be directed exclusively to persons of the same sex,"[13] he rejected the suggestion also attributed to Schopenhauer that "nature seeks to prevent old men (i.e., over fifty years of age) from begetting children . . . [by] turn[ing] the sexual instinct in old men toward their own sex."[14]

For his part, however, Freud always downplayed the significance of Schopenhauer for the development of psychoanalysis. In "On the History of the Psychoanalytic Movement" (1914), Freud insisted that the theory of repression—"the corner-stone on which the whole structure of psychoanalysis rests"—came to him "quite independently of any other source": "I know," he claimed, "of no outside impression which might have suggested it to me, and for a long time I imagined it to be entirely original, until Otto Rank[15] showed us a passage in Schopenhauer's *World as Will and* Idea, in which the philosopher seeks to give an explanation of insanity."[16] Ten years or so later, in "An Autobiographical Study" (1925), Freud reiterated that "the large extent to which psychoanalysis coincides with the philosophy of Schopenhauer—not only did he assert the dominance of the emotions and the supreme importance of sexuality but he was even aware of the mechanism of repression—is not to be traced to my acquaintance with his teaching," and added: "I read Schopenhauer very late in my life."[17]

Yet in a short paper entitled "The Resistances to Psychoanalysis" written at the same time, Freud seemed to concede the priority of Schopenhauer, writing that the views of psychoanalytic theory were "not entirely new" and that "the incomparable significance of sexual life had been proclaimed by the philosopher Schopenhauer in an intensely impressive passage."[18] The passage in question, it has been suggested, is WWR2, chapter 42, entitled "The Life of the Species."[19] In this chapter, Schopenhauer argues that "the sexual impulse is the kernel of the will-to-live, and consequently the concentration of all willing...therefore, I have called the genitals the focus of the will," and he declares "indeed, it may be said that man is concrete sexual impulse" (WWR2$_{[P]}$, 512). At the same time, Freud had identified Schopenhauer as an intellectual predecessor of the notion of *Thanatos* or the death-drive, an idea Freud had introduced in 1920 in *Beyond the Pleasure Principle* as a counteracting force to sexuality or *Eros*: in positing the existence of two "instinctual impulses," the life instincts and the death instincts, Freud conceded he had "unwittingly steered [a] course into the harbour of Schopenhauer's philosophy," since for him death is the "true result and to that extent the purpose of life" (cf. PP1$_{[P]}$, 197).[20]

In her account dated February 23, 1913, of a visit to Freud's house, Lou Andreas-Salomé (1861–1937) related how she and Freud had discussed "his resistance to pure philosophy" and "his notion that it is really essential to struggle against the need peculiar to thinkers for an ultimate unity in things, recognizing this need as the product of a profoundly anthropomorphic root and custom and, furthermore, as a possible hindrance or distraction in the detailed research of positive science."[21] In turn, in a letter to Lou Andreas-Salomé of August 1, 1919, where Freud signaled that he was working on *Beyond the Pleasure Principle* by saying that "for my old age I have chosen the theme of death," he remarked how he had "stumbled on a remarkable notion based on my theory of the instincts" and now had to read "all kind of things relevant to it," claiming that he was reading Schopenhauer "for the first time"—or so he wrote.[22]

In some respects Freud was right to distance himself from Schopenhauer. Although Richard Wollheim has compared Freud's conception of a "bodily ego" to Schopenhauer's notion of the will,[23] Freud regards it as characteristic of the "primitive" mental state to project feelings into a bodily form, whereas Schopenhauer argues that the will does not just represent itself as bodily form—thanks to the *principium individuationis* that structures our perception in space and time, the will actually *is* represented in bodily form. And although R. K. Gupta has highlighted the "striking similarity" between, on the one hand, the Schopenhauerian will, and, on the other, Freud's concept of the id (*das Es*), as "the real driving force behind [human] action in the dark depths of the unconscious,"[24] the *id* is a function of the individual human psyche, whereas the Will is a universal, supraindividual force.

Overall one could assess Schopenhauer's contributions to the development of psychoanalysis as residing in his emphasis on desire. In WWR1, Schopenhauer describes the genitals as "the real *focus* of the will" and as "the life-preserving principle assuring to time endless life" (WWR1$_{[P]}$, 330) and in WWR2, chapter 42 ("The Life of the Species"), he writes that "the sexual impulse" is "the desire that constitutes even the very nature of man," as "the most complete manifestation of the will-to-live, its most distinctly expressed type" and as "the most vehement of cravings, the desire of desires, the concentration of all our willing" (WWR2$_{[P]}$, 512–14). More fundamental, however, is Schopenhauer's emphasis on unconscious motivation. In WWR2, chapter 14 ("On the Association of

Ideas"), he compares consciousness to "a sheet of water of some depth" and maintains that "the distinctly conscious ideas are merely the surface" (WWR2$_{[P]}$, 135). Finally, there is an important affinity of temperament between Schopenhauer and Freud. At the end of WWR2, chapter 45 ("On the Affirmation of the Will-to-Live"), Schopenhauer asks the question, "Is the game worth the candle?" (WWR2$_{[P]}$, 572), answering, in the following chapter ("On the Vanity and Suffering of Life"), it would seem, in the negative: "The present is always inadequate, but the future is uncertain, and the past irrecoverable" (WWR2$_{[P]}$, 573). It is entirely in line with this outlook that Freud, in the conclusion to an early paper on "The Psychotherapy of Hysteria" (1893), described the goal of therapy as being to "transform hysterical misery into common unhappiness."[25]

30.4 GENDER AND MISOGYNY

In his (in)famous essay on women, Schopenhauer described women as "the stunted, narrow-shouldered, broad-hipped and short-legged sex,"[26] thereby earning himself a reputation as one of the great philosophical misogynists of all time. Even though Schopenhauer's dismissal of women as "the *unaesthetic* sex" is implicitly a defense of the artistic values of Greek antiquity, his argument is no more acceptable. Yet even Schopenhauer's anti-female diatribe was outstripped by that of Otto Weininger (1880–1903), the author of *Sex and Character* (1903). This work, an "abstruse mixture of biological theories and Platonic conceptions,"[27] gained massive popularity after its author's suicide (in the house where Beethoven had died) and represents an even more extreme version of Schopenhauer's or Nietzsche's misogyny.[28] On one occasion, Weininger praises Schopenhauer for his "infinitely profound, lasting insight" that "soul, personality, character is...identical with the free will or at least that the will coincides with the ego insofar as the latter is considered in relation to the absolute."[29] Overall Weininger is indebted to Schopenhauer in two respects: first and most obviously, his misogyny, and second, his Platonism.

The Platonic Ideas play an important role in Schopenhauer's philosophical system as helping to explain why the phenomenal world is characterized by multiplicity whereas the noumenal world is identified with the one, single, universal Will. Weininger drew on the Platonic myth of the *Symposium* that male and female were ideal types that were forever seeking to unite, but in vain, and modified it by presenting male and female as inimically opposed: the female is entirely focused on sexuality, but the male is only in part. Consequently, the female is constitutionally incapable of intellect, ethics, logic, value, and the desire for immortality; in this way, Weininger takes Schopenhauer's misogyny to new heights (or new depths). But other Schopenhauerian approaches to the feminine were possible.

Born in Lemberg (now Lviv), the capital of the Kingdom of Galicia and Lodomeria (now part of Ukraine, but formerly a province of the Austrian Empire), Leopold von Sacher-Masoch (1836–1895)—whose father had been ennobled by the Austrian

Emperor—is probably best known today as the author of *Venus in Furs* (1870). This novella was intended to form part of what turned out to be an unfinished cycle, entitled *The Legacy of Cain* (*Love*, 1870; *Property*, 1877; to be followed by further volumes provisionally entitled *The State*, *War*, *Work*, and *Death*), and formed part of its first volume dedicated to "love"—or more precisely sexuality—a highly Schopenhauerian theme.

In *The Wanderer*, Sacher-Masoch's prologue to this epic cycle, a number of other Schopenhauerian themes are struck: the world as a place of "painful testing," pleasure as nothing more than "a redemption from gnawing desire," and the figure of the hermit as a symbol of renunciation and the triumph of knowledge over the will.[30] Sacher-Masoch agrees with Schopenhauer that "pain as such is inevitable and essential to life" (WWR1$_{[P]}$, 315) and affirms "the fact that all happiness is only of a negative, not a positive nature, and that for this reason it cannot be a lasting satisfaction and gratification, but always delivers us only from a pain or want that must be followed either by a new pain or by languor, empty longing, and boredom" (WWR1$_{[P]}$, 320). Sacher-Masoch's work illustrates Schopenhauer's thesis of "the impossibility of attaining lasting satisfaction and the negative nature of all happiness," the inevitable conclusion from the view that "the will, whose objectification is human life like every phenomenon, is a striving without aim or end" (WWR1$_{[P]}$, 320–21).

Schopenhauer's essentially negative representation of the female and the feminine finds its counterpart in the figure of the Magna Mater in Ludwig Anzengruber's short story with a prehistoric setting, *Jaggernaut* (c. 1865) or the various "cruel women" that populate Sacher-Masoch's writings, from Catherine the Great (in the collection of novellas placed under her name)[31] to the whip-bearing, fur-clad Wanda of *Venus in Furs*. As the narrator of *The Capitulant* (or *The Man Who Re-Enlisted*), the second part of volume 1 of *The Legacy of Cain*, puts it, "everything yields to necessity, everything living feels how sad existence is and nevertheless each struggles desperately to stay alive and the human being struggles with nature and with fellow humans, and the man with the woman and even their love is only a struggle for existence."[32] Sacher-Masoch's literary work reflects the foregrounding of sexuality in the work of Schopenhauer, for whom not just every plant and every animal but every individual human being are "concrete sexual impulse" and for whom "the sexual impulse is therefore the most complete manifestation of the will-to-live, its most distinctly expressed type" (WWR2$_{[P]}$, 514) and who devoted an entire chapter to "The Metaphysics of Sexual Love" (WWR2, chapter 44). Similarly, Sacher-Masoch's "The Wanderer" echoes the Schopenhauerian theme of renunciation, embodied in the figure of the wanderer, even if it is for his descriptions of sexual ecstasy and sexual excess that Sacher-Masoch is otherwise justly celebrated.[33]

30.5 LITERATURE

As Dietmar Goltschnigg has argued, the worldview of the bourgeoisie was shaped after the failed revolution of 1848 by primarily two contradictory tendencies: where it maintained an unbroken optimism, it had recourse to Feuerbach; where it descended into skeptical-pessimistic resignation, it found a leading teacher in Schopenhauer. Since the 1860s, a pessimistic outlook had been decisively determining the cultural and political consciousness alike of the conservative bourgeoisie or middle classes.[34] Yet, according to Burkhard Bittrich, the influence of Schopenhauer on Austrian thought (not least because of the absorption of Schopenhauerian and Darwinian ideas by such writers as Ferdinand von Saar and Sacher-Masoch) was even greater than the events of 1848.[35] In the wake of the stock market crash of 1873, the optimistic belief in progress began to decline at the same time as the liberal era in Austria came to an end in 1879, reflected in a growing skepticism that articulated itself as an adoption of Schopenhauerian pessimism.[36] In times such as those, parody and satire flourished, and nowhere more than in Vienna.

According to Edward Timms, the philosopher whom Karl Kraus (1874–1936)—that "apocalyptic satirist"—most admired was Schopenhauer, despite the sharp contrast in their personalities.[37] Indeed, on Janik and Toulmin's account, "if Kraus's views have a philosophical ancestry, this comes most assuredly from Schopenhauer," and as a significant point of affinity between the two they identify Schopenhauer's view on gender, which had been such an influence on Weininger, even if Kraus's view was less devastatingly negative.[38] For Kraus and his admirers, the Krausians, Schopenhauer's influence and popularity was due not least to "the epigrammatic punch and elegant literary style which set him off from his academic and professional colleagues in philosophy," especially the Hegelians.[39] In Die Fackel, the satirical journal or "anti-newspaper" which Kraus published and largely wrote himself between 1899 and 1936, Schopenhauer was mentioned on numerous occasions (see Adamy 1985, who points out that Kraus was a highly critical reader of Schopenhauer),[40] including one text called "The World as Representation" (Die Fackel 18, nos. 426–30 [June 15, 1916]), a satire on military claims that had been made by the Chief of Staff of the Italian Army, Luigi Cadorna.

Consulting the Austrian Academy Corpus digital edition of Die Fackel suggests Schopenhauer was mentioned on around 150 occasions (i.e., not particularly often over a period of thirty-seven or so years), but Schopenhauer's influence is more often felt in the use of such vocabulary and terminology as "will" and "representation" and in an acerbic, satirical writing tone of writing that may certainly be said to be analogous to Schopenhauer's. Kraus's attitude toward women in general and prostitutes (who played an important social role in the life of fin-de-siècle Vienna) in particular differed from Schopenhauer's: in fact, Kraus considered prostitutes to be more heroic than soldiers.[41]

As Peter Sprengel has suggested, the pantheistic view of nature as an essentially benevolent locus of harmony between all beings (including humans), as found in the monistic celebration of a self-regulating nature offered by Ernest Haeckel's General Morphology of the Organisms (1866), began to give way, under the combined influence of Schopenhauer and Darwin, to a darker vision of nature as a site of interminable conflict.[42] Foreshadowed in Werther's letter of August 18, in Goethe's novel The Sufferings of Young Werther with its reference to the "consuming power of nature," in the notion in Romantic Naturphilosophie of an "evil principle" in nature, and in Henrich Steffen's remarks in his Christian Religion-Philosophy about the "terrible passion" and the "anger, unbounded wrath" of some mammals, this view found its classic expression in Schopenhauer.[43] In WWR1, §27, for instance, Schopenhauer writes that "everywhere in nature we see contest, struggle, and the fluctuations of victory," citing the ichneumon fly, the hydra, and the Australian bull-dog ant as examples of nature's savage cruelty (WWR1$_{[P]}$, 146–47).

In his essay "By the Grave of a Suicide or the Despair of the Cheerful and the Cheerfulness of the Despairing" (1875), the Austrian writer Ferdinand Kürnberger (1821–1879) turns against the optimistic outlook that expects life to have meaning and one's subjective wishes to find fulfilment.[44] In other essays from the 1860s and 1870s, Kürnberger makes repeated reference to the "princely" or "masterful" Schopenhauer, praising the "teachings of the master" and the "intellectually weighty tree-top" of WWR.[45] And on two occasions, Kürnberger explicitly thematized the affinity of Schopenhauer and Darwin, in an essay on "The Axes of Optimism and Pessimism" (1867) and in a review (1877) of a study by Emerich du Mont (b. 1846–1911) of *Progress in the Light of the Doctrines of Schopenhauer and Darwin* (1876).[46] Yet is Kürnberger typical in this respect of Austrian writers? David Luft has suggested that Schopenhauer seems to have been "little more than a backdrop" for some leading figures in *fin de siècle* Austria.[47]

For instance, Arthur Schnitzler (1862–1931) told Olga Waissnix on September 26, 1886, that he was "throwing himself into the philosophers" by becoming a friend of Kant and "especially Schopenhauer."[48] Yet, two years later, he responded to Olga's enthusiastic praise for Schopenhauer with a critique of his doctrine of renunciation.[49] And some twenty years later, in a letter of 1917 to Richard Beer-Hofmann (1866–1945), Schnitzler expressed an idiosyncratic skepticism about philosophy in general, adding that "it is not that I 'underestimate' philosophy—it's just that I rank it differently from how its adepts usually like to."[50] Nevertheless, Ivett Guntersdorfer has identified a Schopenhauerian influence on two of Schnitzler's best-known novellas, *Die Toten schweigen* (1897) and *Leutnant Gustl* (1900), in their treatment of the theme of honor.[51] The concept of honor was described by Schopenhauer as having an "objective" side (because it is "other people's opinion of what we are worth") and a "subjective" one ("the respect we pay to this opinion") (PP1$_{[P]}$, 364 [translation modified]). Of course, Schopenhauer's belief that "it is part of a man's honour to resent a breach of the marriage tie on the part of his wife, and to punish it, at the very least by separating from her" (PP1$_{[P]}$, 369) reflects precisely the sort of value system that Schnitzler, in his works, was seeking to question.

Then again, in 1891, Hugo von Hofmannsthal (1874–1929) had told a correspondent (once again, Beer-Hofmann) that he, too, was reading Schopenhauer,[52] although the sparseness of subsequent references to him suggests that Hofmannsthal may have shared the kind of antipathy toward the philosopher that was expressed by Schnitzler in a letter to Hofmannsthal in 1895. Here Schnitzler described Schopenhauer as someone for whom it is "as though the world had ceased to exist... once he had summarized it in a formula,"[53] which is in some ways a fairly accurate summary of Schopenhauer's position in the concluding sentences of WWR1.[54] Later, Hofmannsthal found an direct route of sorts into Schopenhauer, thanks to reading *Mysticism, the Artists, and Life* (1900) by Rudolf Kassner (1873–1959), as Hofmannsthal declared in a letter to Kassner of

December 22(?), 1901: "Never were continuous thoughts of Schopenhauer, of Nietzsche or others like them, capable of giving me such inner happiness, such illumination of my self right into its very depths, such an understanding of why one writes poetry, *of what is happening when one writes poetry*, and what it has to do with existence."[55]

In fact, as David Luft has suggested, Kassner and his like—the essayists, novelists, and thinkers who "reached creative maturity" in the first decade of the twentieth century, such as Karl Kraus (1874–1936), Martin Buber (1878–1965), Grete Meisel-Hess (1879–1922), Otto Weininger (1880–1903), Robert Musil (1880–1942), Ferdinand Ebner (1882–1931), Hermann Broch (1886–1951), and Ludwig Wittgenstein (1889–1951)—were responsible for the sudden surge in "philosophical irrationalism" represented by Schopenhauer as well as by Nietzsche and by Kierkegaard in *fin de siècle* Austria.[56] As Hofmannsthal's remark to Kassner suggests, however, what provoked such a deep fascination with Schopenhauer and Nietzsche was their aesthetic theories.

In *Mysticism, the Artists, and Life*, Kassner identified the following maneuver by Schopenhauer as key to understanding his influence on shaping the modern conception of the individual, as reflected in Nietzsche, Jens Peter Jacobsen (1847–1885), Henri-Frédéric Amiel (1821–1881) Maurice Maeterlinck, Gabriel d'Annunzio, and Max Klinger (among others).[57] In the final chapter of WWR2, entitled "Epiphilosophy," Schopenhauer says: "From the most ancient times, man has been called the microcosm. I have reversed the proposition, and have shown the world as the macranthropos" (WWR$_{[P]}$, 642). On this account, will and representation exhaust the true nature of the world and of the human individual alike, and Austrian modernity reflects this sense that, by investigating the individual, one is discovering the world as well.

There is a continuity between the Schopenhauerian tenor of *fin de siècle* Austria and the more explicit engagement with Schopenhauer's philosophy to be found in its leading Modernists. For instance, Manfred Durzak has argued that Hermann Broch (1886–1951) found his way to Plato and to Kant via Schopenhauer and that Schopenhauer conditioned Broch's conception of art as essentially metaphysical in function.[58] An example of how Broch's great novel, *The Death of Virgil* (1945), bears witness to this interest is its appropriation and conflation of two Schopenhauerian images: first, the relation between microcosm and macrocosm, and second, the predicament of human existence as being like a man in a boat (WWR1, §63). In this episode, the protagonist attains to a key Schopenhauerian insight into the nature of existence: "He himself as he lay here was image, and steering toward the most real reality, carried by invisible waves, immersed in them, the image of the ship was his own image, coming out of darkness, moving into darkness, sinking into darkness, he himself was the immense [*unermeßlich*] ship that at the same time is immensity, and he himself was the flight that aims at this immensity, he himself was the fleeing ship, he himself was the goal, he himself was immense."[59] The Schopenhauerian theme of the human being as resuming the world and being a world, and the image of "the boatman [who] sits in his small boat, trusting his frail craft in a stormy sea that is boundless [*unbegrenzt*] in every direction" (WWR1$_{[P]}$, 352–53) are here skillfully combined.

Born in 1880, the beginning of the *fin de siècle*, much of the work of Robert Musil (1880–1942), especially his great novel, *The Man Without Qualities* (1930–1943), falls outside the period considered here. Yet Musil's engagement with Schopenhauer at the start of his literary career coincides with the heyday of the *fin de siècle*, even if that engagement appears to have been sporadic. Nevertheless, Musil's approach to Schopenhauer through Nietzsche and Eduard Hartmann (1842–1906), and the development of his thinking about art and the unconscious in this philosophical context,[60] testify to the widespread, if diffuse, presence of Schopenhauer in Viennese intellectual circles in the *fin de siècle*. Kelly Coble has suggested that Musil's writings, both published and unpublished, reveal "the subtle presence of a Schopenhauerian reasoning," even or especially when Schopenhauer "seems to have been the last thing on Musil's mind."[61] To this extent Musil's debt to Schopenhauer as a "great writer" as well as a "splenetic genius,"[62] together with the sense that, when investigating irrational motives for our actions or seeking to unite ethics and aesthetics, then Schopenhauer "is never far away,"[63] serves as a paradigm for the influence, often indirect yet nevertheless palpable, of Schopenhauer on *fin de siècle* Austria.

30.6 Philosophy

On Janik and Toulmin's account, there were three significant philosophical traditions at work in the Viennese milieu of the 1890s and 1900s: first, the neo-empiricism of Ernst Mach (1838–1916), with its emphasis on "sense impressions" and natural science; second, the anti-intellectualist approach to morality and aesthetics as proposed by the "anti-philosopher," Søren Kierkegaard (1813–1855) and as reflected in the novels and essays of Leo Tolstoy (1828–1910); and the Kantian analysis of reality in terms of "representation" (*Vorstellung*), an analysis which underpinned and was developed by Schopenhauer's philosophy.[64]

The Kantian background is crucial for understanding the essence of Schopenhauer's philosophy and its intellectual influence. In the preface to the first edition of WWR and again in the preface to the second, Schopenhauer himself emphasized that his philosophy "starts from Kant's, and therefore presupposes a thorough knowledge of it," since Kant's philosophy "produces a fundamental change in every mind that has grasped it" (WWR1$_{[P]}$, xxiii). This fundamental change is an insight into the limits of human reason, as a corrective to the way reason often "falls into obscurity and contradictions" (*Critique of Pure Reason*, Preface, A viii).[65] Schopenhauer accepts Kant's reasoning, but modifies it in two significant respects. First, he argues against Kant that it *is* possible to know the thing-in-itself, using the faculty of intuition. Second, he identifies the thing-in-itself with the metaphysical will and describes it as something essentially irrational, exhibiting all those obscurities and contradictions Kant had sought to abjure.

The fact that, in *fin de siècle* Vienna, Kantianism met in a confluence with neo-empiricism and anti-intellectualism meant that Schopenhauer tended to be read with a particular inflection. The philosopher Fritz Mauthner (1849–1923) is a case in point. As well as being a novelist, critic, and editor of the *Berliner Tageblatt*, Mauthner espoused philosophical skepticism and presented himself as a critic of language in his *Contributions to a Critique of Language* (3 vols., 1901–1903). In this respect, Mauthner identified himself with the British of tradition of empiricism, exemplified by John Locke's *Essay Concerning Human Understanding*, and in this way sharing the intellectual Anglophilia of Schopenhauer (Janek and Toulmin 1973: 123). Yet Schopenhauer was Mauthner's predecessor in another respect, inasmuch as Mauthner took his philosophical stance on the epistemological position formulated by Schopenhauer's dissertation, *On the Fourfold Root of the Principle of Sufficient Reason* (Janik and Toulmin 1973: 23, cf. 124–25). In *On Linguistics* (1901), the second volume of his *Contributions to a Critique of Language*, Mauthner praised Schopenhauer as a worthy successor to Kant and a fierce opponent of Hegel. While conceding there was a weakness in Schopenhauer's system, Mauthner's encomium did not shy away from comparing his significance to Plato's, and declaring that "anyone who demands no more from philosophy than the highest conceivable degree of clarity [*Anschaulichkeit*], the liveliest metaphorical presentation of abstract concepts, has to call him a powerful philosophical poet [*Denkdichter*]."[66] In his four-volume study of the history of atheism, Mauthner declared that he, Schopenhauer, rather than Spinoza, deserved to be honored as a prince of atheism.[67]

Today Mauthner is more or less forgotten, which cannot be said for Ludwig Wittgenstein. Arguably the most important point of contact between Wittgenstein and Schopenhauer lies in the micro–macrocosmic tendencies of both thinkers (i.e., the extent to which both men draw on a medieval or post-classical trend, exemplified by such thinkers as Jakob Böhme [1575–1624]), to consider the human being as a microcosm of a macrocosm created by God and hence as having in miniature the same structure as a slice through the macrocosm. Schopenhauer draws on this idea in various ways, arguing that the individual will tells us something about the universal will or that art can have a cognitive value by telling us something about one aspect of the world and hence revealing the inner truth of the world as a whole. Similar microcosmic tendencies can be found in the thought of Wittgenstein, such as his declaration in *Tractatus logico-philosophicus* that "*the limits of my language* mean the limits of my world" (§5.6), and hence that "I am my world. (The microcosm)" (§5.63).[68]

Furthermore, as Robert Wicks has suggested, Schopenhauer's philosophy involves a kind of "philosophy-transcending aspect," inasmuch as understanding how our consciousness is constructed in and through the *principium rationis sufficientis* (or "principle of sufficient reason," i.e., that for everything there is a reason or cause) allows us to transcend that principle and, in so doing, transform both our consciousness—and our lives.[69] "To those in whom the will has turned and denied itself, this very real world of ours with all its suns and galaxies, is—nothing," as Schopenhauer asserts (WWR1$_{[P]}$, 412). A similar move is intimated in the famous conclusion of Wittgenstein's *Tractatus*—"My propositions are elucidatory in this way: he who understands me finally recognizes them as senseless, when he has climbed out through them, on them, over them. (He must so to speak throw away the ladder, after he has climbed up on it.) He must surmount these propositions; then he sees the world rightly" (§6.54)—and its celebrated last words, "Whereof one cannot speak, thereof one must be silent" (§7).[70]

There are other parallels, too. The role in Schopenhauer's thought has already been noted; in WWR1, §52, he maintains that "music is by no means like the other arts, namely a copy of the Ideas, but a *copy of the will itself*," that it "expresses the metaphysical to everything physical in the world," and that therefore "we could just as well call the world embodied music as embodied will" (WWR1$_{[P]}$, 257, 263, 262–63). In his later life, Wittgenstein used to praise the expressive power of music, as well as performing music on the piano with a quasi-ritualistic precision. And Wittgenstein's espousal of an ethical, even existential, dimension of philosophy sits well with Schopenhauer's impatience with academic philosophy; according to Theodore Redpath, Wittgenstein once remarked of Schopenhauer, "Well, he *was* a philosopher," adding that a philosopher was, above all, "a teacher of manners."[71]

30.7 VISUAL ART

According to Carl E. Schorske, the works of the Symbolist painter Gustav Klimt (1862–1918) presented a "Schopenhauerian universe of boundaries liquefied and rational structures undermined" and thus "limned in allegorical and symbolic language the suffering psyche of modern man impotently caught in the flow of fate."[72] On his account, Klimt's "vision of the universe" is identical to Schopenhauer's of the world "as Will, as blind energy in an endless round of meaningless parturience, love and death."[73] Nowhere can we see this vision more clearly than in his painting, "Philosophy," a work commissioned, along with paintings of "Medicine" and "Jurisprudence", by the University of Vienna and displayed on the ceiling of its Great Hall—an ensemble Klimt himself described as follows: "On the left a group of figures: the beginning of life, fruition, decay. On the right, the globe as mystery. Emerging below, a figure of light: knowledge."[74] In Peter Vergo's view, Klimt's knowledge of Schopenhauer was mediated to him by Wagner, specifically the summary of Schopenhauerian philosophy in his essay on *Beethoven*, and he suggests that the iconography and the message of his painting "Philosophy" were influenced by *Das Rheingold*; the implication here is—the more Wagnerian, the more Schopenhauerian.[75] Yet David S. Luft has contended that Klimt's "erotic vision of reality" in these paintings "drew on the inspiration of Schopenhauer and Nietzsche" inasmuch as it challenged "the liberal view of reason, science, and medicine" advocated by Friedrich Jodl (1849–1914), an influential Vienna-based philosopher who championed the values of the Enlightenment.[76] For Schorske, "Philosophy" ultimately owes more to Nietzsche than it does to Schopenhauer;[77] while Allan Janik has in turn taken issue with Schorske's understanding of the role played by Nietzsche in turn-of-the-century Vienna.[78] To a certain extent, this can seem like hair-splitting, inasmuch as Klimt moved, as Schorske notes, "in social and intellectual circles in which the interlocked figures of Wagner, Schopenhauer, and Nietzsche were all admired," and so it is equally likely that Klimt could have "drawn inspiration for his cosmic vision from any one of them."[79]

Moreover, it points to the difficulty in being able clearly to identify a precise intellectual influence in any work of the kind that is as suggestive and symbolic as Klimt's. Just as one can point with equal validity to Goethe's influence on Klimt's *Beethoven Frieze* and to Nietzsche's,[80] so one could see this late, great work in the Vienna Secession Building, originally designed to accompany a sculpture by the German Symbolist Max Klinger (1857–1920), as thoroughly Schopenhauerian in temperament. The dreaming, will-less genii who float their way along the top of the frieze, most notably in the first painting in the frieze, are surely an evocation of those who have given up the will, while the naked figures in the middle of the first wall, hands clasped in supplication to a stern knight, represent the need for the body to subdue itself through reason. On the end wall, the three gorgons; the three women representing sickness, madness, and death; the mythical, ape-like figure of Typhoeus; three women representing lasciviousness, wantonness, and intemperance; and, finally, the figure of gnawing grief depict the lure of sensual desire and willing and their disastrous consequences. And on the final wall, the gold-draped figure playing a lyre represents the salvation of humankind to be found in art, converting the hitherto horizontal genii into vertical figures, while the final phallic representation of the words in Schiller's ode, "To Joy," set to music by Beethoven, captures the transcendence which only love of art can deliver; behind stand figures in meditative, ecstatic silence, who have in all likelihood abolished the will and (in the words of the conclusion of WWR1) discovered that "to those in whom the will has turned and denied itself, this very real world of ours with all its suns and galaxies is—nothing" (WWR1$_{[P]}$, 412). Whether or not this work is directly influenced by Schopenhauer, it is surely soaked in a Schopenhauerian (rather than Nietzschean) temperament through its visual symbolism of a redemption-through-renunciation mediated by art.

30.8 CONCLUSION

According to the Presocratic philosopher Heraclitus, "a man's character is his fate" (ἦθος ἀνθρώπῳ δαίμων) (DK 22 B 119),[81] and the notion of "character" is clearly an ancient one. Weininger claimed that the notion of "characterology" has its intellectual origins in the thought of Plato, Kant, and Schopenhauer[82]: in Aristophanes's speech in the *Symposium*, in Kant's notion in his *Idea of a Universal History* of an individual's "intelligible character" as something outside time, and in Schopenhauer's "metaphysics of sexual love." In fact, characterology was very much in the air at the time of the *fin de siècle*; in Munich, Ludwig Klages (1872–1956) was developing his theory of *Charakterkunde*, and after the First World War, one of the most successful works of popular neo-Kantian literature was a work by the philosopher and psychologist Eduard Spranger (1882–1963) entitled *Lebensformen* (1914) (translated as *Types of Men*).[83]

In WWR1, §55, Schopenhauer takes over from Kant the distinction between the "empirical" and the "intelligible" character, but he introduces a third kind which he calls "acquired" character. Schopenhauer defines (acquired) character as "the character we obtain in life, through contact with the world," arguing that it is this character we mean "when anyone is praised as a person who has character, or censured as one without character" (WWR1$_{[P]}$, 303). The acquired character is of importance, he says, not so much for "ethics proper," as for *das Weltleben*—or for "life in the world" (WWR1$_{[P]}$, 307). To the extent that the thinkers, writers, and painters of *fin de siècle* Austria regarded their intellectual, cultural, and artistic deeds as, in Schopenhauer's words, "the impression or copy of the character, the mirror of the will," they participated in his project of "looking into this mirror" and "recogniz[ing] our innermost self, the kernel of our will" (WWR1$_{[P]}$, 302). In this respect one could speak of a deep affinity between Schopenhauer and *fin de siècle* Austria which is more significant than any specific details of his reception.

NOTES

1. Philipp Mainländer, *Philosophie der Erlösung*, vol. 1 [*Schriften*, edited by Winfried H. Müller-Seyfarth] (Hildesheim, Zureich, New York: Olms, 1999), 216.

2. For further discussion, see Wolfgang Schömel, *Apokalyptische Reiter sind in der Luft: Zum Irrationalismus und Pessimismus zwischen Nachmärz und Jahrhundertwende* (Opladen: Westdeutscher Verlag, 1985).

3. Peter Kampitz, *Zwischen Schein und Wirklichkeit: Eine kleine Geschichte der österreichischen Philosophie* (Vienna: Österreichischer Bundesverlag, 1984), 74.

4. David S. Luft, "Schopenhauer, Austria, and the Generation of 1905," *Central European History* 26 (1983), 53–75, at 61.

5. Allan Janik and Stephen Toulmin, *Wittgenstein's Vienna* (New York: Simon & Schuster, 1973), 18.

6. Roger Hollinrake, "Philosophical outlook," in *The Wagner Compendium: A Guide to Wagner's Life and Music*, edited by Barry Millington (New York: Schirmer, 1992), 143–46, at 144.

7. Richard Wagner, *My Life* (London: Constable, 1994), 509–10.

8. Friedrich Nietzsche, *The Gay Science*, translated by Walter Kaufmann (New York: Vintage, 1974), 152–56.

9. Friedrich Nietzsche, *Basic Writings*, edited and translated by Walter Kaufmann (New York: Modern Library, 1968), 620.

10. Hollinrake, "Philosophical Outlook," 145.

11. Thomas Mann, "Schopenhauer," in *Schriften und Reden zur Literatur, Kunst und Philosophie*, vol. 2 [*Das essayistische Werk*, edited by Hans Bürgin] (Frankfurt am Main/Hamburg: Fischer, 1968), 251–90, at 288. For further discussion, see Edo Reents, *Zu Thomas Manns Schopenhauer-Rezeption* (Würzburg: Königshausen & Neumann, 1998).

12. See also Richard von Krafft-Ebing, *Psychopathia Sexualis, with especial reference to the Antipathic Sexual Instinct: A Medico-Forensic Study*, translated by F. J. Rebman (New York: Rebman, 1899), v.

13. Ibid., 59.

14. Ibid., 341.

15. Otto Rank, "Schopenhauer über den Wahnsinn," *Zentralblatt für Psychoanalyse: Medizinische Monatsschrift für Seelenkunde* 1, no. 1/12 (1911), 68–71.

16. Sigmund Freud, *Historical and Expository Works on Psychoanalysis* [Penguin Freud Library, vol. 15], edited by Albert Dickinson, translated by James Strachey (Harmondsworth: Penguin, 1993), 72–73.

17. Ibid., 244.

18. Ibid., 268–69.

19. See WWW2, 510–16 (esp. 513–14).

20. Sigmund Freud, *On Metapsychology: The Theory of Psychoanalysis* [Pelican Freud Library, vol. 11], edited by Angela Richards, translated by James Strachey (Harmondsworth: Penguin, 1984), 322; see Schopenhauer's comments on "death, the actual result and insofar the purpose of life," in "Transcendent Speculation on the Apparent Deliberateness in the Fate of the Individual," in PP1, 177–97, at 197. For further discussion, see Stephan Atzert, "Zwei Aufsätze über Leben und Tod: Sigmund Freuds 'Jenseits des Lustprinzips' und Arthur Schopenhauers 'Transscendente Speculation über die anscheinende Absichtlichkeit im Schicksal des Einzelnen,'" *Schopenhauer-Jahrbuch* 86 (2005), 179–94.

21. Lou Andreas-Salomé, *The Freud Journal*, translated by Stanley A. Leavy (New York: Basic Books, 1964), 104.

22. Sigmund Freud and Lou Andreas-Salomé, *Letters*, edited by Ernst Pfeiffer, translated by William Robson-Scott and Elaine Robson-Scott (New York/London: Norton, 1985), 99.

23. Richard Wollheim, "The Bodily Ego," in *Philosophical Essays on Freud*, edited by Richard Wollheim and James Hopkins (Cambridge: Cambridge University Press, 1982), 124–38.

24. R. K. Gupta, "Freud and Schopenhauer," in *Schopenhauer: His Philosophical Achievement*, edited by Michael Fox (Sussex: Harvester Press, 1980), 226–35, at 226.

25. Sigmund Freud and Josef Breuer, *Studies on Hysteria* [Pelican Freud Library, vol. 3], edited by Angela Richards, translated by James and Alix Strachey (Harmondsworth: Penguin, 1974), 393.

26. Schopenhauer, *Essays and Aphorisms*, edited and translated by R. J. Hollingdale (Harmondsworth: Penguin, 1970), 85.

27. Kampitz, *Zwischen Schein und Wirklichkeit*, 147.

28. Chandak Sengoopta, *Otto Weininger: Sex, Science, and Self in Imperial Vienna* (Chicago/London: University of Chicago Press, 2000), 30.

29. Otto Weininger, *Geschlecht und Charakter: Eine prinzipielle Untersuchung*, 9th ed (Vienna/Leipzig: Braumüller, 1920), 260.

30. Peter Sprengel, "Darwin oder Schopenhauer? Fortschrittspessimismus und Pessimismus-Kritik in der österreichischen Literatur (Anzengruber, Kürnberger, Sacher-Masoch, Hamerling)," in *Literarisches Leben in Österreich 1848–1890*, edited by Klaus Amann, Hubert Lengauer, and Karl Wagner (Vienna, Cologne, Weimar: Böhlau, 2000), 60–93, at 73–74.

31. Leopold von Sacher-Masoch, *Katharina II: Russische Hofgeschichten* (Berlin: Knaur, n.d.).

32. Leopold von Sacher-Masoch, *Don Juan von Kolomea; Galizische Geschichten*, edited by Michael Farin (Bonn: Bouvier, 1985), 97; cited in Sprengel, "Darwin oder Schopenhauer?," 75.

33. Sprengel, "Darwin oder Schopenhauer?," 77. For further discussion, see Christoph Dolgan, *Poesie des Begehrens: Textkörper und Körpertexte bei Leopold von Sacher* (Würzburg: Königshausen & Neumann, 2009), 289; and Svletjana Milojević, *Die Poesie des Dilettantismus: Zur Rezeption und Wirkung Leopold von Sacher-Masochs* (Frankfurt am Main: Lang, 1998), 137–39.

34. Dietmar Goltschnigg, "Vorindustrieller Realismus und Literatur der Gründerzeit," in *Geschichte der deutschen Literatur vom 18. Jahrhundert bis zur Gegenwart*, vol. 2, edited by Viktor Žmegač (Königstein im Taunus: Athenäum, 1980), 1–108, at 16–17.

35. Burkhard Bittrich, "Biedermeier und Realismus in Österreich," in *Handbuch der deutschen Erzählung*, edited by Karl Konrad Pohlheim (Düsseldorf: Bagel, 1981), 356–81, at 371.

36. Sprengel, "Darwin oder Schopenhauer?," 61.

37. Edward Timms, *Karl Kraus: Apocalyptic Satirist: Culture and Catastrophe in Habsburg Vienna* (New Haven/London: Yale University Press, 1986), 170.

38. Janik and Toulmin, *Wittgenstein's Vienna*, 74.

39. Ibid., 164 and 150.

40. Bernard Adamy, "Schopenhauer-Rezeption bei Karl Kraus," *Schopenhauer-Jahrbuch* 66 (1985), 85–102.

41. Janik and Toulmin, *Wittgenstein's Vienna*, 70.

42. Sprengel, "Darwin oder Schopenhauer?," 63–65.

43. Ibid., 64–65.

44. Ibid., 67.

45. Ibid., 68.

46. Ibid., 69–70. See Ferdindand Kürnberger, *Fünfzig Feuilletons: Mit einem Präludium in Versen* (Vienna: Daberlow, 1905), 217–27; and *Die Heimat: Illustrirtes Familienblatt* 2, no. 3 (1877), 775–75.

47. Luft, "Schopenhauer, Austria, and the Generation of 1905," 66.

48. Arthur Schnitzler and Olga Waissnix, *Liebe, die starb vor der Zeit: Ein Briefwechsel* (Vienna, Munich, Zurich: Molden, 1970), 36.

49. Ibid., 121–22.

50. Arthur Schnitzler, *Briefe 1913–1931*, edited by Heinrich Schnitzler and Therese Nickl (Frankfurt am Main: Fischer, 1981), 139.

51. Ivett Guntersdorfer, "'Habe die Ehre!' Schnitzlers Novellen 'Die Toten schweigen' und 'Leutnant Gustl' alla Schopenhauer," in *Auf dem Weg in die Moderne: Deutsche und österreichische Literatur und Kultur*, edited by Roswitha Burwick, Lorely French, and Ivett Rita Guntersdorfer (Berlin/Boston: de Gruyter, 2013), 101–23.

52. Hugo von Hofmannsthal and Richard Beer-Hofmann, *Briefwechsel*, edited by Eugene Weber (Frankfurt am Main: Fischer, 1972), 3.

53. Hugo von Hofmannsthal and Arthur Schnitzler, *Briefwechsel*, edited by Therese Nikl and Heinrich Schnitzler (Frankfurt am Main: Fischer, 1964), 57.

54. See WWR1$_{[P]}$, 411–12.

55. Hugo von Hofmannsthal and Rudolf Kassner, *Briefe und Dokumente, samt ausgewählten Briefen Kassners an Gerty und Christiane von Hofmannsthal*, edited by Klaus E. Bohnenkamp (Freiburg im Breisgau/Berlin: Rombach, 2005), 16.

56. David S. Luft, *Eros and Inwardness in Vienna: Weininger, Musil, Doderer* (Chicago/London: University of Chicago Press, 2003), 33.

57. Rudolf Kassner, *Die Mystik, die Künstler und das Leben: Über englische Dichter und Maler im 19. Jahrhundert* (Leipzig: Diederichs, 1900), 187.

58. Manfred Durzak, "Hermann Brochs Anfänge: Zum Einfluß Weiningers und Schopenhauers," *Germanisch-Romanische Monatsschrift* [NF] 17 (1967), 293–301.

59. Hermann Broch, *Der Tod des Vergil* (Frankfurt am Main: Suhrkamp, 1976), 72. For further discussion of this passage, see Vassilaki Papanicolaou, "'Free-Forming' the German Historical Novel: The Paradigmatic Cases of Hermann Hesse's *Siddhartha* (1922) and Hermann Broch's *Der Tod des Vergil* (1945)," in *The German Historical Novel Since the Eighteenth Century: More than a Bestseller*, edited by Daniela Richter (Cambridge: Cambridge Scholars Publishing, 2016), 127–57.

60. See David S. Luft, *Robert Musil and the Crisis of European Culture: 1880–1942* (Berkeley/Los Angeles: University of California Press, 1980).

61. Kelly Coble, "Positivism and Inwardness: Schopenhauer's Legacy in Robert Musil's *The Man Without Qualities*," *The European Legacy* 11, no. 2 (April 2006), 139–53, at 139.

62. Robert Musil, *Prosa und Stücke – Kleine Prosa – Aphorismen – Autobiographisches – Essays und Reden – Kritik* [*Gesammelte Werke*, vol. 2] (Hamburg: Rowohlt, 1978), 648 and 1016.

63. Luft, "Schopenhauer, Austria, and the Generation of 1905," 74.

64. Janik and Toulmin, *Wittgenstein's Vienna*, 119.

65. Immanuel Kant, *Critique of Pure Reason*, edited and translated by Paul Guyer and Allen W. Wood (Cambridge: Cambridge University Press, 1997), 99.

66. Fritz Mauthner, *Beiträge zu einer Kritik der Sprache*, vol. 2, *Zur Sprachwissenschaft* (Stuttgart: Cotta, 1901), 494–95.

67. Fritz Mauthner, *Der Atheismus und seine Geschichte im Abendlande*, 4 vols. (Stuttgart/ Berlin: Deutsche Verlags-Anstalt, 1922–1923), vol. 4, 176; cited in *Die Deutung der Welt: Jörg Salaquardas Schriften zu Arthur Schopenhauer*, edited by Konstantin Broese, Matthias Koßler, and Barbara Salaquarda (Würzburg: Königshausen & Neumann, 2007), 119.

68. Wittgenstein, *Tractatus Logico-Philosophicus*, translated by C. K. Ogden (London: Kegan Paul, Trench, Trubner, 1922), 74.

69. Robert Wicks, *Schopenhauer* (Malden, MA/Oxford: Blackwell, 2008), 37–38.

70. Wittgenstein, *Tractatus Logico-Philosophicus*, 90.

71. Theodore Redpath, *Ludwig Wittgenstein: A Student's Memoir* (London: Duckworth, 1990), 41; cited in Severin Schroeder, "Schopenhauer's Influence on Wittgenstein," in *A Companion to Schopenhauer*, edited by Bart Vandenabeele (Chichester, UK: Wiley-Blackwell, 2012), 367–84, at 367.

72. Carl E. Schorske, *Fin-de-siècle Vienna: Politics and Culture* (Cambridge: Cambridge University Press, 1961), 85.

73. Ibid., 228.

74. Cited in Gilles Néret, *Gustav Klimt 1862–1918* (Cologne: Taschen, 2005), 21.

75. Peter Vergo, "Gustav Klimts 'Philosophie' und das Programm der Universitätsgemälde," *Mitteilungen der Österreichischen Galerie* 66–67 (1978–1979), 69–100, at 94–97.

76. Luft, *Eros and Inwardness in Vienna*, 33.

77. Schorske, *Fin-de-siècle Vienna*, 228–31. According to Schorske, "Klimt's philosophic priestess betrays in her eerily luminous eyes a different attitude: a wisdom, at once wild and icy, affirming the World of Will," and this points in Schorske's view to Nietzsche's rather than Wagner's view of Schopenhauer's existential metaphysics (*Fin-de-siècle Vienna*, 228).

78. Allan Janik, *Wittgenstein's Vienna Revisited* (New Brunswick/London: Transaction Publishers, 2001), 92–95.

79. Schorske, *Fin-de-siècle Vienna*, 228.

80. See Clare A. P. Willsdon, "Klimt's Beethoven Frieze: Goethe, *Tempelkunst* and the fulfilment of wishes," *Art History* 19, no. 1 (March 1996), 44–73; and Timothy W. Hiles, "Gustav Klimt's *Beethoven Frieze*, Truth, and *The Birth of Tragedy*," in *Nietzsche, Philosophy, and the Arts*, edited by Salim Kemal, Ivan Gaskell, and Daniel W. Conway (Cambridge: Cambridge University Press, 1998), 162–86.

81. Jonathan Barnes, *Early Greek Philosophy* (Harmondsworth: Penguin, 1987), 124.

82. Cf. Janik and Toulmin, *Wittgenstein's Vienna*, 71.

83. Ibid., 230.

FURTHER READING

Adamy, Bernard. "Schopenhauer-Rezeption bei Karl Kraus." *Schopenhauer-Jahrbuch* 66 (1985): 85–102.

Andreas-Salomé, Lou. *The Freud Journal*, translated by Stanley A. Leavy. New York: Basic Books, 1964.

Atzert, Stephan. "Zwei Aufsätze über Leben und Tod: Sigmund Freuds 'Jenseits des Lustprinzips' und Arthur Schopenhauers 'Transscendente Speculation über die anscheinende Absichtlichkeit im Schicksal des Einzelnen,'" *Schopenhauer-Jahrbuch* 86 (2005): 179–94.

Barnes, Jonathan. *Early Greek Philosophy*. Harmondsworth: Penguin, 1987.

Bittrich, Burkhard. "Biedermeier und Realismus in Österreich." In *Handbuch der deutschen Erzählung*, edited by Karl Konrad Pohlheim. Düsseldorf: Bagel, 1981, 356–81.

Broch, Hermann. *Der Tod des Vergil*. Frankfurt am Main: Suhrkamp, 1976.

Broese, Konstantin, Matthias Koßler, and Barbara Salaquarda, eds. *Die Deutung der Welt: Jörg Salaquardas Schriften zu Arthur Schopenhauer*. Würzburg: Königshausen & Neumann, 2007.

Coble, Kelly. "Positivism and Inwardness: Schopenhauer's Legacy in Robert Musil's *The Man Without Qualities*." *The European Legacy* 11, no. 2 (April 2006): 139–53.

Dolgan, Christoph. *Poesie des Begehrens: Textkörper und Körpertexte bei Leopold von Sacher*. Würzburg: Königshausen & Neumann, 2009.

Durzak, Manfred. "Hermann Brochs Anfänge: Zum Einfluß Weiningers und Schopenhauers." *Germanisch-Romanische Monatsschrift* [NF] 17 (1967): 293–301.

Freud, Sigmund, and Josef Breuer. *Studies on Hysteria* [Pelican Freud Library, vol. 3], edited by Angela Richards, translated by James and Alix Strachey. Harmondsworth: Penguin, 1974: 335–93.

Freud, Sigmund, and Lou Andreas-Salomé. *Letters*, edited by Ernst Pfeiffer, translated by William Robson-Scott and Elaine Robson-Scott. New York/London: Norton, 1985.

Freud, Sigmund. *Historical and Expository Works on Psychoanalysis* [Penguin Freud Library, vol. 15], edited by Albert Dickinson, translated by James Strachey. Harmondsworth: Penguin, 1993: 57–128.

Freud, Sigmund. *On Metapsychology: The Theory of Psychoanalysis* [Pelican Freud Library, vol. 11], edited by Angela Richards, translated by James Strachey. Harmondsworth: Penguin, 1984: 271–335.

Goltschnigg, Dietmar. "Vorindustrieller Realismus und Literatur der Gründerzeit." In *Geschichte der deutschen Literatur vom 18. Jahrhundert bis zur Gegenwart*, vol. 2., edited by Viktor Žmegač. Königstein im Taunus: Athenäum, 1980, 1–108.

Guntersdorfer, Ivett. "'Habe die Ehre!' Schnitzlers Novellen 'Die Toten schweigen' und 'Leutnant Gustl' alla Schopenhauer." In *Auf dem Weg in die Moderne: Deutsche und österreichische Literatur und Kultur*, edited by Roswitha Burwick, Lorely French, and Ivett Rita Guntersdorfer. Berlin and Boston: de Gruyter, 2013, 101–23.

Gupta, R. K. "Freud and Schopenhauer." in *Schopenhauer: His Philosophical Achievement*, edited by Michael Fox. Sussex: Harvester Press, 1980, 226–35.

Hiles, Timothy W. "Gustav Klimt's *Beethoven Frieze*, Truth, and *The Birth of Tragedy*." In *Nietzsche, Philosophy, and the Arts*, edited by Salim Kemal, Ivan Gaskell, and Daniel W. Conway. Cambridge: Cambridge University Press, 1998, 162–86.

Hofmannsthal, Hugo von and Arthur Schnitzler. *Briefwechsel*, edited by Therese Nikl and Heinrich Schnitzler. Frankfurt am Main: Fischer, 1964.

Hofmannsthal, Hugo von, and Richard Beer-Hofmann. *Briefwechsel*, edited by Eugene Weber. Frankfurt am Main: Fischer, 1972.

Hofmannsthal, Hugo von, and Rudolf Kassner. *Briefe und Dokumente, samt ausgewählten Briefen Kassners an Gerty und Christiane von Hofmannsthal*, edited by Klaus E. Bohnenkamp. Freiburg im Breisgau/Berlin: Rombach, 2005.

Hollinrake, Roger. "Philosophical Outlook." In *The Wagner Compendium: A Guide to Wagner's Life and Music*, edited by Barry Millington. New York: Schirmer, 1992, 143–46.

Janik, Allan, and Stephen Toulmin. *Wittgenstein's Vienna*. New York: Simon & Schuster, 1973.

Janik, Allan. *Wittgenstein's Vienna Revisited*. New Brunswick/London: Transaction Publishers, 2001.

Kampitz, Peter. *Zwischen Schein und Wirklichkeit: Eine kleine Geschichte der österreichischen Philosophie*. Vienna: Österreichischer Bundesverlag, 1984.

Kant, Immanuel. *Critique of Pure Reason*, edited and translated by Paul Guyer and Allen W. Wood. Cambridge: Cambridge University Press, 1997.

Kassner, Rudolf. *Die Mystik, die Künstler und das Leben: Über englische Dichter und Maler im 19. Jahrhundert*. Leipzig: Diederichs, 1900.

Krafft-Ebing, Richard von. *Psychopathia Sexualis, with especial reference to the Antipathic Sexual Instinct: A Medico-Forensic Study*, translated by F. J. Rebman. New York: Rebman, 1899.

Krauß, Ingrid. *Studien über Schopenhauer und den Pessimismus in der deutschen Literatur des 19. Jahrhunderts*. Berne: Haupt, 1931.

Luft, David S. "Schopenhauer, Austria, and the Generation of 1905." *Central European History* 26 (1983): 53–75.

Luft, David S. *Eros and Inwardness in Vienna: Weininger, Musil, Doderer*. Chicago/London: University of Chicago Press, 2003.

Luft, David S. *Robert Musil and the Crisis of European Culture: 1880–1942*. Berkeley/Los Angeles: University of California Press, 1980.

Mainländer, Philipp. *Philosophie der Erlösung*, vol. 1 [*Schriften*, edited by Winfried H. Müller-Seyfarth, vol. 1]. Hildesheim, Zureich, New York: Olms, 1999.

Mann, Thomas. "Schopenhauer." In *Schriften und Reden zur Literatur, Kunst und Philosophie*, vol. 2 [*Das essayistische Werk*, edited by Hans Bürgin]. Frankfurt am Main and Hamburg: Fischer, 1968, 251–90.

Mauthner, Fritz. *Beiträge zu einer Kritik der Sprache*, vol. 2, *Zur Sprachwissenschaft*. Stuttgart: Cotta, 1901.

Mauthner, Fritz. *Der Atheismus und seine Geschichte im Abendlande*, 4 vols. Stuttgart/Berlin: Deutsche Verlags-Anstalt, 1922–1923.

Milojević, Svletjana. *Die Poesie des Dilettantismus: Zur Rezeption und Wirkung Leopold von Sacher-Masochs*. Frankfurt am Main: Lang, 1998.

Musil, Robert. *Prosa und Stücke – Kleine Prosa – Aphorismen – Autobiographisches – Essays und Reden – Kritik* [*Gesammelte Werke*, vol. 2]. Hamburg: Rowohlt, 1978.

Néret, Gilles. *Gustav Klimt 1862–1918*. Cologne: Taschen, 2005.

Nietzsche, Friedrich. *Basic Writings*, edited and translated by Walter Kaufmann. New York: Modern Library, 1968.

Nietzsche, Friedrich. *The Gay Science*, translated by Walter Kaufmann. New York: Vintage, 1974.

Papanicolaou, Vassilaki. "'Free-Forming' the German Historical Novel: The Paradigmatic Cases of Hermann Hesse's *Siddhartha* (1922) and Hermann Broch's *Der Tod des Vergil* (1945)." In *The German Historical Novel Since the Eighteenth Century: More than a Bestseller*, edited by Daniela Richter. Cambridge: Cambridge Scholars Publishing, 2016, 127–57.

Rank, Otto. "Schopenhauer über den Wahnsinn." *Zentralblatt für Psychoanalyse: Medizinische Monatsschrift für Seelenkunde* 1, no. 1/12 (1911): 68–71.

Redpath, Theodore. *Ludwig Wittgenstein: A Student's Memoir*. London: Duckworth, 1990.

Reents, Edo. *Zu Thomas Manns Schopenhauer-Rezeption*, Würzburg: Königshausen & Neumann, 1998.

Rofes, Aina Vega I. "La recepió de Schopenhauer a la Vienna *fin-de-siècle*." *Revista forma* 3 (Spring 2011): 123–37.

Sacher-Masoch, Leopold von. *Don Juan von Kolomea; Galizische Geschichten*, edited by Michael Farin. Bonn: Bouvier, 1985.

Sacher-Masoch, Leopold von. *Katharina II: Russische Hofgeschichten*. Berlin: Knaur, n.d.

Schnitzler, Arthur and Olga Waissnix, *Liebe, die starb vor der Zeit: Ein Briefwechsel*. Vienna, Munich, Zurich: Molden, 1970.

Schnitzler, Arthur. *Briefe 1913–1931*, edited by Heinrich Schnitzler and Therese Nickl. Frankfurt am Main: Fischer, 1981.

Schömel, Wolfgang. *Apokalyptische Reiter sind in der Luft: Zum Irrationalismus und Pessimismus zwischen Nachmärz und Jahrhundertwende*. Opladen: Westdeutscher Verlag, 1985.

Schorske, Carl E. *Fin-de-siècle Vienna: Politics and Culture*. Cambridge: Cambridge University Press, 1961.

Schroeder, Severin. "Schopenhauer's Influence on Wittgenstein." In *A Companion to Schopenhauer*, edited by Bart Vandenabeele. Oxford: Blackwell, 2012, 367–84.

Sengoopta, Chandak. *Otto Weininger: Sex, Science, and Self in Imperial Vienna*. Chicago/London: University of Chicago Press, 2000.

Sorg, Bernard. *Zur literarischen Schopenhauer-Rezeption im 19. Jahrhundert*. Heidelberg: Winter 1975.

Sprengel, Peter. "Darwin oder Schopenhauer? Fortschrittspessismismus und Pessismismus-Kritik in der österreichischen Literatur (Anzensgruber, Kürnberger, Sacher-Masoch, Hamerling)," in *Literarisches Leben in Österreich 1848–1890*, edited by Klaus Amann, Hubert Lengauer, and Karl Wagner. Vienna, Cologne, Weimar: Böhlau, 2000, 60–93.

Timms, Edward. *Karl Kraus: Apocalyptic Satirist: Culture and Catastrophe in Habsburg Vienna*. New Haven/London: Yale University Press, 1986.

Vandenabeele, Bart, ed. *A Companion to Schopenhauer*. Chichester, UK: Wiley-Blackwell, 2012.

Vergo, Peter. "Gustav Klimts 'Philosophie' und das Programm der Universitätsgemälde." *Mitteilungen der Österreichischen Galerie* 66–67 (1978–1979): 69–100.

Wagner, Richard. *My Life*. London: Constable, 1994.

Weininger, Otto. *Geschlecht und Charakter: Eine prinzipielle Untersuchung*, 9th ed. Vienna/Leipzig: Braumüller, 1920.

Wicks, Robert. *Schopenhauer*. Malden, MA/Oxford: Blackwell, 2008.

Willsdon, Clare A. P. "Klimt's Beethoven Frieze: Goethe, *Tempelkunst* and the Fulfilment of Wishes." *Art History* 19, no. 1 (March 1996): 44–73.

Wittgenstein, Ludwig. *Tractatus Logico-Philosophicus*, translated by C. K. Ogden. London: Kegan Paul, Trench, Trubner, 1922.

Wollheim, Richard. "The Bodily Ego." In *Philosophical Essays on Freud*, edited by Richard Wollheim and James Hopkins. Cambridge: Cambridge University Press, 1982, 124–38.

CHAPTER 31

....

THE NEXT
METAPHYSICAL
MUTATION

Schopenhauer as Michel Houellebecq's Educator

....

CHRISTOPHER A. HOWARD

ANYONE with even a passing familiarity with the philosophy of Schopenhauer will almost immediately see its stamp on France's most significant contemporary author, Michel Houellebecq. The aim of this chapter is to explore the philosophical, biographical, and temperamental affinities between the two authors, demonstrating how Houellebecq serves as an ambassador of Schopenhauerian philosophy in the new millennium. As surveyed herein, Houellebecq reaffirms Schopenhauer's doctrine of the Will and his Buddhistic diagnosis of *life as suffering* (see WWR1$_{[P]}$, 310) while also endorsing his moral philosophy. In agreement that the problem is willing, driven by need and lack, the two thinkers propose different solutions to human suffering.

While Schopenhauer as philosopher sees aesthetic contemplation as providing the only relief from the tyranny of the Will, Houellebecq as a fiction writer imagines worlds where the (flawed) human condition has been overcome by techno-scientific advancements. A concern with the future of humanity—based on a profoundly cynical view of human nature and all hitherto forms of social organization, especially neoliberal capitalism—lies at the core of Houellebecq's major novels, each of which plot different utopian/dystopian trajectories, from eugenics to human extinction and the submission of Europe to Islamic rule. In doing so, Houellebecq carries out a devastating critique of the present age from the standpoint of various post-human futures.

After a brief review of Schopenhauer's influence on literature, the chapter discusses a range of Houellebecq's novels, poetry, essays, and interviews before turning to two of his major novels: *The Elementary Particles* (1998) and *The Possibility of an Island* (2005). Both implicitly and explicitly, these and other works grapple with Schopenhauerian problems, arguably taking them further than any other author thus far.

31.1 SCHOPENHAUER AND LITERATURE

Schopenhauer's impact on literature, music, and art in general is extensive, arguably even more so than in the realm of professional philosophy. Along with the powerful philosophical system erected around the doctrine of the Will, Schopenhauer seems to appeal to artists and authors for his extraordinary writing style, as well as for his elevation of aesthetics to the highest realm of experience.[1] Schopenhauer's work has been shown to have had a decisive impact on the thought and writings of major literary figures ranging from Tolstoy and Turgenev to Thomas Hardy, D. H. Lawrence, William Gissing, Joseph Conrad, Machado de Assis, Borges, Kafka, Thomas Mann, and Herman Hesse, among others.[2] It is well known that Schopenhauer had a profound influence on Richard Wagner and Nietzsche, both of whom have exerted tremendous influence of their own. In France, Schopenhauer made a substantial impact on celebrated authors such as Zola, J. K. Huysmans, Maupassant, Proust, and Samuel Beckett.[3] An explicit literary engagement with Schopenhauer seems to taper off by the mid to late twentieth century, at the same time as his philosophy became less widely discussed.[4] In the new millennium, however, there are signs of renewed interest and appreciation of Schopenhauer, not only in philosophy but in fields as diverse as feminist care ethics, ecology, and literary studies.[5] Outside the academe, arguably the most influential and enthusiastic supporter of the Schopenhauer renaissance is the (in)famous French author, Michel Houellebecq.

31.2 *LA MONDE DE HOUELLEBECQ*

Since the late 1990s, Houellebecq has been widely acknowledged as not only France's most prominent contemporary writer, but the most significant French author since Céline and Camus. This elevated status is not without controversy; Houellebecq garners scorn, contempt, even hatred by many who see his work and public persona as distasteful at best, a complete abomination at worst. He is often called the *enfant terrible* of his generation (sometimes referred to as the "depressionists"), an unflinching provocateur, pessimist, and misanthrope of the highest degree. Nevertheless, since the late 1990s, Houellebecq has been hugely popular, both in his native France and internationally. His books have been translated into twenty-five languages, and there is an amassing body of critical commentary around his work.[6] He has also directed and acted in films, exhibited and published books of his photography, curated art exhibitions, and released a rap album. He is an improbable media celebrity in France, a drunken anti-hero who, over the years, has taken every opportunity to speak his mind.

Houellebecq's fame came with the publication of his best-selling second novel, *The Elementary Particles*, in 1998. The Peruvian novelist and Nobel laureate Mario Vargas Llosa, who was on the committee that awarded the book the prestigious Prix Novembre prize, attributes Houellebecq's success to his "insolence." Also on the panel was the British novelist Julian Barnes, who explains the term was meant in praise. The power of Houellebecq's books, writes Barnes, lie in their ability to "systematically affront our current habits of living, and treat our presumptions of mind as the delusions of the cretinous."[7] He cites Voltaire's *Candide* as the epitome of literary insolence, as well as the works of authors such as La Rochefoucauld and Beckett. Inasmuch as books of insolence target notions of a "purposeful God, a benevolent and orderly universe, human altruism, and the existence of free will," Schopenhauer would also seem to belong to the family of insolence.

Houellebecq's writing style has been the subject of sharp critique by the French literary establishment for being unrefined and obscene. The author appears unconcerned, writing, "I often repeat this phrase of Schopenhauer's: 'The first—and virtually the only—condition for a good style is to have something to say.'"[8] Beginning as a poet, his books resist easy classification. Writing in a flat, realist style, aptly described by one critique as "depressive realism,"[9] his novels utilize marginal genres such as millennial, apocalyptic, utopian writing and science fiction.[10] Houellebecq's narratives, typically based around alienated, middle-aged male protagonists (often named Michel), are interspersed with poetry, pornography, and detached scientific and sociological digressions. Despite the many literary hats Houellebecq wears, he is perhaps above all a satirist. While often labeled a provocateur, an author who seeks to insult and annoy as many people as possible, the literary critic Adam Gopnick sees Houellebecq's critical agenda centered on taking what is happening now and imagining what would happen if it kept on happening.[11] Reading a single page of Houellebecq, it is obvious that the author is not happy with how things are going.

In the opening of his first book, a long essay on the life and work of American horror writer H. P. Lovecraft, Houellebecq states: "No matter what might be said, access to the artistic universe is more or less entirely the preserve of those who are a little *fed up* with the world." He continues,

> Life is painful and disappointing. It is useless, therefore, to write new realistic novels. We generally know where we stand in relation to reality and don't care to know any more. Humanity, such as it is, inspires only an attenuated curiosity in us. All these prodigiously refined "notations," "situations," anecdotes.... All they do, once a book has been set aside, is reinforce the slight revulsion that is already nourished by any one of our "real life" days.[12]

Being a satirist places Houellebecq in the company of authors like Jonathan Swift, George Orwell, and Aldous Huxley. As Gopnick points out, Houellebecq is not just a satirist, but "a *sincere* satirist, genuinely saddened by the absurdities of history and the madness of mankind." The tone of his writing, from his first novel, *Whatever* (1994) to, *Serotonin (2019)*, is more melancholic than polemic, conveying a deep sense despair over what he sees as the senseless cruelty not only of human life, but life in general. Like Schopenhauer and Buddhism, life for Houellebecq is synonymous with suffering. Yet suffering is also the wellspring of poetic creativity, as he proclaims in his literary manifesto, entitled "To Stay Alive: A Method."

The world is suffering unfolded. At its origin it is a node of suffering. All existence is
an expansion, and a crushing. All things suffer into existence. Nothingness vibrates
with pain until it arrives at being, in an abject paroxysm. Beings diversify and
become complex without losing anything of their original nature. Once a certain
level of consciousness is reached, the cry is produced. Poetry derives from it.
Articulate language, equally. The first step for the poet is to return to the origin; that
is, to suffering. The modalities of suffering are important; they are not essential.
All suffering is good. All suffering is useful. All suffering bears fruit. All suffering is
a universe.[13]

Such a pronouncement bears clear resemblance to Schopenhauer's metaphysical conception of an indifferent, all-conquering Will that produces "perpetual struggle" and
an "eternity of suffering." Like Houellebecq, Schopenhauer also sees the potential for
transcendence and sanctification through suffering.

Because all suffering is mortification and a call to resignation, it has the potential to
be a sanctifying force; this explains why great unhappiness and deep pain in themselves inspire a certain respect. But the sufferer only becomes truly awe-inspiring
when he reviews the course of his life as a chain of suffering, or laments a great and
incurable pain, without actually looking at the concatenation of circumstances that
have plunged his particular life into sorrow.... He only becomes truly awe-inspiring
when he lifts his gaze from the particular to the universal, when he views his own
suffering as a mere example of the whole and becoming a genius in the ethical sense,
treats it as *one* case in a thousand, so that the whole of life, seen essentially as suffering, brings him to the point of resignation.   (WWR1, 423)

Both Houellebecq and Schopenhauer agree that, in the face of universal suffering, the
only thing a person can do is become resigned to this fact, knowing that life is transitory.
Life as suffering is by no means limited to the human world, however; examples abound
in nature. Take, for instance, the following fragment of a poem from Houellebecq's 1996
collection, entitled *The Art of Struggle*.

> Plant life is depressing
> It just spreads everywhere
> In the meadow the glow-worm
> Shines for a night and then goes.[14]

Although he considers himself a romantic, like Schopenhauer, Houellebecq does not
expect to find solace in the alleged beauty of the natural world. For both, organic life
simply follows the deterministic dictates of the Will. In another poem from *The Art of
Struggle*, he writes,

Swallows are not free. They are conditioned by repeating their orbits geometrically.
They slightly modify the angle of attack of their wings and describe spirals that grow
further and further away from the established circle of the globe. In short, there is
nothing we can learn from swallows.[15]

Writing before Darwin's "struggle for existence" entered the modern lexicon, Schopenhauer does believe we can learn much from the natural world, but what we learn should terrify, bewilder, and convince us not of nature's sublime beauty, but rather of its senseless brutality. For instance, in WWR2, he renders the following scene from field reports from Java by the German-Dutch naturalist F. W. Junghuhn:

> He saw an immense field entirely covered with skeletons, and took it to be a battle-field. However, they were nothing but skeletons of large turtles, five feet long, three feet broad, and of equal height. These turtles come this way from the sea, in order to lay their eggs, and are then seized by wild dogs (*canis rutilans*); with their united strength, these dogs lay them on their backs, tear open their lower armour, the small scales of the belly, and devour them alive. But then a tiger often pounces on the dogs. Now all this misery is repeated thousands and thousands of times, year in, year out. For this then, are these turtles born. For what offence must they suffer this agony? What is the point of the whole scene of horror? The only answer is that the will-to-live thus objectifies itself.   (WWR2$_{[P]}$, 354)

Elsewhere he uses the example of the Australian bulldog-ant, which if cut in half will proceed to attack its own severed body.

> The head catches hold of the tail with its teeth, and the tail fearlessly defends itself by stinging the head. The struggle lasts usually for half an hour, until they die or are dragged away by other ants. This happens every time.   (WWR1$_{[P]}$, 147)

Schopenhauer considers this a metaphor for the world, described as a "playground of tortured and anguish-ridden beings that endure only by eating one another, where consequently every vicious animal is the living grave of thousands of others, and where its self-sustenance is a chain of torturing deaths" (WWR2$_{[P]}$, 581).

If plants and animals are trapped in the struggle for existence as dictated by life's negative character, this does not mean human beings are placed on a higher pedestal; in fact, it appears to be a worse fate. As Schopenhauer writes: "People surpass animals as much in power as in suffering" (WWR1, 59). Fundamentally, the extra and unique capacity for suffering appears to be rooted in the human capacity for time consciousness, and hence, mortality. Like all life forms, human existence is finite, characterized by what Heidegger calls "Being-towards-death." Yet it is not so much the event of death itself, but the conscious awareness of its looming inevitability that causes human beings profound anxiety and suffering. In the worst case, consciousness of death empties life of all meaning, causing our actions, attachments, and very existence to appear as purposeless ephemera. In his fiction and poetry, Houellebecq often dwells on life's transience. He is especially preoccupied with the loss of physical attractiveness and the opportunities that fade with age, which serve as painful reminders of our decline toward death.

> Insects run about between stones
> In the prison of their morphing
> We're prisoners as well

And some nights
Life is just a procession of things
Their whole presence
Shapes and models our decay
Gives it a place, an unfolding and a meaning;

Like the dishwasher that lived through your first marriage
And your separation,
Like the teddy bear which lived through fits of anger
And when you gave up.

Social animals live in a set number of relations
In which their desires are born, develop, and sometimes
Become very powerful,
Then die.

Sometimes they die all of a sudden,
Some evenings
There were the habits which make up life and suddenly
there is nothing at all
The sky once bearable is suddenly blackened
Pain once tolerable is suddenly piercing
Only the objects are left, like objects we wait, we cannot move,

We're a thing among things,
A thing more fragile than things
A very poor thing
Always waiting for love
For love, or a metamorphosis.[16]

Although Houellebecq does appear sincere, his sincerity is often offset by irony and a philosophical stance that wavers between Schopenhauer's Buddhistic life negation and Nietzsche's Dionysian affirmation. Before exploring Houellebecq's ambiguous position in the debate, let us consider some biographical details and the development of his writing career, including some similarities and overlaps with Schopenhauer.

31.3 Houellebecq and Schopenhauer: Philosophical and Biographic Affinities

Michel Thomas was born in 1958 on the remote island of Réunion, off the southeast coast of Africa. He spent the first five years of his life in Algiers with his maternal grandparents, before being sent to live with his paternal grandparents in Dicy, a rural village in central France. He claims to have had a happy childhood there, under the care of his grandmother (whose maiden name, Houellebecq, he adopted as his penname). His father, a mountain guide, he occasionally saw in the summers, while he rarely saw his mother during his childhood and adult life. The sense of maternal abandonment has been discussed by Houellebecq in interviews and is a point literary critics are eager to exploit in explaining Houellebecq's scornfulness and misogyny. While Schopenhauer was not abandoned by his mother, there has been much speculation that the problematic, unloving relationship between them is also key to understanding the genesis of his pessimism.[17] In *Public Enemies*, a book composed of letters between Houellebecq and fellow French provocateur-philosopher Bernard-Henri Lévy, Houellebecq is skeptical.

> When Nietzsche uses Schopenhauer's poor relationship with his mother to explain away his misogyny, he is committing an intellectually terrible act, one that prefigures many others; but at least he has the excuse of plausibility. It is possible to imagine that someone who spent his childhood and adolescence in daily contact with a mother he despised would be unlikely, later in life, to appreciate a woman's qualities. But what about someone who barely knew his mother? One might imagine he would be particularly determined to seek out the company of women; that he would try with all his might to be reunited with this thing that, to him, will forever remain a mystery. Does this mean I should be a *sex maniac*? Looking back over my life, I have my doubts. I have certainly been one at times, but at other times I find I have been inexcusably offhand. I think that in this, as in everything, I have been bipolar.[18]

This last point is of particular relevance not only for understanding Houellebecq's ambiguous treatment of women and sexuality but his philosophical position, which swings from the utopian to the nihilistic, the pathetic to the clinical.[19] He makes no apology for his bipolarity or the blatant political incorrectness for which he is known. Indeed, these trademarks may help explain his popular appeal, given that contradictions are a salient feature of late capitalist society.[20]

Houellebecq did not grow up in an intellectual environment, though he became an avid reader during his adolescence and began writing poetry while at university. Perhaps due to his rural youth and his keen interest in science and the natural world, he took a technical degree in agronomy (specializing in vegetal ecology). Periods of unemployment followed, intercut with periods of work (first to do with agronomics; then mostly for IT service providers). The year 1991 saw him publish his first book while working as an administrative secretary at the Assemblée Nationale. There, he had a brief career in the IT department, taking unpaid leave for personal reasons in 1996, and finally resigning in 2008. During the early 1990s, Houellebecq published poems and articles for the magazine *Les Incorupibles*, where he was also an editor. It was after the cult success of his 1994 novel, *Extension du Domaine de la Lutte* (*Extension of the Domain of Struggle*, but succinctly entitled *Whatever*, in English), at the age of thirty-six, that Houellebecq was able to devote himself fully to writing. His true fame arrived four years later with the publication of *The Elementary Particles* (1998), which sold half a million copies and ignited fierce public debate around its controversial subject matter, misogyny, and overall despairing vision. His next novels, *Lanzarote* (2000) and *Platform* (2003), continued a preoccupation with themes of sex, love, and social disintegration. *The Possibility of an Island* appeared in 2005, followed by a film version directed by Houellebecq himself in 2008. The next novel, *The Map and the Territory*, was published in 2010 and *Submission* in 2015. In 2016, Houellebecq held a major art exhibition at the Palais de Tokyo in Paris, entitled "Rester Vivant" (Stay Alive), made up of sounds, photographs, installations, and films. Houellebecq was awarded France's Legion of Honour in 2019, a month after his latest best-selling novel, *Serotonin*, was published. Within a narrative of a depressed agricultural scientist whose doctor diagnoses as 'dying from sorrow', the novel depicts French farmers struggling to survive in the face of globalisation, agribusiness and European Union regulations.

Besides troubled maternal relations, a passion for scientific understandings of nature appears to be another biographical affinity Houellebecq and Schopenhauer share. More than perhaps any other major contemporary writer, Houellebecq's books display a sophisticated knowledge of science, especially biology and genetics. *The Elementary Particles* (1998), for instance, the novel which brought him fame, while ostensibly about the ruinous love lives of two brothers—one a brilliant scientist, the other a sexually frustrated writer—was apparently inspired by developments in quantum physics.

> The real inspiration was the experiments of Alain Aspect in 1982. They demonstrated the EPR paradox: that when particles interact, their destinies become linked. When you act on one, the effect spreads instantly to the other, even if they are great distances apart. That really struck me, to think that if two things are connected once, they will be forever. It marks a fundamental philosophical shift. Ever since the disappearance of religious beliefs, the current reigning philosophy has been materialism, which says we are alone and reduces humanity to biology. Man as calculable as billiard balls and completely perishable. That worldview is undermined by the EPR paradox. So the novel was inspired by this idea of what could be the next metaphysical mutation. It has to be less depressing than materialism. Which, let's face it, is pretty depressing.[21]

Schopenhauer himself was a man of science and a polymath, probably more so than many of his philosophical contemporaries and precursors (perhaps with the exception of Goethe). Beyond intensive study of the Western philosophical canon, the young Schopenhauer read fervently and attended lectures in everything from botany to astronomy and other scientific fields. Even after completing his formal studies, he remained a firm believer that a philosopher must keep pace with the latest scientific developments,[22] a view that Houellebecq, as a poet and fiction writer, appears to share. It is perhaps due to Schopenhauer's voracious appetite for diverse branches of knowledge and his prescient philosophical vision that lead him to anticipate, first in *The World as Will and Representation* and the follow-up, *The Will in Nature*, three monumental developments in modern science: evolutionary biology as initiated by Darwin, quantum mechanics following Max Planck and Einstein, and Freud's development of psychoanalysis.[23] Schopenhauer's metaphysical conception of *matter as energy* is perhaps the most striking of his observations to be confirmed by modern science.[24]

If Houellebecq sees a welcome departure from atomized materialism to quantum entanglements, Schopenhauer played an important role in initiating what he calls the "next metaphysical mutation." According to Peter Sloterdijk, Schopenhauer's central contribution was leaving the "Western Church of Reason."

> With him there begins the long agony of the good foundation; he bids a concise farewell to the Greek and Judeo-Christian theologies. For him, what was most absolutely real had ceased to be a godlike, reasonable, and just spiritual being. With this doctrine of the Will, the theory of the foundation of the world leaps from the kind of pious rationalism that had prevailed since the days of Plato to a recognition—characterized by horror and amazement—of the arational. Schopenhauer was the first who identified Being's energetic and instinctive nature which is free or reason. In that, he is one of the fathers of the century of psychoanalysis; in the future he could turn out to be a distant patron of and kin to the age of chaos theory and systemics. And over the long term his most important contribution to intellectual history could be that he opened the European doors to the Asian wisdom traditions, especially Buddhism, with the utmost respect.[25]

Entering the doors opened by Schopenhauer, Buddhism is also important for Houellebecq, as will be explored later.

31.4 SCHOPENHAUER AS HOUELLEBECQ'S EDUCATOR

Whereas Schopenhauer's reception can be exhumed in authors such as Proust, Mann, or Conrad, and strong thematic and ethical parallels have drawn between Schopenhauer and contemporary South African writer J. M. Coetzee,[26] in no author is the engagement more explicit than in Houellebecq. Schopenhauer's philosophy, both in its systematic presentation in *The World as Will and Representation* and in the more topical writings of *Parerga and Paralipomena*, bears a highly visible mark on Houellebecq's writing. Beyond overlapping themes—namely, life as struggle, the cunning of desire, and the vanity of human existence—Houellebecq discusses and quotes Schopenhauer in nearly all of his published works. In 2014, he published five essays on Schopenhauer in the French literary magazine *Le Figaro*, later collected in a book entitled *In the Presence of Schopenhauer*.[27] The first essay begins with Houellebecq discussing his literary-intellectual development, for which Schopenhauer marked a turning point.

My childhood was focused on re-reading (Baudelaire, Dostoyevsky, Lautréamont, Verlaine, the Bible, Pascal's *Pensees*, *The Magic Mountain*) versus actually reading. And then everything changed....

My first "intellectual shock" in philosophy came when I found *The World as Will and Representation*, "the most important book of the world." Regarding philosophy, I had only gone as far as Nietzsche, finding his philosophy immoral and revolting, however, his intellectual power was imposing. I would have liked to destroy Nietzscheanism, but I had not the intellectual knowledge to do so. I no longer despise Nietzsche, as simply as Nietzsche had the bad luck to come after Schopenhauer and even of crossing paths (in music) with Wagner.

The second shock, we are told, came a dozen years later when Houellebecq read the mystical humanism of Auguste Comte, who led him in another direction.

After reading both Schopenhauer and Comte, I feel a sort of unhappy (unfulfilled) enthusiasm which has made me become more positive. This has, in the same way, decreased my level of Schopenhauerism even though I take no real pleasure in re-reading Comte, though no other person has influenced me like Schopenhauer. In Nietzsche's third book, *Untimely Mediations*, he borrows Schopenhauer's profound honesty, probity and righteousness, he speaks magnificently of his tone, this surly bonhomie which gives you the disgust of stylists. All in all, the aim of this volume is for me to attempt at showing, using my favorite passages, why Schopenhauer's intellectual attitude remains in my eyes a model for all future philosophy; and also why, even if we find ourselves disagreeing with him, we can do nothing but feel a deep sense of gratitude for him. To cite Nietzsche again, "[t]he burden of living on this Earth is lighter, now that such a man has written."

Although Schopenhauer and Comte are key thinkers for Houellebecq, Nietzsche is another important interlocutor. More precisely, it is in the Schopenhauer–Nietzsche debate that Houellebecq likes to think.

The Schopenhauer-Nietzsche conflict was inarguably a structuring factor in my intellectual life. I think that Nietzsche's thought has won out now, I think we're living in a low-quality Nietzschean world. And this is something I regret.[28]

The so-called debate between Nietzsche and Schopenhauer begins with Nietzsche's essay, "Schopenhauer as Educator," in *Untimely Meditations* (1875). Here Nietzsche expresses his admiration for Schopenhauer's penetrating insights into the elusive yet all-pervading Will but seeks to break with his educator's life-denying philosophy, or his "resignationism." Rather than denying life meaning and value, Nietzsche wants to affirm life, to say yes to all that is, beyond all moral categories and values. An implicit dialogue with Schopenhauer persists through Nietzsche's entire *oeuvre* up to *Ecce Homo*. Analysis of the relationship between the two thinkers is carried on by Georg Simmel (1908), Thomas Mann (1930), and Jorge Luis Borges (1965), and in hundreds of philosophical commentaries.[29] It also continues to play out in the literature of Michel Houellebecq, where Schopenhauer tends to prevail, though not always.[30] In places we see Houellebecq wavering between Nietzschean yea-saying and Schopenhauerian resignation.

> In moments of rare good humor, I have subscribed to Nietzsche's famous dictum: That which does not kill me makes me stronger (most of the time I would be tempted, more prosaically, to think, That which does not kill me hurts me, and eventually weakens me).[31]

As noted earlier, despite his apparent sincerity, Houellebecq is nonetheless an ironist with a shifting philosophical and political stance. Citing Wittgenstein's famous proposition in the *Tractatus*, "Whereof one cannot speak, thereof one must remain silent," Houellebecq reflects on his own philosophical uncertainty in *Public Enemies*, for which he pardons himself by upholding an ethics of compassion.

> The rights of man, human dignity, the foundations of politics, I'm leaving all that aside, I have no theoretical ammunition, nothing new that would allow me to validate such standards. This leaves ethics, and there I do have something. Only one thing, to be honest, luminously identified by Schopenhauer, and that is *compassion*. Rightly exalted by Schopenhauer and rightly vilified by Nietzsche as the source of all morality. I sided—and this is hardly news—with Schopenhauer.
>
> It remains a mystery that Schopenhauer alludes only with a vague terror to the origin of *compassion*. For after all compassion is merely a feeling, something fragile on the face of it, although it seems to be reborn, naturally from generation to generation. Not to mention its logical corollary: What if compassion disappeared? I think, in that case, humanity would disappear. And the disappearance of such humanity would be a good thing. And that we would have to wait for the arrival of another intelligent species, more cooperative, better adapted by its original tribal organization to ascend toward moral law (by which I mean a species rather superior to primates).[32]

If an ethics of compassion is something to be promoted and cultivated for Houellebecq and Schopenhauer, desire is precisely what should be eliminated. In an interview, Houellebecq explains how he favors stillness.

> I don't like desire or movement. It's not only that I don't like them, actually, I wish they would disappear.... [M]y disgust with desire comes from the fact that deep down, I am with the utopians, people who think that the movement of History must conclude in an absence of movement.[33]

As with Houellebecq, Schopenhauer's project can also be seen an act of resistance against the Will's drive toward movement and differentiation. For instance, in his essay, "On the vanity and suffering of life," Schopenhauer writes,

> Awakened from life out the night of unconsciousness, the will finds itself an individual, in an endless and boundless world, among innumerable individuals, all striving, suffering, erring; and as if through a troubled dream it hurries back to its

old unconsciousness. Yet till then its desires are limitless, its claim inexhaustible, and every satisfied desire gives rise to a new one.   (WWR2$_{[P]}$, 573).

Like Schopenhauer, Houellebecq is a metaphysical pessimist. For the metaphysical pessimist, life and the universe could justifiably be called malevolent were they a product of an intelligent creator, but for atheists this cannot the case. For Schopenhauer, the Will is "endless striving" (WWR1$_{[P]}$, 164), but this striving manifests "an absence of goals" (WWR2$_{[P]}$, 404). Houellebecq shares this view of the Will's blind impulse, but, more pronouncedly than Schopenhauer, he is also a cultural pessimist. He is well known for his especially critical views on the liberal social movements of 1960s and the May '68 generation, which he sees as paradoxically intensifying individualism, nihilism, and consumerism, bringing forth a society of the spectacle driven by libidinal capitalism. The metaphysical Will manifests in the neoliberal market economy, which Houellebecq aims to show, has colonized, commodified, and hallowed every aspect of contemporary life, including romantic relationships, sex, and our most intimate spheres. In one essay, "Approches du désarroi," Houellebecq updates Schopenhauer's *The World as Will and Representation* to "The world as supermarket and derision" to highlight the degradation of meaning in consumer society. Houellebecq's novels, from *Whatever* (1994) to *Submission* (2015) may be seen as chronicling the degeneration of Western society, the exhaustion of desire in a system no longer capable of producing meaning or pleasure.

> The West, in my opinion, is an entity that is disappearing, but its disappearance is really a good thing. Its historical role is finished. That doesn't mean I know what's going to come out of all of this. I'm describing a phase of decline, but without seeing this decline as tragic. It's only tragic for these individuals, not for the history of humanity.
>
> ... [I]t's true, I'm openly insulting to the sixty-eight generation, and the twentieth century in general. But all this is inescapable. It's their own fault, but it's inescapable. I think the only viable solution is Buddhism, which has always been hostile towards desire; it aims for suppression of desire through asceticism; which is not exactly the solution I suggest. I don't really propose a solution, anyway, but at least we have a common goal: the destruction of desire. The best thing that could happen to the West would be to obliterate itself in Buddhism. Something that Nietzsche effectively sought to avoid, in his confrontation with Schopenhauer. I'm taking up a position in a debate between Schopenhauer and Nietzsche, an old one, but hardly obsolete, in my opinion.[34]

Like Schopenhauer, Houellebecq agrees with the Buddhist emphasis on the universality of suffering. With his Buddhist inclinations and the inertia of his protagonists, Houellebecq is clearly not a tragic author, insofar as "Buddhism and tragedy represent two utterly different responses to suffering."[35] While the Dutch philosopher of technology Jos de Mul celebrates Houellebecq's "tragic humanism," his project also can be read as dystopian post-humanism. In two of his major novels, *The Elementary Particles* (1998) and *The Possibility of an Island* (2005), Houellebecq envisages future worlds in which the human species has been redesigned along Schopenhauerian and Buddhistic lines.

31.5 THE NEW HUMAN IN
THE ELEMENTARY PARTICLES

Within a polarized narrative of two brothers, Bruno and Michel, *Elementary Particles* explores typical Houellebecqian themes such as alienation, sexual frustration and unrealized love, the horrors of aging, and a paradoxical death drive. Given that Houellebecq is a more philosophical than literary author (that is to say, his plots and characterizations are less interesting than the ideas behind them), for the purpose of this chapter, let us focus on the book's epilogue, where the author lays his cards on the table. The novel ends with the disappearance (most likely a suicide) of the male protagonist, the disaffected biologist Michel Djerzinski. Toward the end of his life, he takes refuge on a remote coastline in Ireland (where Houellebecq lived for some time) to compose his final writings. His groundbreaking work, published posthumously in a 2009 volume of the journal *Nature* in a separate section entitled "Towards Perfect Reproduction," presents an algorithm that will allow scientists to re-engineer the human genome, allowing humanity to reach its next evolutionary phase. Not coincidentally, *Elementary Particles* was published in 1998, shortly before the completion of the Human Genome Project.

Building on Djerzinski's theory, the new human is designed to eliminate the instinctual drives and psychological traits that are the source of previous humanity's suffering, as exemplified by the brothers Bruno and Michel. Desire, the fundamental cause of suffering, is to be eliminated in the new human, who is asexual and androgynous. If aging and an awareness of death are also major sources of suffering, the new human is designed to remain forever youthful and immortal. Sex is decoupled from reproduction, which now takes place via cloning. The perils of individuality, separation, and evolution by natural selection are to be solved by Djerzinski's technical solution. Although sexually undifferentiated, the new humanity is designed to be more feminine. Eradicating the masculine will to power is intended to give rise to a species that is "overall happier and capable of love."

The project, which came to be overseen by UNESCO, was met with hostility by defenders of the three monotheisms—Judaism, Christianity and Islam—but tellingly, was embraced by Buddhists: "the Buddha's teachings were founded on the awareness of the three impediments of old age, sickness and death, and that the Enlightened One, if he meditated on it, would not necessarily reject a technical solution."[36] The project, we are told, also had the "support of neo-Kantians who, making use of the sudden unpopularity of Nietzschean ideas, had taken control of the well-springs of power among the intelligentsia, the universities and press."[37] As Djerzinski had only provided the theory, it was a young biochemist named Hubczejak who promoted and oversaw the project. It is not difficult to surmise that Hubczejak is Houellebecq's alter ego.

Hubczejak, we learn, goes on to found the "Movement for Human Potential," recycling New Age themes such as Gaia and the Feminine Divine and proposing a world government whose slogan boldly declares, "The Future Is Feminine." Under Hubczejak's direction, the first members of the "new intelligent species" arrive in 2029, twenty years after Michel Djerzinski's disappearance. Over the next fifty years, the population of the new humans fills in while the old species faces its extinction without much fanfare.

> Contrary to the doomsayers, this extinction is taking place peaceably, despite the occasional acts of violence, which also continue to decline. It has been surprising to note the meekness, resignation, perhaps even secret relief with which humans have consented to their own passing.[38]

The new species is described as peaceful and less passionate.

> Men consider us happy; it is certainly true that we have succeeded in overcoming the forces of egotism, cruelty and anger which they could not. We live very different lives. Science and art are still a part of our society; but without the stimulus of personal vanity, the pursuit of Truth and Beauty has taken on a less urgent aspect. To humans of the old species, our world seems a paradise. We have even been known to refer to ourselves—with a certain humor—by the name they so long dreamed of: gods.[39]

The book ends with the narrator, a member of the new species writing in the future, paying tribute to "the brave and unfortunate species which created us." He continues in the distanced, deploring tone of Schopenhauer.

> This vile, unhappy race, barely different from the apes, which nevertheless carried within such noble aspirations. Tortured, contradictory, individualistic, quarrelsome and infinitely selfish, it was sometimes capable of extraordinary explosions of violence, but never quite abandoned its belief in love.

Bio-engineering as *the only solution* for alleviating humankind's endemic suffering continues in Houellebecq's next major work, *The Possibility of an Island*. The novel continues to explore the new human, but comes to a different, less utopian conclusion than *The Elementary Particles*.

31.6 *THE POSSIBILITY OF AN ISLAND*

Published in 2005, *The Possibility of an Island* takes place both in the present and approximately two thousand years in the future. The narrative shifts back and forth between Daniel1, a successful, irreverent comedian, and Daniel24 and Daniel25, his clones in the distant future. As in *Elementary Particles*, the utopian solution to the suffering that defines human existence is improved clones, called "neohumans." The techno-scientific breakthrough was brought about by Elohimites, a fictitious global cult based on the Raelians, an actual new religious movement with strong beliefs in scientific progress.

Traveling to the remote island of Lanzarote (where Houellebecq has also lived, photographed, and written about), Daniel1 participates in the early activities of the Elohimite sect, including their realization of human cloning.

As in *Elementary Particles*, old humanity is regarded as an inherently flawed species, destined to suffer from the same sense of isolation, separateness, and contradictory desires already diagnosed and analyzed by Schopenhauer. Daniel24 explains why the advent of neohumans was necessary to overcome the "failures" that defined previous humanity.

> The subject-object separation is triggered, in the course of cognitive processes, by a convergent mesh of failures....It is in failure, and through failure, that the subject constitutes itself, and the passage of humans to neohumans, with the disappearance of all physical contact that is its correlative, has in no way modified this basic onto-logical given....It has, however, been shown countless times that the physical pain that accompanied the existence of humans was consubstantial with them, that it was the direct consequence of an inadequate organization of their nervous system, just as their inability to establish interindividual relations in a mode other than that of con-frontation resulted from a relative insufficiency of their social instincts in relation to the complexity of the societies that their intellectual means enabled them to found.[40]

The sexual impulse as a manifestation of pure desire or Will is a major theme of the novel, as it is for Schopenhauer, who writes: "The *affirmation of the will-to-live* is seen to be concentrated in the act of procreation, which is its most decided expression" (PP2$_{[P]}$, 414). Reading as a synthesis of Schopenhauer and Darwin, the narrator of *Possibility* points to the utilitarian nature of the sex drive, which aims at nothing more than the propagation of the species.

> All energy is sexual, not exclusively but primarily, and when the animal is not good to breed it is absolutely good for nothing. It is the same for men. When the sexual instinct is dead, wrote Schopenhauer, the real core of life is consumed; as he notes in a metaphor of terrifying violence, "human existence like a play which started by live actors, would be completed by automatons dressed in the same costumes."[41]

Sex, for Houellebecq and Schopenhauer, is one of nature's cruel tricks, arguably the cruelest of all. Whether human or non-human, living organisms are essentially co-opted by the Will, driven by an overpowering sex drive, the objectification of the will-to-live itself. The result is offspring who perpetuate the endless cycle of suffering. Unsurprisingly, both Houellebecq and Schopenhauer share the pessimistic belief, also found in the Bible (Matthew 26:24, Ecclesiastes 4:2–3) and in philosophers from Seneca to Montaigne and more recently, David Benatar, that in the final assessment, non-existence is preferable to existence.

Like most of Houellebecq's protagonists, Daniel1 is constantly craving sex, and *The Possibility of an Island* is replete with pornographic detail. The sex drive will be left behind with the advent of neohumans, who live in isolated cells and have no physical contact. They communicate solely through electronic messaging and do not need to eat, subsisting instead on capsules of mineral salts. As in *Elementary Particles*, the neohumans no longer experience the violent emotions and contradictory desires of old humanity. Unlike the previous novel, however, the future Houellebecq envisions is a dystopia. The neohumans are in fact an intermediary being, existing between old humanity and the perfected beings to come, called the "the Future Ones." Guided by the Buddhistic teachings of the "Supreme Sister," the neohumans are responsible for studying the lives of their originals in preparation for the final transition. Having never experienced desire, love, or emotion, they observe previous humanity with wonder and curiosity, and, in the case of Daniel25, a growing sense of envy.

As with *Elementary Particles*, after a meandering plot, the book's long epilogue is where Houellebecq's philosophical conclusions are laid bare. Neither celebrating the placid neohumans, nor reaffirming old humanity, *The Possibility of an Island* ends in a double bind.[42] Taking Schopenhauer and Buddhist philosophy to their logical extremes, the neohuman future Houellebecq paints is a dystopia: "The life of the neohumans was intended to be peaceful, rational, remote from pleasure as well as suffering, and my departure would bear witness to its failure."[43] Although the neohumans do not suffer, they are also incapable of connection and joy; the possibility of an island turns out to be an impossibility (or at least an undesirable possibility).

> Planning the extinction of desire in Buddhist-like terms, the Supreme Sister had banked on the maintenance of a weakened, non-tragic, energy, purely conservative in nature, which would have continued to enable the functioning of thought—a thought less quick but more exact because more lucid, a thought that knew *deliverance*. This phenomenon had only been produced in significant proportions, and it was, on the contrary sadness, melancholy, languid and finally mortal apathy that had submerged our disincarnated generations. The most patent indicator of failure was that I ended up envying the destiny of Daniel1, his violent and contradictory journey, the amorous passions that had shaken him—whatever his suffering and tragic end.[44]

Fascinated by his original's tempestuous quest for love, Daniel25 begins to develop something akin to feelings for Marie23, who is similarly becoming drawn to the idea of love. After Marie23 disappears and with a growing suspicion that neohumans are mere "software fictions," Daniel25 decides to leave his isolated cell in the neohuman compound. With a rucksack and his beloved dog, Fox (a clone of Daniel1's faithful companion), he ventures beyond the fenced enclosure, setting off on foot in the direction of Lanzarote. With a six-month supply of mineral salts, he realizes that unless he finds seawater (if it still existed, the Earth had gone through a dramatic climatic shift known as "the Great Drying Up"), he will die. This prospect does not concern him.

> My attachment to life was not very strong, by the standards of human criteria, everything in the teachings of the Supreme Sister was oriented towards the idea of detachment; on rediscovering the original world, I had the impression of being an

incongruous, contingent presence, in the middle of a universe where everything was oriented towards survival and perpetuation of the species.[45]

Somewhere in the forests of Spain, Daniel25 encounters a small tribe of old humans. He is repulsed by the "savages" who kill his faithful companion, Fox. Traveling on in solitude, he realizes, "definitively this time, that my desire was no longer, and probably never had been, to join some kind of primate community."[46] In the end, he is at home nowhere.

> I had more and more difficulty understanding why I had left the abstract and virtual community of the neohumans. Our existence, devoid of passions, had been that of the elderly; we looked on the world with a gaze characterised by lucidity without benevolence. The animal world was known, human societies were known; no mystery was hidden in it, and nothing could be expected from it, except the repetition of carnage.[47]

Eventually reaching the sea, which had been reduced by the "Great Drying Up" to a string of puddles and ponds, Daniel25 comes to the end of his journey. Realizing he has about sixty years to live out his "obscure existence as an improved monkey,"[48] he resigns himself to the twenty-thousand or so identical days of complete solitude that await him.

In the end, Daniel25 concedes that it will only be with the arrival of an entirely new being, the "Future Ones," that true deliverance will be possible. Approvingly, the narrator suggests that the Future Ones will be a purely technological being. The neohumans, like their human predecessors and all organic life, will disappear.

> [C]arbon biology had had its day, and the Future Ones would be beings made of silicon, whose civilization would be built through the progressive interconnection of cognitive and memory processors.[49]

Inspired by the stand Schopenhauer takes against the tyranny of the Will and Buddhists against desire and attachment, Houellebecq has taken these ideas to their extremes in *Possibility of an Island*. The conclusion he arrives at, however, is that it is not enough to eliminate desire in human beings. It is the entire *modus operandi* of biological life, the will-to-live, defined by negativity and differentiation, that must be transcended.

31.7 CONCLUSION

Literary critics, academics, and the reading public often wonder if Houellebecq is an author whose ideas and writing should be taken seriously. In the realm of philosophy, Schopenhauer has often endured a similar fate. For both thinkers, desire is the problem. Because the Will drives desire, which in turn causes pain and suffering, the solution proposed by Schopenhauer and Buddhism is the cultivation of a conscious defense against it. For Schopenhauer, "unwilling" is facilitated by aesthetic contemplation and experiences of the sublime. In Buddhism, stillness is achieved through meditation and ascetic practices. Houellebecq approves the goal of these approaches—the elimination of desire—but his solution is a technical one. Since life is biologically programmed for reproduction and the survival of a species, yet is subject to the contingent processes of nature, he embraces techno-scientific interventions, saying in an interview: "I don't see why allowing for chance would be of a higher moral order than control by human beings."[50]

Houellebecq is a sincere satirist, but his literature also belongs to the "foresight genre" that begins in the early twentieth century, initiated by a number of quantum leaps in science.[51] In the new millennium, despite ethical debates, all signs point to the inevitability of a post-human future. Driven by innovations in genetics and stem cell research, as well as the economics of public health, by the middle of the twenty-first century, bio-engineered "neohumans" will be a reality. Writing on the cusp of this genetic revolution, Houellebecq may come to be seen as a prophetic author who used literature to explore the potential of evolution by artificial selection. However he is to be seen, an informed view will be mindful of his direct genealogical linkage to Schopenhauer, a visionary who occupies an central place in the next metaphysical mutation.

NOTES

1. Peter Bishop, "Schopenhauer's Impact on European Literature," in *A Companion to Schopenhauer*, edited by Bart Vandenabeele (Hoboken: Wiley-Blackwell, 2012), 333–48.

2. Bryan Magee, *The Philosophy of Schopenhauer* (Oxford: Clarendon Press, 1996); Owen Knowles, "Who's Afraid of Arthur Schopenhauer? A New Context for Conrad's Heart of Darkness," *Nineteenth-century Literature* 49, no. 1 (1994), 75–106; Robert Wicks, "Arthur Schopenhauer," *Stanford Encyclopedia of Philosophy*, http://plato.stanford.edu/entries/schopenhauer/#8.

3. Thomas G. West, "Schopenhauer, Huysmans and French Naturalism," *Journal of European Studies* 1, no. 4 (1971), 313–24.

4. An exception is the British poet Ted Hughes, who was a great admirer of Schopenhauer. See Dwight Eddins, "Ted Hughes and Schopenhauer: The Poetry of the Will," *Twentieth Century Literature* 45, no. 1 (1999), 94–109.

5. Richard Alan Northover, "Schopenhauer and Secular Salvation in the Work of JM Coetzee," *English in Africa* 41, no. 1 (2014), 35–54.

6. Delphine Grass, "Domesticating Hierarchies, Eugenic Hygiene and Exclusion Zones: The Dogs and Clones of Houellebecq's La Possibilité d'une île," *L'Esprit Créateur* 52, no. 2 (2012), 127–40; John McCann, *Michel Houellebecq: Author of our times* (Bruxelles: Peter Lang, 2010); Gerald Moore, "Gay Science and (no) Laughing Matter: The Eternal Returns of Michel Houellebecq," *French Studies* 65, no. 1 (2011), 45–60; Christian Moraru, "The Genomic Imperative: Michel Houellebecq's The Possibility of an Island," *Utopian Studies* (2008), 265–83; Douglas Morrey, *Michel Houellebecq: Humanity and its Aftermath* (Liverpool: Liverpool University Press, 2017); Carole Sweeney, *Michel Houellebecq and the Literature of Despair* (London: A&C Black, 2013); Ashley Harris, "Michel Houellebecq's Transmedial Œuvre: Extension of the Realm of Creative Intervention," *Itinéraires. Littérature, textes, cultures* 2 (2017).

7. Julian Barnes, "Hate and Hedonism: The Insolent Art of Michel Houellebecq," *The New Yorker* 7 (2003).

8. Michel Houellebecq, *Interventions 2: Traces* (Paris: Flammarion, 2010), 153.

9. Ben Jeffery, *Anti-matter: Michel Houellebecq and Depressive Realism* (Winchester, UK: Zero, 2011).

10. Snyman, E., "The Possibility of an Island; or, The Double Bind of Houellebecq's Apocalypse: When the End Is Not the End," *Literator: Journal of Literary Criticism, Comparative Linguistics and Literary Studies* 29, no. 2 (2008), 25–45.

11. Adam Gopnik, "The Next Thing: Michel Houellebecq's Francophobic Satire," *The New Yorker* 26 (2015).

12. Michel Houellebecq, *H. P. Lovecraft: Against the World, Against Life* (San Francisco, CA: Believer Books, 1991/2005), 29–30.

13. Michel Houellebecq, *To Stay Alive: A Method*, http://www.houellebecq.info/popdivers.php?id=13

14. Michel Houellebecq, *The Art of Struggle* (London: Herla, 2010), 127.

15. Ibid., 145.

16. Ibid., 77–79.

17. David E. Cartwright, *Schopenhauer: A Biography* (New York: Cambridge University Press, 2010).

18. Michel Houellebecq and Bernard-Henri Lévy, *Public Enemies* (New York: Random House, 2011), 279.

19. Nancy Huston, "Michel Houellebecq: The Ecstasy of Disgust," *Salmagundi* 152 (2006), 20–37, at 32.

20. See, for instance: Zygmunt Bauman, *Liquid Modernity* (Cambridge: Polity Press, 2000); Daniel Bell, *The Cultural Contradictions of Capitalism* (New York: Basic Books, 1976).

21. Michel Houellebecq, "Michel Houellebecq: The Art of Fiction, No. 206," interviewed by Susannah Hunnewell, *Paris Review* 194 (2010).

22. Cartwright, *Schopenhauer*, 170.

23. Magee, *Philosophy of Schopenhauer*, 403–17.

24. This is an idea already present in all of the world's mystical traditions, but especially well-developed in the major Asian traditions of Hinduism, Buddhism, and Taoism. The EPR paradox, for instance, was already addressed (if not mathematically "proven") in Buddhism with the concept of *pratītyasamutpāda* ("dependent co-arising").

25. Peter Sloterdijk, *Philosophical Temperaments: From Plato to Foucault* (New York: Columbia University Press), 64–65.

26. Richard A. Northover, "Schopenhauer and Secular Salvation in the Work of J. M. Coetzee," *English in Africa* 41, no. 1 (2014), 35–54.

27. Michel Houellebecq, *En présence de Schopenhauer* (Paris, Éditions de L'Herne, 2017). The 2014 essays can be found at https://blogs.mediapart.fr/edition/bookclub/article/010210/en-presence-de-schopenhauer-15. The translations are my own, with assistance from Alexander Stanton.

28. *En présence de Schopenhauer* (see previous note)

29. See, for instance, Ken Gemes and Christopher Janaway, "Life-Denial versus Life-Affirmation," in *A Companion to Schopenhauer* (2012), 280–99.

30. Moore, "Gay Science and (no) Laughing Matter," 45–60.

31. Houellebecq and Lévy, *Public Enemies*, 23.

32. Ibid., 168–69.

33. Nicolas Bourriaud, Jean-Yves Jouannais, and Jacques-François Marchandise, "Presentations/ Interviews/Selections: Michel Houellebecq," *Sites* 3, no. 2 (1999), 239–61, at 244.

34. Ibid., 246.

35. Walter Kaufmann, *Tragedy and Philosophy* (New York: Anchor Books, 1968), 339.

36. Michel Houellebecq, *The Elementary Particles* (New York: Knopf), 258.

37. Ibid., 259.

38. Ibid., 263.

39. Ibid.

40. Michel Houellebecq, *The Possibility of an Island* (New York: Knopf, 2005), 97.

41. Ibid., 154.

42. Snyman, "The Possibility of an Island; or, The Double Bind of Houellebecq's Apocalypse: When the End Is Not the End," 25–45.

43. Houellebecq, *The Possibility of an Island*, 337.

44. Ibid., 313.

45. Ibid., 317.

46. Ibid., 321.

47. Ibid., 331.

48. Ibid., 336.

49. Ibid., 343.

50. Jos De Mul, "The Possibility of an Island: Michel Houellebecq's Tragic Humanism," *Journal of Aesthetics and Phenomenology* 1, no. 1 (2014), 91–110, at 99.

51. Hub Zwart, "From Utopia to Science: Challenges of Personalised Genomics Information for Health Management and Health Enhancement," *Medicine Studies* 1, no. 2 (2009), 155–66.

FURTHER READING

Benatar, David. *Better Never to Have Been: The Harm of Coming Into Existence*. Oxford: Oxford University Press, 2006.

Bess, Michael. *Our Grandchildren Redesigned: Life in the Bioengineered Society of the Near Future*. Boston: Beacon Press, 2016.

Dienstag, Joshua F. *Pessimism: Philosophy, Ethic, Spirit*. Princeton, NJ: Princeton University Press, 2006.

Fukuyama, Francis. *Our Posthuman Future: Consequences of the Biotechnology Revolution*. New York: Farrar, Straus and Giroux, 2002.

Greely, Henry T. *The End of Sex and the Future of Human Reproduction*. Cambridge, MA: Harvard University Press, 2016.

Mann, Thomas. *Essays of Three Decades*. New York: Knopf, 1948.

Nietzsche, Friedrich. *Daybreak: Thoughts on the Prejudices of Morality*, translated by Maudemarie Clark and Brian Leiter (Cambridge: Cambridge University Press, 1997).

Simmel, Georg. *Schopenhauer and Nietzsche*. Amherst: University of Massachusetts Press, 1986.

Wicks, Robert. *Schopenhauer*. Malden, MA: Blackwell Publishers, 2008.

Young, Julian. *Willing and Unwilling: A Study in the Philosophy of Arthur Schopenhauer*. Dordrecht: Nijhoff, 1987.

Index